Writing Today

CANADIAN EDITION

Writing Today

CANADIAN EDITION

Richard Johnson-Sheehan
Purdue University

Charles Paine
University of New Mexico

Cathi Shaw

Jordan Stouck
University of British Columbia, Okanagan

PEARSON

Toronto

Vice-President, Editorial Director: Gary Bennett
Editor-in-Chief: Michelle Sartor
Acquisitions Editor: David S. Le Gallais
Marketing Manager: Jennifer Sutton
Supervising Developmental Editor: Suzanne Schaan
Project Manager: Marissa Lok
Production Editor: Cindy Miller, Element LLC
Copy Editor: Carolyn Zapf
Proofreaders: Leanne Rancourt, Cy Strom, Marcia Gallego
Compositor: Cenveo Publisher Services
Photo and Permissions Researcher: Debbie Henderson
Art Director: Julia Hall
Cover and Interior Designer: Anthony Leung
Cover Image Credit: Fotolia

Credits and acknowledgments of material borrowed from other sources and reproduced, with permission, in this textbook appear on the appropriate page within the text and on pp. 571–572.

10 9 8 7 6 5 4 3 2 1 WC

Library and Archives Canada Cataloguing in Publication

 Writing today / Richard Johnson-Sheehan . . . [et al.].
— Canadian ed.

Includes index.
ISBN 978-0-205-20303-1

 1. English language—Rhetoric—Textbooks.—2. Report writing—Textbooks.—I. Johnson-Sheehan, Richard

PE1408.W7798 2013   808'.042   C2012-905478-X

ISBN 978-0-205-20303-1

Brief Contents

PART 1 GETTING STARTED 2

1 Writing and Genres 4
2 Topic, Angle, Purpose 16
3 Readers, Contexts, and Rhetorical Situations 26

PART 2 USING GENRES TO EXPRESS IDEAS 38

4 Summaries 40
5 Reviews 58
6 Rhetorical Analyses 85
7 Literary Analyses 116
8 Position Papers and Arguments 148
9 Proposals 169
10 Research Papers 210

PART 3 DEVELOPING A WRITING PROCESS 254

11 Developing Ideas and Prewriting 256
12 Organizing and Drafting 269
13 Choosing a Style 276
14 Designing 287
15 Revising and Editing 303

PART 4 STRATEGIES FOR SHAPING IDEAS 320

16 Drafting Introductions and Conclusions 322
17 Developing Paragraphs and Sections 331
18 Using Basic Rhetorical Patterns 343
19 Using Argumentative Strategies 357
20 Working Collaboratively with Other Writers 376

PART 5 DOING RESEARCH 386

21 **Starting Research** 388
22 **Finding Sources and Collecting Information** 398
23 **Quoting, Paraphrasing, and Citing Sources** 415
24 **Using MLA Style** 429
25 **Using APA Style** 454

PART 6 GETTING YOUR IDEAS OUT THERE 478

26 **Using the Internet** 480
27 **Creating a Portfolio** 488
28 **Succeeding on Essay Exams** 498
29 **Presenting Your Work** 509

PART 7 HANDBOOK 522

1 **Sentences** 524
2 **Verbs** 540
3 **Pronouns** 545
4 **Style** 550
5 **Punctuation, Mechanics, and Spelling** 554

Contents

Thematic Contents   xv
Preface   xvi

PART 1

Getting Started   2

1 Writing and Genres   4

What Are Genres?   4

Using Genres to Write Successfully   5
> Writing with Genres • Genres in Movies • Genres in Writing

Genre and the Writing Process   9
> Using a Writing Process • Using Genre as a Guiding Concept

Using Genres in Your Education and in Your Career   12

Quick Start Guide   13

Talk About This • Try This Out • Write This   14–15

2 Topic, Angle, Purpose   16

Topic: What Am I Writing About?   17

Angle: What Is New About the Topic?   19

Purpose: What Should I Accomplish?   20

Choosing the Appropriate Genre   22

Quick Start Guide   23

Talk About This • Try This Out • Write This   24–25

3 Readers, Contexts, and Rhetorical Situations   26

Profiling Readers   27
> A Brief Reader Profile • An Extended Reader Profile

Analyzing the Context   31
> Place • Medium • Social and Political Influences

Genres and the Rhetorical Situation   33

Quick Start Guide   35

Talk About This • Try This Out • Write This   36–37

PART 2

Using Genres to Express Ideas   38

4 Summaries   40

At-a-Glance: Summaries   41

Overview   42

One Student's Work: Rebecca Gillespie, "Summary of 'Boys and Violence: A Gender-Informed Analysis'"   43

Developing Your Summary's Content   44
> Inquiring: Reading and Understanding Your Text • Inquiring: Distinguishing Abstractions from Details • Researching: Finding Out About Context

Organizing and Drafting Your Summary   46
> Articulating the Main Argument • Finding an Appropriate Length and Level of Detail

Structuring Your Summary   48
> Inserting Reporting or Signalling Phrases and Citations

Choosing an Appropriate Style   49
> Using a Formal Versus an Informal Style

Revising and Editing Your Summary   49
Quick Start Guide   51
Readings
Anne Kingston, "Outraged Moms, Trashy Daughters: How Did Those Steeped in the Women's Lib Movement Produce Girls Who Think Being a Sex Object Is Powerful?" (excerpt)   52
Jordan Stouck and Cathi Shaw, "Summary of David Bartholomae's 'Inventing the University'"   54
Talk About This • Try This Out • Write This   56–57

5 Reviews   58

At-a-Glance: Reviews   59
Overview   60
One Student's Work: Kurosh Amoui Kalareh, "Double Googlization: A Review of *The Googlization of Everything (And Why We Should Worry)* by Siva Vaidhyanathan"   60
Developing Your Review's Content   62
Inquiring: Finding Common Expectations • Inquiring: Finding Academic Expectations • Researching: Gathering Background Information • Researching: Go Experience It
Organizing and Drafting Your Review   66
The Introduction • Description or Summary of the Subject • Discussion of Strengths and Shortcomings • Conclusion
Choosing an Appropriate Style   68
Use Detail • Set the Appropriate Tone • Change the Pace
Applying the Genre: Literature Review   70
Designing Your Review   71
Revising and Editing Your Review   71
Quick Start Guide   73
Readings
Brian D. Johnson, "Bare-Knuckled Knockout"   74
James Kendrick, "The Many Shades of Red"   76
Z. Lawrie, E. A. Sullivan, P. S. W. Davies, and R. J. Hill, "Media Influence on the Body Image of Children and Adolescents" (excerpt)   81
Talk About This • Try This Out • Write This   83–84

6 Rhetorical Analyses   85

At-a-Glance: Rhetorical Analyses   86
Overview   87
One Student's Work: Sahil Sidhu, "Analysis of a Canadian Association of Petroleum Producers (CAPP) Advertisement"   87
Developing Your Rhetorical Analysis's Content   91
Inquiring: Highlighting Uses of Proofs ARGUMENT • Rhetorical Patterns: Understanding How the Topic Achieves Its Effects • Researching: Finding Background Information
Organizing and Drafting Your Rhetorical Analysis   95
The Introduction • Explanation of Rhetorical Concepts • Historical Context and Summary • Analysis of the Text • The Conclusion
Choosing an Appropriate Style   99
Applying the Genre: Ad Critique   99
Designing Your Rhetorical Analysis   100
Revising and Editing Your Rhetorical Analysis   101
Quick Start Guide   102
Readings
Liza Featherstone, "What's a Girl to Read?"   103
Emily Martin, "The Egg and the Sperm: How Science Has Constructed a Romance Based on Stereotypical Male-Female Roles" (excerpt)   106
Talk About This • Try This Out • Write This   114–115

7 Literary Analyses   116

At-a-Glance: Literary Analyses   117
Overview   118
One Student's Work: Max Doran, "'Border' Crossings in Thomas King's Narrative"   118
Developing Your Literary Analysis's Content   121
Read, Reread, Explore • Inquiring: What's Interesting Here? • Researching: What Background Do You Need?
Organizing and Drafting Your Literary Analysis   124
The Introduction • The Body of Your Analysis • The Conclusion
Choosing an Appropriate Style   126
Use the "Literary Present" Tense • Integrate Quoted Text • Move Beyond Personal Response

Applying the Genre: Reading Response   128

Designing Your Literary Analysis   128

Revising and Editing Your Literary Analysis   130

Quick Start Guide   131

Readings

Thomas King, "Borders"   132

Jennifer Andrews and Priscilla L. Walton, "Rethinking Canadian and American Nationality: Indigeneity and the 49th Parallel in Thomas King" (excerpt)   140

Talk About This • Try This Out • Write This   146–147

8 Position Papers and Arguments ARGUMENT   148

At-a-Glance: Position Papers and Arguments   149

Overview   150

One Student's Work: Kurosh Amoui Kalareh, "Watching Movies at Home or Going to the Cinema?" ARGUMENT   150

Developing Your Position Paper's Content   152

Inquiring: Identifying Points of Contention ARGUMENT • Researching: Finding Out What Others Know

Organizing and Drafting Your Position Paper   154

The Introduction • Summary and Limitations of Your Opponents' Position ARGUMENT • Your Understanding of the Issue • Reasons Why Your Understanding Is Stronger • Conclusion

Choosing an Appropriate Style   155

Use Plain Style to Describe Your Opponents' Position • Use Similes, Metaphors, and Analogies When Describing Your Position • Use Top-Down Paragraphs • Define Unfamiliar Terms

Applying the Genre: The Rebuttal   157

Designing Your Position Paper   157

Revising and Editing Your Position Paper   158

Quick Start Guide   160

Readings

Kate Dailey, "Friends with Benefits: Do *Facebook* Friends Provide the Same Support as Those in Real Life?" ARGUMENT   161

Russ Walker and David Roberts, "Letter to the Editor on Climate Story" ARGUMENT   165

Talk About This • Try This Out • Write This   167–168

9 Proposals ARGUMENT   169

At-a-Glance: Proposals   170

Overview   171

One Student Group's Work: Fahmida Ahmed, Jeff Brown, David Felix, Todd Haurin, and Betty Seto, "Changing the Campus Climate: Strategies to Reduce Greenhouse Gas Emissions at the University of California, Santa Barbara"   173

Developing Your Proposal's Content   181

Inquiring: Defining the Problem • Inquiring: Analyzing the Problem • Researching: Gathering Information and Sources • Inquiring: Planning to Solve the Problem • Researching: Finding Similar Projects

Organizing and Drafting Your Proposal   184

The Introduction • Description of the Problem, Its Causes, and Its Effects • Description of Your Plan • Discussing the Costs and Benefits of Your Plan • The Conclusion

Choosing an Appropriate Style   190

Applying the Genre: Academic Proposals   191

The Introduction • The Literature Review • The Plan and Methodology • The Conclusion

Designing Your Proposal   192

Revising and Editing Your Proposal   192

Quick Start Guide   194

Readings

Derek Rasmussen, "Forty Years of Struggle and Still No Right to Inuit Education in Nunavut" (excerpt) ARGUMENT   195

M. H. Saier Jr. and J. T. Trevors, "Tell the Awful Truth: It's Not Just Global Warming, It's Global Disaster!" ARGUMENT   203

Talk About This • Try This Out • Write This   208–209

10 Research Papers   210

At-a-Glance: Research Papers   211

Overview   212

One Student's Work: Holly Wylie, "The CNN Effect: How Media Can Influence Government Foreign Policy" 212

Developing Your Research Paper's Content 218

Inquiring: Defining Your Topic, Angle, Purpose • Inquiring: Finding Out What You Already Know • Researching: Creating a Research Plan • Researching: Gathering Sources and Revisiting Your Thesis

Organizing and Drafting Your Research Paper 223

Abstract • Introduction • The Body • Conclusion • References or Works Cited

Choosing an Appropriate Style 226

Applying the Genre: The Annotated Bibliography 227

Designing Your Research Paper 229

Revising and Editing Your Research Paper 230

Quick Start Guide 232

Readings

Piers Robinson, "The CNN Effect Revisited" 233

June Feder, Ronald F. Levant, and James Dean, "Boys and Violence: A Gender-Informed Analysis" 239

Talk About This • Try This Out • Write This 252–253

PART 3

Developing a Writing Process 254

11 Developing Ideas and Prewriting 256

Prewriting 257

Concept Mapping • Freewriting • Brainstorming or Listing • Storyboarding

Using Heuristics 259

Asking the Journalist's Questions • Using the Five Senses • Investigating *Logos, Ethos, Pathos* ARGUMENT • Cubing

Exploratory Writing 263

Journaling, Blogging, or Microblogging • Writing an Exploratory Draft • Exploring with Presentation Software

Taking Time to Prewrite and Develop 266

Quick Start Guide 267

Talk About This • Try This Out • Write This 268

12 Organizing and Drafting 269

Using Genres to Organize Your Ideas 269

Drafting Introductions, Bodies, and Conclusions

Sketching an Outline 270

Creating a Basic Outline • Filling Out Your Outline

Drafting Through Writer's Block 272

Drafting (Almost) Every Day • Overcoming Writer's Block

Quick Start Guide 274

Talk About This • Try This Out • Write This 275

13 Choosing a Style 276

Writing in Plain Style 276

Guideline 1: Clarify What or Who the Sentence Is About • Guideline 2: Make the "Doer" the Subject of the Sentence • Guideline 3: Put the Subject Early in the Sentence • Guideline 4: State the Action in the Verb • Guideline 5: Reduce Nominalizations • Guideline 6: Boil Down the Prepositional Phrases • Guideline 7: Eliminate Redundancies • Guideline 8: Use Sentences That Are Breathing Length

Establishing Your Voice 281

Get into Character • Imitate Other Writers

Writing Descriptively with Tropes 282

Use Similes and Analogies • Use Metaphors • Use Onomatopoeia

Improving Your Writing Style 284

Quick Start Guide 285

Talk About This • Try This Out • Write This 286

14 Designing 287

Before You Begin Designing 287

Five Basic Principles of Design 288

Design Principle 1: Balance 288

Balancing a Page • Using Columns

Design Principle 2: Alignment 290

Design Principle 3: Grouping 291

Design Principle 4: Consistency   292

Choosing Typefaces • Using Headings Consistently

Design Principle 5: Contrast   294

Using Photography and Images   295

Downloading Photographs and Images from the Internet • Labelling a Photograph or Image

Using Graphs and Charts   296

Creating a Graph or Chart • Choosing the Appropriate Graph or Chart

Quick Start Guide   301

Talk About This • Try This Out • Write This   302

15 Revising and Editing   303

Level 1: Global Revision   304

Challenge Your Draft's Topic, Angle, and Purpose • Think About Your Readers (Again) and the Context

Level 2: Substantive Editing   309

Determine Whether You Have Enough Information (or Too Much) • Reorganize Your Work to Highlight Major Ideas • Look for Ways to Improve the Design • Ask Someone Else to Read Your Work

Level 3: Copyediting   313

Review Your Title and Headings • Edit Paragraphs to Make Them Concise and Consistent • Revise Sentences to Make Them Clearer • Revise Sentences to Make Them More Descriptive

Level 4: Proofreading   315

Read Your Writing Out Loud • Read Your Draft Backwards • Read a Hard Copy of Your Work • Know Your Grammatical Weaknesses • Use Your Spellchecker

Peer Review: Asking for Advice   316

Quick Start Guide   318

Talk About This • Try This Out • Write This   319

PART 4

Strategies for Shaping Ideas   320

16 Drafting Introductions and Conclusions   322

Drafting Introductions   322

Five Introductory Moves • Using a Grabber to Start Your Introduction • Using a Lead to Draw in the Readers • Using the State of Existing Research

Drafting Conclusions   326

Quick Start Guide   329

Talk About This • Try This Out • Write This   330

17 Developing Paragraphs and Sections   331

Creating a Basic Paragraph   332

Transition or Transitional Sentence (Optional) • Topic Sentence (Needed) • Support Sentences (Needed) • Point Sentence (Needed)

Getting Paragraphs to Flow (Cohesion)   335

Subject Alignment in Paragraphs • Given-New in Paragraphs

Deciding on Paragraph Length   337

Supersized Paragraphs • Rapid-Fire Paragraphs • Paragraph Length Variety

Organizing a Section   338

Opening, Body, Closing • Organizational Patterns for Sections • Using Headings in Sections

Using Sections and Paragraphs Together   339

Quick Start Guide   341

Talk About This • Try This Out • Write This   342

18 Using Basic Rhetorical Patterns   343

Narrative   343

Description   344

Describing with the Senses • Describing with Vocabulary and Rhetoric

Definition   346

Classification   348

Step One: List Everything That Fits into the Whole Class • Step Two: Decide on a Principle of Classification • Step Three: Sort into Major and Minor Groups

Cause and Effect   349

Comparison and Contrast   351

Combining Rhetorical Patterns   352

Quick Start Guide   354

Talk About This • Try This Out • Write This   355–356

19 Using Argumentative Strategies [ARGUMENT]   357

What Is Arguable?   358

Arguable Claims • Four Sources of Arguable Claims

Using Reason, Authority, and Emotion   361

Reason (*Logos*) • Authority (*Ethos*) • Emotion (*Pathos*)

Avoiding Argumentative Fallacies   365

Rebuttals and Refutations   367

Summarize Your Opponents' Position Objectively • Recognize When the Opposing Position May Be Valid • Concede Your Opponents' Minor Points • Refute or Absorb Your Opponents' Major Points • Quality Your Claims

Using an Argumentative Form   370

Classical Argument Form • Rogerian Form • The Toulmin Model

Quick Start Guide   374

Talk About This • Try This Out • Write This   375

20 Working Collaboratively with Other Writers   376

Working with a Group of Other Writers   377

Choosing Group Roles • Figuring Out What the Group Needs to Do • Getting the Work Done

Working with a Team   379

Forming: Planning a Project • Storming: Overcoming Differences • Norming: Getting Down to Work • Performing: Working as a Team

Quick Start Guide   383

Talk About This • Try This Out • Write This   384–385

PART 5

Doing Research   386

21 Starting Research   388

Starting Your Research Process   389

Step One: Define Your Research Question • Step Two: Develop a Working Thesis • Step Three: Devise a Research Plan

Doing Start-Up Research   392

Assessing a Source's Reliability   392

Is the Source Credible? • How Biased Are the Author and the Publisher? • How Biased Are You? • Is the Source Up to Date? • Can You Verify the Information in the Source?

Managing Your Research Process   394

Creating a Research Schedule • Starting Your Bibliography File

Following and Modifying Your Research Plan   395

When Things Don't Go as Expected

Quick Start Guide   396

Talk About This • Try This Out • Write This   397

22 Finding Sources and Collecting Information   398

Evaluating Sources with Triangulation   398

Using Primary and Secondary Sources   399

Finding Electronic and Online Sources   401

Using Internet Search Engines • Using the Internet Cautiously • Using Documentaries and Television/Radio Broadcasts • Using Wikis, Blogs, and Podcasts

Finding Print Sources   405

Locating Books at Your Library • Finding Articles at the Library

Using Empirical Sources 407
Interviewing People • Using an Informal Survey • Doing Field Observations
Developing an Annotated Bibliography 411
Quick Start Guide 413
Talk About This • Try This Out • Write This 414

23 Quoting, Paraphrasing, and Citing Sources 415

Common Knowledge: What You Don't Need to Cite 416
Quoting 416
Brief Quotations • Long Quotations
Paraphrasing and Summarizing 419
Paraphrasing • Summarizing
Framing Quotes, Paraphrases, and Summaries 422
Avoiding Plagiarism 424
Academic Dishonesty • Patchwriting • Ideas and Words Taken Without Attribution • The Real Problem with Plagiarism
Quick Start Guide 427
Talk About This • Try This Out • Write This 428

24 Using MLA Style 429

Parenthetical Citations 430
When the Author's Name Appears in the Sentence • Citing More Than One Source in the Same Sentence • Citing a Source Multiple Times • Other Parenthetical References

Preparing the List of Works Cited 432
Including More Than One Source from an Author • Formatting a List of Works Cited
Citing Sources in the List of Works Cited 436
MLA List of Works Cited • Citing Journals, Magazines, and Other Periodical Publications • Citing Books and Other Nonperiodical Publications • Citing Web Publications • Citing Other Kinds of Sources
A Student's MLA-Style Research Paper: Katelyn Turnbow, "Lives Not Worth the Money?" 446

25 Using APA Style 454

Parenthetical Citations 454
When the Author's Name Appears in the Sentence • Citing More Than One Source in the Same Sentence • Citing a Source Multiple Times • Other Parenthetical References
Preparing the List of References 457
Formatting a List of References in APA Style
Citing Sources in the List of References 460
APA List of References • Citing Journals, Magazines, and Other Periodical Publications • Citing Books and Other Nonperiodical Publications • Citing Web Publications • Citing Other Kinds of Sources
A Student's APA-Style Research Paper: Coralee Miller, "Is Organically Produced Food Better in Terms of Nutrition, Sensory Appeal, and Safety Than Conventionally Produced Food?" 468

PART 6

Getting Your Ideas Out There 478

26 Using the Internet 480

Is this Writing? 480
Creating a Social Networking Site 481
Choose the Best Site for You • Be Selective About Your "Friends" • Add Regularly to Your Profile
Starting Your Own Blog 482
Choose a Host Site for Your Blog • Begin Your Blog • Personalize Your Blog

Writing Articles for Wikis 484
Write the Article • Add Your Article to the Wiki
Putting Videos and Podcasts on the Internet 484
Create Your Video or Record Your Podcast • Edit Your Work • Upload Your Video or Podcast
Quick Start Guide 486
Talk About This • Try This Out • Write This 487

27 Creating a Portfolio   488

Two Basic Kinds of Portfolios   488
Getting Started on Your Portfolio   489
Step One: Collecting Your Work   490
   Archiving for a Specific Course • Archiving for Your Post-Secondary Career • Archiving for Your Professional Career
Step Two: Selecting the Best Artifacts   491
Step Three: Reflecting on Your Work   492
   Your Reflection as an Argument
Step Four: Presenting Your Materials   492
   Creating an E-Portfolio
Keeping Your Portfolio Up to Date   495
Quick Start Guide   496
Talk About This • Try This Out • Write This   497

28 Succeeding on Essay Exams   498

Preparing for an Essay Exam   498
   Work in Study Groups • Ask Your Professor About the Exam • Pay Attention to Themes • Create Your Own Questions and Rehearse Possible Answers
Starting Your Essay Exam   500
   Review the Exam Quickly to Gain an Overall Picture • Budget Your Time

Answering an Essay Exam Question   501
   Organize Your Answer
Finishing Your Essay Exam   502
One Student's Essay Exam   503
Quick Start Guide   507
Talk About This • Try This Out • Write This   508

29 Presenting Your Work   509

Getting Started   509
   Ask a Few Key Questions to Get Started • Choose the Appropriate Presentation Technology • Allot Your Time
Organizing Your Presentation's Content   512
   Introduction: Tell Them What You're Going to Tell Them • The Body of Your Talk: Tell Them • Conclusion: Tell Them What You Told Them • Question and Answer
Designing Your Visual Aids   515
   Format Your Slides
Delivering Your Presentation   516
   Body Language • Voice and Tone
Practising and Rehearsing   518
   Practise, Practise, Practise • Rehearse, Rehearse, Rehearse
Quick Start Guide   519
Talk About This • Try This Out • Write This   520–521

PART 7

Handbook   522

1 Sentences   524
2 Verbs   540
3 Pronouns   545

4 Style   550
5 Punctuation, Mechanics, and Spelling   554

Credits   571
Index   573

Thematic Contents

CONSUMER CULTURE

Liza Featherstone, "What's a Girl to Read?" POPULAR 103

Brian D. Johnson, "Bare-Knuckled Knockout" POPULAR 74

Kurosh Amoui Kalareh, "Watching Movies at Home or Going to the Cinema?" STUDENT 150

Anne Kingston, "Outraged Moms, Trashy Daughters: How Did Those Steeped in the Women's Lib Movement Produce Girls Who Think Being a Sex Object Is Powerful?" (excerpt) POPULAR 52

Z. Lawrie, E. A. Sullivan, P. S. W. Davies, and R. J. Hill, "Media Influence on the Body Image of Children and Adolescents" (excerpt) ACADEMIC 81

Coralee Miller, "Is Organically Produced Food Better in Terms of Nutrition, Sensory Appeal, and Safety Than Conventionally Produced Food?" STUDENT ACADEMIC 468

Sahil Sidhu, "Analysis of a Canadian Association of Petroleum Producers (CAPP) Advertisement" STUDENT ACADEMIC 87

Katelyn Turnbow, "Lives Not Worth the Money?" STUDENT ACADEMIC 446

ENVIRONMENT AND SUSTAINABILITY

Fahmida Ahmed, Jeff Brown, David Felix, Todd Haurin, and Betty Seto, "Changing the Campus Climate: Strategies to Reduce Greenhouse Gas Emissions at the University of California, Santa Barbara" STUDENT ACADEMIC 173

Coralee Miller, "Is Organically Produced Food Better in Terms of Nutrition, Sensory Appeal, and Safety Than Conventionally Produced Food?" STUDENT ACADEMIC 468

M. H. Saier Jr. and J. T. Trevors, "Tell the Awful Truth: It's Not Just Global Warming, It's Global Disaster!" ACADEMIC 203

Sahil Sidhu, "Analysis of a Canadian Association of Petroleum Producers (CAPP) Advertisement" STUDENT ACADEMIC 87

Russ Walker and David Roberts, "Letter to the Editor on Climate Story" POPULAR 165

GENDER ISSUES

Liza Featherstone, "What's a Girl to Read?" POPULAR 103

June Feder, Ronald F. Levant, and James Dean, "Boys and Violence: A Gender-Informed Analysis" ACADEMIC 239

Rebecca Gillespie, "Summary of 'Boys and Violence: A Gender-Informed Analysis'" STUDENT ACADEMIC 43

Brian D. Johnson, "Bare-Knuckled Knockout" POPULAR 74

James Kendrick, "The Many Shades of Red" ACADEMIC 76

Anne Kingston, "Outraged Moms, Trashy Daughters: How Did Those Steeped in the Women's Lib Movement Produce Girls Who Think Being a Sex Object Is Powerful?" (excerpt) POPULAR 52

Z. Lawrie, E. A. Sullivan, P. S. W. Davies, and R. J. Hill, "Media Influence on the Body Image of Children and Adolescents" (excerpt) ACADEMIC 81

Emily Martin, "The Egg and the Sperm: How Science Has Constructed a Romance Based on Stereotypical Male-Female Roles" (excerpt) ACADEMIC 106

MEDIA AND COMMUNICATION

Kate Dailey, "Friends with Benefits: Do *Facebook* Friends Provide the Same Support as Those in Real Life?" POPULAR 161

Liza Featherstone, "What's a Girl to Read?" POPULAR 103

Brian Johnson, "Bare-Knuckled Knockout" POPULAR 74

Kurosh Amoui Kalareh, "Double Googlization: A Review of *The Googlization of Everything (And Why We Should Worry)* by Siva Vaidhyanathan" STUDENT ACADEMIC 60

Kurosh Amoui Kalareh, "Watching Movies at Home or Going to the Cinema?" STUDENT 150

James Kendrick, "The Many Shades of Red" ACADEMIC 76

Anne Kingston, "Outraged Moms, Trashy Daughters: How Did Those Steeped in the Women's Lib Movement Produce Girls Who Think Being a Sex Object Is Powerful?" (excerpt) POPULAR 52

Z. Lawrie, E. A. Sullivan, P. S. W. Davies, and R. J. Hill, "Media Influence on the Body Image of Children and Adolescents" (excerpt) ACADEMIC 81

Piers Robinson, "The CNN Effect Revisited" ACADEMIC 233

Jordan Stouck and Cathi Shaw, "Summary of David Bartholomae's 'Inventing the University'" ACADEMIC 54

Holly Wylie, "The CNN Effect: How Media Can Influence Government Foreign Policy" STUDENT ACADEMIC 212

MIGRATION AND ETHNICITY

Jennifer Andrews and Priscilla L. Walton, "Rethinking Canadian and American Nationality: Indigeneity and the 49th Parallel in Thomas King" (excerpt) ACADEMIC 140

Max Doran, 'Border' Crossings in Thomas King's Narrative" STUDENT ACADEMIC 118

Thomas King, "Borders" CREATIVE 132

Derek Rasmussen, "Forty Years of Struggle and Still No Right to Inuit Education in Nunavut" (excerpt) ACADEMIC 195

Preface

The Canadian edition of *Writing Today* began with a few basic assumptions. First, we believe that students want to learn writing skills that will help them succeed in academic environments and subsequently in their careers. Second, students need a writing guide that presents relevant information clearly, simply, and in a way that is easy to reference. Third, writing instructors prefer teaching tools that are both practical and flexible, allowing them to adapt content to their own pedagogical approaches and teaching styles. And finally, both students and instructors need an approach that addresses writing in context, inviting students to compare and contrast academic and popular writing, and so better understand the particular requirements of each discourse.

To help students with the kinds of writing they do in their courses and in their lives outside of the classroom, *Writing Today* provides tools they can use to respond effectively to many different writing situations. This book teaches *genres* of writing (summaries, reviews, analyses, arguments, proposals, and research papers) and *strategies* for writing (causality, comparison, classification, definition, and argumentation) as well as *processes* for writing (planning, drafting, researching, and revising). It is designed to be a comprehensive text that includes thorough discussion and examples of current MLA and APA citation styles as well as a Handbook covering key grammatical concepts.

Writing Today is an easy-to-use book that addresses the way today's students read, learn, process, and disseminate information through media and technology. We believe they respond best to the interactive writing style of *Writing Today*: the instruction is brief and to the point; key concepts are immediately defined and reinforced; sections and paragraphs are short; important points are clearly labelled and supported by instructional visuals. This straightforward presentation of complex information creates a reading experience in which students can access information *when they are ready for it*.

This textbook, moreover, draws attention to the expectations for academic writing in Canadian universities and colleges. It teaches students the distinctions between popular and academic forms, and directly addresses ways in which students can transform the popular forms of argumentation, analysis, research, or evaluation with which they may be more familiar into styles appropriate for academic contexts.

The readings were selected and organized to offer content with Canadian references and interest points, as well as to address five themes: consumerism, environment and sustainability, gender, media and communication, and migration and ethnicity. This organization will allow instructors to create assignments more easily and students to explore these large topics from multiple perspectives and in relation to both academic and popular genres. The professional academic readings were selected for accessibility as well as content. As instructors, we believe that students in the first and second years of their post-secondary studies need to be exposed to professional academic essays, beginning with more accessible examples such as these, in order to meet the research requirements of more advanced courses.

We know from our own experiences as teachers and writing program administrators that pedagogical approaches and teaching styles vary—and that the best writing guides support a range of instructors. The variety of writing purposes (expressive, informative, persuasive, popular, and academic) and writing projects in *Writing Today* support a broad range of curricular goals. Writing instructors can choose the order in which they teach these chapters and combine them into units that fit their course designs. Custom versions can also support individual course designs.

We have found that writing instructors want to help students understand that genres are not rigid templates but are rather a set of versatile tools that guide every aspect of the writing process. In other words, instructors want students to develop *genre awareness* and *genre know-how*. We emphasize paying attention to how communities get things done with words and images. We also believe that people learn best by doing; therefore, we emphasize inquiry, practice, production, and active research. Students need to become versatile writers who can respond effectively to a changing world.

The approach we take in the book is informed by personal experience and by much of the best research done in the field of writing studies over the last twenty years. Surveys have found that when faculty assigned challenging and diverse writing assignments, students reported deeper learning, increased practical competence, and greater personal and social gains. The Canadian version of *Writing Today* is designed to facilitate these goals.

How This Book Is Organized

PART 1

Getting Started

Purposefully brief, the first three chapters are designed to inform students about genres and start them thinking about the different requirements of academic versus popular writing contexts. They introduce the five elements of rhetorical situations (topic, angle, purpose, readers, and context) and explain why and how using genres will help students to write successfully.

PART 2

Using Genres to Express Ideas

These chapters help students master seven commonly assigned kinds of writing that form the foundation of an adaptable portfolio of skills. Readings emphasize Canadian content and ways that both student and professional writers have used summary, review, analysis, argumentation, proposal, and research genres. These samples, along with the information presented in each chapter, will help students respond effectively to a majority of academic writing situations.

PART 3

Developing a Writing Process

Stand-alone chapters on planning, organization, style, design, and revision offer strategies students can apply to any writing situation. Instructors can assign them alongside the genre chapters.

PART 4

Strategies for Shaping Ideas

Straightforward chapters on drafting introductions and conclusions, developing paragraphs and sections, and incorporating rhetorical strategies (such as narration, classification, and comparison and contrast) provide resources for writing those sections of papers where students often find themselves stuck. A chapter on argument explores appeals and fallacies, and a chapter on collaboration helps students work effectively in groups.

PART 5

Doing Research

The ability to research effectively is critical to students' success in classes and in their careers. Students learn to engage in inquiry-driven research, evaluate sources, and work with sources by paraphrasing, quoting, and synthesizing. Up-to-date coverage of MLA and APA styles includes citation examples and model papers.

PART 6

Getting Your Ideas Out There

Today's students have more opportunities to present their work publicly than ever before. Students learn how to use social networking and other Web applications for rhetorical purposes. Students learn best practices for creating a portfolio of their work. Basics such as succeeding on essay exams and giving presentations are covered in depth as well.

PART 7

Handbook

Designed to be as accessible and usable as possible, the handbook gives students a quick resource for issues of grammar, usage, and punctuation. This handbook covers the core grammatical concepts relevant to most kinds of writing assignments and can be supplemented with instruction and exercises on MyCompLab.

Ways to Fit This Book to Your Teaching Approach

Flexibility is a chief strength of *Writing Today*. The first three chapters form a foundation, but remaining chapters can be taught in any order or combination to suit individual teaching approaches and objectives.

A Process Approach. A process-based approach can be particularly helpful to students in the early years of an undergraduate degree. The chapters in Part 2 tailor the writing process with strategies specific to informative, persuasive, analytical, and research genres. Part 3, "Developing a Writing Process," provides additional chapters on prewriting, drafting, designing, revising, and editing that can be assigned with any project.

A Genre-Based Approach. Genres help students better understand and respond to the expectations, audiences, and purposes of diverse writing situations. Yet genres aren't templates into which writers simply pour words: they are tools writers can use to help them develop ideas and plan, research and draft, design and edit. *Writing Today* covers summaries, reviews, analyses, arguments, proposals, and research formats that help students solve real problems and achieve specific goals.

A Purposes or Aims-Based Approach. Instructors who teach an aims approach to writing encourage students to be aware of their audience and purpose as they write to express, inform, analyze, or persuade. This approach works hand-in-hand with a genre-based approach: knowing the genre helps writers better understand a text's purpose, readers, and context.

A Strategies or Patterns-Based Approach. Instructors who teach rhetorical patterns (narrative, description, comparison and contrast, cause and effect, etc.) will find them embedded in this book. Part 4, "Strategies for Shaping Ideas," shows how strategies work with and within genres to help students organize and shape their ideas. *Writing Today* applies the strengths of a patterns-based approach to diverse writing situations.

An Academic Approach. Students learn the kinds of writing common in first-year curricula, such as summaries, rhetorical analyses, literary analyses, and argument essays. They also learn the foundations of advanced academic writing, such as proposals and research papers. Strategies for writing from sources—including paraphrasing, quoting, citing, and documenting sources—are covered in Part 5.

An Argument-Based Approach. *Writing Today* presents a rhetorical approach to writing. Several genres in Part 2, such as rhetorical analyses, position papers, and proposals, are purposefully designed to be argument-based, this content is labelled with ARGUMENT in the table of contents. Chapter 19 helps students determine what is arguable and anticipate opposing points of view while also explaining the classical appeals and argumentative fallacies.

An Integrated, Multimodal Approach. Instructors teaching multimodal composition courses know there are few writing guides that teach critical twenty-first century composing skills and even fewer that offer multimodal assignments. *Writing Today* assumes that students compose electronically and research online, and it offers strategies for writers to plan and collaborate online, create visual texts, create media projects, and post compositions to the Web.

Distance Learning and Online Teaching. *Writing Today* was designed to be easily adaptable to online and hybrid learning environments. The book's comprehensiveness and flexibility provide strong scaffolding on which distance learning, online, and hybrid courses can be developed. Its highly accessible design allows students to quickly find the information they need while learning on their own and composing at their computers. MyCompLab provides an eText version of the book and additional writing, research, and grammar resources.

Features of This Book

Interactive writing style. Instruction is brief and to the point. Key concepts are immediately defined and reinforced. Paragraphs are short and introduced by heads that preview content. This interactive style helps students locate information, ask questions, and access concepts when they are ready for them—putting students in control of their learning.

At-a-Glance. Each Part 2 chapter opens with a diagram that shows one or two common ways to organize a genre's key elements, giving an immediate and visual orientation to the genre. Students learn to adapt this organization to suit their rhetorical situation as they read the chapter.

End-of-Chapter Activities. Exercises conclude every chapter in the book to help students understand and practise concepts and strategies.

- **Talk About This** questions prompt classroom discussion.
- **Try This Out** exercises suggest informal writing activities students can complete in class or as homework.
- **Write This** prompts facilitate longer, formal writing assignments.

One Student's Work. A student-written example in each writing project chapter shows the kinds of issues students might explore in a specific genre of writing as well as the angles they might take. Annotations highlight the writer's key rhetorical decisions so the reading can be used either for discussion or as a model.

Features of This Book

Applying the Genre. In Part 2, some chapters include examples of how writers apply features of major genres to specific academic situations. For example, Chapter 5 on reviews applies the elements of summary and evaluation to a specific academic format, the literature review; in Chapter 10, the annotated bibliography is discussed as a potential component of a research paper.

Quick Start Guide. This practical review includes action steps and appears in each chapter to get students writing quickly. Students spend less time reading about writing and more time working on their own compositions. They can also use the Quick Start Guide as a quick way to gain familiarity with a genre before reading the chapter.

Readings and Prompts. Two to three professional readings in each chapter of Part 2 offer models of each genre. Annotations identify the key moves in each reading for better student comprehension. Question sets after each reading encourage critical engagement.

- **A Closer Look** questions facilitate analytical reading.
- **Ideas for Writing** questions prompt responses, analyses, and different genres of writing.

MyCompLab

MyCompLab Icons. Icons in the text margins direct students to related material within MyCompLab:

Explore icons link to writing samples.

Watch icons link to video simulations and animated lessons.

Listen icons link to instruction and practice questions that can be downloaded and listened to on an MP3 player.

Instructor Supplements

Instructor's Manual. The Instructor's Manual offers teaching strategies and support for each chapter in the book, including support for teaching the readings, and additional resources. The manual is available for download from a password-protected section of Pearson Education Canada's online catalogue (www.pearsoncanada.ca). Navigate to your book's catalogue page to view a list of those supplements that are available. See your local sales representative for details and access.

MyCompLab

The moment you know. Educators know it. Students know it. It's that inspired moment when something that was difficult to understand suddenly makes perfect sense. Our MyLab products have been designed and refined with a single purpose in mind—to help educators create that moment of understanding with their students.

MyCompLab delivers **proven results** in helping individual students succeed. It provides **engaging experiences** that personalize, stimulate, and measure learning for each student. And, it comes from a **trusted partner** with educational expertise and an eye on the future.

MyCompLab can be used by itself or linked to any learning management system. To learn more about how MyCompLab combines proven learning applications with powerful assessment, visit www.mycomplab.com

MyCompLab—the moment you know.

CourseSmart for Instructors. CourseSmart goes beyond traditional expectations—providing instant, online access to the textbooks and course materials you need at a lower cost for students. And even as students save money, you can save time and hassle with a digital eTextbook that allows you to search for the most relevant content at the very moment you need it. Whether it's evaluating textbooks or creating lecture notes to help students with difficult concepts, CourseSmart can make life a little easier. See how when you visit **www.coursesmart.com/instructors.**

Technology Specialists. Pearson's Technology Specialists work with faculty and campus course designers to ensure that Pearson technology products, assessment tools, and online course materials are tailored to meet your specific needs. This highly qualified team is dedicated to helping schools take full advantage of a wide range of educational resources by assisting in the integration of a variety of instructional materials and media formats. Your local Pearson Canada sales representative can provide you with more details on this service program.

Pearson Custom Library. For enrollments of at least 25 students, you can create your own textbook by choosing the chapters that best suit your own course needs. To begin building your custom text, visit **www.pearsoncustomlibrary.com**. You may also work with a dedicated Pearson custom editor to create your ideal text—publishing your own original content or mixing and matching Pearson content. Contact your local Pearson representative to get started.

Student Supplements

MyCompLab. Visit **www.mycomplab.com** to access diverse resources for composition in one easy-to-use place:

- Sections on **writing**, **research**, and **grammar** cover all the key topics in the text, providing additional instruction, examples, and practice. **Exercises** offer the opportunity to practise the skills learned in class and include both self-grading quizzes and writing activities. **Writing samples** provide examples of different types of writing and different documentation styles; some are annotated to highlight key aspects or to stimulate reflection and discussion. **Videos** illustrate aspects of the writing process through scenarios, or provide grammar and editing tutorials through onscreen revision.

- **Pearson eText** gives you access to the text whenever and wherever you have access to the internet. eText pages look exactly like the printed text, offering powerful new functionality for students and instructors. Users can create notes, highlight text in different colours, create bookmarks, zoom, click hyperlinked words and phrases to view definitions, and view in single page or two page view. Pearson eText allows for quick navigation to key parts of the eText using a table of contents and provides full-text search. Icons in the eText are hotlinked to related material within MyCompLab:

Explore icons link to writing samples.
Watch icons link to video simulations and animated lessons.
Listen icons link to instruction and practice questions that can be downloaded and listened to on an MP3 player.

- An online **composing** space includes tools such as writing tips and editing FAQs, so you can get the help you need when you need it, without ever leaving the writing environment. Within this space, you'll find access to **EBSCO's ContentSelect**, a database of articles from academic journals that can be used for research and reference.

- The **portfolio** feature allows you to create an e-portfolio of your work that you can easily share with your instructor and peers. Use the access code packaged with new copies of this textbook to log on to MyCompLab, or purchase separate access through your campus bookstore or directly through the website.

A student access card for MyCompLab is packaged with every new copy of the text. Access codes can also be purchased through campus bookstores or at **www.mycomplab.com**

Study on the Go. Featured at the end of each chapter, you will find a unique QR code providing access to Study on the Go, an unprecedented mobile integration between text and online content. Students link to Pearson's unique Study on the Go content directly from their smartphones, allowing them to study whenever and wherever they wish! Go to one of the sites below to see how you can download an app to your smartphone for free. Once the app is installed, scan the code with your phone and link to Pearson's Study on the Go website, which includes Quizzes, Glossary Flashcards, and Videos, and which can be accessed at any time.

ScanLife
http://getscanlife.com/

NeoReader
http://get.neoreader.com/

QuickMark
http://www.quickmark.com.tw/

CourseSmart for Students. CourseSmart goes beyond traditional expectations—providing instant, online access to the textbooks and course materials you need at an average savings of 60%. With instant access from any computer and the ability to search your text, you'll find the content you need quickly, no matter where you are. And with online tools like highlighting and note-taking, you can save time and study efficiently. See all the benefits at **www.coursesmart.com/students.**

Acknowledgments

Of course, a book like this one is never the work of one or two people, even though our names appear on the cover. We would like to thank our editors, Lauren Finn, Meg Botteon, and Joe Opiela, for their great ideas and persistence. We would also like to thank our colleagues, Scott Sanders, Susan Romano, Wanda Martin, Michelle Kells, Karen Olson, David Blakesley, Irwin Weiser, and Shirley Rose, for their feedback on our ideas. We also want to thank our students, especially our graduate students, for trying out some of these materials in their classes and helping us refine the ideas and approaches in this book. Mark Pepper, Danielle Cordaro, Leigh Johnson, and Katie Denton were very helpful with choosing readings and finding student texts to include as examples. We are appreciative of our thoughtful and enthusiastic reviewers, whose feedback over years of writing helped us articulate, shape, and sharpen our vision.

And finally, we would like to thank our families for their patience and support while we worked on this project. Thank you, Susan, Kellen, Dana, Tracey, Emily, and Collin.

Richard Johnson-Sheehan
Charles Paine

We would like to thank our editors and project managers—David Le Gallais, Suzanne Schaan, and Marissa Lok at Pearson Canada, as well as Katie Monrea'L and Carolyn Zapf—for their guidance and helpful advice. We would also like to thank our colleagues, Laura Patterson, Allison Hargreaves, Melissa Jacques, and especially Janet Giltrow, for their suggestions and inspiration.

We thank our students in first- and second-year courses at the University of British Columbia, whose willingness to test out these readings and generosity in offering their work for publication have been invaluable. We would like to thank in particular our graduate teaching and research assistants, whose work has enabled us to further clarify these approaches and collect student writing samples. We would like to express our appreciation to our families, whose patience made this adaptation possible. Finally, we are indebted to our reviewers, whose feedback helped us focus and improve the Canadian edition:

Geraldine Arbach, University of Ottawa
Timothy Chamberlain, Camosun College
Jill Goldberg, Langara College
Elizabeth Gooding, Kwantlen Polytechnic University
Brigid Kelso, George Brown College
Marie H. Loughlin, University of British Columbia Okanagan Campus
Rachel Mines, Langara College
Paul Ohler, Kwantlen Polytechnic University
Jennifer Payson, University of British Columbia Okanagan Campus
Jillian Skeffington, Grant MacEwan University
Dat Tran, University of Ottawa
David West, Douglas College
Sarah Whyte, University of Waterloo
Trisha Yeo, George Brown College
— and others who choose to remain anonymous.

Cathi Shaw
Jordan Stouck

About the Authors

Richard Johnson-Sheehan is a Professor of Rhetoric and Composition at Purdue University. At Purdue, he has directed the Introductory Composition program, and he has mentored new teachers of composition for many years. He teaches a variety of courses in composition, professional writing, and writing program administration, as well as classical rhetoric and the rhetoric of science. He has published widely in these areas. His prior books on writing include *Technical Communication Today,* now in its fourth edition, and *Writing Proposals,* now in its second edition. Professor Johnson-Sheehan was awarded 2008 Fellow of the Association of Teachers of Technical Writing and has been an officer in the Council for Writing Program Administrators.

Charles Paine is a Professor of English at the University of New Mexico, where he teaches undergraduate courses in first-year, intermediate, and professional writing as well as graduate courses in writing pedagogy, the history of rhetoric and composition, and other areas. At UNM, he directed the Rhetoric and Writing Program and the First-Year Writing Program. He is an active member of the Council of Writing Program Administrators and currently serves on its Executive Board. He cofounded and coordinates the Consortium for the Study of Writing in College, a joint effort of the National Survey of Student Engagement and the Council of Writing Program Administrators. The Consortium conducts general research into the ways that undergraduate writing can lead to enhanced learning, engagement, and other gains related to student success.

Cathi Shaw is a faculty member in the Departments of Communications and English at Okanagan College. Over the last ten years, she has taught technical, professional, and academic writing at Simon Fraser University, the University of British Columbia, and Okanagan College. Her research focus is on the development of voice and critical thinking in university and college student writers. She is a member of the Canadian Association for the Study of Discourse and Writing and the Canadian Authors Association.

Jordan Stouck is an Instructor of Composition at the University of British Columbia Okanagan Campus. She has taught composition for the past decade at both UBC and the University of Lethbridge, and in 2007–2008 coordinated the University of Lethbridge's Academic Writing Program. Her publications and presentations have focused on how discourse and language are context-driven. She is an active member of the Canadian Association for the Study of Discourse and Writing and of the Modern Languages Association.

Writing Today

CANADIAN EDITION

1 Getting Started

PART OUTLINE

CHAPTER 1
Writing and Genres   4

CHAPTER 2
Topic, Angle, Purpose   16

CHAPTER 3
Readers, Contexts, and Rhetorical Situations   26

Sometimes the hardest part about writing is **GETTING STARTED.** *In these chapters, you will learn strategies for discovering a topic, identifying your purpose, profiling your readers, and adapting to your context.*

1

Writing and Genres

In this chapter, you will learn how to:

- use genres to communicate with readers.
- begin to distinguish between popular and academic forms of writing.
- use "genre know-how" to become a versatile writer in post-secondary studies and in the workplace.
- develop a writing process that will help you write efficiently and effectively.

Writing gives you the power to get things done with words and images. It allows you to respond successfully to the events and people around you, whether you are trying to improve your community, write an academic essay, pitch a new idea at work, or just text with your friends.

The emergence of new writing situations—new places for writing, new readers, and new media—means writing today involves more than just getting words and images onto a page or screen. Writers need to handle a wide variety of situations with diverse groups of people and multiple technologies. Learning to navigate among these complex situations is the real challenge of writing in today's world.

What Are Genres?

In this book, you will learn how to use writing *genres* to interpret these complex situations and respond to them successfully. Defining the word *genre* is difficult. Mistakenly, genres are sometimes defined by their structure alone (e.g., "A report has five parts: introduction, methods, results, discussion, and conclusion"). But this understanding of genre is a bit misleading. Genres are not fixed or rigid patterns to be followed mechanically. They are not forms into which we insert sentences and paragraphs.

Genres are ways of writing and speaking that help people interact and work together. In other words, genres reflect the things people do, and they are always evolving because human activities change over time to suit new social situations and new challenges. Genres *do* offer somewhat stable patterns for responding to typical situations. More importantly, though, they reflect how people act, react, and interact in these situations. Genres are meeting places—and *meaning* places.

In university and college, you will need to master and write in a variety of genres that help you to achieve different kinds of goals. This book will help you develop this "genre know-how," which you can use to strengthen your writing in post-secondary courses and in your career. You will also master a useful "genre set" that will allow you to respond successfully to a variety of important situations.

With this book, you will learn how to recognize and adapt genres for your own needs. You will become a more agile writer with a greater awareness of the differences among readers and contexts. You will become more proficient at analyzing specific writing situations and at adapting your writing to them. In particular, this text invites you to compare and contrast popular genres, written for general audiences, with academic genres, written for fellow post-secondary researchers and professors. This kind of comparison and contrast will help you better define the purposes, audiences, and contexts for each writing situation.

Using Genres to Write Successfully

For writers, genres offer flexible approaches to writing that reflect how people in communities interact with each other. They provide strategies for analyzing and interpreting what is happening around you. Once you understand your current situation, you can then use genres to focus your creativity, generate new ideas, and present those ideas to others. You can use words and images to mould reality to your advantage.

Readers use genres, too. They use them as guideposts to orient themselves to a text, helping them to anticipate what they are likely to find in the document and how they can use the information in it. Readers are never passive spectators. They bring specific expectations with them and they respond to your writing, in part, according to those expectations. As a writer, when you understand what your readers expect to find, you can make strategic choices about what information you will include and how you will present your ideas. Knowing what your readers expect of a particular genre gives you insight about how to compose your text. It gives you power.

Writing with Genres

As a writer, you can use a genre to help you make sense of a complex situation, develop your ideas, and write a text that achieves your purpose and meets the expectations of your readers. Here are the most important things to remember about genres:

Genres Are Flexible. It is helpful to identify the common features of each genre so you can use it to help you interpret and write, but keep in mind that genres reflect human activities. As a result, genres should be viewed as potentially flexible and adaptable to the evolving reality around you.

Genres Adjust to Fit Various Situations. When the audience or context changes, a genre needs to be adjusted to suit the new situation. An argument that worked previously with some readers or in a particular context might not work with different readers or in another context. If you decide to go against your readers' expectations, do so consciously and for a specific purpose.

Genres Suit Various Fields. Each discipline adapts common genres to its own needs and purposes. A report written by a biologist, for example, will share many characteristics with a report written by a manager at a corporation, but there will also be notable differences in the content, organization, style, and design of the text.

Genres Shape Situations and Readers. When you choose a particular genre, you are deciding what kinds of issues will be highlighted and what role your readers will play. For instance, readers know that when they encounter a short story (a type of literary genre), they should read thoroughly and follow the story line. Quite differently, when readers encounter a proposal, they assume they can "raid" the text for the specific information they need; that is, they can follow headings and read for the key ideas.

Genres in Movies

Most forms of entertainment are categorized by genre so that audiences can easily locate the kinds of works they are interested in. Music, for example, includes genres like hip hop, rap, country, classical, blues, folk, and rock. Television includes genres like news, sports, sitcoms, reality shows, dramas, and soap operas. To more fully illustrate how genres work, let's take a look at how they function in the movie industry. Movies can be sorted by the genres that were used to make them (Figure 1.1). Movie genres include romantic comedies, action films, documentaries, murder mysteries, musicals, science fiction and fantasy, horror, thrillers, and others. These genres aren't formulas that the writers and directors must follow. Instead, they are familiar patterns that audiences will recognize and understand.

Once the audience recognizes the genre of the movie, they form specific expectations about what kinds of things they will—and will not—experience. For example, a romantic comedy usually explores the amusing awkwardness and pratfalls of a new relationship. Two people meet and feel an attraction to each other. But then, events beyond their control keep them apart and cause humorous misunderstandings. Eventually, the two star-crossed lovers realize they truly do love each other and find a way at the end of the movie to be together.

Directors of successful romantic comedies use the boundaries and conventions of this genre to help them work creatively and produce something that is both recognizable and new. Genres aid the director's creativity by providing guidelines about how the movie should be structured, scripted, visually designed, musically scored, and even edited. Genres also constrain movies by helping directors determine what is "in bounds" and what is "out of bounds." Good directors work creatively within a genre to create something original.

Movies that flop often don't follow a recognizable genre or—even worse—formulaically follow a common genre in a trite way. A movie that strictly uses a genre

FIGURE 1.1 Movie Genres

Usually, moviegoers recognize the genre of a movie even before they step into the theatre. Movie studios use posters and previews to help audiences know what to expect and how to interpret the movie.

formulaically feels painfully predictable and shallow. The people in the audience get bored and tune out when they realize that the movie is mechanically following a genre in a predictable way.

Like successful movie directors, effective writers need to fully understand the genres they are using. Genres help writers figure out where to start and how to proceed. They allow writers to create something fresh and new, while also helping them to organize and control their message in a way that readers will recognize and comprehend. In this sense, good writers (like good movie directors) are always balancing the old, familiar, and stable with the new, creative, and dynamic.

Genres in Writing

Like movies, different kinds of writing have different generic conventions and expectations. A recipe, for instance, needs to give a full list of ingredients, give instructions on how to make the dish, and do so in an ordered and concise way. A recipe, in other words, is a genre. To write successfully in that genre, one must fulfill its basic expectations. If a writer does not write a recipe in an ordered, step-by-step fashion, as sometimes happens, then the reader will likely end up confused and perhaps with a poorly cooked dish. The reader is unlikely to follow other recipes or buy other cookbooks by that writer because the reader's expectations have not been met. On the other hand, if the recipe is nicely organized with clear steps leading to a tasty result, then the reader is likely to fol-low other recipes by that writer because the genre has been used successfully.

In this textbook we discuss academic or research genres in some depth, because those are the genres you are expected to use in post-secondary studies. We realize, however, that you are still becoming familiar with academic genres and, when not doing coursework, probably read popular genres, such as magazines or newspapers, for entertainment or general information. Since comparison is a good way to distin-guish between popular and academic genres, we offer a number of comparative examples throughout this book, showing for instance a popular movie review along with an academic book review in Chapter 5. Here is an example of an introduction from a popular magazine article on advertising followed by an introduction from an academic journal article, also on advertising:

> Blonder hair, faster cars, newer and cooler video games. Why is it that the same things that tantalize a consumer in San Francisco, California, are also what those in Sao Paulo or Singapore aspire to? The answer is in advertising: instead of catering to the cultures that it targets, advertisers are shaping the minds of global consumers to think like a North American consumer.
>
> —Lynne Ciochetto, "The Meme Machine," *Adbusters*
> Sept.-Oct. 2006

> Many anthropologists argue that popular culture is not an appropriate domain of study as what is being studied is not society but the international culture (Powers). The postmodern thesis holds that the economic realm has bled into the cultural (D. Harvey; Jameson). Products of all kinds (including advertising) are thus standardized in order to produce a homogenized, decontextualized, mish-mash of popular culture. This perspective holds that it is not possible to study a mass culture artifact, such as advertising, because the artifact has been "spoiled" by foreign influences. This standpoint, how-ever, neglects the role of national cultures in resisting globalization through a process of assimilating and appropriating meanings. Foreign cultures are quite capable of being imported into and being remade in a given national culture. There is little literature, however, that addresses how global adver-tising works in the context of transnational symbols and popular culture. This article attempts to explicate a process by which global advertisers use cultural metaphors and symbols from a cultural tool kit to promote new con-sumption habits for globally available consumer goods.
>
> —Noel M. Murray, "Pepsiman! Toward a Theory of Symbolic Morphosis in Global Advertising," *Journal of Popular Culture* 39.6 (2006): 1077-92

Looking at these excerpts, you can see that the academic piece is longer and more detailed than the popular piece. The academic piece uses sophisticated and techni-cal wording, while the popular piece is easier to read. The academic piece is scrupu-lous in citing its sources, while the popular piece does not include any sourced material. The academic genre carries expectations for detail, formality, and accuracy, while the popular genre is expected to be easily understood by a general audience and to provide information that will satisfy the less rigorous needs of everyday readers. Both of these excerpts effectively fulfill the genres in which they are written, but the genres themselves are quite different. As we progress through the following chapters, we will keep in mind and continue to explore the distinctions between academic and popular genres of writing. We will also discuss a variety of written genres that you may be asked to use in educational and professional settings.

Genre and the Writing Process

So, how can genres help you write better? Think of something you already do well. Perhaps you are a good swimmer or a solid basketball player. Maybe you are a great video game player. Do you play the guitar, or do you like to make pottery? Have you learned a martial art? Do you like to do yoga?

To do something well, you first needed to learn the *process* for doing it. Someone else, perhaps a teacher, coach, parent, or friend, showed you the process and helped you get better at it (Figure 1.2). Then, once you knew that process, you worked on improving and refining your skills. You gained confidence. Before long, you developed the "know-how" for that activity—not just the skill to do it, but also an ability to be innovative and original. When you reached this point, you could then start being creative and trying out new ideas.

Writing is similar to the other things you enjoy doing. To write well, you first need to develop your own writing process. Strong writers aren't born with a special gift,

FIGURE 1.2 Learning to Do Something Involves Learning a Process

In order to do something you enjoy, you first had to learn a step-by-step process for doing it. Once you mastered the process and it became second nature, you could make it yours by refining and adapting it.

and they aren't necessarily smarter than anyone else. Strong writers have simply learned and mastered a reliable writing process that allows them to generate new ideas and shape those ideas into something readers will find interesting and useful. Strong writers are also aware of the context they write in and of the expectations their readers hold.

Using a Writing Process

A writing process is a series of steps that leads you from your basic idea to a finished document. Over time, you will develop your own unique writing process, but the following six steps work well as a starting place:

Analyze the rhetorical situation. Identify the genre you are being asked to use or the genre that fits the needs of your project. Then define your topic, state your purpose, and analyze your readers and the contexts in which your text will be read or used.

Develop your ideas. Use inquiry and research to generate your own ideas and discover what others already know about your topic.

Organize and draft your paper. Arrange and compose your ideas into familiar patterns that your readers will recognize and find useful.

Choose an appropriate style. Use techniques of plain and persuasive style to clarify your writing and make it more compelling.

Design your document. Develop an appropriate page layout and use visuals to make your ideas more accessible and attractive to readers.

Revise and edit your work. Improve your writing by rewriting, reorganizing, editing, and proofreading your work.

Experienced writers tend to handle each of these steps separately, but a writing process shouldn't be followed mechanically from one step to the next. Instead, experienced writers tend to move around among these steps as needed (Figure 1.3). For instance, while drafting your paper, you may find you need to develop more content. Or, while revising, you may decide that you need to rethink the style of the text.

Why bother with a writing process at all? Can't you just write the paper? Truth is, as projects grow more complex and important, you need to give yourself time to generate and refine your ideas. A reliable writing process helps you do things one step at a time. In the long run, following a writing process will save you time and will help you to write something that is more relevant and interesting to your readers.

Watch
Genre

Using Genre as a Guiding Concept

The genre you are using should influence each stage of your writing process, as shown in Figure 1.3. The genre will help you make decisions about the content of your paper, how your paper should be organized, what style would be appropriate,

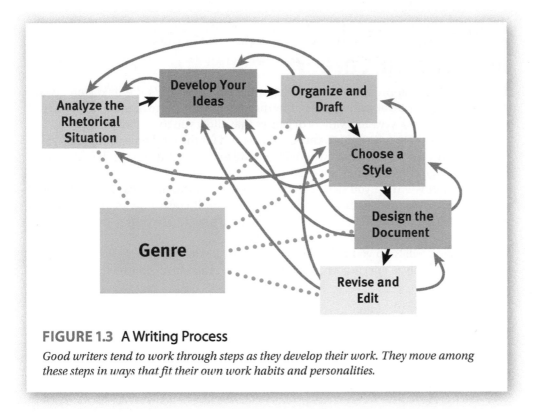

FIGURE 1.3 A Writing Process

Good writers tend to work through steps as they develop their work. They move among these steps in ways that fit their own work habits and personalities.

and what kind of design would work best. Then, as you revise and edit your paper, you can use the genre to guide any changes to the text. As you write, keep the genre you are following in mind. Use the genre as a source for creativity.

For example, if you are writing a movie review, the "review genre" (discussed in Chapter 5, "Reviews") will help you make decisions about what kinds of information your readers will expect. Should you tell them the plot of the movie? Should you describe the characters? Should you give away the ending? The genre will provide you with a model organization, so you can arrange your ideas in a pattern that your readers will expect. The genre also helps you to make informed decisions about what kind of style and design would work.

The purpose of a genre is to help you figure out how people tend to act, react, and interact in the situation in which you are writing. So if you tell your readers you are giving them a "movie review," they will have some expectations about the content, organization, style, and design of that text. If you meet those expectations, they will probably find the review useful and easy to read. If you bend those expectations, they might find your review creative or unique. However, if you completely violate their expectations for a movie review, your readers will likely be confused or frustrated with your work.

Using Genres in Your Education and in Your Career

This genre-based approach to writing might be new to you. It's the next step toward developing higher-level writing skills. Now that you are in college or university, you will need to master and write in a variety of genres that allow you to achieve new goals. You need to learn how to write for advanced courses and for the workplace situations you'll encounter in your future career, where the ability to incorporate research and specialized knowledge is increasingly important.

This book will help you develop genre know-how, the practical knowledge and skill to write effectively with research genres. You will learn how to recognize and adapt genres for your own needs, and you will learn how to use your genre know-how to adjust to unique situations and specific readers.

This book will help you to become a versatile, flexible, and agile writer. You will learn how to analyze specific writing situations and then take action with words and images.

At the end of each chapter in this book, you will find something called the "Quick Start Guide." The purpose of the Quick Start Guides is to help you get up and running as soon as possible. You can use these guides for review or to preview the essential information in the chapter. Here is the essential information in this chapter.

KNOW What a Genre Is

Genres are ways of writing and speaking that help people communicate and work together in specific situations. Genres offer relatively stable patterns for writing, but more importantly, they reflect how humans act, react, and interact in everyday situations. Genres are meeting places—and *meaning* places.

GET Some "Genre Know-How"

Genre know-how is the ability to use genres to analyze and interpret what is happening around you. When you have genre know-how, you can use genres to focus your creativity, generate new ideas, and present those ideas to others.

KEEP in Mind That Genres Are Flexible

Genres may need to be adjusted to suit evolving situations. They can be stretched and messed around with, to a degree.

DEVELOP Your Writing Process

A writing process is a series of steps that leads you from your basic idea to a finished document. Developing and refining your writing process will save you time and effort in the long run.

USE Genres in Your Education and in Your Career

A genre-based approach to writing helps you master a "genre set" that can be used in advanced post-secondary courses and in the workplace. The genre set taught in this book will cover most of the texts you will write in college or university and in your career.

1. In a group, first ask each person to talk briefly about his or her favourite movie genre; then, as a group, choose one of those genres to discuss. Describe the genre and its characteristics: What do all or most movies in this genre include? What kinds of characters do they have? What happens in them? Then talk about some of the best and worst movies that fit the genre. What do the best movies do well? Why do the worst movies fail?

2. Go to the periodicals section of your institution's library and find an example of an academic journal. Brainstorm about its qualities. What does it look like? How does it differ from a regular magazine? How long are the articles? Are there any advertisements? Who wrote the articles? What kinds of titles do they have? How were the articles accepted for publication? Then look at an article in more depth. What kind of wording does it use? Does the author cite sources? Who do you think was the intended audience? Why do you think the article was written? What does it tell you about the expectations for academic writing?

   If you are unable to view a hard copy of an academic journal, go online to your library's databases and call up an academic journal article. What does it look like and how does it differ from an online magazine or newspaper article? How long is the article and who wrote it? How did it get published? What kinds of wordings and citations does it use? Who do you think was the intended audience? Why do you think the article was written? What does it tell you about the expectations for academic writing?

3. With your group, brainstorm and list all the restaurant genres you can think of. Then choose one restaurant genre to explore further. (For instance, one restaurant genre might be the coffee shop, which could include Starbucks, Tim Hortons, and a variety of local coffee shops.) Describe the characteristics that all or most of the restaurants in the genre share. What guideposts signal to customers what kind of restaurant they are in? How are restaurant customers expected to behave, and how do the restaurants' characteristics encourage or require such behaviours?

1. On the Internet, find a webpage or website that conforms to a familiar website genre. For your professor (who may not know about this genre), write a one page document that describes the website and explains the genre and how it works (how people use websites like this one, the genre's general features, how and why writers create texts in that genre, how and why readers come to such texts). You should also explain whether you think the website uses the genre properly and highlight any places where you think it could be improved by using the genre better.

2. When a movie uses the well-known features of a genre to make fun of that genre, it's called a parody. For instance, the *Scary Movie* movies are parodies of horror films. *Get Smart* is a parody of spy movies. Think of other parodies that use a genre in order to poke fun at it. For your professor or your group, write a one page description of a movie that parodies a particular genre, the genre it makes fun of, and the features of genre that are specifically targeted by the parody.

3. Consider a kind of writing activity that you do frequently and are good at. It might be texting your friends, e-mailing people, working on a social networking profile, writing college or university application essays, or composing the five paragraph essay. Write informally about the features of this writing and how those features affect the people who use this kind of writing (both writers and readers). Describe the setting of such writing (where it occurs and in what medium). Finally, describe the writing itself: What kind of content is typical, how is that content organized, what kind of language is used? In what ways does the genre determine who the participants can and cannot be?

4. Imagine that you have been asked to direct a movie that crosses two very different genres. For example, you might be asked to tell a horror story as a romantic comedy, or you might be asked to convert a historical documentary into an action movie. In a one page paper written for your professor, explain how this merging of genres might offer some creative opportunities. What kinds of problems would it cause? Do you know of any movies that do this kind of genre bending or genre merging? Are these movies successful, and do you find them entertaining?

1. **Describe a genre.** Find a longer nonfiction document that seems to be using a specific genre. Write a three page analysis in which you describe the document's content, organization, style, and design. Then explain how its genre highlights certain kinds of information and ignores other kinds of information. Show how the style and design of the document is well suited (or ill suited) for the intended readers.

2. **Review a movie for a website or blog.** Write a three page review of a movie you saw recently for a blog or movie review website. In your review, identify the genre of the movie and the common characteristics of that genre. Then show your readers how the movie exhibited those characteristics. Toward the end of your review, tell your readers whether you thought the movie was good or not by discussing how well it worked within its genre. Compare it to other successful movies in that genre. See Chapter 5 for more information on reviews.

CHAPTER 2

Topic, Angle, Purpose

In this chapter, you will learn how to:

- develop and narrow your topic to respond to any writing situation.
- develop your angle, the unique perspective you'll bring to the topic.
- identify your purpose (what you want to accomplish).
- use your identified purpose to develop a thesis statement (or main point).
- identify the most appropriate genre for the writing task at hand.

Imagine that one of your professors has given you a new writing assignment. What should you do first? Of course, you should read the assignment closely. Take a deep breath. Then ask yourself a few specific questions about what you are being asked to do:

What am I being asked to write about? (Topic)

What is new or has changed recently about this topic? (Angle)

What exactly is the assignment asking me to do or accomplish? (Purpose)

Who will read this document and what do they expect? (Readers)

Where and when will they be reading this document? (Context)

These kinds of questions are also helpful in the workplace. When you are writing something for a client or your supervisor, you can use these five questions to help you figure out what you need to accomplish.

These questions are the basic elements of what we will be calling the "rhetorical situation" throughout this book (Figure 2.1). Before you start writing any text, you should first gain an understanding of your rhetorical situation: topic, angle, purpose, readers, and context. In this chapter, we will discuss the first three of these elements. Then, in Chapter 3, "Readers, Contexts, and Rhetorical Situations," we will discuss techniques and strategies for profiling your readers and anticipating the contexts in which they will experience your document.

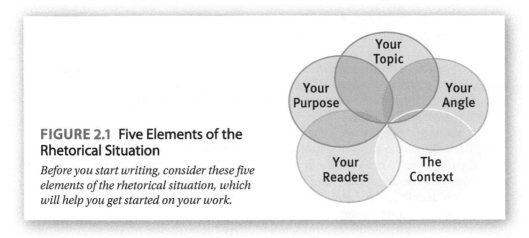

FIGURE 2.1 Five Elements of the Rhetorical Situation

Before you start writing, consider these five elements of the rhetorical situation, which will help you get started on your work.

Gaining a clear understanding of your topic, angle, and purpose will help you decide which genre is most appropriate for your writing project.

Topic: What Am I Writing About?

In university and college, either the topics for your papers will be assigned or you will be asked to come up with your own topics to write about. When your professor supplies the topic, he or she might say something like this:

> For this paper, I want you to write about the Constitution Act of 1982.

> Shakespeare's *King Lear* is often held up as a masterpiece of Renaissance tragedy. We will explore why this play is still popular today.

> Our next subject will be "mating and dating" in college, and we will be using our own campus for field research.

If your professor does not supply a topic, you will need to decide for yourself what you are writing about. In these cases, you should pick a topic that intrigues you and one about which you have something interesting to say.

In the workplace, the topics of your documents will be different than the ones you write about in university or college, but you should still begin by identifying clearly what you are writing about. A client or your supervisor may request a written document from you in the following way:

> Our organization is interested in receiving a proposal that shows how we can lower our energy costs with sustainable energy sources, especially wind and solar.

> Please write a report that explains the sociological causes behind the sudden rise in violence in our city's south side neighbourhoods.

Evaluate these three road surfaces to determine which one would be best for repaving 2nd Street in the downtown area.

Once you have clearly identified your topic, you should explore its boundaries or scope, trying to figure out what is "inside" your topic and what is "outside" the topic. A good way to determine the boundaries of your topic is to create a concept map like the one shown in Figure 2.2.

To make a concept map, start out by writing your topic in the middle of your computer screen or a sheet of paper. Circle it, and then write down everything connected with it that comes to mind. For example, let's say your sociology professor wants you to write about the romantic relationships of college students. Put "dating and mating in college" in the middle of a sheet of paper and circle it. Then start mapping around that topic, as shown in Figure 2.2.

Write down all the things you already know about your topic. Then, as you begin to run out of ideas, go online and enter some of the words from your map

FIGURE 2.2 Creating a Concept Map About Your Topic

A concept map is a helpful way to get your ideas onto the screen or a piece of paper.

into a search engine like *Google Scholar* or an online scholarly database. The search engine will bring up links to numerous other ideas and sources of information about your topic. Read through these sources and add more ideas to your concept map.

As your map fills out, you might ask yourself whether the topic is too large for the amount of time you have available. If so, pick the most interesting ideas from your map and create a second concept map around them alone. This second map will often help you narrow your topic to something you can handle.

Angle: What Is New About the Topic?

Completely new topics are rare. On just about every issue, someone has said something about it already. That's fine. You don't need to discover a completely new topic for your writing project. Instead, you need to come up with a new *angle* on a topic. Your angle is your unique perspective or view on the issue. Academics often deliberately address areas where there is debate or disagreement on a topic. These contentious areas suggest that research is not complete or conclusive and so indicate an angle on the topic worth pursuing.

One way to come up with your angle is to ask yourself, "What has changed recently about this topic that makes it especially interesting right now?" For example, let's say you are searching the Internet for articles about college dating trends. You find a 2001 report from the Institute for American Values called "Hooking Up, Hanging Out, and Hoping for Mr. Right: College Women on Dating and Mating Today." The report is both American in content and getting a little out of date, but you mostly agree with the sociologists who wrote it, especially the part about students wanting marriage but shying away from commitment.

Your experiences as a Canadian university or college student, however, give you some additional insights or "angles" into this topic. Plus, times have changed a little since the report came out. You believe that the hooking-up culture has been replaced by a culture of "serial monogamy" in which many students now go through a series of short-term emotional and physical relationships while they are in college. These so-called monogamous relationships may last a few months or perhaps a year, but most people don't expect them to lead to marriage. That's your angle.

You decide to do a little freewriting to see if your angle works. Freewriting involves opening a new page in your word processor and writing anything that comes to mind for about five minutes (Figure 2.3, page 20). When freewriting, don't stop to correct or revise. Just keep writing anything that comes into your head.

Dating and mating in university and college is a very large topic—too large for a five to ten page paper. But if you write a paper that explores a specific angle (e.g., the shift from a hooking-up culture to a culture of serial monogamous relationships) you can say something really interesting about how college students date and mate.

FIGURE 2.3
Freewriting to Find Your Angle

Freewriting about your topic helps you test your new angle. Just write freely for five to ten minutes without making revisions or corrections.

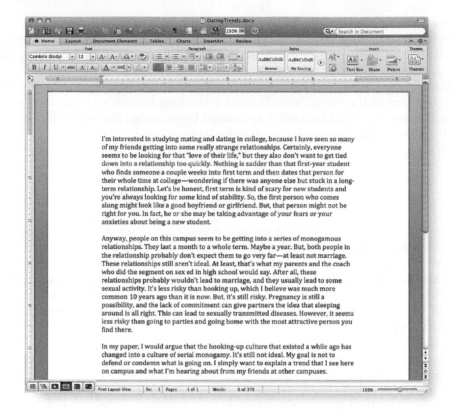

I'm interested in studying mating and dating in college, because I have seen so many of my friends getting into some really strange relationships. Certainly, everyone seems to be looking for that "love of their life," but they also don't want to get tied down into a relationship too quickly. Nothing is sadder than that first-year student who finds someone a couple weeks into first term and then dates that person for their whole time at college—wondering if there was anyone else but stuck in a long-term relationship. Let's be honest, first term is kind of scary for new students and you're always looking for some kind of stability. So, the first person who comes along might look like a good boyfriend or girlfriend. But, that person might not be right for you. In fact, he or she may be taking advantage of your fears or your anxieties about being a new student.

Anyway, people on this campus seem to be getting into a series of monogamous relationships. They last a month to a whole term. Maybe a year. But, both people in the relationship probably don't expect them to go very far—at least not marriage. These relationships still aren't ideal. At least, that's what my parents and the coach who did the segment on sex ed in high school would say. After all, these relationships probably wouldn't lead to marriage, and they usually lead to some sexual activity. It's less risky than hooking up, which I believe was much more common 10 years ago than it is now. But, it's still risky. Pregnancy is still a possibility, and the lack of commitment can give partners the idea that sleeping around all all right. This can lead to sexually transmitted diseases. However, it seems less risky than going to parties and going home with the most attractive person you find there.

In my paper, I would argue that the hooking-up culture that existed a while ago has changed into a culture of serial monogamy. It's still not ideal. My goal is not to defend or condemn what is going on. I simply want to explain a trend that I see here on campus and what I'm hearing about from my friends at other campuses.

Purpose: What Should I Accomplish?

Your purpose is what you want to accomplish—that is, what you want to explain or prove to your readers. To this point, figuring out your topic and angle has helped you determine *what* you are writing about. Now, you need to clearly state your purpose— *why* you are writing. In academic writing, your purpose often develops into your main argument or thesis. A purpose identifies your main focus, while a thesis presents your complete argument about the topic.

Your professor may have already identified a purpose for your paper in the assignment sheet, so check there first. Assignments based on the topics given on page 17 might look like this:

Your objective in this paper is to show how Pierre Trudeau's "bringing home" of the Canadian Constitution in 1982 gave Canada its sovereignty but also highlighted some ongoing divides in this country (most notably the French-English divide, illustrated by Quebec's rejection of the Constitution Act).

In your paper, show how Shakespeare's *King Lear* is similar to and different from his other tragedies. Then discuss why the themes in *Lear* still resonate with today's audiences.

I want you to use close observation of students on our campus to support or debunk some of the common assumptions about dating and mating in college.

If you need to come up with your own purpose for the paper, ask yourself what you believe and what you would like to prove about your topic.

At the end of the freewrite in Figure 2.3, a thesis statement is starting to form:

In my paper, I would argue that the hooking-up culture that existed a decade ago has changed into a culture of serial monogamy. It's still not ideal. My goal is not to defend or condemn what is going on. I simply want to explain a trend that I see here on campus and what I'm hearing about from my friends at other campuses.

This statement is still a bit rough and it lacks a clear focus, but the project's thesis is starting to take shape.

Your thesis statement also defines what genre you are likely to follow. For example, the word "argue" in the rough thesis statement above signals that the author will likely be writing a position paper, a proposal, or a research paper. It helps to remember that documents in university or college and in the workplace tend to be written for two primary reasons: to *inform* and to *persuade*. So your thesis statement will usually be built around some of the verbs shown in Figure 2.4.

You can consult this list of verbs if you are having trouble coming up with your thesis statement. Start by determining whether you are trying to *inform* your readers or trying to *persuade* them. Then pick the key word that best describes what you are trying to accomplish. See Chapter 10 for more discussion of thesis statements.

Informative Papers	Persuasive Papers
to inform	to persuade
to describe	to convince
to define	to influence
to review	to argue
to notify	to recommend
to instruct	to change
to advise	to advocate
to announce	to urge
to explain	to defend
to demonstrate	to justify
to illustrate	to support

FIGURE 2.4
Common Verbs Used in Thesis Statements

Choosing the Appropriate Genre

Once you have sketched out your topic, angle, and purpose, you can choose which genre would be appropriate for your project. The appropriate genre depends on what you are trying to do and whom you are writing for. Perhaps your professor has already identified the genre by asking you to write a "research paper," a "literary analysis," or a "proposal." If so, you can turn to that chapter in this book to learn about the expectations for that genre (Chapters 4–10). If you are writing in a genre that has both popular and academic applications, remember to adapt the genre to the expectations of your audience.

If you are allowed to choose your own genre, or if you are writing something on your own, the best way to figure out which genre would work best is to look closely at your purpose statement and working thesis. Keep in mind, though, that genres are not formulas or recipes to be followed mechanically. Instead, each one reflects how people in various communities and cultures do things with words and images. They are places where people make meaning together. Figure 2.5 shows how your purpose can help you figure out which genre is most appropriate for your writing situation.

The genre that fits your purpose will help you make strategic decisions about how you are going to generate the content of your document, organize it, develop an appropriate style, and design it for your readers.

FIGURE 2.5
Identifying the
Appropriate
Genre

My Purpose	The Appropriate Genre
"I want to write a summary of an article I read while researching."	Summary
"I need to critique something I saw, experienced, or read."	Review
"I need to explain why a text or speech was effective or persuasive, or not."	Rhetorical Analysis
"I need to explain and interpret a work of literature or art."	Literary Analysis
"I want to argue for my beliefs or opinions."	Position Paper
"I want to propose a solution to a problem."	Proposal
"I need to explain an issue by doing research about it."	Research Paper

Ready to start right now? Here are some techniques and strategies for identifying your topic, angle, and purpose.

IDENTIFY Your Topic

Your topic will be assigned by your professor or you will need to come up with it yourself. Either way, figure out what interests you about the topic. Then use a concept map to determine what issues are related to your topic.

NARROW Your Topic

Ask yourself whether the topic is too large for the amount of time you have available. If it might be too large, pick the most interesting ideas from your map and create a second concept map around them. This second map should help you narrow your topic to something you can handle.

DEVELOP Your Angle

Your angle is your unique perspective on the topic. A good way to develop an angle is to ask yourself, "What has changed recently about this topic that makes it especially interesting right now?" You might also ask what unique perspective you could offer on this issue.

WRITE Down Your Purpose

Your purpose is what you want to accomplish—that is, what you want to explain or prove to your readers. Decide whether you are *informing* your readers or *persuading* them. Then write a thesis statement that says exactly what you are going to do. The verbs shown in Figure 2.4 might help.

CHOOSE the Appropriate Genre

The best way to figure out which genre would work best for your project is to look closely at your purpose and thesis statement. The chart in Figure 2.5 will help you decide which genre would work for the document you want to write. In some cases, your professor will tell you which genre to use.

1. With a small group, list some topics that people often discuss and argue about. For example, what do people talk about on television or the radio? What do they argue about at local gathering places like cafés, restaurants, or bars? What are some things people discuss with their friends or families? What topics have your professors presented as debatable or controversial? With your group, come up with ten things that you yourselves have discussed or argued about over the last few days.

2. Take a look at today's news on websites like *cbc.ca/news*, *Canada.com*, or *theglobeandmail.com*. What are some of the topics in the news today? You will notice that totally new topics aren't all that common. However, there are new angles developing all the time. With your group, discuss the new angles you notice on these topics. How do the reporters come up with these new angles? What has changed recently to create some of these new angles?

1. List five topics that you might be interested in writing about this term. They can include anything that captures your imagination. Then, for each of these topics, ask yourself, "What is new or has changed recently about this topic?" Using your answers to this question, write down two possible angles for each topic.

2. Think of a topic that catches your interest. For five minutes, create a concept map that includes everything you can think of about this topic. Now, look at your concept map and find a part of this topic that you would like to explore further. Then freewrite on that part for five more minutes and see what kinds of ideas begin to emerge. Would this "narrower" topic be easier to write about than the topic you started with?

3. Pick a topic and angle that interests you and develop a thesis statement for a paper about that topic. Your thesis statement doesn't need to be perfect right now, but try to describe what you want to say in your paper. Do you want to inform your readers about your topic or do you want to persuade them? Build your thesis statement around one of the words shown in the chart in Figure 2.4.

4. Using the topic and thesis statement from the exercise above, identify which genre would be most appropriate for writing about this topic. Figure 2.5 provides a chart that shows how to use your purpose and thesis statement to figure out which genre you should use. Once you've determined which genre to use, turn to that chapter in Part 2, "Using Genres to Express Ideas," to see what that genre usually involves.

1. **Identify a topic, angle, and purpose.** Choose a writing assignment from one of your professors. Using the steps and concepts discussed in this chapter, determine the topic you are being asked to write about and come up with a unique angle on it. Then draft a thesis statement for your assignment. Write an e-mail to your professor in which you identify the topic, angle, purpose, and main point of the paper you will be writing. Then discuss which genre would be appropriate for this assignment and why.

2. **E-mail your professor about a new angle on a topic.** Pick any topic that interests you and find a new angle on that topic. Use concept mapping to explore and narrow your topic. Then write a rough thesis statement that shows what you want to achieve in your paper.

   Using the chart in Figure 2.5, choose a genre that would help you to say something meaningful and interesting about this issue. Turn to the chapter in Part 2 that discusses the genre you chose. Using the diagram that appears early in the chapter, sketch a brief outline on this topic.

   Finally, write an e-mail to your professor in which you explain how you would go about writing an argument on this topic. Explain your topic, angle, purpose, readers, and the genre you would use. Tell your professor why you think your approach to the topic would be effective for your readers.

3

Readers, Contexts, and Rhetorical Situations

In this chapter, you will learn how to:

- profile your readers to understand their expectations, values, and attitudes.
- figure out how context—the place readers read and the medium you use—shapes your readers' experience.
- use the rhetorical situation (topic, angle, purpose, readers, and context) to help you respond to both popular and academic writing situations.

In your post-secondary courses and in your career, you will need to write to real people who will read and use your documents in specific times and places. Your writing needs to inform them, persuade them, achieve your purpose, and get something done.

In the previous chapter, you learned how to identify your topic, angle, and purpose. In this chapter, you will learn how to achieve your purpose by developing *reader profiles* and sizing up the *contexts* in which people will read your work. Together, this information makes up the *rhetorical situation*—that is, the topic, angle, purpose, readers, and context. Each rhetorical situation is unique, because every new situation puts into play a specific writer with a purpose, writing for specific readers who are encountering the work at a unique time and place.

When you have sized up the rhetorical situation, you can use genres more successfully to accomplish what you want to achieve. Identifying your topic, angle, and purpose allows you to figure out which genre would work best. Understanding your readers and the contexts in which they will experience your text will help you adjust the genre to fit their expectations.

Profiling Readers

❋─⌐ **Explore** Boys and Girls: Understanding the Rhetoric of Audience

In university or college and in the workplace, you will usually be writing for other people, not yourself. So before writing, you need to develop a reader profile that helps you adapt your ideas to their expectations and the situations in which they will use your document.

A profile is an overview of your readers' traits and characteristics. At a minimum, you should develop a *brief reader profile* that gives you a working understanding of the people who will be reading your text. If time allows, you should create an *extended reader profile* that will give you a more in-depth view of their expectations, values, and attitudes.

A Brief Reader Profile

To create a brief reader profile, you can use the Five-W and How questions to help you describe the kinds of people who will be reading your text (Figure 3.1).

Who Are My Readers? What are their personal characteristics? How old are they? What cultures do they come from? Do they have much in common with you? Are they familiar with your topic already or are they completely new to it?

What Are Their Expectations? What do they need from you and your document? What do they want, exactly? What are their potential concerns or questions? What ideas excite them, and what things bore them? What information do they need to help them accomplish their personal and professional goals?

Where Will They Be Reading? In what locations might they read your document? Will your readers be sitting at their desks, in a meeting, or on an airplane? Will they be reading from a printed page, a computer screen, or a small-screen reading device like a smartphone?

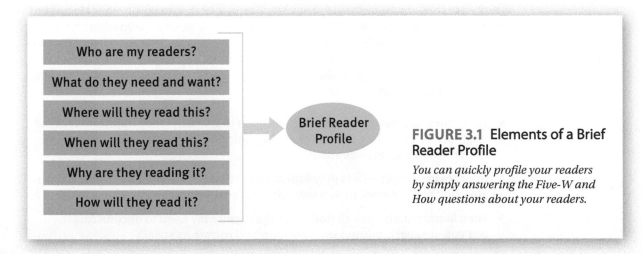

Who are my readers?

What do they need and want?

Where will they read this?

When will they read this?

Why are they reading it?

How will they read it?

→ Brief Reader Profile

FIGURE 3.1 Elements of a Brief Reader Profile

You can quickly profile your readers by simply answering the Five-W and How questions about your readers.

When Will They Be Reading? Does the time of day affect how they will read your document? Will they be reading it when the issues are hot and under discussion? Will they be reading it at a time when they can think about your ideas slowly and carefully?

Why Will They Be Reading? Why will they pick your document up? Do their reasons for reading the document match your purpose in writing it? Do they want to be informed, or do they need to be persuaded?

How Will They Be Reading? Will they read slowly and carefully? Will they skip and skim? Will they read some parts carefully and some parts quickly or not at all?

Your answers to the Five-W and How questions will give you a brief reader profile to help you start writing. For simple documents, a brief profile like this one might be enough. For larger, more complex documents, you will need to dig a little deeper to develop a more thorough understanding of your readers.

An Extended Reader Profile

You should always remember that your readers probably understand issues differently than you do. Their expectations, values, and attitudes will be unique, and sometimes even contradictory to yours. Meanwhile, complex genres, like the ones discussed in this book, usually require a more thorough understanding of the people who will be reading the text.

To write successfully in these complex rhetorical situations, you might find it helpful to create an *extended reader profile* that goes beyond answering the Who, What, Where, When, Why, and How questions. An extended reader profile will help you to better anticipate what your readers expect, what they value, and what their attitudes are toward you and your topic. Since you may not yet be familiar with academic readers, we have included some explanations of their expectations, values, and attitudes here alongside general questions you can apply to all readers.

What Are Their Expectations? Your readers probably picked up your document because they *expect* or *need* something. Do they need to know something specific? What do they need in order to do something or achieve a goal? Make a list of the two to five items that your readers expect you to address in your document for it to be useful to them. Depending on the genre you are using, your readers will be looking for various kinds of information:

- For a summary, your readers will expect you to give a detailed description of the original text, providing them with enough information so they can understand what the original text was about.

- For a review, your readers may expect you to define and explain the criteria you are using and the reasons you have chosen those criteria.

- For a literary analysis or rhetorical analysis, you may need to deconstruct the text you are analyzing and use examples to illustrate its style.

- For a position paper, they will expect you to back up your claims with facts, examples, and solid reasoning.

- For a research paper or a proposal, your readers will expect you to provide background information to allow them to understand the current situation. They will also be looking for specific plans and recommendations to help them solve problems.

- In all situations, academic readers will expect a formal tone, accurate information, detailed analysis, and carefully documented research.

If you can figure out your readers' expectations, you are well on your way to knowing what to include in your document and how to present it.

What Are Their Values? *Values* involve personal beliefs, social conventions, and cultural expectations. Your readers' values have been formed through their personal experiences, family or religious upbringing, and social/cultural influences.

Personal values. Your readers' personal beliefs can be hard to predict, but you can take a few educated guesses. Think about your readers' upbringings and experiences. What are their core beliefs? What makes your readers different or unique? How are your readers similar to you and what personal values do you and your readers likely hold in common? Academic readers, for example, are people who have dedicated at least part of their lives to the pursuit of higher learning. They are likely to value knowledge, critical thinking, and thorough research, and less likely to value emotional reactions in a piece of writing.

Social values. Your readers' values are also shaped by the conventions, practices, and customs of their society. How do people do things in their social circles? What expectations does their society place on them? What traditions or codes govern their behaviour?

A university or a college is a kind of society, so you will need to consider some of the customs of this society. For instance, academics usually take a critical stance. They are expected to question rather than simply accept ideas. Academics in the social science and science disciplines tend to qualify rather than exaggerate claims, because there is a common expectation that further research may prove those claims right or wrong. Academics also write and speak in formal, often technical, language. Their society is a professional one, engaged in international research about very specialized topics. Technical terms allow academics to communicate very precisely, while formal language ensures that scholars from other societies and cultures will understand key points.

Cultural values. Your readers' culture may influence their behaviour in ways even they don't fully understand. What do people in your readers' culture value? How are these cultural values similar to or different from your cultural values? Academic readers in particular value objectivity, so avoid cultural assumptions. If your topic involves cultural values, address them in a way that allows an international academic audience to appreciate and fully understand the context.

Mistakenly, writers sometimes assume that their readers hold the same values they do. Even people very similar to you in background and upbringing may hold values that are different from yours. Meanwhile, people whose cultures and upbringings are different from yours may have distinctly different ways of seeing the world.

What Is Their Attitude Toward You and the Issue? Your readers will also have a particular *attitude* about your topic and, perhaps, about you. As far as you are able, assess their existing attitudes. Are they excited, or are they bored? Are they concerned or apathetic, happy or upset about your topic? Do they already accept your ideas, or are they deeply skeptical? Are they feeling positive toward you or negative? Will they welcome your views or be hostile to them?

If your readers are positive and welcoming toward your views, you will want to take advantage of their goodwill by giving them persuasive reasons to agree with you. If they are negative or resistant, you will want to use solid reasoning, ample examples, and good style to counter their resistance and win them over.

Anticipating all of your readers' expectations, values, and attitudes can be especially difficult if you try to do it all in your head. That's why professional writers often like to use a Reader Analysis Worksheet like the one shown in Figure 3.2 to help them create an extended profile of their readers.

Using the Reader Analysis Worksheet is easy. On the left, list the types of readers who are likely to read your document, ranking them by importance. Then fill in what

Types of Readers	Expectations	Values	Attitudes
Most Important Readers:			
Second Most Important Readers:			
Third Most Important Readers:			

FIGURE 3.2 A Reader Analysis Worksheet

A Reader Analysis Worksheet is a helpful tool for understanding your readers and making good decisions about the content, organization, style, and design of your document.

you know about their expectations, values, and attitudes. If you don't know enough to fill in a few of the squares on the worksheet, just put question marks (?) there. Question marks signal places where you may need to do some additional research on your readers.

An extended reader profile blends your answers to the Five-W and How questions with the information you added to the Reader Analysis Worksheet. These two reader analysis tools should give you a strong understanding of your readers and how they will interpret your document.

Analyzing the Context

((•—[**Listen** Audio Lesson Section 1: Big Ideas—Writing Successfully in Other Courses

The *context* of your document involves the external influences that will shape how your readers interpret and react to your writing. It is important to remember that readers react to a text moment by moment. So the happenings around them can influence their understanding of your document.

Your readers will be influenced by three kinds of contexts: place, medium, and social and political issues.

Place

Earlier, when you developed a brief profile of your readers, you answered the Where and When questions to figure out the locations and times in which your readers would use your document. Now go a little deeper to put yourself in your readers' place.

What are the physical features of this place?

Who else is in this place, and what do they want from my readers?

What is the history and culture of this place, and how does it shape how people view things?

A place is never static. Places are always changing. So figure out how this changing, evolving place influences your readers and their interpretation of your text.

The genre of your document may help you to imagine the places where people are likely to read your document. Proposals tend to be read in office settings, and they are often discussed in meetings. Professors tend to grade analyses, position papers, or research essays in their offices so they can give full attention to the ideas. Reviews and evaluations may be read in more casual settings.

While locations are physical, remember that they can also involve cultural and historical positions. North American society, for instance, has been accused of privileging certain religious, ethnic, and gender identities over others and, while much of that is changing, the history or cultural norms of a place can still affect people's reading processes. If you are writing about a historically controversial topic, you may need to address that context and consider how it influences your readers.

Once you know the genre of your document, you can make decisions about how it should be designed and what would make it more readable in a specific place.

Medium

The medium is the technology that your readers will use to experience your document. Each medium (e.g., paper, website, public presentation, video, podcast) will shape how they interpret your words and react to your ideas:

Paper documents. Paper documents are often read more closely than onscreen documents. With paper, your readers may be more patient with longer documents and longer paragraphs. Document design, which is discussed in Chapter 14, "Designing," makes the text more attractive and helps your readers read more efficiently. While graphics can enhance and reinforce ideas, be sure to use them appropriately. Academic documents rarely include visuals. Paper documents are also less accessible than onscreen documents, because they are harder to store and keep track of.

Electronic documents. When people read text on a screen, like a website or a blog, they may scan it, reading selectively for the information they need. In other words, your onscreen readers may prefer a shorter document with specific facts and information. They will appreciate any visuals, like graphs, charts, and photographs, that you can add to enhance their understanding. You can turn to Chapter 26, "Using the Internet," for more ideas about how to write for the screen.

Presentations. Presentations tend to be much more visual than onscreen and print documents. A presentation made with *PowerPoint* or *Keynote* usually boils an original text down to bullet points that highlight major issues and important facts. Your readers will focus on the items you choose to highlight, and they will rely on you to connect these items and expand on them. Turn to Chapter 29, "Presenting Your Work," for more ideas about how to make great presentations.

Podcasts or videos. A podcast or video needs to be concise and focused. Hearing or seeing a text can be very powerful in this multimedia age; however, amateurs are easy to spot. So your readers will expect a polished, tight presentation that is carefully produced. Your work should get to the point and not waste their time, or they will turn to something else. You can turn to Chapter 26, "Using the Internet," to learn how to make podcasts and videos and upload them to the Internet.

Paper is no longer the only medium for writing. So you should always keep in mind that your texts will likely appear in electronic media. These various media shape how readers will experience your text and interpret your ideas.

Social and Political Influences

Now, think about how current trends and events will influence how your readers interpret what you are telling them. Always keep in mind that your readers will encounter your writing in specific and real contexts that are always undergoing change. The change can be quick and dramatic, or it can be slow and almost imperceptible.

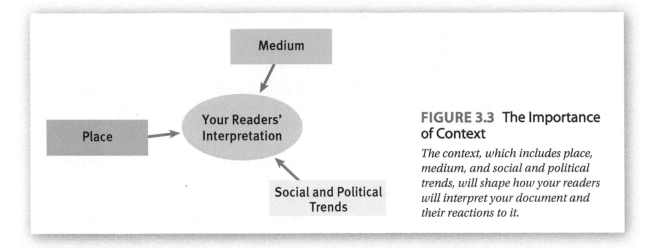

FIGURE 3.3 The Importance of Context

The context, which includes place, medium, and social and political trends, will shape how your readers will interpret your document and their reactions to it.

Social trends. Pay attention to the social trends that are influencing you, your topic, and your readers. You originally decided to write about this topic because you believe it is important right now. What are the larger social trends that will influence how people in the near and distant future understand this topic? What is changing in your society that makes this issue so important? Are economic trends likely to be a factor? Most importantly, how do these trends directly or indirectly affect your readers? Remember that academic readers are more likely to be affected by recent developments in knowledge and research than other readers.

Political trends. Also, keep any political trends in mind as you analyze the context for your document. On a micropolitical level, how will your ideas affect their relationships with you, their families, their colleagues, or their supervisors? On a macropolitical level, how will political trends at the local, provincial, federal, and international levels shape how your readers interpret your ideas? For instance, a conservative government's cutbacks in education might make academic readers more sympathetic to liberal views.

Readers, naturally, respond to the immediate context in which they live (Figure 3.3). If you understand how place, medium, and social and political trends influence your readers, you can better adapt your work to their specific expectations, values, and attitudes.

Genres and the Rhetorical Situation

We threw quite a bit of material at you in this chapter and in the previous one. Here's the point and a brief overview: Genres are used to respond to specific types of rhetorical situations. So when choosing the appropriate genre, you first need to completely understand the situation to which you are responding:

Explore The War Around Us: Understanding the Rhetorical Situation

Watch Genres and the Rhetorical Situation

Topic. What is the exact topic your document is going to discuss? What information is "inside" the topic's boundaries and what is "outside" those boundaries? Have you sharpened your topic enough to allow you to handle it in the time and space you have available?

Angle. What is new or different about your approach to this topic? What has happened recently that makes your topic especially interesting to you and your readers right now? What makes your ideas about this topic different than the ideas of others?

Purpose. What exactly do you want to achieve in this document? What do you want your readers to believe or do after they are finished reading it? What are your goals in writing this text?

Readers. What are your readers' expectations, values, and attitudes? How do these characteristics shape the content, organization, style, and design of your document?

Contexts. In what places do you expect your readers to encounter your document? How does the medium of your text shape how they will read it? What social-political trends will influence how they react to what you are saying?

It might seem like a lot of work to figure all these things out, especially when the deadline is not that far away. In reality, though, analyzing the rhetorical situation only takes a few minutes for most documents. Once you have developed a full understanding of the rhetorical situation, you will find that writing the document is faster and more efficient. In other words, you will save time, because you won't go down dead ends and spend time collecting information you don't need. A few minutes invested at the beginning will pay off with better writing that takes less time and effort.

Need to quickly analyze your readers and the context for your document? Here are some steps to help you get started.

CREATE a Brief Profile of Your Readers

Using the Five-W and How questions, figure out *who* your readers are, *what* they need, *where* and *when* they will be reading the document, *why* they are reading it, and *how* they will be reading it. A sentence or two for each question should be enough to develop a brief profile.

KNOW Your Readers' Expectations

On a basic level, what are the two to five pieces of information your readers *expect* or *need* you to tell them for your document to be useful?

FIGURE OUT Your Readers' Values

Write down your readers' personal, social, and cultural values, and try to anticipate how these values will shape your document.

ANTICIPATE Your Readers' Attitudes About You and Your Topic

Try to figure out what your readers' mindset will be. Are they already convinced or deeply skeptical? Are they feeling positive toward you or negative? Will they welcome your views or be hostile to them? Are they glad or angry, optimistic or pessimistic?

THINK About How Place and Medium Affect Your Readers

The physical and cultural-historical place may affect how closely they are reading and dictate what they need you to highlight for them. The medium of your document (e.g., paper, screen, presentation, podcast) will also shape how they interpret your ideas.

CONSIDER Social and Political Trends

Identify any current trends or events that might colour your readers' understanding of your writing. What social trends affect your topic? How does your project touch on micropolitical and macropolitical trends?

1. Choose an advertisement from a magazine or a newspaper. In a group, figure out the advertisement's purpose, target readers, and the contexts in which it was used. Be as specific and thorough as you can as you define the following:

   • *Purpose:* What is the advertisement trying to do? Use key words like *persuade, inform, entertain,* and others to describe its objectives.

   • *Readers:* What are the expectations, values, and attitudes of the target readers? How does the advertisement try to use those expectations, values, and attitudes to its advantage?

   • *Context:* Describe the place and medium of the advertisement as well as the social and political trends that might influence how it is interpreted. How do these contextual factors influence how readers respond to this ad?

   Finally, do you think the ad is effective in persuading or influencing its intended readers? For which readers would it be most effective, and for which ones would it not?

2. Think of a time when you did not communicate effectively. With your group, discuss why the communication failed. What happened? Describe how you misread the situation, and why the audience or readers reacted as they did. How could you have better handled the situation if you had known the expectations, values, and attitudes of the audience or readers? If you had better understood the social and political issues, how might you have been more successful?

3. With your group, make a list of ten things that motivate people to agree with others or to take action. Discuss how these motives influence the ways people make decisions in real life. What are some ways you could use these motivations in your written work to persuade or influence people?

1. Imagine that you are an advertising specialist who has been asked to develop an advertising campaign to sell digital audio players (MP3, iPod, or other audio device) to people over 60 years old. Figure out these customers' expectations, values, and attitudes toward the product. Then figure out how place and social and political factors shape their decisions about buying this kind of product. In a one page memo to your professor, explain how you might use this knowledge to create an advertising campaign for this new market.

2. For your next project in this class, do a brief reader analysis in which you answer the Five-W and How questions about your readers. Then do an expanded reader analysis in which you explore their expectations, values, and attitudes. In a one page memo to your professor, explain the differences between your brief analysis and the extended analysis. What does the extended analysis reveal that the brief analysis didn't reveal? Would the brief analysis be enough for this project? Why? Or do you think the extended analysis would help you write a more effective document?

1. **Evaluate an argument.** Find an opinion article about an issue that interests you and write a two page evaluation in which you discuss how well the writer has adapted his or her article for its context. You can find a variety of opinion articles in your local or school newspapers (in the "opinion" section) or on the Internet (blogs, personal pages, online newspaper opinion sections and the responses to them). Mark up the text, paying attention to how the writer addresses the following contextual issues:

   - *Place:* First, note how the place in which the article was published and where it will likely be read influences the way readers interact with it.

   - *Medium:* How does the medium shape the way people read the text and what they will focus on?

   - *Social and Political Trends:* What have people been saying about the issue? If it's a hot topic, what makes it hot? What larger trends have motivated the writer to write this argument?

   In your evaluation, explain how the author of this opinion article adjusted his or her argument to the context in which it appears. Discuss whether you felt the opinion article succeeded. How might it be improved?

2. **Rewrite an online text for an academic reader.** Find a brief document on the Internet that is aimed at a general reader. You might choose a movie or concert review, or an online newspaper article. Then rewrite the document for your professor. To complete this assignment, you will need to do an extended reader analysis of your academic reader. When you are finished rewriting the document, write a brief paragraph on how the change in readers altered the content, organization, style, and design of your rewrite. Hand in your new version of the text and your explanatory paragraph to your professor.

Write This

2
Using Genres
to Express
Ideas

PART OUTLINE

Writing well means responding effectively to diverse situations.
In these chapters, you will learn how to use seven GENRES *that will help you write critically, take a stand, use sources effectively, and argue with others.*

CHAPTER 4
Summaries   40

CHAPTER 5
Reviews   58

CHAPTER 6
Rhetorical Analyses   85

CHAPTER 7
Literary Analyses   116

CHAPTER 8
Position Papers and Arguments   148

CHAPTER 9
Proposals   169

CHAPTER 10
Research Papers   210

Summaries

> **In this chapter, you will learn how to:**
> - analyze and identify main points in a text and organize them into an original and accurate summary.
> - develop an appropriate tone or voice for your summary.
> - contextualize and accurately document the summary.
> - begin an extended comparison/contrast of popular and academic genres.

Summarizing may seem like a skill you have already mastered in everyday life. If someone asks how your weekend was, for instance, you summarize the highlights (such as how you saw a great movie or went to dinner at a good restaurant) rather than recount moment by moment what you did, thought, and felt.

In written communication and particularly academic communication, summary takes on new importance, because it allows writers to situate themselves in relation to current debates and existing research. For this reason, many professors assign summaries, either as separate exercises or as components of academic research papers. Indeed, summary is a major part of the scholarly literature review, which we will discuss in Chapter 5. Another form of summary, called the abstract, often precedes scholarly research papers. An abstract is a 50–150 word summary created by an article's author to identify the main argument and research methods. You can turn to Chapter 10 for a fuller description and example of an academic abstract. The ability to summarize, then, is a fundamental skill for new scholars to acquire, both for its research applications and for its multiple uses within academic writing.

Articles written for general audiences also use summary to inform readers about new publications or existing ideas. In the workplace, employees may be asked to summarize meetings or lengthy documents, and the ability to do so clearly and accurately is considered an important asset. In this chapter, we have included examples of academic summaries as well as a summary written for a general audience. Through examining these two types of summaries, we will show you how they differ in their use of detail and citation, and begin the comparison and contrast of academic versus popular forms of communication that informs this entire section. This comparative approach will allow us to distinguish between popular and academic writing and better equip you to complete writing assignments in academic contexts.

Summaries

This diagram shows one organization for a summary, but other arrangements will work too. Many summaries follow the organization of the original text or debate, since the authors of those communications had a carefully thought-out structure for their ideas. For instance, a summary of a lab report might begin with a description of the hypothesis, continue to methods and results, and end with discussion and conclusions, as in the original document. Other summaries choose to rearrange information to avoid repetition or to highlight major points in the argument.

Introductory description of the main argument

Background/key terms necessary to the argument

Description of the author's point 1

Description of the author's point 2

:

Conclusion: Implications of the main argument

Overview

The purpose of summaries, as you probably know, is to highlight the main points or ideas in relation to a topic. Summarizing an argument means that you will highlight the major concepts and eliminate much of the supporting evidence or details. In scholarly research, the discussion of key points allows writers to explain where they stand in a debate, whether they agree with one person or another, and how they build on previous work. Indeed, some writing instructors (such as Gerald Graff at the University of Illinois and Janet Giltrow at the University of British Columbia) have likened the use of summary in research to a scholarly conversation or dialogue. Although a summary is largely neutral in tone, the words used to describe the major concepts of a debate or text can subtly shape the information and prepare readers for your own ideas. For this reason, you shouldn't simply quote a pre-existing abstract or online summary (as students sometimes would like). Quoting someone else's summary does not allow you to incorporate or integrate the material into your own writing.

The process of summarizing begins with a careful analysis or reading of the material in order to locate the main ideas. Those ideas are then described in a new format to serve the needs of the writer. All summaries tend to have these main features:

- **Accurate restatements of the topic's main argument and support,** given in the summary writer's own words.

- **Greater brevity than the original,** achieved by retaining key abstractions and minimizing supporting details/evidence.

- **Reporting or signalling phrases,** which clarify the speaker and put the information in context.

- **A logical structure** that either follows the original or emphasizes key ideas in the argument.

Academic summaries also include another important feature:

- **Thorough citations** that allow readers to locate the original text, pursue further reading, and advance their knowledge about the topic.

Summaries tend to include these features and follow a pattern like the one shown on page 41. Later in this chapter, we will go over each of these features in more depth. Keep in mind that the summary pattern, as with all genres, should not be followed mechanically. Instead, you should adjust the organization, style, and design to fit your purpose, readers, and the context in which your summary will be read.

ONE STUDENT'S WORK
Summary

The following student summary describes June Feder, Ronald Levant, and James Dean's essay, "Boys and Violence: A Gender-Informed Analysis." See Chapter 10 for the original essay. Please note that the page numbers and citations here come from the article published in its original format. The side notes indicate where to find each idea on pages 239–251 of Chapter 10.

Summary of "Boys and Violence: A Gender-Informed Analysis"

Rebecca Gillespie

In the article "Boys and Violence: A Gender-Informed Analysis," June Feder, Ronald F. Levant, and James Dean (2007) discuss the alarming rates of violence and aggressive behaviour amongst young people. The focus of the research is the effect of gender on violence, the associated traditional norms, and possible solutions. Boys appear to be particularly affected, because their socialization isolates them from making emotional connections with others and understanding themselves. Feder et al. believe that this issue may lead young men astray into the world of violence (p. 385).

The authors open their article by examining the trend of youth violence, ranging from harming others with harassment and homicide to harming themselves (Feder et al., 2007, p. 385). They look at causative factors including the availability of weapons. Easy access to weapons is a concern, particularly in the United States of America, where the number of privatized firearms could equip approximately three out of four Americans (Portner, as cited in Feder et al., 2007, p. 386). Other issues include the impact of media, teasing and bullying, and parental and caretaker influences (Feder et al., 2007, pp. 386–387).

The main focus of Feder et al.'s argument is the effect of sex and gender on violence among young males. According to Garbarino, "ninety-five percent of juvenile homicides are caused by boys" (as cited in Feder et al., 2007, p. 387). The traditional ideals of masculinity and the social involvements of boys in aggressive contexts are major risk factors. Vulnerability is viewed as weak and is punished; boys are encouraged to act tough, portray aggression and dominance, and avoid emotional behaviour (Feder et al., 2007, p. 387). Levant discussed *normative male alexithymia*, or "the inability to put emotions into words" (as cited in Feder et al., 2007, p. 387) as a key factor. Other researchers, who focus on sex differences and gender-based emotional stereotyping, have argued that Levant's theories do not contain substantial evidence and therefore are inconclusive. Levant's work relates to what Pollack calls the "boy code," a form of containment of feelings.

Identification of article, authors, and topic, taken from paragraphs 1–3 of the original.

Key ideas are cited in APA format throughout the summary and a full end reference is provided. See Chapter 25 for a full explanation of APA style.

Concise restatement of the factors that contribute to youth violence, taken from paragraphs 4–12 of the original essay.

(continued)

Discussion of the key issue of gender socialization, condensed from paragraphs 13–22 of the article.

Summary of the authors' proposals for treatment from paragraphs 23–33 of the original.

Brief restatement of Feder et al.'s conclusion from paragraph 34 of the original essay.

If boys cannot portray the masculine ideal, they suffer in multiple ways, such as experiencing disapproval and taunting from others, which can be a catalyst for violence (as cited in Feder et al., 2007, p. 387). Feder et al. (2007) clarify these issues may contribute to boys' aggressive attitudes, including punishment of nonconformity, and hostility toward homosexuals and women (p. 388).

Feder et al. developed ideas to free young males from this perpetuation of violence. Early intervention, with potential revision of existing programs, is important to hinder aggressive behaviours and promote positive social and emotional conducts. Having a father, mentor, or other adult is important; their support can boost self-esteem and reduce violent acts. Schools are significant in children's development; however, teachers need to be more aware of "boys' particular learning styles and unique educational, social, and emotional needs" (pp. 388–389). Modification of clinical practices could encourage boys to express their emotions. Activities involving humour and action, and open discussions can inspire boys to connect with their thoughts and feelings, and express them in healthy ways (Pollack, as cited in Feder et al., 2007, p. 389).

In conclusion, Feder et al. (2007) recognize that violence among youth is a multifaceted issue, and gender is a critical aspect in understanding what leads boys to their belligerent behaviours. By encouraging communication and giving boys channels for their anxiety, sorrow, and pain, as well as access to adult role models, the risk of violence and aggression can be reduced (p. 390).

Reference

Feder, J., Levant, R. F., & Dean, J. (2007). Boys and violence: A gender-informed analysis. *Professional Psychology: Research and Practice, 38*(4), 385–391. doi: 10.1037/0735-7028.38.4.385

Developing Your Summary's Content

Your goal in a summary is to concisely state the text's main ideas for yourself and your readers. When starting out, you do not need to be too concerned about your attitude toward the text. Instead, be clear on what the author or participant is saying and how the argument is proven.

Inquiring: Reading and Understanding Your Text

The first step in summary is a careful reading of the text. Most writers do an initial reading to be sure they understand the literal meaning of the argument. Locating the topic sentences in each paragraph can be useful at this point, because the topic sentence (frequently located near the beginning of the paragraph) tells you what the main idea of each paragraph is. A second or even third reading reinforces understanding and reveals some of the subtleties and further implications of the text. On an initial reading, you might wish to highlight or underline what seem to be key points or passages in the original. On subsequent readings, you might make marginal notes, beginning the process of translating the original into your own words. Be sure to distinguish your wording from the wording of the original, should you repeat any of it. What you, as a reader, find key in the original also begins to personalize the summary and make it useful for your own research.

Inquiring: Distinguishing Abstractions from Details

A second step in preparing your summary involves clarifying the length and amount of detail required for your writing situation. Sometimes you will be asked to write a short summary of one to two sentences. Other times, your professor or editor will expect a longer, more in-depth summary of a paragraph or even one to two pages. Typically, the length of a summary signifies the importance of the text being summarized. The content of all summaries condenses the original and so consists primarily of abstractions and omits supporting details and examples. For this reason, you will want to distinguish abstractions from details in your understanding of the text.

Separate Details from Abstractions. An abstraction is a large, non-specific concept, while a detail is concrete and generally very specific. For example, feminism is an abstraction, while the historical point that women were not granted personhood in Canada until 1929 is a concrete fact or detail. Most writers present their main ideas as abstractions and then support those abstractions with details. You will want to retain and restate the main abstraction for a shorter summary, and the main plus some supporting abstractions and a small number of key details for a longer summary. Figure 4.1 shows a breakdown of details and abstractions identified in a paragraph on Canadian feminist history in preparation for writing a summary.

Retrace the Structure of the Argument. A final way to understand your text and prepare to write a summary involves looking at the structure of the original essay or debate. You will want to locate features like the thesis statement, the literature review or discussion of previous research (if there is one), the methodology or approach taken, and the major divisions of the paper or argument. Identifying these features will ensure you include the major ideas (which can sometimes be complex in scholarly research) and can evaluate their relative importance to the argument (see Chapter 10 for more discussion of the features found in research papers).

Researching: Finding Out About Context

Research, although not required for all summaries, can help you better understand how the text you are condensing fits into existing knowledge on the topic. For instance, a writer summarizing an essay on feminism in Canada may find it useful to research other writings on that topic to see if the essay being summarized agrees or

FIGURE 4.1
Distinguishing Abstractions from Details

This figure demonstrates how an abstract concept (seen on the left) can be supported with a fact or detail (seen on the right). Locating the key abstractions will help you identify important ideas to include in your summary, while many of the supporting details can be omitted.

Abstraction	Supporting Details
Women's Rights in Canada	"Famous Five" led by Emily Murphy and Nellie McClung petitioned for women's personhood
	1929 women granted personhood
	1977 Canadian human rights act guaranteed pay equity, freedom from discrimination
Enfranchisement	1917 women granted limited voting rights
	1919 vote extended to all women
Government	1921 Agnes MacPhail first woman voted into Canadian parliament
	2011 men continue to outnumber women as elected officials

disagrees with work by other researchers. This research is a starting point for a literature review (see Chapter 5). If you decide to research your topic, you should try to find information from the following types of sources:

Online Sources. Use Internet search engines and library databases to help you find recent, related essays.

Print Sources. At your campus or public library, look for books or journal articles in the field to better understand the scholarly context.

Empirical Sources. Research doesn't only happen on the Internet and in the library. Your professors can likely help you identify ongoing research or explain how the text you are summarizing relates to other work in the field.

Organizing and Drafting Your Summary

To create a good summary, you will need to go through a series of drafts in order to accurately articulate the main argument, decide on a structure and appropriate level of detail versus abstraction, adopt a suitable tone, and insert any situating expressions and citations. On a first draft, focus on representing the content of the original accurately in your own words. In subsequent drafts, you can work on phrasing, details, and situating the material.

Articulating the Main Argument

Now it's time to transform the notes you made when reading and analyzing your topic into your summary. Use your notes as a starting point, but draft complete sentences for the main argument and any additional information you want to include in your summary, keeping in mind the following elements.

Accuracy. Be accurate in your representation of the text you are summarizing. Misrepresentation in summary is like misquoting or taking information out of context; it can cause misunderstandings and distortions of the material. Be clear on the ideas in the original and be careful that your rewriting of them, while allowing you to highlight key ideas and prepare for your own discussion, does not deviate from the essence of the original.

Originality. As suggested above, the summary should be mainly in your own words. Using your own words allows you to integrate the summary with your own ideas and to assimilate the information. It is not enough to simply change some vocabulary and sentence structures; instead, you want to fully translate the ideas into your own wording (see page 422 on avoiding "patchwriting" or the replacement of only the occasional word). However, if the wording is truly significant or you want to invoke the authority of the original, you may choose to include a brief quotation in a longer summary. Quotations should be formatted and cited according to the appropriate style guide.

Finding an Appropriate Length and Level of Detail

One challenge as you draft your summary will be to achieve the appropriate length.

Condensing. Once you have represented the main idea of the text you are summarizing, you will need to decide on the level of detail you can use to represent the supporting points and evidence. If you are writing a one or two sentence summary, then you can probably stop with a clear representation of the main argument. In this case, your summary will be primarily composed of abstractions. However, if you are writing a longer summary, you will need to include some description of the evidence supporting the main idea. You may choose to select a quotation (cited and correctly formatted) or an example as details for clarification. This means you will want to distinguish abstractions from details in the original text, retain the key abstractions, and then carefully select one or two details that illustrate the concepts you are summarizing. Keep in mind that in a summary length indicates significance. Here is an eighty word summary of a recently published book that condenses, but also retains some illustrating explanation and a brief quotation:

> Andrew Nikiforuk's 2008 book, *Tar Sands: Dirty Oil and the Future of a Continent*, argues that Alberta's oil fields are creating devastating environmental and social problems. Nikiforuk travelled to Fort McMurray to study the effects of bitumen mining and found that the Conservative government has not fully revealed the costs associated with extracting and refining the oil sands. Unless the Canadian people break their "dirty addiction" to oil, Nikiforuk claims the environment and the nation's long-term well-being are at risk (31).
>
> —Nikiforuk, A. (2008), *Tar sands: Dirty oil and the future of a continent*, Vancouver, BC: Greystone Books

Structuring Your Summary

Once you have drafted the content of your summary, you will want to decide on an organization. As mentioned above, many summaries simply follow the format of the original text, since the author of the text would have carefully planned his or her argument. However, some texts contain repetition or a circular structure that can be edited in summary. In those cases, writers may choose to reorganize the material so that the summary follows a logical order or eliminates duplications. In summarizing a scientific study, for example, many writers find that having distinct results and discussion sections is redundant and so combine them into one clear statement of the study's findings.

Inserting Reporting or Signalling Phrases and Citations

The final step in formatting a summary is to properly acknowledge where the ideas come from. None of the ideas are your own, even though you have put them in your own words, so they must be acknowledged as belonging to the original author. Acknowledging the original author is accomplished through the following two devices.

Reporting or Signalling Expressions. In summary, it is important not only to acknowledge the original author and so guide the reader to your sources, but also to clearly demarcate your own original ideas from those of your sources. Reporting or signalling expressions such as "Jones explains . . . ," "Peterson, in contrast, argues . . . ," or "Researchers report . . ." allow writers to do this. You will find these kinds of expressions in both general and academic summaries. Note that reporting expressions typically consist of a directly or indirectly named subject and a present- or past-tense verb. The following opening paragraph from the student summary above now shows the reporting expressions in bold:

> **In the article "Boys and Violence: A Gender-Informed Analysis," June Feder, Ronald F. Levant, and James Dean (2007) discuss** the alarming rates of violence and aggressive behaviour amongst young people. The focus of the research is the effect of gender on violence, the associated traditional norms, and possible solutions. Boys appear to be particularly affected, because their socialization isolates them from making emotional connections with others and understanding themselves. **Feder et al. believe** that this issue may lead young men astray into the world of violence (p. 385).

From this excerpt, you can see that the initial reporting set up typically contains more detail, such as the article title and full names of the researchers. Later reporting expressions use last names only and, depending on the citation style, may abbreviate lists of multiple authors. When you move from summary as an end in itself to summary as part of a review or research paper, you will also find that the neutral reporting verbs you have been using (such as "state" or "explain") may be replaced by more value-laden words as you set up your agreement, qualification, or disagreement with the text you are summarizing. Verbs such as "contends" or "claims," for instance, effectively prepare your reader for your reservations about the text.

Citations. In academic summaries, it is considered essential not only to report the original author's name but also to provide a full citation so that the source can be located. A full citation allows the reader to pursue research on the topic and adds a further level of authenticity to the writing. Your professor and/or discipline will determine which citation style you use (see Chapters 24 and 25 for full explanations of MLA and APA styles). Typically, citations follow quotations or appear at the ends of summaries and, again, this can help demarcate the end of a summary from the ideas that follow. See Chapter 23 on avoiding plagiarism.

Choosing an Appropriate Style

A summary's style and tone depend on the context you are writing for. If you are writing for a general audience, then use accessible language and a more casual style and tone. If you are writing for an academic audience, then you may wish to retain any key technical terms found in the original (as those will have special meaning for your audience) and adopt a more formal style and tone.

Using a Formal Versus an Informal Style

Formal Style. In addition to the technical or more complex terms that establish the academic tone of a research summary, you will want to adopt a formal writing style. You will need to avoid abbreviations, use gender-neutral language, and strive for grammatical correctness. Academics typically avoid clichéd or slang language as well, because they want their work to be widely disseminated to specialists in their field who may not be familiar with local or culturally specific slang terms.

Informal Style. Summaries written for general audiences tend to use a less formal style than research summaries. Writers in these contexts may use some abbreviations and non-technical, popularized language to make the ideas more accessible and interesting to the audience.

Revising and Editing Your Summary

A good summary is concise, with little or no extra detail. After drafting your content, work toward a final version that is as polished and concise as possible. Cut out any non-essential pieces of information and fine tune your phrasing for clarity and conciseness.

Re-evaluate the Details and Eliminate Wordiness. Look at every aspect of the summary and take out what is not absolutely necessary. If you are writing a longer summary, carefully evaluate any details or quotations you have chosen to retain to be sure they clarify the main points.

Clarify Who Says What. Once you have finalized the content of your summary, review it one more time to be sure it is clear whose ideas are being discussed at each point in the summary. You will likely need to begin with a signalling expression, remind your reader at key points what you are summarizing, and include citations for any quotations from the text itself.

Leave plenty of time to rework your descriptions. In some cases, you might need to "re-vision" your whole summary because you figure out something important as you are writing. If so, have the courage to make those changes. The effort will be worth it.

Here's one basic approach for creating a clear and concise summary.

READ the Material You Need to Summarize

Review the material on a literal level, and then highlight and make notes as you begin to understand the major arguments and implications.

LOCATE Key Elements of the Text

Identify topic sentences, main abstractions, and major sections of the material you are reading. Use these to guide your summary and ensure that you include the important ideas.

RESEARCH the Context

If you find you need more information about the text you are summarizing and how it relates to existing research, do some background research.

DRAFT the Summary

Write a description of the text, condensing the material accurately in your own words, using a logical structure, and considering the context in which you are writing. If you are writing a longer summary, you will want to select details for clarification and illustration.

ADD Reporting or Signalling Expressions and Citations

Remember to clearly identify the author(s) of the original and to cite in academic situations so that you acknowledge whose ideas are whose.

DEVELOP an Appropriate Tone or Voice

Identify whether you are writing for a general or academic audience and choose your vocabulary appropriately.

EDIT the Summary to Achieve Greater Clarity and Conciseness

A first draft is usually longer than needed; take the time to edit, polish your phrasing, and ensure that your tone and situating devices are appropriate for the writing situation.

Outraged Moms, Trashy Daughters: How Did Those Steeped in the Women's Lib Movement Produce Girls Who Think Being a Sex Object Is Powerful?

ANNE KINGSTON

The previous examples of summary in this chapter have all been academic as the use of summary in research writing is a key concern. However, summary can be used in non-academic contexts as well. Here is an example excerpted from an article by Anne Kingston, who describes the current state of feminism in Canada before going on to summarize a recent publication on how feminism has shifted in recent years.

Identification of topic, along with the book and author.

Author's credentials are noted.

Communications professor Susan Douglas, the mother of a 22-year-old daughter, compares popular culture targeted at young women to junk food. "I feel like Julia Child forced to eat at Hooters," she writes in her new book *Enlightened Sexism: The Seductive Message that Feminism's Work is Done.* Douglas, the chair of communication studies at the University of Michigan, articulates the plight of the progressive mom back in the late 1990s observing her little girl watch the Spice Girls: "Should she be happy that they're listening to bustier feminism instead of watching Barbie commercials on Saturday morning TV? Or should she run in, rip the CD out of the player, and insist that they listen to Mary Chapin Carpenter or Ani DiFranco instead?"

Enlightened Sexism charts how the wedge between mothers and daughters increased during the first decade of the 21st century as so-called "millennials"—girls born in the late 1980s and early 1990s—became the most sought-after advertising demographic in history. The desire for power and change that coursed through Douglas's generation was recast for their daughters as "empowerment" through conspicuous consumption and sexual display, she writes. Activist outlets like *Sassy* magazine, published from 1988 to 1997, and "riot grrrl," the feminist punk move-ment of the early 1990s, were eclipsed by *Buffy the Vampire Slayer* and *Xena: Warrior Princess*, along with a tribe of female action heroes. These "warriors in thongs," as Douglas dubs them, paved the way for the retro "girliness" championed by *Legally Blonde*, *Ally McBeal*, and *Bridget Jones's Diary*. And from there it was a heartbeat to reality shows like *The Bachelor* and *Say Yes to the Dress*, which depicted young women as obsessed with boys and getting married when they weren't engaged in catfights with one another.

> Concise restatement of the history described in Douglas's book.

  "If you did not know anything about American culture or American life other than what you saw on reality TV, it would be extremely easy to believe that the women's rights movement never happened, that the civil rights movement never happened, that the gay rights movement never happened," says Jennifer Pozner, the director of Women In Media & News in New York City, whose book *Reality Bites Back: The Troubling Truth About Guilty Pleasure TV*, is to be published in November. "Reality TV producers have achieved what the most ardent fundamentalists and anti-feminists haven't been able to achieve," she says. "They've concocted a world in which women have no choices and they don't even want choices."

> Supporting quotations from an author who writes on similar issues. This places Douglas's book in a larger cultural context.

5 "Enlightened sexism" is Douglas's term for this new climate, one based on the pre-sumption that women and men are now "equal," which allows women to embrace formerly retrograde concepts, such as "hypergirliness," and seeing "being decorative [as] the highest form of power," she writes. What really irks her is how a *Girls Gone Wild* sensibility has been sold to women as "empowerment," that old feminist mantra. But in this version, men are the dupes, "nothing more than helpless, ogling, crotch-driven slaves" of "scantily clad or bare-breasted women [who] had chosen to be sex objects."

> Definition of a key term coined by Douglas to describe the social situation.

  Douglas says she was inspired to write the book after noticing what seemed to be a glaring disconnect between the prime-time shows aimed at her generation—*Grey's Anatomy*, *CSI*, *The Closer*, all featuring tough-talking, assured women who don't use their sexuality to get what they want—and the programming aimed at her daughter. Eventually she came to believe both kinds of shows were perpetuating the myth that feminism's work was over: "both mask, even erase how much still remains to be done for girls and women. The notion that there might, indeed, still be an urgency to feminist politics? You have to be kidding."

> Implications of the book's ideas and a real-life example. Examples are important in a popular review to explain why the information is summarized and how it might affect the reader.

A CLOSER LOOK AT
Outraged Moms, Trashy Daughters

1. Consider the content summarized in Kingston's passage: What does the excerpt suggest is the cur-rent state of feminism in Canada? What are the problems? What are the positive changes that have occurred since the 1960s?

2. Identify the reporting or signalling expressions used in the excerpt. How many voices are incor-porated? Is it always clear who is speaking? Is the intended audience mothers or daughters?

3. Kingston's piece offers an example of summary written for a general or popular audience. Com-pare this to the academic summaries you read earlier in the chapter. What similarities and dif-ferences do you see between the popular and aca-demic summaries? Consider the content and style, as well as the use of reporting and citations.

IDEAS FOR
Writing

1. Now that you have read and considered Kingston's passage, summarize its position on feminism as if you were writing for an academic paper on popular perceptions of feminism. What are the excerpt's key points? What position in the debate does it lean toward and how do you know? How can you indicate that in your summary? How will you cite the excerpt? Do you think that young women would agree with the perspective it summarizes?

2. Look up "third wave feminism" in a dictionary or encyclopedia and summarize its key concepts in three or four sentences. Could this term be used in *Kingston's* article? Does it apply to the situation described there and could it be used to understand the generational differences the excerpt cites?

Summary of David Bartholomae's "Inventing the University"

JORDAN STOUCK AND CATHI SHAW

The following is a summary of "Inventing the University" by David Bartholomae, a founding figure in modern composition studies and author of several well-known texts on writing. In the essay, Bartholomae discusses some of the difficulties students encounter in learning to write academic papers. Please see below for a reference to the original essay. Your university or college library will likely have a copy or be able to order one for you. Here is an online version (please note the page numbers differ slightly): http://www4.ncsu.edu/~catonell/documents/D.Bartholomae.pdf

---

Identification of the author, essay, and focus, taken from paragraphs 1–2 of the original.

In David Bartholomae's essay "Inventing the University" (1988), he argues that students must learn to take on the various voices of the university community. They must learn to speak, write, and reason in a range of academic discourses, taking on a professional persona before they have the knowledge behind that profession. This requirement, Bartholomae notes, inevitably causes problems (p. 273).

Bartholomae's essay develops through an examination of the kinds of writing students produce as they begin this process of adapting to university discourse. He notes that one misjudgment students can make involves failing to speak as a fellow researcher and instead addressing readers in a teaching tone, offering a "life lesson" or instructions rather than scholarly findings (p. 275). Bartholomae refers to composition theorist Linda Flower in describing this as a difficulty in moving from "writer-based prose," which focuses on the needs of the writer, to "reader-based prose," which is able to successfully anticipate the needs of the reader or audience (as cited in Bartholomae, 1988, p. 276). In an academic context, this audience awareness requires the student to take on the reader's position of privilege and write as an academic "insider" (Bartholomae, 1988, p. 277).

> Explanation of Bartholomae's method.

> Restatement of Bartholomae's key findings from paragraphs 4–15 of the original.

Bartholomae continues to propose that students be made more familiar with, in Pat Bizzell's words, "the academic discourse community" (as cited in Bartholomae, 1988, p. 278). This means that students must learn the commonplaces or conventions of academic vocabulary, formats, and reasoning processes. After further analysis of first semester university essays, Bartholomae (1988) states that these commonplaces include taking on an objective analytic stance and questioning received knowledge. Unlike a general community, Bartholomae writes, a university "is the place where 'common' wisdom is only of negative value; it is something to work against" and to replace with "a more specialized discourse" (p. 283). Finally, the essay cautions that this development of a scholarly voice can be accompanied by increased levels of grammatical error, but that this is symptomatic of the struggle to write more authoritatively and should not be used as a marker of writing ability (pp. 283–284). Ultimately, Bartholomae concludes, while students may roughly imitate academic discourse at first, their progress will be marked by their eventual facility in speaking from a position of intellectual privilege (p. 284).

> Summary of Bartholomae's points on academic conventions from paragraphs 17–32 of the original article.

> Restatement of Bartholomae's position on grammar and conclusion from paragraphs 33–39 of the article.

Bartholomae, D. (1988). Inventing the university. In E. R. Kintgen, B. M. Kroll, & M. Rose (Eds.), *Perspectives on literacy* (pp. 273–285). Carbondale, IL: Southern Illinois University Press.

> APA end reference.

A CLOSER LOOK AT
Summary of David Bartholomae's "Inventing the University"

1. Consider the description of Bartholomae's thesis found in paragraph 1 of the summary. Do you agree with his assessment of the expectations students encounter on entering university? How have you negotiated the writing assignments you have been asked to do so far?

2. The end of the summary describes Bartholomae's opinion on grammar or what he terms "sentence-level error." What is his opinion of the role grammar plays in good writing? Do you agree with his ideas? Do you find most professors stress grammatical correctness or accept a certain level of error?

IDEAS FOR
Writing

1. Describe your experiences, both positive and negative, on entering university. In particular, consider the writing assignments you have been asked to do. In two to three paragraphs, summarize the expectations those assignments entailed and the level of difficulty you experienced fulfilling those expectations.

2. Write a formal, academic summary of a recent article on the Canadian university experience. You may select an academic article from the library databases or use a popular article, such as one from *Maclean's* magazine's annual special issue on universities. Be sure to locate the key abstractions or main ideas, to use reporting expressions, and to cite the article in APA or MLA style. Aim for 250 to 300 words.

Talk About This

1. Ask each member of your group to summarize a recent vacation or movie plot. What events do they highlight? What events do they omit? How does this shape your understanding?

2. With a group of people in your class, talk about your favourite novel or story. Summarize the general narrative for your classmates. Consider how much detail you want to give and the ideas in the narrative you want to highlight.

Try This Out

1. Find an abstract that precedes an academic paper. Does it give you a clear idea of what the paper is about? What is the paper's main argument and method? Write an abstract for your next research paper to help you clarify your argument and approach.

2. Read a body paragraph first from an academic essay and then from a popular essay. Identify the main abstractions in each, and then consider how each abstraction is supported by details. How convincing is each paragraph in its use of details to support the main ideas? Does one paragraph contain more details than another? Is there any difference in the kind of details offered as evidence?

1. **Write a summary.** Write a two page formal summary on a book that has been important to you. It could be a book on a topic you are particularly interested in, a textbook, or even a novel. Be sure to include the main idea and then carefully select your other points. Before you finish, add reporting expressions and citations as needed.

2. **Write a "six-word narrative."** A six-word narrative tries to tell a story in just six words and is an excellent way to practise conciseness. For instance, when the famous writer Ernest Hemingway was challenged to tell a story in just six words, he responded: "For sale: baby shoes, never worn." Work on your summarizing skills by developing your own six-word narrative on any topic you find to be of interest.

MyCompLab

For support in meeting this chapter's objectives, follow this path in MyCompLab:

Student Resources → Writing → Writing Samples → Writing Samples: Abstracts. Review the Multimedia resources on abstracts; then complete the Exercise and click on the Gradebook to measure your progress.

5

Reviews

In this chapter you will learn how to:

- develop and organize a review.
- determine common expectations with readers.
- improve your writing style for both popular and academic readers.

While in school and during your career, you will be asked to write reviews in which you discuss whether something was successful or not. Reviews offer critical discussions of books, movies, software, music, products, services, performances, and many other items, helping readers to understand the subject's strengths and limitations.

In essence, a review expresses the reviewer's informed opinion about the subject and explains why the reviewer came to that opinion. Reviewers need to do more than simply state whether they liked or didn't like something. Instead, they need to base their opinions on some *common expectations* that they share with their readers. When writing a review, your opinion is important, but it needs to be based on your shared assumptions with readers about what makes something successful or not.

Reviews are found in both academic and popular publications, such as academic journals, magazines, newspapers, and on the Internet. You probably check out the reviews before deciding to see a movie, pick up a book, go to a performance, or download some music. Reviews help you determine whether you would enjoy or use something before you buy it. Sometimes, people also like to read reviews after they experience something to see if others agree with their opinion about it.

In academic settings, professors will use reviews to give you a chance to express your opinion about the arts, architecture, books, politics, education, fashion, and other issues. When assigning a review, professors are typically looking for your ability to support your opinions by discussing something in a knowledgeable way. Reviews give you a chance to demonstrate your understanding of a subject, while also allowing you to express your opinion in an informed way. For example, literature reviews, explained at the end of this chapter, summarize and evaluate a range of current research on a topic, allowing you to situate your work in relation to existing research.

Reviews

These diagrams show two possible organizations for a review, but other arrangements of these sections will work too. You should alter these organizations to fit your topic, angle, purpose, readers, and context.

Introduction	Introduction
Description or summary of the subject	Description or summary of the subject
Strengths and weaknesses of the first feature of the subject	Strengths of the subject
Strengths and weaknesses of the second feature of the subject	Weaknesses of the subject
Strengths and weaknesses of the third feature of the subject	Weighing the strengths of the subject against its weaknesses
⋮	Conclusion
Conclusion	

Overview

A review typically has the following features:

- **An introduction** that identifies the subject being reviewed or evaluated.

- **A description** or summary of the subject.

- **A discussion** of the subject that determines whether it meets, exceeds, or falls short of expectations.

- **A conclusion** that offers an overall judgment of the subject.

Two typical patterns for a review are shown on page 59. Keep in mind, though, that reviews come in a variety of shapes and sizes. You will need to adjust the genre's pattern to fit the needs of your topic, angle, purpose, readers, and the context in which the review will be read. Be sure to consider whether your audience will consist of the general public or academic readers, since scholars often have particular expectations and needs (see page 64 for more explanation).

ONE STUDENT'S WORK
Reviews

The following student book review was written for a class on cultural studies. It identifies the reader's expectations as a student researcher and assesses the book in line with those expectations.

Double Googlization: A Review of *The Googlization of Everything (And Why We Should Worry)* by Siva Vaidhyanathan

Kurosh Amoui Kalareh

Key ideas are cited in MLA format throughout the review and a full end reference is provided.

"We are not Google's customers: we are its product" (Vaidhyanathan 3). This statement could be read as the main argument of *The Googlization of Everything (And Why We Should Worry)*. Published in 2011, the 260-page book aims to criticize a company that has received high praise for its various innovations throughout the last decade. The purpose of this book, therefore, contrasts that of previous works on Google, which have focused on the "company's rise and triumph" (Vaidhyanathan xii). What

Opening description of author, title, and topic.

author Siva Vaidhyanathan (Professor of Media Studies and Law at the University of Virginia) intends to do in his book is challenge people's common, optimistic percep-tions of Google, and also question Google's motto "Don't be evil"; however, it seems

Identification of expectations and overall assessment.

as though he has failed to accomplish these goals.

The Googlization of Everything provides new and precise information about Google as an advertising company. The book delivers several arguments on how Google advertises products by tracing users' activities. Through analyzing and archiving a user's previous records, Google anticipates on some level what one might want to see or consume. Questioning Google's search engine algorithm is one of the strong points of this book. In addition, by ascribing a negative sense to the word "Googlization," Vaidhyanathan attempts to demonstrate the three areas most affected by Google: us or agents, the world, and knowledge. "Us" refers to the users' information and records archived by Google. Since this information could be potentially deployed against the users, Google should be regarded as a medium of surveillance with considerable effect on "us." The Googlization of "the world" is a bit problematic though, because Vaidhyanathan has not defined what he means by "the world." He seems to be referring to all the governments that have interacted with Google in different ways throughout the last decade. Thus, using the term "the world" could be regarded as a false generalization, since the world is not merely a sum of governments. In my opinion, Vaidhyanathan has selected this phrase to exaggerate the influence of Google. Finally, the book analyzes the influence of Google on "knowledge." While this subject could have easily become the highlight of the book, Vaidhyanathan has missed many recent arguments on the relation between power and knowledge by limiting himself to the Google Books project and the copyright issue. The book can also be criticized for its argument on memory. The text makes the assumption that remembrance is superior to forgetting and that being productive has more value than laziness. These evaluations are debatable. It does not seem as though productivity and remembrance are the prevailing values in all cultures throughout history—especially productivity, which is a concept that a company like Google is built upon. Vaidhyanathan has employed these concepts without defining them accurately; therefore, the book has failed to achieve a coherent theoretical framework.

> Concedes one strength.

> Summarizes and assesses three key points in the book.

Although *The Googlization of Everything* firmly criticizes Google for its advertising role, the book itself implicitly advertises Google. This argument can be supported by looking at the title and also the cover of the book. Googlization of "everything" puts an emphasis on the importance and dominance of Google. One of Vaidhyanathan's main stated goals in writing this book is to reduce people's reliability on Google; however, he is in fact empowering Google by describing it as something extraordinary which can consume users. By employing the expression "why we should worry," the writer is pushing us to fear this colossal power. We should be aware that creating fear is a strategy employed to maintain dominance. Also, the Google logo is reproduced on the book's cover. The author is benefiting from Google's popularity to sell the book, while at the same time advertising Google by promoting its logo on a larger scale. In addition, the term "Google" is repeated on almost every page of the book, usually more than once, thus making the term stick in the readers' minds. If we search "Googlization" in Google, it guides us directly to

> Discusses an additional weakness

> Summary and elaboration of central criticism, confirming the negative tone of the review.

(continued)

Vaidhyanathan's work. This result is no accident, since Vaidhyanathan's manner of criticizing Google is also a means of advertising it.

In conclusion, it seems we cannot regard Vaidhyanathan's book as an anti-Google one. Analyzing Google as a company, not as a communication and research tool, has turned this book into a journalistic text rather than a theoretical one. The book's only real accomplishment is its analysis of Google's role in surveillance and Google's method of advertising. However, generally speaking, both Google and *The Googlization of Everything* are using the same marketplace logic, known as new liberalism. This review is entitled "Double Googlization," since apparently Vaidhyanathan has Googlized Googlization. If we consider Google as an enemy or as something evil, we should be aware that no tool or weapon can easily make it weaker. Maybe Friedrich Nietzsche was right after all: "What does not kill it, makes it stronger."

Work Cited

Vaidhyanathan, Siva. *The Googlization of Everything (And Why We Should Worry)*. Los Angeles: University of California Press, 2011. Print.

> Strong conclusion repeating the overall judgment and framing the review with an explanation of its title and return to the introductory reference to evil.

> MLA citation. See Chapter 24 for more discussion of MLA style.

Developing Your Review's Content

Of course, in order to write a review of something, you need to spend some time experiencing it. If you're reviewing a movie, you need to go see it. If you're reviewing a book, you need to read it. If you're reviewing a product or service, you need to use it. That's the fun part.

But wait. Before you see the movie, read the book, or use the product, you should do a little inquiry and background research to help you view your subject from a critical perspective. Inquiry will help you determine what you and your readers expect of your subject. Background research will help you develop a fuller understanding of your subject's history and context.

Inquiring: Finding Common Expectations

The foundation of a good review is the set of common expectations that you and your readers share about what makes something successful or not. Those expectations are not usually stated directly in the review itself. Instead, the reviewer assumes his or her readers share some assumptions about the thing being reviewed.

For example, let's say you want to write a review of an action movie that just arrived in the theatres. Your first challenge is to decide what features make an action movie successful. In other words, you need to figure out what moviegoers, namely you and your readers, expect from a movie like the one you are going to review.

So use an invention strategy like brainstorming to help you list all the things most people would expect from the kind of movie you are reviewing. As fast as you can, write out a list like the one shown in Figure 5.1. Then put a star or asterisk next to the three to six items that are most important to you.

More than likely, if you asked a group of people to make their own lists of expectations for an action movie, they would produce lists similar to yours. They might use different words and they might put stars next to a few other items, but most people would agree on what makes a good action film. That's what we mean by "common expectations." They are expectations that you and your readers already share.

Once you have identified the features you believe are most important, sort the unstarred items on your list under the starred ones. For example, the list shown in Figure 5.1 could be sorted into six major categories:

- Noble but Flawed Hero
- Complex and Sinister Villain
- A Romantic Relationship
- Fast-Paced Plot
- Stunts and Chase Scenes
- Music That Enhances Scenes

Features of a Good Action Movie

*Great hero
Memorable lines
Love interest that doesn't sidetrack movie
Real or potential victims of villain
Character evolution, especially hero
Suspense
Interesting setting
Something unexpected
Chase scenes
Use of weapons
*Complex and sinister villain
*Fast-paced plot
Fighting scenes
Some irony, but not too much
Hero needs to be flawed in some way
Mystery to be solved
*Amazing stunts

Cool special effects
Unexpected humour
Intense music soundtrack
Strong set of values
Villain is brilliant
*Music that sets the moods for scenes
Hero's desire for revenge
Opening scene that grabs audience
Social pressures on hero to give up
Good friends for hero
Low expectations for hero
Recognizable actors
Dark lighting
Somewhat realistic, even if fantasy
Characters worth caring about
Rivalry between hero and villain
Violence that has purpose and meaning

FIGURE 5.1
Using Brainstorming to List Common Expectations

Brainstorming is a good way to come up with a list of elements that you and your readers would expect the subject of your review to have.

Having created your list of common expectations, you will have a better idea about what you and your readers will be looking for in this kind of movie.

Inquiring: Finding Academic Expectations

Academic expectations for a review are a bit harder to identify in the beginning. Scholarly writers have different needs and expectations from those of the general public. Rather than building on or confirming common knowledge as popular writers do, scholars are engaged in the pursuit of new knowledge. This goal creates a demand for originality and for awareness of existing work in the field. Similarly, scholarly writers must be careful to use technical and formal language to prevent misunderstandings and to enable foreign scholars to read their work. They must also provide sufficient evidence to support any claims and be careful not to make assumptions. The following list outlines the academic expectations for a book or article you are reviewing:

Displays Originality. Is the work you are reviewing original? Does it develop a new topic or take a different stance on an existing topic?

Advances Knowledge and Addresses an Important Topic. Does the book or article advance existing knowledge? If so, in what way? Is the topic important in relation to current debates? (If you are doing a literature review, this last question is particularly important.)

Shows Existing Knowledge in the Field and Compares to Similar Texts on Similar Topics. Does the book or article you are reviewing acknowledge or refer to existing work in the field of study?

Uses a Formal Style. Is it written in a formal style, as indicated by word choice, sentence length, and grammatical correctness?

Contains Detailed, In-Depth Analysis and Sufficient Research and Evidence. Does the book or article show a depth of thought about the topic? Does it offer sufficient research and evidence? Is the information presented accurate?

Makes a Sound Argument and Takes a Reasoned Critical Stance. Does the logic in the book or article make sense? Does it take a reasoned and critical tone, avoiding hyperbole and unsupported claims? Does the author write from an unbiased position?

Researching: Gathering Background Information

The best reviewers do some background research before they experience their subject to help them understand its finer points.

Answer the Five-W and How Questions. Using the Internet, library databases, or print sources like magazines and newspapers, find out as much about your subject as possible. When collecting information to write a review, you might start out with an

Internet search, typing your subject's name or title into the search line. Look for answers to the Five-W and How questions:

- Who were its creators or original developers?
- What exactly are you reviewing?
- When and where was it created?
- Why was it created—for what purpose?
- How was it made?

After you've got an overview of the subject from the Internet, do a specific database search to locate more scholarly information about the topic. Then follow up with print or electronic articles, which are available through your campus library. In magazines, newspapers, and academic journals, look for more background information on your subject and the people who participated in it.

Locate Other Reviews of Your Subject. You might also use your library's indexes and databases or an Internet search engine to help you find other reviews on your subject. What have others said about the book, movie, album, performance, restaurant, or product that you are reviewing? Other reviewers might bring up issues that you hadn't thought about.

Be very careful not to use the words or ideas of another reviewer without citing them. In academic settings, borrowing ideas without citation is plagiarism. In professional settings, it could violate copyright laws. Of course, it is not uncommon for reviews to arrive at similar conclusions and even to refer to each other, but your review needs to be original in wording and presentation.

Interview or Survey Others. Depending on your subject, you might find an expert you could interview. On almost any university or college campus, someone is an expert about your subject. This person might help you understand what to look for when you experience your subject. You could also survey others who have already read the book, seen the movie, eaten at the restaurant, listened to the music, and so on. What did they think of your subject? How did they react to it? What did they like and dislike about it? If you use this information in your review, be aware that you will need to obtain consent from your participants to publish an interview and your institution's ethics approval to publish survey results.

Prepare to Do Field Observations. Grab your laptop or notebook and get ready to do some field observations of your subject. In a field observation, you would watch your subject closely *and* pay attention to how others react to it. For example, while watching an action movie, take notes about how the audience reacted to particular scenes. Did they laugh? Did they groan? Did they seem to enjoy themselves, or were they dismissive of the film?

Remember, informal observation is fine, but always be aware of privacy issues when participating in field research.

Researching: Go Experience It

This might sound obvious, but part of your research involves experiencing your subject. Go see the movie. Go eat at the restaurant. Read the book. Your inquiry and background research should help you experience your subject from an informed and critical perspective.

Being critical means being aware of your own reactions to your subject. For example, when you are reviewing a movie, allow yourself to experience the movie as a regular moviegoer. But also step back and experience the movie critically as a reviewer. If something in the movie is funny, go ahead and laugh, but then ask yourself *why* you laughed. If you thought the book was biased, ask yourself *why* you had that reaction.

It helps if you can take down some notes as you are experiencing your subject. Your inquiry, critical reading, and research should have given you some things to keep in mind as you experience your subject. During the experience, keep notes about whether your subject measures up to common or academic expectations. Also keep notes about why you came to these conclusions.

After you experience your subject, you might also spend some time playing the Believing and Doubting Game to draw out some ideas for your review:

Believing. First, imagine that you are going to write an overly positive review. What did you like? What were your subject's strengths? What stood out as superior? How did your subject exceed your expectations?

Doubting. Now imagine that you are going to write a very negative review. What didn't you like? What didn't work? What were the weakest aspects of your subject? What annoyed or irritated you? What didn't fit your expectations or the genre?

Synthesizing to Find Common Ground. Now examine the two sides of the game to consider which features are most important to you and your readers. Where do they agree, and where do they strongly disagree? Which side do you think is right?

While synthesizing, try to figure out how you really feel about your subject. Where do you stand among the people who would totally dislike your subject or would totally love it?

Organizing and Drafting Your Review

The organization of a review tends to be rather straightforward, so drafting these kinds of documents is often easier than drafting other documents.

The Introduction

In your introduction, you should identify your topic (the subject of your review) and offer enough background information to familiarize your readers with it. You should also identify your purpose directly or indirectly. You don't need to say something like

"My purpose is to review . . ." but it should be clear to your readers that you are writing a review.

> Reviewing a classic action movie like *The Bourne Identity* is always challenging, because these kinds of movies develop a cult following of fans who are no longer able to watch from a critical perspective.

> Film scholars will be both informed and intrigued by this new book of criticism.

Later in the introduction, you may want to tell your readers your overall assessment of your subject (your main point). In some reviews, though, you may not want to tell your readers your verdict up front. Reviewers of movies, music, and performances, for instance, will often wait until the conclusion before they finally give their overall judgment.

Description or Summary of the Subject

Now you need to familiarize your readers with the subject of your review. Begin by assuming that your readers have not seen the movie, read the book, eaten at the restaurant, or gone to the performance, so you will need to give them a brief description or summary of your subject. You have a couple of options:

Chronological Description or Summary. Describe or summarize your subject by leading your readers through the major scenes of the movie, book, or performance. At this point in your review, you should offer an objective description without making any evaluative comments. Your goal is to describe or summarize your subject well enough that your readers do not need to actually see your subject or read it to understand your review.

Feature-by-Feature Description. If you are reviewing something that is stationary, like a building or a piece of artwork, your best approach would be to describe your subject feature by feature. Divide your subject into two to five major parts and then describe each part separately. Make sure you use your senses to include plenty of detail. What does it look like? How does it sound, taste, smell, and feel?

In most reviews, this description or summary tends to be one substantial paragraph. This part of the review rarely goes over three paragraphs unless the review or evaluation is particularly long.

Discussion of Strengths and Shortcomings

Earlier, you generated a list of three to six common expectations that you and your readers have about your subject. Point out its strengths—how the subject met these expectations—and any shortcomings—how the subject failed to meet these expectations—and explore why.

> The primary strength of *The Bourne Identity* is the characters of Jason Bourne and his reluctant partner, Marie. Both Jason and Marie have typical desires and fears

that make them very human. Jason seems like a regular guy, even though he discovers that he has unexplainable fighting abilities and expertise with weaponry. The audience wants Jason and Marie to survive and escape. . . .

On the downside, the absence of a great villain means *The Bourne Identity* lacks some of the intensity of a typical action movie. The forces of evil in this movie are mostly faceless bureaucrats who send one-dimensional assassins to kill Jason Bourne. The audience has trouble focusing its anger on one person or a few people, because there is no single evil-doer in the movie. Instead . . .

Early in each paragraph, make a direct claim about a strength or shortcoming of your subject. Then, in the rest of the paragraph, support that claim with reasoning, examples, quotes, facts, and any other evidence you need to prove your point.

In this part of the review, go ahead and express your opinion. That's what readers expect from you. They want you to tell them exactly how you felt about the movie, the book, the restaurant, or the performance.

Conclusion

The conclusion of your review will usually be brief, perhaps a few sentences. In your conclusion, you should state or restate your overall assessment of the subject. Then you might offer a look to the future.

Overall, I found *The Bourne Identity* to be a thoroughly entertaining film, despite its few weaknesses. Matt Damon carries the film with one of his best performances. The film also leaves plenty of loose ends to be explored in its two equally entertaining sequels, *The Bourne Supremacy* and *The Bourne Ultimatum*. This movie certainly deserves to be listed among the classics of action movies.

Avoid introducing any new information in the conclusion. Your conclusion should bring your readers around to your main point.

Choosing an Appropriate Style

The style of your review depends on your readers and the places where they will encounter your review. Most readers will expect your review to be entertaining as well as factually correct. A review written for a mainstream newspaper, magazine, or website should use a lively style that matches your reaction to the movie, book, or performance. A review written for academic purposes should use a formal style.

Use Detail

Reviews need detail. Whether you are reviewing a movie or a restaurant, you need to provide descriptive detail to help your readers envision what you are discussing. For example, when you are summarizing a movie, you want to describe the characters and the action by selecting key details. You want the readers to be able to imagine what the movie actually looked and sounded like. Similarly, if you are reviewing a new restaurant, you want your readers to imagine the taste of the food, while hearing the same sounds you heard and smelling the same smells.

One way to add detail to your review or evaluation is to concentrate on your senses:

Sight: What colours did you see? How were people dressed and how did they behave? What objects did you notice as you were observing? What were the reactions of other people around you?

Hearing: What sounds did you hear? How did people talk? What sounds did you enjoy and which noises irritated you? Were people laughing? If you closed your eyes, what did you hear?

Taste: If you had a chance to sample some food or drink, what did it taste like? Did you enjoy the taste? If so, what made it pleasurable? Did something taste awful? Use specific details to tell your readers why you felt that way.

Touch: How did things feel? Did you brush your hands over any surfaces? What did that feel like? Were surfaces rough or smooth, cold or hot, hard or soft?

Smell: What scents did your nose pick up? Did you enjoy the smells, or did they turn you off? What smells came through the strongest and which ones were not immediately obvious?

Of course, you don't need to use something from all five senses in your review, and some reviews require you to consider the argument, examples, and ideas. Movie reviews are about what you saw and heard, not what you smelled or touched. Book reviews are about the argument and the analysis you read. Keep all your senses open, your critical stance engaged, and take notes on what you detected. You never know what kinds of details might be useful as you draft and revise your review.

Set the Appropriate Tone

The tone of your review should reflect your reaction to the subject, and your voice should be entertaining to your readers. If you were really excited by the movie you saw, the tone of your review should reflect your excitement. If you thought a book was particularly informative, your review should reflect your increased knowledge. A concept map can help you set a specific tone in your writing. See Chapters 2 and 11 for examples and explanations of concept mapping.

If you occasionally slip words from your concept map into your writing, your readers will sense the tone you are trying to set. So if you thought a movie like *The Bourne Identity* was intense, using words associated with intensity will give your readers that feeling too. If you thought a book was informative, using words from a cluster around "information" will signal that to your readers.

Change the Pace

You might also pay added attention to pace in your review. Typically, shorter sentences will make the pace of your writing feel faster, because they increase the heartbeat of the text. So if you are describing action scenes in a movie, you might try using shorter sentences to increase the intensity of your writing. Longer sentences slow the pace down. So if you are describing an idea from a book that involved lengthy, painstaking research, use longer sentences to slow down the pace of your writing.

Applying the Genre: Literature Review

A literature review is a kind of review that uses summary and evaluation (as do the other examples in this chapter), but also compares sources to each other to gain a better understanding of the overall state of research or of the general opinion on a topic. For an example of a literature review, see the excerpt from "Media Influence on the Body Image of Children and Adolescents" in the readings at the end of the chapter. In academic essays, literature reviews are necessary to situate the researcher in relation to existing ideas.

If you are asked to write a literature review, here are some guidelines to follow (you will notice that they are expansions of techniques for review already covered in this chapter):

Use Academic Expectations. You will need to use academic expectations regarding originality, significance, formality, objectivity, analysis, and research (see above). Also consider your own expectations regarding the topic as you begin. Your ideas may change as you write, but a literature review is designed to assess the various merits of existing research and to use that research to develop your own ideas.

Ensure You Consider a Representative Range of Key Texts. One of the most significant elements of the literature review involves ensuring you consider a representative range of key texts. Be sure to research thoroughly, using triangulation and assessing the validity and influence of your sources. See Chapters 21 and 22 for more tips on researching. Your professor may also be able to point you toward some important sources on the topic.

Use Summary Techniques to Locate and Restate Key Points of Important Sources. Once you have identified several important sources, use the techniques of summary to locate and restate the main points of each. These summaries will be brief (likely one to two sentences), but you want to clearly state the main argument of each source.

Compare and Contrast the Sources. How are the sources similar and different in their claims about your topic? Are there key debates between researchers? If so, where do you stand in those debates?

Combine Your Summaries and Comparative Assessments into Paragraphs. Put your summaries and comparative assessments together into formally written paragraphs on the current state of research. The length will depend on your assignment, but two to five paragraphs are typical for first- and second-year papers. Integrate the sources you read with your own position and identify the advantages and disadvantages of each argument. Consider what directions or methods for future research are indicated and how your work might use or relate to those.

Designing Your Review

Typically, the format and design of reviews depend on where they will appear or be used. A review written to appear in a newspaper, magazine, academic journal, or on a blog should be designed to fit that setting.

Choose the Appropriate Medium. Paper is fine, but you should consider other media, like a website, a blog, or even a podcast, for making your review available to the public. Today, the vast majority of movie, book, and product reviews appear on the Internet.

Add Photographs, Audio, or Video Clips. Depending on what you are reviewing, you might consider adding a photograph of the item, such as a book cover, a still from the movie, or a picture of the product. In some cases, such as a movie, you might be able to add in a link to a trailer or a clip from a scene. If you plan to publish your review or post it on a website, though, make sure you ask permission to use any photos or screenshots. Please note that academic journals rarely use graphics. If you are asked to write an academic book or film review, graphics are generally not necessary.

Revising and Editing Your Review

When you are finished drafting and designing your review, leave yourself at least an hour (preferably more) to revise and edit your work. Revising and editing are integral parts of the writing process and will help you sharpen your claims and develop better support for your opinions.

Determine Whether Your Opinion Has Evolved. Sometimes while you are reviewing something, your opinion will evolve or change. Watching a movie closely or reading a book carefully, for example, might cause you to gain more respect for it, or you might see some flaws that you did not notice before. If your opinion has evolved, you will need to rewrite and revise the review to fit your new opinion.

Review Your Expectations. Now that you are finished reviewing your subject, look at your list of common or academic expectations again. Did you cover all these expectations in your review? Did any new expectations creep into your draft?

Improve Your Tone. The tone of a review is important, because readers expect to be entertained or informed while reading. Look for places where your voice seems a little flat or inappropriate for your audience and revise those parts of the review to add appeal for readers.

Edit and Proofread. As always, carefully check your work for grammar mistakes, typos, and misspellings. Your credibility with readers will be harmed if they notice mistakes in your writing. Errors make you look careless at best, and uninformed and unintelligent at worst.

While you are finishing up your review or evaluation, put yourself in your readers' place. What kinds of information and details would help you make a decision about whether to see a movie, eat at a restaurant, or read a book? Keep in mind that your readers have not seen or experienced your subject. Your job is to let them experience it through you, so they can make a decision about whether they want to see it, read it, or buy it. If you are writing a literature review, your readers will want to know exactly where you stand in relation to existing research and debates.

Need to write a review? Here's what you need to get going.

FIND Something You Want to Review

Your professor may tell you what you should review. If not, choose something that you can analyze critically, not something you absolutely adore or detest. You want to pick something you can assess fairly.

FIGURE OUT Your and Your Readers' Common or Academic Expectations

List two to seven qualities that you and your readers would expect something like your subject to have.

GATHER Background Information on Your Subject

Using online and print sources, collect background information on your subject and read other reviews. You might interview an expert.

GO Experience It

As you are experiencing your subject, pay attention to your own reactions as a regular participant and as a critical observer.

DRAFT Your Review

Introduce your subject and describe it. Then describe its strengths and weaknesses. Finish with a conclusion that offers your overall judgment.

DEVELOP an Appropriate Writing Style

The style of your review depends on where it will appear and who will read it. Most reviews use a lively tone that is entertaining or informative depending on the readers.

ADD Graphics to Support Your Written Text if Appropriate

A few graphics, like photographs and movie stills, will help you to visually illustrate what you are talking about in popular reviews. Graphics are not necessary in academic reviews.

REVISE and Edit

Keep in mind that your opinion of the subject may have changed while you were reviewing it. If so, you may need to revise the whole argument to fit your current opinion.

Bare-Knuckled Knockout

BRIAN D. JOHNSON

The movie Fight Club *received mixed responses when it first came out, as this review from* Maclean's *magazine exemplifies. Many viewers and critics were unsure how to interpret its violence and social critique. Since 1999, however, the movie has gained cult status, generating numerous popular references and scholarly analyses. See the second to last paragraph of the book review of* New Hollywood Violence *(following this review) for an example of how this film has been discussed by academics for its portrayal of masculinity and violence.*

Engages readers, identifies topic, and gives overall assessment.

"First rule of Fight Club: You do not talk about Fight Club. Second rule of Fight Club: You do not talk about Fight Club." That's the mantra for a cult of bare-knuckled boxers who relieve their ennui by beating each other to a pulp. It is also the mantra being used to promote the movie: not talking about *Fight Club* is part of a clever anti-hype campaign that seems destined to make it one of the most talked-about movies of the year. It is certainly one of the most incendiary.

In some respects, *Fight Club* recalls David Cronenberg's *Crash* (1996), another story of a cult devoted to the existential kick of self-mutilation—people smashing into each other. *Fight Club* is far more accessible than *Crash*—brashly iconoclastic instead of coolly hermetic. And its subversive wit even extends to the marketing: *Fight Club's* press kit includes a mock fashion catalogue of costumes from the film, lavishly presented with lines such as "hand-crafted in an Indonesian sweatshop by Frida, a single mother of seven whose monthly salary is equivalent to six American dollars."

Gives background context on the film and its marketing.

Fight Club is a "grande" Molotov cocktail pitched at the comfort zone of consumer culture, the cozy capitalism of Starbucks and Ikea. At the same time, with Brad Pitt and Edward Norton leading the cast, it is as much a part of that culture as everything else—an ultra-hip Hollywood movie that is ferociously entertaining. Based on the 1996 novel by Chuck Palahniuk, *Fight Club* is directed by David Fincher (*Seven*) who has created a diabolical satire that mixes flamboyant gamesmanship with visceral brutality. It drags on too long, and the violence gets excessive. But Norton is brilliant in a role that deftly exploits his range. And Pitt scuffs up his pretty boy image with a show of gaudy malevolence.

Discusses strengths and weaknesses of the movie.

Norton plays an unnamed narrator who works for a major auto manufacturer. His job is to help calculate whether it costs more to recall defective cars or settle the death and injury claims arising from accidents. He is an insomniac. Stumbling across a support group for men with testicular cancer, he finds some solace, and soon he is spending all his spare time in group therapy for diseases and addictions he does not have—until he meets a rival imposter (Helena Bonham Carter) who is doing the same thing.

5   The narrator's life is turned upside down when a mysterious explosion destroys his Ikea-furnished condo. He spends the night getting drunk with an aggressive weirdo named Tyler (Pitt), who introduces him to the joys of fistfighting. Taking a beating becomes the narrator's new addiction. He moves into Tyler's rotting carcass of a house, a leaky ruin on the edge of town. And in a derelict basement they start the Fight Club, which is not about winning but about getting creamed—savouring self-destruction in a culture obsessed with self-improvement.

The club expands into a terrorist franchise, a Weather Underground for the '90s devoted to blowing up icons of consumer culture. To reveal more would not only break the Fight Club rules but spoil the plot, which has a wonderfully unpredictable twist. What can be said is that *Fight Club* throws down the gauntlet in the debate over screen violence in a way that will inflame the moral majority and give others pause. Even more disturbing than the violence is the film's giddy nihilism. There are nasty racial overtones to a Quentin Tarantino-like scene of Tyler holding a gun to the head of a whimpering Asian convenience-store clerk, making him aware of death so he will do something better with his life. Women, meanwhile, barely exist. Bonham Carter's character is just a blip in the narrator's peripheral vision.

> Summary of the film without revealing the ending.

> Identification of potential criticisms.

But this is, after all, a movie about men, men seeking their inner warrior. And there are uncanny parallels to *American Beauty*, another satirical drama about the perceived crisis of American manhood. In both films, a guy with his brain on fire rebels against conformity, tells his boss to shove it and discovers the meaning of muscle. In *American Beauty*, Kevin Spacey threatens to frame his boss for sexual harassment; in *Fight Club*, Norton frames his boss for assault by beating himself up in the man's office.

> Dismisses those potential criticisms.

Fight Club is an uglier, bloodier *American Beauty*. Susan Faludi, the feminist author of *Stiffed: The Betrayal of the American Male*, must be on to something: the year's two hottest movies are about white-collar weaklings who get tough, then go crashing through the looking glass as they try to get even.

> Concludes with an overall positive assessment of the film.

A CLOSER LOOK AT
Bare-Knuckled Knockout

1. The writer of the review, Brian Johnson, summarizes the plot of the movie in paragraphs 4–6. What aspects of the movie does he highlight for readers? What aspects does he leave out? If you haven't seen the movie, does the review's summary offer you enough information to give you an overall sense of the plot and themes?

2. What are some common expectations that the reviewer assumes his readers share for an action-based, social commentary movie like *Fight Club*? List three to five criteria that the reviewer uses to evaluate the movie. Do you think those are fair expectations?

IDEAS FOR
Writing

1. Compare this review to two or three other reviews of *Fight Club* that came out in 1999 (when the movie was first released). Use the library databases to find the largest range of reviews on the film. Then write a brief comparison of the reviews. Based on the sources you looked at, what was critics' general opinion of the film? Are there repeated criticisms or praise for certain elements? What you have written is a version of a literature review, which surveys and evaluates multiple sources. You may wish to look at pages 70–72 and 81–82 for more information and an example which compares sources.

2. One of the most interesting aspects of *Fight Club* is its portrayal of masculinity. The movie suggests that traditional male roles and occupations are being lost or discarded, but that there is a lack of viable new roles for men to play in society. Write a three page description and evaluation of a male role or occupation (you might consider the cowboy, the provider, the businessman, and so forth). Are these roles still relevant or have they changed? How has consumer culture exploited or altered these roles in its own interests?

The Many Shades of Red

JAMES KENDRICK

In this scholarly book review, James Kendrick discusses New Hollywood Violence, *Steven Jay Schneider's collection of essays about violence in Hollywood films. Kendrick both summarizes and evaluates the usefulness of the collection from an academic perspective, offering information that would be particularly relevant to a scholar in the field of film studies or new media.*

While there is a great deal of talk about violence in the media and much ink has been spilled in various newspapers and magazines, until about 10 years ago there had been surprisingly little significant humanistic scholarship done on the topic. Recent book publications like the Depth of Field Series' *Screening Violence* (2000; edited by Stephen Prince) and the American Film Institute's *Violence and the American Cinema* (2001; edited by J. David Slocum), as well as conferences like the 2001 meeting held at the University of Missouri–St. Louis titled "Violence, Cinema, and American Culture" have provided much-needed academic context to what otherwise often devolves into political brow-beating and social-scientific number crunching.

> *Context and significance of topic.*

New Hollywood Violence, which is part of Manchester University Press' diverse "Inside Popular Film" series and includes several essays first presented at the 2001 "Violence, Cinema, and American Culture" conference, is a welcome addition to this growing literature, especially as it places front and center the complex and often contradictory roles of screen violence in contemporary American cinema. Drawing from Murray Smith and Thomas Schatz, editor Steven Jay Schneider

> *Positive introduction and initial assessment of the collection of essays on violence in Hollywood.*

defines the "New Hollywood" as "a return to genre filmmaking following America's flirtation with European art cinema in the late 1960s and early 1970s, albeit a return 'now marked by greater self-consciousness, as well as supercharged by new special effects, saturation booking, engorged production budgets and, occasionally, even larger advertising budgets'" (xiv).

> Definition of New Hollywood.

The breadth of Hollywood cinema covered in the book's 15 essays is quite broad, ranging from the new ghettocentric films of John Singleton, to Terrence Malick's elegiac *The Thin Red Line* (1998), to the action spectacles of Arnold Schwarzenegger, to the homosocial cinematic world of Quentin Tarantino. Oddly enough, not a single essay is devoted exclusively to that most violent of genres, the horror film, which is perhaps reflective of how that genre had fallen on hard times in the mid-1990s prior to its resurgence following the smash success of *The Sixth Sense* (1999) and the new wave of '70s horror classic remakes. The writers contributing to the volume are also intriguingly varied, running the gamut from established voices in the realm of cinematic violence such as J. David Slocum, Stephen Prince, and Martin Barker, to a number of doctoral students making their first significant dent in academic publishing.

> Explanation of the range of topics covered and identification of one topic not covered.

Following an introduction by Thomas Schatz that lays out the familiar story of how screen violence has evolved in Hollywood filmmaking from the silent era to the modern blockbuster, the book is clearly organized into four main sections: "Surveys and Schemas," "Spectacle and Style," "Race and Gender," and "Politics and Ideology."

> Summary of book's structure.

5 The "Surveys and Schemas" section contains essays that offer broad historical, political, and ideological contexts for the role of screen violence in Hollywood. J. David Slocum's opening essay, "The 'Film Violence' Trope: New Hollywood, 'the Sixties,' and the Politics of History," offers an impressive start, cutting through the obvious and questioning the very historical and analytical foundations of the concept of "film violence," which Slocum argues is "a shorthand that circumscribes meaning and authorizes delimited explanations of a wide range of phenomena" (29).

This second essay, "Hitchcock and the Dramaturgy of Screen Violence" by Murray Pomerance, is an attempt to make sense of different forms of screen violence by categorizing them, an approach utilized in previous publications by Henry Giroux (1995) and Devin McKinney (1993), among others. Pomerance devises a taxonomy based on probability and irony of presentation, which results in four categories of screen violence: mechanical, mythic, idiomorphic, and dramaturgical. While critics might find gray areas between and among these categories, they still hold the potential to help explain and illustrate the flexibility of screen violence as a signifier.

The next chapter, Martin Barker's "Violence Redux," covers very familiar ground for those who have read Barker's other publications. His primary point is that violence is a social concept, not an object, which emerged in the late 1950s and early 1960s and has maintained surprising explanatory force in relation to the mass media while its meanings have become fractured and questionable in virtually every other realm. Barker takes to task the seemingly objective conclusions of social scientific research regarding media effects, especially as it relies on the social concept of "violence" as if it were an empirically testable object instead of, as he argues, "a central repository for a set of fears about social change, which at the same time proffers an understanding of those changes in an ideologically-skewed way" (73).

The final chapter in the opening section, "The Big Impossible: Action-Adventure's Appeal to Adolescent Boys" by Theresa Webb and Nick Browne, attempts to connect the culture of action films to American adolescent boys' "culture of cruelty" by examining closely 14 action films released in 1994 and arguing that they function primarily to socialize boys by providing role models and focusing male adolescent aggression toward possible military service. It makes for an intriguing companion piece to Todd Onderdonk's chapter "Tarantino's Deadly Homosocial," which appears much later in the book and suggests that Tarantino's *Pulp Fiction* (1994) is a "seminal example" of a film whose male homosocial relations support and encourage "the gender bias and homophobia of American capitalism" (287). Pairing the chapters together suggests that action films begin the task of socializing adolescent boys while Tarantino's crime capers solidify the work in young adulthood.

Despite the title of the second section, "Spectacle and Style," the only area *New Hollywood Violence* doesn't address as thoroughly as one might hope is the area of film aesthetics. For example, Fred Pfeil's chapter "Terrence Malick's War Film Sutra: Mediating on *The Thin Red Line*" has little to do with film aesthetics, or even film violence for that matter, but is rather an examination of Malick's film as a Buddhist meditation on singularity based on how his film presents death in comparison to Steven Spielberg's *Saving Private Ryan* (1998) and Stanley Kubrick's *Full Metal Jacket* (1987).

As Stephen Prince rightly points out at the end of his Afterword, "without close attention to formal design—to what filmmakers are actually doing with the audiovisual elements of cinema—we will be unable to explain the elemental pull that violence has within the history of cinema" (322). A number of the essays in the "Spectacle and Style" section do mention formal film elements as part of their larger ideological and historical discussions, but the only essay that puts aesthetics front and center is editor Steven Jay Schneider's "Killing in Style: The Aestheticization of Violence in Donald Cammell's *White of the Eye*." Schneider's close textual analysis is thorough and interesting, and he makes a compelling argument about Cammell's use of violence to conflate himself as director with the film's killer. However, the general obscurity of the film and the cult status of Cammell as an auteur keep the piece from providing anything more than an intriguing and isolated case study.

There is also some discussion of cinema aesthetics in Geoff King's " 'Killingly Funny': Mixing Modalities in New Hollywood's Comedy-With-Violence," which argues that mixing comedy with graphic violence is a specific contribution of the New Hollywood. King shows how this can be used to make violence both pleasurable and disturbing, and he offers formal analysis of several example films, including *American Psycho* (2000), *Very Bad Things* (1998), and *Series 7: The Contenders* (2001).

The mixing of comedy and violence, especially in the films of Arnold Schwarzenegger, is also addressed later in the book in David Tetzlaff's "Too Much Red Meat!" Perhaps because he is mounting a vigorous argument to recuperate the critical standing of Schwarzenegger's much-maligned *Commando* (1985), Tetzlaff adopts a somewhat cheeky writing style, one that effectively matches the comic-book excesses of his object of study, but without compromising his own critical insight and alleged seriousness. On the other hand, Thomas Leitch's "Aristotle v. the Action Film" argues that the action genre has evolved (perhaps backwards) from its Aristotelian roots of

---

Margin notes:

Summary of the essays in the first section of the book, with positive assessments.

Identification and discussion of the book's one weakness, a failure to discuss aesthetics in real depth.

Summary of the remaining essays in section two and explanation of what they do offer.

tragedy, logical causation, and ethical consequences and replaced "human insight" with artless "spectacle."

The last two sections, "Race and Gender" and "Politics and Ideology," place film violence into social contexts, thereby foregrounding cultural studies issues such as identification, representation, and hegemony. Paula J. Massood tackles race directly in "From Homeboy to *Baby Boy*: Masculinity and Violence in the Films of John Singleton," showing how black masculinity is constructed in Singleton's films in relation to justified violence, often at the expense of the invisibility or marginalization of black women. The role of female characters in violent films is addressed in Jacinda Read's chapter on the kitschy postmodern *Charlie's Angels* (2000), which she effectively shows to be much more complex in merging issues of femininity, violence, and culture than most would assume. Using a history of female protagonists as her foundation, Read shows how the three "Angels" resist essentialist notions of gender and instead construct femininity as performance.

Several chapters explore the social function of violence in contemporary Hollywood films, most notably Sylvia Chong's "From 'Blood Auteurism' to the Violence of Pornography: Sam Peckinpah and Oliver Stone" and Ken Windrum's "*Fight Club* and the Political (Im)Potence of Consumer Era Revolt." Chong's chapter uses Peckinpah's *The Wild Bunch* (1969) and Oliver Stone's *Natural Born Killers* (1994) to talk about the shifting discourses around film violence from the 1960s to the 1990s. Interestingly, she ends by suggesting that the problem with film violence is not in the films themselves, but rather in their reception, particularly by those who reify violence by either celebrating or condemning it, thus "collapsing the differences between types of violence and their deployment" (265), a grave mistake that Martin Barker would argue happened a long time ago. Windrum's chapter uses the deployment of heavily masculinized violence in *Fight Club* (1999) to question whether any product of Hollywood can successfully present a critique of "the franchised, corporate culture of late consumer-era capitalism" (304). Windrum finds *Fight Club* to be an essentially incoherent text, and for that reason it fails to work as critique and sustain any revolutionary potential.

> Summary of the third and fourth sections of the book, with positive assessments. Ends with a critical discussion of *Fight Club*.

15   As a whole, *New Hollywood Violence* presents an intriguing and multifaceted overview of the ways in which screen violence can be deployed in contemporary films. The book will work well as a primer for thinking about screen violence in the modern age, and the inclusion of a wide range of genres and critical approaches strengthens the oft-heard, but still frequently ignored argument that screen violence is not a simple object, but rather a complex set of signifying practices that can be deployed for purposes both reactionary and progressive. The book in no way reaches any kind of consensus about how screen violence should be treated by either Hollywood producers or film scholars, not that such a consensus could possibly be expected given the complexities of screen violence both formal and cultural. This is a topic whose surface has only begun to be scratched.

> Conclusion on the value of the book and need for more studies on Hollywood violence.

Bibliography

Giroux, H. A. (1995). Racism and the aesthetic of hyper-real violence: *Pulp Fiction* and other visual tragedies. *Social Identities, 1*(2), 333–355.

McKinney, D. (1993). Violence: The strong and the weak. *Film Quarterly, 46*(4), 16–22.

> APA style references. See Chapter 25 for more discussion of APA style.

A CLOSER LOOK AT
The Many Shades of Red

1. In this review of an academic text, Kendrick asserts that the book successfully gives an overview of violence in contemporary American films. Kendrick argues that violence as portrayed in films is often "complex and contradictory." How does Kendrick's review of the book illustrate these contradictions? Find two or three examples of how violence is analyzed in the book. Do you find them convincing? Are there other examples of onscreen violence you can think of that are not discussed in the book Kendrick is reviewing?

2. Kendrick uses a scholarly tone in reviewing this book. What determines the tone he uses (look for sentence length, word choice)? Now compare the style he uses to the style used in Brian Johnson's *Fight Club* review from *Maclean's* magazine. Is there a difference in sentence length, word choice, and format of the document? What other differences can you identify?

IDEAS FOR
Writing

1. Think of two different genres of television programs you might watch. Now think of the degree of violence in each. Write a brief comparative review of the level of violence in two contemporary television programs. As you write, consider how the different programs use the violence. Are they trying to elicit a specific response from the audience? Is the violence used to portray a more realistic scene?

2. Review Kendrick's review in two to three paragraphs. Do you find it to be successful? Does it give you a clear sense of what the book is about? Does it address a scholarly audience's likely expectations for a book review (see page 64 for a list of those expectations)? Does it provide enough background context?

Media Influence on the Body Image of Children and Adolescents

Z. LAWRIE, E. A. SULLIVAN, P. S. W. DAVIES, AND R. J. HILL

The following excerpt is an example of a literature review from an essay on how media affects children and often leaves them with distorted body images. As outlined in this chapter, literature reviews situate the researcher in relation to existing ideas, which is what Lawrie, Sullivan, Davies, and Hill do below in their overview and comparison of previous research.

In today's society, children are bombarded with constant exposure to the media in many different modes. These include television, magazines, radio, newspaper, movies, and, more recently, the Internet. Contemporary issues surrounding body awareness in children and adolescents have increased with several researchers suggesting the media to be a significant contributor to this phenomenon (Park, 2005). A historical perspective of the media's portrayal of the ideal body size and shape demonstrates change over the last century. The ideal body size and shape for men has changed from a larger body to become more muscular with a physically fit appearance (Lien, Pope, & Gray, 2001; McCabe & Ricciardelli, 2004). The ideal shape for women has changed from a curvaceous shape in the mid 1900s to become noticeably leaner and slimmer to align with current fashion trends (Katzmarzyk & Davis, 2001). The implications of childhood exposure to the mass media, which portrays these particular images of body size and shape, are concerning, as there is an increased probability of the child becoming discontent with his or her body if his or her appearance differs from the so-called norm (Stice, Schipak-Neuberg, Shaw, & Stein, 1994).

The pressures placed on children to attain the "perfect body" may be completely unachievable for their individual genetically determined shape and may explain the obsessive nature that some children develop as they are so engrossed with achieving this ideal. According to Wertheim and colleagues (Wertheim, Paxton, Schultz, & Muir, 1997) the strongest pressure on 15-year-old girls to be thin was the presentation of the thin ideal by the media.

Internalization of the thin ideal has been identified as a key component in the development of body dissatisfaction (Cusumano & Thompson, 2001; Sands & Wardle, 2003). Internalization often occurs before adolescence (Cusumano & Thompson, 2001; Sands & Wardle, 2003; Stice et al., 1994; Stice & Shaw, 1994) and has been linked to dieting motivation in pre-adolescents (Sands & Wardle, 2003).

> Identification of topic.

> Literature review begins with a discussion of historical perspectives supporting increased media influence and changing ideals.

> Early study supporting media pressure on girls.

> Discussion of research from 1994–2003, which shows that children internalize a thin ideal.

Field et al. (1999) studied 6,928 girls aged 9 to 14 years and found that attempting to emulate the appearance of females on television, in movies, and in magazines was predictive of beginning purging behaviour at least on a monthly basis and that the risk for this behaviour increased per category increase in frequency of trying to look like females in the media. A further study by Field et al. (2001) in boys and girls aged 9 to 14 years showed that children who were trying to imitate the appearance of same-sex media personalities were more likely to develop weight concerns and become constant dieters. Sands and Wardle (2003) reported that media exposure, in the form of reading magazines that reflect the thin ideal, as well as awareness of a standard for appearance, increased with age in their sample of 356 girls aged 9 to 12 years. Thomsen et al. (2002) observed that restricting calories and taking diet pills were associated with reading beauty and fashion magazines in female high school students 15 to 18 years of age, and similarly, Utter et al. (2003) found that weight control behaviours and binge eating increased in middle and high school students as their frequency of reading magazines containing diet related information increased.

> Summary of key points on thinness as an ideal for females and the progressive and dramatic influence of the media.

> Based on the preceding literature review, Lawrie et al. explore children's perceptions (rather than just the effects) of media influence toward thinness and ideals of beauty.

Thinness is promoted as a standard for female beauty (Tiggemann & Slater, 2004) and the images presented by the media of the so-called ideal shape have become progressively thinner in recent years (Spitzer, Henderson, & Zivian, 1999). Children are particularly vulnerable to the messages the media portray and during youth become accustomed to the images conveyed. This paper investigates children's beliefs about what the media messages are regarding body size and shape.

A CLOSER LOOK AT
Excerpt from "Media Influence on the Body Image of Children and Adolescents"

1. What does current research indicate about media and body image? How do unrealistic media images affect children and adolescents? Why do Lawrie et al. feel that the effects of media on children in particular should be studied?

IDEAS FOR
Writing

1. Look at two or three images of women's bodies found in a popular magazine. Write a short commentary on these images. Do they portray unrealistic ideals? How do you feel looking at the images? Are you negatively or positively affected by them or do you feel unaffected?

2. Write a short literature review on a topic of your choosing, summarizing and evaluating three sources in relation to each other. Begin by collecting three sources that present important ideas on the topic; then decide on your key criteria. Write in formal, scholarly style using reporting expressions and citations to clarify which text you discuss in each part of the review. After you finish, think about how this review could lead in to your own ideas on the topic.

1. With a group in your class, discuss a movie that you all have seen. What did you like about the movie, and what were some of its limitations? As you discuss the movie, take note of the issues that seem to be part of the discussion. What are some expectations that your group members seem to have in common? Are there any issues that some members seem to care about but others don't? When people disagree, what do they disagree about?

2. In class, talk about what you want a reviewer to discuss in a typical book review. How much do you want the reviewer to reveal about the book? What kinds of reviews do you find most helpful when you are considering whether to buy or read a particular book? Do you like reviewers whose work reveals their personalities, or do you prefer objective reviewers who seem to stick to the facts? Are there any book, movie, or music reviewers that you seem to trust more than others? Why?

3. Examine and critique the following passage, which is taken from a review of a Greek restaurant. Describe which aspects of the review work well. Explain how it could be improved so that it meets the expectations readers have for reviews.

    > Among the appetizers, everybody in the group agreed that the spanako-pita was by far the best but that the hummus was not up to par. There was some disagreement about the entrees. Personally, I liked the chicken souv-laki and dolmades plate, but two members of the group preferred the "Greek Combo," which includes dolman, spanakopita, souvlaki, broiled scampi, and mousaka.

1. On the Internet, find a video advertisement that you can review. Most companies put their most recent advertisements on their websites, or you can find them on video-sharing websites like *YouTube*. Write a review of the advertisement in which you critique its effectiveness. Tell your readers why you thought it worked, failed, or just irritated you. Your review should run about two pages.

2. Choose a movie and write two, one page reviews for it. Your first review should be positive. Focus on your and your readers' common expectations and say mostly positive things about the movie. The second review should be negative. Focus on elements that would cast the movie in a negative light. Then, in a memo to your professor, explore how your decisions about what to consider changed your review and what you had to say about the movie. Could you reconcile these two reviews into one that is balanced?

3. Compare the content of a movie review found in an academic journal to one found in a popular magazine or newspaper (if the reviews are on the same film, this will make your comparison even easier). Consider the reviewers' expectations and how those are related to the audiences for whom they write. How are the expectations similar or different? What expectations do academics have that a popular audience does not and vice versa?

1. **Write a review for your campus newspaper.** Imagine that you are a reviewer for your campus newspaper or another local newspaper. You can review music, books, poetry, movies, video games, television, sports teams, or just about anything that you enjoy doing. Write a three to four page review of a subject you choose. Be sure to summarize your subject for your readers, who probably haven't seen, heard, or experienced it. Then discuss your subject based on expectations that you and your readers share. Explain to your readers why you are giving your subject a positive or negative review.

2. **Write an opposing review.** Find a review on the Internet that you disagree with. Then in a brief response to the website, write an opposing review. Your review should be written as a response to the original review, showing why you felt differently about the subject. Next, write a one page cover memo to your professor in which you explain your strategy for rebutting the original review. Also, discuss why you believe someone might find your review of the subject stronger than the original review.

MyCompLab

For support in meeting this chapter's objectives, follow this path in MyCompLab:

Student Resources → Writing → Writing Purposes → Writing to Evaluate. Review the Instruction resources about writing to evaluate; then complete the Exercises and click on Gradebook to measure your progress.

Rhetorical Analyses

In this chapter, you will learn how to:

- analyze rhetorical elements of a text.
- use *logos, ethos, pathos,* and other rhetorical patterns as modes of development and persuasion.
- use voice appropriately in both academic and popular analyses.

The purpose of a rhetorical analysis is to determine how and why forms of communication are influential, or not. Advertisers, marketing analysts, and public relations agents use rhetorical analyses to understand how well their messages are influencing target audiences and the general public. Political scientists and consultants use rhetorical analyses to determine which ideas and strategies will be most persuasive to voters and consumers. Meanwhile, historians and rhetoricians use rhetorical analyses to study historic speeches and documents to understand how and why they were influential in their day and perhaps are still influential today.

Ultimately, the objective of a rhetorical analysis is to show why a text was *effective* or *persuasive.* Although you may associate the word "text" solely with written forms of communication, when we refer to texts in this chapter we mean communication that can be written, verbal, or visual. By studying texts closely, we can learn how writers and speakers sway others and how we can be more persuasive ourselves. If you are asked to analyze a novel or short story, you will want to consult the next chapter on literary analysis.

In your university or college courses, you may be asked to write rhetorical analyses that explore historical and present-day documents, advertisements, and speeches. These assignments are not always called "rhetorical analyses" but any time you are being asked to analyze a nonfiction text, you are probably being asked to write a rhetorical analysis. In this chapter, we have included a rhetorical analysis of teen magazines written for a general audience, as well as an academic analysis of the language used in scientific textbooks so that you can better observe some of the requirements of academic analysis through comparison. The readings also show a variety of texts (using our expanded definition) that can be analyzed, including magazines, books, and, in a student example, advertisements.

Rhetorical Analyses

Here are two possible organizations for a rhetorical analysis, but other arrangements of these sections will work too. You should adjust these organizational patterns to fit your topic, angle, purpose, readers, and context.

Introduction	Introduction
Explanation of rhetorical concepts	Historical context and summary of the text
Historical context and summary of the text	Explanation of first rhetorical concept followed by analysis of text
Analysis of *logos*-related (reasoning) proofs in subject	Explanation of second rhetorical concept followed by analysis of text
Analysis of *ethos*-related (credibility) proofs in subject	Explanation of third rhetorical concept followed by analysis of text
Analysis of *pathos*-related (emotion) proofs in subject	• • •
Conclusion	Conclusion

Overview

Rhetorical analyses can be written a variety of ways. Nevertheless, they tend to have some common features:

- **An introduction** that identifies the subject of your analysis, states your purpose and main point, offers background information on the subject, and stresses its importance.

- **An explanation of the rhetorical concepts** that you will use to analyze the subject.

- **A description or summary of your subject** that sets it in a historical context.

- **An analysis of the subject** through the chosen rhetorical concepts.

- **A conclusion** that states or restates your main point and looks to the future.

Rhetorical analyses come in many forms and sizes. For the sake of simplicity, the diagram on page 86 shows two common patterns used for rhetorical analyses. The pattern on the left examines the uses of reasoning (*logos*), credibility (*ethos*), and emotion (*pathos*) in a text. This is one of the most common types of rhetorical analysis; however, other kinds of rhetorical concepts can be used as the basis of a rhetorical analysis, including metaphor, narrative, genre, style, definition, classification, and others. Consult Chapter 18 for further discussion of rhetorical patterns.

ONE STUDENT'S WORK
Rhetorical Analyses

The following ad analysis was written for a first- composition course. It examines a Canadian Petroleum Producers ad, available through the CAPP website (www.capp.ca) under "Canada's Industry/Oil Sands/Innovation/TV and Print ads."

Analysis of a Canadian Association of Petroleum Producers (CAPP) Advertisement

Sahil Sidhu

Over the past decade, the Alberta oil sands have become the nation's largest source of harmful greenhouse gas emissions (Woynillowicz, Severson-Baker, & Raynolds, 2005, p. 19). However, the 2011 ad "Patrick Moore, PhD, Environmentalist and Co-founder of Greenpeace," produced by the Canadian Association of Petroleum Producers (CAPP) both as a video and as a poster, depicts the oil sands development site as a clean, natural location. The ad, which this review will call the "Reclamation" ad, associates CAPP with maintaining natural diversity. Using the technique of cause marketing, it is designed to appeal to eco-conscious viewers.

Explore
Oil-Soaked Cove Photograph

Background information contextualizes the topic.

(continued)

The text is carefully chosen and formatted to mask the mining operation's damage to the environment and, instead, to focus on and emphasize environmental renewal or "reclamation." Further, the images in the ad direct the audience's attention toward scenes of nature and away from devastated mining sites. With the use of cause marketing, manipulative text, and deceptive images, the ad is effective and may help the oil companies convince the public to abandon negative perceptions about the oil sands and to accept them as a clean source of energy.

Charles Doyle (2011) defines cause marketing, or cause-related marketing, as a marketing approach in which a company or organization associates itself with a relevant social cause for the benefit of both the company and the cause. Typically, this term refers to instances in which a corporation donates funds to a social cause or charity. However, cause marketing can also refer to an organization's sponsorship of a cause, even if no actual funds are donated. When employed correctly, this marketing technique can help corporations strengthen public relations and stimulate sales by appealing to consumers interested in the supported cause (Marconi, 2002, pp. 1–3). Cause marketing can also benefit the sponsored party through increased publicity and funding (Marconi, 2002, p. 2). In this case, CAPP's "Reclamation" ad links CAPP to the cause of maintaining biodiversity in Canadian ecosystems. However, this example of cause marketing only minimally meets the requirements of the term, because the cause (biodiversity) cannot receive its benefits (reclamation) until after its benefactor has destroyed it by mining. Still, by associating CAPP with the cause of biodiversity, the "Reclamation" ad strengthens CAPP's public relations by appealing to environmentally conscious viewers and readers. This tactic is a particularly effective method of manipulating the public, considering that environmental sustainability has become an issue of such critical importance in recent years (De, 2004, p. 1). With sources of pollution, such as industry, rapidly destroying the planet's ecosystems, people readily support parties or organizations that promise to repair or prevent environmental damage. Therefore, by identifying CAPP with the urgent cause of maintaining biodiversity, this ad helps to convince the public that further developing the oil sands is healthy, not harmful, for the environment (CAPP, 2011).

Similarly, the text of both the print and video versions of the "Reclamation" ad (CAPP, 2011) is selected to convince the public to accept the oil sands development. The print version emphasizes the term "reclamation," which appears in the centre of the page in a distinct orange hue. It is written in lowercase letters, giving the impression of a friendly appeal. Another important textual aspect is the ad's title, which uses the name of environmentalist Patrick Moore, PhD, and openly displays it in the first shot of the video ad and again in the print ad. By focusing on Moore, the ad employs the persuasive technique of expert testimony or *ethos* appeal. Although Greenpeace (2008) describes Moore as an advocate of

---

Division of topic into key components of text and image.

Here is the author's main point or thesis.

Extended definition of the ad's marketing approach.

Analysis of the CAPP ad's use of cause marketing.

anti-environmental views, this ad portrays him as an environmental expert and co-founder of Greenpeace (CAPP, 2011). By doing so, the ad uses Moore to give its claims authority. Notably, Moore is shown "signing off" on the video ad, as if endorsing the validity of its message. Another interesting detail in the video is the phrase "new ideas" (CAPP, 2011). Although "new ideas" actually refers to newly developed sustainable practices, the phrase could indirectly influence viewers to adopt a new perspective. While the above components of the ad are emphasized to help persuade readers and viewers that the oil sands are environmentally friendly, other textual elements are placed so as to downplay their significance. For example, the CAPP logo, situated in the bottom right corner of the print ad, is the last part of the ad a reader would notice, effectively minimizing the reader's awareness that the oil companies themselves have funded the ad. Thus, by emphasizing positive environmental messages and de-emphasizing the CAPP logo, the text of this ad attempts to persuade the public to adopt a more positive view of the oil sands.

> Text of the ad is described and analyzed for its *ethos* appeal. See page 91 for explanations of *ethos, logos,* and *pathos.*

The "Reclamation" ad also effectively conveys its message through focusing on images that show thriving natural environments (CAPP, 2011). The print ad immediately makes viewers believe they are wading through a sea of flowers and bushes, giving the sense that Canada's oil sands are in harmony with nature rather than harmful to it. Nature is in the foreground, while the remnants of a tailings pond are confined to the background. The pond is further disguised by a blanket of sunlight, which makes it appear almost like an oasis inviting the public to accept the oil sands' false purity. Visuals in the "Reclamation" video ad (CAPP, 2011) use similar techniques. Shots of the mining operation's barren landscape are shown only fleetingly and are often slightly blurred, directing the audience's attention to Moore. CAPP's ad allots the most time to Moore as he walks through a lush green hillside while discussing the oil sands. This image misguides viewers into associating the mining operations with the beautiful landscape. Thus the images of the "Reclamation" ad link the oil sands to nature and thereby help to further persuade the public that the oil sands are a clean source of energy.

> Contrast between the ad's logical (*logos*) and ethical (*ethos*) elements.

> Detailed description of the ad's visuals with reference to their *pathos* or emotional appeal.

> Analysis of the ad's imagery.

Finally, the success of the "Reclamation" ad (CAPP, 2011) in promoting a positive view of the oil sands through the use of the manipulative techniques is further highlighted by comparing it with another CAPP ad produced by Cenovus Energy (2011). The 2011 Cenovus ad, entitled "Our Wedge Well™ Technology," shows an oil sands operations and field coordinator discussing more sustainable approaches for designing pipelines. Both the "Reclamation" ad (CAPP, 2011) and the Cenovus ad (2011) show CAPP as concerned about the environment in an attempt to win the support of eco-friendly viewers and readers. However, the "Reclamation" ad is more likely to succeed in winning some support, because

(continued)

it effectively conceals the barren mining sites. The Cenovus ad, on the other hand, makes the mistake of allowing viewers a clear view of the treeless land immediately surrounding the oil plant (CAPP, 2011; Cenovus, 2011). This weakens the ad, because the destruction of Alberta's forests is directly associated in most people's minds with a negative environmental impact from the oil sands (Woynillowicz, Severson-Baker, & Raynolds, 2005, p. 39). Despite this discrepancy though, both the Cenovus (2011) and "Reclamation" (CAPP, 2011) ads are effective in encouraging a positive view of the oil sands.

Ultimately, CAPP's "Reclamation" ad (2011) is a highly effective tool in the oil companies' ongoing campaign to persuade the public to see Canada's oil sands as a clean, environmentally friendly source of energy. The manipulative text and images used in this ad are designed to convince viewers and readers that the environmental impact of the oil sands is insignificant and easily repairable. Over the past fifteen years, the oil companies have worked hard to change the public's perception of oil production in northern Alberta, including rebranding the "dirty-sounding 'tar sands'" with a "new brand name," "oil sands," and framing them as "a national prize" (Woynillowicz, Severson-Baker, & Raynolds, 2005, p. 3). This strategy has undoubtedly had an effect, but whether the public will finally accept the "Reclamation" ad's message remains to be determined.

Comparison which discusses the *ethos* and *pathos* appeals of two energy company ads.

Conclusion on the implications of the ad.

List of APA style references.

References

Canadian Association of Petroleum Producers. (2011). *Patrick Moore, Ph.D., environmentalist and Greenpeace co-founder* [Video & Poster]. Retrieved from http://www.capp.ca/canadaIndustry/oilSands/Innovation/media/Pages /PatrickMoore.aspx

Cenovus Energy. (2011). Our Wedge Well™ technology [Video]. Retrieved from http://www.cenovus.com/news/our-videos.html

De, A. K. (2004). *Environmental education.* Delhi, India: New Age International.

Doyle, C. (2011). Cause-related marketing. *A dictionary of marketing* (3rd ed.). London, England: Oxford University Press. Retrieved from http://www .oxfordreference.com

Greenpeace USA. (2008, October). *Greenpeace statement on Patrick Moore* [News release]. Retrieved from http://www.greenpeace.org/usa/en/media-center /news-releases/greenpeace-statement-on-patric/

Marconi, J. (2002). *Cause marketing.* Chicago, IL: Dearborn Trade.

Woynillowicz, D., Severson-Baker, C., & Raynolds, M. (2005). *Oilsands fever: The environmental implications of Canada's oil sands rush.* Drayton Valley, AB: The Pembina Institute. Retrieved from http://www.pembina.org/pub/203

Developing Your Rhetorical Analysis's Content

Explore All in the Family: Understanding the Rhetoric of Occasion

When preparing to write a rhetorical analysis, the first thing you need to do is closely examine the text you are analyzing. Read through it at least a couple of times, taking special note of any places where the author seems to make important points or perhaps misses an opportunity to do so.

Explore Plug It In: Understanding the Rhetoric of Proof

Inquiring: Highlighting Uses of Proofs

Now, do some analysis. When looking closely at the text, you will notice that authors tend to use three kinds of *proofs* to persuade you:

Reasoning (*logos*): appealing to readers' common sense, beliefs, or values

Credibility (*ethos*): using the reputation, experience, and values of the author or an expert to support claims

Emotion (*pathos*): using feelings, desires, or fears to influence readers

Rhetoricians often use the ancient Greek terms *logos, ethos,* and *pathos* to discuss these three kinds of proofs, so we have used them here. Let's look at these concepts more closely.

Highlighting Uses of Reasoning (*Logos*).

The word *logos* in ancient Greek means "reasoning" in English. This word is the basis for the English word "logic," but *logos* involves more than using logic to prove a point. *Logos* also involves appealing to someone else's common sense and using examples to demonstrate a point. Here are some common ways people use reasoning to influence the beliefs and opinions of others:

If . . . then: "If you believe X, then you should believe Y also."

Either . . . or: "Either you believe X, or you believe Y."

Cause and effect: "X is the reason Y happens."

Costs and benefits: "The benefits of doing X are worth/not worth the cost of Y."

Better and worse: "X is better/worse than Y because . . ."

Examples: "For example, X and Y demonstrate that Z happens."

Facts and data: "These facts/data support my argument that X is true or Y is false."

Anecdotes: "X happened to these people, thus demonstrating Y."

As you analyze the text, highlight these uses of reasoning so you can figure out how the writer uses *logos* to influence people.

Highlighting Uses of Credibility (*Ethos*). The Greek word *ethos* means "credibility," "authority," or "character" in English. It's also the basis for the English word "ethics." *Ethos* could mean the author's credibility or the use of someone else's credibility to support an argument.

Highlight places in the text where the author is using his or her authority or credibility to prove a point:

Personal experience: "I have experienced X, so I know it's true and Y is not."

Personal credentials: "I have a degree in Z" or "I am the director of Y." "So I know about the subject of X."

Good moral character: "I have always done the right thing for the right reasons, so you should believe me when I say that X is the best path to follow."

Appeal to experts: "According to Z, who is an expert on this topic, X is true and Y is not true."

Identification with the readers: "You and I come from similar backgrounds and we have similar values; therefore, you would likely agree with me that X is true and Y is not."

Admission of limitations: "I may not know much about Z, but I do know that X is true and Y is not."

Expression of good will: "I want what is best for you, so I am recommending X as the best path to follow."

Use of "insider" language: Using special terminology or referring to information that only insiders would understand.

When you are looking for *ethos*-related proofs, look carefully for places where the author is trying to use his or her character or experience to sway readers' opinions. Also consider that accurate, carefully edited work is itself a form of *ethos* in making the writer appear trustworthy and knowledgeable to the reader.

Highlighting Uses of Emotion (*Pathos*). Finally, look for places where the author is trying to use *pathos*, or emotions, to influence readers. The psychologist Robert Plutchik suggests there are eight basic emotions: joy, acceptance, fear, surprise, sadness, disgust, anger, and anticipation. As you analyze the text, highlight places where the author is using these basic emotions to persuade readers.

Promise of gain: "By agreeing with us, you will gain trust, time, money, love, advancement, reputation, comfort, popularity, health, beauty, or convenience."

Promise of enjoyment: "If you do things our way, you will experience joy, anticipation, fun, surprises, enjoyment, pleasure, leisure, or freedom."

Fear of loss: "If you don't do things this way, you risk losing time, money, love, security, freedom, reputation, popularity, health, or beauty."

Fear of pain: "If you don't do things this way, you may feel pain, sadness, grief, frustration, humiliation, embarrassment, loneliness, regret, shame, vulnerability, or worry."

Expressions of anger or disgust: "You should be angry or disgusted because X is unfair to you, me, or someone else."

Some other common emotions that you might find are annoyance, awe, calmness, confidence, courage, disappointment, delight, embarrassment, envy, frustration, gladness, grief, hate, happiness, hope, horror, humility, impatience, inspiration, joy, jealousy, loneliness, love, lust, nervousness, nostalgia, paranoia, peace, pity, pride, rage, regret, resentment, shame, sorrow, shock, suffering, thrill, vulnerability, worry, and yearning.

Frequently, writers will not state emotions directly. Instead, they will inject feelings by using emotional stories about others or by incorporating images that illustrate the feelings they are trying to invoke. Advertisements, for example, rely heavily on using emotions (*pathos*) to sell products. Academic arguments, on the other hand, prioritize *ethos* and *logos* appeals and use *pathos* sparingly, because their focus is on providing intellectual proofs.

Rhetorical Patterns: Understanding How the Topic Achieves Its Effects

The major rhetorical patterns used both to develop and to analyze topics are description, classification and division, definition, comparison and contrast, example or illustration, process analysis, and cause and effect. Most of these patterns are discussed in more detail in Chapter 18, so here we offer only brief explanations of these patterns. However, we elaborate further on process analysis—those forms of analysis that can be applied to topics which go through change and development, such as speeches, essays, films, or television commercials.

Description. Observes the key parts or details of a topic. Description is the starting point for most analyses. The analysis of the CAPP ad begins by describing how the ad represents "the oil sands as a clean, natural location."

Classification and Division. Classification places a topic into a larger category or grouping, while division separates the topic into parts most relevant to that category. The two processes typically work together. The CAPP ad analysis classifies the ad as a form of cause marketing and as deceptive. It divides the ad into text and image.

Definition. Definition offers the literal meaning of a concept and can also include its function and extended, contextual meanings. See the definition of *pathos* on pages 92–93 of this chapter or the definition of cause marketing in the CAPP analysis for examples, and consult Chapter 18 for a fuller discussion.

Comparison and Contrast. Explore the similarities and differences between two topics that have an underlying likeness or basis for comparison. The CAPP analysis compares two ads within the same campaign on pages 89–90 of this chapter.

Example or Illustration. Show how a concept is used within the speech, advertisement, or other text under consideration. Examples are key forms of evidence in analysis. In the CAPP analysis, Moore's signature is offered as an example of *ethos* appeal.

Process Analysis. Linear processes describe a step-by-step or sequential series of events. Occasionally, within a linear process, events occur simultaneously; this is important to note so as not to distort your description. For instance, within the writing process you may follow a linear series of steps to create an essay, but during the research stage you may be both finding sources and making final decisions about your topic. Narrative is a form of process in that it describes a sequence (sometimes linear, sometimes not) of events. See Chapter 18 for more discussion of narrative.

Cause and Effect. Events lead to or cause other events. Often, a cause may have more than one effect or an effect may result from multiple causes. For instance, an advertisement may succeed both because it addresses the audience appropriately and because it highlights an important feature of the product. See Chapters 18 and 19 for further discussion of causation.

Researching: Finding Background Information

Once you have highlighted the proofs (i.e., *logos, ethos, pathos*) and located the rhetorical patterns used in the text, it's time to do some background research on the author, the text, and the context in which the work was written and used.

Online Sources. Using Internet search engines and electronic databases, find out as much as you can about the person or company who wrote the text and any issues that he, she, or they were responding to. What historical events led up to the writing of the text? What happened after the text was released to the public? What have other people said about it? Remember to check any site you use for reliability and accuracy.

Print Sources. Using your library's catalogue and article databases, dig deeper to understand the historical context of the text you are studying. How did historical events or pressures influence the author and the text? Did the author need to adjust the text in a special way to fit the audience? Was the author or organization that published the text trying to achieve particular goals or make a statement of some kind?

Empirical Sources. In person or through e-mail, you might interview an expert who knows something about this text, its author, or the context of the text you are analyzing. An expert can help you gain a deeper understanding of the issues and people involved in the text. You might also show the text to others and note their reactions to it. You can use surveys or informal focus groups to see how people respond to the text.

As always, keep track of your sources. You will need to cite them in your text and list them in the works-cited or references list at the end of your rhetorical analysis.

Organizing and Drafting Your Rhetorical Analysis

At this point, you should be ready to start drafting your rhetorical analysis. As mentioned earlier, rhetorical analyses can follow a variety of organizational patterns, but those shown on page 86 are good models to follow. You can modify these where necessary as you draft your ideas.

Keep in mind that you don't actually need to use rhetorical terms, such as *logos, ethos,* and *pathos*, in your rhetorical analysis, especially if your readers don't know what these terms mean. Instead, you can use words like "reasoning," "credibility," and "emotion," which will be more familiar to your readers.

The Introduction

Usually, the introduction to a rhetorical analysis is somewhat brief. In this part of your analysis, you want to include up to five items:

- Identify the subject of your analysis (the text you are analyzing).

- State the purpose of your analysis (e.g., to explain why this text was effective or persuasive, or not).

- State your main point about the text (e.g., "This text was persuasive because . . .").

- Provide some background information on the text, its author, and the historical context in which it was produced and received.

- Stress the importance of the text, telling readers why its rhetorical strategies are significant.

These items can be arranged in just about any order in your introduction, so write them down and then figure out what order best suits your rhetorical analysis and your readers.

Explanation of Rhetorical Concepts

After the introduction, you should define and explain the rhetorical concepts you are using to analyze the text. So if you are using *logos, ethos,* and *pathos*, you would need to explain how these concepts are defined. For example, here is how a student defined *pathos* in her rhetorical analysis:

> *Pathos,* which involves using emotion to influence someone else, is a commonly used rhetorical tactic in advertisements aimed at teenage girls. Emotional scenes and images are used to grab the teen's attention and often make her feel

something negative, like less confident, insecure, undesirable, unattractive, anxious, or dependent (Holt et al. 84).

Of course, the product being pushed by the advertiser is then put forward as a solution to that supposed inadequacy in the teen's life. For example, as psychologist Tina Hanson points out, teenage girls don't really need a cabinet full of haircare products (73). The typical teenage girl's hair is already healthy, shiny, full, and rich in colour. Yet, television and magazine advertisements from haircare companies, which make shampoo, conditioner, and dye, routinely show frustrated teens unsatisfied with their hair. Usually the message being sent to a teen is "You don't even know you need this product, but everyone *else* knows you do, especially guys." The images show a discouraged girl who risks losing friends or being embarrassed because her hair isn't perfect.

In your rhetorical analysis, you don't need to use all of the rhetorical tools mentioned in this chapter. Instead, you might decide to concentrate on just one of them, like *pathos*, so you can develop a fuller definition of that concept for your readers.

Also as mentioned earlier, keep in mind that other rhetorical concepts besides *logos, ethos,* and *pathos* are available. For instance, you could choose to study the metaphors used in a text, or perhaps its genre, style, or use of comparison and contrast. If you choose one of these other rhetorical concepts, you may need to define and explain that concept to your readers.

Historical Context and Summary

To give your readers an overall understanding of the text you are analyzing, give them some historical background on it. Then summarize the text with an emphasis on the elements most important to your analysis.

Historical Context: Tell your readers the history of the text. Who wrote it or presented it? Who was the target reader or audience? Where and when did the text appear? Why was the text produced or written?

Summary: Summarize the content of the text. You can place your summary either as a separate section of the analysis, which ends with a restatement of your main point, or at the beginning of each paragraph, when you describe the particular parts of the text you are discussing. Your summary should be completely in your own words, with select quotes taken from the text. When summarizing, do not express your own opinions about the text or its message. Instead, just give the readers an objective overview of the content of the text with a focus on the parts most important to your discussion.

The aim of this historical context section is to give your readers enough background to understand the text you are analyzing. For example, here is the historical context and a summary of an advertisement for Red Bull:

Advertisements for energy drinks rely heavily on emotion to make sales to university students. These unique soft drinks, which usually contain high amounts of caffeine and calories, began to grow in popularity in the late 1990s.

Red Bull, one of the most popular brands, actually was invented in the 1970s in Thailand, and it was first exported to the United States in 1997 (FundingUniverse). From the beginning, Red Bull's advertising has been squarely aimed at university students, telling them that they need to have extra energy to get through their hectic days. One of its recent advertising campaigns, which is called "Red Bull Gives You Wings," began in 2005 with simple hand-drawn movies like the one shown in Figure 1.

In this advertisement, a bird relieves himself on a man who looks a lot like a professor. The man then drinks a can of Red Bull and sprouts wings. He flies above the bird, pulls down his pants, and proceeds to return the favour (off-screen, thankfully). The viewer hears the bird screech in horror as an image of a can of Red Bull fills the screen, but we can all imagine what happened.

FIGURE 6.1
"Red Bull Gives You Wings."

During the span of the 30-second advertisement, the man transforms from being a seemingly helpless victim to a superheroic figure who can take vengeance on the bird. Drinking Red Bull is shown to be the way he gains this new power.

The extent of your summary depends on your readers. If they are already familiar with the text you are analyzing, your summary should be brief. You don't want to bore your readers by telling them something they already know. If, however, they are not familiar with the text, your summary should be longer and more detailed.

Analysis of the Text

Now analyze the text for your readers. Essentially, you are going to interpret the text for them, using the rhetorical concepts you defined earlier in the rhetorical analysis.

There are two main ways to organize this section:

- You can follow the organization of the text you are analyzing, starting from the beginning and working to the end of the text. Apply the rhetorical concepts to each major section of the text you are analyzing.

- You can discuss the text through each major point separately. For instance, if you are arguing that the text uses *logos, ethos*, and *pathos* you would separately discuss the text's use of each kind of proof.

For example, here is a discussion of *pathos* in the Red Bull advertisement:

Using Emotion to Sell Red Bull

Like much advertising aimed at young people, the Red Bull advertisement uses emotions to bring home its argument. In this advertisement, the use of humour is what gives the message its emotional punch.

Many young people feel like the professor in this advertisement, because they perceive that they are ultimately powerless in society. So when someone else treats them badly, young people usually assume they need to just take it. In this case, the Red Bull advertisement shows the bird relieving itself on the professor-like character. In most situations, the man would simply need to suffer that humiliation. But, he has a secret weapon, Red Bull. He drinks a can, sprouts wings, and humorously takes revenge on the bird.

The story itself is an emotional parable that reflects the life of most young people. The bird represents all the things in young people's lives that humiliate and embarrass them but that they cannot fix. The professor-like man, though not young, is a figure that students can relate to, because he is still in the educational system and seems powerless in his own ways. So when he is able to actually use a product like Red Bull to take revenge, young people not only laugh but also feel an emotional release of their own frustration. The emotional message to young people is, "Drink Red Bull, and you can get back at all those people who crap on you."

The humour, coupled with the revenge theme, makes the advertisement's use of emotion very effective. According to Mark Jefferson, a professor at Penn State who studies advertisements, the use of revenge is very effective for university students. "Students often feel powerless in a world that tells them they are adults but refuses to give them power. Advertisements that tap into that frustration in a humorous way are very powerful" (23).

In this discussion of emotion, the writer is applying her definition of *pathos* to the advertisement. This allows her to explain the use of emotion to sell Red Bull. She can now go on to discuss the use of *logos* and *ethos* in the ad. Or, if she has more to say about *pathos*, she might make her rhetorical analysis about the use of *pathos* alone.

The Conclusion

When you have finished your analysis, wrap up your argument. Keep this part of your rhetorical analysis brief. A paragraph should be enough. You should answer one or more of the following questions:

- Ultimately, what does your rhetorical analysis reveal about the text you studied?
- What does your analysis tell your readers about the rhetorical concept(s) you used to analyze the text?
- Why is your explanation of the text or the rhetorical concept(s) important to your readers?
- What should your readers look for in the future with this kind of text or this persuasion strategy?

Minimally, the key to a good conclusion is to restate your main point about the text you analyzed.

Choosing an Appropriate Style

The style of a rhetorical analysis depends on your readers and where your analysis might appear. If you are writing your analysis for a website like *Slate* or a magazine like *The Walrus*, readers would expect you to write something colourful and witty. If you are writing the argument for an academic journal, your tone would need to be more formal. Here are some ideas for using an appropriate style in your rhetorical analysis:

Use Lots of Detail to Describe the Text. Whether writing for a popular or academic context, tell readers the *who, what, where, when, how,* and *why* of the text you are analyzing. Also, use details to describe what the text looks like, sounds like, and feels like. Above all, you want readers to experience the text, even if they haven't seen or read it themselves.

Use Appropriate Language. When analyzing something, you might be tempted to puff up your language with lots of specialized terminology and complex words. While academic pieces may occasionally use specialized language for greater accuracy, any such terminology should be necessary, not stylistic. In analyses written for general audiences, these kinds of complex words will unnecessarily make your text harder to read.

Improve the Flow of Your Sentences. Rhetorical analyses are designed to explain a text as clearly as possible, so you want your writing to flow easily from one sentence to the next. The best way to create this kind of flow is to use the "given-new" strategies that are discussed in Chapter 17, "Developing Paragraphs and Sections." Given-new involves making sure each new sentence takes something like a word, phrase, or idea from the previous sentence.

Pay Attention to Sentence Length. If you are writing a lively or witty analysis, you will want to use shorter sentences to make your argument feel more active and fast-paced. If you are writing for an academic audience, longer sentences will make your analysis sound more formal and proper. Keep in mind that your sentences should be "breathing length."

As mentioned earlier in this chapter, rhetorical terms like *logos, ethos,* and *pathos* do not need to appear in your rhetorical analysis. If you are writing for readers who probably don't know what these terms mean, you are better off using words like "reasoning," "credibility," or "emotion." If you want to use the actual rhetorical terms, make sure you define them for readers.

Applying the Genre: Ad Critique

An ad critique, such as the student example earlier in this chapter on pages 87–90, is a kind of rhetorical analysis that evaluates an advertisement to show how it works and to consider why it was or was not effective. Today, ad critiques are becoming common. They give people a way to express their reactions to the kinds of advertisements being thrown at them. Here are some strategies that are particularly useful in writing an ad critique:

Targeted Summary. For clarity, summarize the ad objectively, but with a focus on the parts that are particularly relevant to your critique.

Description. Is there something remarkable about the ad? What is it? What makes it stand out from other ads?

Comparison and Contrast. Discuss why this ad is better or worse than its competitors. Or, identify the three to five common features that are usually found in this type of advertisement. You can use examples of other ads to explain how a typical ad would look or sound.

Examples and Detail. Throughout your critique, use plenty of detail to help your readers visualize or hear the ad. You want to replicate the experience of seeing or hearing it.

Designing Your Rhetorical Analysis

Analyses for general audiences sometimes include visuals, such as downloaded images or links to further information. Academic analyses, however, rarely include visuals, and further information should be cited in a recognized format. If you are writing a popular analysis or if your professor has asked you to include visuals, here are some options:

Download Images from the Internet. If you are reviewing a book or a historical document, you could download an image of its cover and include that image in your rhetorical analysis. That way, readers can actually see what you are talking about.

Add a Screenshot. If you are writing about an advertisement from the Internet, you can take a picture of your screen (i.e., a screenshot). Then include that screenshot in your analysis. On a PC, you can push the Print Screen button to capture a screenshot. Then you can use the cropping tool to remove the parts of the image you don't want. On a Mac, just type Command-Shift-3 for a shot of the whole screen or Command-Shift-4 for a cursor that allows you to take a picture of part of the screen.

Include a Link to a Podcast. If you are analyzing a video or audio text (perhaps something you found on *YouTube*), you can put a link to that text in your analysis. Or you can include the Web address so readers can find the text themselves. If your analysis will appear online, you can use a link to insert the podcast right into your document.

Make a Website. Your rhetorical analysis could be made into a website. The homepage could be the introduction, and you could provide links to the rest of your analysis. You could add images and links to other sites, which will allow readers to better experience the text you are analyzing. Why not be creative? Look for ways to use technology to let your readers access the text you are analyzing.

Revising and Editing Your Rhetorical Analysis

Rhetorical analyses tend to be medium-sized documents, so they are easy to revise and edit. Consult Chapter 15 for a full discussion of the revision and editing process, as well as checklists to help you edit thoroughly. One of the challenges of editing a rhetorical analysis is keeping your definitions of key terms consistent throughout the argument. If you aren't careful, your definitions of rhetorical concepts will evolve as you analyze a text. So you want to make sure you are using your terms consistently.

Recheck Definitions of the Rhetorical Concepts. Early in the analysis, you defined one or more rhetorical concepts you used to analyze the text. Now that you have finished drafting your analysis, make sure you actually used those definitions as you described them. You might find that you need to revise or refine your definitions, or you might need to rewrite parts of your analysis to fit those original definitions.

Expand Your Analysis. Did you cover all the angles? Could you say more? Look for gaps in your analysis of the text. For example, if you were talking about the use of emotion in a Red Bull ad, are there some additional emotional elements you didn't talk about or could expand on?

Copyedit for Clarity Take a closer look at your paragraphs and sentences. Can you make them clearer and more concise? Can you put better claims at the beginnings of paragraphs? Can you work on improving the flow of the sentences?

Read Your Work Out Loud. Your ears are more sensitive to phrasing problems than your eyes. So read your rhetorical analysis out loud to yourself, or have someone read it to you. Mark any places where something sounds odd or makes you stumble. Then edit those marked places.

As always, a solid effort at proofreading will only improve your work (and your professor's response to it). Some people find it helpful to print out the document, so they can proofread on paper. Errors are often easier to find on paper than they are on the screen.

Need to write a rhetorical analysis? Here are some steps to get you going.

FIND a Text You Want to Analyze

Pick something you find intriguing. The best texts are ones that seem curiously persuasive to you (or not persuasive at all). You might also look for texts that are historically important.

HIGHLIGHT the Uses of Rhetorical Devices

Read or examine the text, marking places where the author uses reasoning (*logos*), credibility (*ethos*), emotion (*pathos*), or other rhetorical patterns.

RESEARCH the Context

Use a variety of sources to do background research on the text you are analyzing. Find out as much as you can about the author and the historical context in which he or she created the text. Use interviews or surveys to measure how others react to the text you are studying. Interview experts who know about this kind of text.

DRAFT Your Rhetorical Analysis

A rhetorical analysis typically has the following sections: Introduction, Definitions of Rhetorical Concepts, Historical Context and Summary, Analysis, and Conclusion. Draft each section separately.

CHOOSE an Appropriate Style

Your style depends on your readers, the place where your analysis will appear, and the text you are analyzing. Use ample details and good pacing to match your analysis's style to the place where it could be published. Add graphics if they help advance the reader's understanding and are appropriate.

REVISE and Edit

You have gone this far. Now, finish the job. Do some revising and editing to make your rhetorical analysis shine. Look for any inconsistencies. Fill out places where more information might be helpful.

What's a Girl to Read?

LIZA FEATHERSTONE

In this article written for a general audience, Liza Featherstone discusses the current magazines available to teenage girls. Traditionally, these kinds of magazines have been about image, fashion, and relationships. Featherstone detects a shift, with some magazines changing for the better and others repackaging the same old themes. In this rhetorical analysis, pay attention to how she criticizes and applauds the ways some magazines use emotion and credibility to attract young women.

Trying to seduce as many underage girls as possible, corporate publishing has adopted the buzzword "real" as its come-on of the moment. Rightly sensing that there is a vacuum in the teen magazine market—the fastest-growing segment of the population has, like, nothing to read—publishers have dreamed up *Jump, Teen People, Twist* and *Glossy. Teen People*, which hit the newsstands this month, promises "real teens, real style." *Jump*'s slogan is "For girls who dare to be real." It makes sense that realness should become a market niche—existing teen magazines like *Seventeen* and *YM* being so decidedly unreal.

Identification of topic and examples.

But how much realer is this new crop? "Reality" is a place where bodies come in all shapes and sizes, and girls have a political, intellectual and creative life of their own. Despite their pretenses, commercial teen magazines' reality bureaus are still pretty short-staffed.

Main point stated.

Time Inc.'s Joe Camel, *Teen People*, deserves some credit for putting out a model-free magazine. Only a third of *Teen People* is devoted to fashion and beauty, and it has refreshingly little advice about how to find a boyfriend. *Teen People* also nods to the not-so-girly girls with profiles of girl sportclimbers and in-line streetskaters. But it's a sad commentary on the state of the glossies that these achievements are even worth mentioning, since *Teen People* is clearly nothing more than a way to hook future *People* readers on celebrity worship—and on a made-in-Hollywood world view (movies are praised for making you "believe in love"). Worse, *Teen People* trivializes girls' achievements; a profile of *Party of Five*'s Jennifer Love Hewitt is almost entirely dedicated to her clothes and her love life. But *Teen People*'s most heinous crime is unskeptically quoting—just five pages away from a full-page *Dawson's Creek* ad, but who's noting such minutia—one of the cast members of *Dawson's Creek* as claiming, "We're a mouthpiece for real teens." Did *Teen People* even "watch" that show? Talk to the hand.

Example 1 analyzed positively and negatively.

Jump, just a few issues old, from the fitness-oriented Weider Publishing, is a refreshing paean to the active girl—"stylin' snowboarders" and girl hockey players fill its pages; nail polishes recommended are quick-drying (which assumes you have something better to do than sit around and fan your nails). *Jump* clearly has feminist intentions; a first-person story by a girl who suffered from chronic acne offers a powerful indictment of how girls are made to suffer over any physical flaw.

Example 2 analyzed positively and negatively.

But at points *Jump* reads like a 90s *Cosmo:* Pressure to be skinny is replaced by pressure to be "buff," and a plea to girls not to worry about being model-perfect is written by a boy. The message is clear: It's OK that boys and magazines still have the last word on what makes you sexy.

Twist, a bimonthly launched this month by Bauer Publishing, fails at realness 5 even more dismally. It does try to boost girls' body images; "Do our bellies really need busting?" is an eloquent plea for self-acceptance, and the magazine commendably names "Anti-Waifs" as a "Trend We Love . . . Finally! Hollywood is recognizing that you don't have to be scary skinny to shine." But check out their wussy examples—Jewel, Jennifer Aniston, Neve Campbell—no Janeane Garofalo or, hello, Kate Winslet, who was the romantic lead in the blockbuster of the year? Is it too utopian to hope that actresses with real meat on their bones could be presented as sexy icons in a commercial teen magazine? *Twist* shows some models of color, and recently ran a short item on how Janet Jackson gets her "rad red highlights," but these half-hearted hi-fives to multiculturalism are dwarfed by a full-page feature on "How can I get smooth silky hair"—in which the strived-after tresses shown are, you guessed it, blonde.

Example 3 critically analyzed and compared to previous two.

Aggravating as these body problems are, *Twist*'s assault on girls' minds is even worse. We know only one thing for certain about a girl who picks up a magazine: She doesn't spend every single minute of her life watching TV. So what else does *Twist* recommend she read? Books that might as well be TV shows because they are: the *Party of Five*, *Buffy the Vampire Slayer*, *Moesha* and *X-Files* book series. *Twist* also plugs supermodel autobiography *Veronica Webb Sight*. Whatever. *Twist* manages to have even less respect for readers' intelligence than its older sister glossies; while *Seventeen*, to its credit, has always featured fiction-writing contests, *Twist*'s idea of reader participation is—no joke—a "love quiz" contest.

Then there's *Glossy,* a Web magazine newly launched in print, which doesn't remotely aspire to realness. It makes *YM* look like the Seneca Falls Declaration.

OK, OK. My catty sniping is all very well, but ultimately, what's a girl to read?

Alternative examples endorsed.

Luckily there are a number of alternatives to these mind-numbing infomercials: independently published magazines written by and for teenage girls. These magazines are not only more feminist than their glossy counterparts, they're far smarter, more racially diverse, and yes, more real.

Alternative example 1 analyzed positively.

Rochester, N.Y.-based *Blue Jean*, an ad-free bimonthly, offers, to use its own words, an "alternative to the fashion and beauty magazines targeting young women." Ani "I-refuse-to-sell-out-to-the-McMusic-industry" diFranco graces the cover of the January/February "Women We Love" issue with gritty style—not your father's *Esquire*'s "Women We Love": in addition to Ani, *Blue Jean* loves Third Wave activist Rebecca Walker, soccer star Mia Hamm, tennis pro Venus Williams (and "the sassy swing of her beaded hair"), author Veronica Chambers, teen novelist Jean Crowell and Hard Candy nail polish entrepreneur Dineh Mohajer, and features interviews with both Missy "Misdemeanor" Elliott and Rosa Parks.

Alternative example 2 analyzed positively.

Teen Voices, a national quarterly run out of Boston that roughly estimates its 10 readership at 45,000, focuses on urban girls—taking on issues from teen pregnancy and body mutilation to "Snowboarding on the Cheap!" Articles ask: Was the court decision in the Boston Latin affirmative action case fair? Are cartoons sexist? Do animals have rights? How do you get over shyness? Should you get a tattoo? *Teen Voices* has a fine mix of politics, personal stuff, book and record reviews, fiction and poetry.

Hues, a feisty, multi-cultural quarterly, has a high-quality, attractive, innovative layout—on shiny paper (none of this hard-to-read, self-marginalizing newsprint). Its current issue features "Get On the Bus!" an account of Philadelphia's little-covered Million Woman March; "Making It Big," a profile of a successful and gorgeous 190-pound model who's outspoken in her criticism of the fashion industry; advice on looking for a good job "before you give up and accept a lifetime position at Minimum-Wages-R-Us"; an undercover look at phone sex; and a cultural dialogue between two young Indian women about arranged marriage. They've also run pieces on "Ghetto Feminism" and a "Swimsuit Issue" featuring women of all colors, shapes and sizes. *Hues* was recently acquired by New Moon publishing, the creator of the younger girls' magazine *New Moon*; it will go bimonthly next year.

Reluctant Hero is a Canadian quarterly with some serious feminist analysis—"Birds do it, Bees do it, Boys sure do. Why is it so taboo for girls to have a libido?"—asking why boys on TV shows don't listen to girls' desires (they pursue girls who aren't interested, harass them endlessly, and end up winning them over in the end). *Reluctant Hero* also explores cliques, sexual harassment and peer mediation, and asks that timeless question that you will probably never see in a commercial teen magazine—"Why Are Girls So Mean?" Other features cheer girls' creativity and ambitions: "Be a Mega Zine Queen," "Does Science Have a Gender?" and "Getting a Record Deal."

These magazines are so good that re-reading them actually made me dislike *Jump, Teen People* and *Twist* even more. Though these commercial ventures are, considering the territory, a step in the right direction, girls themselves can do so much better. It's too soon to say for sure how many readers the mainstream newcomers have attracted, but *Teen People* is reportedly selling like the Titanic. The independents don't attract Gap ads, and, at least in *Blue Jean*'s case, wouldn't even if they could; they need support. Subscribe, request them at your bookstore or library, make a contribution, show them to your favorite teenager—or millionaire investor. Let's hope the talent behind this girls' alternative press gets the encouragement it deserves to keep on keeping it real.

> Alternative example 3 analyzed positively.

> Alternative example 4 analyzed positively.

> Conclusion with call to action.

A CLOSER LOOK AT
What's a Girl to Read?

1. In her article, Featherstone says this about these new magazines: "The message is clear: It's OK that boys and magazines still have the last word on what makes you sexy." What does Featherstone believe is the alternative to this common theme in magazines aimed at teenage girls? How do the magazines she supports change this dynamic?

2. How does image, especially images of the body, become an issue of credibility (*ethos*) in teen magazines? How do these magazines use or misuse images of celebrities and models to promote a specific ideal of what teenage girls should aspire to?

3. According to Featherstone, how do these kinds of magazines play on the emotions of teenage girls? Does she suggest that there are good ways to use emotional arguments aimed at girls? What are some of the inappropriate ways that emotions are used in these magazines and their advertisements?

IDEAS FOR
Writing

1. At your campus library or local library, find a magazine that is aimed toward women. Write a two page review in which you use the concepts of *logos, ethos,* and *pathos* to discuss how this magazine tries to persuade its readers. Your review should be aimed at the target audience for the magazine. Tell them whether the magazine is effective or not.

2. Choose a magazine aimed at university-age men or women. Pick an advertisement from it and write a rhetorical analysis of the ad. Be sure you first define and describe the ad's intended audience. Then explore how the ad tries to appeal to that audience. Consider what rhetorical tactics you wish to focus on and use an academic tone.

The Egg and the Sperm: How Science Has Constructed a Romance Based on Stereotypical Male-Female Roles

EMILY MARTIN

The following discussion is an excerpt from a scholarly rhetorical analysis. Anthropologist Emily Martin analyzes the language in biological texts surrounding the female egg and male sperm to discover that the descriptions used advance stereotypical ideas about femininity and masculinity. This analysis has been widely discussed among academics and has drawn into question some of the supposed objectivity of scientific language.

The theory of the human body is always a part of a world-picture. . . . The theory of the human body is always a part of a *fantasy.*

—James Hillman, *The Myth of Analysis*[1]

As an anthropologist, I am intrigued by the possibility that culture shapes how biological scientists describe what they discover about the natural world. If this were so, we would be learning about more than the natural world in high school biology class; we would be learning about cultural beliefs and practices as if they were part of nature. In the course of my research I realized that the picture of egg and sperm drawn in popular as well as scientific accounts of reproductive biology relies on stereotypes central to our cultural definitions of male and female. The stereotypes imply not only that female biological processes are less worthy than their male counterparts but also that women are less worthy than men. Part of my goal in writing this article is to shine a bright light on the gender stereotypes hidden within the scientific language of biology. Exposed in such a light, I hope they will lose much of their power to harm us.

Identification of topic and thesis.

Egg and sperm: A scientific fairy tale

At a fundamental level, all major scientific textbooks depict male and female reproductive organs as systems for the production of valuable substances, such as eggs and sperm.[2] In the case of women, the monthly cycle is described as being designed to produce eggs and prepare a suitable place for them to be fertilized and grown—all to the end of making babies. But the enthusiasm ends there. By extolling the female cycle as a productive enterprise, menstruation must necessarily be viewed as a failure. Medical texts describe menstruation as the "debris" of the uterine lining, the result of necrosis, or death of tissue. The descriptions imply that a system has gone awry, making products of no use, not to specification, unsalable, wasted, scrap. An illustration in a widely used medical text shows menstruation as a chaotic disintegration of form, complementing the many texts that describe it as "ceasing," "dying," "losing," "denuding," "expelling."[3]

Analysis of terms used to describe female reproduction.

Male reproductive physiology is evaluated quite differently. One of the texts that sees menstruation as failed production employs a sort of breathless prose when it describes the maturation of sperm: "The mechanisms which guide the remarkable cellular transformation from spermatid to mature sperm remain uncertain. . . . Perhaps the most amazing characteristic of spermatogenesis is its sheer magnitude: the normal human male may manufacture several hundred million sperm per day."[4] In the classic text *Medical Physiology*, edited by Vernon Mountcastle, the male/female, productive/destructive comparison is more explicit: "Whereas the female sheds only a single gamete each month, the seminiferous tubules *produce* hundreds of millions of sperm each day" (emphasis mine).[5] The female author of another text marvels at the length of the microscopic seminiferous tubules, which, if uncoiled and placed end to end, "would span almost one-third of a mile!" She writes, "In an adult male these structures produce millions of sperm cells each day." Later she asks, "How is this feat accomplished?"[6] None of these texts expresses such intense enthusiasm for any female processes. It is surely no accident that the "remarkable" process of making sperm involves precisely what, in the medical view, menstruation does not: production of something deemed valuable.[7]

Contrasting analysis of terms used to describe male reproduction.

One could argue that menstruation and spermatogenesis are not analogous processes and, therefore, should not be expected to elicit the same kind of response. The proper female analogy to spermatogenesis, biologically, is ovulation. Yet ovulation does not merit enthusiasm in these texts either. Textbook descriptions stress that all of the ovarian follicles containing ova are already present at birth. Far from being *produced*, as sperm are, they merely sit on the shelf, slowly degenerating and aging like overstocked inventory: "At birth, normal human ovaries contain an estimated one million follicles [each], and no new ones appear after birth. Thus, in marked contrast to the male, the newborn female already has all the germ cells she will ever have. Only a few, perhaps 400, are destined to reach full maturity during her active productive life. All the others degenerate at some point in their development so that few, if any, remain by the time she reaches menopause at approximately 50 years of age."[8] Note the "marked contrast" that this description sets up between male and female: the male, who continuously produces fresh germ cells, and the female, who has stockpiled germ cells by birth and is faced with their degeneration.

Nor are the female organs spared such vivid descriptions. One scientist writes 5 in a newspaper article that a woman's ovaries become old and worn out from ripening eggs every month, even though the woman herself is still relatively young: "When you look through a laparoscope . . . at an ovary that has been through hundreds of cycles, even in a superbly healthy American female, you see a scarred, battered organ."[9]

Further analysis of terms used to describe female reproduction.

To avoid the negative connotations that some people associate with the female reproductive system, scientists could begin to describe male and female processes as homologous. They might credit females with "producing" mature ova one at a time, as they're needed each month, and describe males as having to face problems of degenerating germ cells. This degeneration would occur throughout life among spermatogonia, the undifferentiated germ cells in the testes that are the long-lived, dormant precursors of sperm.

Alternative language proposed.

But the texts have an almost dogged insistence on casting female processes in a negative light. The texts celebrate sperm production because it is continuous from puberty to senescence, while they portray egg production as inferior because it is finished at birth. This makes the female seem unproductive, but some texts will also insist that it is she who is wasteful.[10] In a section heading for *Molecular Biology of the Cell*, a best-selling text, we are told that "Oogenesis is wasteful." The text goes on to emphasize that of the seven million oogonia, or egg germ cells, in the female embryo, most degenerate in the ovary. Of those that do go on to become oocytes, or eggs, many also degenerate, so that at birth only two million eggs remain in the ovaries. Degeneration continues throughout a woman's life: by puberty 300,000 eggs remain, and only a few are present by menopause. "During the 40 or so years of a woman's reproductive life, only 400 to 500 eggs will have been released," the authors write. "All the rest will have degenerated. It is still a mystery why so many eggs are formed only to die in the ovaries."[11]

The real mystery is why the male's vast production of sperm is not seen as wasteful.[12] Assuming that a man "produces" 100 million (10^8) sperm per day (a conservative estimate) during an average reproductive life of sixty years, he would produce well over two trillion sperm in his lifetime. Assuming that a woman "ripens" one egg per lunar month, or thirteen per year, over the course of her forty-year reproductive life, she would total five hundred eggs in her lifetime. But the word "waste" implies an excess, too much produced. Assuming two or three offspring, for every baby a woman produces, she wastes only around two hundred eggs. For every baby a man produces, he wastes more than one trillion (10^{12}) sperm.

Further comparison and contrast of terms applied to male and female reproduction.

How is it that positive images are denied to the bodies of women? A look at language—in this case, scientific language—provides the first clue. Take the egg and the sperm.[13] It is remarkable how "feminincly" the egg behaves and how "masculinely" the sperm.[14] The egg is seen as large and passive.[15] It does not *move* or *journey*, but passively "is transported," "is swept,"[16] or even "drifts"[17] along the fallopian tube. In utter contrast, sperm are small, "streamlined,"[18] and invariably active. They "deliver" their genes to the egg, "activate the developmental program of the egg,"[19] and have a "velocity" that is often remarked upon.[20] Their tails are "strong" and efficiently powered.[21] Together with the forces of ejaculation, they can "propel the semen into the deepest recesses of the vagina."[22] For this they need "energy," "fuel,"[23] so that with a "whiplashlike motion and strong lurches"[24] they can "burrow through the egg coat"[25] and "penetrate" it.[26]

More detailed language analysis.

10   At its extreme, the age-old relationship of the egg and the sperm takes on a royal or religious patina. The egg coat, its protective barrier, is sometimes called its "vestments," a term usually reserved for sacred, religious dress. The egg is said to have a "corona,"[27] a crown, and to be accompanied by "attendant cells."[28] It is holy, set apart and above, the queen to the sperm's king. The egg is also passive, which means it must depend on sperm for rescue. Gerald Schatten and Helen Schatten liken the egg's role to that of Sleeping Beauty: "a dormant bride awaiting her mate's magic kiss, which instills the spirit that brings her to life."[29] Sperm, by contrast, have a "mission,"[30] which is to "move through the female genital tract in quest of the ovum."[31] One popular account has it that the sperm carry out a "perilous journey" into the "warm darkness," where some fall away "exhausted." "Survivors" "assault" the egg, the successful candidates "surrounding the prize."[32] Part of the urgency of this journey, in more scientific terms, is that "once released from the supportive environment of the ovary, an egg will die within hours unless rescued by a sperm."[33] The wording stresses the fragility and dependency of the egg, even though the same text acknowledges elsewhere that sperm also live for only a few hours.[34]

In 1948, in a book remarkable for its early insights into these matters, Ruth Herschberger argued that female reproductive organs are seen as biologically interdependent, while male organs are viewed as autonomous, operating independently and in isolation:

> At present the functional is stressed only in connection with women: it is in them that ovaries, tubes, uterus, and vagina have endless interdependence. In the male, reproduction would seem to involve "organs" only.
>
>   Yet the sperm, just as much as the egg, is dependent on a great many related processes. There are secretions which mitigate the urine in the urethra before ejaculation, to protect the sperm. There is the reflex shutting off of the bladder connection, the provision of prostatic secretions, and various types of muscular propulsion. The sperm is no more independent of its milieu than the egg, and yet from a wish that it were, biologists have lent their support to the notion that the human female, beginning with the egg, is congenitally more dependent than the male.[35]

Bringing out another aspect of the sperm's autonomy, an article in the journal *Cell* has the sperm making an "existential decision" to penetrate the egg: "Sperm are cells with a limited behavioral repertoire, one that is directed toward fertilizing eggs.

To execute the decision to abandon the haploid state, sperm swim to an egg and there acquire the ability to effect membrane fusion."[36] Is this a corporate manager's version of the sperm's activities—"executing decisions" while fraught with dismay over difficult options that bring with them very high risk?

There is another way that sperm, despite their small size, can be made to loom in importance over the egg. In a collection of scientific papers, an electron micrograph of an enormous egg and tiny sperm is titled "A Portrait of the Sperm."[37] This is a little like showing a photo of a dog and calling it a picture of the fleas. Granted, microscopic sperm are harder to photograph than eggs, which are just large enough to see with the naked eye. But surely the use of the term "portrait," a word associated with the powerful and wealthy, is significant. Eggs have only micrographs or pictures, not portraits.

One depiction of sperm as weak and timid, instead of strong and powerful—the only such representation in western civilization, so far as I know—occurs in Woody Allen's movie *Everything You Always Wanted To Know About Sex* *But Were Afraid to Ask*. Allen, playing the part of an apprehensive sperm inside a man's testicles, is scared of the man's approaching orgasm. He is reluctant to launch himself into the darkness, afraid of contraceptive devices, afraid of winding up on the ceiling if the man masturbates.

The more common picture—egg as damsel in distress, shielded only by her sacred garments; sperm as heroic warrior to the rescue—cannot be proved to be dictated by the biology of these events. While the "facts" of biology may not *always* be constructed in cultural terms, I would argue that in this case they are. The degree of metaphorical content in these descriptions, the extent to which differences between egg and sperm are emphasized, and the parallels between cultural stereotypes of male and female behavior and the character of egg and sperm all point to this conclusion.

> Contextualization of analysis within research.

> Single alternative depiction acknowledged.

> Concluding paragraph (to this section of the essay) making final point and linking scientific language to cultural stereotypes.

15

1. James Hillman, *The Myth of Analysis* (Evanston, Ill.: Northwestern University Press, 1972), 220.

2. The textbooks I consulted are the main ones used in classes for undergraduate premedical students or medical students (or those held on reserve in the library for these classes) during the past few years at Johns Hopkins University. These texts are widely used at other universities in the country as well.

3. Arthur C. Guyton, *Physiology of the Human Body*, 6th ed. (Philadelphia: Saunders College Publishing, 1984), 624.

4. Arthur J. Vander, James H. Sherman, and Dorothy S. Luciano, *Human Physiology: The Mechanisms of Body Function*, 3d ed. (New York: McGraw Hill, 1980), 483–84.

5. Vernon B. Mountcastle, *Medical Physiology*, 14th ed. (London: Mosby, 1980), 2:1624.

6. Eldra Pearl Solomon, *Human Anatomy and Physiology* (New York: CBS College Publishing, 1983), 678.

7. For elaboration, see Emily Martin, *The Woman in the Body: A Cultural Analysis of Reproduction* (Boston: Beacon, 1987), 27–53.

8. Vander, Sherman, and Luciano, 568.

9. Melvin Konner, "Childbearing and Age," *New York Times Magazine* (December 27, 1987), 22–23, esp. 22.

10. I have found but one exception to the opinion that the female is wasteful: "Smallpox being the nasty disease it is, one might expect nature to have designed antibody molecules with combining sites that specifically recognize the epitopes on smallpox virus. Nature differs from technology, however: it thinks nothing of wastefulness. (For example, rather than improving the chance that a spermatozoon will meet an egg cell, nature finds it easier to produce millions of spermatozoa.)" (Niels Kaj Jerne, "The Immune System," *Scientific American* 229, no. 1 [July 1973]: 53). Thanks to a *Signs* reviewer for bringing this reference to my attention.

11. Bruce Alberts et al., *Molecular Biology of the Cell* (New York: Garland, 1983), 795.

12. In her essay "Have Only Men Evolved?" (in *Discovering Reality: Feminist Perspectives on Epistemology, Metaphysics, Methodology, and Philosophy of Science*, ed. Sandra Harding and Merrill B. Hintikka [Dordrecht: Reidel, 1983], 45–69, esp. 60–61), Ruth Hubbard points out that sociobiologists have said the female invests more energy than the male in the production of her large gametes, claiming that this explains why the female provides parental care. Hubbard questions whether it "really takes more 'energy' to generate the one or relatively few eggs than the large excess of sperms required to achieve fertilization." For further critique of how the greater size of eggs is interpreted in sociobiology, see Donna Haraway, "Investment Strategies for the Evolving Portfolio of Primate Females," in *Body/Politics*, ed. Mary Jacobus, Evelyn Fox Keller, and Sally Shuttleworth (New York: Routledge, 1990), 155–56.

13. The sources I used for this article provide compelling information on interactions among sperm. Lack of space prevents me from taking up this theme here, but the elements include competition, hierarchy, and sacrifice. For a newspaper report, see Malcolm W. Browne, "Some Thoughts on Self Sacrifice," *New York Times* (July 5, 1988), C6. For a literary rendition, see John Barth, "Night-Sea Journey," in his *Lost in the Funhouse* (Garden City, N.Y.: Doubleday, 1968), 3–13.

14. See Carol Delaney, "The Meaning of Paternity and the Virgin Birth Debate," *Man* 21, no. 3 (September 1986): 494–513. She discusses the difference between this scientific view that women contribute genetic material to the fetus and the claim of long-standing Western folk theories that the origin and identity of the fetus comes from the male, as in the metaphor of planting a seed in soil.

15. For a suggested direct link between human behavior and purportedly passive eggs and active sperm, see Erik H. Erikson, "Inner and Outer Space: Reflections on Womanhood," *Daedalus* 93, no. 2 (Spring 1964): 582–606, esp. 591.

16. Guyton (n. 3 above), 619; and Mountcastle (n. 5 above), 1609.

17. Jonathan Miller and David Pelham, *The Facts of Life* (New York: Viking Penguin, 1984), 5.

18. Alberts et al., 796.

19. Ibid., 796.

20. See, e.g., William F. Ganong, *Review of Medical Physiology*, 7th ed. (Los Altos, Calif.: Lange Medical Publications, 1975), 322.

21. Alberts et al. (n. 11 above), 796.

22. Guyton, 615.

23. Solomon (n. 6 above), 683.

24. Vander, Sherman, and Luciano (n. 4 above), 4th ed. (1985), 580.

25. Alberts et al., 796.

26. All biology texts quoted above use the word "penetrate."

27. Solomon, 700.

28. A. Beldecos et al., "The Importance of Feminist Critique for Contemporary Cell Biology," *Hypatia* 3, no. 1 (Spring 1988): 61–76.

29. Gerald Schatten and Helen Schatten, "The Energetic Egg," *Medical World News* 23 (January 23, 1984): 51–53, esp. 51.

30. Alberts et al., 796.

31. Guyton (n. 3 above), 613.

32. Miller and Pelham (n. 17 above), 7.

33. Alberts et al. (n. 11 above), 804.

34. Ibid., 801.

35. Ruth Herschberger, *Adam's Rib* (New York: Pelligrini & Cudaby, 1948), esp. 84. I am indebted to Ruth Hubbard for telling me about Herschberger's work, although at a point when this paper was already in draft form.

36. Bennett M. Shapiro, "The Existential Decision of a Sperm," *Cell* 49, no. 3 (May 1987): 293–94, esp. 293.

37. Lennart Nilsson, "A Portrait of the Sperm," in *The Functional Anatomy of the Spermatozoan*, ed. Bjorn A. Afzelius (New York: Pergamon, 1975), 79–82.

A CLOSER LOOK AT
The Egg and the Sperm

1. In this analysis, what kind of language does Emily Martin find biology texts attach to eggs? To sperm? Do you agree that these are problematic representations? What stereotypes, if any, do they perpetuate?

2. Some of Martin's later points suggest that the language used to describe sperm and egg is also language used in fairy tales. Consider Martin's points about how sperm are portrayed as active and decisive, while eggs are portrayed as passive and inactive, and think about how this would relate to a well-known fairy tale like "Snow White," "Sleeping Beauty," or "Cinderella."

IDEAS FOR
Writing

1. Locate an article on pregnancy in a women's or parenting magazine, or look online for an article offering pregnancy advice. What kind of language does the article use? Does it replicate some of the passive, "feminine" terminology that Martin describes? Write a two page rhetorical analysis of the article.

2. Decide on a film, topic, book, or story that particularly interests you and write a short rhetorical analysis of the language and ideas used in that work. What kinds of descriptions are offered? Do you see any biases to the language? How is the work formatted?

1. With a group in your class, discuss the ways people try to persuade you. How do family members try to persuade you? How do your friends try to persuade you? In what ways do their persuasive strategies differ from the ways advertisers try to persuade people?

2. List some ways people try to use their credibility (*ethos*) or emotion (*pathos*) to persuade others. Supposedly, using reason (*logos*) is the most reliable way to persuade someone, and yet we use credibility and emotion all the time to get our points across. Why? When are arguments from credibility and emotion even more persuasive than arguments that rely on reason?

3. With a group, make a list of your favourite five commercials on television and a list of five commercials you cannot stand. Why do people in your group find some of these commercials interesting and worth watching? Why are some commercials so irritating that you want to turn the television off? As a group, create a list of ten dos and don'ts of advertising to post-secondary students.

1. Find a commercial online that you think is persuasive (or not). Then write a one page analysis of the commercial in which you discuss why you think it is effective (or not). Look closely at its uses of reasoning, credibility, and emotion. What kinds of support does the advertiser rely on most? What other rhetorical patterns does the advertisement use? What do these rhetorical strategies say about the people the advertiser is targeting?

2. Find a political satire, cartoon, or attack ad based on Canadian politics. You may wish to search the editorial pages of major newspapers, clips from shows like *This Hour Has 22 Minutes* or the *Rick Mercer Report*, or *YouTube* postings of attack ads from every Canadian election dating back to 1993. In one or two pages analyze the rhetoric of the satire, cartoon, or attack ad. What is it mocking/criticizing? How does it make its point? Does it use *ethos*, *pathos*, or *logos*? How effective is the ad, satire, or cartoon in persuading you of its position?

3. Find a rhetorical analysis on the Internet that you can study. These documents are rarely called "rhetorical analyses." Instead, they tend to be critiques of advertisements, speeches, or documents. You can find good examples on websites like *Slate.com* and *Straight.com* or on newspaper sites like the *National Post* (www.nationalpost.com) or the *New York Times* (www.nytimes.com). Write a one page discussion in which you study the organization, style, and design of the rhetorical analysis. How does it work? What kinds of rhetorical elements does the reviewer pay attention to? Do you agree with the reviewer's analysis?

1. **Analyze a text.** Choose a historical, nonfiction text you find interesting and write a five page rhetorical analysis of it. Your analysis should define the rhetorical concepts you will use to study the document. It should summarize the text and offer some historical background on it. Then offer a close analysis of the text, explaining why it is effective or not.

2. **Analyze something else as a rhetorical text.** Find something other than a written text for your rhetorical analysis. You could study the architecture of a building, the design of a sculpture, the way someone dresses, or perhaps how someone acts. Discuss how designs or people can be persuasive in nonverbal ways. Write a five page paper or create a website in which you explain the ways in which reason, credibility, and emotion can be conveyed without using words.

3. **Critique an advertisement or advertising campaign.** Choose an advertisement or a series of advertisements that you enjoy or detest. Then write a formal, academic rhetorical analysis in which you explain why the ad or series is effective or ineffective.

MyCompLab

For support in meeting this chapter's objectives, follow this path in MyCompLab:

Student Resources → Writing → Writing Purposes → Writing to Analyze. Review the Instruction and Multimedia resources about writing to analyze; then complete the Exercises and click on Gradebook to measure your progress.

Literary Analyses

┌─ In this chapter, you will learn how to: ──────────────────────────────
- analyze literary texts by exploring genre, plot, characters, setting, theme, language, and tone.
- organize your literary analysis to highlight your interpretations of the text.
- write in an academic style and use quotations to add authority to your analysis.

A literary analysis poses an *interpretive question* about a literary text and then answers that question to explain the text, its author, or the cultural context in which it was written. Your aim in a literary analysis is to provide your readers with new and interesting insights into the work by examining it closely.

Literary analyses explain the meaning of a text, analyze its structure and features, and examine it through the lenses of historical, cultural, social, biographical, and other contexts. An effective literary analysis helps readers understand what makes a literary work thought-provoking, revealing, or enjoyable. Literary analyses also contribute to the larger scholarly conversation about the meaning and purpose of literature.

When writing a literary analysis, you shouldn't feel like you need to prove that you have the only "correct" or "right" interpretation. Instead, your literary analysis should invite your readers to consider the work from new and interesting angles, while showing them how a particular angle can lead to fresh insights. Just keep in mind that all interpretations are based on specific evidence found in the text.

The literary analysis genre overlaps in many ways with the rhetorical analysis genre, which was discussed in Chapter 6. Both genres study forms of communication closely to understand why they have particular effects on readers. Rhetorical analyses, however, tend to study all forms of communication and to focus on how arguments or ideas are constructed, while literary analyses usually examine fictional or poetic texts, often using them as ways to understand humanity and culture.

Literary analyses are used in a variety of courses, not just English courses. For example, a history class studying Arctic exploration might read Margaret Atwood's story "The Age of Lead." A class examining aboriginal history might read a short story by Thomas King (one of which is included in this chapter). Professors across the disciplines assign literary works that provide insights into the subjects they want to explore with their students. While extensive literary analysis is primarily an academic genre and the examples in this chapter reflect that, you may also find analyses of fiction, drama, or poetry in popular essays and reviews.

Literary Analyses

These diagrams show two possible basic organizations for a literary analysis, but other arrangements will work too. You should adjust these organizational patterns to fit your topic, angle, purpose, readers, and context.

Introduction

Targeted summary or description of the text

Analysis: First point

Analysis: Second point

Analysis: Third point

•
•
•

Conclusion

Introduction

Targeted summary and analysis of first part of text

Targeted summary and analysis of second part of text

Targeted summary and analysis of third part of text

•
•
•

Conclusion

Overview

Literary analyses have these features:

- **An introduction** that identifies the literary work you are analyzing and its background. The introduction should also identify an interpretive question that will drive the analysis and provide a thesis or main idea you will follow as you interpret the story for your readers.

- **Targeted summaries or descriptions of the text** that focus *only* on the events or features that play a key role in your interpretation. These summaries and descriptions are usually brief.

- **Quoted material** taken directly from the text that helps to move your interpretation forward and illustrate your points.

- **Support for your interpretation** that uses solid reasoning to show how your interpretation makes sense and offers insights into the interpretive question. Evidence, including quotes and descriptive examples, is taken from the work itself (and sometimes other places) to support your interpretation.

- **A conclusion** that helps readers understand the big picture by describing the significance of the interpretation or by pointing out the additional questions that need to be addressed.

Literary analyses are written in a variety of ways. The diagram on page 117 shows a couple of useful organizations that you can alter to fit the needs of your topic, angle, purpose, readers, and context.

ONE STUDENT'S WORK
Literary Analyses

The following student analysis considers the historical implications of Thomas King's short story "Borders." You will want to read "Borders," found on pages 132–139, before you read this example.

"Border" Crossings in Thomas King's Narrative

Max Doran

The writer begins with a clear introduction of the literary work under consideration.

Thomas King's short story "Borders," from his collection *One Good Story, That One*, uses an innocent, child-like narrator to describe the continuing legacy of colonialism on Canada's aboriginal peoples. The story recounts a young boy and his mother's attempt to cross the Canada-US border in order to visit his older sister who is living in Salt Lake City. The mother, however, refuses to declare herself either Canadian or American, insisting on her Blackfoot identity (which crosses both borders) and revealing how the Blackfoot nation was divided by colonialists who never considered aboriginal territories or identities in marking their national boundaries. This refusal creates a "standoff" at the border, gaining media attention, until finally the border guards are ordered to capitulate and let the pair through. Why tell this politically loaded story from a child's point of view? While the narrative does make a point about aboriginal rights, it uses its youthful narrator to explore the tensions between past, present, and future. The story suggests aboriginal peoples must move forward, a future embodied by the child speaker, but only with a full and clear awareness of the past.

King's story is set in Southern Alberta. The mother and son claim to be from "Standoff," which is both a town on the Kanai reserve west of Lethbridge and a description of their experience at the border. The Blackfoot confederacy consists of four tribes; the Kanai, Piikuni, and Siksika have territories in Canada, while the Blackfeet[1] have a reserve in Montana (Blood Tribe). Traditional Blackfoot territory thus crosses the US-Canadian border, a fact that colonialists ignored in 1818 when dividing the countries and an issue that still divides some Blackfoot families who, like the characters in King's story, find themselves with relatives on both sides of the border. Such divisions can serve political ends, in that it becomes harder to argue for rights or autonomy when dealing with two very different federal governments. By dividing the Blackfoot people, the Canadian and US governments limit aboriginal political power (McManus). As on many Canadian reservations, the Kanai people contend with poverty and addiction even as they work towards autonomous government. How future generations deal with this situation is significant for the Blackfoot people.

The past is represented in "Borders" as both harmful and formative, a source of colonial legacies and of Kanai identity. The border dispute which forms the main conflict in the story is clearly a legacy of colonialism. Blackfoot identity is not recognized at the border because both Canada and the United States remain bound to colonial concepts of nationhood. As one customs officer says, "I'd be proud of being Blackfoot if I were Blackfoot. But you have to be American or Canadian" (King 138-139). Indeed, the real antagonist in the narrative is the border which divides the Blackfoot people. The border guards and duty-free store manager are generally sympathetic and polite, but bound to their duties as colonial officers. King's description of two border guards even plays on their association with Western history as he describes them, "swaying back and forth like two cowboys headed for a bar or a gunfight" (135). They may be polite and non-violent in this instance, but the guards' role in suppressing aboriginal identity is clear. While this harmful past is criticized in King's narrative, the boy and his mother also draw on their Blackfoot heritage as a source of strength during their ordeal. Stuck between the Canada-US border for two days, the mother

[1]The US community uses the term "Blackfeet," while the Canadian tribes prefer "Blackfoot."

Margin annotations:

A targeted summary focuses only on aspects of the narrative that are crucial to this essay's interpretation.

Interpretive question.

The main claim or thesis explains or interprets the narrative, answering the interpretive question.

This paragraph provides background information used to contextualize the analysis.

Topic sentence identifies a key point supporting the thesis.

Example supported by a quotation from the story.

Second example described and supported with a quotation.

Reiteration of the claim or paragraph topic.

(continued)

Example described and explained.	tells her son Coyote stories, "repeating parts as she went, as if she expected me to remember each one" (King 142). The mother's connection to traditional Blackfoot territory also suggests a positive link to the past. She struggles to understand why her daughter wishes to leave and what urban environments have to offer. Ultimately, the past carries two meanings in this narrative, so that the mother shows her son how to reject colonialism, as well as educating him about their Blackfoot heritage.

Analysis linking the examples and ideas in the paragraph to the main interpretation or thesis.

Topic sentence identifies a second key support for the thesis.

The story's juvenile narrator represents a present and future for the Kanai people. As a child, he naively yet tellingly recounts the actions of the border guards, the media, and the government official who finally resolves the situation. By seeing what happens at the border, and through the education which his mother gives him, the narrator will grow up with an awareness of his people's past and how it has created their present situation. As a representative of his people, the narrator may well work to change that situation. Moreover, King's child narrator makes the political commentary at once less threatening to a non-aboriginal reader and more poignant. As the duty-free store manager tells the boy and his mother that "justice was a damn hard thing to get, but that we shouldn't give up" (King 143), the reader is invited to see the injustice that colonial and contemporary governments continue to impose on aboriginal peoples. In fact, the secondary conflict in the story, between sister Laetitia and the mother, is over the present reality of Blackfoot people. While the mother clings to tradition, Laetitia seeks a modern, urban experience only to become disillusioned. At the end she says she is "thinking about moving back" (144) and King seems to be suggesting that it is not possible to simply start over in Salt Lake City and forget the past. Ultimately, the narrator embodies the future, but it is a future fully informed by history.

Example explained and supported by a quotation.

Analytic sentence linking the evidence to the thesis.

Marker of ending.

In conclusion, King's story makes an important point about the relationships between past, present, and future. The experience at the border gives King's child narrator a political education and an awareness of both his people's history and present situation. Rather than forget the past, the story suggests Blackfoot people must remember both the good and the bad, and move forward from there to grow up as an autonomous, independent people. Although fictional, the narrative clearly has real-life implications.

Restatement of key argument and application of ideas to society at large.

MLA style citations.

Works Cited

Blood Tribe – Kanai. Homepage. 2012. Web. 24 May 2012.

King, Thomas. "Borders." *One Good Story, That One.* Toronto: HarperCollins, 1993. 129-46. Print.

McManus, Sheila. "Mapping the Alberta-Montana Borderlands: Race, Ethnicity and Gender in the Late Nineteenth Century." *Journal of American Ethnic History*, 20.3 (2001): 71–88. Web. 24 May 2012.

Developing Your Literary Analysis's Content

The first challenge in writing a literary analysis is finding an interesting *interpretive question* about the work you are studying. Ideally, when considering a literary work you want to pose a question that explores what is not immediately evident and then attempt to answer that question. For instance, the student analysis of the King text focuses on the unusual situation of a child narrating a politically charged story and attempts to explain why that is a significant element. As you read and research the text, look for signs and evidence that might offer insights that go beyond the obvious.

Read, Reread, Explore

If the literary work is a short story or novel, read it at least twice. If it is a poem, read it again and again, silently and aloud, to get a feel for how the language works and how the poem makes you feel. As you read the text, mark or underline anything that intrigues or puzzles you. Write observations and questions in the margins.

Inquiring: What's Interesting Here?

As you are reading and exploring the text, try to come up with an interesting question that focuses on the work's genre, plot, characters, or use of language. The goal here is to find your interpretive question, which will serve as your angle into the text, and then to answer that question as you interpret.

Explore the Genre. In your literature classes, your professors will use the term *genre* somewhat differently than it is used in this book. Literary works fall into four major genres: fiction, poetry, drama, and literary nonfiction.

Literary Genre	Subgenres
Fiction	short stories, novellas, novels, detective novels, science fiction, romance, mysteries, horror, fantasy, historical fiction
Poetry	limericks, sonnets, ballads, epic poems, haikus, villanelle, odes, sestinas, open verse
Drama	plays, closet dramas, comedies, tragedies, romances, musicals, operas
Literary nonfiction (or nonfiction prose)	memoirs, profiles (of people, places, events), biographies, histories, essays, nature writing, religion, politics

While examining the text, identify the genre and ask yourself why the author chose this genre or subgenre of literature and not another one. Why a poem rather than a story? Why a short story rather than a novel?

Also, look for places where the author follows the genre or strays from it. How does the genre constrain what the author can do? How does the author bend the genre to fit the story that he or she wants to tell? How does the author use this genre in a unique or interesting way? If you are unsure of the conventions of a specific literary genre, look them up on the Internet or consult your literature textbook or professor. You may wish to attempt exercise 2 in the "Try This Out" section at the end of this chapter.

Explore the Plot. Plot refers not just to the sequence of events but also to how the events arise from the main conflict in the story. How do the events in the story unfold? Which events are surprising or puzzling? What is the complication or conflict on which the narrative is based? How do the characters react to it? And how is this conflict resolved?

Keep in mind that conflict often arises from characters' values and beliefs and from the setting in which the characters reside. What conflicts do you sense in the story as you read? Are there conflicts between characters, between characters and their surroundings, between characters' aspirations, or between competing values and beliefs? Are there inconsistencies in the plot?

Finally, pay special attention to the critical moment in the story, called the *climax*. What happens and why is this moment so crucial? How is the conflict resolved, for better or worse?

Explore the Characters. The characters are the people who inhabit the story or poem. Who are they? What kinds of people are they? Why do they act as they do? What are their values, beliefs, and desires? How do they interact with each other, or with their environment and setting?

You might explore the psychology or motives of the characters, trying to figure out the meaning behind their decisions and actions. Are there inconsistencies in characters' voices, actions, or motives (such as a juvenile character using a word that a typical child wouldn't know)? Identify them. Do you think the author intended them? Why would the author do this? Also consider point of view. From what perspective is the narrative told?

Explore the Setting. What is the time and place of the story? What is the broader setting—culture, social sphere, historical period? What is the narrow setting—the details about the particular time and place? How does the setting constrain the characters by establishing their beliefs, values, and actions? How does the setting become a symbol that colours the way readers interpret the work? Is the setting realistic, fantastical, ironic, or magical?

Explore the Theme. What is the story's central message or idea? How is it conveyed? Where can you see it being addressed directly and indirectly in the story? Is the theme successfully developed? Keep in mind that theme goes beyond the sequence of events in the narrative, which is the plot, and instead articulates an abstraction or larger concept, which is the story's main message.

Explore the Symbolism. Symbols are objects, concepts, language, or events that carry meaning beyond the literal. For instance, in "Borders" the author refers to

Canadian and American flags as symbols of those nations. When considering a story, ask yourself whether any objects, actions, or ideas carry deeper meaning. What are those deeper meanings? How does the symbol link to other parts of the story, such as theme, characters, and plot? How are those symbols conveyed and developed throughout the story?

Explore the Language and Tone. How does the author's tone or choices of words colour your attitude toward the characters, setting, or theme? What feeling or mood does the work's tone evoke, and how does that tone evolve as the story or poem moves forward?

Also, pay attention to the author's use of metaphors, similes, and analogies. How does the author use these devices to deepen the meaning of the text or bring new ideas to light? What images are used to describe the characters, events, objects, or setting? Do those images become metaphors or symbols that colour the way readers understand the work, or the way the characters see their world?

Literary works usually cannot be broken down into simple tidy messages or lessons, but authors want their work to affect readers in some way. They want their words to influence the way readers view the world and what they believe.

Researching: What Background Do You Need?

While many literary analyses focus primarily on the literary text itself, you should also research the historical and cultural background of a work or author. Depending on the assignment and where you want to take it, you can use Internet or print sources to find resources that provide insights into the work, its impact, and the author's intentions.

Research the Author. Learning about the author can often lead to interpretive insights. The author's life experiences may help you understand the context of the work. You might study the events that were happening in the author's time, because the work itself might directly or indirectly respond to them.

Research the Historical Setting. You could also do research about the text's historical setting. If the story takes place in a real setting, you can read about the historical, cultural, social, and political forces that were in play at that time and in that place.

Research Possible Theoretical Contexts. Human and physical sciences can often give insights into human behaviour, social interactions, or natural phenomena. Sometimes additional research into psychology, sociology, biology, and other sciences can give you interesting insights into characters and events.

Some professors may ask you to consider literary works from a theoretical perspective. This means that they want you to enter existing discussions that highlight certain ideas or themes in literary works. Theoretical perspectives seek to explore the varying assumptions and perspectives we use when we read a work of literature and make readers aware of which assumptions they may be applying in particular instances. For example, a reader using a feminist perspective will focus on gender relationships and issues of gender equality as represented in a text. The following are some of the major theoretical approaches used in literary analysis:

Formalism/new criticism considers the narrative's structural elements such as plot, characters, setting, or other components (see above).

New historicism considers the historical context of the literary work, such as events or prevailing ideas that may have influenced the author (see above on researching historical setting). Critics Stephen Greenblatt and Stephen Orgel have demonstrated the particular value of this approach in relation to Renaissance literature.

Marxism applies the work of Karl Marx to analyze issues of class and economic power as represented in texts. Contemporary Marxist critics such as Terry Eagleton and Frederic Jameson focus on material culture and the structures of twentieth century capitalism. Your professor may be able to give you more information and suggestions on using this approach.

Feminism/gender studies consider representations of women (and now men in the growing area of masculinity studies) with a focus on issues of equality, sexuality, and social construction. Julia Kristeva and Elaine Showalter are two founding feminist critics, while Judith Butler and Lee Edelman led the expansion into queer and gender theory. See the Kingston, Featherstone, Martin, and Feder, Levant, and Dean readings in this section for more background and examples of gender analysis.

Deconstruction, based on the work of Jacques Derrida, considers the use of oppositions, both ideological and language-based, in literary works. Deconstructivist critics often seek to subvert prevailing ideas; first-year writers typically find this approach difficult.

Cultural studies/post-colonialism studies literature and society with a particular focus on defining and understanding cultural differences. Post-colonialism, led by critics such as Homi Bhabha and Gayatri Spivak, develops this approach in relation to former European colonies. King's narrative in this chapter could be read as post-colonial for its representation of aboriginal issues.

Organizing and Drafting Your Literary Analysis

So far, you have read the literary work carefully, taken notes, done some research, and perhaps written some informal responses. Now, how should you dive in and begin drafting? Here are some ideas for getting your ideas down on the page.

The Introduction

Introductions in literary analyses usually include a few common features:

Include Background Information That Leads to Your Interpretive Question. Draw your reader into your analysis by starting with information that your reader is already familiar with, and then move steadily toward your interpretive question. Show your reader why this is an interesting question that will lead to new insights about the work or other broader concerns.

State Your Interpretive Question Prominently and Clearly. Make sure your reader understands the question that your analysis will investigate. If necessary, make it obvious by saying something like, "This analysis will explore why . . ." That way, your readers will clearly understand your purpose.

State Your Thesis at or Near the End of the Introduction. State your main claim or thesis about the literary work. Your main claim should answer your interpretive question. Figure 7.1 shows how a few interpretive questions might be answered by some possible claims. See Chapter 21 for a fuller discussion of thesis statements.

The Body of Your Analysis

In the body paragraphs, you should take your reader point by point through your analysis, showing them that your interpretation makes sense and leads to interesting new insights. Each paragraph should offer a major concept in support of your interpretation, along with some or all of the following components.

Interpretive Questions	Interpretive Claims
What does the border represent for the narrator and his mother?	The border represents their colonial history, how the Blackfoot nation continues to be divided, how they are at least somewhat powerless, and how they are continually being asked to negate their identity.
Why does King use a child narrator to tell an adult-themed story?	The child makes the story less alienating for non-aboriginal readers, introduces a certain innocent humour, and suggests the future for aboriginal people because children are the next generation who will be making political decisions.
How does the setting further the theme?	Land is vital to aboriginal identity. The border "Standoff" shows the restrictions placed on the Blackfoot people, and the setting in the West recalls North American history.

FIGURE 7.1
Interpretive Questions and Interpretive Claims

Summarize and Describe Key Aspects of the Work. You can assume that your readers will be familiar with the literary work, so you don't need to provide a complete summary or fully explain who characters are. But there may be aspects of the work that are crucial to your analysis and that need to be brought to your readers' attention. You may wish to focus on a particular scene, or on certain features, such as a character, interactions between characters, language, symbols, plot features, and so forth. Discuss *only* those aspects of the work that are crucial to understanding your analysis.

Build Your Case, Step by Step. Keep in mind that the goal of a literary analysis is not to prove that your interpretation is correct but to show that it is plausible and leads to interesting insights into the text and related matters. Take your readers through your analysis point by point. Back up each key point with detailed reasoning and evidence, and make connections to your main claim or thesis.

Cite and Quote the Text to Back Up and Illustrate Your Points. The evidence for your interpretation should come mostly from the text itself. Show your readers what the text says by quoting and citing it.

Include Outside Support, Where Appropriate. Although you can bring in concepts and ideas from outside the text, make sure your ideas are anchored by what is actually written in the text you are studying. Don't just use the text as a springboard to dive off into some other topic. Stay focused on what happens in the literary work.

The Conclusion

Your conclusion should bring your readers around to the main point that you expressed in the introduction. Your conclusion should also point the reader in new directions. Up to this point in the literary analysis, your readers will expect you to closely follow the text. In the conclusion, though, they will allow more leeway. In a sense, you've earned the right to speculate and consider other ideas, although any speculations should of course follow from the points you have proven in the body of the analysis.

So, if you want, take on the larger issues that were dealt with in this literary work. What conclusions or questions does your analysis suggest? What challenges does the author believe we face? What is the author really trying to say about people, events, and the world we live in?

Choosing an Appropriate Style

Literary analyses invite readers into a conversation about a literary work. Therefore, the style should be straightforward but also inviting and encouraging.

Use the "Literary Present" Tense

The literary present tense involves talking about the work and the characters as though they live in the present day. For example, you might say,

> King's narrator is loyal to his mother, but he is also aware of her
> uncompromising nature.

When discussing the author historically, however, use the past tense.

> Thomas King published the story "Borders" in 1993, when aboriginal land rights
> were first being re-negotiated.

Integrate Quoted Text

Weave words and ideas from the literary text into your words and ideas, and avoid quotations that are detached from your ideas. For example, you can include a quotation at the end of your own sentence:

> In her poem "Sunset," Apryl Leaf describes the seal as beautiful in death. For
> instance, she writes that its body is "a mystery of dark red diffusion" (6).

You could also take the same sentence from the story and weave a "tissue" of quotations into your words:

> In her poem "Sunset," Apryl Leaf describes the seal as beautiful even in death.
> Its body is "a mystery" and its fur is a "dark red diffusion," creating a strong
> visual image (6).

Make sure any sentences that include quotations remain grammatically correct. When you omit words from your quotation, use ellipses.

When You Quote, Tell Readers What You Want Them to Notice. Whenever you take a quote from the text, explain how the quotation supports your point and your overall claim. Don't leave your readers hanging with a quotation and no commentary. Tell them what the quote means.

Move Beyond Personal Response

Literary analyses may develop from a personal reaction, but they are not merely personal. Your literary analysis will need to move beyond any initial personal response to a discussion of the literary work itself. In other words, describe what the text does, not just what it does to you, and be sure to support your interpretation with examples and quotations.

Cast Interpretations as Speculative. Literary analyses are interpretive, not absolute and final. When you want your readers to understand that you are interpreting, use words and phrases such as "perhaps," "it could be," "may," "it seems clear that," "seems," and "probably."

> King seems to be suggesting that it is not possible to simply start over and
> forget the past. The narrator may embody the future, but it is a future fully
> informed by history.

Applying the Genre: Reading Response

The reading response is a form of literary analysis that is used in a variety of post-secondary situations. Your professor may assign a reading response as "informal writing." A literature professor, for instance, might ask you to write about your first reaction to a poem to help you explore its meaning. An anthropology professor might ask you to describe your reactions to the rituals of a different culture.

Your professors may assign a wide variety of reading response assignments, but no matter what the specific assignment, make sure you do the following:

Read the Prompt Carefully. Make sure you understand exactly what your professor wants you to do. Pay attention to the verbs. Are you supposed to summarize, explore, speculate, analyze, identify, explain, define, evaluate, apply, or something else?

Try Out New Ideas and Approaches. Informal writing can be your chance to speculate, explore, and be creative. Be sure you understand what your professor expects, but reading responses can allow you to stretch your thinking into new areas.

Show that You Have Read, Understand, and Can Work with the Material. Ground your response in the material you are being asked about. When writing about a story or poem, come back to the text with quotations, summaries, and descriptions. If the reading involves a concept, make sure your response shows that you understand or can use the concept to address the prompt.

Branch Out and Make Connections (if Appropriate). Look for the broader implications and for connections with other issues from the course. With informal writing like reading responses, you're usually allowed, or even encouraged, to take risks and speculate. If you're not sure whether your professor wants you to do this, ask.

Figure 7.2 is an example of a reading response based on a poem. The response prompt asked students to write a one paragraph reaction to the poem that considers the main theme or meaning. Note that even in this informal writing, the student is careful to support her responses with evidence from the poem. Reactions can begin subjectively, but to develop into a valid interpretation those reactions must be solidified and backed up by the text.

Designing Your Literary Analysis

Typically, literary analyses use a simple and traditional design, following the MLA format for manuscripts: double-spaced, easy-to-read font, one inch (2.5 cm) margins, MLA documentation style (see Chapter 24). Always consult with your professor about which format he or she wants you to use.

If you want to use headings, ask your professor if they are allowed. Headings will help you organize your analysis and make transitions between larger sections. Design features like headers and page numbers are usually welcome, because they help professors and your classmates keep the pages in order. Also, if you discuss your work in class, page numbers help your readers easily find what is being discussed.

Sunset

Against blue stones
at calm high tide
you came upon it first
and warned me
Harbor Seal whole and freshly dead
mystery of dark red diffusion
through its mottle fur
I guessed to be red algae
its voids for eyes unnerving
obvious health of fanged teeth and flippers
prompted me to look for
a propeller cut a killer whale bite
you moved it and crouched beside
its broad neck
big bullet holes you say
peering at the gruesome gapes
yahoos I guess or so-called salmon lovers
you know a few skippers like that
we push on and away from
western colors and the seal abandoned
no scavenger bird around
Walking drift logs to the trail
I saw that people do such things
to each other these things and worse
as if that is any consolation

Sample Reader Response:
My first reaction to this poem is anger and sadness. Why would someone randomly shoot such a beautiful creature? Phrases that really prompt this feeling are "obvious health of fanged teeth and flippers" and "gruesome gapes," which capture the unnecessary and brutal nature of the act. Then, as I read on with the image of the seal still in mind, the phrase "walking drift logs to the trail" makes the experience seem more real and heartbreaking. I've walked on beaches like this. The other aspect of the poem that stands out on a first reading is what is not told—we do not know who "I" or "you" are, and we don't know why the seal was really shot or what kinds of things the speaker is thinking people do to each other at the end. I think some of this poem works off the idea of making a connection to the reader and then having the reader fill in these gaps with his or her own experiences. Maybe what really evokes emotion in this poem is that the situation is possible, even similar to experiences most people have had.

FIGURE 7.2
A Reading Response
The author of this poem, Apryl Leaf, is a contemporary poet from British Columbia who has worked in marine ecology and writes on landscapes and environmental issues. "Sunset" is from her 2010 collection, Grass Widow.

Revising and Editing Your Literary Analysis

Once you have drafted your literary analysis, take the time to make sure that you have created a piece that will lead readers to new and interesting insights about the literary work you are analyzing. Here are some issues to consider as you revise and edit your draft:

Make Sure the Interpretive Question and Its Importance Are Clearly Stated. If your readers are to engage with you in a conversation about the literary work, they first need to understand your interpretive question and the angle you are exploring. They also need to understand why your interpretive question is important or interesting and how answering it will lead to insights about the work that go beyond a surface reading.

Check Your Thesis, or What Your Interpretation Reveals About the Work. Your reader will also want to completely understand what your interpretation reveals about the work. State your main claim or thesis clearly, prominently, and completely near the end of your introduction. You may have already written a working thesis early in the drafting process, but as you fill out your analysis, you will get a better sense of exactly what your interpretation is about and why it is interesting and important. Return to your thesis again to adjust and refine it.

Check Whether Your Analysis Remains Focused on Your Interpretive Question and Thesis. Every paragraph should further develop your interpretation. Examine your topic sentences and make sure each paragraph moves your interpretation further along. If you find yourself going off on a tangent, revise or eliminate that part of the analysis.

Make Sure You Cite, Quote, and Explain Specific Parts of the Literary Text. Use the text as evidence to support your thesis. Although you may wish to bring in ideas and sources from outside the text, make sure your reader understands exactly how the material in the literary text itself leads you to your interpretation.

Verify that You Have Cited the Text Appropriately. When you quote the text or describe a specific part of it, your readers will want to know exactly where in the text they can find that material. So use MLA documentation style to cite any quotes or sources. Also, include a "Works Cited" page that identifies the edition of your literary text and any other sources you consulted.

Make sure you spend ample time revising and editing your work. The real reader of your literary analysis is probably a professor, perhaps an English professor. That kind of reader is more sensitive than most to good (and bad) organization and style. So the extra time spent revising and editing will greatly improve his or her impression of your work.

Here are some quick steps to get you going on your literary analysis.

READ the Literary Work at Least Twice and Narrow Your Topic

Make sure you're very familiar with the work you'll be analyzing so you can examine the text closely. Make notes if necessary.

STATE Your Interpretive Question

In one sentence, try to write down the question that you want to answer in your analysis. This will probably change as you draft your analysis and continue delving deeply into the text, so don't worry about making it perfect. This is just to get you started; you'll refine this later.

DO Some Inquiry and Research

Using your reading notes, decide what intrigues you most about the work. Then do some outside research on the text, its author, the theoretical context, and the historical period in which it was written.

IDENTIFY Your Main Claim or Thesis

Come up with a main claim or thesis statement that answers your interpretive question. Your main claim will probably change and evolve, so just write it down as clearly as possible at this point.

DRAFT Your Analysis

Take your reader step by step through the analysis. Use targeted summaries and quotes to direct readers' attention to specific aspects of the text (not the whole text).

REVISIT Your Introduction and Conclusion

After drafting, go back to your introduction and refine your interpretive question and interpretive claim. After reading through your analysis once more, go to your conclusion and make sure that it brings readers back to your main claim and then branches out in new directions.

DESIGN, Revise, and Edit

Make sure you format the document the way your professor requests. Then revise by sharpening your topic sentences and making sure each paragraph stays focused on answering your interpretive question. Make sure you use the literary present tense and cite the text properly.

Borders

THOMAS KING

Thomas King was born in California in 1943 and is of Cherokee and Greek descent. He has lived and worked in Canada since 1980 and has been a strong advocate for aboriginal culture and rights. He is widely known for his novels and short stories and as the creator of the CBC series The Dead Dog Café. *In 2003, King became the first aboriginal Massey lecturer.*

When I was twelve, maybe thirteen, my mother announced that we were going to go to Salt Lake City to visit my sister who had left the reserve, moved across the line, and found a job. Laetitia had not left home with my mother's blessing, but over time my mother had come to be proud of the fact that Laetitia had done all of this on her own.

"She did real good," my mother would say.

Then there were the fine points to Laetitia's going. She had not, as my mother liked to tell Mrs. Manyfingers, gone floating after some man like a balloon on a string. She hadn't snuck out of the house, either, and gone to Vancouver or Edmonton or Toronto to chase rainbows down alleys. And she hadn't been pregnant.

"She did real good."

I was seven or eight when Laetitia left home. She was seventeen. Our father was   5
from Rocky Boy on the American side.

"Dad's American," Laetitia told my mother, "so I can go and come as I please."

"Send us a postcard."

Laetitia packed her things, and we headed for the border. Just outside of Milk River, Laetitia told us to watch for the water tower.

"Over the next rise. It's the first thing you see."

"We got a water tower on the reserve," my mother said. "There's a big one in   10
Lethbridge, too."

"You'll be able to see the tops of the flagpoles, too. That's where the border is."

When we got to Coutts, my mother stopped at the convenience store and bought her and Laetitia a cup of coffee. I got an Orange Crush.

"This is real lousy coffee."

"You're just angry because I want to see the world."

"It's the water. From here on down, they got lousy water."   15

"I can catch the bus from Sweetgrass. You don't have to lift a finger."

"You're going to have to buy your water in bottles if you want good coffee."

There was an old wooden building about a block away, with a tall sign in the yard that said "Museum." Most of the roof had been blown away. Mom told me to go and see when the place was open. There were boards over the windows and doors. You could tell that the place was closed, and I told Mom so, but she said to go and check anyway. Mom and Laetitia stayed by the car. Neither one of them moved. I sat down on the steps of the museum and watched them, and I don't know that they ever said anything to each other. Finally, Laetitia got her bag out of the trunk and gave Mom a hug.

I wandered back to the car. The wind had come up, and it blew Laetitia's hair across her face. Mom reached out and pulled the strands out of Laetitia's eyes, and Laetitia let her.

"You can still see the mountain from here," my mother told Laetitia in Blackfoot. 20

"Lots of mountains in Salt Lake," Laetitia told her in English.

"The place is closed," I said. "Just like I told you."

Laetitia tucked her hair into her jacket and dragged her bag down the road to the brick building with the American flag flapping on a pole. When she got to where the guards were waiting, she turned, put the bag down, and waved to us. We waved back. Then my mother turned the car around, and we came home.

We got postcards from Laetitia regular, and, if she wasn't spreading jelly on the truth, she was happy. She found a good job and rented an apartment with a pool.

"And she can't even swim," my mother told Mrs. Manyfingers. 25

Most of the postcards said we should come down and see the city, but whenever I mentioned this, my mother would stiffen up.

So I was surprised when she bought two new tires for the car and put on her blue dress with the green and yellow flowers. I had to dress up, too, for my mother did not want us crossing the border looking like Americans. We made sandwiches and put them in a big box with pop and potato chips and some apples and bananas and a big jar of water.

"But we can stop at one of those restaurants, too, right?"

"We maybe should take some blankets in case you get sleepy."

"But we can stop at one of those restaurants, too, right?" 30

The border was actually two towns, though neither one was big enough to amount to anything. Coutts was on the Canadian side and consisted of the convenience store and gas station, the museum that was closed and boarded up, and a motel. Sweetgrass was on the American side, but all you could see was an overpass that arched across the highway and disappeared into the prairies. Just hearing the names of these towns, you would expect that Sweetgrass, which is a nice name and sounds like it is related to other places such as Medicine Hat and Moose Jaw and Kicking Horse Pass, would be on the Canadian side, and that Coutts, which sounds abrupt and rude, would be on the American side. But this was not the case.

Between the two borders was a duty-free shop where you could buy cigarettes and liquor and flags. Stuff like that.

We left the reserve in the morning and drove until we got to Coutts.

"Last time we stopped here," my mother said, "you had an Orange Crush. You remember that?"

"Sure," I said. "That was when Laetitia took off." 35

"You want another Orange Crush?"

"That means we're not going to stop at a restaurant, right?"

My mother got a coffee at the convenience store, and we stood around and watched the prairies move in the sunlight. Then we climbed back in the car. My mother straightened the dress across her thighs, leaned against the wheel, and drove all the way to the border in first gear, slowly, as if she were trying to see through a bad storm or riding high on black ice.

The border guard was an old guy. As he walked to the car, he swayed from side to side, his feet set wide apart, the holster on his hip pitching up and down. He leaned into the window, looked into the back seat, and looked at my mother and me.

"Morning, ma'am."   40

"Good morning."

"Where you heading?"

"Salt Lake City."

"Purpose of your visit?"

"Visit my daughter."   45

"Citizenship?"

"Blackfoot," my mother told him.

"Ma'am?"

"Blackfoot," my mother repeated.

"Canadian?"   50

"Blackfoot."

It would have been easier if my mother had just said "Canadian" and been done with it, but I could see she wasn't going to do that. The guard wasn't angry or anything. He smiled and looked towards the building. Then he turned back and nodded.

"Morning, ma'am."

"Good morning."

"Any firearms or tobacco?"   55

"No."

"Citizenship?"

"Blackfoot."

He told us to sit in the car and wait, and we did. In about five minutes, another guard came out with the first man. They were talking as they came, both men swaying back and forth like two cowboys headed for a bar or a gunfight.

"Morning, ma'am."   60

"Good morning."

"Cecil tells me you and the boy are Blackfoot."

"That's right."

"Now, I know that we got Blackfeet on the American side and the Canadians got Blackfeet on their side. Just so we can keep our records straight, what side do you come from?"

I knew exactly what my mother was going to say, and I could have told them if   65
they had asked me.

"Canadian side or American side?" asked the guard.

"Blackfoot side," she said.

It didn't take them long to lose their sense of humor, I can tell you that. The one guard stopped smiling altogether and told us to park our car at the side of the building and come in.

We sat on a wood bench for about an hour before anyone came over to talk to us. This time it was a woman. She had a gun, too.

"Hi," she said. "I'm Inspector Pratt. I understand there is a little misunderstanding." 70

"I'm going to visit my daughter in Salt Lake City," my mother told her. "We don't have any guns or beer."

"It's a legal technicality, that's all."

"My daughter's Blackfoot, too."

The woman opened a briefcase and took out a couple of forms and began to write on one of them. "Everyone who crosses our border has to declare their citizenship. Even Americans. It helps us keep track of the visitors we get from the various countries."

She went on like that for maybe fifteen minutes, and a lot of the stuff she told us 75 was interesting.

"I can understand how you feel about having to tell us your citizenship, and here's what I'll do. You tell me, and I won't put it down on the form. No-one will know but you and me."

Her gun was silver. There were several chips in the wood handle and the name "Stella" was scratched into the metal butt.

We were in the border office for about four hours, and we talked to almost everyone there. One of the men bought me a Coke. My mother brought a couple of sandwiches in from the car. I offered part of mine to Stella, but she said she wasn't hungry.

I told Stella that we were Blackfoot and Canadian, but she said that that didn't count because I was a minor. In the end, she told us that if my mother didn't declare her citizenship, we would have to go back to where we came from. My mother stood up and thanked Stella for her time. Then we got back in the car and drove to the Canadian border, which was only about a hundred yards away.

I was disappointed. I hadn't seen Laetitia for a long time, and I had never been 80 to Salt Lake City. When she was still at home, Laetitia would go on and on about Salt Lake City. She had never been there, but her boyfriend Lester Tallbull had spent a year in Salt Lake at a technical school.

"It's a great place," Lester would say. "Nothing but blondes in the whole state."

Whenever he said that, Laetitia would slug him on his shoulder hard enough to make him flinch. He had some brochures on Salt Lake and some maps, and every so often the two of them would spread them out on the table.

"That's the temple. It's right downtown. You got to have a pass to get in."

"Charlotte says anyone can go in and look around."

"When was Charlotte in Salt Lake? Just when the hell was Charlotte in Salt Lake?" 85

"Last year."

"This is Liberty Park. It's got a zoo. There's good skiing in the mountains."

"Got all the skiing we can use," my mother would say. "People come from all over the world to ski at Banff. Cardston's got a temple, if you like those kinds of things."

"Oh, this one is real big," Lester would say. "They got armed guards and everything."

"Not what Charlotte says." 90

"What does she know?"

Lester and Laetitia broke up, but I guess the idea of Salt Lake stuck in her mind.

• • •

The Canadian border guard was a young woman, and she seemed happy to see us.

"Hi," she said. "You folks sure have a great day for a trip. Where are you coming from?"

"Standoff."

"Is that in Montana?"   95

"No."

"Where are you going?"

"Standoff."

The woman's name was Carol and I don't guess she was any older than Laetitia.
"Wow, you both Canadians?"

"Blackfoot."   100

"Really? I have a friend I went to school with who is Blackfoot. Do you know
Mike Harley?"

"No."

"He went to school in Lethbridge, but he's really from Browning."

It was a nice conversation and there were no cars behind us, so there was no rush.

"You're not bringing any liquor back, are you?"   105

"No."

"Any cigarettes or plants or stuff like that?"

"No."

"Citizenship?"

"Blackfoot."   110

"I know," said the woman, "and I'd be proud of being Blackfoot if I were
Blackfoot. But you have to be American or Canadian."

• • •

When Laetitia and Lester broke up, Lester took his brochures and maps with him,
so Laetitia wrote to someone in Salt Lake City, and, about a month later, she got a
big envelope of stuff. We sat at the table and opened up all the brochures, and
Laetitia read each one out loud.

"Salt Lake City is the gateway to some of the world's most magnificent skiing.

"Salt Lake City is the home of one of the newest professional basketball fran-
chises, the Utah Jazz.

"The Great Salt Lake is one of the natural wonders of the world."   115

It was kind of exciting seeing all those color brochures on the table and listening to
Laetitia read all about how Salt Lake City was one of the best places in the entire world.

"That Salt Lake City place sounds too good to be true," my mother told her.

"It has everything."

"We got everything right here."

"It's boring here."

"People in Salt Lake City are probably sending away for brochures of Calgary   120
and Lethbridge and Pincher Creek right now."

In the end, my mother would say that maybe Laetitia should go to Salt Lake
City, and Laetitia would say that maybe she would.

• • •

We parked the car to the side of the building and Carol led us into a small room on
the second floor. I found a comfortable spot on the couch and flipped through some
back issues of *Saturday Night* and *Alberta Report*.

When I woke up, my mother was just coming out of another office. She didn't say
a word to me. I followed her down the stairs and out to the car. I thought we were

going home, but she turned the car around and drove back towards the American border, which made me think we were going to visit Laetitia in Salt Lake City after all. Instead she pulled into the parking lot of the duty-free store and stopped.

"We going to see Laetitia?" 125

"No."

"We going home?"

Pride is a good thing to have, you know. Laetitia had a lot of pride, and so did my mother. I figured that someday, I'd have it, too.

"So where are we going?"

Most of that day, we wandered around the duty-free store, which wasn't very 130 large. The manager had a name tag with a tiny American flag on one side and a tiny Canadian flag on the other. His name was Mel. Towards evening, he began suggesting that we should be on our way. I told him we had nowhere to go, that neither the Americans nor the Canadians would let us in. He laughed at that and told us that we should buy something or leave.

The car was not very comfortable, but we did have all that food and it was April, so even if it did snow as it sometimes does on the prairies, we wouldn't freeze. The next morning my mother drove to the American border.

It was a different guard this time, but the questions were the same. We didn't spend as much time in the office as we had the day before. By noon, we were back at the Canadian border. By two we were back in the duty-free shop parking lot.

The second night in the car was not as much fun as the first, but my mother seemed in good spirits, and, all in all, it was as much an adventure as an inconvenience. There wasn't much food left and that was a problem, but we had lots of water as there was a faucet at the side of the duty-free shop.

. . .

One Sunday, Laetitia and I were watching television. Mom was over at Mrs. Manyfingers's. Right in the middle of the program, Laetitia turned off the set and said she was going to Salt Lake City, that life around here was too boring. I had wanted to see the rest of the program and really didn't care if Laetitia went to Salt Lake City or not. When Mom got home, I told her what Laetitia had said.

What surprised me was how angry Laetitia got when she found out that I had 135 told Mom.

"You got a big mouth."

"That's what you said."

"What I said is none of your business."

"I didn't say anything."

"Well, I'm going for sure, now." 140

That weekend, Laetitia packed her bags, and we drove her to the border.

. . .

Mel turned out to be friendly. When he closed up for the night and found us still parked in the lot, he came over and asked us if our car was broken down or something. My mother thanked him for his concern and told him that we were fine, that things would get straightened out in the morning.

"You're kidding," said Mel. "You'd think they could handle the simple things."

"We got some apples and a banana," I said, "but we're all out of ham sandwiches."

"You know, you read about these things, but you just don't believe it. You just 145 don't believe it."

"Hamburgers would be even better because they got more stuff for energy."

My mother slept in the back seat. I slept in the front because I was smaller and could lie under the steering wheel. Late that night, I heard my mother open the car door. I found her sitting on her blanket leaning against the bumper of the car.

"You see all those stars," she said. "When I was a little girl, my grandmother used to take me and my sisters out on the prairies and tell us stories about all the stars."

"Do you think Mel is going to bring us any hamburgers?"

"Every one of those stars has a story. You see that bunch of stars over there that 150 look like a fish?"

"He didn't say no."

"Coyote went fishing, one day. That's how it all started." We sat out under the stars that night, and my mother told me all sorts of stories. She was serious about it, too. She'd tell them slow, repeating parts as she went, as if she expected me to remember each one.

Early the next morning, the television vans began to arrive, and guys in suits and women in dresses came trotting over to us, dragging microphones and cameras and lights behind them. One of the vans had a table set up with orange juice and sandwiches and fruit. It was for the crew, but when I told them we hadn't eaten for a while, a really skinny blonde woman told us we could eat as much as we wanted.

They mostly talked to my mother. Every so often one of the reporters would come over and ask me questions about how it felt to be an Indian without a country. I told them we had a nice house on the reserve and that my cousins had a couple of horses we rode when we went fishing. Some of the television people went over to the American border, and then they went to the Canadian border.

Around noon, a good looking guy in a dark blue suit and an orange tie with little 155 ducks on it drove up in a fancy car. He talked to my mother for a while, and, after they were done talking, my mother called me over, and we got into our car. Just as my mother started the engine, Mel came over and gave us a bag of peanut brittle and told us that justice was a damn hard thing to get, but that we shouldn't give up.

I would have preferred lemon drops, but it was nice of Mel anyway.

"Where are we going now?"

"Going to visit Laetitia."

The guard who came out to our car was all smiles. The television lights were so bright they hurt my eyes, and, if you tried to look through the windshield in certain directions, you couldn't see a thing.

"Morning, ma'am."   160

"Good morning."

"Where you heading?"

"Salt Lake City."

"Purpose of your visit?"

"Visit my daughter."   165

"Any tobacco, liquor, or firearms?"

"Don't smoke."

"Any plants or fruit?"

"Not any more."

"Citizenship?" 170

"Blackfoot."

The guard rocked back on his heels and jammed his thumbs into his gun belt. "Thank you," he said, his fingers patting the butt of the revolver. "Have a pleasant trip."

My mother rolled the car forward, and the television people had to scramble out of the way. They ran alongside the car as we pulled away from the border, and, when they couldn't run any farther, they stood in the middle of the highway and waved and waved and waved.

We got to Salt Lake City the next day. Laetitia was happy to see us, and, that first night, she took us out to a restaurant that made really good soups. The list of pies took up a whole page. I had cherry. Mom had chocolate. Laetitia said that she saw us on television the night before and, during the meal, she had us tell her the story over and over again.

Laetitia took us everywhere. We went to a fancy ski resort. We went to the tem- 175 ple. We got to go shopping in a couple of large malls, but they weren't as large as the one in Edmonton, and Mom said so.

After a week or so, I got bored and wasn't at all sad when my mother said we should be heading back home. Laetitia wanted us to stay longer, but Mom said no, that she had things to do back home and that, next time, Laetitia should come up and visit. Laetitia said she was thinking about moving back, and Mom told her to do as she pleased, and Laetitia said that she would.

On the way home, we stopped at the duty-free shop, and my mother gave Mel a green hat that said "Salt Lake" across the front. Mel was a funny guy. He took the hat and blew his nose and told my mother that she was an inspiration to us all. He gave us some more peanut brittle and came out into the parking lot and waved at us all the way to the Canadian border.

It was almost evening when we left Coutts. I watched the border through the rear window until all you could see were the tops of the flagpoles and the blue water tower, and then they rolled over a hill and disappeared.

A CLOSER LOOK AT
Borders

1. Make a list of specific words and phrases that describe the story's setting, characters, and interpersonal relationships. Consider the border, Salt Lake City, the reserve, the narrator, his mother, his sister Laetitia, and the relationships among family members. Put the descriptions together and come up with an interpretation of setting, character, or relationships based on the text. If you form groups, each group can take on one of these topics and present their description and interpretation to the class.

2. If you were going to produce a movie based on King's short story, how would you do it? What key ideas would you want to highlight? Which actors would you choose to play the roles of each character and why? How would you portray the setting? What camera angles, lighting, costume, and visual effects would you use to capture the tone of the story? Is there anything you would add to the story and why?

1. Research the details of Thomas King's biography. What do his personal history, education, political beliefs, or cultural contexts tell you about him? How does this information help you understand the story or see aspects to it you didn't before? How does knowing the author's background help you to appreciate a literary work? Write a paragraph on King that you could incorporate into a literary analysis as background information.

2. Begin your own interpretation of "Borders" by writing a one paragraph reading response to the short story. What is the main theme or message of the narrative in your reading? Ground your response in the text itself by describing or summarizing key aspects or quoting from it. This is an informal response so feel free to explore, but remember to make connections to the story.

Rethinking Canadian and American Nationality: Indigeneity and the 49th Parallel in Thomas King

JENNIFER ANDREWS AND PRISCILLA L. WALTON

The following reading is an excerpt from a published literary analysis by critics Jennifer Andrews and Priscilla Walton. This scholarly analysis examines Thomas King's story "Borders," along with some of his other work, to make an argument about how indigenous perspectives complicate discussions of nationalism. Their interpretive question focuses on "what might constitute 'identity, citizenship, and belonging' within and beyond the borders of the nation-states that constitute the Americas." They argue that King's writings "demonstrate that the simultaneous need for and undermining of nation-state structures go hand-in-hand for indigenous peoples." Please note that the citations refer to King's story in its original format, so page numbers do not correspond with the above.

As King's 1993 short story "Borders" demonstrates, the 49th parallel can be used as a site of resistance to imperialist definitions that preclude Native self-definition, although, again, such challenges seem to bring about only temporary, not fundamental, changes. In this story, King pointedly subverts the concept of border "in-between-ness" by reminding readers that such utopian ideals and spaces ignore the daily realities of Native peoples, whose identities have been fractured by the lasting effects of colonialism on the local populations.

A (deceptively) simple tale, "Borders" recounts the adventures of a Native family divided by the border between Canada and the US. It begins with its unnamed young male narrator recounting how members of his family came to disperse, and then telling of the difficulties engendered by their efforts to reunite. Specifically, the narrator's sister, Laetitia, has moved to Salt Lake City, forsaking her life in a small Alberta town for residence south of the border, a move that is facilitated by her father's American citizenship. Despite the disagreements between mother and daughter over the move, the narrator's mother finally decides to pay a visit to Utah and takes her young son along on this driving trip: "she bought new tires for the car and put on her blue dress with the green and yellow flowers. . . . We made sandwiches and put them in a big box with pop and potato chips and some apples and bananas and a big jar of water" (135). Complications arise, however, when mother and son drive over the Canadian border, past the duty-free shop, and reach the American border checkpoint. After an initial discussion with an official, the vacationers are approached by two border guards and are asked their nationality:

> "Now I know that we got Blackfeet on the American side and the Canadians got Blackfeet on their side. Just so we can keep our records straight, what side do you come from?"
> I knew exactly what my mother was going to say, and I could have told them if they had asked me.
> "Canadian side or American side?" asked the guard.
> "Blackfoot side," she said. (137–38)

Because the narrator's mother refuses to recognize the demarcated national borders, she and the narrator are denied entry to the US and return to the Canadian side. But they must cross the Canadian border checkpoint before entering their country, and in doing so, encounter further difficulties:

> "Citizenship?"
> "Blackfoot."
> "I know," said the woman, "and I'd be proud of being Blackfoot if I were Blackfoot. But you have to be American or Canadian." (141)

Refusing to accept the standard categorizations, the protagonists become trapped between the borders and are forced to camp in front of the duty-free shop for three nights. During this time, the mother relays her own series of narratives to her son, tales from the old days that celebrate the beauty of the natural world and the power of Native storytelling. But her description of the trickster Coyote's attempts to fish for stars also offers an ironically charged undermining of the nationalist and capitalist agendas of Canada and the US, countries that refuse to recognize

Statement of interpretive focus relates the analysis of this particular story to the essay's thesis on the complexity of nation-states.

Quotations direct the reader to particularly significant moments in the text.

the priority of the First Nations and the legitimacy of their hemispheric tribal status, in the way that it contests the presumption of homogeneity under a nationalist rubric through its insistence on the multiplicity of stories:

> "Every one of those stars has a story. You see that bunch of stars over there that look like a fish? . . . Coyote went fishing, one day. That's how it all started." We sat out under the stars that night, and my mother told me all sorts of stories. She was serious about it, too. She'd tell them slow, repeating parts as she went, as if she expected me to remember each one. (144)

By the third day, mother and son have begun to attract media interest, and reporters start to descend on the border towns to interview the First Nations people caught between the countries. Eventually, the media accounts capture government attention and an official appears on the scene to question the mother. When, shortly after, mother and son approach the border, their interrogation takes a different turn:

> "Citizenship?"
>   "Blackfoot."
>   The guard rocked back on his heels and jammed his thumbs into his gun belt.
>   "Thank you," he said, his fingers patting the butt of the revolver. "Have a pleasant trip." (146)

Finally passing into the US, the two drive down to Salt Lake City for a visit with Laetitia. As the visit draws to a close, they head back to Alberta and are permitted to recross the border into Canada. "Borders" concludes with the narrator's last glimpse of this troubled contact zone: "I watched the border through the rear window until all you could see were the tops of the flagpoles and the blue water tower, and then they rolled over a hill and disappeared" (147). The landscape eventually overpowers the artificial border, blocking it from the narrator's line of vision. In so doing, the regimented demarcations of the 49th parallel are replaced by the natural flow of the hills.

King's story depicts the work of a Native woman who resists identifying herself as American or Canadian and instead insists upon the validity of her tribal heritage as a legitimate third term. She literalizes her status as "an Indian without a country" (indeed, with only a duty-free shop), which paradoxically gains her free access, without any sacrifice of pride or principle, to the *commodities* of both countries. But she refuses these commodities, instead bringing food for herself and her child, along with tales of the days when borders did not separate Native peoples. Her decolonizing border crossing, then, is a crossing with a difference. The mother's narratives undermine the authoritative narratives by raising questions about their primacy. Indeed, her storytelling, which occurs literally between the borders, functions within King's story as an appeal to understand the complex workings of borders and boundaries—what they admit, what they impede, and how they mediate what crosses or doesn't cross them in very different ways.

Situated between the Canadian and American borders, the Native mother tells counter-narratives—narratives that readers do not always "hear," but narratives

---

The preceding targeted summary of the narrative is designed to focus on the cultural meanings of borders and border crossings.

Point on the economic and subversive implications of the narrative.

that, because they are of "the old days," operate as an alternative to the narratives of nation that she undermines by refusing to acknowledge them. Intriguingly, the governmental and border officials do not know how to cope with her accounts and ultimately refuse to ask the question that will destabilize the borders they defend. Their very refusal to ask the question, however, underscores the importance of the position she maintains.

The counter-narratives or alternative visions within King's texts also perform a political purpose, for they create a gap that induces cultural resistance to the dominance of nation. King's texts, as they critique the nation-state in which they are situated, problematize the object of colonization and thus emerge as cross-cultural texts that demand cross-cultural readings. They encourage a resistance to political amnesia and insist on the importance of acknowledging and exploring the contradictions of colonizing histories, especially when relayed by those under colonial rule.

> The analysis is situated as post-colonial, addressing cultural difference as experienced in Canada, a former British colony.

10   King's "Borders," however, is cautious about merely embracing the utopian dimensions of such textual resistance. The story explicitly presents a doubled vision, informed both by a postmodern desire to move beyond the confines of nation and national borders and by the reality of ongoing Native colonization. Though Mel, the white manager of the duty-free shop in "Borders," where mother and son pass several days, eventually becomes sympathetic to their cause, providing peanut brittle and encouraging words, he is initially dismissive of their presence in the store, insisting that they "should buy something or leave" (142). Wearing a name tag with "a tiny American flag on one side and a tiny Canadian flag on the other," which epitomizes an ideally harmonious relationship between the two nations, Mel soon discovers that an unimpeded passage through this contact zone is not as simple as he might think. The idealizing myths and official history of Canada–US relations are undermined by the tangible experiences of mother and son; as he tells them, "You know, you read about these things, but you just don't believe it. You just don't believe it" (144).

> The authors note that, for indigenous peoples, borders cannot be easily crossed or overcome (as some literary analyses suggest) because they still carry oppressive historical meaning.

Mel's gradual recognition of the ludicrousness of border operations and the power of the nation-state to define one's identity is juxtaposed with the arrival of television reporters who, in covering the story, tend to ignore the stories that the young boy, in particular, provides. Although he is repeatedly asked how it feels "to be an Indian without a country," the answers he offers go unheard precisely because they do not accord with the reporters' expectations. The youth's description of the family's "nice house on the reserve" and the horses that "we rode when we went fishing" (145) complicate the fixity of colonizing histories by offering a vision of identity in which border politics are altogether irrelevant. Rather than recognizing and giving space for other ways of reading the border and by implication notions of "nation"—as epitomized by the young boy's answers—the reporters' presence and their focus on the 49th parallel serve as a reminder of how the patrolling of geopolitical and cultural boundaries occurs in a myriad of forms. Even the outcome of this border standoff resists utopian alterity. Although the female protagonist of "Borders" may finally succeed in visiting Laetitia without having to declare her citizenship as Canadian, there is no promise that such exceptions will be permitted in the future; the possibility of unimpeded transnational journeys in a larger hemispheric space without personal sacrifice are indeed absent from King's texts generally.

> Despite the subversive implications of King's story, the authors note that borders remain fixed and highly significant in current North American society.

> The authors refer to a new area, "hemispheric studies," which discusses borders and their cultural meanings throughout North America.

The structure of this story, then, accords with Winfried Siemerling's term "re-cognition" (2), which he develops in his recent *The New North American Studies* (2005) and which he explains in relation to King's positioning in "Godzilla vs. Post-colonial":

> King's argument, while it is counter-discursive in its critique of the notational colonialism of the term "postcolonial," clearly seeks to avoid the logic of "reverse discourse" . . . ; it uses the tradition of orality as a frame and ground that bypasses "recognition" of Native culture on the basis of "postcolonial" assumptions. While it is possible to see Native cultural practices as responses to the imposition of colonialism, King's "re-cognition" casts European contact as an imbalance to be recognized and balanced according to Native explanatory principles that continue their reaction and are not grounded in this event. (69–70)

In keeping with Siemerling's definition, King's short story (and his fiction generally) repositions "authoritative" accounts and upsets, in form and content, the historical linearity and construction of traditional Western narratives. King also expands on his argument, first developed in "Godzilla vs. Post-colonial," in *The Truth About Stories*. There, he notes, "The difference [between oral and written literature] is this: instead of waiting for you to come to us, as we have in the past, written literature has allowed us to come to you" (114). His fictions thus can be seen as potential models for balancing the indigenous need for alternate forms of nationalism with the reality of the continued existence of nation-states.

> The authors conclude that borders and their meanings cannot be simply reversed or dismissed, but must be negotiated in more complex ways.

Works Cited

King, Thomas. "Borders." *One Good Story, that One*. Toronto: HarperCollins, 1993. 129–46. Print.

———. *The Truth About Stories: A Native Narrative*. Toronto: Anansi Press, 2003. Print.

Siemerling, Winfried. *The New North American Studies: Culture, Writing, and the Politics of Re/Cognition*. New York: Routledge, 2005. Print.

A CLOSER LOOK AT
Rethinking Canadian and American Nationality

1. Why do you think Thomas King uses the genre of short fiction to express his ideas rather than a poem, play, or novel? What about the short story form helps him deliver his message? What, if anything, do you think might be limiting about the short story versus another literary genre? Is this form effective for you as a reader?

2. Do you agree with Jennifer Andrews and Priscilla Walton's interpretation of King's story? Is the main point of this story to demonstrate the arbitrariness yet significance of national borders? Do you see other ideas in the story? How would you interpret it if you were writing your own literary analysis? What ideas do you find key in the narrative? You may wish to continue this exercise by posing a full interpretive question, as discussed in "Ideas for Writing" question 3 below.

IDEAS FOR
Writing

1. Practise summarizing and quoting. Summarize Andrews and Walton's interpretation of King's story in a short, 200 word paragraph. If you need to quote briefly for evidence or because the phrasing is important, be sure to incorporate the quotation into your own writing. Then consider how you would use the summary to set up your own interpretation. Will you agree or disagree with Andrews and Walton or qualify their reading? (For help with quotation, consult Chapter 23, "Quoting, Paraphrasing, and Citing Sources.")

2. Write a short story on an event or experience that has affected your life. What settings, form, and language will you use? What characterizations will you make? Will you use metaphors, similes, or symbolism? How can you effectively express the key ideas or theme in your story?

3. Re-read Thomas King's story "Borders." Generate an "interpretive question" about the narrative. Ask yourself, "What do I want to understand by going beneath the surface of the story?" Focus on just one question and delve deeply into it, so that you can begin to answer it in your thesis statement.

   a. Address your interpretive question by noting the specifics of the story. Focus at first on the story itself rather than what you might know about the author or the context in which it was written. Finally, come up with one aspect of the story that makes a plausible case about its message, what makes it effective, thought provoking, revealing, or enjoyable.

   b. In a single sentence, write down your interpretive question. In another single sentence, write down your main claim or thesis statement.

1. In a group, consider how you could analyze a movie in the same way that you analyze a literary work. Start out by selecting a movie that most of you have seen or are familiar with. Then generate an "interpretive question" about the movie. Ask yourself, "What do I/we want to understand by going beneath the surface of the movie?" In a single sentence, write down your interpretive question, and in another single sentence, write down your interpretive claim or thesis.

2. Ask each member of your group to bring in a short poem. Discuss the poem as a literary work by paying attention to its genre, plot, characters, setting, and use of language and tone. What intrigues you about each poem? What makes them interesting and worth talking about?

3. Find a literary analysis in your library databases. Point to specific places in the analysis where the author makes the following moves:

   a. Identifies an interpretive question

   b. Makes an interpretive claim that addresses that question

   c. Examines the text itself to support the interpretation

   d. Goes outside the text (with information about the author, the social or historical setting, etc.) to develop the interpretation

   e. Provides insights that go beyond the obvious

1. Practise summarizing, describing, and quoting by choosing a scene or feature (character, plot, setting, etc.) from "Borders" that you find interesting. First, summarize that scene or feature as clearly and efficiently as possible in two or three sentences. Refer to Chapter 4 for more information on summary. Second, rework what you've written to weave in quoted words and phrases that are particularly important to the summary. Be sure to use quotation marks and parenthetical citations to show which words are quoted and where they came from.

2. Search the Internet to find literary definitions of the word "genre." Cut and paste those definitions into a single file. Now, look back at the definition of genre in Chapter 1, "Writing and Genres." How are the literary definitions of genre different than the one used in this book? Are there any similarities? In a response to your professor, try to reconcile these two definitions of genre in a way that makes both useful.

1. **Analyze a short story or poem.** Write a literary analysis of a short story or poem that poses an interesting interpretive question and offers an interpretive claim or thesis that explains the work's message or significance, or that analyzes its structure and features (character, symbol, setting, etc.). Be sure that you focus on the text itself for your interpretation.

2. **Create a multimedia literary analysis of song lyrics or a poem.** Drawing on a variety of media (images, sound, or text), create an electronic multimedia presentation of a song or poem. Choose whatever medium you are comfortable with (or

that you want to learn), such as a podcast, webpage, or *PowerPoint* slide presentation. Combine these media to provide your audience with an experience that goes beyond the text and presents them with something new—a new insight, analysis, or interesting juxtaposition.

3. **Turn a review into a literary analysis.** Write an informal review of a book or play. Then transform the review into a more formal literary analysis using the strategies described in this chapter. Pose an interpretive question and make a claim or thesis statement that answers the question. Quote and describe the text. Then explain the message or significance of the work you are analyzing. Your literary analysis should use an academic tone, so make changes to the style where appropriate.

MyCompLab

For support in meeting this chapter's objectives, follow this path in MyCompLab:

Student Resources → Writing → Writing Purposes → Writing to Analyze. Review the Instruction and Multimedia resources about writing to analyze; then complete the Exercises and click on Gradebook to measure your progress.

8

Position Papers and Arguments

In this chapter, you will learn how to:
- develop an argumentative thesis about a controversial issue.
- describe the strengths and limitations of opposing viewpoints.
- use evidence and reasoning to back up your thesis.

If you like to engage with the ideas of others, you will enjoy writing position papers. The purpose of a position paper is to explain both sides of a controversy and then argue for one side over the other. This two-sided approach is what makes position papers and argument essays different from writing merely from your own viewpoint or opinion. Rather than only expressing the author's personal opinion about a current issue or event, a position paper explains both sides and discusses why one is stronger or better than the other.

Your goal is to fairly explain your side and your opponents' side of the issue, while highlighting the differences between these opposing views. You need to use solid reasoning and factual evidence to persuade your readers that your view is more valid or advantageous than your opponents' view. These argumentative skills are important when used on their own, as in the position papers we offer as readings for this chapter, but they are also skills used in research papers and proposals to establish a position on existing ideas.

In college and university, your professors will ask you to write position papers that analyze and evaluate both (or all) sides of an issue and then argue for one side or another. In the workplace, corporate position papers are used to argue for or against business strategies or alternatives. The ability to argue effectively is a useful skill that will help you throughout your life.

Position Papers and Arguments

This diagram shows two basic organizations for a position paper or argument essay, but other arrangements of these sections will work too. In the pattern on the left, the opponents' position is described up front with its limitations; then your own position is explained with its strengths. In the pattern on the right, you make a point-by-point comparison, explaining why your position is better than your opponents.' You should alter this organization to fit your topic, angle, purpose, readers, and context.

Introduction	Introduction
Summary of opponents' position	Major point of difference Opponents' position Your position
Limitations of opponents' position	Major point of difference Opponents' position Your position
Your understanding of the issue	• • •
Reasons why your understanding is better than your opponents' understanding	Reasons why your understanding is better than your opponents' understanding
Conclusion	Conclusion

Overview

Arguing can be fun, but you need to argue fairly and reasonably if you want to win over your readers. The strongest position papers and argument essays present both sides of an issue as objectively as possible and then persuade readers that one side is superior to the other. They tend to have the following features:

- **An introduction** that states the issue being debated, identifies the issue's two or more sides, and usually makes an explicit claim (thesis) that the position paper will support.

- **An objective summary** of your opponents' understanding of the issue.

- **A point-by-point discussion** of the limitations of your opponents' understanding.

- **A summary** of your understanding of the issue.

- **A point-by-point discussion** of why your understanding is superior to your opponents' understanding.

- **A conclusion** that drives home your main point and looks to the future.

This genre tends to be organized in two ways, as shown on page 149. With some topics, you may need to show that there are more than two sides to the argument. In these cases, the pattern on the left can be expanded to include discussions of these other positions. It is best, though, to try to narrow the issue down to two major sides. Otherwise, your readers will find it difficult to keep the sides of the argument straight.

ONE STUDENT'S WORK
Position Papers and Arguments

The following student sample uses the principles of argumentation to take a stand on an issue that would interest a general audience.

Watching Movies at Home or Going to the Cinema?

Kurosh Amoui Kalareh

Writer sets the scene to focus the reader's attention.

Here is his main point.

The phone rings. It is your friend asking you out to a movie. Prior to this, you have read some reviews of the film and intended to watch it. Now you have to decide whether to go to the cinema or wait for the DVD to be released and watch the movie at home. You weigh your options: which one would be more exciting? This is a kind of dilemma that happens to many of us nowadays. Although going to the cinema can be an enjoyable experience, there are many advantages to watching movies at home.

Primarily, this dilemma is a matter of cost and quality. Those who prefer going to the cinema obviously find the quality superior to that of the DVD. The screen is much bigger and the sound is also superior. These moviegoers argue that films are naturally meant to be seen at cinemas. However, to benefit from this high-quality experience, one must pay more. A regular moviegoer may have a hard time balancing his or her budget in order to watch several films every month. And with technology progressing faster each day, high-quality devices are becoming more and more available at home. The increase in the number of home theatres attests to this ever-growing availability.

Secondly, audience reactions during a film bear a major significance for some people. They argue that sitting in huge movie theatres while hearing other people laugh, cry, and scream adds an extra value to the film. It is as though a type of collective spirit is being made in the huge halls. This phenomenon applies to live concerts as well. On the other hand, sitting next to strangers can be a bit risky. More often than not there are some inconsiderate audience members in the theatre, annoying others by talking to each other, answering their cell phones, going back and forth to the washroom, making out, and so on. Although such interruptions could also happen at home, there is always the choice of pausing the film, and even rewinding it. Thus, one won't miss a scene while watching a movie at home, and there is the possibility of watching an exciting or important scene over and over. For many, this less distracting, more convenient home environment takes precedence over the collective experience of going to the cinema.

Moreover, some people state that movie-going is a great opportunity to hang out with friends and get out of the house. They believe that technology is turning us into stay-at-home individuals, a phenomenon that we ought to resist by all means including going to the cinema. This argument, however, does not seem reasonable, as while watching a movie, we are not focusing on our friends. Activities such as going to restaurants, shopping, walking in streets, or participating in sports seem like better opportunities for socializing because there are more opportunities to communicate with one another. So if the purpose is communication, inviting friends over, watching the movie together, and perhaps discussing it afterwards would be a better idea.

Finally, according to Theatrical Market Statistics of 2010, US/Canada movie admissions (or tickets sold) for that year dropped by 10% to 1.34 billion, in comparison to 2002 when 1.57 billion people went to cinemas. These statistics are in spite of the introduction of 3D technology to movie theatres. All in all, it seems that people in North America have found their houses more relaxing and appropriate for watching films.

Work Cited

Motion Picture Association of America. *Theatrical Market Statistics*. 2010. Web. 23 Oct. 2011.

> Point-by-point comparison of the two positions, with an argument for at-home viewing winning throughout.

> The main point is restated and supported with statistics.

> MLA style citation. See Chapter 24 for more discussion of MLA style.

Developing Your Position Paper's Content

When writing a position paper, you should try to summarize both sides of the issue as fairly as possible. If readers sense that you are distorting your opponents' view, they might doubt whether your views are trustworthy. So let your facts and reasoning do the talking for you. If your position is truly stronger, you should be able to explain both sides fairly and then demonstrate to readers why your side is the stronger one.

Inquiring: Identifying Points of Contention

To begin generating content for your position paper, first identify the major points on which you and your opponents disagree. A brainstorming list like the one shown in Figure 8.1 is often the best way to identify these major points.

Use two columns. In the left column, write "My position" and list all the arguments you can think of to support your case. In the right column, write "My opponents' position" and list your opponents' best arguments for their side of the case. When listing your opponents' ideas, you should do so from their perspective. What are their strongest arguments? What would they likely say to defend their position?

My position: More North Americans prefer viewing movies at home than in the cinema	My opponents' position: Viewing films in the theatre offers a unique experience that can't be replicated with home viewing
It is more cost effective to view movies at home	Theatres offer a better quality experience for viewing movies (better sound, larger screens)
It is more convenient to view movies at home	Movies are designed to be viewed in a theatre rather than at home
Home theatre technology is approaching the same quality as one achieves in a theatre	Collective experience with other movie viewers is an important part of viewing a film
Viewing films with strangers in a theatre can be dangerous and annoying	Physically going to the cinema is an opportunity for socializing with friends
Films can be paused at home to deal with interruptions	
Important or exciting scenes can be replayed over and over again at home	

FIGURE 8.1 Brainstorming to Identify Major Points of Contention

When brainstorming about your topic, write down key points as they come to mind.

When you have filled out your brainstorming lists, put checkmarks next to the two to five most important points on which you and your opponents seem to disagree. These are called "points of contention" between your side and your opponents' side of the argument.

Researching: Finding Out What Others Know

Now it is time to do some research. You can use your two-column brainstorming list as a guide to doing research on your topic. Collect sources that support both sides of the argument. You should look for a variety of database, online, print, and empirical sources.

Again, put yourself in your opponents' place as you research their side of the issue. If you were your opponent, how would you build your argument? What would be your best points? What kinds of sources would you use to support your points? After all, if you only look for sources that support your side of the argument, there is a good chance you will miss your opponents' best reasons for holding their opinion. Then it would be easy for your opponents to undermine your argument by showing that you have not considered one or more important ideas.

Online Sources. The Internet can be helpful for generating content, but you need to be especially careful about your sources when you are preparing to write a position paper. Countless people will offer their opinions on blogs and websites, but these sources are often heavily biased and may provide little support to back up their opinions. When researching, you should look for factual sources on the Internet and avoid sources that are too biased. Also, keep an eye out for credible television documentaries and radio broadcasts on your subject, because they will often address both sides of the issue in a journalistic way.

Print Sources. Print documents will likely be your most reliable sources of factual information. Look for magazines, academic journals, and books, because these sources tend to be more careful about their facts and have less bias. Through your library's website, try using the *Readers' Guide* to find magazine articles and *periodical indexes* to find academic articles. Your library's *online catalogue* is a good place to search for books.

Empirical Sources. Facts you generate yourself will be very useful for backing up your claims about your topic. Set up an interview with an expert on your topic, or create a survey that will generate some data. Do some field observations. If you really want to dig up some interesting information, interview an expert who holds an opposing view to your own. This kind of interview will help you understand both sides of the issue much better.

Remember, you are looking for information that is credible and not biased. It is fine to use sources that make a strong argument for one side or the other, but you need to make sure these sources are backed up with facts, data, and solid sources.

Organizing and Drafting Your Position Paper

The key to organizing a position paper is to remember that you need to tell both sides of the story. As you are drafting your argument, it might help to imagine yourself in a debate with another person. If you were in a public debate, how would you express your best points and win over the audience? Meanwhile, try to anticipate your opponents' best arguments for their position.

The Introduction

Identify your topic and offer some background information to help your readers understand what you are writing about. State your purpose clearly by telling readers that you are going to explain both sides of the issue and then demonstrate why yours is stronger. You might offer your main point (thesis) here in the introduction, although some popular writers save it for the conclusion if they think readers might resist the argument. Your introduction should both gain the readers' attention and establish your credibility as an author.

Summary and Limitations of Your Opponents' Position

Here is the tough part. Try to explain your opponents' side of the issue in a straightforward way. You do not need to argue for their side, but you should explain their side in a way that your readers would consider fair and reasonable. Where possible, use quotes from your opponents' arguments to explain their side of the issue. Paraphrasing or summarizing their argument is fine too, as long as you do it fairly.

As straightforwardly as possible, explain the limitations of your opponents' position. What exactly are they missing? What have they neglected to consider? What are they ignoring in their argument? Again, you want to highlight these limitations as objectively as possible. This is not the place to be sarcastic or dismissive. You want to fairly point out the weaknesses in your opponents' argument.

Your Understanding of the Issue

Then it's your turn. Explain your side of the argument by taking your readers through the two to five points of contention, showing them why your side of the argument is stronger. Here is where you need to use your sources to back up your argument. You need to use good reasoning, examples, facts, and data to show readers why your position is more credible.

In argumentative contexts, points that are supported by specific and accurate evidence are typically described as claims rather than opinions. Opinions suggest subjective views, while the term "claim" connotes a researched position. As you present your understanding, your professor will expect your ideas to be at the level of claims rather than opinions.

Reasons Why Your Understanding Is Stronger

Before moving to your conclusion, you might spend a little time comparing and contrasting your opponents' views with your own. Briefly, go head to head with your opponents, showing readers why your view is stronger. At this point, it is all right to concede some points to your opponents. Your goal is to show readers that your view is stronger *on balance.* In other words, both sides probably have their strengths and weaknesses. You want to show that your side has more strengths and fewer weaknesses than your opponents' side.

Conclusion

Bring your argument to a close by stating or restating your thesis and looking to the future. Here is where you want to drive your main point (thesis) home by telling your readers exactly what you believe. Then show how your position leads to a better future than your opponents' position. Overall, your conclusion should be brief (a paragraph in most position papers).

The diagram on page 149 shows two possible patterns for organizing your position paper, but as you draft, you may come up with another pattern that fits your topic better. The key is to present both sides of the issue as fairly as possible.

Choosing an Appropriate Style

The style of your position paper will help you distinguish your side from your opponents' side. Even though your goal is to be *factually* fair to your opponents, there is nothing wrong with using style to make your side sound more appealing and exciting.

Use Plain Style to Describe Your Opponents' Position

You should not be sarcastic or dismissive of your opponents' side of the argument. Instead, describe the other side's argument as plainly as possible. In Chapter 13, "Choosing a Style," you will find helpful strategies for writing plainly, like putting the subjects of your sentences up front and using active verbs. You will also find techniques for writing better paragraphs that use clear topic sentences. If you use these plain style techniques to describe your opponents' side of the argument, it will sound like you are fairly and objectively summarizing their views.

Use Similes, Metaphors, and Analogies When Describing Your Position

When you are describing your side of the argument, you want to present your case as visually as possible. Similes, metaphors, and analogies are a great way to help your readers visualize your argument. Note, however, that these figures of speech are used sparingly in academic writing, although they are common in popular style.

A simile compares something unfamiliar to something familiar:

Simile (X Is Like Y)

Watching movies at home is like hearing about a book from a friend.

Sharing music is like lending a good book to a friend, not pirating a ship on the high seas.

Metaphor (X Is Y)

Viewing movies in theatres is a drain on your bank account.

The purpose of the music industry's lawsuits is to throw a few unfortunate university and college students to the lions. That way, they can hold up a few bloody carcasses to scare the rest of us.

Analogy (X Is to Y Like A Is to B)

For some people, viewing a movie at home is like hibernating; it allows them to regroup and restore their energy for another hard day at work.

Try some of these "persuasive style" techniques to enhance the power of your argument. Similes, metaphors, and analogies will make your writing more visual and colourful, and they will also help you come up with new ways to think and talk about your topic. You can learn more about persuasive style in Chapter 13, "Choosing a Style."

Use Top-Down Paragraphs

Your argument needs to sound confident, and your readers should be able to find your major points easily. In your paragraphs, put each major point in the first or second sentence. Don't put your major points in the middle of your paragraphs or at the end because your readers won't find them easily. A top-down style will make you sound more confident, because you are stating your major claims and then proving them.

Define Unfamiliar Terms

Your readers may or may not be familiar with the topic of your argument. If you use any specialized or technical terms, you should provide quick parenthetical or sentence definitions to explain them.

Sentence Definition

Peer-to-peer file sharing involves using a network of computers to store and share files without charge.

Parenthetical Definitions

Music sharing should become illegal when a person *burns* the songs (i.e., puts them on a CD) and sells them to someone else.

Applying the Genre: The Rebuttal

A rebuttal counters or refutes an argument. Rebuttals often appear as letters to the editor. For an example of a rebuttal, see the reading "Letter to the Editor on Climate Story" at the end of the chapter. They are also used in the workplace to argue against potentially damaging reviews, evaluations, position papers, and reports. Knowing how to write a rebuttal is an important part of defending your beliefs, projects, and research.

The main difference between a rebuttal and a position paper is that a rebuttal responds directly to the points made in the original argument. After responding to your opponent's argument point by point, you then offer a better counterargument. Here are some strategies for writing a successful rebuttal:

Review Your Opponent's Argument Briefly. Objectively summarize the original argument's main point and its major claims.

Challenge Any Hidden Assumptions Behind Your Opponent's Claims. Look for unstated assumptions in each major claim of your opponent's argument. These are weak points that you can challenge.

Challenge the Facts. If the author cites any facts, locate the original source to see if any data or details are outdated, inaccurate, exaggerated, or taken out of context. If the author has no supporting facts, then you can point that out in your rebuttal.

Challenge the Authority of the Sources. If possible, question whether the author's sources are truly authoritative on the issue. Unless a source is rock solid, you can question the reliability of the information taken from it.

Examine Whether Emotion Is Overcoming Reason or Evidence. If the author is allowing his or her feelings to fuel the argument, you can suggest that these emotions are clouding his or her judgment on the issue.

Look for Argumentative Fallacies. Argumentative fallacies are forms of weak reasoning that you can use to challenge your opponents' ideas. You can learn more about fallacies in Chapter 19, "Using Argumentative Strategies."

Offer a Solid Counterargument. Offer a different understanding of the issue supported by authoritative research.

Designing Your Position Paper

More and more, you will find that your professors appreciate the use of good page design. If your work looks professional, it will likely make a more favourable impression on your audience.

Use Descriptive Headings. Each of the major sections in your position paper should start with a clear heading that identifies what the section is about. For example, you could use headings like these:

The Costs of Theatre Going

The Drawbacks of Public Viewing

The Benefits of Home Viewing

Conclusion: Why Many People Now View Movies at Home

You might use bold type to help your headings stand out, and you might use a larger font size where appropriate. Make sure your headings are formatted consistently.

Include Helpful Graphs, Diagrams, and Charts. Position papers often discuss trends in our society, so you might look for ways to use graphs that illustrate those trends. If you collected data or found data on the Internet, you might create a graph or chart to present that data visually. Or, if you found a helpful graph on the Internet, you could use it in your own document, as long as you cite it properly. Graphs and charts should have a title, and you should use figure numbers in your written text to refer readers to the visual (e.g., "In Figure 2, the graph shows . . .").

Number Pages. Page numbers might seem like a simple thing, but they are helpful when discussing a position paper with other students or with your professor. Your word processor can add them automatically to the top or bottom of each page.

Explore
Report 11:
Position Paper
(interactive)

Revising and Editing Your Position Paper

As you draft your position paper, your ideas will evolve. Some shift in your understanding is natural because writing about something gives you the opportunity to think about it in greater depth and consider other viewpoints. Drafting your argument will also force you to back up your claims, which may cause you to rethink your position a little.

Now that you are finished drafting, you need to spend time revising and "re-visioning" your argument to make sure the whole paper holds together. In other words, you don't want to argue one thing at the beginning of the position paper and then argue something a little different at the end. The whole argument needs to work together to prove your main point or thesis.

Remove Any Digressions. When arguing, you might find yourself temporarily drifting off topic. These moments are called *digressions*, and you should remove them from the final version of your paper. Check each paragraph to make sure you are discussing your topic and not going off in a direction that expands or sidetracks your argument.

Back-Check the Evidence for Your Claims. Make sure your claims are backed up with solid support. If you make a claim about your position or your opponents' position, that statement should be followed up with facts, data, examples, reasoning, or quotations. Short paragraphs are usually a signal that you are not backing up your claims, because such paragraphs typically include only a claim with minimal support. See Chapter 19 for a discussion of argumentative fallacies and ensure that you are not using any of these in your arguments.

Improve the Flow of Your Sentences. Try reading your draft out loud to yourself or someone else. Mark any places where you stumble or hear something that doesn't sound right. Then use the "plain style" methods discussed in Chapter 13, "Choosing a Style," to make your sentences flow better.

Make Your Writing More Visual. If you are writing in popular style, rather than academic style, look for places where you can use more detail and colour to bring your writing to life. Describe things and people. Look for places where you can use similes and metaphors to add a visual component to your writing.

Ask a friend or roommate to read through your position paper to highlight places where you could revise. Also, your university or college may have a Writing Lab where you can get help with locating places in your essay that need revision.

Revising and editing are critical to developing solid position papers and argument essays because your readers (i.e., your professors or supervisors) place a high value on clear, thoughtful writing. If they sense that you did not revise and edit your work, they will rate your work lower.

Here are some quick steps for writing a position paper or argument.

IDENTIFY a Debatable Topic

A debatable topic has at least two sides. Choose the side that you agree with. Then narrow your topic to something suitable for a position paper. Think about what is new or has changed about your topic recently.

IDENTIFY the Points Separating Your Views from Opponents' Views

Using brainstorming or another prewriting tool, put down everything you know about your topic. Then write down everything your opponents believe about this issue. When you are finished, put stars or checkmarks next to the issues on which you and your opponents disagree.

RESEARCH Both Sides of the Topic

Collect materials that support both sides of the issue, because you want to discover your opponents' best reasons for supporting their side. You can authoritatively counter their position as you support your own.

ORGANIZE Your Materials and Draft Your Argument

Position papers are organized to explain both sides of the issue. Be sure you give fair and adequate space to explaining as well as refuting your opponents' argument.

CHOOSE Your Style

When explaining your opponents' position, use a "plain style" with simple sentences and paragraphs. If you are not writing an academic paper, consider adding energy to your argument by using similes, metaphors, and analogies.

DESIGN the Document

Position papers tend to be rather plain in design. However, you might look for opportunities to add visuals to support your argument. Consider using headings and other elements to make the document more attractive.

REVISE and Edit

As you draft your argument, your position may evolve. Give yourself time to modify your argument and refine your points. Proofreading is critical because readers will see errors as evidence that your argument has not been fully thought through.

Friends with Benefits: Do *Facebook* Friends Provide the Same Support as Those in Real Life?

KATE DAILEY

Social networking sites like Facebook *and* MySpace *have challenged our ideas about what it means to be a "friend." Today, people can keep in touch with others who might otherwise have faded into the past. Also, we can be "friends" with people we barely know who share common interests or backgrounds. In this position paper, pay attention to how Dailey builds her argument and notice where she summarizes the other side of the debate.*

I have a friend named Sue. Actually, "Sue" isn't her real name, and she isn't really a friend: she's something akin to a lost sorority sister—we went to the same college, participated in the same activities and had a lot of mutual respect and admiration for one another. But since graduation, we've fallen out of touch, and the only way I know about Sue, her life and her family is through her *Facebook* updates. That's why I felt almost like a voyeur when Sue announced, via *Facebook*, the death of her young son. I was surprised she had chosen to share something so personal online—and then ashamed, because since when did I become the arbiter of what's appropriate for that kind of grief?

> Author sets the background to her position in a manner that captures the readers' attention.

The more I thought about it, the more I realized *Facebook* might be the perfect venue for tragic news: it's the fastest way to disseminate important information to the group without having to deal with painful phone calls; it allowed well-meaning friends and acquaintances to instantly pass on condolences, which the family could read at their leisure, and it eliminated the possibility that were I to run into Sue in the supermarket, I'd ask unknowingly about her son and force her to replay the story over again.

Numerous studies have shown that a strong network of friends can be crucial to getting through a crisis, and can help you be healthier in general. But could virtual friends, like the group of online buddies that reached out to Sue, be just as helpful as the flesh-and-blood versions? In other words, do *Facebook* friends—and the support we get from them—count? These questions are all the more intriguing as the

> Author clearly states her position.

number of online social-network users increases. *Facebook* attracted 67.5 million visitors in the U.S. in April (according to ComScore Inc.), and the fastest-growing demographic is people over 35. It's clear that connecting to friends, both close and distant, via the computer will become more the norm than novelty.

Researchers have yet to significantly study the social implications of *Facebook*, so what we do know is gleaned from general studies about friendship, and some of the emerging studies about online networking. First, a definition of "friend": In research circles, experts define a friend as a close, equal, voluntary partnership—though Rebecca G. Adams, a professor of sociology at the University of North Carolina, Greensboro, says that in reality, "friendships don't have to be equal or close, and we know from research that friendships aren't as voluntary as they seem," because they're often constricted by education, age and background. Friends on *Facebook* seem to mimic, if not replicate, this trend—there are people online that you are more likely to chat with every day, while others only make an appearance once or twice a year, content to spend the rest of the time residing silently in your friend queue. (Though the *Facebook* friends with whom you have frequent social interaction might not be people you interact with often in "real life.")

In life, having 700 people in your circle of friends could get overwhelming, but 5 that's less of an issue online. "Research suggests that people are only intermittently in touch with many of their online 'friends' but correspond regularly with only a few good friends," says Shelley E. Taylor, professor of psychology at the University of California, Los Angeles. "That said, creating networks to ease the transition to new places can be hugely helpful to people, offsetting loneliness until new friends are made."

In other words, *Facebook* may not replace the full benefits of real friendship, but it definitely beats the alternative. I conducted a very informal poll via my *Facebook* status update, asking if *Facebook* makes us better friends. A high-school pal, with whom I haven't spoken in about 10 years, confessed that since she had her baby, corresponding via *Facebook* has been a lifeline—and even if she wasn't actively commenting, it was nice to know what people were up to. "Any electronic communication where you don't have to be in the same physical space is going to decrease feelings of isolation," says Dr. Adams.

Several people in my online network admit that *Facebook* doesn't make them a better friend, but a better acquaintance, more likely to dash off a quick happy birthday e-mail, or to comment on the photo of a new puppy. But that's not a bad thing. Having a large group of "friends" eager to comment on your daily life could be good for your self-esteem. When you get a new job, a celebratory lunch with your best friends will make you feel good and make for a fantastic memory. But the boost you get from the 15 *Facebook* friends who left encouraging comments can also make you happy.

"The way to think of this is before the Internet, we wouldn't see our acquaintances very often: every once in a while, we might show up at a wedding and suddenly have 100 of our closest friends around," says James Fowler, associate professor of political science at the University of California, San Diego. "With *Facebook*, it's like every day is a wedding." And just like leaving a wedding may leave you feeling energized and inspired by reconnecting to old pals, so can spending time on *Facebook*, says Fowler.

While Fowler's research also shows that bad habits like smoking and weight gain can be contagious among close friends, emotions like happiness and sadness

Opposing side is alluded to.

Informal research that supports the author's position. Notice the use of *pathos* in this example.

Further support for author's position.

Expert support for author's position

are easily transferable through acquaintances. The good news? "Because happiness spreads more easily than unhappiness, getting positive comments from your *Facebook* friends is more likely to make you happy than sad," he says.

10   Shy people who may not always be able to engage friends in the real world are finding solace in the structure of *Facebook*. Though people who identify as shy have a smaller circle of *Facebook* friends than those who don't, they are better able to engage with the online friends they do have. "Because people don't have to interact face-to-face, that's why we're seeing them having relationships: they can think more about what they have to say and how they want to say it," says Craig Ross, a graduate student in psychology at the University of Windsor who studies online social networks.

And what of my "friend" "Sue"? Can the support she received from *Facebook* friends upon learning about the death of her son replicate the support that would come from friends stopping by the house? It's impossible to replace the warm feelings—or brain-boosting endorphins—that come from human-on-human contact, and you can't send someone a casserole through *Facebook*. But grieving online can have powerful and productive benefits. Diana Nash, professor of psychology at Marymount Manhattan College, who has studied how college students use *MySpace* to deal with grief, notes that, "One of the primary desires that we all have is for someone to really listen to us in a deep kind of way. They want to be listened to," she says. Her research shows that by sharing their grief on *MySpace*, her subjects felt more listened to and more visible, and doing so helped them heal.

Posting personal experiences, no matter how painful, also allows acquaintances who have lived through similar experiences to reach out, either with information about support groups or just an empathetic ear. "The idea of sharing a commonality helps make it a little more bearable. You're not alone, and there are others going through what you went through," says Nash. "It doesn't take away the pain, but it can lessen the pain and make you feel not so alone."

The majority of times we reach out on *Facebook*, however, it's not about a tragedy, but a smaller problem for which we need advice: good movers in the San Francisco area, a copy of yesterday's newspaper, answers to a question about taxes. This is another place where the large *Facebook* networks come in handy. In real life, people tend to befriend people who think thoughts and live very similar lives to their own, but because on *Facebook* people often "friend" classmates, people met at parties, and friends-of-friends, the networks include individuals who wouldn't make the "real friend" cut. Having that diversity of opinion and experience available online increases the diversity of responses received when posting a question, which allows you to make a better-informed decision.

Still, there are experts who worry that too much time online keeps us from living satisfying lives in the real world. "It's great to have a lot of *Facebook* friends, but how many of those friends will show when you're really in trouble?" asks Michael J. Bugeja, a professor of communications at Iowa State University of Science and Technology and author of *Interpersonal Divide: The Search for Community in a Technological Age*. He notes the world of difference between someone typing a frowny emoticon upon hearing that you've been in a car crash and showing up to help you get home. He also says that *Facebook*, with its focus on existing relationships—and its ability to codify and categorize those relationships—in some ways

Author shows both sides of the debate but emphasizes her position.

Reflects back to her opening point and uses it and expert opinion to reinforce her position.

States the other side of the argument in full.

Moves from opposition point of view to a conclusion that clearly restates the author's position.

belies the promise of the Internet. "Rather than opening us up to a global community, it is putting us into groups," he says.

That's why *Facebook* works best as an amplification of a "real life" social life, 15 not a replacement—even as time and technology progress and the lines between online interactions and real-world experiences continue to blur.

A CLOSER LOOK AT
Friends with Benefits

1. In this position paper, the definition of the word "friend" seems open for debate. Dailey offers a couple of different definitions of a friend: a traditional definition and a social networking site definition. How are these two types of friends similar, and how are they different?

2. This position paper talks about how habits can be contagious among friends, like smoking and weight gain. Dailey, however, sees this kind of contagiousness as a good thing because of *Facebook*. Why?

3. A good position paper fairly describes the other side of the debate, usually early in the argument. However, in this position paper, Dailey waits until the end to fully explain her oppositions' argument. What do these people find wrong with calling people on *Facebook* "friends"?

IDEAS FOR
Writing

1. Write a three page commentary in which you discuss the future of friendships in an electronically networked world. Do you think people will lose touch with each other because they are mostly interacting through texting, social networking sites, or e-mail? Or do you think electronic networking is actually making relationships stronger? What are some of the benefits of friendships through electronic networking? What are some of the downsides?

2. Find one of your childhood friends on *Facebook, MySpace*, or another social networking site. Write a two page profile of your friend using only evidence drawn from his or her page. On his or her page, your friend has tried to project a particular image. What is that image? How is that image similar to or different from the person you know or knew personally?

Letter to the Editor on Climate Story

RUSS WALKER AND DAVID ROBERTS

The following reading is an example of a rebuttal, a kind of position paper that responds to a previous argument. The original article by Erika Lovley is available at http://www.politico.com/news/stories/1108/15938.html.

Politico did a disservice to its readers in publishing the Nov. 25 story, "Scientists urge caution on global warming." It reports that "climate change skeptics"—the too-charitable name given those who deny the existence of climate change in the face of overwhelming evidence and the testimony of every reputable scientific organization—are watching "a growing accumulation of global cooling science and other findings that could signal that the science behind global warming may still be too shaky to warrant cap-and-trade legislation."

> Opponent's position is reviewed.

While reasonable people may debate the value of cap-and-trade legislation, and it is certainly worth reporting on how its congressional opponents are strategizing to block it, it is simply false to point to a "growing accumulation" of evidence rendering basic climate science "shaky." There is no such accumulation; there is no such science. If there were, perhaps the author would have cited some of it—it is telling that she did not.

Instead, she relies on the work of Joseph D'Aleo, a meteorologist (meteorology is the study of weather, not climate). D'Aleo's lack of qualifications in climate science would be less relevant if he had published his work on "global cooling" in peer-reviewed scientific journals. Instead, it appears in the *Farmers' Almanac*.

> Challenges authority of sources.

Incidentally, D'Aleo's professional association, the American Meteorological Association, is one of dozens of leading national and international scientific groups to endorse the broad consensus on anthropogenic climate change. For some reason, the author did not reference or quote a single one of the hundreds if not thousands of scientists who might have vouchsafed that consensus (inexplicably, the one countervailing quote is given to Al Gore's spokeswoman). If she had spoken with mainstream climate scientists, she would have discovered that they are not "urging caution" on global warming—they are running around, to paraphrase ex-CIA chief George Tenet, with their hair on fire, increasingly radicalized by the ignorance and delay of the world's governments in the face of the crisis.

> Points out that the original article missed key sources of information.

Also glossed over is the fact that the organizations backing D'Aleo's work—National Consumer Coalition, Americans for Tax Reform, the National Center for Policy Analysis and Citizens for a Sound Economy—are (for better or worse) conservative interest groups, not science organizations. Similarly, the "Global Warming Petition Project" the author cites is one of the oldest, most discredited hoaxes in the "skeptic" handbook. It first emerged in 1998, when it was promptly disavowed and disowned by the Academy of Sciences. The petition is deceptive: Only a handful of signatories come from relevant scientific disciplines, it is open to signature by anyone willing to fill out an online form and there is no clear way to document the scientific credentials of those who have signed. (One clever blogger signed up his dog.) The petition is rereleased every few years and debunked all over again, inevitably after snookering a few journalists.

> Offers a counter-argument.

Meanwhile, respected and nonpolitical scientific bodies are firmly united when it comes to climate change—humanity's reliance on carbon-based fuels is pumping dangerous amounts of CO_2 into the atmosphere, leading to a steady rise in average global temperature and attendant ill effects including droughts, the spread of infectious diseases, and sea level rise. This basic consensus is as well-established in mainstream science as any finding in biology or chemistry, endorsed with a greater than 90 percent degree of confidence by the reports of the Intergovernmental Panel on Climate Change.

Journalists working on climate issues will recognize the bogus evidence and outlier scientists featured in *Politico*'s piece; they are regularly highlighted by the office of Sen. James Inhofe. Though Inhofe's long campaign of disinformation on climate science is eagerly consumed and propagated by political allies dead set on opposing any government action on global warming, mainstream science and climate journalists have long since learned to disregard it. There's a reason Inhofe's campaign is waged via press conferences and online petitions rather than peer-reviewed science.

> Here is the main point with an ending that snaps.

Climate change is an incredibly complex topic; the policy prescriptions for addressing it are wide open for debate; the maneuverings of various industries and interest groups are well worth documenting. But the basic science is quite clear, and *Politico* should take the subject seriously enough not to equate the views of a small group of ideological deniers with a consensus reached over decades of intense data collection, study, and peer review.

A CLOSER LOOK AT
Letter to the Editor on Climate Story

1. What are Walker and Roberts' major objections to Erika Lovley's original article? Do they present their objections in a useful manner? Why or why not?

2. What are the key elements of Walker and Roberts' counterargument; in other words, what do they say is the correct perception to hold on climate change research? Do you agree or disagree with them and why?

IDEAS FOR
Writing

1. Find a published rebuttal to a published argument (use your library database or ask your librarian for assistance). After reading through the original argument and the rebuttal, write a short position paper on the piece you find more persuasive. Be sure to use examples from each text to support your position.

2. Write a rebuttal. Find an article in a newspaper or on a website that you disagree with. Analyze the original argument and then write a two page rebuttal in which you refute the original argument and offer a counterargument. Your goal is to convince readers of your position.

1. With a small group, make a list of some challenging issues facing our society today. Pick an issue and explore both sides. What are the two to five major points of contention between the two sides of the issue? What are the strengths of each side? What are the limitations of each side?

2. With your class, list ten effective and ineffective ways to argue. What is the best way to get your point across to someone else? What are your most effective strategies? Then list some of the worst ways to argue. What are some of the annoying ways in which other people have tried to persuade you? How did you react to some of these less effective methods?

3. Think about arguments you have had with friends, family members, and other people you care about. With a small group, discuss why these arguments are sometimes more difficult than arguments with people who are not so close to you. Do you have any strategies for arguing effectively with people you care strongly about? Do you avoid these kinds of arguments? If so, why?

1. Look at the opinions section of your local newspaper. Pick one of the issues that is being discussed in the editorials, commentaries, or letters to the editor. On your screen or a piece of paper, list the positions and the kinds of support offered by one of the writers. Then list the points the opponents might make to counter these positions and support their own opinions. In a memo to your professor, explain both sides of the argument as fairly as possible. Then show why you think one side or the other has the stronger argument.

2. Find a position paper or argument essay on the Internet. You might look for these arguments in the online versions of newspapers or magazines. In a two page memo to your professor, analyze the argument and explain whether you think the author is arguing effectively or not. Did the author fairly represent both sides of the issue? Is the author too biased, or does he or she neglect any strengths of the opponents' position or the limitations of his or her own position?

3. Pick a topic that you feel strongly about. Create a two column brainstorming list that explores the issues involved with this topic. Then identify the two to five main points of contention that separate you from someone who disagrees with you about this topic. In a one page memo to your professor, discuss the strengths and limitations of your side of the issue and your opponents'. Explain what kinds of information you would need to collect to support your best arguments and highlight the limitations of your opponents' views.

1. **Write a position paper on a local issue.** Write a five page position paper in which you explore both sides of a contentious local issue. Pick an issue that affects you directly and try to fairly represent both sides of the issue. Explain your opponents' side of the issue as clearly and fairly as possible. Then point out the limitations of their side. Explain your side of the issue and concede any limitations of your side. Then persuade your readers that your understanding of the issue is stronger and more reasonable than your opponents' understanding.

2. **Create a multimedia presentation.** Illegal downloading of music has been an important issue on campuses recently. Some students are being sued by the music industry, and they are being forced to pay thousands of dollars in damages and fines. Create a ten slide presentation in which you state your opinion about downloading music "illegally" off the Internet. Explain your opponents' understanding of the issue. Then explain your side and show why you think your understanding is stronger than your opponents'. Your presentation could be made with *PowerPoint*, *Keynote*, or any other presentation software. Try adding photographs, charts, video, and audio, where appropriate.

3. **Argue that something bad for people is really good for them.** In a five page position paper, argue that something people traditionally assume is "bad" (e.g., playing video games, being overweight, seeing violence in movies, watching television, cramming for an exam) is actually good. Summarize the conventional assumptions about why something is bad. Then use research to show that it is actually good for people.

MyCompLab

For support in meeting this chapter's objectives, follow this path in MyCompLab:

Student Resources → Writing → Writing Purposes → Writing to Argue or Persuade. Review the Instruction and Multimedia resources about writing to argue or persuade; then complete the Exercises and click on Gradebook to measure your progress.

Proposals

In this chapter, you will learn how to:

- use proposals to develop your ideas and explain them clearly and persuasively to your readers.
- analyze problems in terms of their causes and effects.
- synthesize your ideas into well-defined and workable plans.

People write proposals to explore problems and offer plans for solving those problems. In your advanced post-secondary courses, your professors will ask you to write proposals that explain how to improve your community or that describe research projects you want to do. In the workplace, proposals are used to develop new strategies, take advantage of new opportunities, and pitch new projects and products.

A proposal is a form of persuasive writing. The aim of a proposal is to help readers understand the *causes* and *effects* of a problem and to persuade them that your step-by-step plan offers the best solution for that problem. Your readers will expect your proposal to be clearly written and convincing. They expect you to try to win them over with strong reasoning, good examples, and appropriate appeals to authority and emotion.

In today's workplace, the proposal is one of the most common genres. Any time someone wants to solve a problem or present new ideas, he or she will be asked to "write the proposal." In university and college, proposals are popular as a genre. Advanced courses often require students to write research proposals before embarking on a research project. These courses are also becoming more team-oriented and project-centred. Your professors may put you into teams and ask you to write proposals that describe the projects you want to pursue. This chapter will show you how to use proposals to develop your ideas and explain them clearly and persuasively to your readers.

Proposals

This diagram shows a basic organization for a proposal, but other arrangements of these sections will work too. You should alter this organization to fit your topic, angle, purpose, readers, and context.

Introduction

Problem analysis
  Major causes
  Evidence
  Effects of the problem

Plan for solving the problem
  Major steps
  Support
  Deliverables

Benefits of the plan
  Costs-benefits analysis

Conclusion

Overview

A proposal is one of the more complicated genres you will be asked to write. Here are a proposal's typical features:

- **An introduction** that defines a problem and stresses its importance.

- **An analysis** of the problem, discussing its causes and its effects. For a research proposal, this section may include a brief overview of the literature on the topic.

- **A detailed plan** that shows step by step how to solve the problem.

- **A costs-benefits analysis** that measures the benefits of the plan against its costs.

- **A conclusion** that looks to the future and stresses the importance of taking action.

Proposals tend to follow an organization like the one shown on page 170, but this pattern can be changed to suit your topic, angle, purpose, readers, and context. For each unique situation, sections can be merged or moved around to address the needs of the specific readers and the situations in which the proposal will be used.

There are several kinds of proposals. A *solicited proposal* is written when someone requests it. For example, your professor may request that you write a research proposal before settling on a topic for a research paper. *Unsolicited proposals* are not requested by the readers. They are often used to pitch new ideas. For example, you may choose to write a proposal to your professor suggesting an alternate topic for an assigned research paper. In such cases, your professor is more likely to allow you to write on your suggested topic if you can show in your proposal that it is a relevant and worthy project.

Proposals are also used "internally" and "externally." *Internal proposals* are written to people within an organization. They might pitch a new idea to a supervisor or to management. *External proposals* are written to people outside the organization.

Another type of proposal is the grant proposal, which researchers and nonprofit organizations use to obtain funding for their projects.

ONE STUDENT GROUP'S WORK
Proposals

An executive summary, which often accompanies very long reports, is written for the convenience of decision-makers and includes all of the structural features of the full proposal. This is the executive summary of a proposal written by students at the University of California–Santa Barbara in May 2006. It describes a plan for transforming their campus into a carbon-neutral site.

While this example is from an American institution and outlines a local problem the students at the University of California–Santa Barbara recognized, the problem is by no means unique to their university. As you read through this proposal, think of how you might write a similar proposal for your campus, based on a recognized problem your institution faces.

CHANGING THE CAMPUS CLIMATE:
Strategies to Reduce Greenhouse Gas Emissions at The University of California, Santa Barbara

Fahmida Ahmed I Jeff Brown I David Felix I Todd Haurin I Betty Seto

May 2006

Descriptive title tells readers what the proposal is about.

A Bren School of Environmental Science and Management Master's Project

Sponsored by
National Association of Environmental Law Societies

EXECUTIVE SUMMARY

Background & Significance

Anthropogenic climate change is arguably the most significant problem of our generation. Unfortunately, its drivers – greenhouse gas (GHG) emissions from energy use and land use changes – are among the most integral inputs to the current economic system. Furthermore, the range of possible effects of climate change – from rising sea levels to increases in extreme weather events – makes addressing the consequences of climate change especially challenging and important.

Recognizing this, much of the world (and almost all "developed" countries) is starting to act to reduce GHG emissions, with both the Kyoto Protocol coming into force and the European Union (EU) implementing its Emissions Trading Scheme recently. Unfortunately, the United States has no equivalent national GHG emissions reduction regulation. Given this lack of leadership at the federal level, action at the state and local level is all the more important, and a number of initiatives are underway (e.g., Northeastern State's Regional Greenhouse Gas Initiative, U.S. Mayors Climate Protection Agreement) that will help reduce GHG emissions and demonstrate that doing so need not be detrimental to local and state economies.

Indeed, California is already leading the way with a number of policies enacted (e.g., Assembly Bill 1493 (Pavley), Renewable Portfolio Standard) or in the development stages that directly or indirectly address global warming. With the Governor's new executive order (S-3-05) committing California to eighty percent reductions below 1990 levels by 2050, California is likely to continue to be a leader into the future.

Set against this background is the University of California (UC), an institution that educates tomorrow's business, political, and intellectual leaders. As the main higher education institution within California, the UC system is well positioned to play a pivotal role in California's climate strategy. UCSB, with its history of environmental stewardship, can serve as a model to public universities and other UC schools to show that greenhouse gas emissions mitigation is the right thing to do. Furthermore, universities can reap the following benefits from prioritizing the reduction of greenhouse gas emissions:

- Reduce campus energy costs;
- Hedge against future climate regulations and energy price volatility;
- Transform markets for low-cost climate mitigation technologies through their large purchasing power; and,
- Improve the reputation of the University.

Ultimately, UCSB, and the wider UC system, has the responsibility of producing tomorrow's leaders and citizens who will significantly influence California's and the U.S.'s response to global warming. Therefore, commitments to reduce greenhouse gas emissions from campuses are of great importance.

5

Margin annotations:

Introduction defines the topic and links it to the larger, global issue.

The problem and its causes are described.

The purpose of the proposal is stated here.

The benefits of implementing the plan are described up front.

Approach

This Group Project encourages UCSB to be a leader, and to provide lessons learned to other universities with a similar vision. Our efforts can be divided into two inter-related tracks – analysis and implementation. In the analysis phase, we characterize the main sources of GHG emissions on campus and how they are likely to change in the future, identify mitigation strategies, develop criteria for selecting mitigation strategies, and analyze the feasibility of several prominent emissions reductions targets. In the implementation phase, we seek to understand UCSB as a complex organization and to both identify institutional obstacles that constrain the implementation of the previously described mitigation strategies and opportunities to maneuver around the obstacles. These two parallel and complementary tracks are aimed at inducing UCSB to actually reduce its net GHG emissions over time and to receive the associated benefits previously discussed.

Opening for plan section.

UCSB GHG Emissions Inventory

We use the Greenhouse Gas Inventory Calculator (volume 4.0), developed by Clean Air – Cool Planet specifically for universities, to create a GHG inventory for UCSB. The inventory includes emissions from electricity consumption, natural gas consumption, the UCSB fleet, student, faculty and staff commuting, faculty and staff air travel, fugitive emissions of coolants, and solid waste. However, for the purposes of our primary analysis, we only consider the first *three* emissions sources on the list; this is because these are the emissions sources for which the University is committed to measuring and certifying with the California Climate Action Registry (CCAR), and the other emissions are highly uncertain because of poor data quality.

Major step 1.

Figure 1 displays UCSB's GHG emissions by source over the past 15 years. Electricity is the single largest source of GHG emission at UCSB, representing roughly two thirds of total emissions, followed by natural gas, representing roughly one third of total emissions, and the campus fleet, which is almost negligible.

Figure 1: UCSB GHG Emissions by Source

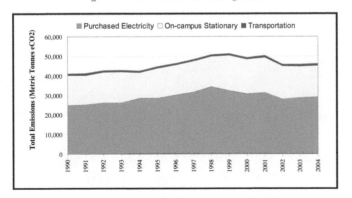

The use of colour draws readers' attention to this graph.

In 2004, the most recent year for which we have complete data, total GHG emissions were approximately 46,000 metric tons of carbon dioxide equivalent ($MTCO_2e$). Interestingly, total emissions peak in 1999 and shrink by approximately two percent per year through 2004. This emissions reduction was not caused by a reduction in enrollment or building square footage; rather it was largely due to significant new investments in energy efficiency on campus precipitated by the California energy crisis. This is a promising finding and suggests that UCSB has the potential to reduce its climate footprint without reducing enrollment or campus size.

Emissions Targets Applied to UCSB

Major step 2.

Determining an appropriate reduction target for GHG emissions is a critical first step towards long term emissions reductions. We analyze what three separate emissions targets would look like as applied to UCSB through 2020 – the U.S. targets from the first commitment period of the Kyoto Protocol (7% below 1990 levels by 2010), the first two California state targets (2000 levels by 2010, 1990 levels by 2020), and Climate Neutrality (net zero GHG emissions by 2020).

First, we project UCSB's GHG emissions through 2020 given current emissions levels and assumptions about campus growth. Given historical emissions levels of roughly 2.25 $MTCO_2e$ per student and anticipated growth of approximately 300 students per year through 2020, we project total emissions through 2020 (see solid red line in Figure 2). Second, we apply the three potential targets to UCSB in order to understand the scale of emissions reductions that would be required to meet the specific targets (displayed in Figure 2 as the vertical distance between the projected emissions line and any particular target line).

Figure 2: Projected Emissions and Potential Targets

Line graph tells a simple story that readers can understand at a glance.

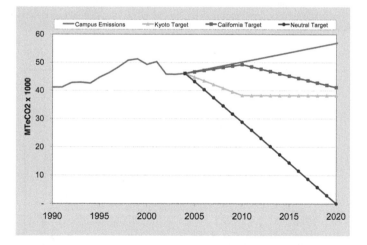

Mitigation Strategies

We profile a range of mitigation strategies available to UCSB, including energy efficiency and conservation projects, on campus renewable energy projects, alternative fuel vehicles, and external mitigation options (e.g., carbon offsets, renewable energy credits).[1] For each mitigation mechanism we provide the capital cost, associated savings (e.g., energy), annual GHG reduction potential, net cost per unit of GHG reduced[2], and payback period.

Major step 3.

Feasibility Analysis of Meeting Specific Targets

We identify the specific combination of mitigation mechanisms that would enable UCSB to meet the previously discussed emissions targets. We assume a consistent mechanism choice logic that reflects UCSB priorities – we first select projects with no capital costs that yield savings, then we select projects that yield the highest savings over time (best in terms of $/ $MTCO_2e$), and finally, once all mechanisms with costs below the price of external offsets (an estimated average of $11/$MTCO_2e$) have been exhausted, the University meets all additional emissions reductions through the purchase of carbon offsets (see Figure 3).

Major step 4.

Figure 3: Mitigation Mechanism Schedule for CA Targets

Year Stage	Mechanisms	Potential MT/year	Capital Cost	NPV/MT	Annual Saving
ASAP Stage A	**Energy star computer settings**	310	$0	196	**$94,000**
	Fleet smaller vehicles	33	$0	215	**$9,545**
	Fleet ethanol	1	$0		**$0**
2011 Stage B	**HVAC Upgrade – Air Handlers 1**	573	$200,000	245	**$112,000**
	HVAC Commissioning	340	$120,000	241	**$71,159**
	HVAC Upgrade – Filters	607	$372,323	196	**$184,053**
	EE – Fume Hoods	55	$80,000	156	**$14,298**
	Building baseline awards	14	$15,000	127	**$4385**
2012 Stage C	**HVAC Upgrade – Fans**	914	$1,574,464	125	**$277,048**
	Lighting Upgrades	835	$1,797,762	97	**$252,919**
2013 Stage D	**HVAC Upgrade – Air Handlers 2**	174	$550,000	42	**$45,328**
	Reduce fleet driving – bikes	1	$2500	11	**$27**
	Begin purchasing offsets	763	$8,091	-11	**$0**

Table presents complex data in an accessible way.

Figure 4 illustrates the specific four stage emissions reduction path that UCSB could take to meet the first two California targets – the 2010 and 2020 standards (see dashed line in Figure 4). The solid trend line shows how UCSB can reduce its GHG emissions through time with the implementation of on-campus projects with costs lower than the external offset price; these on campus emissions reduction opportunities keep UCSB on track with the California goals through 2012. After that point, the most inexpensive mitigation mechanisms have been exhausted, and

---

[1] The mitigation mechanisms profiled in this section represent examples of the types of projects UCSB could implement to reduce its emissions, rather than an exhaustive or fully comprehensive survey of the University's mitigation options.

[2] This includes the upfront capital cost and the discounted savings over the lifetime of the project.

purchasing offsets becomes the next cheapest alternative. Therefore, we assume that UCSB purchases external offsets to make up the difference in subsequent years.

Figure 4: Four Stage Emissions Reduction Path

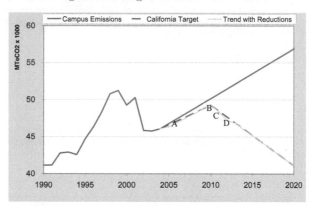

Graphs show trends.

This combination of mechanisms has a net present value (NPV) of $2.6 million, including the cost of offsets through 2020, suggesting that the University could meet the California targets through 2020 according to the previously described emissions path and save a significant amount of money in the process. This emissions trajectory does require some significant capital investments after 2010 (when the emissions target increases in stringency); but, as the cash flow analysis below illustrates, these capital investments are recouped quickly through energy savings (see Figure 5).

Figure 5: Cash Flow for CA Targets

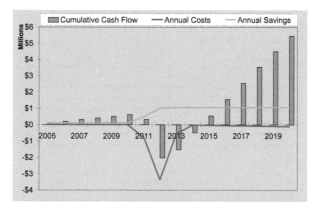

9

According to our analysis, meeting the California targets not only appears feasible through 2020 despite significant campus growth, it also appears to be justified solely on the economics. We performed similar analyses for two additional targets – the Kyoto Protocol and Climate Neutrality – and observe similar findings. These targets imply more aggressive emissions reductions, both in timing and the absolute level of emissions reductions. In terms of NPV, this turns out to increase the savings associated with the mitigation strategies – because they are implemented earlier, which captures more years of energy savings – and to increase the number of offsets purchased. We find the NPV of the savings to be $5.8 million for the Kyoto targets and $4.3 million for Climate Neutrality. Finally, as a sensitivity analysis, we perform the same calculations using an offset price of $30/MTCO_2e$, which is similar to the current price of carbon in the EU market; we find a NPV of savings equaling $4.3 million, $2.1 million, and -$0.2 million for the Kyoto, California, and Climate Neutrality targets, respectively.

Implementation

Given the previous analysis, it would seem that UCSB should already be implementing GHG mitigation strategies. To some extent it is – through the energy efficiency projects implemented by the Facilities Management team, the efforts to green UCSB buildings by a virtual Office of Sustainability, and efforts to reduce the use of single occupancy vehicles through the Transportation Alternative Program, among others – and the results of these efforts can be seen in the declining aggregate GHG emission trend over the past 5 years (see Figure 1). Although, UCSB has typically done so with energy savings or reduced traffic congestion in mind, not GHG emissions. We argue that reduction in GHG emissions is another important reason for UCSB to consider – one that points towards increasing the overall scale and the immediacy of their current efforts.

Notwithstanding their significant previous efforts, there are a number of institutional obstacles that constrain UCSB from implementing more GHG mitigation projects, and from doing so more immediately. These include:
- The state funding allocation system, which allots separate funds for capital projects and for operations and prevents borrowing from the operations budget to fund capital projects;
- Lack of funding in general and restrictions on UCSB's access to capital;
- Lack of an information management system for GHG emissions, which hinders efforts to understand emissions sources and trends; and,
- Institutional inertia and risk averseness.

Addressing these barriers is integral to the implementation of any significant GHG reduction policy.

Our Group's Direct Contribution to GHG mitigation:
• Facilitation of UCSB membership with California Climate Action Registry.
• Design of The Green Initiative Fund (a student fee based revolving fund for environmental projects on campus), which passed on April 24, 2006.
• Participation in the development of the Campus Sustainability Plan

Authors look ahead to the next phase of the project.

Final Recommendations and Conclusion

Based on our mitigation and institutional analyses, and from our experience engaging with the relevant decision makers at UCSB over the past year, we identify a main recommendation and five supporting recommendations that would put UCSB on track to be a leader in responding to climate change.

Key Recommendation

With consideration to the financial findings of our research and evaluation of institutional barriers, **UCSB should make a firm commitment to meet the California GHG reduction targets**.

In order to accomplish this, UCSB should:
1. Use aggregate GHG emissions targets as a metric in long-term campus planning documents.
2. Turn the "Sustainability Working Team" of the Campus Planning Committee's Sub-Committee on Sustainability into a real Office of Sustainability.
3. Implement zero cost emissions reduction projects first, followed by the most cost effective (i.e., highest $/ MTCO$_2$e) projects.
4. Focus on identifying additional cost-effective GHG mitigation opportunities on campus, such as energy efficiency.
5. Work with administrators at other UC schools to press UCOP and the state legislature for capital budget funding reform as one of the top priorities.

These recommendations should allow UCSB to reap the multiple benefits previously discussed, including significant dollar savings, improved environmental performance, and positive public relations opportunities. Furthermore, UCSB's leadership on addressing climate change has the potential to have significant impacts beyond the UCSB campus, including:
- Mobilizing other public universities, in the UC system and beyond, to address climate change;
- Demonstrating the feasibility – indeed benefits – of meeting the first two commitments of the California targets; and,
- Educating the students of UCSB, as future consumers, investors, professionals, and leaders.

Ultimately, it is these longer term and broader scale implications of UCSB's actions today that make climate mitigation so important. As David Orr (2000), a professor of Environmental Studies at Oberlin College puts it: "*Education is done in many ways, the most powerful of which is by example.*" It is time for UCSB to educate – its students, other universities, and California businesses – by example.

Using this Group Project as a model, NAELS is working to implement a nationwide campaign to develop bottom-up climate leadership through its Campus Climate Neutral (CCN) program – an ambitious and unprecedented grassroots effort to mobilize graduate students around the United States to lead the way to aggressive, long-term climate solutions.

11

Margin annotations:

Conclusion wraps up by stating the argument concisely.

Summarizes main point(s).

Discussion of benefits.

A look to the future.

Developing Your Proposal's Content

When writing a proposal, your first challenge is to fully understand the problem you are trying to solve. Then you can come up with a plan for solving it.

Inquiring: Defining the Problem

You should start out by figuring out the boundaries of your topic and what you want to achieve with your proposal.

State Your Proposal's Purpose. A good first step is to state the purpose of your proposal in one sentence. A clear statement of your purpose will help you focus your research and save you time.

> The purpose of this proposal is to show how university students can help fight global climate change.

Narrow Your Topic and Purpose. Make sure you aren't trying to solve a problem that is too big. Look at your purpose statement again. Can you narrow the topic to something more manageable? Specifically, can you take a local approach to your subject by discussing how the problem affects people where you live or in your province? Can you talk about your topic in terms of recent events?

> The purpose of this proposal is to show how our campus can significantly reduce its greenhouse gas emissions, which are partly responsible for global climate change.

Find Your Angle. Figure out what might be unique or different about how you would approach the problem. What is your new angle?

> We believe attempts to conserve energy offer a good start toward cutting greenhouse emissions, but these effects will only take us part of the way. The only way to fully eliminate greenhouse gas emissions here on campus is to develop new sources of clean, renewable energy.

Inquiring: Analyzing the Problem

Now you need to identify and analyze the major causes of the problem, so you can explain them to your readers.

Identify the Major and Minor Causes of the Problem. A good way to analyze a problem is to use a concept map to determine what you already know about the causes of the problem. To create a concept map, put the problem you are analyzing in the middle of your screen or a sheet of paper. Then write the two to five major causes of that problem around it (Figure 9.1).

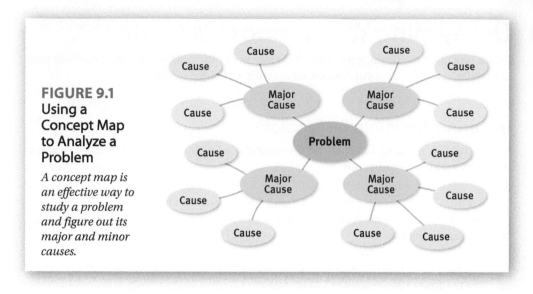

**FIGURE 9.1
Using a
Concept Map
to Analyze a
Problem**

*A concept map is
an effective way to
study a problem
and figure out its
major and minor
causes.*

Keep Asking "What Changed?" As you explore the problem's major causes, keep asking yourself, "What has changed to create this problem?" If you pay attention to the things that are changing about your topic, you will find it easier to identify what is causing the problem itself.

Analyze the Major and Minor Causes. Once you have identified two to five major causes, find the "minor causes" that are causing them. Ask yourself, "What are the two to five minor causes of each major cause? What has changed recently that created each of the major causes or made them worse?" Figure 9.1 shows how a concept map can illustrate both major and minor causes, allowing you to develop a comprehensive analysis of the problem.

Researching: Gathering Information and Sources

Your concept map will give you a good start, but you are going to need to do some solid research on your topic. When doing research, you need to collect information from a variety of sources. You should "triangulate" your research by drawing material from online, print, and empirical sources.

Online Sources. Choose some keywords from your concept map, and use Internet search engines to gather background information on your topic. Pay special attention to websites that identify the causes of the problem you are exploring. Also, look for documentaries, podcasts, or broadcasts on your subject. You might find some good sources on *YouTube* or the websites of television networks.

Print Sources. Your best print sources will usually be newspapers and magazine articles, because most proposals are written about current or local problems. You can run keyword searches in newspaper and magazine archives on the Internet, or you can use the Canadian Newsstand database through your institution's library. On your library's website, you might also use research indexes to find articles in academic journals. These articles tend to offer more empirically grounded discussions of issues in our society.

Empirical Sources. Set up interviews, do field observations, or survey people to gather empirical evidence that supports or challenges your online and print sources. Someone on your campus, perhaps a professor or a staff member, probably knows a great amount about the topic you have chosen to study. So send that person an e-mail to set up an interview. If you aren't sure who might know something about your topic, call over to the department that seems closest to your topic. Ask the person who answers the phone if he or she can tell you who might know something about your topic.

As always, you should use a combination of online, print, and empirical sources to gather information. While doing your research, you will probably find ideas that you can add to the concept maps you made earlier, or you will discover that some of the causes you originally came up with are not really causes at all.

Solid research is the backbone of any proposal. If you don't fully research and understand the problem, you will not be able to come up with a good solution. So give yourself plenty of time to gather and triangulate your sources.

Inquiring: Planning to Solve the Problem

With your preliminary research finished, you are now ready to start developing a plan to solve the problem. A plan is a step-by-step strategy for getting something done. Essentially, when writing a plan, you are telling your readers, "If we take these steps, we will solve the problem I just described to you."

Map Out Your Plan. Again, a concept map is a useful tool for figuring out your plan. Start out by putting your best solution in the middle of your screen or a piece of paper. Then ask yourself, "What are the two to five major steps we need to take to achieve this goal?" Write those major steps around your solution and connect them to it with lines (Figure 9.2).

Explore Each Major Step. Now, consider each of the major steps one at a time. Ask yourself, "What are the two to five steps we need to take to achieve each of these major steps?" For example, if one of your major steps is "develop alternative sources of energy," what steps would your university need to take to do that?

1. The university might look for grants or donations to help it do research on converting its campus to renewable energy sources like wind power or solar energy.

2. The university might explore ways to replace the inefficient heating systems in campus buildings with geothermal heating and cooling systems.

3. The university might convert its current fleet of buses and service vehicles to biodiesel or plug-in hybrids.

Each major step can be broken down further into minor steps that offer more detail.

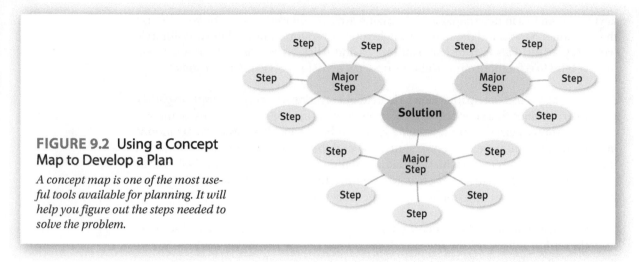

FIGURE 9.2 Using a Concept Map to Develop a Plan

A concept map is one of the most useful tools available for planning. It will help you figure out the steps needed to solve the problem.

Figure Out the Costs and Benefits of Your Plan. With your plan mapped out, you should now identify its costs and benefits. Essentially, your goal is to determine whether the benefits of your plan outweigh the costs. After all, nothing is free. So someone, probably your readers, will need to give up something (like money) to put your plan into action. You want to prove to your readers that the benefits are worth the costs. When figuring out the costs and benefits, brainstorming is an especially helpful tool. You can use it to list all the costs of your plan and then use it to list all the benefits (Figure 9.3).

Researching: Finding Similar Projects

Now that you have developed your plan, do some more research. Again, you should gather information from online, print, and empirical sources. This time, though, look for projects similar to the one you are proposing. There is a good chance that someone else has already been trying to solve this problem.

Of course, you don't want to copy their solution—their plan probably won't work for your situation anyway—but you might learn what others have tried before, what has worked, and what hasn't worked.

As you do your research, also try to find sources that will help you fill out and support your plan. More than likely, your research is going to uncover new strategies and complications that you would not have thought of yourself. Incorporate those strategies into your own plan, and try to come up with ways to work around the complications. Always make sure you keep track of your sources, so you can cite them in your proposal.

Be prepared to alter your plan as you come across new strategies and new information. Research will almost always bring new ideas to your attention that you might want to use in your proposal.

Organizing and Drafting Your Proposal

Organizing and drafting a large document like a proposal can be challenging, but here is where your hard work doing inquiry and research will finally pay off. The best

Benefits of My Plan to Make Our Campus Carbon Neutral

Help save humanity from apocalyptic end (!)

Reduce this university's dependence on foreign oil

Help clean up local air, water, and soil

Widely distributed power sources, which will make us less vulnerable to energy system failures

Not contribute to ecological destruction involved with mining coal and drilling for oil

Help create more local jobs for a "green economy"

Millions of dollars in energy savings, starting in 10 years

Be ahead of energy policy changes that are coming anyway

Make our campus modern and forward thinking, which is attractive to top students

Costs of My Plan

Transformation costs will be high, perhaps even $100 million

University will need to invest in energy research and training

Need to retrain current power plant employees

University will need to stress energy conservation as system evolves

FIGURE 9.3 Costs and Benefits of Your Plan

Brainstorming can help you list the costs and benefits of your plan. Your goal is to show your readers that the benefits of your plan outweigh the costs.

way to draft a proposal is to write each of its major sections separately. Draft each major section as though it is a small argument on its own.

The Introduction

An introduction to a proposal will typically make up to five moves, which can be made in just about any order:

State the topic. Tell your readers what the proposal is about.

State the purpose. State the purpose of your proposal in one or two sentences.

State the main point. Briefly, tell readers your solution.

Provide background information. Give readers just enough historical information to understand your topic.

Stress the importance of the topic to the readers. Tell readers why they should care about this topic.

In the introduction to a proposal, you should almost always state your topic, purpose, and main point. The other two moves are optional, but they become more important and necessary in larger proposals.

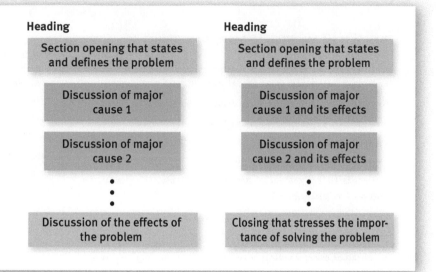

FIGURE 9.4 Drafting the Problem Section

An effective analysis of the problem will discuss its causes and effects. Make sure you offer good support for your statements. Here are two possible ways to organize this section of the proposal.

Description of the Problem, Its Causes, and Its Effects

You should now describe and analyze the problem for your readers, showing them its causes and effects. Look at your concept map and your research notes to identify the two to five major causes of the problem. Then draft this section of the proposal around those causes (Figure 9.4).

Opening Paragraph. Use the opening paragraph to clearly describe the problem and perhaps stress its importance.

> The problem we face is that our campus is overly dependent on energy from the Anderson Power Facility, a 20-megawatt coal-fire plant on the east side of campus that belches out many tons of carbon dioxide each year. At this point, we have no alternative energy source, and our backup source of energy is the Bentonville Power Plant, another coal-fire plant 50 miles away. This dependence on the Anderson Plant causes our campus's carbon footprint to be large, and it leaves us vulnerable to power shortages and rising energy costs.

Body Paragraphs. Explain the causes of the problem, providing plenty of support for your claims. Here is an example discussion of one cause among a few others that the writers want to include.

> The primary reason the campus is so reliant on coal-fire energy is the era when the campus was built. Our campus is like many others in the United States. The basic infrastructure and many of the buildings were built in the early twentieth century when coal was the cheapest source of energy and no one could have anticipated problems like global warming. A coal-fire plant, like the one on the east side of campus, seemed like the logical choice. As our campus has grown, our energy needs

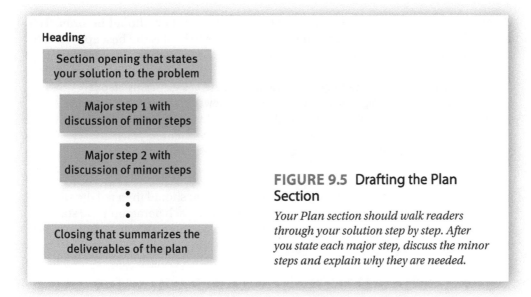

Heading

Section opening that states your solution to the problem

Major step 1 with discussion of minor steps

Major step 2 with discussion of minor steps

• • •

Closing that summarizes the deliverables of the plan

FIGURE 9.5 Drafting the Plan Section

Your Plan section should walk readers through your solution step by step. After you state each major step, discuss the minor steps and explain why they are needed.

have increased exponentially. Now, on any given day, the campus needs anywhere from 12 to 22 megawatts to keep running (Campus Energy Report 22).

Closing Paragraph. You might consider closing this section with a discussion or summary of the effects of the problem if no action is taken. In most cases, problems grow worse over time, so you want to show readers what will happen if they choose not to do anything. Be sure to support your claims with source material.

> Our dependence on fossil fuels for energy on this campus will begin to cost us more and more as the United States and the global community are forced to address global climate change. More than likely, coal-fire plants like ours will need to be completely replaced or refitted with expensive carbon capture equipment (Gathers 12). Also, federal and state governments will likely begin putting a "carbon tax" on emitters of carbon dioxide to encourage conservation and conversion to alternative energy. These costs could run our university many millions of dollars. Moreover, the costs to our health cannot be overlooked. Coal-fire plants, like ours, put particulates, mercury, and sulfur dioxide into the air that we breath (Vonn 65). The costs of our current coal-fire plant may seem hidden now, but they will eventually bleed our campus of funds and continue to harm our health.

Figure 9.4 shows two of the more common patterns for the Problem section, but other patterns will work, too. You can use whichever pattern helps you best explain the causes and effects of the problem to your readers.

Description of Your Plan

Draft the Plan section next. In this section, you want to describe step by step how the problem can be solved (Figure 9.5). The key to success in this section is to tell your readers *how* you would solve the problem and *why* you would do it this way.

Opening Paragraph. The opening paragraph of this section should be brief. Tell the readers your solution and give them a good reason why it is the best approach to the problem. Give your plan a name. For example:

> The best way to make meaningful cuts in greenhouse gas emissions on our campus would be to replace our current coal-fire power plant with a 12-turbine wind farm and install solar panels on all campus buildings. The "Cool Campus Project" would cut greenhouse gas emissions by half within ten years, and we could eliminate all greenhouse emissions within twenty years.

Body Paragraphs. The body paragraphs for this section should then tell the readers step by step how you would carry out your plan. Usually, each paragraph will start out by stating a major step. You can use subtitles for each step, although they are not necessary.

Step Three: Install a 12-Turbine Wind Farm at the Experimental Farm

The majority of the university's electricity needs would be met by installing a 12-turbine wind farm that would generate 18 megawatts of energy per day. The best place for this wind farm would be at the university's Experimental Farm, which is two miles west of campus. The university already owns this property and the area is known for its constant wind. An added advantage to placing a wind farm at this location is that the Agriculture Department could continue to use the land as an experimental farm. The turbines would be operating above the farm, and the land would still be available for planting crops.

Closing Paragraph. In the closing paragraph of this section, you should summarize the *deliverables* of the plan. Deliverables are the things you will deliver to the readers when the project is completed:

> When the Cool Campus Project is completed, the university will be powered by a 12-turbine wind farm and an array of solar panels mounted on campus buildings. This combination of wind and solar energy will generate the 20 megawatts needed by campus on regular days, and it should be able to satisfy the 25 megawatts needed on peak usage days.

Don't get locked into the pattern shown in Figure 9.5. You might find other, more effective patterns for describing your plan, depending on the solution you are proposing.

Discussing the Costs and Benefits of Your Plan

A good way to round out your argument is to discuss the costs and benefits of your plan. You want to show readers the two to five major benefits of your plan and then argue that these benefits outweigh the costs.

In the long run, the benefits of the Cool Campus Project will greatly outweigh the costs. The major benefits of converting to wind and solar energy include—

- A savings of $1.2 million in energy costs each year once the investment is paid off.
- The avoidance of millions of dollars in refitting costs and carbon tax costs associated with our current coal-fire plant.
- The improvement of our health due to the reduction of particulates, mercury, and sulfur dioxide in our local environment.
- A great way to show that this university is environmentally progressive, thus attracting students and faculty who care about the environment.

We estimate the costs of the Cool Campus Project will be approximately $20 million, much of which can be offset with government grants. Keep in mind, though, that our coal-fire plant will need to be refitted or replaced soon anyway, which would cost millions. So the costs of the Cool Campus Project would likely be recouped within a decade.

Costs do not always involve money, or money alone. Sometimes, the costs of the plan will be measured in effort or time. Be sure to mention any nonmonetary costs, so they are not a surprise to your readers.

The Conclusion

Your proposal's conclusion should be brief and to the point. By now, you have told the readers everything they need to know, so you just need to wrap up and leave your readers in a position to say yes to your plan. Here are a few moves you might consider making in your conclusion:

Restate your main claim. Again, tell the readers what you wanted to prove in your proposal. Your main claim first appeared in the introduction. Now bring the readers back around to it, showing that you proved your argument.

Restress the importance of the topic. Briefly, tell the readers why this topic is important. You want to leave them with the sense that this issue needs to be addressed as soon as possible.

Look to the future. Proposal writers often like to leave readers with a description of a better future. A "look to the future" should only run a few sentences or a brief paragraph.

Offer contact information. Tell readers who to contact and how to contact that person if they have questions, want more information, or are interested in discussing the proposal.

Your conclusion should not be more than a couple of brief paragraphs, even in a large proposal. The goal of your conclusion is to wrap up quickly.

Choosing an Appropriate Style

Proposals are persuasive documents by nature, so your style should be convincing to match your proposal's content. In Chapter 13, "Choosing a Style," you can learn about how to use persuasive style techniques. For now, here are some easy strategies that will make your proposal sound more convincing.

Create an Authoritative Tone. Pick a tone that expresses a sense of authority. Then create a concept map around it (Figure 9.6). You should weave these terms from your concept map into your proposal, creating a theme that sets the desired tone.

Use Metaphors and Similes. Metaphors and similes allow you to compare new ideas to things that are familiar to your readers. For example, you might use a metaphor to discuss your wind turbines in terms of "farming" (e.g., harvesting the wind, planting wind turbines in a field, reaping the savings) because that will sound good to most people.

Pay Attention to Sentence Length. Proposals should generate excitement, especially at the moments when you are describing your plan and its benefits. To raise the heartbeat of your writing, shorten the sentences at these key places in your proposal. Elsewhere in the proposal, keep the sentences regular length (breathing length). See Chapter 13, "Choosing a Style," for more on sentence length and style.

Minimize the Jargon. Proposals can get somewhat technical, depending on the topic. So look for any jargon words that could be replaced with simpler words or phrases. If a jargon word is needed, make sure you define it for readers.

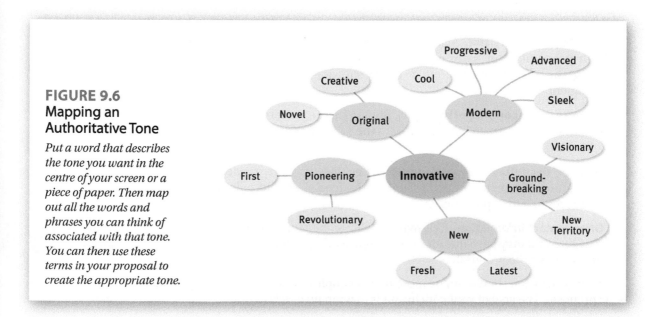

FIGURE 9.6
Mapping an Authoritative Tone

Put a word that describes the tone you want in the centre of your screen or a piece of paper. Then map out all the words and phrases you can think of associated with that tone. You can then use these terms in your proposal to create the appropriate tone.

Applying the Genre: Academic Proposals

The examples and discussion so far in this chapter have addressed technical proposals and proposals written for a more general audience. Sometimes, however, proposals are also required in academic contexts. For examples of an academic proposal, see the readings at the end of the chapter: the excerpt from "Forty Years of Struggle and Still No Right to Inuit Education in Nunavut" and "Tell the Awful Truth: It's Not Just Global Warming, It's a Global Disaster!" In those situations, some variations on the format discussed previously are required. A standard academic proposal includes the following elements.

The Introduction

In addition to identifying the topic and purpose, an academic proposal introduction includes a rationale for the choice of topic, showing why it is important or useful within the discipline. For instance, an academic study on whether Canadian immigrants experience prejudice may explain its rationale by addressing how social scientists and policy makers could develop tactics to redress prejudice, if indeed it occurs.

The Literature Review

The description of the problem is typically framed within a literature review. A literature review summarizes and evaluates existing studies in relation to the proposed research. See Chapter 5 for more discussion of the scholarly literature review. An academic study on experiences of prejudice would, for instance, need to be contextualized in relation to existing research on that topic.

The Plan and Methodology

An academic proposal also frames the plan differently, emphasizing and justifying the intended approach or methodology. Costs, resources needed, and a timeline might be included. Ethics issues may need to be addressed. The plan may also identify hypotheses and outline a design or structure for the proposed research based on existing studies. For example, a study on immigrants and prejudice would need to identify data collection and analysis methods and assure readers that human ethics regulations would be met. It might identify a hypothesis that prejudice does occur and explain how the research plan seeks to test that hypothesis.

The Conclusion

An academic conclusion restates the main topic and purpose, but with emphasis on the significance of the study. A full reference list is always included at the end of an academic proposal. Some professors may ask for an annotated bibliography. See Chapter 10 for more information on the annotated bibliography.

Designing Your Proposal

Your proposal needs to be attractive and appropriate for your audience, so leave yourself some time to design the document. Good design will help your proposal stand out, while making it easy to read. Your readers may also appreciate graphics that enhance and support your message.

Create a Look. Figure out what image your proposal should project to the readers. Is it appropriate for your proposal to appear progressive or conservative? Do you want it to look exciting or traditional? Then make choices about fonts, columns, and photographs that reflect that design. See the preceding student proposal for an example.

Use Meaningful Headings. When they first pick up your proposal, your readers will likely scan it before reading. So your headings need to be meaningful and action-oriented. Don't just use headings like "Problem" or "Plan." Instead, use specific headings like "Our Campus's Global Warming Problem" or "Introducing the Cool Campus Initiative."

Include Relevant, Accurate Graphics. Proposals often talk about trends, so you should look for places where you can use charts or graphs to illustrate those trends. Where possible, put data into tables. Photographs can help you explain the problem or show examples of your solution.

Use Lists to Highlight Important Points. Look for places in your proposal where you list key ideas or other items. Then, where appropriate, put those ideas into bulleted lists that are more scannable for readers.

Create White Space. You might want to expand your margins to add some white space. Readers often like to take notes in the margins of proposals, so a little extra white space is useful. Also, extra white space makes the proposal seem more welcoming and easier to understand.

Explore Research Proposal 1

Explore Research Proposal 2 (interactive)

Revising and Editing Your Proposal

Proposals are often large, complex documents, so make sure you save time for revising and editing. Since proposals are designed to persuade others, you need to make sure that your proposal is well written and nearly flawless. Solid revision and careful editing will help you raise the quality of your document to a higher level.

Let Someone Else Edit Your Work. Your professor may set up a "peer editing" session in which you can let someone else look over your work. Ask your editor to pay special attention to the content, organization, style, and design of your proposal. If peer editing is not available in class, ask a friend or a roommate to look over your work. Tell him or her to be critical and challenge your ideas.

Look for Inconsistencies in Content. As you drafted your proposal, your ideas about the topic probably evolved and changed as you learned more about it. So make sure your analysis of the problem matches up with your plan for solving it. In your Costs and Benefits section, make sure you have summarized the most important benefits mentioned in your plan and listed the costs. Finally, your introduction and conclusion should be consistent with each other in both content and style.

Get Rid of the Extra Stuff. Look for places where you have included material that goes beyond the readers' need to know. It is always tempting to tell the readers everything you know about your topic, but they only need information that will help them make a decision. So cut out any extra information they probably don't need or want.

Tweak the Design. When the whole proposal is put together, look for places where the design is inconsistent or looks odd. Then make adjustments to get rid of those problems. Check the headings to make sure they are consistent. Look over the graphics to ensure that they are properly placed and easy to read.

Don't Forget to Proofread! Proofreading is always important, but it is essential for proposals. If your readers see misspellings and grammatical errors, they are going to doubt the soundness of your ideas. Even small problems like typos will sabotage your entire proposal. So read it through carefully, and have others look it over as well.

As you are editing your proposal, keep in mind that you are trying to persuade readers to trust you and your ideas. A professional, polished proposal will build their confidence in you and your ideas. Inconsistencies and small errors will undermine your whole argument.

Here are some quick steps to get you working on your proposal.

IDENTIFY the Problem You Want to Solve

In one sentence, write down the topic and purpose of your proposal. Then narrow the topic to something you can manage.

ANALYZE the Problem's Causes and Effects

Use a concept map to analyze the problem's two to five major causes. Then use another concept map to explore the effects of the problem if nothing is done about it.

DO Your Research

Search the Internet and your library to collect sources. Then use empirical methods like interviews or surveys to help you support or challenge the facts you find.

DEVELOP Your Plan for Solving the Problem

Using a concept map, figure out the two to five major steps needed to solve the problem. Then figure out what minor steps will be needed to achieve each of these major steps.

FIGURE OUT the Costs and Benefits of Your Plan

Look at your Plan section closely. Identify any costs of your plan. Then list all the benefits of solving the problem your way. You want to make sure the benefits of your solution outweigh the costs.

DRAFT the Proposal

Try drafting each major section separately, treating each one like a small document on its own.

DESIGN Your Proposal

Your proposal needs to look professional and easy to read. Make choices about fonts, graphics, and document design that best suit the materials you are presenting to your readers.

REVISE and Edit

Proposals are complicated documents, so you should leave plenty of time to revise and edit your work.

Forty Years of Struggle and Still No Right to Inuit Education in Nunavut

DEREK RASMUSSEN

In this excerpt from an academic proposal, Derek Rasmussen outlines the obstacles that have stood in the way of Inuit education. He uses the proposal genre as a way to organize his argument and make his case. First he both identifies the problem and outlines the socio-historical factors that have led to it. He then proposes a number of precise solutions that, if enacted, will support Inuit education rights.

After 40 years of negotiating a land claim, a new territory, and a new government, how is it possible that Inuit still do not have their own school system in Nunavut?

What do you think of when you hear the word *Nunavut*? Polar bears? The Canadian Arctic? Perhaps you think of Inuit, the majority population, 85% of the people in the new territory?

> Article starts with a series of questions that both capture the attention of and prepare the reader for the proposal that follows.

But do you think of an entire school system that does not operate in the Inuit language? Do you think of Inuit language students studying an Alberta curriculum in English schools run by Ontario and Newfoundland teachers?

That is the sad reality. There is no school in Nunavut that offers K-12 education in the Inuit language, the mother tongue spoken by 75% of Inuit (Nunavut Tunngavik Incorporated, 2007, p. 18). There is one Francophone school board in Nunavut which gets to operate its own K-12 French school, but there are no Inuit school boards. There are district education "authorities" with no authority, merely carrying out instructions sent by the Minister of Education of Nunavut—the same Nunavut government spending $3,400 each year for language education for each Francophone in the territory and only $48.50 on Inuktitut education for each Inuk (p. 19).

> Problem is outlined in detail with supporting evidence.

5　What should be obvious is that Nunavut's 10,000 Inuit students do not have the same rights as their 40 or so Francophone schoolmates.[1] As a French parent, your child can go to the new $5 million French school in Iqaluit. And as an English parent, you will be able to send your kids to any one of the other 41 schools in Nunavut where they will get instruction in their own language from mostly southern teachers. But for an Inuk parent, your child will be going to school in the English language because only two schools offer Inuktitut instruction beyond Grade 3 (and then only to Grade 6), and the remaining schools offer only 45 minutes a day of Inuktitut (Nunavut Tunngavik Incorporated, *Saqqiqpuq*, 2007, p. 18). Despite living in a territory with the highest number of aboriginal language speakers in Canada, as an Inuk parent you will likely have to watch your child lose that language and culture because the new Education Act passed in the territory last September virtually guarantees that there will not be enough Inuit language teachers or Inuit curriculum until 2019 or later.

The long time-lag is precarious because the erosion of the Inuit language may be at a tipping point. Census Canada's most recent study noted that Inuit language usage in Nunavut had declined 7% from 1991–2001, most likely due to "in-migration of English-speaking individuals" and the "continued prevalence of the English language in public service jobs" (Sorensen & Aylward, 2002, p. 21). If this trend continues, by the time the Government of Nunavut (GN) finally implements an Inuit curriculum and 85% Inuit teacher employment (two big "ifs"), targeted for 2019, the Inuit language will likely be a minority language in Nunavut, spoken by less than half the population.

Timely importance of the issue is outlined.

How did this happen? Wasn't Nunavut supposed to be the answer to the dreams of Inuit? Yes it was. Have Inuit ever told Canada that they want their own education system? Yes, they have, repeatedly. . . . So, if Inuit have asked for their own school system, why can't they get one? And is there anything we can do to help?

• • •

The Struggle for Inuit Language and Education Rights: 1972–1990

In 1972, Canadian Inuit held their own conference on education organized by the Eskimo Brotherhood under President Tagak Curley; at that time Inuit said they wanted their own teacher credential process which reflected their values, and an education system which passed on the Inuit way of life and emphasized the oral tradition of teaching. That same year, Inuk teacher Elizabeth Quaki delivered the following warning to a national meeting of Inuit in Pangnirtung: "As long as southern teachers and southern courses dominate schools, the Eskimo culture and heritage will continue to erode" (Nunavut Tunngavik Incorporated—*Saqqiqpuq*, 2007, p. 12).

Detailed background to the problem is provided.

During the 1970s, Nunavut Inuit put forth dozens of reports and efforts to protect their language and education rights,[2] and by the 1980's these efforts had coalesced into a battle to enshrine Inuit language and education rights, along with other rights, within a Nunavut land claim agreement. To this end, Inuit had organized themselves into the Tunngavik Federation of Nunavut (TFN), the group that would eventually sign a land claim with Canada (and then change its name to Nunavut Tunngavik Incorporated—NTI). TFN's first education and language clauses for their proposed land claim were presented to Canada in 1981, and then again in 1984 and 1986.

The Department of Indian Affairs was alarmed by Inuit insistence on putting protections for their language and culture into a constitutionally protected land claim—the consequences of extending constitutional protection to a language other than French or English were unknown. Quietly, behind the scenes, Ottawa commissioned research in 1983 into the cost of making Inuktitut an official language within Nunavut, while at the same time telling Inuit negotiators that this goal was a constitutional impossibility. Indian Affairs wanted to know the cost of an Inuit language school system "using Inuktitut as a language of instruction in school at all levels," while recognizing that this would require "language training for all teachers" and "standardized

Inuktitut curriculum development for all school levels including adult education."[3] Whatever the results of the research, it was not shared with Inuit negotiators.

The Inuit continued pressing Canada to acknowledge their language and education rights. During negotiations on August 24, 1987, TFN retabled this position:

> An Inuk resident in Nunavut has the right to have his or her child receive primary and secondary school instruction in Inuktitut, and has the right to participate in the management of schools in Nunavut through the election of local committees and regional boards. (Tunngavik Federation of Nunavut, 1987, *Language Rights Position Paper.* Ottawa: TFN)

Donat Milortuk, President of TFN, followed that up three months later with a letter to Indian Affairs Minister Bill McKnight thanking him for meeting with TFN but reminding him that "It is TFN's position that language rights must be negotiated within the context of the land claim agreement." And TFN re-tabled their position—yet again including the Inuit right to Inuit education—in negotiations with Canada on April 11, 1988.

A year later (November 25, 1988), Minister McKnight wrote back to Milortuk, noting that in their November 1987 meeting, "we discussed at some length the importance of protecting and promoting Inuktitut. This is certainly an objective which I support, and a land claim settlement could contribute to that goal in a number of ways. However, the language guarantees which you are seeking go beyond the scope of comprehensive land claims policy."

Whatever the outcome of the secret costing exercises,[4] the federal government chose to block all Inuit efforts to put protections for their language and education rights into their land claim with Canada. It seemed then (and now) that Canada wanted access to Inuit land and the minerals underneath it, but was not interested in protecting the Inuit language and culture. As the Indian Affairs Minister said in his 1988 letter, the government's position was that "the primary purpose of land claims negotiations is to provide certainty and clarity of rights with respect to lands and resources." For other things, like language and education, the Indian Affairs Minister urged Inuit to appeal to lower levels of government, telling them "to cooperate with the territorial government in designing practical measures to promote the use of your language."

Rebuffed but not discouraged, Inuit leaders decided to sign an Agreement-in-Principle with Canada in 1990, confident that they could secure language and education guarantees before a Final Agreement. Inside a massive igloo built for the historic AIP signing, TFN President Paul Quassa told Canada's Indian Affairs Minister Tom Siddon that:

> The Inuit agenda is comprehensive and still evolving . . . it includes issues that the federal government has not been prepared to discuss. For example, we assert the right to use Inuktitut in all facets of life in Nunavut. . . . We insist too that our children have the constitutional right to be educated in Inuktitut.

And Quassa warned Siddon that "TFN's position remained that any constitution for a Nunavut Territory" must ensure that "residents of the Nunavut territory whose first language learned and still understood is Inuktitut have the right to have their children to receive primary and secondary school instruction in Inuktitut in Nunavut."[5]

• • •

But in the end, all the carefully worded provisions to protect Inuit language and [15] education rights were blocked by Ottawa. When Inuit leaders signed the final Nunavut Land Claim Agreement (NLCA) in 1993, all that was left to protect Inuit language and education was one clause, Article 32, saying that "Inuit have the right to participate in the development, design and delivery of social and cultural policies in Nunavut."[6]

• • •

What Can Be Done to Support Inuit Education Rights?

It is evident that Nunavut Inuit have had a very difficult time establishing their own education system in their homeland. But there may finally be some hope. A new Nunavut government has been elected, led by a Premier who has been a strong advocate for Inuit language rights. Before becoming Premier, during her tenure as Nunavut's Languages Commissioner, Eva Aariak pushed for Inuit language rights under the Education Act, saying that "parents who speak Inuktitut and Inuinnaqtun must be given the same rights as French and English speakers. . . . It simply isn't good enough to teach Inuktitut only as a subject beyond Grade 4."[7] Since becoming Premier, she has gone on record saying that education is "an underlying solution to many of the issues that we're dealing with today."[8] But she may face an uphill battle trying to convince the largely non-Inuit senior management[9] that dominates the Nunavut Department of Education to return responsibility for the education of Inuit children to Inuit parents and Inuit school boards.

In 1990, the Supreme Court of Canada in its Mahé decision listed all the education protections that must be put in place to prevent a people's culture from being wiped out.

> The minority language representatives should have exclusive authority to make decisions relating to the minority language instruction and facilities, including:
>
> (a) expenditures of funds provided for such instruction and facilities;
> (b) appointment and direction of those responsible for the administration of such instruction and facilities;
> (c) establishment of programs of instruction;
> (d) recruitment and assignment of teachers and other personnel; and
> (e) making of agreements for education and services for minority language pupils.

All the things the Mahé decision said must be done to protect a culture and language *are* happening in Nunavut, it's just that they are being done for the Francophone population, not Inuit. So here are some proposed solutions:

Solution Number One: Implement Mahé Rights for Inuit

It's wrong to pursue justice only for European-Canadians while ignoring the people who've been here for 5000 years. This means local control:

• Inuit school boards must be re-instated, along with Inuit curriculum—no more teaching math using examples full of trains and grain silos (two things never seen in Nunavut).

[margin note] Proposed solution is introduced.

[margin note] Supreme Court decision is used to introduce the solution, increasing credibility of proposal.

[margin note] Solutions are systematically listed.

Solution Number Two: Implement Thomas Berger's Recommendations

In June 2005, Justice Thomas Berger was appointed by the federal government as conciliator between Nunavut Inuit and Ottawa. Berger recommended that Ottawa—at a minimum—should immediately pay $20 million for six near-term initiatives to tackle the drop-out rate by improving bilingualism in the schools. In his final report, Berger noted rhetorically: "What did we expect? When we agreed to the establishment of Nunavut, it cannot have escaped our notice that the overwhelming majority of the people of the new territory would be Inuit, speaking Inuktitut."

20   Berger's six near-term initiatives ($20 million per year):

- Nunavut Sivuniksavut expansion: $1.3 million per year;
- summer student program: $950,000 per year;
- internship expansion: $40 million over five years or $8 million per year;
- community career counselor program: $3.3 million in the first year and $2.6 million each year thereafter;
- mature graduation/returning student program: $1.85 million in startup costs and $5.225 million each year thereafter; and
- scholarship program: $1.5 million per year.[10]

Solution Number Three: Revise the Education Act

Nunavut has recently elected a new group of legislators; this new government should re-open the Education Act for revisions by Inuit. Let Inuit finally exercise their Article 32 land claim rights to design the law to suit their needs (starting with the points listed in Mahé).

Solution Number Four: Form an Inuit Teachers' Union

There's nothing wrong with having a Newfoundvut—oops, sorry!—*Nunavut* Teachers' Association, but Inuit need a union that will speak with them and for them in the Inuit language.

Solution Number Five: Enforce Article 23 Job Descriptions

This means write job descriptions for teachers and principals that include the requirements listed under Article 23.4.2: "An understanding of the social and cultural milieu of Nunavut including: knowledge of Inuit culture, society and economy; community awareness, fluency in Inuktitut and/or Inuinnaqtun, and knowledge of the environmental characteristics of Nunavut."

Solution Number Six: Employ 85% Inuit Teachers and Principals

This is required under Article 23 of the land claim, therefore Canada must help pay for this.[11] Nunavut can also help by shifting spending from recruiting southern teachers to training Inuit teachers in their home communities. This means it should core-fund community-based Inuit teacher training, with good trainers on long-term contracts, and then guarantee all graduates teaching jobs in their home communities (replacing non-Inuktitut-speaking teachers). Nunavut's new Premier has openly called for training "more teachers, many more teachers." But Eva Aariak has also warned that "we need money to do these things. We need a collective effort, both our government and Canada, to work together."[12]

Arctic Sovereignty: Protecting the Land, but What About the People?

Conclusion both sums up the problem and emphasizes the importance of the solution.

The historical record lists the enormous efforts Inuit have waged to try to regain control over the education of their children. But, 16 years after signing their land claim there is still no Inuit education system in Nunavut. [25]

It's not that Canada can't afford to pay for an Inuit education system. Last summer, the Prime Minister announced plans for a $720 million icebreaker[13] to patrol *our* Arctic (enough to pay for Berger's $20 million education initiatives 36 times over). This summer he flew up to Nunavut to highlight an expensive series of military exercises designed to assert our Arctic sovereignty. But if Canada had not signed a land claim with Inuit who have actually lived there for 5,000 years, its Arctic assertions would be laughed at by other nations.

A land claim is a contract between two parties; Inuit have been doing their part to honour this—we have to do ours. Write to the federal Minister of Indian Affairs and insist that Canada financially support the development of Inuit curricula and the training of Inuit teachers so that we can live up to our side of the deal in the Nunavut Land Claim. Up to this point, Canadian sovereignty has focused almost exclusively on getting access to Inuit land and the minerals beneath it, while on top of it priceless Inuit languages and culture remain unvalued and unprotected. We call it *our* Arctic; let's not forget the people who live there.

Notes

1. In the rush to create Nunavut ten years ago, Parliamentarians neglected to notice that they were creating a territory that would relegate both English and French to minority language status, thus not conforming to Canada's Charter of Rights and Freedoms and Canada's Official Languages Act. The Official Languages Act and Section 23 of the Charter say that the minority official language group can be English or French, but apparently cannot be both. For the past ten years, Ottawa has allowed these two minority groups to get almost all the public education money in the new territory, depriving the majority of essential funds to build up an Inuit language school system. See *Rabble.ca:* "Nunavut's promise still lost in translation," by Derek Rasmussen, April 6, 2009. Retrieved August 31, 2009 from: http://www.rabble.ca/news/2009/04/nunavuts-promise-still-losttranslation.

2. Some of these are archived at InuitEducation.com; others are listed in *Saqqiqpuq*, (Nunavut Tunngavik Incorporated, 2007, pp. 7–8), and in Darnel, F. & Hoem, A. (1996), *Taken to Extremes: Education in the Far North*. Oslo: Scandinavian University Press.

3. Letter from B. Heidenreich, Northern Political Development Group, Indian and Northern Affairs Canada to J. Hucker, Director General, Northern Policy and Coordination branch, INAC, Dec. 2, 1983.

4. Although INAC has not made public the 1983 Inuktitut cost studies, a later estimate made by INAC in 1998 at the request of Federal official Maryantonett Flumian, estimated the cost to the federal government of funding Inuktitut as a language of government within the Nunavut Territory at $8–10 million per year. See April 30, 1998 *OIC Report from Louis Langois to Maryantonett Flumian*. OIC: Iqaluit.

5. Tunngavik Federation of Nunavut. (1990). *Notes for an Address by Paul Quassa, President, TFN, on the Signing of the Nunavut Agreement in Principle between the Inuit of the Nunavut Settlement Area and Her Majesty in Right of Canada.* Igloolik, April 30, 1990.

6. John Bainbridge, interview with the author. August 10, 2009. John Bainbridge has lived in and worked for Aboriginal communities and organizations throughout the Canadian arctic and sub-arctic regions for 22 years as a school principal and lawyer. Until recently he was the Senior Policy Advisor for Nunavut Tunngavik Inc. (NTI). The full text of this interview is posted at http://www.policyalternatives.ca

7. October 1, 2002. Media Release from the Office of the Languages Commissioner of Nunavut: *Education Bill denies Inuktitut speakers equal rights.*

8. March 31, 2009. CBC report: *Education key to Nunavut's next decade: Premier.* Retrieved from http://www.cbc.ca/canada/north/story/2009/03/31 /education-nunavut.html

9. Across the entire Nunavut Government, senior and middle-management averages 74–78% non-Inuit; in Education, senior management is 88% non-Inuit, according to December 31, 2008 statistics. See pages 2 and 7, *Towards a Representative Public Service,* Prepared by Inuit Employment Planning office of GN Department of Human Resources, Dec. 31, 2008.

10. Berger, T. (2006). *Conciliator's Final Report: Nunavut Land Claims Agreement Implementation Planning Contract Negotiations for the Second Planning Period,* pp. 54–59. Retrieved August 25, 2009 from http://www.tunngavik.com/documents /publications/2006-0301%20Thomas%20Berger%20Final%20Report%20ENG.pdf

11. NTI has filed a lawsuit to force Canada to implement Article 23 and other provisions of the Nunavut Land Claim Agreement. Their statement of claim is posted here: http://www.tunngavik.com/documents/publications /2006-1200%20Statement%20of%20Claim.pdf

12. March 31, 2009. CBC report: *"Education key to Nunavut's next decade: Premier."* Retrieved from http://www.cbc.ca/canada/north/story/2009/03/31 /education-nunavut.html

13. Office of the Prime Minister, 28 August 2008, *Backgrounder,* The John G. Diefenbaker National Icebreaker Project. Retrieved from http://pm.gc.ca/eng/media .asp?category=5&id=2252

References

Darnel, F. & Hoem, A. (1996). *Taken to extremes: Education in the far north.* Oslo, NO: Scandinavian University Press.

Nunavut Tunngavik Incorporated. (2007). *Saqqiqpuq: Kindergarten to grade 12 education in Nunavut. The annual report on the state of Inuit culture and society.* Iqaluit: Nunavut Tunngavik Incorporated. Retrieved August 5, 2009 from http:// www.tunngavik.com/documents/publications/2005-2007-AnnualReport-on -the-State-of-Inuit-Culture-and-Society-Eng.pdf

Rasmussen, D. (2009). *Rabble.ca.* Retrieved August 31, 2009 from http://www .rabble.ca/news/2009/04/nunavuts-promise-still-losttranslation

Sorensen, M. & Aylward, J. (2002). *Nunavut profile: A ten year census analysis 1991-2001*. Ottawa, ON: Rural Secretariat, Agriculture and Agri-Food Canada. Available at http://dsp-psd.pwgsc.gc.ca/collection_2007/agr/A114-13-13-2001E.pdf

Tunngavik Federation of Nunavut. (1987). *Language rights position paper*. Ottawa: TFN.

A CLOSER LOOK AT
Forty Years of Struggle and Still No Right to Inuit Education in Nunavut

1. Rasmussen argues that the Inuit people should be entitled to education in their native language. According to Rasmussen, what are the barriers to a Nunavut Inuit school system?

2. This proposal includes several examples that support Rasmussen's argument. How does he use these examples to bring the problem to life and make his solution sound more persuasive?

3. Find Rasmussen's plan in this proposal. What exactly is he proposing and what are the steps in his plan? What are the benefits for the Inuit in Nunavut if they accept his proposal?

IDEAS FOR
Writing

1. Write a commentary in which you describe the future of education in Nunavut. Use the arguments in Rasmussen's proposal to help you come up with your own suggestions for supporting Inuit education rights.

2. Write a report in which you study the loss of Aboriginal languages in Canada. Do you see public education as playing a role in preserving these languages? What other options are there for the preservation of Aboriginal heritage in our country?

Tell the Awful Truth: It's Not Just Global Warming, It's Global Disaster!

M. H. SAIER JR. AND J. T. TREVORS

In this article, Saier and Trevors outline a multitude of problems facing our planet and propose solutions for dealing with them. Notice how the authors, after introducing the topic, systematically list the main problems facing humanity followed by a clear listing of proposed solutions to effectively address those problems.

The awful truth (and a most inconvenient truth) is that the present and future global warming of our common, shared, biosphere represents a global disaster in progress. The last 100 years (and the years of the immediate future) will be written in history (as long as the human race survives) as the period when some humans carelessly jeopardized the security of life on our planet. It will be recorded that we carelessly destroyed our oceans, fisheries and forests while removing immense amounts of carbon in the form of fossil fuels from the Earth and placing the combustion products into the atmosphere and the planet's waterways. The last century (and this one) will also be remembered as a period of immense human population growth, to the overshoot level, exceeding the capacity of our common biosphere to provide even the essentials for the universal quality of life. The awful, inconvenient truth is that we have created a global preventable disaster without identifying the correct solutions. Solutions other than preventative ones may in fact be impossible to achieve.

To correct the ills of our generations may be beyond the capabilities of all of science and technology. We do not know the life span of a technological society. Such corrective solutions may never be brought forward and implemented precisely because the problems we are creating are too immense and complex. Problems are typically created at a much simpler level than the solutions, which are several orders of magnitude higher in complexity and cost. We may have already passed the global tipping point for humanity. A reasonable planetary quality of life—for humans and for other species—may be beyond achievement with our continued population growth. The consequences will be continuously increasing poverty and misery for large segments of the world's human population, and increasing rates of species extinction. And the faster we destroy nature and use up the available resources, the more pervasive these conditions will become. The end of nature as we think we

> Introduction both introduces the topic and puts the problem in socio-historical context.

> Causes of the overall problem are outlined in detail.

know it, is completely possible. Good examples include the rainforests, oceans and the drought conditions throughout areas of the world including the USA and Australia. The average standard of living will decline, and resource wars will be commonplace. Even the wealthiest and most greedy industrialists will lose their security. There will be no place for sympathy and humanistic feelings; survival will be the only goal.

Let's list the most important, complex, global problems facing humanity in today's world and the future world of our children. We are not borrowing our children's future world from them, we are destroying it for them. How can any current political leader (the term leader is used in the general sense as many so called leaders are not leaders but part of the problem) who claim they love their children, act in the way they presently do? Do they not understand that the sum of all human activities has taken us to the tipping point for humanity?

1. First and foremost: the excessive human population and its continued expansion
2. Climate change/global warming and the environmental consequences including: drought and water shortage, crop and livestock failure, food shortages, species extinction and the loss of biodiversity. Three crops—rice, corn and wheat—stand between humans and hunger
3. Poverty, misery, inadequate infrastructure and health care and increasingly frequent premature death
4. Infectious diseases and pandemics affecting humans and other species as well as their food sources
5. Loss of democratic principles with increasingly fascist regimes prevailing; failure of governments to create transparency and represent the people
6. The rise of pervasive discrimination and intolerance at the hands of specific power groups
7. A lack of intelligent, informed, visionary and morally correct leadership
8. An inability of well intending governments to ameliorate local, national and global problems
9. Failure of individuals and nations to alter their actions for conservation of the biosphere
10. Inefficiency, insufficient funding, incompetence and graft in educational systems, resulting in decreased quality and quantity of learning
11. A lack of competent research and innovation that could facilitate the formulation of correct solutions
12. Rapid urbanization without adequate infrastructure; loss of public communication and travel; increasing prevalence of slum cities within cities
13. Intentional perpetration of misinformation by individuals, agencies, governments and industries
14. Lawlessness, corruption, crime, discrimination, violence and war; unequal and unjust allocation of scarce resources
15. Lack of participation by some countries in international accords
16. Religious leaders who should be educating their membership on the moral responsibility they have to ensure a common future for all of humanity

Developing countries have argued they want to improve their standards of living to match those of existing developed countries. This is to be achieved via economic growth and an increase in consumption of energy and other natural resources. In some cases it is to be achieved without restricting population growth. Some of these countries may approach this objective, but if so, there will be no future for the next generations because the fundamental laws of thermodynamics will prevail. Increased resource consumption is nothing more than a temporary solution to one of our many problems. It will increase the time of onset of the pending global biosphere disaster.

5   Developed countries, on the other hand, naturally want to maintain their high standards of living. However, without careful planning, this too, will promote global disaster. More, more, more—using the same destructive means of resource consumption accompanied by pollution production—is simply not acceptable. The awful truth is that humans are creating a global disaster and will continue to do so unless universal birth control is implemented so that the human population can first stabilize and then begin its requisite decline. Our population must decrease by several billions until we achieve sustainability. The alternative is immense human suffering and death. This is true because Natural Selection is cruel and will continue until a sustainable population emerges, if this ever becomes possible. The weak, young, old and undernourished members of society will be the first to die. However, no country or economic class of people will be spared. And no one wants to experience this consequence.

The most immediate, rationally, recognized solutions are:

1. To make universal birth control available, with the financial means provided by the richest countries of the world—so that the human population can stabilize and then decline

> Parallel listing of solutions is provided.

2. To implement conservation measures involving the three environmental Rs—reduce, reuse and recycle—as applied to every aspect of society including energy, transportation, local organic farming, construction of green residential and commercial buildings, preservation of existing forests and marine habitats and restoration of destroyed ecosystems. Transportation of food products over immense distances must also be reduced, unless absolutely necessary

3. To use alternative energy sources such as wind, solar, wave, tidal, fuel cells and geothermal power, each of these alternatives being used when and where most practical

4. To DECREASE economic growth while INCREASING prosperity, a goal that is possible only with a decrease in the human population, better planning, and the instigation of universal health care with proper disease control programs

5. To improve the quality of education for all world citizens, attempting to eliminate ignorance, irrationality and planetary irresponsibility

6. To create urban and rural infrastructure, permitting a gradual decrease in city size while maintaining accurate information transfer and allowing requisite travel

7. To promote research and innovation leading to more sustainable ways of life for humans and other species on the planet

8. To establish responsible governments based on democratic principles with intelligent, environmentally well-educated officials at the helm

9. To maintain financial responsibility at all levels with taxation according to ability to pay in order to empower governments to fulfill their responsibilities to their citizens and the world

10. Cessation of discrimination, threats, violence and wars with implementation of measures that insure international cooperation with international law dominant over national law

> **Restatement of the gravity of the problem and the necessity of change.**

The awful truth we must recognize is that there are too many humans on the planet, consuming too many irreplaceable resources and producing too much pollution. The fundamental laws of thermodynamics rule in the natural world, not human-made artificial, economic rules. Human-made rules can be broken, but the laws of nature cannot. Every living organism must obey them, from the simplest bacterium to a complex human being. The laws that govern energy and matter transformations and the production of heat as a waste product spare no living organism. For example, a gasoline-powered vehicle is at best 20% efficient with the remainder of the fuel being converted to heat and gaseous pollutants. And to squeeze out this 20% efficiency, a massive amount of oxygen must be consumed for every liter of fuel used.

> **Conclusion reminds the reader of the problem and solution, and relies on *pathos* to make the final points.**

No unwanted child should ever be born, and every woman should have the right to make her own reproductive choices. No rational, thinking human being can believe that our current human activities can continue indefinitely. Corrective measures are paramount. Technology cannot provide solutions for the billions of humans on this small planet with guarantees of a reasonable quality of life. We must embrace change and decrease our human numbers. This one goal must be our number one priority. Then and only then can humans work towards the ultimate goal of sustainability.

A CLOSER LOOK AT
Tell the Awful Truth

1. This article follows the organization of a traditional proposal. Look through the article and identify the places where Saier and Trevors describe (a) the problem, its causes, and its effects, (b) a solution to the problem, including any major and minor steps, and (c) the benefits of accepting their proposal.

2. Saier and Trevors do not support their major points with empirical evidence. Do you think the use of empirical evidence in this proposal would have made parts of their argument more credible? Why or why not? Even though they have not backed up their argument with empirical sources, do you find their arguments reasonable and solid? Why or why not?

3. In your opinion, what are Saier and Trevors's three strongest arguments against humanity maintaining the status quo and what are their two weakest arguments? What are their three best ideas for solving the problems facing our planet? What are the two ideas in their plan that you are most skeptical about?

IDEAS FOR
Writing

1. Write a letter to the editor of *Water, Air and Soil Pollution* in which you agree or disagree with Saier and Trevors's argument. If you agree with their argument, how do your experiences as someone who is living on this planet match up with Saier and Trevors's descriptions? What parts of their plan do think would work? If you disagree with them, where do their criticisms and ideas fall short? Do you think they are wrong or do you have a better way to address the global disaster they argue is approaching for our planet?

2. Write a position paper in which you argue for or against one or more of the solutions Saier and Trevors propose. If you are arguing for one of their solutions, can you think of additional ways to implement the solution? If you are arguing against one of their solutions, do you have an option that you think would work better than Saier and Trevors's approach?

1. What are some of the problems on your institution's campus? With a group in your class, list them and pick one that seems especially troublesome. What do you think are the causes of this problem? What has changed recently to bring this problem about or make it worse? Discuss this problem with a group of other people in your class.

2. Now try to figure out a way to solve this campus problem. What would be a good solution to this problem? Can you think of a few other solutions? With a small group, discuss the costs and benefits of solving the problem in different ways.

3. With a group in class, find a proposal on the Internet that you can discuss. Look closely at the proposal's content, organization, style, and design. Do you think the proposal is effective? What are its strengths? What are its weaknesses? If you were going to revise this proposal, what are some of the things you would change?

1. Find a proposal on the Internet by entering keywords like "Proposal and (Topic)" into a search engine. Write a one page analysis of the proposal, describing how it explains the problem and offers a plan for solving it. In your analysis, tell your readers whether you think the proposal is or is not effective. Explain why you think so, and offer suggestions about how the proposal could be improved.

2. List five problems that are facing our society right now. Pick one that interests you and then try to narrow the topic down to something you can manage in a small proposal. Use a concept map to explore what you already know about the problem, its causes, and its effects. Then do research on the subject by collecting online and print sources on it. Draft a one or two page analysis of the problem that explores its causes and effects.

1. **Propose your own solution.** Write a proposal that solves a problem in our society or in your life. Explore the causes of the problem and then come up with a plan that solves it. Then identify all the benefits that would come about if the problem were solved according to your plan. The best topics for proposals are ones that affect your life in some way. Pick a problem that you feel strongly about or something that affects your everyday life. Your proposal should run about seven to ten pages. Include graphics and make sure the document is well designed.

2. **Remake a proposal into a multimedia presentation.** Using a search engine, find a proposal available on the Internet. Transform the proposal into a presentation that incorporates multimedia features. You can use presentation software, overhead projector slides, flipcharts, or posters. Then write a one page rhetorical analysis for your professor that introduces the proposal and describes how you altered the original proposal's content, organization, style, and design to make it work as a multimedia presentation.

MyCompLab

For support in meeting this chapter's objectives, follow this path in MyCompLab:

Student Resources → Writing → Writing Samples → Writing Samples: Proposals. Review the Multimedia resources for writing proposals; then complete the Exercises and click on Gradebook to measure your progress.

10

Research
Papers

CHAPTER

In this chapter, you will learn how to:

- figure out what kind of research paper your professor is asking for.
- develop a topic and angle for an effective research paper.
- adopt an appropriate style, structure, and format for your research paper.

Research papers are used to deeply examine topics, thoroughly analyze issues, and demonstrate students' ability to enter into an academic dialogue. When writing a research paper, you need to do more than just present facts. You also need to critically examine issues and ideas in a way that helps your reader understand your interpretation of the topic.

The main format of a research paper is the academic essay. Essays are often assigned in university and college settings as a way for students to expand their understanding of a topic and develop their critical thinking and writing skills. However, you will also find research papers and essays in a variety of publications, from academic journals to popular magazines.

Different disciplines and different professors may have different expectations about the content, organization, style, and format of a research paper. For example, some professors may ask you to write an "expository" research paper. In this case, you will be expected to explain an issue without making an overt argument for one or the other side. Other professors may ask you to write an "argumentative" research paper in which you take a side on an issue and use your research to support your position. When you are assigned a research paper, one of your first tasks is to find out what kind of research paper—expository or argumentative—your professor expects.

In post-secondary studies, your professors will ask you to write research papers on a variety of important issues and topics. As you take more advanced courses, the topics for your research papers will become more complex, creative, and critical. Professors in your advanced courses will ask you to analyze intricate issues specific to your field of study and to present your critical evaluation of those topics. The readings in this chapter offer three examples of academic research writing.

Research Papers

Research papers can be organized in a variety of ways. These models demonstrate two basic patterns that you can adjust to fit your topic, angle, purpose, readers, and context.

Abstract (Optional)	Abstract (Optional)
Introduction	Introduction
First Issue or Time Period	Factual Overview of Issues
Second Issue or Time Period	Explanation of Opposing Views
Third Issue or Time Period	Argument for Your View
⋮	⋮
Conclusion	Conclusion
Works Cited/References	Works Cited/References

Overview

The research paper genre is flexible, allowing it to be used in a variety of ways. Different disciplines have different requirements for research papers. For instance, a research paper in a scientific discipline may require a formal methods or results section. A typical research paper, however, tends to have the following features:

- **Abstract** that summarizes the paper. Shorter research papers (less than four pages) may not have this feature.

- **Introduction** that defines a research question or problem and explains why it is important to the reader and society. The introduction should define the topic and go on to explain why the selected topic is important. Most research papers will close the introduction with a thesis statement. The thesis statement both informs the reader of the content of the paper and clearly states the writer's position.

- **Body paragraphs** that use an issue-by-issue or chronological pattern to present the results of your research; the body is divided into sections with headings.

- **Conclusion** that restates the thesis or main point of the research paper and offers a brief discussion of the implications of research. Often a call to action is included in this section.

- **References** that provide a list of references or works cited in a standardized citation style (usually MLA or APA style).

ONE STUDENT'S WORK
Research Paper

This paper was written for a class that assigned topics on media influence. Students were asked to focus on a particular situation and explore the nature, extent, and implications of media intervention in that situation.

The CNN Effect: How Media Can Influence Government Foreign Policy

Holly Wylie

This paper is written using APA citation style. See Chapter 25, "Using APA Style," for correct APA citation style.

The mass media has become one of the most powerful forces in our society. As Bernard Cohen wrote, "The press may not be successful in telling people what to think, but it is stunningly successful in telling its readers what to think about" (Cate, 1996, p. 17). Broadcasts from countries worldwide can now be viewed in the comfort of our own living rooms. Iconic moments, like Tiananmen Square and the tearing down of the Berlin Wall, captured audiences around the globe (Robinson, 1999, p. 301). It is commonly known that images such as these can influence the minds of individuals, but are they powerful enough to change governmental decisions? The ability of the media to alter a country's foreign policy, or the "CNN effect," has been intensely debated by scholars, with varying conclusions. Although claims about the CNN effect are often exaggerated, there is substantial evidence that suggests it has played a part in key events. By examining the case study of Iraq, and comparing it with those of Somalia and Sudan, this paper will demonstrate that the media can influence governmental intervention in humanitarian crises.

> Introduction begins by establishing the topic that the paper will discuss, touching on the background to the CNN effect, and closing with a strong thesis statement.

> Thesis statement is fully developed, both explaining how the writer will examine the topic (through a case study) and what she ultimately will show in the paper (that media can influence government interventions).

The term "CNN effect" is used interchangeably with media control over a government's foreign policy. As each author uses the term in a slightly different sense, its use leaves room for uncertainty. Livingston and Eachus give this term a political sense by defining the CNN effect as "elite decision makers' loss of policy control to the news media" (as cited in Gilboa, 2005, p. 328). This paper will refer to the CNN effect in this sense, as the ability of the news media to control the formation of foreign policy. The "CNN effect" was first used to describe CNN's coverage in the Gulf War, but became a reality with the Kurdish crisis following the Gulf War (Gilboa, 2005, p. 328). Originally, Western powers were extremely opposed to intervention. Bush himself stated, "But we are not there to intervene. That is not our purpose; it never was our purpose. . . I am not going to commit our forces to something of this nature" (as cited in Robinson, 2002, p. 64). The influence of the media was crucial in turning Bush from such a firm stance against providing military aid to deploying troops to Iraq.

> The author provides a brief overview of the relevant literature on her topic.

Media pressure and intervention in Iraq in 1991

Through emotional framing of the situation juxtaposed with relentless criticism of government, the media pinned responsibility for the Kurdish emergency directly on Western leaders and forced military intervention (Shaw, 1996). Disturbing images were featured on the nightly news that urged both the public and government to take action. In Shaw's study on television and newspaper coverage during the Kurdish crisis, the description of the images that were broadcast is horrifying: scenes of men fighting over the remains of a donkey in the streets and starving, freezing children (Rees, as cited in Shaw, 1996, p. 89). When President Bush gave his statement on April 16 about why the American government had decided to send military aid to the Kurds, his reason was that "hunger, malnutrition, disease and exposure" had taken their toll (as cited in Robinson 2002, p. 66). These ills were all regularly featured on the news, suggesting that the media had played a role in the American decision. Along with the pictures and videos that shocked viewers, the news featured commentary that

> Background to the current issue is provided to orient the reader to the topic being discussed.

(continued)

was intensely critical of Western leaders. In a segment filmed in Dahuk, there are images of children with burnt, mutilated faces and a man crying in the background, "George Bush, why don't you interfere with this?" (Shaw, 1996, p. 90). The American newspapers were equally unforgiving. In the *New York Times*, 16 out of 22 editorials on the Kurdish situation, published between April 1 and 15, 1991, were either highly critical of President Bush's response or demanded aid be sent to the Kurds; in the *Washington Post*, 9 out of 15 took the same stance (Robinson, 2002, p. 68). This direct criticism of the US government disproves the theory that the executive controlled the response to the Kurdish crisis. If they were looking to gain public favour by intervening in Iraq and were using the media to that end, why would the media publish such ruthless and unforgiving articles? In one instance, an editorial by William Safire accused President Bush of fishing instead of ordering a halt to Saddam Hussein's movement of aircraft and weapons, which could have saved thousands of lives (as cited in Robinson, 2002, p. 68). As a result of these editorials, articles, and broadcasts, the public's interest in the situation grew exponentially. The sheer volume of news features attests to this: between March 26 and April 15, 1991, the *New York Times* published over six articles a day on the crisis, and the *Washington Post* published (on average) four articles daily (Robinson, 2002, p. 67). On April 3 in Britain, this topic occupied almost a whole BBC bulletin (Shaw, 1996, p. 87). The explosion of media on this topic, with its unforgettable imagery and brutal criticism, overwhelmed politicians and forced them to take assertive action quickly. Shaw argued that the imagery and commentary manufactured a "nexus of responsibility" which governments simply could not ignore (Shaw, 1996, p. 156). After a few weeks of intense coverage, government caved in to the demands of the media and the public.

A discussion of other issues that could be attributed to this example is included, along with an explanation (with scholarly support) as to why media influence is the most likely answer.

Other explanations have been proposed as to why Western society decided to intervene in the Kurdish crisis, but none are as likely as media influence. Natsios (1996) acknowledges that the news media did play a significant role, but argues that a more likely reason was America's political support of groups opposing Saddam Hussein. However, what Natsios fails to recognize by drawing this conclusion is that the American government was adamantly opposed to interfering only a few weeks prior to the launching of "Operation Provide Comfort." This argument neglects to mention the timing of intervention relative to media coverage. President Bush's announcement that America would provide military aid took place on April 16, after a month of massive media pressure. It is unlikely that he would have changed his mind so quickly without that intense pressure. Robinson (2002, p. 69) concludes that the risk of damaging relations with Turkey was more important than media influence. However, analysis of this assumption completely neglects the relationship between the decision to intervene and news coverage. By assuming that Turkish foreign relations drove the American and British governments to intervene, one is assuming that the decision to send troops after a few weeks of media pressure and criticism is simply coincidental. Based on the evidence presented, this seems highly unlikely. Overall, although foreign relations with Turkey may have contributed to the decision to send military aid into Iraq in 1991, news coverage is the more likely factor. Although the media's role on intervention in Iraq may not exactly be the "clear cut case" that Shaw (1996, p. 156) suggests, it is most likely the factor that compelled the governments to action.

Media influence and intervention in Somalia and the Sudan

By attacking the conscience of both the public and government officials, media coverage resulted in military intervention in Somalia in 1992. As John Shattuck, former US Assistant Secretary of State, wrote, "The media got us into Somalia and then got us out" (as cited in Gilboa, 2005, p. 329). The situation in Somalia was dire: the United Nations and the International Committee for the Red Cross estimated between 300,000 and 500,000 people had died from war, starvation, or disease (Livingston, 1996, p. 71). News features made the suffering in Somalia explicit for the Western world. Livingston's (1996) analysis of newspaper coverage on Somalia from 1990 to 1994 in the *Washington Post* shows a significant increase between 1991 and 1992, from approximately 30 to 200 articles per year. Rosenblatt commented that images of suffering and starving Somalis were an integral part of the nightly news (1996, p. 142). This did not go unnoticed by powerful policy officials. Diplomat and scholar George Kennan believes that intervention was an error in American policy and was only accepted by Congress because of television coverage, "[T]he reason for this acceptance lies primarily with the exposure of the Somalia situation by the American media, and above all, television. . . . The reaction was an emotional one, occasioned by the sight of the suffering of the starving people in question" (as cited in Gilboa, 2005, p. 332). Similarly, Mandelbaum's study on Somalia led him to the conclusion that there was no national interest behind the American involvement in the Somali famine and that it was propelled by these emotional images (as cited in Gilboa, 2005, p. 224). Many high-ranking policy officials have made no attempt to deny the influence of television's gruesome images in the Somali situation. The American ambassador to the United Nations, Madeline Albright, publicly stated, "Television's ability to bring graphic images of pain and outrage into our living rooms has heightened the pressure for both immediate engagement in areas of international crisis and immediate disengagement when events do not go according to plan" (as cited in Gilboa, 2005, p. 328). Even President Bush himself stated that television was what urged him to call for troops to be sent to Somalia. The heart-wrenching images of children, starving and desperately searching for a small amount of rice, was what forced Bush to call for this decision (Hines, as cited in Robinson, 2002, p. 50).

> Further discussion of media influence (with scholarly support) extends the critical examination of the CNN effect.

(continued)

As with Iraq in 1991, there has been much debate about which factor was the primary influence prompting government aid to Somalia. Robinson presents a number of other explanations: Bush's opportunity for glory with the Somali campaign, his own Christian nature, and American fear of "losing face" over Somalia (2002, p. 51). However, Robinson also notes that these explanations could all be associated with media. The media was a major agent in advancing the concept of "loss of face" over Somalia and in creating the idea of Bush's supposed glory. And the images that appealed to Bush's Christian nature could only be viewed through the newspaper and television. Another argument Robinson (2002) presents is that Bush had no real power at the time of the Somali crisis. This argument implies that Bush was the only policy official affected by the television broadcasts; but numerous other high-ranking officials, including Shattuck, Kennan, and Albright, have published statements that point to the media's influence on the policy-making process. The true measure of the impact the media had on the Somali crisis is best understood when seen in comparison with the Sudan.

The Sudanese civil war is an instance where lack of media coverage resulted in lack of intervention. Sudanese losses were equal to or greater than those of the Somalis; between 1992 and 1993, 300,000 people died in southern Sudan from disease, starvation, and war (Livingston, 1996, p. 71). Interestingly, the Somalis received faster, more successful aid than the Sudanese (Rosenblatt, 1996, p. 136). Media attention here was the critical factor that separated the two. Rosenblatt directly attributes this difference in support given to Sudan compared with Somalia to the CNN effect (1996, p. 136). Somalia and Sudan can be compared because they both occupied the same place in American foreign policy and were largely ignored by the media before 1991 (Livingston, 1996, pp. 72–73). Therefore, the only major difference between these two situations was the amount of media coverage. Livingston's comparison of newspaper articles featuring Somalia with those featuring Sudan confirms this: between 1990 and 1994, there was a vast difference in the number of newspaper articles covering the two crises. At its peak in 1993, the *Washington Post* was publishing approximately 400 articles a year on Somalia and only approximately 20 on Sudan (1996, p. 75). Statistically speaking, the Sudan was ignored by the media. Therefore, the Western public knew little to nothing about the suffering of the Sudanese (Rosenblatt, 1996, p. 141). As a result, the Somalis received faster, more successful aid in larger amounts (Rosenblatt, 1996, p. 136). Sudan was not the only example of a "forgotten war;" other conflicts ignored at this time include Azerbaijan, Angola, and Liberia (Rosenblatt, 1996, p. 136).

In conclusion, this paper argues that based on the evidence presented, military intervention in the Kurdish crisis in Iraq in 1991 and the famine in Somalia in 1992 was directly influenced by media, while the lack of aid to Sudan in 1992 was due to a lack of media attention. Coverage of the Kurdish crisis featured not

The author brings both examples together in this section and discusses other plausible explanations for the Somalia situation. She then goes on to show how media influence is once again the most likely culprit.

only emotionally moving images but harsh criticism of government (Shaw, 1996). The graphic images shown in the coverage on Somalia appealed to the public's consciences, and especially to those of high-ranking officials. In contrast, the crisis in the Sudan, which was just as terrible as the famine in Somalia, received little news coverage. As a result, there was no intervention by Western forces (Rosenblatt, 1996). These three case studies represent situations where the media can influence military intervention in humanitarian crises. This is not always true, but in times of uncertainty and lack of political leadership, the CNN effect can take place (Robinson, 2002). Understanding the power of the media on governmental foreign policy is essential in improving aid to foreign countries (Hawkins, 2011). This paper demonstrates that the growing power of the media can not only shape individual opinions, but can also influence the decisions of governments.

> Conclusion clearly and concisely sums up the author's main points, relating them back to the thesis statement. The paper comes to a close with several comments on the power of the media to affect humanitarian actions and leaves the reader with critical thinking points.

References

Cate, F. H. (1996). Communications, policy-making, and humanitarian crises. In R. I. Rotberg & T. G. Weiss (Eds.), *From massacres to genocide: The media, public policy, and humanitarian crises* (pp. 15–44). Washington, DC: The Brookings Institution.

Gilboa, E. (2005). Global television news and foreign policy: Debating the CNN effect. *International Studies Perspectives, 6,* 325–341. doi:10.1111/j.1528-3577.2005.00211.x

Hawkins, V. (2011). Media selectivity and the other side of the CNN effect: The consequences of not paying attention to conflict. *Media, War & Conflict, 4*(1), 55–68. doi:10.1177/1750635210396126

Livingston, S. (1996). Suffering in silence: Media coverage of war and famine in the Sudan. In R. I. Rotberg & T. G. Weiss (Eds.), *From massacres to genocide: The media, public policy, and humanitarian crises* (pp. 68–89). Washington, DC: The Brookings Institution.

Natsios, A. (1996). Illusions of influence: The CNN effect in complex emergencies. In R. I. Rotberg & T. G. Weiss (Eds.), *From massacres to genocide: The media, public policy, and humanitarian crises* (pp. 149–169). Washington, DC: The Brookings Institution.

Robinson, P. (1999). The CNN effect: Can the news media drive foreign policy? *Review of International Studies, 25,* 301–399. doi:10.1017/S0260210599003010

Robinson, P. (2002). *The CNN effect: The myth of news, foreign policy and intervention.* London, UK: Routledge.

Rosenblatt, L. (1996). The media and the refugee. In R. I. Rotberg & T. G. Weiss (Eds.), *From massacres to genocide: The media, public policy, and humanitarian crises* (pp. 136–146). Washington, DC: The Brookings Institution.

Shaw, M. (1996). *Civil society and media in global crises: Representing distant violence.* London, UK: Pinter.

> Correct APA reference list is included. See Chapters 24 and 25 for an overview of both MLA and APA citation styles.

Developing Your Research Paper's Content

When starting a research project, you first need to figure out your topic, your research question, and your thesis. Then you need to discover what you already know about your topic and come up with a systematic way to find out what others know. And finally, you need to use your research skills to generate findings, critically analyze those findings, and develop your conclusions. In other words, much needs to happen before you sit down to draft your paper.

The content of your research paper will be primarily based on your research at your campus library. Remember that your professor will want to see that you've used sources to back up your claims and statements. Your professor does *not* want you to simply write your opinion and then sprinkle in a few citations to make it look like you did research. Professors know the difference between a research paper that is grounded in solid research and one that merely mentions a few sources.

Inquiring: Defining Your Topic, Angle, and Purpose

Start out by identifying what kind of research paper you are being asked to write. There are two major types of research papers:

Expository Research Paper. Expository means to "exhibit" or "explain" what you have discovered about your topic. Expository research papers explain an issue, event, or trend, without making an overt argument for one side.

Argumentative Research Paper. Argumentation involves choosing one side of the issue and using your research to support your side while disputing opposing views.

If it's not clear whether you are *explaining* something (exposition) or *arguing* a point (argumentation), you should ask your professor to clarify the assignment.

Next, identify your topic, angle, research question, and thesis.

Topic. Define your topic and then narrow it down to something you can handle in the time you have available. Research papers tend to be large compared to other documents, so you may be tempted to pick a topic that is very large (e.g., violence, eating disorders, alternative energy, etc.), but these topics are too broad. Instead, you need to choose a narrower topic within a larger topic (e.g., recent incidents of violence on campus, how first-year university students with eating disorders adapt to dorm food, using wind energy to power your dormitory). Some ways to narrow your topic might be to consider a certain time period, a political ideology, or a specific group of individuals. A narrower topic will allow you to focus your research and come up with a more critical evaluation and discussion of the topic.

Angle. The best way to narrow down your topic is to find the *angle* you want to pursue. Completely new topics are rare, but there are always new angles you can explore on existing topics. To help you find your angle, ask yourself: What has changed about this topic recently? How does this topic affect us locally?

Research Question.   Now, it's time to develop your *research question*. Your research question should state your topic and identify an issue that your research will address. As discussed in Chapter 21, "Starting Research," your research question also needs to be as focused as possible.

Too Broad: Why do people eat so much fast food?

Focused Research Question: Why do university and college students turn to fast food as a way to help them handle stressful situations?

Too Broad: Why do crows behave the way they do?

Focused Research Question: Why do crows tend to live here on campus in the winter and how can we encourage them to go somewhere else?

Too Broad: Are children becoming more violent?

Focused Research Question: Do violent video games cause children to act out more violently in their everyday lives?

Thesis.   Once you have figured out your research question, you should turn it into a *thesis* that will guide your research. Your thesis is the central guiding idea behind your paper. Your thesis will evolve into a fully developed thesis statement as you complete your research. The thesis statement is the anchor for all the points you will make in your paper. It should be supported by the research and developed by your critical assessment of the research you complete.

My thesis is that fast food contains ingredients like salt, protein, carbohydrates, and fat that give our bodies short-term fuel for overcoming threatening moments. This craving is due to evolution. Our minds, when anxious or stressed, start thinking about the needs of short-term survival, not long-term health.

My hunch is that crows congregate on our campus in the winter because there is ample food available and sources of warmth. Also, they are intelligent birds and have strong social bonds, so campus provides a consistent safe place for them to live together through the winter.

My thesis is that today's children fantasize more about violence due to video games, but these games actually make children less violent because they can work through their aggression in a virtual environment.

Your thesis is your main idea for now, and it will probably change as you move forward with your research. You're not committed to it. Instead, you are going to find evidence that extends and develops your thesis into a fully developed thesis statement. Then you will need to revise it to fit your findings. You can turn to Chapter 21, "Starting Research," for help with creating a good thesis.

Inquiring: Finding Out What You Already Know

There is a good chance you already know quite a bit about your topic. That's why you or your professor chose it in the first place. So first discover what is already stored away in your grey matter about your topic.

Begin by brainstorming about your topic (Figure 10.1). Put your topic at the top of a piece of paper. Then list everything you know about that topic. Do this for five minutes or more. When you are finished brainstorming, identify two to five major

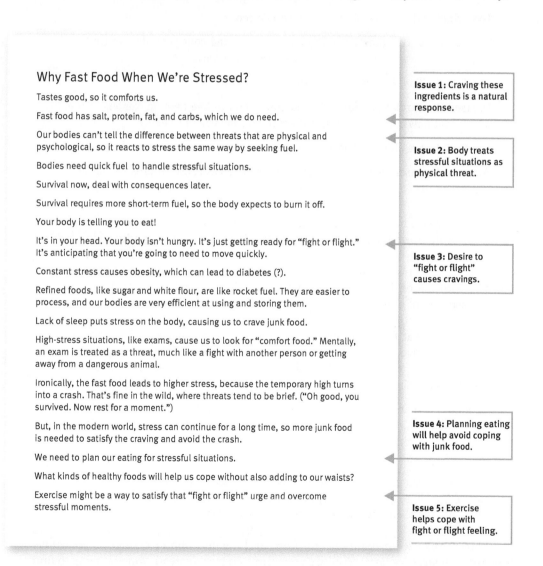

Why Fast Food When We're Stressed?

Tastes good, so it comforts us.

Fast food has salt, protein, fat, and carbs, which we do need.

Our bodies can't tell the difference between threats that are physical and psychological, so it reacts to stress the same way by seeking fuel.

Bodies need quick fuel to handle stressful situations.

Survival now, deal with consequences later.

Survival requires more short-term fuel, so the body expects to burn it off.

Your body is telling you to eat!

It's in your head. Your body isn't hungry. It's just getting ready for "fight or flight." It's anticipating that you're going to need to move quickly.

Constant stress causes obesity, which can lead to diabetes (?).

Refined foods, like sugar and white flour, are like rocket fuel. They are easier to process, and our bodies are very efficient at using and storing them.

Lack of sleep puts stress on the body, causing us to crave junk food.

High-stress situations, like exams, cause us to look for "comfort food." Mentally, an exam is treated as a threat, much like a fight with another person or getting away from a dangerous animal.

Ironically, the fast food leads to higher stress, because the temporary high turns into a crash. That's fine in the wild, where threats tend to be brief. ("Oh good, you survived. Now rest for a moment.")

But, in the modern world, stress can continue for a long time, so more junk food is needed to satisfy the craving and avoid the crash.

We need to plan our eating for stressful situations.

What kinds of healthy foods will help us cope without also adding to our waists?

Exercise might be a way to satisfy that "fight or flight" urge and overcome stressful moments.

Issue 1: Craving these ingredients is a natural response.

Issue 2: Body treats stressful situations as physical threat.

Issue 3: Desire to "fight or flight" causes cravings.

Issue 4: Planning eating will help avoid coping with junk food.

Issue 5: Exercise helps cope with fight or flight feeling.

FIGURE 10.1 Brainstorming on Your Topic

A brainstorming list is a great way to put your ideas on the screen or a piece of paper. It will also help you identify the two to five major issues you will probably explore as you do research for your paper.

issues on your list that you could explore further in your research. Circle these issues or make a special mark next to them. At this point, you could do some freewriting or Internet research to see which issue might make a good topic for your paper.

Researching: Creating a Research Plan

When you are finished writing down what you already know, you should have a good idea about where your research project is going. Now it's time to figure out how you are going to do your research (i.e., your research methods).

You will need to develop a step-by-step plan for finding information. A concept map is an especially helpful tool for developing your research methods. It will help you figure out the steps you need to take when you are doing your research (Figure 10.2). You can map out your research methods like this:

1. In the middle of the screen or page, write down your research question.

2. Write down the two to five *major steps* you will need to take to answer that research question. Circle them.

3. For each major step, write down two to five *minor steps* that you would need to take to achieve that major step. Circle them and draw lines to connect them to the major steps.

The key question you should keep asking yourself is, "How?" "*How* am I going to answer that question? *How* am I going to find that information? *How* am I going to generate that data?" To help you answer these questions, you might turn to Chapter 21, "Starting Research," for ideas about doing your research.

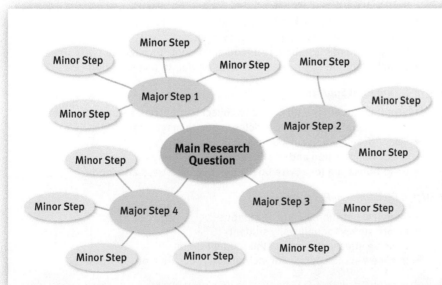

FIGURE 10.2 Developing Your Methods with a Concept Map

Even the most experienced researchers find it difficult to develop their research methods. Making a concept map allows you to get your thoughts down in front of you and to organize them spatially.

You can then turn your concept map into an outline, as shown in Figure 10.3. Your methodology can include all three kinds of sources (i.e., online, print, and empirical) so you can "triangulate" the facts you discover while doing your research. However, in most humanities courses you will answer your research question by drawing on published work rather than completing experiments. Triangulation, as discussed in Chapter 22, "Finding Sources and Collecting Information," is a way to cross-reference your sources to determine the strength and the usefulness of the information they offer.

Researching: Gathering Sources and Revisiting Your Thesis

Your research will inevitably turn up new ideas and concepts that you didn't know about when you started the project. That's good. When doing research for a paper, your objective is *not* to simply find sources that prove what you believed at the start of the project. Instead, your objective is to do open-ended inquiry into your topic, letting the facts *lead* you to answers.

As you do research for your paper, you will probably find information and facts that challenge your thesis. That's not a bad thing. Your original thesis was only your best guess when you began your research. Now that you know more about your topic, you should be willing to modify or even completely change your thesis based on the research you've conducted and your critical analysis of those secondary sources.

FIGURE 10.3
Outlining a Methodology

A concept map can easily be turned into an outline like the one shown here. List your major steps and then arrange the minor steps beneath them.

Research Question: Why Do Stressed Out People Eat So Much Fast Food?

Major Step 1: Search for Online Sources

- Review hospital websites for information about fast food
- Look on *WebMD* and other medical websites
- Find documentaries about fast food at library or through Netflix
- Search fast food companies' websites for nutrition information

Major Step 2: Find Print Sources

- Visit the Student Health Centre to collect pamphlets on stress and diet
- Use *Readers' Guide* to find articles in health magazines
- Find articles in medical journals at library
- Check out nutrition and health textbooks in library
- Go to bookstore to browse books that discuss stress and food

Major Step 3: Do Empirical Research

- Interview nutritionist here on campus
- Create survey for university students
- Observe stressed people at the Student Union
- Interview spokesperson for McDonald's, Taco Bell, or Tim Hortons

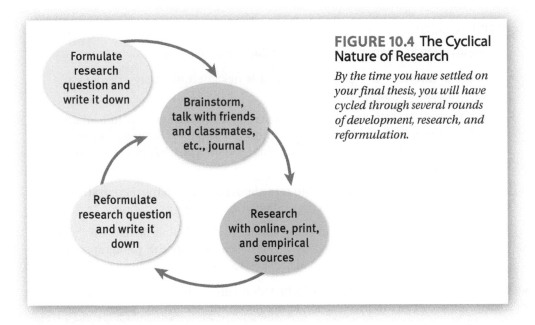

FIGURE 10.4 **The Cyclical Nature of Research**

By the time you have settled on your final thesis, you will have cycled through several rounds of development, research, and reformulation.

Formulate research question and write it down

Brainstorm, talk with friends and classmates, etc., journal

Reformulate research question and write it down

Research with online, print, and empirical sources

Good research is a cyclical process (Figure 10.4). You should keep returning to your thesis to see if you have changed your mind about how you will answer your research question. Your ideas will evolve as you figure things out. Eventually, as you finish doing your research, your thesis will solidify and become the main point of your paper. At that point, you can start drafting your paper with confidence.

Organizing and Drafting Your Research Paper

After collecting your sources, you might feel a little overwhelmed by the amount of information available on your topic. How will you fit all these facts into your paper and still write something worth reading? Don't panic. It's not that difficult.

When you begin the drafting phase, your first task is to figure out which issues you want to cover and how you want to organize your research paper. The models in the At-a-Glance at the beginning of this chapter should give you a few ideas about how you might organize your paper.

Abstract

Abstracts, if required by your discipline, tend to be only one paragraph, devoting a sentence or two to each section of the research paper. The abstract should be written after you have finished drafting the rest of the paper.

Introduction

An introduction in a paper will typically include the following sections:

Point of interest. The point of interest is designed to engage readers and draw them into your paper.

Brief summary of the topic. The summary provides background information to help the reader understand the context of the paper. Sometimes a quote or paraphrase from a scholarly source (as seen in "The CNN Effect") is added to this section.

Explanation of why readers should care about the topic. This section stresses the importance of the topic to the audience and society as a whole.

Thesis statement. The introduction should include a well-developed thesis statement, usually positioned as the last sentence in the paragraph. See Chapter 21 for more discussion of the thesis statement.

These sections can be included in just about any order, and they are not all necessary. Minimally, your introduction should tell your readers the paper's topic, purpose, and main point.

The Body

The body of your research paper can be organized in a variety of ways. It will often begin with a review of existing literature on your topic. Here are three common ways to organize the remainder of your draft:

Issue. Divide your information into two to five major issues that you want to discuss in your research paper. Specifically, pay attention to issues on which people tend to disagree or major points that people tend to discuss when they consider a topic.

Chronology. Divide your information into two to five historical time periods (e.g., 1980s, 1990s, 2000s; or before the event, start of the event, during the event, end of the event, aftermath of the event). Then, arrange your information by sorting out what happened in each of those time periods.

Argumentation. Divide your information into three categories: Review of the facts; discussion of how others, especially people with opposing views, interpret the facts; discussion of how you and people who agree with you interpret the facts.

Once you have decided on an overall strategy (as described above), the body of your research paper will probably have two to five major sections. These major sections will then have several paragraphs each. Each section in your research paper can follow a variety of patterns. The following organizational strategies can be helpful for organizing the material in each section:

Description. Divide something into its major parts and describe them separately.

Cause and effect. Explain the causes of a problem and the effects.

Classification. Divide something into major and minor categories.

Comparison and contrast. Identify similarities and differences between two things.

Chapter 17, "Developing Paragraphs and Sections," offers other ideas about how to organize information in sections.

Using and Citing Your Sources. While drafting the body of your research paper, you need to carefully quote and thoroughly cite your sources. Chapter 23, "Quoting, Paraphrasing, and Citing Sources," will help you use your sources properly. Here is a quick review on citing sources:

In-text parenthetical citations. Each time you take an idea or quote from a text, you need to use an in-text citation to signal where it came from. In-text MLA citations will usually include the author's last name and the page number, for example (Author 34). In-text APA citations will usually include the author's last name, the year published, and a page number, for example (Author, 20XX, p. 43).

Quotations. Using quotes from experts is encouraged in research papers. Brief quotations can appear within a sentence and are highlighted with quotation marks. Longer quotations (more than four lines of text for MLA and more than forty words for APA) should be put into block quotes that are indented.

Paraphrasing and summarizing. You can also paraphrase or summarize your sources. When paraphrasing, you should follow the structure of the source, putting the ideas or information in your own words. When summarizing, you should organize the information from most important to least important, using your own words.

Refer to Chapter 23 for more help with using your sources. In a research paper, it's critical that you properly quote, paraphrase, and cite your sources.

Conclusion

The conclusion of your paper should be brief. A research paper's conclusion typically makes all or some of the following moves:

Restate your thesis. One more time, state the paper's overall main point or thesis.

Re-emphasize the importance of the topic. Explain briefly why your readers should care about this topic and take action. A discussion of the implications of the issues discussed in the paper is often included here.

Look to the future. Research papers often end with a few sentences that describe what will happen in the near and distant future.

Your conclusion should be brief, often only one paragraph in length. Your goal is to leave your readers with a clear sense of what you discovered and what should be done about it.

References or Works Cited

Provide bibliographic information for any sources you have cited. For APA style, they should be listed under the title "References." For MLA style, call them "Works Cited." Turn to Chapters 24 and 25 for help with your references.

Choosing an Appropriate Style

Expository research papers tend to be written in the plain style, while argumentative research papers use both plain and persuasive styles. The plain style is especially helpful for explaining the facts about your topic and discussing what happened. The persuasive style should be used when you are trying to influence readers to accept your point of view. See Chapter 13 for more discussion of style and Chapter 19 for tips on persuasion.

Strike an Objective, Academic Tone. Write efficiently and authoritatively and focus on presenting information to your readers as clearly as possible. You should let the information be the main attraction of the paper, not you. Generally, you will avoid using first person in a research paper.

Use Top-Down Paragraphs. Consistently put each paragraph's main claim or statement in the first or second sentence of the paragraph (i.e., the topic sentence). Then use the remainder of the paragraph to prove or support that claim or statement. Putting topic sentences at the top of each paragraph will help your readers locate the most important information.

Use Concise Sentences. Your sentences should be concise and straightforward. In each sentence, move your subject (i.e., what the sentence is about) to an early position, and use active verbs where possible. Look for ways to minimize your use of excessive prepositional phrases.

Minimize Passive Voice as Much as Possible. Passive voice is common in research papers (e.g., "These interpretations are reinforced by the existing literature."). However, active voice is often stronger and easier to read, so you should look for places where you can turn passive sentences into active sentences. Active voice will help your readers understand who or what did the action (e.g., "The existing literature confirms these interpretations.").

Reduce Nominalizations. Because research papers are sometimes technical, they may overuse nominalizations, which can cloud the meaning of sentences. A nominalization happens when the action in the sentence appears as a noun rather than a verb. *Hint:* Look for words that end in "-tion."

Nominalization: This paper offers a presentation of the existing literature on the CNN effect.

Revised: This paper presents an overview of the existing literature on the CNN effect.

Nominalizations make your writing less clear because they hide the action in a sentence. If you move the action into the sentence's verb, your meaning will be much clearer to your readers.

Define Jargon and Other Technical Terms. In research papers jargon words and technical terms are common and often unavoidable. When you use a jargon word or a technical term for the first time, give your readers a sentence definition or parenthetical definition to clarify its meaning.

Sentence Definition: Low-density lipoprotein cholesterol (LDL) is a waxy substance that causes fat to build up in the walls of larger arteries.

Parenthetical Definition: The extreme amount of salt in most fast food can cause hypertension, a condition in which a person's blood pressure rises to an abnormally high level and potentially does damage to the heart.

In moderation, jargon and technical terms are fine. Just define these words so your readers understand what you are talking about.

In Chapter 13, "Choosing a Style," you can find additional helpful advice about how to write clearly and plainly. Plain style will make your research paper sound authoritative and objective.

Applying the Genre: The Annotated Bibliography

Your professor may ask you to prepare an *annotated* bibliography that summarizes and evaluates the sources you collected for your research paper. An annotated bibliography is an alphabetical list of your sources that briefly summarizes and sometimes assesses how each will be useful in your research paper. See Figure 10.5 for an example of an annotated bibliography.

An annotated bibliography is a great way to collect and better understand the print and electronic sources on your topic. It is a good way to sort out the facts of a topic and identify the larger arguments and trends that influence your topic. Here are the key steps in writing an annotated bibliography:

Collect the Required Number of Sources. Begin by collecting the required number of sources and selecting those which are most relevant to your research. Be sure to obtain complete and correct bibliographic information on your sources.

Annotated Bibliography
Sultan Ullah, Applied Science 176

Moniz, E. (2011). Why we still need nuclear power. *Foreign Affairs, 90*(6), 83–94.

    In this peer-reviewed article, Ernest Moniz describes how the Fukushima power plant failure contributed to people's skepticism over whether nuclear energy can be considered a safe energy source. Moniz points out the benefits of using nuclear energy and compares nuclear energy to other energy sources such as wind, solar, and hydro. The author also examines the costs of nuclear energy use, which include safety hazards, high maintenance fees, and waste disposal. The author outlines each negative aspect and notes how these negatives were highlighted by the public after the disaster at Fukushima. Munoz gives concise details about why the Fukushima power plant failed, as well as lessons that can be learned from this disaster about the safety of future power plants.

    This is a useful article because it highlights the impact of Fukushima, not only in Japan, but around the world. This article will be helpful for my own project because it details the societal importance of the incident at Fukushima and how the disaster changed the way society views nuclear energy.

Wakeford, R. (2011). And now, Fukushima. *Journal of Radiological Protection, 31*(2), 167–176. doi:10.1088/0952-4746/31/2/E02

    This article describes in detail the events that occurred before and during the disaster at Fukushima and the results of the disaster. The operations of the power plant are also detailed. The author explains exactly how the two natural disasters occurred that resulted in the failure of the power plant. The effects of both the tsunami and earthquake on the temperature and pressure of the reactors inside the power plant, which ultimately led to the hydrogen explosion, are analyzed. The radiation emitted from the disaster as well as the long term effects on the environment are considered.

    Many details of the Fukushima disaster are discussed in this article and will be useful in writing a technical description of the failure. As well, the factors that caused the eventual explosion and the reasons for the failure are outlined in detail. In short, this article provides important technical information and background that will be helpful for the research paper I am writing.

Wheeler, B. (2011). Understanding Fukushima. *Power Engineering, 115*(8), 12. Retrieved from http://ezpro xy.library.ubc.ca/login?url=http://search productrquest.com/docview/887542601?a

    This article includes a brief description of what happened at Fukushima; however, its great usefulness comes from the expert witnesses who are interviewed. The president of the American Nuclear Society, a representative of the Tokyo Institute of Technology, and the commissioner of the Japan Atomic Energy Commission give their explanations and points of view concerning this disaster. The United States, unlike other countries, did not stop nuclear power after the disaster. Instead the US made improvements to their regulations on nuclear power plants.

    This article is important because the reactions and comments about the Fukushima disaster from many professionals can be analyzed. Relevant quotes can be taken from this article and cited to further understand the failure at Fukushima and the reactions to it.

Levendis, J., Block, W., & Morrel, J. (2006). Nuclear power. *Journal of Business Ethics, 67*(1), 37–49. doi:10.1007/s10551-006-9003-y

    This article describes the history and the processes of nuclear energy. Nuclear power affects both government and industry. Statistics outlining the enormous cost that comes with the use of nuclear power are given in this article. The authors also outline the many regulations that have been added to the use of nuclear energy throughout the years in order to decrease the risks associated with it. The problem of waste is also addressed, along with the impact of nuclear power on industry.

    This article will be helpful because it provides background information about nuclear energy and nuclear power plants, and about the effect nuclear power has on government and business. An overview of the history of nuclear energy can give readers a better idea of what occurred at Fukushima and help them to understand the analysis of the Fukushima failure.

Margin annotations:

- APA citation style is used.
- The writer gives a summary of the article he is evaluating.
- Writer gives his positive evaluation of the piece as an acceptable research article for informing his paper.
- Note the use of passive sentences in this applied science writing.
- Writer discusses the specific uses for this article.
- Writer explains the additional perspectives that this article provides, making it an important complement to the previous research.
- The writer begins to identify recurring issues surrounding the use of nuclear power.
- The uses for this article are clearly identified.

FIGURE 10.5 An Annotated Bibliography

In this annotated bibliography, the student writer has used APA documentation to list his sources. Each source is briefly summarized and related to the student's research project on nuclear power.

Read the Sources Carefully and Make Marginal Notes. This step is an important preparation for the brief summaries that will be the first component of your annotated bibliography. Draft the summary notes into complete sentences and consult Chapter 4 on writing a summary.

Assess the Information in Each Source. What criteria will you use for assessing the utility and applicability of each source? How does each source relate to the others you assess? Draft two to three sentences assessing the source and its place in your research.

Finalize the Citations and Edit Your Annotations. Each entry in an annotated bibliography should begin with a complete reference in the appropriate style. Then take a few minutes to edit your annotation for a concise and formal academic tone.

Designing Your Research Paper

Research papers usually aren't flashy documents, but that doesn't mean they should look unattractive and be difficult to read. Your paper should be presented in a neat and clear manner. Focus on your audience and always pay attention to your professor's preferences for formatting (often professors will include acceptable formats on the assignment guideline sheet).

Use an Academically Acceptable Format. At university, your professors will generally want you to use the academic style acceptable to your discipline. Usually that will be either MLA or APA style. Regardless of which style you use, clear headings to highlight key sections and important information are essential.

Include a Cover Page. A cover page can add a professional touch to your research paper. Your cover page should include the title of your paper, your name and student identification number, your professor's name, the name and number of the course, and the date the research paper was submitted. Academic research papers generally do not include images on the cover page.

Use Meaningful Headings. Your paper's headings should give readers a clear idea about what is in each section of the paper. You don't need to use *Literature Review, Analysis, Discussion,* and *Conclusion* as headings. Instead, you can give readers a sense of what they will find in each section with descriptive and interesting headings:

Media pressure and intervention in Iraq in 1991

Media influence and intervention in Somalia and the Sudan

Use Page Numbers and a Header or Footer. All multi-page documents should have page numbers, but this guideline is especially true with research papers. Due to their length, research papers need page numbers to make them easier to discuss. You might also consider adding a header or footer with your name and student identification number.

Whatever you do, keep your paragraphs brief and to the point and use headings to give your readers access points into the text. Designing a research paper does not take long, and your readers will appreciate a document that is attractive and easy to use.

Revising and Editing Your Research Paper

Because research papers tend to be large documents, the revising and editing phase is critical to improving your paper's quality. Here are some guidelines that will help you revise and edit your document:

Clarify the Purpose of the Paper. In your introduction, make sure your thesis statement is stated clearly and prominently. Does this statement clearly identify the paper's main point and position? Now that you are finished drafting, would it be possible to state your thesis in an even clearer, more direct way? Did your thesis evolve while you were drafting your paper? If so, rewrite your thesis to reflect what your paper actually achieves.

Look for Gaps in Content. Search out places where you are making any unsupported statements or claims. Each major point needs to be backed up with some evidence that you have drawn from online, print, or empirical sources. If you find a gap in your support, look in your notes for evidence to fill that gap. If you don't have any evidence, you need to do more research or you will have to remove that statement or claim.

Find Nonessential Information That Can Be Cut. Include only need-to-know information and locate any places where your paper goes off topic. Keep in mind that you probably found more information than you need. Not all of that material needs to go into your paper. So slash any information that does not help you support or prove your major points in the paper.

Pay Special Attention to Your Paper's Paragraphs. Strong paragraphs are essential in a research paper because they help people scan and read quickly (research papers are rarely read for enjoyment). Spend some extra time making sure you use good topic sentences early in your paragraphs. Then improve the readability of your paragraphs by weaving their sentences together better.

Proofread Carefully. Research papers are typically large, complex documents, so there are plenty of opportunities for typos, garbled sentences, spelling mistakes, and grammatical errors. Proofread carefully. Read your paper out loud to help you find errors and weak sentences. Ask your friends to read your paper carefully. Proofreading is especially important because errors in your paper will signal shoddy research to your readers. If they find errors, they will be less likely to trust your findings.

Yes, time is short when you reach the revision and editing phase. The deadline is here. But don't skimp on revising and editing your paper. Your hard work doing research, drafting, and designing will be undermined if your paper isn't thoroughly revised.

Here are some quick strategies to get you going on that research paper.

DEVELOP Your Research Question and Thesis Statement

Write down an interesting research question about your topic—a question you would like to answer with some research. Then turn that question into a thesis statement (your best guess about how that research question will be answered).

FIND Out What You Already Know

Use prewriting tools to get your ideas out on the screen or a piece of paper. Star or highlight your best ideas. Then share your ideas with your friends and classmates.

FIND Out What Others Know

Develop a research plan that uses a combination of online, print, and empirical sources to find information. Interview experts on campus to find out more.

REVISIT Your Thesis Statement

After you have done a good amount of research, look at your thesis again. Does it need to be modified or refined?

ORGANIZE and Draft Your Research Paper

A variety of organizations are available for your research paper. They almost always include an introduction and conclusion. The body should be organized in a way that allows you to present your research in a logical manner.

CHOOSE an Appropriate Style

Research papers are almost always written in plain style, because this style sounds objective and authoritative. Use plain sentences and top-down paragraphs with solid topic sentences. The best style is one that sounds neutral and objective. Add persuasive elements if you have been asked to argue.

DESIGN the Document

Create an academically acceptable and accessible page layout. Use active headings to help readers locate important information.

REVISE and Edit

Revise headings so they clearly state the points you want to make. Pay special attention to your paragraphs, especially topic sentences. Also, your research paper needs to be error-free if you want your readers to take your work seriously.

The CNN Effect Revisited

PIERS ROBINSON

Piers Robinson is an internationally renowned researcher in the areas of communications, media, and international politics. In this research paper, he gives an overview of previous studies on the CNN Effect, a popular debate in the 1990s. Robinson goes on to argue that post 9/11 the ideology of the "war on terror" has muted the freedom of the press and resulted in a mainstream media that mimics government rhetoric.

For policy-makers and academics, the 1990s appeared to be an era of media empowerment. The ending of the Cold War anti-communist consensus between journalists and policy-makers and the spread of real-time news reporting technology seemed to disrupt traditional patterns of media deference to foreign policy elites and expand the power of the media. Interventions during humanitarian crises in northern Iraq 1991, Somalia 1992, Bosnia 1995, and Kosovo 1999, often preceded and accompanied by emotive media attention to human suffering, confirmed to some the thesis that media was driving foreign policy formulation.

> Introduction sets the stage for the rest of the paper, giving a historical overview.

CNN, with its global reach, 24-hour news cycle, and foreign affairs agenda, came to encapsulate the idea of a media-driven foreign policy, creating the so-called "CNN effect." In the wake of 9/11 and the Bush administration's "war on terror," however, the geopolitical landscape has been dramatically transformed. U.S. foreign policy has come to be dominated by the perceived threat of global terrorism, rogue states, and the proliferation of weapons of mass destruction (WMDs). In this essay I discuss the impact of both 9/11 and the subsequent shifts in U.S. foreign policy upon the CNN effect thesis. I start by assessing the extent to which foreign policy was indeed driven by the CNN effect during the 1990s. I then discuss how developments since 9/11, specifically the "war on terror," a "humanitarian war" discourse inherited from the 1990s, and strengthened media management by government, have undermined the CNN effect and ushered in a new era of media deference to government reminiscent of the Cold War era.

> Author gives an overview of the organization of the paper.

> Paragraph ends with thesis statement.

The 1990s and Media-Inspired Humanitarianism?

> Headings are used to organize points of paper.

Controversy has always surrounded the validity and scope of the CNN effect (for a thorough review of the literature see Gilboa, 2005). But a number of studies have found evidence for the effect in decisions to use force during humanitarian crises. For example, both Nik Gowing (1994) and Royce Ammon (2001) argued that the U.S. intervention in northern Iraq 1991 during the Kurdish crisis was in part a consequence of the CNN effect. My own research (Robinson, 2002) found evidence of media influence during decisions both to threaten and to use force during the 1992–1995 war in Bosnia.

A frequently cited cause of the CNN effect was policy uncertainty. Many scholars (Entman, 2004; Gowing, 1994; Minear, Scott, & Weiss, 1997; Robinson, 2002;

Shaw, 1996, Strobel, 1997) agree that as policy certainty decreases, news media influence increases and that, conversely, as policy becomes more certain, the influence of news media coverage is reduced. During the 1990s policy uncertainty manifested itself at the micro-level, when shocking images from conflicts such as Bosnia caught policy-makers off-guard or in a state of panic (see in particular Gowing, 1994). At the macro-level, U.S. foreign policy was characterised by a loss of direction following the end of the Cold War (Shaw, 1996).

At the same time, most researchers agreed that initial estimates of the CNN [5] effect overstated its importance (Gowing, 1994; Robinson, 2002). This was, at least in part, because focus on media tended to obscure other, more self-interested, motivations underpinning Western humanitarianism. For example, Livingston (1997) pointed out that the intervention in northern Iraq was driven in part by geo-strategic concerns over Kurdish refugees "threatening" the interests of Turkey, a key U.S. ally. Moreover, the selective nature of media-inspired humanitarianism was highlighted by the dismal performance of the international community when it withdrew UN forces during the 1994 genocide in Rwanda, where up to one million civilians were subsequently murdered. This "non-response" was accompanied by an equally dismal performance on the part of Western media who presented the genocide as a "cease-fire breakdown" and simply another round of unstoppable tribal blood-letting (Livingston & Eachus 1999; Myers, Klak, & Koehl, 1996; Robinson, 2002). These events stood in stark contrast to optimistic debates surrounding the power of media to promote humanitarian concern amongst Western foreign policy elites and publics.

Placing these sceptical points to one side, the idea of humanitarian intervention did appear to gain ground among foreign policy elites during the course of the 1990s. In the U.S., early realist concerns over the loss of elite control over foreign policy gave way to a foreign policy community more amenable to humanitarian intervention. In part, this reflected the internationalist and Wilsonian temperament of many U.S. Democrats. In the U.K., the Labour government proclaimed the arrival of an "ethical foreign policy" and, in his 1999 speech to the Economic Club of Chicago, British Prime Minister Tony Blair publicly advocated humanitarian intervention, albeit in circumstances where the national interest would also be served. By 1999, the NATO air campaign against Serbia during the Kosovo crisis appeared to be the culmination of a decade in which humanitarian intervention had become firmly established on both media and foreign policy agendas.[1] In 2000, UN Secretary General Kofi Annan called on the international community to forge a consensus regarding when and how the "right of humanitarian intervention" should be exercised and, in response, the Canadian government instigated the International Commission on Intervention and State Sovereignty (ICISS).

9/11 and the Death of the CNN Effect?

The events of 9/11, however, marked a major turning point for the direction of U.S. foreign policy as President Bush declared a "war on terrorism" and fought two wars in quick succession against Afghanistan and Iraq. With respect to the CNN effect thesis, three developments have occurred, all of which tend to reduce the likelihood of its occurrence.

Overview of existing literature and research with respect to the CNN effect.

Author points to a flaw in early research—that the CNN effect was actually overstated.

Author outlines humanitarian intervention in both the media and in foreign policy.

Clearly indicates the organization of this section around three main developments.

First and foremost, the "war on terror" has pushed humanitarian concerns down, if not off altogether, the U.S. foreign policy agenda. Indeed, former advisor to the British government David Clark argued in 2003 that the Iraq war has "wrecked the case for humanitarian wars" by making it unlikely an international consensus regarding humanitarian intervention could be achieved due to the mistrust caused by U.S. unilateralism. Certainly, the question of humanitarian intervention has been subservient to U.S. objectives aimed at containing and eliminating the al-Qaeda network.

First point explained.

More important is the impact of policy certainty within the current U.S. administration. If the 1990s were marked by a lack of policy certainty, events since 9/11 have witnessed a U.S. administration determinedly promoting and pursuing a foreign policy underpinned by the idea of a "war on terror." In this situation of policy certainty, the Bush administration has sought to lead both media and public opinion. Indeed, Bush's speechwriter Michael Gerson believed 9/11 provided the Bush administration with a "plastic, teachable moment" (Woodward, 2004, p. 84).

10   Not only does this mean that the CNN effect is unlikely to occur, but also that media coverage has become far more deferential and constrained, thereby reducing the chances of an adversarial or oppositional media that might influence policy. Certainly, the "war on terror" frame provides journalists with a template with which to understand global events and policy-makers with a powerful rhetorical tool with which to justify a more aggressive and interventionist foreign policy agenda (Domke, 2004; Jackson, 2005).

For example, David Domke's recent work, *God Willing? Political Fundamentalism in the White House, The War on Terror and the Echoing Press*, provides empirical support for the existence of the ideological constraints now active in U.S. journalism. He argues that the Bush administration imposed a hegemonic discourse on the American public sphere between September 2001 and the end of "major combat operations" in Iraq in 2003. The central feature of this discourse was its fundamentalist nature, created by a conjunction of "nation-challenging crisis," religiously conservative political leadership skilled in strategic communication, and media tending to reproduce the views of the leadership. According to Domke, the Bush administration's fundamentalism is characterised by binary discourses opposing good and evil and security and peril (see also Jackson, 2005). Overall, it is reasonable to conclude that the "war on terror" has helped create an ideological bond between journalists and policy-makers akin to that of anti-communism during the Cold War era.

A second reason for the fading of any CNN effect: In addition to the "war on terror" framework, the humanitarian war discourse of the 1990s has functioned as a further legitimating device employed by both British and U.S. political elites when justifying military action in Afghanistan and Iraq. In particular, the British Prime Minister Tony Blair advocated war against Iraq on grounds both of national security due to a perceived threat from WMD and of the claim that regime change could be justified in humanitarian terms in order to save the Iraqi people from Saddam Hussein. Importantly, however, as David Clark (2003) pointed out, such a claim is spurious because the situation in Iraq did not meet the criteria by which humanitarian war is justified—i.e., large-scale human suffering that cannot be averted by other means (for more on humanitarian war and intervention see Ramsbotham & Woodhouse, 1996). As has recently been disclosed, the British Attorney General Lord Goldsmith also made clear that war in Iraq could not be justified in humanitarian terms.

Second point explained.

In short, if the 1990s witnessed a more influential media that helped persuade policy-makers to engage in humanitarian intervention, post 9/11 has seen the concept of humanitarian intervention used as a policy tool that Western leaders employ in order to justify interventions driven by national interest and not altruistic concern for the humanitarian needs of 'other' people.

The third development mitigating the CNN effect concerns the accelerated attempts by government to manage the information environment. Since the Kosovo conflict, U.S. and U.K. military operations have been accompanied by a transnational media management operation that seeks to co-ordinate national information activities. These techniques explicitly draw on "war room" models developed during domestic election campaigns (Brown, 2002) and use publicity rather than "censorship" to shape coverage.

Taking advantage of the limited capacity of news agendas, political administrations encourage coverage of particular issues through the provision of information and access. These techniques are explicitly designed to influence media agendas by promoting coverage of some issues over others and to influence the framing of stories in ways that support official policy. For example, during the 2003 Iraq war, key themes promoted by the coalition included frequent reiteration of the official justifications for war, including the threat of WMD, the argument for regime change, and the broader "war on terror" narrative. In addition, the coalition sought to promote its agenda on a daily basis by highlighting humanitarian activities (such as the delivery of drinking water), identifying potential WMD sites uncovered by advancing coalition forces, and stressing the past brutality of Saddam's regime. The coalition also sought to minimise the impact of bad news, involving civilian casualties and military setbacks, by accenting such Iraqi tactics as the use of human shields while emphasising the precision targeting employed by coalition forces and promoting upbeat prognoses regarding the likelihood of rapid victory.[2]

Overall, it appears that, at least during the 2003 Iraq war, these attempts at media management were generally quite successful. For example, a recent, comprehensive study by Sean Adey, Steve Livingston, and Maeve Herbert (2005) concluded that "none of the networks ran many stories about or pictures of U.S. or civilian casualties. FNC and CNN's *Lou Dobbs Show* ran virtually none. In addition, all of the American networks largely ignored any antiwar sentiment" (p. 17).

Conclusion

Viewed from the post-9/11 perspective, the CNN effect debate of the 1990s and associated interventions during humanitarian crises appear as an aberration, during an era in which greater media autonomy and a loss of policy direction following the Cold War led to greater potential for media to shape politics. Today, there are strong grounds for concluding that the threat of communism, which helped create an ideological bond between journalists and policy-makers during the Cold War, has been replaced by the "war on terror," pursued with determination by the Bush administration and forging a new consensus between journalists and policy-making elites.

In addition, the discourse of humanitarian warfare and contemporary approaches to media management have strengthened the ability of foreign policy elites to influence media. In these circumstances of policy certainty, debate within mainstream media is likely to remain bounded within the terms set by the U.S.

Marginal notes:

Third point explained.

Author restates the thesis at the start of the conclusion.

Sums up the main points of the paper.

government and, moreover, the chance of it having an impact upon the substance of U.S. foreign policy formulation is remote. Put simply, the conditions under which the CNN effect occurred during the 1990s are not present at this point in time.

The danger for U.S. journalism in these circumstances is that, by following and replicating elite debate, it ends up helping manufacture consent (Herman & Chomsky, 1988) for the Bush administration's "war on terror." Free and open discussion about the fundamentals of U.S. foreign policy, terrorism in all its forms, and the wisdom of different approaches to dealing with terrorism is unlikely to surface widely in mainstream media debate. The dominant foreign affairs issue will be derived from the administration: the perceived threat from al-Qaeda and the need for the U.S. to respond through various forms of military action. For political alternatives and fresh perspectives, U.S. citizens will have to look beyond mainstream media.

Paper ends with a call to action.

Notes

1. In fact, the air campaign against Serbia was intended as an act of coercive diplomacy that had the consequence of exacerbating a humanitarian crisis, even though it was promoted and justified to Western publics as a humanitarian war (for further details see Robinson, 2002).
2. Based on initial research for a project funded by the Economic and Social Research Council (ESRC) entitled *Media Wars: News Media Performance and Media Management During the 2003 Iraq War* (award reference RES-000-23-0551).

References

Adey, S., Livingston, S., & Herbert, M. (2005). Embedding the truth: A cross cultural analysis of objectivity and television coverage of the Iraq War. *Press/Politics, 10,* 3–21.

Ammon, R. (2001). *Global television and the shaping of world politics: CNN, telediplomacy, and foreign policy.* Jefferson, North Carolina: McFarland and Company.

Brown, R. (2002). The US and the politics of perception management. *Journal of Information Warfare, I,* 40–50.

Clark, D. (2003, August 11). Iraq has wrecked our case for humanitarian wars. *The Guardian,* p. 20.

Domke, D. (2004). *God willing? Political fundamentalism in the White House, the War on Terror and the echoing press.* London: Pluto Press.

Entman, R. M. (2004). *Projections of power: Framing news, public opinion and U.S. foreign policy.* Chicago: The University of Chicago Press.

Gilboa, E. (2005). The CNN effect: The search for a communication theory of international relations. *Political Communication, 22,* 27–44.

Gowing, N. (1994). *Real-time coverage of armed conflicts and diplomatic crises: Does it pressure or distort foreign policy decisions?* (Harvard working paper). Cambridge, MA: The Joan Shorenstein Barone Center on the Press, Politics, and Public Policy at Harvard University.

Herman, E., & Chomsky, N. (1988). *Manufacturing Consent: The Political Economy of the Mass Media.* New York: Pantheon.

Jackson, R. (2005). *Writing terrorism.* Manchester, UK: Manchester University Press.

Livingston, S. (1997). *Clarifying the CNN effect: An examination of media effects according to type of military intervention* (Research paper R-18). Cambridge, MA:

The Joan Shorenstein Barone Center on the Press, Politics, and Public Policy at Harvard University.

Livingston, S., & Eachus, T. (1999). US coverage of Rwanda. In H. Adelman & A. Suhrke (Eds.), *The path of a genocide* (pp. 122–156). Uppsala: Nordic Institute of Africa Studies.

Minear, L., Scott, C., & Weiss, R. (1997). *The news media, civil wars and humanitarian action*. Boulder, CO, and London: Lynne Rienner.

Myers, G., Klak, T., & Koehl, T. (1996). The inscription of difference: News coverage of the conflicts in Rwanda and Bosnia. *Political Geography*, 15, 21–46.

Ramsbotham, O., & Woodhouse, T. (1996). *Humanitarian intervention in contemporary conflict*. Cambridge, UK: Policy Press and Blackwell.

Robinson, P. (2002). *The CNN effect: The myth of news, foreign policy and intervention*. London and New York: Routledge.

Shaw, M. (1996). *Civil society and media in global crises*. London: St Martin's Press.

Strobel, W. (1997). *Late breaking foreign policy*. Washington, DC: United States Institute of Peace.

Woodward, B. (2004). *Plan of attack*. London and New York: Pocket Books.

A CLOSER LOOK AT
The CNN Effect Revisited

1. The background section of this paper is rather brief (Robinson directs students to a literature review paper on the CNN effect for a detailed overview of the background of this phenomenon). Nevertheless, he does give a brief overview of the literature on the CNN effect. How does Robinson's discussion of the research give an overview of the background of the theory? How does this section provide a backdrop to Robinson's thesis?

2. How does Robinson support this thesis throughout the paper? Find four specific examples (not just main points) he uses to support his main argument. Are these examples successful at convincing you, the reader, of the validity of Robinson's thesis?

IDEAS FOR
Writing

1. How do you feel about the influence of the government on mainstream media? Write a position paper in which you argue for or against the use of mainstream media for government agendas.

Boys and Violence: A Gender-Informed Analysis

JUNE FEDER, RONALD F. LEVANT, AND JAMES DEAN

This research paper offers a discussion of the masculine socialization that occurs in Western society and its effect on boys' engagement in violent acts. The authors review existing literature along with the factors that influence boys' socialization. Consult the abstract that precedes the paper as an example of that feature and for a fuller summary of the article.

This article discusses the phenomenon of youth violence from a psychology of gender perspective. Although other factors are discussed—including gun availability, violence-related media influence, family and caretaker factors, and effects of teasing and bullying—the intention is to highlight new thinking on the potential relationship between boys' traditional masculine socialization experiences and violence. In this new perspective, traditional masculine socialization estranges and isolates many boys from their genuine inner lives and vital connections to others, which is theorized to heighten their risk of engaging in acts of violence. The authors identify school and community programs that may be helpful in counteracting damaging socialization experiences and supporting boys' healthier emotional and psychological development. Finally, the article discusses approaches that psychologists and other mental health professionals can use to help address this vital issue.

> This paper includes an abstract. Note how it concisely summarizes the main points of the article.

Despite data showing reductions in violent crime nationally, youth violence remains a serious problem. Headline stories over the last decade have depicted a spate of horrific acts in numerous locales: Littleton, Jonesboro, Pearl River, Paducah, Springfield, and Columbine. Data from studies about violence in schools between 1994 and 1999 indicate that 172 students ages 5 to 18 were killed on or near school grounds or at school-related activities (Anderson et al., 2001). More recent events have again brought attention to this tragic and disturbing phenomenon. On March 21, 2005, 16-year-old Jeff Weise from Minnesota erupted in a spasm of devastating violence—first shooting and killing his grandfather and grandfather's companion, then entering his school on the Red Lake Indian Reservation and killing nine people, wounding seven, and ending his own life by turning the gun on himself (Davey & Wilgoren, 2005).

> Introduction begins by setting the stage for youth violence.

Overall crime statistics confirm this trend of youth violence. Data from juvenile and criminal justice sources indicate that 10% of the more than 20,000 homicides reported yearly are committed by individuals under 18 (Federal Bureau of Investigation, 1995). In 1999, juveniles accounted for 16% of all violent crime arrests, including 14% of aggravated assaults, 17% of forcible rapes, and 24% of weapons charges. In addition, the data about youths as victims are also cause for concern. In 2001, 5,486 young people ages 10 to 24 were murdered, an average of 15 each day (Centers for Disease Control and Prevention, 2004).

Data about youth suicide are equally chilling. Although there are indications that the overall suicide rate has slowly declined since 1992 (Lubell, Swahn, Crosby, & Kegler, 2004), numbers among youths remain disturbingly high. In 2001, there were 3,971 suicides of young people ages 15–25, making suicide the third leading cause of death in this age group nationwide (Anderson & Smith, 2003). Sells and Blum (as cited in Cleary, 2000) noted that among youths in the United States ages 15–19, the rate of suicide has increased 35% over the past 2 decades. The data on suicide adds significantly to the disturbing picture of escalating trends for overall youth violence. Arias, Anderson, Kung, Murphy, and Kochanek (2003) pointed out that acts of suicide and homicide together account for almost 25% of all deaths involving youths ages 10–24 in the United States. In addition, empirical and anecdotal evidence substantiate a strong link between factors leading to acts of homicide and suicide among youths. In the case of Jeff Weise, for example, newspaper accounts at the time indicated that he had been treated for depression over the previous year. On a blog to which Weise had contributed postings only a few months before the tragedy, he had written, "Right now I feel as low as I ever have. I'm starting to regret sticking around. I should have taken the razor blade express last time around" (as cited in Davey & Wilgoren, 2005, p. A18). Portner (2001), writing about the tragedy at Columbine, noted that "nearly lost in the avalanche of reaction to the massacre was the fact that the young men were also on a suicide mission. The high school seniors had meticulously planned their own deaths—down to the last bullet and explosive—for nearly a year" (p. 1).

Contributory Factors to Youth Violence

The data on youth violence—regarding both acts of destruction against others and self—are disturbing, and there has been much discussion of contributory factors. These include availability of weapons, influence of violence-infused media, teasing and bullying, family factors, and learning problems. All have been extensively documented as significant risk factors.

Availability of Weapons

Data consistently reveal pervasive gun possession nationwide. Garbarino (1999) cited surveys indicating that nearly 40% of all households in the country contain at least one gun and that firearm availability is widely regarded as an important contributing factor in youth homicide rate increases. According to data from the Bureau of Alcohol, Tobacco, and Firearms (Portner, 2001), an estimated 200 million firearms are in the hands of private citizens and, if distributed nationwide, would be enough to arm three out of four Americans. It would then follow that, despite the existence of state and federal laws banning possession of handguns by anyone under the age of 18, "many young people know that getting a firearm is no more complicated than pilfering from a closet" (Portner, 2001, p. 19). Indeed, despite a dramatic drop in violent crime throughout the mid- to late 1990s, youth gun violence has remained a significant issue. Each year, more than 20,000 children and youths under age 20 are killed or injured by firearms in the United States (Fingerhut & Christoffel, 2002).

Problems related to weapons in schools have reverberated across the nation for more than 2 decades. Brener, Lowry, and Barrios (2005) reported that in 2003, 1 in 16 high school students reported carrying a weapon to school. Adato and Genovese (1999) noted that in 1997, 7.4% of high school students indicated they were threatened by a weapon in the previous year. Brener et al. (2005) reported that in 2003, this jumped to 10%. On the other hand, Kopel's (1992) research suggests that gun deaths are more frequent among late adolescents (ages 15–20) and less so among those age 14 and younger. Although, admittedly, access to guns is only one component in the broader landscape of contributory factors, the data suggest it merits special attention.

Influence of Media

A large number of studies conducted over several decades have found that violence in the media is a significant contributor to aggressive behavior in children, adolescents, and adults (Anderson & Bushman, 2001). Children who watch television regularly and are exposed to violent acts that are constantly shown are at much greater risk of aggressive behavior. Furthermore, studies have indicated that children in the United States between the ages of 8 and 18 spend more than 40 hr a week with some form of media (Rideout, Foehr, Roberts, & Brodie, as cited in Anderson & Bushman, 2001). Toomey (1991) cited data indicating that, on the average, an American child by age 16 has viewed more than 200,000 acts of television violence.

Research conducted over the last decade has also investigated the effects of exposure to "new media"—including video games, music videos, and the Internet. These emergent modalities—constituting powerful interactive experiences—have raised serious concern about their effects because current psychological theory suggests they may have far greater impact than that of passive media (U.S. Public Health Service, 2001). Indeed, reports about Jeff Weise indicated that, whereas adults in his life were aware of his emotional travail and helped him seek treatment during the year prior to the shootings, all were apparently surprised by post-tragedy evidence of a prolific Internet life in which the young man found expression and support for stories, drawings, and interchanges that were strikingly revealing and that, in retrospect, proved frighteningly prescient (Davey & Wilgoren, 2005). Anderson and Bushman (2001) noted that the young men who perpetrated the tragedy at Columbine High School had apparently developed their own version of a violent video game that presaged the horrific events that unfolded there.

10 Although, clearly, research on the effects of media points to an array of potential outcomes, it is, nonetheless, widely agreed that exposure to violent media is a significant risk factor for violence. Indeed, Anderson et al. (2003) concluded that "the scientific debate over whether media violence increases aggression and violence is essentially over" (p. 81). However, these investigators noted that it is far from clear how to effectively reduce youths' exposure to violent media.

Parental and Caretaker Factors

Parents and caretakers influence the course of a child's development in every way, including the propensity toward violence. As Steinberg (2000) noted, "I doubt that there is an influence in the development of antisocial behavior among young people that is stronger than that of the family" (p. 31). Some of this influence is indirect and involves the impact of parental decisions that affect a child's life: where a child lives, goes to school, whether there are siblings, and so forth. Other factors stem directly from the parent/caretaker–child relationship. Harsh discipline styles, aggression in the family, and favorable attitudes toward aggression have been linked to increased aggression and violence among youths (Margolin, Youga, & Ballou, 2002). Qualitative studies by Margolin et al. (2002) substantiate the extent to which youths are influenced by aggressive and/or violent behaviors modeled in the family. Pollack (1998) noted that parental connection, that is, the degree to which a child perceives genuine parental involvement and gets adequate emotional care, can significantly impact a potential trajectory to violence. Following events at Columbine, police investigators who searched Eric Harris's room wondered how his parents could not have noticed what Eric was up to because he had made no attempt to hide his plans or preoccupations.

To provide a clinical example, a colleague of Ronald F. Levant described a recent case in which a 16-year-old boy, very bright but getting poor grades, had been engaging in an escalating pattern of vandalism against a teacher (E. Longin, personal communication, April 18, 2005). The father responded to his son's report of his behavior in a family therapy session with laughter. The therapist asked the father what he found so funny. The father replied, "My son is a great put-on, and he really got that teacher." The son's face grew dark during this interaction, clearly indicating that this was not the response he needed. Here was a boy engaging in increasingly extreme acts to get his father to step in and, in effect, say, "No, son, you are ruining your life, and I won't let you do that because I love you too much." Noting this, the therapist turned to the father and said, "You think that's funny? Let me tell you what's not funny. You went to law school, right? Do you think your son is going to go to law school?" The father replied, "Well, probably not." "Right," said the therapist. "Your son will not go to law school and have a nice career like yours because he is going to jail." Sometimes it takes powerful therapeutic interventions like this to effectively confront the psychological forces in families that support violence.

Teasing and Bullying

Just as exposure to physical violence is widely viewed as a significant factor in the perpetration of violence, there is equally compelling evidence about exposure to emotional and psychological violence. Teasing and bullying are cases in point. Garbarino (1999) noted that bullying and teasing are widespread phenomena nationwide, with one third of children in Grades 6–10 reporting experiencing serious, frequent bullying. Pollack (1998) cited a Centers for Disease Control study that indicated that 81% of students admitted to engaging in bullying and 75% said they had been victims of bullying during their teenage years. Cleary (2000) reported that one third of high school students in New York State indicated that they had been bullied during the previous year. He also noted that, in general, such students are at greater risk of suicidal and homicidal behavior. Studies of college students have found that teasing is associated with lower self-esteem and often results in difficulties in establishing intimate interpersonal relationships.

Sex and Gender

Although the factors described provide a partial framework for understanding the problem of youth violence, they do not tell the whole story. In recent years, the lens has shifted to focus on the possible influence of sex and gender on youth violence.[1] Sex seems to be a significant risk factor for violence in that much of youth violence is perpetrated by males (Garbarino, 1999). Young men are about 10 times more likely than young women to commit murder. Ninety-five percent of juvenile homicides are caused by boys. In the Surgeon General's 2001 report (U.S. Public Health Service, 2001), being male is cited as strongly linked to violence among youths ages 15–18. In a National Institute of Mental Health (2000) study on child and adolescent violence, it was noted that "from about 4 years of age on, boys are more likely than girls to engage in both aggressive and nonaggressive antisocial behavior" (p. 3).[2]

> Second major point of paper.

15   Although biological factors may play a role in boys' and men's greater propensity for violence, theorists have identified male childhood socialization experiences that are informed by traditional masculinity ideology as a potential risk factor for violence. A number of writers have hypothesized that socialization practices may predispose boys to violence (Kindlon & Thompson, 1999; Levant, 1998, 2001; Pollack, 1998, 2006). This perspective, based on a social constructionist view of masculinity, has been developed by leading members of the Society for the Psychological Study of Men and Masculinity (Division 51 of the American Psychological Association).

Clinical and empirical research conducted over the past 2 decades has suggested that the socialization of boys to conform to traditional notions of masculinity such as toughness, aggression, dominance, and the restriction of emotional expression may heighten the potential for boys to engage in violence. This is thought to occur through the emotion socialization process by which boys' sense of vulnerability is discouraged, suppressed, and punished. In contrast to girls, who are generally encouraged to express a broad range of emotions, boys "have been left in a box" (Froschl & Sprung, 2005, p. 7). Discouraged from acknowledging and showing feelings of vulnerability and emotional need, boys organize their inner lives around a "tyranny of toughness" (Kindlon & Thompson, 1999, p. 54), which predisposes them to increased aggression.

Several psychologists have discussed this process. Kindlon and Thompson (1999) pointed out that in our culture boys acquire training that "steers them away from their emotional world" (p. xix) to a model of masculinity that emphasizes toughness, stoicism, depersonalization, and dominance over others. They further noted that the requirement to adopt an ethos of manliness for handling responses to feelings of vulnerability results in a state of emotional ignorance for boys, which

---

[1] Following current conventions in the study of sex and gender, we use *sex* to refer to the biological aspects (e.g., whether one is male or female) and *gender* to refer to the behavioral and social aspects (e.g., masculinity, femininity and related constructs).

[2] We do understand that girls can be as aggressive as boys, but we are not aware of any study that finds that they are as violent as boys. Girls' aggression, popularized in media accounts as "relational aggression," is typically enacted verbally rather than physically.

may not only leave them unprepared to adequately deal with the complexities of their own inner lives but also set the stage for social, academic, and other difficulties. For example, data indicate that boys have higher rates of learning problems and increased incidence of attention deficit disorder and behavioral difficulties.

Pollack (1998, 2006) has explored the impact of social attitudes on boys' psychological development, coining the term *boy code* to refer to the gender straitjacket constraining boys from knowing and safely expressing their full range of emotions. According to Pollack, boys view this as an ideal, attempt to reach it, fall short, and suffer in substantial ways, which, in turn, may lead to violence.

Levant (1992) coined the term *normative male alexithymia* to describe the major effect of male emotional socialization informed by traditional masculinity ideology. Alexithymia refers to the inability to put emotions into words. Levant learned from his clients and research participants that they were discouraged as boys from expressing and talking about their vulnerable and caring emotions and hence did not develop a vocabulary for, nor awareness of, many of their emotions. They often had great difficulty finding words to describe their emotions, even when they were in obvious distress. Research on traditional masculinity ideology has found that the requirement to restrict emotional expression is a traditional male role norm (Levant et al., 1992). On this basis, Levant (1992, 1998) theorized that mild-to-moderate forms of alexithymia occur more frequently among men socialized under traditional masculinity ideology.

Levant (1992) reviewed the research literature in developmental psychology on the socialization of masculine emotion when developing his theory. He concluded that although boys start life with greater emotional reactivity and expressiveness than girls, they become less verbally expressive than girls at about the age of 2 years and less facially expressive by age 6. The emotional socialization process leading to this change includes influences from both parents and peers. This leads boys to suppress, channel, and tune out their vulnerable emotions; between a child's fourth and sixth birthday, mothers of boys become less able to identify emotions from their child's facial expression, compared with mothers of girls. In addition, girls' peer group interactions tend to be intimate and to focus on building and maintaining relationships, whereas boys' groups tend to focus on structured games in larger groups, direct competition, teamwork, and toughness. Finally, boys punish each other for deviations from stereotyped expectations of emotional reserve.

Levant's (1992, 1998) theory of normative male *alexithymia* has been challenged by Heesacker et al. (1999) in their research on gender-based emotional stereotyping and by Wester, Vogel, Pressly, and Heesacker (2002) in their review of the literature on sex differences in emotions. Both articles asserted that Levant's theory lacks empirical support. Heesacker et al. (1999) did so by referring to a single study on gender differences in alexithymia, and Wester et al. (2002) did so by referring to two such studies. Neither article systematically reviewed the literature on gender differences in alexithymia. In contrast, Levant et al. (2006) reviewed 32 studies of gender differences in alexithymia with nonclinical samples and found that the overwhelming majority of those studies with significant results found that males scored higher on measures of alexithymia than did females.

Levant (2001) also theorized that the early emotion socialization experiences in which boys learn to shut off their tears and fears set the stage for boys' greater propensity to engage in violence. First, boys are made to feel ashamed about experiencing vulnerable emotions, which blocks them from expressing such feelings. Because aggression is encouraged, it may become boys' only outlet. Second, paternal and peer group socialization are theorized to teach boys to actively transform their vulnerable emotions into aggression and violence.

In summary, there is a clear connection between sex and violence, with boys far more likely than girls to engage in violence, and there is empirical support for the proposition that traditional socialization in masculine gender roles results in emotional problems such as normative male alexithymia. It has been theorized that these results of gender role socialization predispose boys to engage in violence, thus accounting for the sex difference. In partial support of this, it should be noted that some measures of masculinity-related constructs have been found to be associated with hostility and violence in adult males. Levant and Richmond (in press) reported that the endorsement of traditional masculinity ideology (as measured by the Male Role Norms Inventory) was found to be associated with a range of problematic individual and relational variables, including attitudes conducive to sexual harassment and self-reports of sexual aggression. And O'Neill, Good, and Holmes (1995) reported that self-reports of gender role conflict (as measured by the Gender Role Conflict Scale-1) were found to be associated with hostile attitudes toward women and homosexuals. Obviously more research is needed. In particular, it would be important to include gender-related variables in studies of risk factors for boys' violence, which has not usually been done (e.g., gender-related factors are missing from Loeber, 2005).

What Boys Need: Implications for Practitioners

> Final major point of paper, with subsections.

Although it is important to identify and explore aspects of contributory factors, understanding alone will not suffice. Ways to address the problem also need to be considered. Although we discuss in this article a range of factors linked to increased risk of youth violence—including access to weapons, influence of media, parental influence, and exposure to teasing and bullying—our primary goal is to shed some light on the role of gender. In particular, we have reviewed some of the current thinking on how traditional masculine socialization experiences impact boys' emotional functioning in ways that may predispose them to increased risk of aggression and violence. We now need to consider how to intervene to help boys overcome the limitations of such socialization, take off their gender straitjackets, and understand and feel comfortable in seeking support for their emotional needs. To effect change of this magnitude will require the combined effort of policy makers, communities, schools, families, and professionals. In this section we highlight promising new programs in the areas of early intervention; the involvement of fathers, mentors, and adults; the role of schools; and the approaches and techniques psychologists should consider.

Early Intervention

25 The literature has highlighted the value of early intervention experiences in helping boys develop skills and capabilities to manage their emotional lives in healthy, nonaggressive ways. Violence prevention programs have emphasized teaching

specific skills and encouraging development of a range of emotional capacities. Licurse (2003) reported that her Peace-It-Together program for teens gives them skills for developing peaceful relationships with peers. In a 6-week curriculum module that focuses on role plays and simulated dating scenarios, students learn to tackle interpersonal difficulties in nonabusive, supportive ways. Following a wave of violence in Ontario schools, the Canadian government launched a Safe Schools initiative that included expansion of an earlier successful program called Roots of Empathy (Weir, 2005). Elementary schoolchildren were assigned to neighborhood families with babies and provided with instruction in human development, nurturant responding, and social inclusion. Gerst (2005) described a program for nurse practitioners to help teenage youths reduce the likelihood of engaging in hate crimes—those acts of aggression and violence aimed at members of a particular group. Intervention strategies include techniques to manage conflict, promote empathy, and control anger and impulsive behaviors.

Although, in general, these programs and others like them are often cited as examples of how community agencies can help young people curb violent behaviors, empirical evidence of their effectiveness is lacking. In a comprehensive review of a broad range of violence prevention programs involving youths, families, or systems, Kerns and Prinz (2002) noted that most are problem driven rather than theory based and that published evaluation reports generally lack features that would support their efficacy, such as random assignment to condition, the inclusion of comparison groups, reliable and valid assessment instruments, and statistical analyses. In general, most violence prevention programs in current use lack the capacity for sophisticated research and thus may be severely limited in their ability to identify change mechanisms and best practices. As these programs proliferate, there will be an increased need for rigorous evaluations to identify relevant variables related to change and to provide a basis for making evidence-informed decisions. Psychologists working in agencies can play important roles both in designing programs containing empirical evaluation plans and in facilitating the implementation of programs to enhance boys' social, emotional, psychological, and behavioral functioning.

Fathers, Mentors, and Adults

Kindlon and Thompson (1999) discussed ways to help boys access their inner lives and find satisfying venues for self-expression. They emphasized the important roles that family members and, in particular, fathers can play in reducing the damage that results from the emotional gulf separating most boys from their fathers in this culture. As they pointed out, "It is clear to us that the most emotionally resourceful and resilient boys are those whose fathers are part of the emotional fabric of the family, whose fathers care for them and show it in comforting, consistent ways" (Kindlon & Thompson, 1999, p. 96).

Spencer (as cited in Palmer, 2003) examined the impact of mentoring relationships in the Big Brother program and found that boys, particularly those who had limited access to positive male role models, developed strong relationships with adult mentors. Although earlier data had substantiated the general value of these types of relationships, Spencer found that the emotional component of the mentoring relationship appeared to be strongly associated with increased self-esteem and reduced aggression.

Kalogerakis (2003) investigated intervention programs aimed at addressing and preventing youth violence and found that the less effective programs lacked meaningful youth involvement with concerned adults. Margolin et al. (2002) interviewed male juvenile offenders and found that the offenders wanted someone to talk to who could help them address specific problems in their immediate environments. Offenders reported that no one had ever really listened to them and that having a caring adult to talk to would be effective in reducing their aggressive tendencies. The offenders also talked about the impact of parental relationships. Many boys described disorganized families and parents with self-control problems. Social conditions are also important factors. For example, some studies have shown that youths from disorganized and economically disadvantaged families are more likely to turn to the street (Margolin et al., 2002). One implication from this literature is that successful intervention programs need to include individual, family, and community approaches to be most effective. Additionally, practitioners working with boys at risk for violence should consider seeking ways to involve fathers and other caring adults and mentors in their clients' lives.

Schools

30 Schools play vital roles in promoting children's emotional and psychological development. For boys, who face the challenge of developing a strong, resilient sense of self as a prerequisite to realizing their potential as men, schools can be formative influences. The data, however, suggest that schools may fail boys in substantial ways. Boys lag behind girls in reading and writing, are more likely to be diagnosed with attention deficit disorder and learning disabilities (Diller, 1998; Pollack, 1998), and experience far higher numbers of school suspensions due to disruptive behavior (Ferguson, 2000). Schools may also reinforce emotion socialization experiences that inhibit boys' emotional growth and play havoc with their self-esteem. As boys feel compelled to hide their inner selves, they risk threats to their capacity to learn, achieve, and feel successful. Educators may lack insight about boys' particular learning styles and unique educational, social, and emotional needs. Not only may they fail to structure the classroom environment to best support boys' progress and growth but they may unwittingly foster "antiboy" attitudes that undermine their sense of self-worth and healthy development. Kindlon and Thompson (1999) noted the potentially damaging impact of a poor school "fit" on boys' development: "The first two years in school are a critical moment of entry into that world of learning, but boys' relative immaturity and the lack of fit they so often experience in school set them up to fail" (p. 24). This literature makes it clear that practitioners working with boys at risk for violence should consider looking more closely into the boys' experiences in school and perhaps consult with the boys' teachers so that all caregivers are on the same page.

Clinical Practice

Practitioners who work with boys at risk for violence might benefit by viewing the presenting problems in the larger context of the traditional masculine emotional socialization process and its effects. Several authors have described clinical approaches and techniques based on such a perspective that address the socialized learnings that may underpin violent behavior or that may prevent the development of nonviolent methods of conflict resolution.

Pollack (2006) emphasized the importance of the therapist creating a genuine relational connection to support boys' emotional development. He identified strategies for therapists to get behind the mask of masculinity, which include learning to talk to boys in nonshaming ways, understanding what supports boys' emotional responsiveness, connecting with boys through actions, and sharing of oneself when interacting with boys. In his discussion of 15 distinct steps to foster boys' healthy emotional development, Pollack (2000) also stressed the importance of discovering and encouraging boys' unique communication styles, fostering mentoring relationships, and connecting with boys through both actions and words.

Kiselica (2001), a pioneer in this area, has written about a male-friendly therapeutic process for working with school-age boys. He encourages clinicians to think out of the box of the 50-min-hour office practice and use alternative time formats and settings. He also encourages the use of action, humor, selfdisclosure, and other rapport-building techniques. Kiselica discusses how to apply these principles to individual and group therapy, but in our view they are also relevant to teaching and recreation. Thus practitioners who provide in-service education for teachers and coaches might consider incorporating some of his material.

Richmond and Levant (2003) reported an application of the Gender Role Strain Paradigm (Pleck, 1981) to an experimental group treatment program for adjudicated adolescent boys, some of whom had been violent. The focus was on creating a safe and cohesive environment in which the boys could begin to discuss and challenge traditional male role norms, particularly the restriction of emotional expression. A set of 3 in. by 5 in. cards containing neutral themes as well as those that bore directly on gender role norms was used to frame the conversations. Each session began with a boy turning a card face up; the theme written on that card then became the topic of discussion. The boys became so engaged in the process that several stayed in the group beyond their mandated time period.

Conclusion

Conclusion is brief but restates the thesis statement and summarizes the main points of the paper ending on a hopeful note.

As we have tried to demonstrate, although aggression and violence in boys are 35 multidimensional and multidetermined, gender may be a crucial factor in understanding underlying causes and taking necessary steps to address problems. Psychologists can be in the forefront of these efforts. Using insights and data from research and clinical work, psychologists should continue to play key roles in encouraging awareness about boys' emotional needs and finding ways to support them. In developing connections to appropriate role models and having opportunities for healthy emotional expression, including outlets for fear, sadness, and emotional pain, boys can connect to themselves and others in ways that may reduce the risk of violence.

References

Adato, A., & Genovese, C. (1999, March 1). The secret lives of teens. *Life, 22,* 38–43.
Anderson, C. A., Berkowitz, L., Donnerstein, E., Huesman, L. R., Johnson, J. D., Linz, D., et al. (2003). The influence of media violence on youth. *Psychological Science in the Public Interest, 4,* 81–110.

Anderson, C. A., & Bushman, B. J. (2001). Effects of violent video games on aggressive behavior, aggressive cognition, aggressive affect, physiological arousal, and prosocial behavior: A meta-analytic review of the scientific literature. *Psychological Science, 12,* 353–359.

Anderson, C. A., Kaufman, J., Simon, T. R., Barrios, L., Paulozzi, L., Ryan, G., et al. (2001). School-associated violent deaths in the United States, 1994–1999. *Journal of the American Medical Association, 286,* 2695–2702.

Anderson, R. N., & Smith, B. L. (2003). Deaths: Leading causes for 2001. *National Vital Statistics Reports, 52*(9), 1–86. Hyattsville, MD: National Center for Health Statistics.

Arias, E., Anderson, R. N., Kung, H. C., Murphy, S. L., & Kochanek, K. S. (2003). Deaths: Final data for 2001. *National Vital Statistics Reports, 52*(3), 1–100. Hyattsville, MD: National Center for Health Statistics.

Brener, N., Lowry, R., & Barrios, L. (2005). Violence-related behaviors among high school students—United States, 1991–2003. *Journal of School Health, 75,* 81–85.

Centers for Disease Control and Prevention. (2004). *Web-based Injury Statistics Query and Reporting System.* [Data file]. Available from Centers for Disease Control and Prevention Web site, http://www.cdc.gov/ncipc/wisqars

Cleary, S. D. (2000). Adolescent victimization and associated suicidal and violent behaviors. *Adolescence, 35,* 671–682.

Davey, M., & Wilgoren, J. (2005, March 24). Signs of trouble were missed in a troubled teenager's life. *The New York Times,* pp. A1, A18.

Diller, L. H. (1998, November 12). Pills for kids sound alarm bells in suburbs. *USA Today,* p. A15.

Federal Bureau of Investigation. (1995). *1994 Uniform crime report: Supplemental homicide reports.* Washington, DC: U.S. Department of Justice.

Ferguson, A. (2000). *Bad boys: Public schools in the making of black masculinity.* Ann Arbor: University of Michigan Press.

Fingerhut, L. A., & Christoffel, K. K. (2002). Firearm-related death and injury among children and adolescents. *Future of Children, 12*(2), 25–37.

Froschl, M., & Sprung, B. (2005). *Raising and educating healthy boys: A report on the growing crisis in boys' education.* New York: Educational Equity Center.

Garbarino, J. (1999). *Lost boys: Why our sons turn violent and how we can save them.* New York: Free Press.

Gerst, D. (2005). Preventing teen hate crimes: Our role as nurse practitioners. *Nurse Practitioner, 30,* 62–63.

Heesacker, M., Wester, S. R., Vogel, D. L., Wentzel, J. T., Mejia-Millan, C. M., & Goodholm, C. R. (1999). Gender-based emotional stereotyping. *Journal of Counseling Psychology, 46,* 483–495.

Kalogerakis, M. G. (2003). Adolescent violence in America. *Adolescent Psychiatry, 27,* 3–28.

Kerns, S. E., & Prinz, R. J. (2002). Critical issues in the prevention of violence-related behavior in youth. *Clinical Child and Family Psychology Review, 5,* 133–160.

Kindlon, D., & Thompson, M. (1999). *Raising Cain: Protecting the emotional life of boys.* New York: Ballantine Books.

Kiselica, M. S. (2001). A male friendly therapeutic process with school-age boys. In G. R. Brooks & G. Good (Eds.), *The new handbook of counseling and psychotherapy for men* (Vol. 1, pp. 43–58). San Francisco: Jossey-Bass.

Kopel, D. B. (1992). *The samurai, the Mountie, and the cowboy: Should America adopt the gun controls of other countries?* New York: Prometheus Books.

Levant, R. (1992). Toward the reconstruction of masculinity. *Journal of Family Psychology, 5,* 379–402.

Levant, R. (1998). Desperately seeking language: Understanding, assessing and treating normative male alexithymia. In W. Pollack & R. Levant (Eds.), *New psychotherapy for men* (pp. 35–56). New York: Wiley.

Levant, R. F. (2001). The crises of boyhood. In G. R. Brooks & G. Good (Eds.), *The new handbook of counseling and psychotherapy with men: A comprehensive guide to settings, problems, and treatment approaches* (Vol. 1, pp. 355–368). San Francisco: Jossey-Bass.

Levant, R. F., Good, G. E., Cook, S., O'Neil, J., Smalley, K. B., Owen, K. A., & Richmond, K. (in press). *Validation of the Normative Male Alexithymia Scale: Measurement of a gender-linked syndrome.* Manuscript submitted for publication.

Levant, R. F., Hirsch, L., Celentano, E., Cozza, T., Hill, S., MacEachern, M., et al. (1992). The male role: An investigation of contemporary norms. *Journal of Mental Health Counseling, 14,* 325–337.

Levant, R. F., & Richmond, K. (in press). A program of research on masculinity ideologies using the Male Role Norms Inventory. *Journal of Men's Studies.*

Licurse, D. (2003). Teens practice being peaceful in relationships. *Curriculum Review, 42,* 9–12.

Loeber, R. (2005). Can future violence in boys be predicted by traditional 390 risk factors? *Journal of Consulting and Clinical Psychology, 73,* 1074–1088.

Lubell, K. M., Swahn, M. H., Crosby, A. E., & Kegler, S. R. (2004, June 11). Methods of suicide among persons aged 10–19 years—United States, 1992–2001. [Electronic version]. *Morbidity and Mortality Weekly Report, 53*(22), 471–473.

Margolin, A., Youga, J., & Ballou, M. (2002). Voices of violence: A study of male adolescent aggression. *Journal of Humanistic Counseling, Education, and Development, 41,* 215–231.

National Institute of Mental Health. (2000). *Child and adolescent violence research at the NIMH* (DHHS Publication No. 00-4706). Washington, DC: U.S. Government Printing Office.

O'Neil, J. M., Good, G. E., & Holmes, S. (1995). Fifteen years of theory and research on men's gender role conflict: New paradigms for empirical research. In R. F. Levant & W. S. Pollack (Eds.), *A new psychology of men* (pp. 164–206). New York: Basic Books.

Palmer, A. (2003, October). Boys' emotional development addressed. *Monitor on Psychology, 34*(9), 13.

Pleck, J. H. (1981). *The myth of masculinity.* Cambridge, MA: MIT Press.

Pollack, W. S. (1998). *Real boys.* New York: Henry Holt.

Pollack, W. S. (2000). *Real boys' voices.* New York: Random House.

Pollack, W. S. (2006). The "war" for boys: Hearing "real boys'" voices, healing their pain. *Professional Psychology: Research and Practice, 37,* 190–195.

Portner, J. (2001). *One in thirteen: The silent epidemic of teen suicide.* Beltsville, MD: Robins Lane Press.

Richmond, K., & Levant, R. (2003). Clinical application of the gender role strain paradigm: Group treatment for adolescent boys. *Journal of Clinical Psychology: In Session, 59*(11), 1–9.

Steinberg, L. (2000, April). Youth violence: Do parents and families make a difference? *National Institute of Justice Journal* (Office of Justice Programs Publication No. 243, pp. 31–38). Washington, DC: U.S. Department of Justice.

Toomey, M. (1991). The price of masculinity based on violence. *Independent School, 51,* 41–43.

U.S. Public Health Service. (2001). *Youth violence: A report of the Surgeon General.* Retrieved November 7, 2006, from http://www.surgeongeneral.gov/library /youthviolence

Weir, E. (2005). Preventing violence in youth. *Canadian Medical Association Journal, 172,* 1291–1292.

Wester, S. R., Vogel, D. L., Pressly, P. K., & Heesacker, M. (2002). Sex differences in emotion. *The Counseling Psychologist, 30,* 630–652.

A CLOSER LOOK AT
Boys and Violence

1. The article concludes that boys are conditioned to violence through the "traditional masculine emotional socialization process" in modern society. Look closely at this article and identify three to five factors that lead to violent masculine socialization. Then identify three to five strategies for counteracting that socialization.

2. Where and how does the paper define "youth violence"? Based on your own experience, do you agree with this definition? Have you experienced or witnessed youth violence in your own life?

3. Look over the suggested strategies for addressing youth violence. Which of these do you believe would have the greatest impact on violence in society? Which of these strategies do you believe would change the way young men perceive themselves and masculinity in society?

IDEAS FOR
Writing

1. Write a three page reflection describing an event in which you experienced or witnessed youth violence. First, set the scene and describe the event as a complication that disrupts that scene. Then describe how the event was evaluated and resolved. End your reflection by discussing what was learned.

2. Write a two page response to this article in which you react to its findings and suggested strategies. What parts of the article do you agree with? What parts do you disagree with? Would you expand or narrow the article's definition of youth violence? How might you address this issue in more depth?

1. Using an Internet search engine, find a research paper written by a university or college student. With your group, discuss the strengths and weaknesses of this research paper. Determine whether this research paper is an expository research paper or an argumentative one. Can you find a clear purpose statement or thesis? Do you think the writer covered the topic in enough depth, or can you find gaps in his or her research?

2. The research paper is often criticized as a genre that is mostly used in school. With your group, come up with five ways in which a research paper could be used outside of school settings. What kinds of readers would find a research paper interesting and worth reading?

3. After reading the student example in this chapter, discuss with your group how this research paper does or does not match the genre of the research paper. Separately, consider its content, organization, style, and design. What are the strengths of this paper? What could be improved?

1. Make a list of five topics on which you might want to do research. Then pick three of these topics, choose an angle, and narrow them down to something that you could handle in a research paper. When choosing an angle, try to figure out why this issue is interesting right now. Share your topic ideas with your group to see which one they like best.

2. Find an annotated bibliography on the Internet. What kinds of sources did the author include in the bibliography? Do you find the summaries of the sources helpful, or could the writer have described the sources in more depth? Using your library's website, find five additional sources that could have been included in this bibliography. Put them in APA or MLA style and send them to your professor.

3. Even a brief search on the Internet will turn up many of those "Buy a Research Paper" websites. Looking at these websites, write down ten ways that would help you detect whether a research paper was bought or plagiarized. Do these websites promise results that they cannot possibly deliver?

1. **Collect sources and create an annotated bibliography.** For a research paper you are writing, collect ten documents from a variety of print and electronic sources. Read these sources and create an annotated bibliography. Each source should be put into MLA or APA bibliographic format. Then, each should include a three sentence or more summary.

2. **Write a research paper.** To write a research paper, you need to pose a research question, devise a method for answering it, do the research, and analyze your findings. Working on your own or in a small group, do these activities:

   a. Make a list of interesting or urgent issues or questions that your community or country faces. What are some of the more interesting topics that are in the news?

   b. Choose one that seems especially urgent. What has changed recently to bring this problem to a head?

   c. Discuss this problem with a group of other people in your class.

   d. Choose one angle of that issue and turn it into a research question that could be answered by doing research. State that research question briefly but clearly and thoroughly.

   e. Turn your research question into a thesis statement.

   Show your research question and thesis statement to your professor. If he or she approves it, begin your research. Devise your methodology and do your research. Write an eight page research paper on your topic.

MyCompLab

For support in meeting this chapter's objectives, follow this path in MyCompLab:

Student Resources → Research → The Research Assignment → Writing the Research Paper. Review the Instruction and Multimedia resources about drafting and revising a research paper; then complete the Exercises and click on Gradebook to measure your progress.

3 Developing a Writing Process

PART OUTLINE

CHAPTER 11

Developing Ideas and Prewriting 256

CHAPTER 12

Organizing and Drafting 269

CHAPTER 13

Choosing a Style 276

CHAPTER 14

Designing 287

CHAPTER 15

Revising and Editing 303

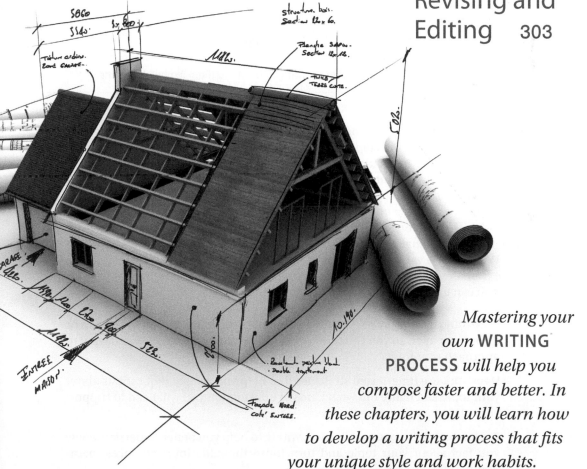

*Mastering your own **WRITING PROCESS** will help you compose faster and better. In these chapters, you will learn how to develop a writing process that fits your unique style and work habits.*

11

Developing Ideas
and Prewriting

┌─ **In this chapter, you will learn how to:** ─────────────────

- use prewriting techniques to get your ideas flowing.
- develop your ideas with heuristics.
- reflect on your ideas with exploratory writing and extend them in new directions.

D evelopment involves generating new ideas and inquiring into topics that you find interesting. Development also helps you discover and create the content of your document. In this chapter, you will learn some simple but powerful strategies that will help you generate original thoughts and perspectives. These strategies will help you figure out what you already know about your topic and get those ideas onto your screen or a piece of paper. In research genres, you will then go on to develop your ideas in relation to existing research. In genres such as analyses or position papers, these original ideas will form the basis of your discussion.

Writers use a variety of techniques to help them develop their ideas and see their topic from new perspectives. In this chapter, we will discuss three types of strategies that you can use to generate new ideas and inquire into your topic:

Prewriting uses visual and verbal strategies to put your ideas on the screen or a piece of paper, so you can think about them and figure out how you want to approach your topic.

Heuristics use time-tested strategies that help you ask good questions about your topic and figure out what kinds of information you will need to support your claims and statements.

Exploratory writing uses reflective writing to help you better understand how you feel about your topic and turn those thoughts into sentences, paragraphs, and outlines.

Some of these strategies will work better for you than others. So try them all to see which ones help you best develop your ideas.

Prewriting

◉─[**Watch** Office Hours Series: Prewriting

Prewriting helps you put your ideas on your screen or a piece of paper, though usually not in an organized way. Your goal while prewriting is to figure out what you already know about your topic and to start coming up with new ideas that go beyond what you already know.

Concept Mapping

One of the most common prewriting tools is *concept mapping*. To create a concept map, write your topic in the middle of your screen or a piece of paper (Figure 11.1). Put a circle around it. Then write down as many other ideas as you can about your topic. Circle those ideas and draw lines that connect them with your original topic and with each other.

The magic of concept mapping is that it allows you to start throwing your ideas onto the screen or a blank page without worrying whether they make sense at the moment. Each new idea in your map will help you come up with other new ideas. Just keep going. Then, when you run out of new ideas, you can work on connecting ideas together into larger clusters.

For example, Figure 11.1 shows a concept map about the pitfalls of male fashion on campus. A student made this concept map for a position paper. She started out by

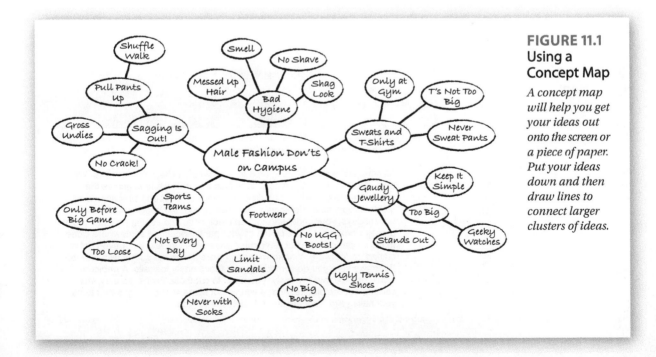

**FIGURE 11.1
Using a
Concept Map**

A concept map will help you get your ideas out onto the screen or a piece of paper. Put your ideas down and then draw lines to connect larger clusters of ideas.

writing "Male Fashion Don'ts on Campus" in the middle of a sheet of paper. Then she began jotting down anything that came to mind about that topic. Eventually, the whole sheet was filled out. She then linked ideas together into larger clusters.

With her ideas in front of her, she can now figure out what she wants to write about. The larger clusters might become major topics in her argument paper (e.g., sweats and T-shirts, jewellery, footwear, hygiene, saggy pants, and sports uniforms). Or she could pick one of those clusters (e.g., footwear) and write her paper about that narrower topic.

If you like concept mapping, you might try one of the free mapping software packages available online, including *Compendium, Free Mind, VUE,* and *XMIND.*

Freewriting

To freewrite, all you need to do is open a page on your computer or pull out a piece of notebook paper. Then write as much as you can for five to ten minutes, putting down anything that comes into your mind. Don't worry about making real sentences or paragraphs. If you find yourself running out of words, try finishing phrases like "What I mean is . . ." or "Here's my point. . . ."

When using a computer, some people like to turn off the monitor or close their eyes as they freewrite. That way, the words they have already written won't keep them from writing down new ideas. Plus, a dark screen will help you avoid the temptation to go back and fix those typos and garbled sentences.

Figure 11.2 shows an example freewrite. The text has typos and some of the sentences make no sense. That's fine.

FIGURE 11.2
Freewriting

When you are freewriting, just let the ideas flow and see where they lead you. In this sample, the writer didn't stop to correct typos. She just moved from one topic to the next. The result is a little chaotic, but now she has several new ideas to work with.

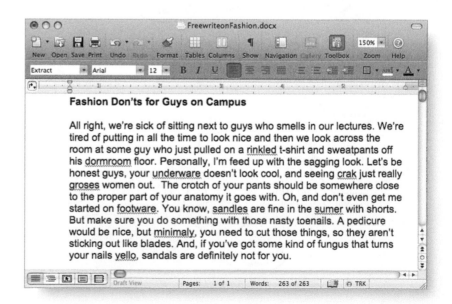

When you are finished freewriting, go through your text, highlighting or underlining your best ideas. Some people find it helpful to do a second, follow-up freewrite in which they concentrate on those best ideas alone.

Brainstorming or Listing

Another kind of prewriting is *brainstorming*, which is also called *listing*. To brainstorm about your topic, open a new page on your screen or pull out a piece of paper. Then list everything that comes to mind about your topic. As in freewriting, you should just keep listing ideas for about five to ten minutes without stopping.

Next, pick your best idea from your list and create a second brainstorming list in a second column. Again, list everything that comes to mind about this best idea. Making two lists will help you narrow your topic and deepen your thoughts about it.

Another option, once you have done some initial brainstorming, is to cluster the ideas, grouping similar ideas together to find themes.

Storyboarding

Movie scriptwriters and advertising designers use a technique called storyboarding to help them sketch out their ideas. *Storyboarding* involves drawing a set of pictures that show the progression of your ideas. Storyboards are especially useful when you are working with genres like reviews or proposals, because they show how something happens or happened step by step. They are useful for helping you visualize the "story."

The easiest way to storyboard about your topic is to fold a regular piece of paper into four or eight panels. Then, in each of the panels, draw a scene or a major idea involving your topic. Stick figures are fine. Don't worry about making your drawings look good. We can't all be artists.

Storyboarding is similar to turning your ideas into a comic strip. You add panels to your storyboards and cross them out as your ideas evolve. You can also add dialogue into the scenes and put captions underneath each panel to show what is happening. Storyboarding often works best for people who like to think in drawings or pictures rather than in words and sentences.

Using Heuristics

You already use heuristics, but the term is probably not familiar to you. A *heuristic* is a discovery tool that helps you ask insightful questions or follow a specific pattern of thinking. Writers often memorize the heuristics that they find especially useful. Here, we will review some of the most popular heuristics, but many others are available.

Asking the Journalist's Questions

The most common heuristic is a tool called the *journalist's questions*, which we like to call the "Five-W and How questions." Writers for newspapers, magazines, and television use these questions to help them sort out the details of a story.

Who was involved?   **When** did it happen?

What happened?   **Why** did it happen?

Where did the event happen?   **How** did it happen?

Write each of these questions separately on your screen or a piece of paper. Then answer each question in as much detail as you can. Make sure your facts are accurate, so you can reconstruct the story from your notes. If you don't know the answer to one of these questions, put down a question mark. A question mark signals a place where you might need to do some more research.

When using the Five-W and How questions, you might also find it helpful to ask, "What has changed recently about my topic?" If you pay attention to what has changed or is changing about your topic, you will likely discover what makes this topic most interesting to your readers. Paying attention to change will also help you determine your "angle" on the topic (i.e., your unique perspective or view).

Using the Five Senses

Writers also like to use their five senses as a heuristic to explore a topic and develop their ideas, especially when they are following descriptive genres, such as reviews or analyses. When trying to describe something to your readers, concentrate on each of your senses one by one:

Sight. What can you see? What does it look like? What colours or shapes do you see?

Hearing. What sounds can you hear? What do people or objects sound like?

Smell. What can you smell? Does anything have a distinctive scent?

Touch. What do things feel like? Are they rough or smooth? Are they cold or hot?

Taste. Are there any tastes involved? If so, are they sweet, salty, sour, stale, delicious?

Some senses will be more important to your writing project than others. Using all five senses will help you experience your topic from a variety of standpoints. These vivid descriptions will give your readers a richer understanding of your subject with added detail.

Investigating *Logos, Ethos, Pathos*

Aristotle, a philosopher and rhetorician, realized that arguments tend to draw on three kinds of proof: reasoning (*logos*), authority (*ethos*), and emotion (*pathos*). Today, writers still use these Greek terms as a heuristic to remind themselves to gather evidence from all three kinds of proof. This three-part heuristic works especially well for argumentative papers, such as position papers and proposals.

Logos. *Logos* includes any reasoning and examples that will support your claims. You can use logical statements to prove your points, or you can use real or realistic examples to back up your claims. Here are some basic strategies that you can use to support your ideas with *logos:*

If . . . then: "If you believe X, then you should believe Y also."

Either . . . or: "Either you believe X, or you believe Y."

Cause and effect: "X is the reason Y happens."

Costs and benefits: "The benefits of doing X are worth/not worth the cost Y."

Better and worse: "X is better/worse than Y because . . ."

Examples: "For example, X and Y demonstrate that Z happens."

Facts and data: "These facts/data support my argument that X is true (or Y is false)."

Anecdotes: "X happened to these people, thus demonstrating Y."

Ethos. *Ethos* involves information that will help you build your authority and reputation with readers. If you are an expert on a particular topic, you can use your own experiences to support your argument. For example, a person majoring in fashion design has more *ethos* about the topic of clothing than others. If you are not an expert on your topic, then you can draw from sources written by experts to add *ethos* to your writing. Here are a few ways to use *ethos* in your writing:

Personal experience: "I have experienced X, so I know it's true and Y is not."

Personal credentials: "I have a degree in Z" or "I am the director of Y." "So I know a lot about the subject of X."

Good moral character: "I have always done the right thing for the right reasons, so you should believe me when I say that X is the best path to follow."

Appeal to experts: "According to Z, who is an expert on this topic, X is true and Y is not true."

Identification with the readers: "You and I come from similar backgrounds and we have similar values; therefore, you would likely agree with me that X is true and Y is not."

Admission of limitations: "I may not know much about Z, but I do know that X is true and Y is not."

Expression of goodwill: "I want what is best for you, so I am recommending X as the best path to follow."

Use of "insider" language: Using jargon words or referring to information that only insiders would understand.

Pathos. *Pathos* relates to emotional support for your argument. To use emotion in your writing, think about the aspects of your topic that make people happy, mad, sad, anxious, concerned, surprised, disgusted, joyful, or fearful. You can appeal to these emotions to persuade people to see things your way. Here are some strategies for using emotion:

Promise of gain: "By agreeing with us, you will gain trust, time, money, love, advancement, reputation, comfort, popularity, health, beauty, or convenience."

Promise of enjoyment: "If you do things our way, you will experience joy, anticipation, fun, surprises, enjoyment, pleasure, leisure, or freedom."

Fear of loss: "If you don't do things this way, you risk losing time, money, love, security, freedom, reputation, popularity, health, or beauty."

Fear of pain: "If you don't do things this way, you may feel pain, sadness, grief, frustration, humiliation, embarrassment, loneliness, regret, shame, vulnerability, or worry."

Expressions of anger or disgust: "You should be angry or disgusted because X is unfair to you, me, or others."

Emotion alone usually won't create the strongest arguments. Instead, you should use emotion to support your *logos*-based or *ethos*-based arguments. Emotion will add power and feeling to your argument, while heightening the intensity for your readers. Figure 11.3 shows the introduction to a first draft in which the author uses emotion to support her *logos* and *ethos* arguments. See Chapter 19 for more discussion of persuasive techniques.

Cubing

A cube has six sides, and cubing asks you to explore your topic through six "sides" or angles.

1. **Describe it.** What does your topic look like? What are its colour and shape? How big or small is it? What is it made of?

2. **Compare it.** What is like? What is it *not* like? In what ways is it similar to or different from things that are more familiar to your readers?

3. **Associate it.** What does it remind you of? What other topics is it related to that you know something about?

4. **Analyze it.** What patterns run through your topic? What are its hidden questions or meanings? Who created it? What has changed that makes it important?

5. **Apply it.** How could you or someone else use it? Who would use it? What good would it do them? What harm might it do?

6. **Argue for or against it.** What arguments could you or someone else make for or against your topic?

As a fashion design major (and a woman), let me offer you guys a little helpful advice about attracting women on campus. Women view campus differently than most men. Guys see campus as a place to go to class and study, perhaps throw a frisbee. So, showing up in a faded T-shirt, sweatpants, and flipflops might seem all right. Quite differently, women see campus as a place to socialize and meet friends, in addition to doing class-related stuff. For women, campus is a place to see people and be seen. Consequently, women don't like to be seen with guys who look like they were just shot out of a wrinkle gun. But, if you guys make a few simple wardrobe changes, women are going to notice you.

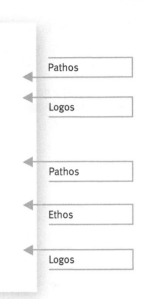

Pathos

Logos

Pathos

Ethos

Logos

FIGURE 11.3 A First Draft That Uses *Logos*, *Pathos*, and *Ethos* for Support

In this first draft of an essay's introduction, the author uses a combination of reasoning, authoritative, and emotional appeals to persuade her readers.

Exploratory Writing

Exploratory writing helps you to reflect on your ideas about a topic and to put down your thoughts for further consideration. Essentially, exploratory writing is "writing about writing" that allows you to think about your writing projects with a little more distance.

Journaling, Blogging, or Microblogging

Some writers find it helpful to keep a regular journal or blog to reflect on their experiences and generate new ideas. You can write down your thoughts and think about your life without the pressure of drafting the full argument.

Journaling. This kind of exploratory writing can be done in a notebook or on your computer. The key to writing a journal is to add something new every day. In your journal, you can talk about the things that happen to you and what is going on in your world.

Blogging. Blogging is very similar to journaling but blogs are public texts (Figure 11.4). You can sign up for a blog at several blogging websites, often for free. You may not want everyone to read your innermost ideas—but then, of course, you might! Some personal blogs develop their own cult followings. For more on blogging, see Chapter 26, "Using the Internet."

FIGURE 11.4 A Blog

Journals or blogs can be helpful for coming up with new ideas and reflections. This blog was found on Blogger.com, a free blogging website.

Microblogging. You can use a microblog like *Twitter, Facebook, Plurk,* or *Tumblr* to describe what is happening to you. Besides keeping your friends informed about where you are and what you are doing, your microblog can track your thoughts and experiences.

Before writing a new entry into your journal or blog, go back and read what you wrote previously. That way, you can build from your previous thoughts or use them as a springboard for coming up with new ideas. If you are writing a blog, you can check out what others have written in response to your posts.

Writing an Exploratory Draft

Sometimes it is helpful to write an "exploratory draft" before you begin trying to write a rough draft. In an exploratory draft, write about how you feel about the topic and what you already know about it. Write down some of the main points you want to make in your paper and what kinds of information or examples you will need to support your points. Your exploratory draft is also a good place to express your concerns about the project and come up with some strategies for handling them.

In this position paper, I want to make an argument that guys should dress nicer on campus. But I don't want to come off as some kind of fashion snob or diva.

I also don't want to give the impression that I think everyone has enough money to buy designer clothes. I strongly believe that looking good is not a matter of money or being physically attractive. It's about making good choices and taking a few minutes to think about what looks good to others. I guess my main goal in this paper is to give guys good reasons to dress nicer on campus. Yeah, I'll need to tweak them a little to get their attention. My writing style will probably need to be funny or even teasing. If they get a little angry, maybe they'll think a little more about how they look. It would be nice if I could find some pictures that demonstrate good fashion choices. Nothing GQ. Just normal guys on campus making good choices about clothing. Maybe I need a digital camera to get some of those kinds of pictures. That would help me show my readers what I mean.

The purpose of an exploratory draft is not to write the paper itself but to use writing to help you explore your topic and sort out your ideas.

Exploring with Presentation Software

Presentation software, such as Microsoft's *PowerPoint,* OpenOffice's *Impress,* or Apple's *KeyNote,* can be a powerful tool for doing exploratory writing about your subject. The software can help you create slides, making a bulleted list of your major subjects and key points. Then you can fill out the slides with details, pictures, and graphs. Presentation software is a fast and easy way to explore your topic and organize your ideas. Try this:

1. Create a new page in your favourite presentation software.

2. On the title slide, type a title for your paper that identifies your topic. In the subtitle area, type in your angle on that topic.

3. Think of two to five major topics that will be discussed in your argument. Create separate slides for each of those major topics.

4. On the slide for each major topic, list two to five issues that you might need to talk about in your paper.

5. As you fill in each slide, look for opportunities to add visuals, such as photographs, charts, and graphs.

If you don't know something about one of your major topics, just leave that slide blank for now. These gaps in slides signal places where you need to do more exploration or research.

When you are finished filling in the slides as best you can, you might find it helpful to change your screen to Slide Sorting View, so you can see an overview of your whole text (Figure 11.5). This view will allow you to move slides around to figure out how to best organize your ideas.

When you are finished exploring your topic with the presentation software, you will have a good outline for writing your paper. Plus, you will have collected the photographs, charts, and other visuals you need to design the document.

Campus Fashion for Guys

Looking like a slob is not fashionable

Hygiene

- Regular shower a baseline
- Shag look is hard to pull off
- Messed up hair isn't as cute as people think
- Shave or trim beard daily

Sweats and T-Shirts

- Only when you're actually working out
- Never wear sweatpants to class
- T-shirts should fit and not be too loose

Footwear

- Tennis shoes are all right
- Decent brown or black shoes are nice
- No UGG boots or other kinds of big boots
- Guys don't look good in flipflops (sorry)

Sports Team Clothing

- Shouldn't be your everyday clothing
- Before the big game is fine
- Not too loose or baggy

Sagging

- No.
- Don't want to see your undies
- Crack is definitely a turnoff
- Pull them up and get a belt

FIGURE 11.5 Outlining with Presentation Software

Presentation software can help you make a quick outline of your argument and insert graphics.

Taking Time to Prewrite and Develop

When writing a paper, it is very tempting to jump straight to the drafting stage of the writing process. After all, time spent prewriting, using heuristics, and doing exploratory writing might seem like time away from your real task—getting that assignment finished. In the end, the secret is to give yourself the time and space to explore your ideas.

Above all, think of development as a separate stage in your writing process. Set aside some time to discover and form your ideas before you start trying to draft your paper. You will be more original. Plus, you will actually save time, because you won't just sit at your computer staring into the screen.

Start developing the content of your document. Here are some techniques for prewriting, using heuristics, and doing some exploratory writing.

DO Some Prewriting to Get the Ideas Flowing

Prewriting uses visual and verbal strategies to help you figure out what you already know about your topic and how you want to approach it. Try making a concept map, freewriting, doing some brainstorming, or making a storyboard on your topic.

USE Heuristics to Draw Out Your Ideas

A heuristic is a discovery tool that helps you ask insightful questions or follow a specific pattern of thinking. Some of the common heuristics are the Five-W and How questions, the five human senses, *logos/ethos/pathos*, and cubing.

REFLECT on Your Topic with Exploratory Writing

Exploratory writing is "writing about writing" that allows you to think about your writing projects with a little more distance. You can do some journaling or blogging. Or you can write an exploratory draft that lets you talk about what you want to write about. Presentation software can be a useful tool for putting your ideas on the screen in an organized way.

GIVE Yourself Time to Develop Your Ideas

It's tempting to jump right to the drafting stage. That deadline is looming. But you will find that you write more efficiently and better if you give yourself time to sort through your ideas first.

1. List three times in your life when you have been especially inspired or innovative. Why did you decide to take the less-travelled path rather than the ordinary path? Tell your group about these moments and how they came about.

2. With your group, list five celebrities who you think are especially original and innovative. Can you find any common characteristics that they all share?

3. What kinds of development strategies have you learned previously, and what has worked for you in the past? With your group, talk about methods you have used in the past to come up with new ideas for projects.

1. Create a concept map about a topic that interests you. What are the one or two most interesting issues in your concept map? Put one of those issues in the middle of your screen or a piece of paper and create a second concept map on this narrower version of the topic. Ask yourself, "What has changed to make this topic interesting right now?" Doing so will help you find a new angle on your topic.

2. Check into some of the free blogging services available online. What are some of the pros and cons of each blogging site? If you don't have a blog of your own, what kind of blog might you enjoy keeping?

1. **Freewrite for five minutes.** Using a topic for your next paper in this class, freewrite for five minutes. When you are finished, pick your best idea and freewrite for another five minutes. This second freewrite will help you develop a solid understanding of the topic, purpose, and angle for your paper.

2. **Start keeping a journal or blog.** For the next two weeks, keep a journal or a blog. Spend a little time each day writing something about the topic of your next paper. Then, as you draft, design, and edit your paper, write about your successes and challenges while developing the document. Hand in your journal or your blog's URL with the final draft of your paper.

MyCompLab

For support in meeting this chapter's objectives, follow this path in MyCompLab:

Student Resources → Writing → The Writing Process → Planning. Review the Instruction and Multimedia resources about freewriting and prewriting; then complete the Exercises and click on Gradebook to measure your progress.

12

Organizing and Drafting

In the previous chapter, you learned how to develop the content of your paper by using prewriting, heuristics, and exploratory writing to find ideas and gather information. In this chapter, you will learn about the second stage in the writing process: how to use genres to organize your ideas and write a draft of your paper.

The genre you choose will help you determine where your ideas and the information you gathered should appear in the text. The genre helps you organize your ideas into a shape that is familiar to you and your readers. Remember, genres are not formulas to be followed mechanically. Instead, genres follow flexible patterns that reflect how people act, react, and interact in the real world. The organization of a genre, in other words, reflects how people get things done.

Using Genres to Organize Your Ideas

As your documents grow longer and more complex, genres will help you dramatically improve your writing. Genres follow organizational patterns that reflect the activities you will do in your classes and in the workplace. For example, the proposal genre (discussed in Chapter 9) reflects the steps that you should follow when proposing the solution to a problem:

1. Define a problem and outline its importance.

2. Analyze the problem and discuss its causes and effects, based on solid research.

3. Develop a detailed plan for solving the problem.

4. Discuss the benefits and costs of the plan.

5. Draw conclusions and stress the importance of taking action.

It's no coincidence, then, that the proposal genre calls for five sections that reflect this research process: *introduction, problem analysis, plan for solving the problem, benefits of the plan*, and *conclusion*. Once you know that a proposal tends to be organized into these five sections, you can arrange the information you have gathered to fit what your readers expect.

Should you mechanically follow a genre as a fixed pattern? Absolutely not. A genre's organization can be adjusted to suit your purpose and the unique characteristics of the rhetorical situation. Genres are flexible and "stretchy," allowing writers to move, combine, and divide sections as needed.

Drafting Introductions, Bodies, and Conclusions

Genres commonly used in university and college and in the workplace have some organizational features that you can commit to memory. Specifically, genres for school and the workplace almost always include an introduction, body, and conclusion.

Introduction. The purpose of the introduction is to set a "context" for the body of the document. The introduction usually tells readers your topic, purpose, and main point. It might also offer background information on your topic and stress its importance to readers. Introductions can range in size from a small paragraph to several paragraphs.

Body. The body presents the "content" of the document. Essentially, the body provides the facts, reasoning, examples, quotations, data, and anything else needed to support or prove your document's main point and achieve its purpose.

Conclusion. At the end of the document, the conclusion re-establishes the context for the document by restating your main point (usually with more emphasis), restating why your topic is important to your readers, and offering a look to the future. Your conclusion should be as brief as possible, from a small paragraph to at most a few paragraphs.

To help you remember this three-part pattern, sometimes it helps to keep the time-tested speechwriter's pattern in mind: "Tell them what you're going to tell them. Tell them. Then tell them what you told them."

In Chapter 16, "Drafting Introductions and Conclusions," you will learn more about how to write strong beginnings and endings for your documents. You can turn there now if you are looking for immediate advice on writing introductions and conclusions.

 **Watch** Office Hours Series: Drafting

Sketching an Outline

An outline can be an important tool for organizing your ideas, especially as the documents you write grow larger and more complex. In the workplace, most people sketch out a rough outline to help them sort out their ideas. Your outline doesn't need to be formal, but it should list the major parts of your document. In academic contexts, you may need to be more detailed in preparing your major points and supporting evidence. Your outline is a map you will follow when drafting your document.

Creating a Basic Outline

When creating a basic outline, you first need to decide which genre you are following and turn to that chapter in Part 2 of this book. At the beginning of each genre chapter, you will see a diagram illustrating one or two organizational patterns that the genre tends to follow. These patterns should give you an overall idea about which sections should appear in your outline.

Here's the easy part. Type or write "I. Introduction" on your screen or a piece of paper. Then type or write "X. Conclusion" at the bottom. After all, you already know your document will need an introduction and a conclusion. For now, use an "X" with the conclusion, because you aren't sure how many sections will be needed for the body of your text.

Filling Out Your Outline

Here's the hard part. Start listing the major sections that will appear in your document. Give each one an uppercase roman numeral (e.g., II, III, IV, V, VI, VII, etc.). The genre you are following should give you a good idea about how many sections you will need (Figure 12.1). *Hint:* If your roman numerals are nearing X (that's ten sections), you probably have too many sections. If that's the case, some of your sections should be combined or removed.

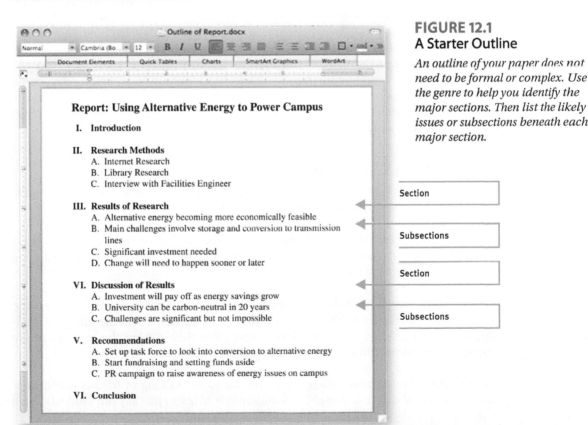

FIGURE 12.1
A Starter Outline

An outline of your paper does not need to be formal or complex. Use the genre to help you identify the major sections. Then list the likely issues or subsections beneath each major section.

When you have finished listing the major sections, list the issues or subsections that will appear in each of these major sections. Each major section should include about two to five issues or subsections.

How will you know what to include in each section? That's where the development strategies you learned about in the previous chapter will help you. Look at the ideas and keywords you came up with during the development phase, and put them into your outline. Research will add to and support your ideas.

Drafting Through Writer's Block

Writer's block happens to everyone, even the most experienced writers. Here are some strategies for keeping the words flowing and for working through those moments of writer's block.

Drafting (Almost) Every Day

The worst thing you can do is start drafting the night before your paper is due. You will often hear people say things like, "I write best under pressure" or "I need to figure out what I'm going to say before I start writing." These kinds of statements are warning signals that a writer is procrastinating. After all, people don't really write well under pressure, and the best way to figure out what you have to say is to write something down.

Our best advice is to do half an hour of drafting every day. Each day, set aside a regular time in the morning or evening to work on your writing assignments. Writing is like exercising at the gym. If you exercise for half an hour every day, you will improve steadily—much more than if you exercised for four hours on one day. In the same way, if you say, "I'm setting aside Sunday afternoon to write that paper," you are not going to do your best work. But, if you write for half an hour every day, you will easily finish your work—and you will write better.

Overcoming Writer's Block

Almost all writers find themselves blocked at some point. Here are some of the most popular techniques for overcoming writer's block:

"What I Really Mean Is. . . ."   Whenever you are blocked, finish the sentence "What I really mean is. . . ." You will discover that simply finishing this sentence will help you get past the temporary block.

Lower Your Standards While Drafting.   Stop trying to get it right on the first try. Instead, put your ideas on the screen without worrying about whether they are intelligent or grammatically correct. Then spend extra time during the revision phase turning those ideas into a document that has the high quality you expect.

Talk It Out.   Professional writers can often be found talking to friends about their work or even talking to themselves. Sometimes it helps to just say out loud what you want to write. Then, after you have rehearsed the text a few times, you should find your ideas easier to write down.

Change How and Where You Write. If you normally draft on a computer, try switching over to pen and paper for a little while. If you normally write in your room, try a change of scenery by going over to the library or out on central campus. Sometimes the change in medium or location will help you loosen up.

Use Both Sides of Your Brain. The right side of your brain is more visual than your left. So use techniques like concept mapping, freewriting, and cubing to tap into that visual creativity. These techniques will help you put your ideas on the screen. Then the left side of your brain can organize them into sentences and paragraphs.

Write an E-mail. Start writing your document as an e-mail to a friend. E-mail is often a more familiar writing environment, allowing you to relax as you write.

Talk to Your Professor. Your professors probably have some helpful ideas about how to draft your papers. Visit your professors during office hours. They are there to help you.

Go to the Writing Centre. If your campus has a writing centre, you should drop by for some help. You can talk your ideas over with an experienced writer who can offer you some advice and strategies.

Stop Procrastinating. Procrastination is the usual culprit behind writer's block. The pressure of a deadline can cause your brain to freeze. So start each project early, and write a little every day. Your writer's block will evaporate.

Your first year of university or college is the best time to develop good writing habits. Don't wait until your advanced courses or your first job to form these habits, because it will be too late.

Organization is the key to presenting your ideas in a meaningful, orderly way. It also allows you to highlight the important information that your readers need.

USE Genres to Organize Your Ideas

Genres are not formulas, but they do offer helpful patterns for organizing the content of your document. Chapters 4–10 will give you a good idea of how each genre is typically organized.

DIVIDE Your Document into an Introduction, Body, and Conclusion

Almost all nonfiction genres include an introduction, body, and conclusion. The introduction "tells them what you're going to tell them." The body "tells them." And the conclusion "tells them what you told them."

SKETCH an Outline

Outlines may seem a bit old-fashioned, but an informal outline is often a good way to sort your ideas into sections of a document.

DRAFT Your Document

Drafting is about putting your rear end in the seat and keeping your hands on the keyboard. Try drafting for half an hour almost every day.

OVERCOME Writer's Block

It happens to everyone. The techniques discussed in this chapter should help you get over those moments.

1. With a group, discuss how you were taught to outline papers in high school. Do you think outlining works well for you? In which situations do outlines seem to work best?

2. Have you ever waited until the last moment to write a paper for one of your classes? If you got a good grade, why do you think you did well despite procrastinating? If you didn't do well, what do you think you should have done differently to avoid waiting until the last moment?

3. When does writer's block happen most frequently to you? Can you think of ways to avoid writer's block in the first place? When writer's block happens, which strategies have you used to get writing again?

1. As you draft your next paper, keep a log of how much time you spend drafting. When you hand your paper in, look at your log. Where have you devoted more or less time to the project? How can you spread your time out better on the project to strengthen your writing?

2. Do some research on the writing habits of one of your favourite contemporary authors. How often does he or she write, and how much time does he or she devote to it each day? Does this writer offer any wisdom about how to overcome writer's block? Write an e-mail to your professor about this author's writing habits.

1. **Analyze your writing process.** In a brief report, describe how you currently draft your documents. How much time do you usually devote to drafting? Which strategies or routines help you draft a paper? Next, offer some ideas for improving how you draft documents. Which techniques for overcoming writer's block in this chapter would be most helpful for you?

2. **Interview a professional through e-mail.** Set up an e-mail interview with a professional in your desired career or a professor in your major. Ask that person about his or her writing process and pay special attention to what he or she says about organizing ideas and drafting documents. Ask how documents are organized in his or her field. Ask how he or she learned how to write those kinds of documents. In a brief profile, describe how your subject uses writing in his or her personal life.

MyCompLab

For support in meeting this chapter's objectives, follow this path in MyCompLab:

Student Resources → Writing → The Writing Process → Drafting. Review the Instruction and Multimedia resources about organizing and outlining; then complete the Exercises and click on Gradebook to measure your progress.

Choosing
a Style

In this chapter, you will learn how to:

- use plain style to write clearly and confidently in all situations.
- establish a scholarly voice or tone in your academic papers.
- use persuasive style to add energy and impact to your writing.

Watch
Writing
in Action
Series:
Exploring
Appropriate
Language

Style is not something you have or you don't have. Instead, style is a way of expressing your attitude and feelings about a topic. It is a way of establishing your character and a sense of authority with your readers. In a word, style is about the quality of your writing.

Style is *not* flowery language or ornamentation. It's *not* about sprinkling in a few adjectives to make dull sentences more interesting or colourful. Sometimes inexperienced writers will talk about "my style," as though each writer possesses one unique voice or way of writing. In reality, the best style for your document depends on your topic, the rhetorical situation, and the genre that you are using.

There is no correct style for a particular genre; however, certain genres are associated with specific styles. For example, scientific reports tend to be written in a plain, objective style. Movie reviews are often more subjective and upbeat. In some circumstances, though, a scientific report could use an upbeat style and a movie review could be serious. Ultimately, the style you choose depends on the rhetorical situation for your document.

In this chapter, you will learn strategies to strengthen your style and improve the power of your writing.

Writing in Plain Style

Plain style is the basis of all other writing styles. The usual advice to writers is to "write clearly" or "write in concrete language" as though making up your mind to do so is all it takes. Actually, using plain style is a skill that requires some practice. Once you learn a few basic guidelines, writing plainly will become a natural strength. Plain style is also the starting point for academic writing; however, keep in mind that academics may occasionally use nominalizations, passive voice, or longer sentences to achieve objectivity and allow them to discuss complex subjects in detail.

Guideline 1: Clarify What or Who the Sentence Is About

Often, difficult sentences simply lack a clear subject. For example, consider the following sentence:

Original:

Seven months after our Spring Break trip to Banff in which a bunch of us travelled around the Rockies, my roommates' fond memories of the trip were enough to ignore the nagging reality that the trip itself had yet to be fully paid for.

What is this sentence about? The word "memories" is currently in the subject position, but the sentence might also be about "months," "vacation," "bunch of us," "my roommates," or "trip." A sentence like this one is hard to understand because readers cannot easily locate the subject of the sentence.

To clarify this sentence, you first need to decide what the sentence is about. Then you can move that subject into the subject position of the sentence. For example, when this sentence is reconstructed around "my roommates and I" it is much easier to understand.

Revised:

Seven months after our Spring Break trip to Banff, my roommates and I still have fond memories of travelling around the Rockies, which helps us ignore the nagging reality that we haven't paid for the trip yet.

This sentence is still lengthy, but it is clearer now because the noun in the subject position (i.e., "my roommates and I") is what the sentence is about.

Guideline 2: Make the "Doer" the Subject of the Sentence

Readers tend to focus on who or what is doing something in a sentence, so whenever possible, try to move the "doer" into the subject position. For example, which of the following sentences is clearer?

On Monday morning, the report was completed just in time by Sheila.

On Monday morning, Sheila completed the report just in time.

Most readers would point to the second sentence, because Sheila, the subject of this sentence, is doing something. Meanwhile, the subject of the first sentence, the report, is just sitting still, not doing anything. In grammatical terms, the first sentence is in passive voice, and the lack of clarity you can see here is why some professors may ask you to avoid passive voice. Professors in the sciences, however, occasionally prefer passive voice for its objective tone.

Guideline 3: Put the Subject Early in the Sentence

Subconsciously, your readers start every sentence looking for the subject. The subject is the anchor of the sentence, so the longer you make them wait for it, the harder the sentence will be to read.

Original:

If the Sandia Mountains ecosystem experiences another drought like the one observed from 2000–2009, black bears will suffer severely from lack of available food and water.

Revised:

Black bears will suffer severely from lack of available food and water if the Sandia Mountains ecosystem experiences another drought like the one from 2000–2009.

The second sentence is easier to read, because the subject arrives early in the sentence. When readers find that anchor, they immediately know how to read the rest of the sentence.

Guideline 4: State the Action in the Verb

In each sentence, ask yourself what the doer is doing. Then move that action into the verb position and put the verb as close to the subject as possible.

Original:

The detective is the person who conducted an investigation into the homicide that happened last night on 4th Avenue.

Revised:

The detective investigated last night's homicide on 4th Avenue.

The original sentence is harder to understand because the action (investigation) is not a verb, and it's buried later in the sentence. The revised sentence is easier to understand because the action (investigate) is in the verb position, and it's close to the subject.

Guideline 5: Reduce Nominalizations

Nominalizations are perfectly good verbs and adjectives that have been turned into awkward nouns:

Original:

Students have an expectation that all professors will be rigorous and fair in the assignment of grades.

Revised:

Students expect all professors to be rigorous and fair when assigning grades.

By turning nominalizations into verbs, you can simplify and shorten a sentence. You also make the sentence more active because the action is being expressed in the verb.

Be aware, however, that nominalization is often used in scientific and business writing to describe complex processes. Here is an example from a student's psychology paper:

Thin ideal internalization has negative effects on women's self-esteem.

In this academic context, the occasional use of nominalization is fine.

Guideline 6: Boil Down the Prepositional Phrases

Prepositional phrases follow prepositions, like *in, of, by, about, over,* and *under.* These phrases are necessary in writing, but they can be overused.

Original:

This year's increase *in* the success *of* the basketball team called the Thunderbirds *of* UBC offered a demonstration *of* the importance *of* a coach *with* a national reputation *for* the purposes *of* recruiting.

Revised:

This year's successful UBC Thunderbirds basketball team demonstrated the importance *of* a nationally known coach *for* recruiting.

In the examples above, the prepositions have been italicized and the prepositional phrases are blue. Notice how prepositional phrases can create "chains" of phrases that make the sentence harder to read.

To eliminate prepositional phrases, try turning some of them into adjectives. For example, "in the success of the basketball team called the Thunderbirds of UBC" was boiled down to "successful UBC Thunderbirds basketball team." You don't need to eliminate all prepositional phrases, but you can simplify a sentence by eliminating some of them.

Guideline 7: Eliminate Redundancies

To stress an important idea, some writers mistakenly turn to redundant phrasing. For example, they might say "unruly mob" as though some mobs are not unruly. Or, they might talk about "active participants" as though people can participate without doing anything. In some cases, they are tempted to use two or more synonyms that mean the same thing to modify a noun.

Original:

We are demanding important, significant changes to university policies.

Revised:

We are demanding significant changes to university policies.

Original:

The London plague of 1665 was especially deadly and lethal for the poor, who could not escape to the countryside.

Revised:

The London plague of 1665 was especially deadly for the poor, who could not escape to the countryside.

Redundancies should be eliminated because they use two or more words to do the work of one. As a result, readers need to do twice the work to understand one basic idea.

Guideline 8: Use Sentences That Are Breathing Length

You should be able to read a sentence out loud in one comfortable breath. If a sentence runs on and on—even if it is grammatically correct—it makes readers feel like they are mentally holding their breath. By the end of an especially long sentence, readers are more concerned about when the sentence will end than what the sentence is saying.

On the other hand, if you only use short sentences, your readers will feel like they are breathing too quickly. Each period at the end of a sentence signals, "Take a breath." So many short sentences together will make readers feel like they are hurrying.

If you are writing in an academic context, you may find that longer sentences are necessary to fully describe your complex ideas. This is an acceptable academic variation on plain style.

Here are two ways to make your sentences the appropriate length in standard writing situations:

- Sentences that cannot be said out loud comfortably in one breath should be shortened or cut into two sentences. (Don't asphyxiate your readers!)

- Sentences that are too short should be combined with other short sentences around them. (Don't make them hyperventilate, either!)

Plain style takes some practice, but writing clearly is not that hard to master. These eight guidelines and the academic adaptations we have noted will help you transform your writing into something that is easy to read. This is the essence of plain style.

Establishing Your Voice

When reading, all of us, including your readers, hear a voice that sounds out the words. The best way to create a specific voice in a text is to decide what *tone* you want your readers to hear as they read your writing.

In other words, think about how you want your voice to sound: excited, angry, joyful, sad, professional, disgusted, objective, happy, compassionate, surprised, optimistic, aggressive, regretful, anxious, tense, affectionate, or sympathetic.

After you choose a specific tone, you can create your voice by getting into character or imitating other writers.

Get into Character

While drafting, one easy way to establish your voice is to imagine yourself playing a role, as in a movie or a play. You need to get into character before you start drafting your paper. This is common advice given to creative writers, but role playing works for writing nonfiction, too.

For instance, you may need to write a review about a funny movie, but since it has been a few days since you saw it you are no longer laughing at the jokes. In that situation, try to recall the feelings you experienced while watching the film and to re-create that excitement and humour in your word choices.

Conversely, if you are writing an academic research essay, you will need to adopt the professional tone and language of a scholar. You may feel unprepared to do so as an undergraduate student, but by getting into character you can work toward developing a more objective, well-informed academic voice.

Imitate Other Writers

Imitation was once a common way for people to learn how to improve their voice and tone. Teachers of speech and writing would regularly ask their students to imitate the style of well-known speakers and writers to practise new stylistic techniques.

Imitation is not widely used to teach writing today, but you can still use it to improve your own style. Choose an author whose work you enjoy or whose work you would like to emulate. Pay close attention to his or her style. How does the choice of words shape what the writer says? How do the writer's sentences convey his or her meaning? As you are drafting or revising your next paper, use some of those word choices and sentence strategies to convey your own ideas. When imitating someone else, you will usually end up blending elements of his or her writing style with elements of yours.

Of course, be careful not to use the exact words or ideas of the writer or text you are imitating. That's plagiarism. To avoid any chance of plagiarism, try imitating the style of a text that was written on a completely different topic than the one you are writing about.

Writing Descriptively with Tropes

Tropes, which are usually referred to as "figurative language," are good devices for helping you write visually. They include analogies, similes, metaphors, and onomatopoeia, which use language in ways that invite readers to see an issue from new and different perspectives. Trope, in ancient Greek, means "turn." While these devices are particularly useful in helping general audiences understand a point, they are used less frequently in academic writing. The professional tone required in academic writing tends to reduce the amount of figurative language, except in some arts or humanities subjects.

Use Similes and Analogies

A *simile* is a figure of speech in which one thing is compared to something that has similar features but is also very different.

> Up ahead, two dozen white pelicans were creating a spiral staircase as they flew. It looked like a feathered DNA molecule. Their wings reflected the sun. The light shifted, and they disappeared. (Terry Tempest Williams, *Refuge*)

A simile makes a comparison, "X is like Y," or "X is as Y," asking the readers to make visual connections between two different things. Comparing flying pelicans to a spiral staircase, for instance, calls up all kinds of interesting visual relationships.

Analogies are similes that work at two levels. When using an analogy, you are saying, "X is like Y, as A is like B."

> Like police keeping order in a city, white blood cells patrol your body's bloodstream controlling viruses and bacteria that want to do you harm.

> In the 17th century, England's reliance on imported salt was similar to the United States' dependence on foreign oil today. England's Queen Elizabeth I was especially anxious about her nation's reliance on salt from France, her nation's old enemy (Kurlansky, *Salt,* 195). So, she pushed hard for increased domestic production and sought to open other, more dependable sources of foreign salt. Indeed, England's build-up of its navy in the 17th century was prompted in part by its need to protect the importation of salt.

Analogies are used to highlight and explain complex relationships. A good analogy allows readers to visualize similar features between two things.

Use Metaphors

Metaphors are much more powerful than similes and analogies, and they tend to work at a deeper level. There are two types of metaphors that you can use to add power and depth to your writing: simple metaphors and cultural metaphors.

A *simple metaphor* states that one thing is something else, "X is Y."

Mr. Lewis's face is an aged parchment, creased and wrinkled from his years of sailing.

Vince, our boss, threw one grenade after another in our meeting.

On the surface, these metaphors say something patently false (i.e., a face is a parchment, the boss threw grenades in the meeting), which urges readers to figure out an alternative meaning that fits the situation. The meaning they come up with will be much more visual than a standard description.

A simple metaphor can be extended:

Mr. Lewis's face is an aged parchment, creased and wrinkled from his years of sailing. In his bronze skin, you can see months spent sailing in the Caribbean. The wrinkles around his eyes reveal many years of squinting into the wind. His bent nose and a scar on his chin bear witness to the storms that have thrown him to the deck. His bright eyes peer out from beneath his white brow, hinting at a lifetime of memories that non-sailors like me will never have.

In this example, you can see the power of a fertile metaphor. You can use it to create a perspective or a unique way of "seeing" something.

There are also larger *cultural* metaphors that shape the way people think about issues. For example, here are some common metaphors that we almost take for granted:

Time is money (e.g., spend time, waste time, saved time, lost time)

Thought is light (e.g., he is bright, she was in the dark, they enlightened me)

Argument is war (e.g., she defended her argument, she attacked my claims)

Cultural metaphors like the "war on cancer" or the "war on drugs" have become so standard that we do not challenge them. And yet, the "war on X" metaphor urges us to think of a subject in a certain way.

Use Onomatopoeia

Onomatopoeia is a big word that stands for a rather simple idea. It means using words that sound like the things you are describing.

The fire *crackled* in the fireplace.

He *shuffled* down the hallway.

The trees *fluttered* in the wind.

Using onomatopoeia isn't difficult. As you draft or revise, think about the sounds that are associated with your subject. Then look for some words that actually capture those sounds.

Improving Your Writing Style

With a little practice, you can dramatically improve the power and intensity of your writing by simply paying attention to its style. You can help your readers "see" and "hear" what you are writing about. You can speed up their reading pace or slow it down—and they won't even realize you're doing it.

But good style takes time and practice. As you draft and revise, look for places to use detail, similes, analogies, metaphors, and onomatopoeia to add intensity to your writing.

If you practise these techniques, they will become a natural part of your writing skills. Then you will be able to use them without even trying.

Remember that style is a choice that you can and should make. Style is a way to express your attitude and feelings about a topic, while establishing your character and a sense of authority.

USE Plain Style

Plain style is the basis of all other writing styles. By choosing an appropriate subject for each sentence and moving it to an early place, you can clarify your writing for readers. Put the action of the sentence in the verb. Then reduce nominalizations, boil down prepositional phrases, and eliminate redundancies.

ESTABLISH Your Voice

Think of a voice or tone that would be appropriate for your text. Then put that voice into your writing by getting into character or imitating other writers. Practise using other writers' styles and adapt their strategies to your own context and purpose.

USE Similes, Analogies, and Metaphors

Similes, analogies, and metaphors highlight relationships among different things and ideas. They allow readers to see your topic in new and interesting ways.

EXPLORE and Challenge Cultural Metaphors

Pay attention to the cultural metaphors that shape how we think. You can use those cultural metaphors or challenge them.

EVOKE Atmosphere with Sound

You can describe something by using sound. An onomatopoeia is a word that sounds like the thing it is describing (e.g., crackling fire, shuffling walk, screeching voice). You can also use shorter and longer sentences to speed up or slow down the pace of the text.

1. With a group of people from your class, make a list of ten authors whose writing style you enjoy. What about their work signals that they have good style?

2. With your group, talk about the ways people adopt a particular style or voice. Are there situations in your life when you need to adopt a different style or voice than you normally would?

3. Find three texts on the Internet that demonstrate three different styles. Have each member of your group explain why he or she likes or dislikes the style of each document. How does the style of each document fit or not fit the needs of its readers and contexts?

1. Find a text or author that you would like to imitate. Then, with that text on your desk or screen, try to write about a different topic but use the style of that text. Try to match its use of tone, metaphors, similes, detail, and sentence length.

2. Searching the Internet, explore the different uses of a common cultural metaphor. What does this cultural metaphor say about how we think about these subjects in our culture?

3. Come up with your own simile or metaphor. Pick any metaphor that comes to mind. Try freewriting for three minutes with your simile or metaphor in front of you. Does the simile or metaphor give you any new insights? At what point does the simile or metaphor become far-fetched or absurd?

1. **Analyze a cultural metaphor.** Find a common cultural metaphor and write an analysis in which you discuss its strengths and weaknesses. Where does the metaphor fail to capture the full meaning of its subject?

2. **Review the style of an academic or well-written popular essay.** Choose a document that exhibits good style and write a review of the document's use of any figurative language, sentence structures, or other stylistic strategies.

MyCompLab

For support in meeting this chapter's objectives, follow this path in MyCompLab:

Student Resources → Writing → The Writing Process → Finishing and Editing. Review the Instruction and Multimedia resources about checking your voice; then complete the Exercises and click on Gradebook to measure your progress.

14

Designing

In this chapter, you will learn how to:

- design documents that suit your paper's purpose, readers, context, and genre.
- use principles of design to lay out a document.
- enhance and reinforce written text with graphs and charts.

Imagine your own reaction to a large document with no pictures, no headings, no graphics, and no lists. If you're like most people, you would feel intimidated by the format and unsure of how to locate the key ideas.

Good design makes the information in a document more accessible, and it makes reading that document more pleasurable. A well-designed text helps readers quickly locate the information they need. If your document looks accessible and attractive, readers are going to want to spend more time reading it. If it looks difficult and unattractive, they might not read it at all.

In this chapter, you will learn some basic strategies for designing your documents and creating graphics. These strategies work with any genre, depending on the kinds of information you want to share with your readers. Just keep in mind that academic documents may use fewer visuals than texts written for general audiences.

Before You Begin Designing

After drafting, spend some time thinking about what kind of design features would work best in this kind of text.

Genre. What design features and graphics are typical for the genre of this document? You might search for examples of the genre on the Internet or in library databases to gain a sense of how they tend to look. The comments about design in Part 2 of this book will also give you some good ideas about how a specific genre uses design and graphics.

Purpose. How can you use design and graphics to achieve your purpose? Think about how your document's page layout (e.g., headings, columns, margin notes, colour) could be used to highlight important information and make it more accessible to readers. Also,

Watch
Writing in Action: How to Format Documents Using a Word Processor

if you are writing for a general audience, look for places where graphics can be used to support the written part of your text.

Readers. What kinds of design features and graphics will your readers expect or prefer? For some genres, like proposals, readers are "raiders," so they expect the design to help them locate the information they need. Other genres, like analyses, are designed to be read in a more leisurely way, so that text doesn't need to be "raidable." If you are writing for an academic audience, be sure to consult the formatting guidelines for the citation style you are using. See Chapters 24 and 25 for examples of MLA and APA formats.

Context. In what situations will readers use the document, and how do these situations shape how it should look? Think about the places where readers will use it and how they will use it.

Now you're ready to design your text. To get you started, we will begin with some basic principles of design.

Five Basic Principles of Design

Good design creates a sense of order and gives your readers *access points* to help them locate the information they need. Here are five basic principles of design that will help you make your documents accessible and attractive:

1. **Balance.** Your text should look balanced from left to right and top to bottom.

2. **Alignment.** Related words and images should be aligned vertically on the page to reveal the text's structure and its hierarchy of information.

3. **Grouping.** Related images and ideas should be put near each other on the page, so readers see them as groups.

4. **Consistency.** Design features should be used consistently and predictably, helping readers quickly interpret the layout of each page and locate the information they need.

5. **Contrast.** Items on the page that are different should *look* different, creating a feeling of boldness and confidence.

These five principles are based on the Gestalt theory of design, which is used by many graphic designers, clothing designers, architects, and artists. Once you learn these principles, you should find it easy—and perhaps even fun—to design your texts.

Design Principle 1: Balance

To balance a text, imagine that a page from your document has been placed on a point, like a pencil point. Everything you add to the left side of the page needs to be balanced with something on the right. If you add a picture to the left side, you will need to add text or perhaps another picture on the right.

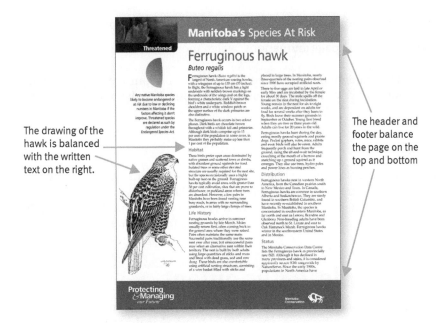

The drawing of the hawk is balanced with the written text on the right.

The header and footer balance the page on the top and bottom

FIGURE 14.1
A Balanced Design

Balance creates a sense of order in documents. This page is balanced both left to right and top to bottom.

For example, look at the page from a report shown in Figure 14.1. On this page, the drawing of a hawk on the left has what graphic designers call "weight." This drawing strongly attracts the readers' eyes to it. So to offset the drawing, the designers decided to put a large block of two-column text on the right. Meanwhile, the heavy green borders at the top and bottom of the sheet balance with each other, making the page feel stable and steady from top to bottom.

Balance is not a matter of making the page look symmetric (the same on the left and right). The items on the left and right of the page should balance, but they don't need to mirror each other.

Balancing a Page

When graphic designers talk about how much the items on the page "weigh," they are talking about how strongly elements will attract the readers' eyes to them. For example, on a webpage, animated images weigh more than images that don't move. (That's why advertisers often use dancing people in their Internet ads.)

Here are some guidelines for balancing the features on a page:

- Pictures weigh more than written text.

- Colour items weigh more than black and white items.

- Big items weigh more than small ones.

- Strange shapes weigh more than standard shapes.

- Things on the right side of the page weigh more than things on the left.

- Things on the top of the page weigh more than things on the bottom.
- Moving features, like webpage animations, weigh more than static ones.

You can use these guidelines to help you balance just about any page. As you design your document, don't be afraid to move items around on the page to see how they look.

Using Columns

You might also try using columns to create a balanced document design. The page shown in Figure 14.1, for example, uses a three-column layout to structure the page and create a sense of balance. The designers of this page decided to devote the left column to graphics, and they saved the right two columns for written text.

Design Principle 2: Alignment

Your readers will subconsciously search for visual relationships among items on the page. If two items line up on the page, they will assume that those two items are related in some way. If a picture, for example, is vertically aligned with a caption, list, or block of text on a page, readers will naturally assume that they go together.

For example, in Figure 14.2, the absence of alignment means the page on the left gives no hint about the levels of information, making it difficult for readers to find what they are looking for in the text. The page on the right, on the other hand, uses vertical alignment to highlight the levels in the text. Most readers would find the text on the right easier to read, because they immediately understand how the information is structured.

FIGURE 14.2
Using Vertical Alignment

Aligning text vertically allows you to show different levels of information in the text, making the document easier to read and scan. The page on the left is harder to read because it has minimal alignment. The page on the right uses alignment to signal the levels of information in the text.

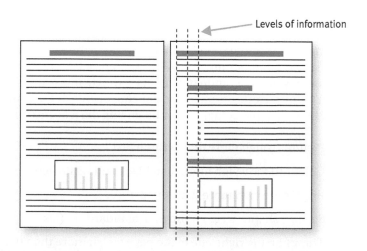

Levels of information

To create vertical alignment in your page design:

- Use margins and indentation consistently to highlight the hierarchy of the information.

- Use bulleted lists or numbered lists whenever appropriate to set off related information from the main text.

- Adjust the placement of any photographs or graphics to align vertically with the text around them, so readers see them as belonging together.

To check alignment on a page, use a straightedge, like a ruler or the edge of a piece of paper, to determine if items on the page line up.

Design Principle 3: Grouping

The design principle "grouping" takes advantage of your readers' tendency to see any items on a page that are close together as belonging to a group. If a photograph appears near a block of text, your readers will naturally assume that the image and text are related. Similarly, if a heading appears near a block of written text, the readers will see the heading as belonging with the written text.

Figure 14.3 shows a page design that uses grouping well. The "BioGems Facts" on the top left of the page is put close to the picture of mountains on the top right, creating a group. Also, the picture and the green headline, "Stop Electrocuting Patagonia,"

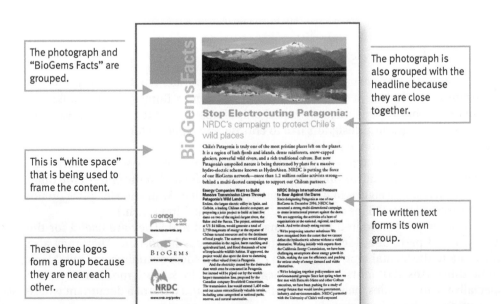

The photograph and "BioGems Facts" are grouped.

This is "white space" that is being used to frame the content.

These three logos form a group because they are near each other.

The photograph is also grouped with the headline because they are close together.

The written text forms its own group.

FIGURE 14.3
Using Grouping

Grouping is a good way to help readers put items together on the page. In this page, for example, you can see four distinct blocks of information that are grouped together, making the text easier to read.

can be seen as one group because they appear close together. Finally, the columns of text are naturally seen as a group, too, because they are so close together on the page.

One key to using grouping well is to be aware of the white spaces in your document's design where no text or images appear. When areas are left blank, they become eye-catching frames around graphics and written words.

Look again at Figure 14.3. Notice how the white space in the left margin creates a frame for the "BioGems Facts." The white space draws the readers' attention to these visual elements by creating a frame around them.

Design Principle 4: Consistency

The principle of consistency suggests that design features should be used consistently throughout the document.

- Headings should be used in a predictable and repeatable way.
- Pages should follow a predictable design pattern.
- Lists should use consistent bullets or numbering schemes.
- Headers, footers, and page numbers should be used to help make each page look similar to the others.

Consistency creates a sense of order in your document's design, so your readers know what to expect. If the page design or features like headings or images are used consistently, your readers will find it easier to understand how your document is structured.

Choosing Typefaces

A good first step toward consistency is to choose appropriate typefaces. A typeface is the design of the letters in your written text (e.g., Times Roman, Arial, Bookman, Helvetica). As a basic guideline, you should only choose one or two typefaces for your document. Many graphic designers like to choose one typeface for the headings and a different typeface for the main text.

There are two basic types of typeface: serif and sans serif. A serif typeface, like Times Roman, Garamond, or Bookman, has small tips (serifs) at the ends of the main strokes in each letter (Figure 14.4). Sans serif typefaces like Arial and Helvetica do not have these small tips. ("Sans serif" means "without serifs" in French.)

Serif fonts are considered more formal and traditional. They are useful for the main text and parts of a document where readability is important. They may also contribute to the formal tone you want to establish in most academic writing. Many people think sans serif fonts, like Helvetica and Arial, look more modern. They are especially useful for titles, headings, footers, captions, and parts of a document where you want to catch readers' eyes.

FIGURE 14.4 Serif vs. Sans Serif Typefaces

Serif fonts, like Times Roman on the left, have serifs, while sans serif fonts, like Arial on the right, do not have them.

Using Headings Consistently

Headings are very useful visual elements in any kind of document, but you need to use them consistently (Figure 14.5). Make some choices up front about the levels of headings you will use.

Title. The title of the document should be sized significantly larger than other headings in the text unless you are preparing an academic paper, in which case a title only slightly larger or in the same size as the rest of the document is appropriate. You

FIGURE 14.5 Levels of Headings

The headings you choose for your document should be clearly distinguishable from the body text and from each other. That way, your readers can see the hierarchy of your text clearly.

> # Document Title: The Best Paper Ever Written
>
> ## First-Level Headings
> These "A heads" divide a document into its major sections. They are usually significantly larger and bolder and use a different font than the body text.
>
> ### *Second-Level Headings*
> These "B heads" divide sections into smaller subsections. While these use the same font as the first-level headings, they should differ significantly in size or style (such as italics).
>
> **Third-Level Headings.** These "C heads" might be the same font and size as the body text (and appear on the same line), but use bold or italics to distinguish them.

might consider using colour to set off the title if you are writing for a general audience, or you could centre it.

First-Level Headings ("A Heads"). These are the most common headings. They divide your text into its major sections. First-level headings are often bold and slightly larger than the text used in the body of the document.

Second-Level Headings ("B Heads"). These are used when you need to divide a large section in your document into even smaller parts. These headings tend to use italics and can be the same size as the body text.

Third-Level Headings ("C Heads"). These are usually the smallest level of headings. They are often italicized or boldfaced and placed on the same line as the body text.

Headings help readers in a few important ways. First, they offer access points into the text, giving readers obvious places to locate the information they need. Second, they highlight the structure of the text, breaking down the larger document into smaller blocks of information. Third, they give readers places to take breaks from reading sentence after sentence, paragraph after paragraph.

Headings are also beneficial to you as the writer, because they help you make transitions between large sections of the document. Instead of a clumsy, "And now, let me move on to the next issue" kind of statement, you can use a heading to quickly and cleanly signal the transition to a new subject. Headings also allow you, as the writer, to easily see the overall structure of your text so you can check the logic and sequence.

Just remember that headings do not take the place of well-constructed topic sentences and should be used to indicate major sections of a document rather than paragraph breaks.

Design Principle 5: Contrast

The fifth and final design principle is *contrast*. Using contrast means making different items on the page look significantly different. Contrast is a common design element in documents written for general audiences, but is used only occasionally in academic documents. In less specialized writing, your headings, for example, should look significantly different than the main text. Your title should also be clearly distinguishable from your headings.

There are a variety of ways to create contrast in your document's design. You can change the size of the font, add colour, use shading, and use highlighting features like boldface, italics, or underlining. The sample report shown in Figure 14.6 uses contrast in several important ways:

- The blue banner across the top, "Geothermal Technologies Program, Colorado," clearly contrasts with the rest of the items on the page because it uses big lettering and a bold colour.

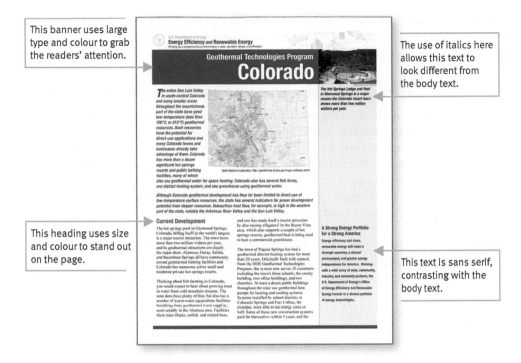

FIGURE 14.6 Using Contrast

Contrast makes a page look more readable and attractive. This page uses several kinds of contrast to capture the readers' attention.

- Below the banner, the italicized text contrasts sharply with the body text, helping it stand out on the page.

- The blue heading "Current Development" is clearly distinguishable from the body text because it is larger and uses colour.

- In the blue screened box on the right of the page, the use of a sans serif font helps to distinguish this text from the body text just to its left.

The secret to using contrast is experimenting with the page design to see how things look. So be daring and explore how items on the page look when you add contrast. Try making visual features larger, bolder, more colourful, or different.

Using Photography and Images

With the design capabilities of today's computers, it's fairly simple to add photography and other images to your document. However, remember that most academic forms of writing do not use photographs. If you want to add figures to a piece of writing, make sure it is because they aid the reader in understanding what you are writing about (rather than just adding a pretty picture to a piece). To add a picture, you can use a digital camera or a mobile phone to snap the picture, or you can download a picture from the Internet.

Downloading Photographs and Images from the Internet

If you find a photograph or image on the Internet that you want to use, save the image to your hard drive and insert it into your document.

When using photographs and images taken from the Internet, remember that almost all of them are protected by copyright law. You will need to consult the terms of use for each image that you plan to include. Some sites, such as *Creative Commons*, allow most images to be used for academic purposes, but other sites have restrictions. You will need to assess copyright on a case-by-case basis.

If you want to publish your document or put it on the Internet, you will need to ask permission to use the photograph or image from the person or organization that owns it. Current Canadian copyright law prohibits public distribution (e.g., online posting or publication) of images without copyright permission. The easiest way to ask permission is to send an e-mail to the person who manages the website on which you found the image. Explain how you want to use the image, where it will appear, and how you will identify its source.

In most cases, the website owner will give you permission or explain how you can get permission. If the owner denies you permission, you will not be able to use the photograph or image.

Labelling a Photograph or Image

You should label each photograph or image by giving it a figure number and a title (Figure 14.7). The figure number should then be mentioned in the written text, so your readers know when to look for the photograph.

Captions are not mandatory, but they can help your readers understand how the image relates to the written text.

Using Graphs and Charts

Graphs and charts can also be helpful additions to your documents, especially if you are presenting data to your readers. Genres like proposals routinely use graphs and charts to illustrate data. These graphics can also be useful in evaluations and position papers to provide support for claims in the written text.

Creating a Graph or Chart

If you need to make your own graph or chart, your best option might be to use the spreadsheet program, such as *Excel* or *Quattro Pro,* that came bundled with your word-processing software (Figure 14.8). Simpler graphs can be made in presentation software, like *PowerPoint* or *Keynote.*

Fig. 1: A Tiktaalik

Figure number and title.

The Tiktaalik was a prehistoric fish that had four legs. Paleontologists think this creature fills the fossil gap between fish and early limbed animals.

Caption and source information.

Source: National Science Foundation,
 Oct. 2008,
 Web, 19 Mar. 2009.

These spreadsheet and presentation software packages can help you create quick graphs and charts from a data set. Then you can insert the graphic right into your document. (Your word processor will probably have a Chart feature that will take you to the spreadsheet program.) Once you have created the graph, you should add a title

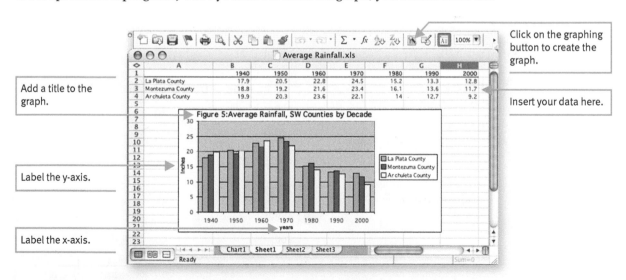

Click on the graphing button to create the graph.

Add a title to the graph.

Insert your data here.

Label the y-axis.

Label the x-axis.

FIGURE 14.8 **Using Spreadsheet Software to Make a Graph**
A spreadsheet is a helpful tool for creating a graph. Enter your data and then click the graphing button to create a graph. Then you can insert the graph into your document.

and label the horizontal x-axis and vertical y-axis (Figure 14.8). These axes need to be clearly labelled, so readers know exactly what they measure.

After you have inserted your graph into your document, make sure you have labelled it properly and provided a citation for the source of the data. To label the graph, give it a number or letter and a title. For example, the graph in Figure 14.8 is called "Figure 5: Average Rainfall, SW Counties by Decade." After you have labelled the graph, include your source below the graph using a common citation style (e.g., MLA, APA).

In the written part of your document, refer to the graphic by its number, so readers know when to refer to it. When you want the readers to consider the graph, write something like, "As shown in Figure 5, the annual rainfall. . . ." Or, you can simply put "(Figure 5)" at the end of the sentence where you refer to the graph.

Choosing the Appropriate Graph or Chart

You can use various kinds of graphs and charts to display your data. Each graph or chart allows you to tell a different story to your readers.

Line Graph. A line graph is a good way to show measurements or trends over time. In a line graph, the vertical axis (y-axis) displays a measured quantity, such as temperature, sales, growth, and so on. The horizontal axis (x-axis) is usually divided into time increments such as years, months, days, or hours. See Figure 14.9.

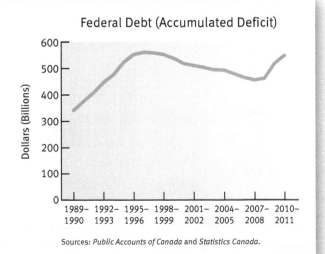

**FIGURE 14.9
Line Graph**

A line graph is a good way to show a trend over time. In this graph, the line reveals a trend that would not be apparent from the data alone.

Federal Debt (Accumulated Deficit)

Sources: *Public Accounts of Canada* and *Statistics Canada*.

Bar Chart. Bar charts are used to show quantities, allowing readers to make visual comparisons among different amounts. Like line graphs, bar charts can be used to show fluctuations in quantities over time. See Figure 14.10.

Pie Charts. Pie charts are useful for showing how a whole quantity is divided into parts. These charts are a quick way to add a visual element into your document, but they should be used sparingly. They take up a great amount of space in a document while usually presenting only a small amount of data. See Figure 14.11.

Tables. Tables provide the most efficient way to display data or facts in a small amount of space. In a table, information is placed in horizontal rows and vertical columns, allowing readers to quickly locate specific numbers or words that address their interests (Figure 14.12).

Diagrams. Diagrams are drawings that show features or relationships, which might not be immediately apparent to readers. The diagram in Figure 14.13, for example, shows the different parts of the human eye.

 With the capabilities of computers to create and add graphs, charts, and diagrams to your documents, you should look for opportunities to use these illustration methods. Readers expect these kinds of visuals, especially in proposals, to reinforce and clarify your main points.

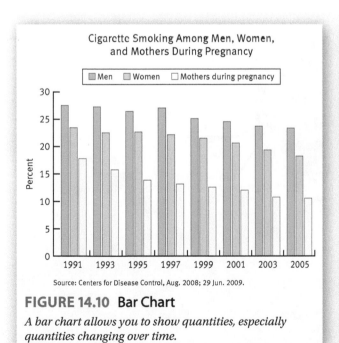

FIGURE 14.10 Bar Chart

A bar chart allows you to show quantities, especially quantities changing over time.

Source: Centers for Disease Control, Aug. 2008; 29 Jun. 2009.

Distribution of Seats by Party in the Canadian 2011 Federal Election

New Democratic Party (103 seats) 33.4%

Conservative Party (166 seats) 53.9%

Liberal Party (34 seats) 11.0%

Bloc Québécois (4 seats) 1.3%

Green Party (1 seat) 0.3%

Source: Adapted from Table 7, Distribution of seats by political affiliation and sex, in *Forty-First General Election 2011: Official Voting Results*, by Elections Canada. Retrieved from http://www.elections.ca/scripts/ovr2011/default.html

FIGURE 14.11 Pie Chart

A pie chart is a good way to show how a whole is divided into parts. When using a pie chart, you should label the slices of the pie and add the numerical information that was used to create the chart.

FIGURE 14.12
Table

A table offers a great way to show data efficiently. This table combines words and data to illustrate differences between boys' and girls' malicious uses of the Internet.

Online Rumours Tend to Target Girls *Have you, personally, ever experienced any of the following things online?*		
	Boys	*Girls*
Someone taking a private e-mail, IM, or text message you sent them and forwarding it to someone else or posting it where others could see it	13%	17%
Someone sending you a threatening or aggressive e-mail, IM, or text message	10%	15%
Someone spreading a rumour about you online	9%	16%
Someone posting an embarrassing picture of you online without your permission	5%	7%
At least one of the forms of cyberbullying listed above	23%	36%

Source: *Few Internet and American Life Project Parents and Teens Survey,* 2006.

FIGURE 14.13
A Diagram

A diagram is only partially realistic. It shows only the most important features and concentrates on relationships instead of showing exactly what the subject looks like.

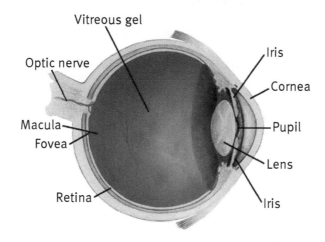

Now it's time to make your document look better. Here are some basic strategies for designing your document.

REVIEW Your Genre, Purpose, Readers, and Context

Your document's design should reflect and reinforce the genre and the overall purpose of your text. Design features should also be appropriate for your readers and the contexts in which your document will be used.

BALANCE the Text

Use design features to balance elements on the left and right as well as on the top and bottom of the page.

ALIGN Items Vertically on the Page

Look for opportunities to vertically align items on the page. Indenting text and aligning graphics with text will help create a sense of hierarchy and structure in your document.

GROUP Related Items Together

Put items near each other that are meant to be seen together. Photos should be near any text they reinforce. Headings should be close to the paragraphs they lead off. Use white space to frame items you want to be seen as a group.

CHECK the Document for Consistency

Your headings and other design features should be used consistently throughout the document. Make sure you use lists consistently.

ADD Some Contrast

Items on the page that are different should look significantly different. Use colour and font size to make written text stand out.

INCLUDE Photographs, Graphs, and Charts

Add your own photographs or images downloaded from the Internet to your document, being sure to follow copyright law. Create graphs or charts to illustrate data and complex ideas. Number, title, and caption these visuals so readers understand how the images connect to your text.

1. Ask each member in your group to bring a favourite magazine. Discuss the magazine's full-page advertisements and their use of design features. Pay special attention to the use of balance, alignment, grouping, consistency, and contrast.

2. Discuss the design of your favourite websites. What kinds of design features make it a favourite? What design features help you access information more easily?

3. On campus or in the community, find a flyer or brochure that you think is a failure in design. With your group, discuss how the document could be redesigned to make it more accessible and attractive.

1. Find a document written for a general audience on the Internet, on campus, or at your workplace that shows minimal attention to design. Then do a "design makeover" to make the document more accessible and attractive to readers.

2. Write a brief critique of the visual elements of a document you found on campus or at your workplace. Show how each of these five design principles makes its design effective or ineffective.

3. Practise downloading photographs and images and inserting them into a document. Add figure numbers and titles to the images. Include captions that explain the images and their relevance to your document. Be sure to check the copyright status of each visual.

1. **Evaluate the design of a document.** Write an evaluation in which you discuss the visual design of a document of your choice. Your analysis should consider whether the design is appropriate for the document's topic, purpose, readers, and context.

2. **Redesign a document on a computer.** Choose a document you wrote earlier in the semester. Redesign the document with your computer, using some of the concepts and principles discussed in this chapter. Then write a brief evaluation in which you discuss your design decisions.

MyCompLab

For support in meeting this chapter's objectives, follow this path in MyCompLab:

Student Resources → Writing → The Writing Process → Finishing and Editing. Review the Instruction and Multimedia resources about designing your document; then complete the Exercises and click on Gradebook to measure your progress.

15

Revising and Editing

In this chapter, you will learn how to:

- revise the overall approach of your document.
- edit the content, organization, and design of your paper.
- copyedit paragraphs and sentences to make them clearer.
- proofread your work efficiently and effectively.

N ow it's time to take your text from "good" to "excellent" by revising and editing it. This chapter shows you how to revise and edit your work at four different levels. Each level asks you to concentrate on different aspects of your text, moving from global issues to small details.

Level 1: Global Revision re-examines and adjusts the document's overall approach, using genre to sharpen its topic, angle, purpose, and appropriateness for the readers and context.

Level 2: Substantive Editing pays attention to the document's content, organization, and design.

Level 3: Copyediting focuses on revising the style for clarity, persuasion, and consistency, paying close attention to paragraphs and sentences.

Level 4: Proofreading examines and revises surface features, such as grammar, spelling, and usage.

As shown in Figure 15.1, you should work from the "global level" (global editing) to the "local level" (proofreading). That way, you can start out making large-scale changes to your document. Then, as the paper gets closer to finished, you can focus exclusively on style and correctness.

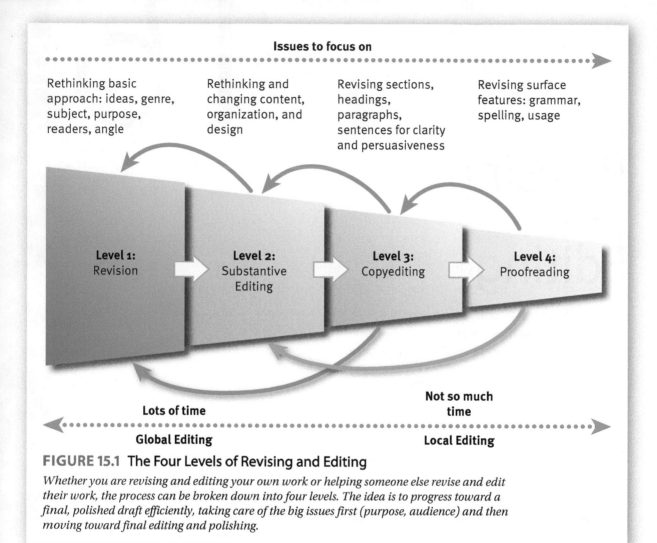

FIGURE 15.1 The Four Levels of Revising and Editing

Whether you are revising and editing your own work or helping someone else revise and edit their work, the process can be broken down into four levels. The idea is to progress toward a final, polished draft efficiently, taking care of the big issues first (purpose, audience) and then moving toward final editing and polishing.

Level 1: Global Revision

All right. You finished your first draft. Now it's time to re-examine and reconsider your project's topic, angle, and purpose, and your understanding of the readers and the context.

Figure 15.2 shows an excerpt of a student's proposal when it was a first draft. Figure 15.3 (on page 307) shows how Brad's original notes helped him challenge his ideas and rethink how he could persuade his readers to agree with him.

North America Is Addicted to Oil

When I hear all the whining about gas prices, it makes me really mad. After all, it's not like we haven't been warned. Economists and environmentalists have been telling people for years that this day of reckoning would come. Now it's here, and everyone is acting like they have been completely caught off guard. They don't have solutions. They just want another hit of their drug.

This crisis reminds me of people trying to quit smoking. I started smoking when I was 16 and I smoked for three years until I started university. Why did I stop? Well, I knew it was bad for me, but mostly I couldn't afford it anymore. That's kind of where North America is right now. We know our addiction to oil is bad for us, but as long as it doesn't cost too much, we keep using. We'll deal with the effects later. So, why can't we break our addiction to oil like a smoker breaks the nicotine addiction?

How do we stop being addicted to oil? One of my friends gave me a book that helped me stop smoking. It is called *Seven Tools to Beat Addiction*, and it's by a social/clinical psychologist who has helped many people beat their addictions to smoking, sex, pornography, drugs, gambling, etc. The seven tools he describes would work well to help North America get off its oil habit, like when I stopped smoking:

1. *Values:* Build a foundation of values—We need to stop being so greedy and selfish.

2. *Motivation:* Activate our desire to quit—It's not going to happen until we admit we have a problem and want to break our addiction.

> Brad notices that his topic is mostly about gasoline prices, not about other oil-related issues (see his notes in Figure 15.3).

> Brad figures out that his best angle is the "Our addiction to oil is like an addiction to nicotine." He decides to stress that angle in the next draft.

FIGURE 15.2 Rough Draft   *(continued)*

With global revision, you need to look at the big picture and rethink your basic approach. Here is an excerpt from student writer Brad's rough draft of a proposal. Figure 15.3 shows part of his global revision.

(continued)

**FIGURE 15.2
Rough Draft**

3. *Reward:* Weigh the costs and benefits of addiction—Imagine all the money we'll save if it's not all going over to Saudi Arabia! Plus, pollution will go down and we'll be more healthy.

4. *Resources:* Identify strengths and weaknesses—We have lots of possible sources of alternative energy. Plus, we already have lots of highly educated people who can figure this stuff out.

> Brad realizes that this list is messy and long. So he decides to trim it down, while expanding on some of the more important concepts.

5. *Support:* Get help from those nearest to us—If other nations see us on the right track, they will probably start working with us, not against us.

6. *A Mature Identity:* Grow into self-respect and responsibility—For the last decade, our continent has been acting like an immature brat on the world stage. It's time to start acting more mature.

7. *Higher Goals:* Pursue and accomplish things of value—Maybe we can strive for a better, cleaner world instead of just trying to figure out how we can keep the cheap gas flowing.

> He sees that he needs to expand on the argument in this paragraph. Right now it's mostly broad statements with minimal concrete support.

Getting over an addiction is tough. I still feel those cravings for nicotine. Getting ourselves off oil is going to be hard and even a little painful. We are going to be tested, and our pushers will be waiting for us to fail. But ending our oil addiction has so many benefits. We will save money, our health, and improve our national securities. We've taken the first step. We admitted we have a problem. Now, let's get to work.

Notes on First Draft (Global Revision)

I'm writing a proposal to fix our dependence on oil as an energy source.

Topic: My topic is how to solve the oil crisis that we are facing right now. I need to concentrate mostly on consumer's need for gasoline to drive. Also, I want to bring in some of the environmental benefits of transitioning to alternative fuels. I want to show how seeing oil as an addiction can be a path to solving the problem.

Angle: My angle is the metaphor "North America is addicted to oil." What happens if we take that metaphor seriously and treat oil as a drug? As someone who was addicted to nicotine, I think I have some insight into how it feels to fight an addiction and what it takes to win.

Purpose: I don't think my purpose is clearly stated in this draft. So, here it is in one sentence: The purpose of my paper is to argue that North America needs to treat oil as a drug and we need to recognize that we are addicted to that drug; so, we need to use drug rehab steps to end our addiction. (That's messy.)

Readers: Mostly, I thought I was writing to everyone, but now I realize that I am writing mostly to younger people who can't afford these gas prices and really want to do something to change the world.

Expectations— First my readers need to understand the real problem. Then they need a clear strategy for solving that problem. The media keeps acting as though this problem is really about gas prices. That's just a symptom of the deeper problem underneath. My readers need to see that the prices are not the real problem.

Values—My values are similar to my readers' values. They care about the environment, but they also like the freedom of driving and travelling. They're also realistic about this problem. They want to do the right thing, but they know an easy solution isn't out there.

Attitudes—They are probably frustrated with the gas prices like most people. I would like to tap into their frustration, turn it into anger, and then get my readers to consider my solution. Get angry at that drug! It's the best way to fight it!

Here are Brad's notes to help him with the global revision process.

Brad realizes that he needs to narrow his topic.

He points out that his purpose is not fully stated in this first draft.

Brad analyzes his readers to figure out how he can use their expectations, values, and attitudes to persuade them.

FIGURE 15.3 Global Revision

Brad's professor asked him to reflect on his first draft. In these notes, Brad is examining what he hopes to accomplish with a global revision of his proposal draft.

Challenge Your Draft's Topic, Angle, and Purpose

You need to challenge your first draft to make sure it's doing what you intended. Reread your draft, paying special attention to the following global issues:

Topic. How has your topic evolved since you started? Do you now have a better understanding of the boundaries of your topic? Can you sharpen the topic, or does it need to be broadened a little? Can you find any places where your paper strays from the topic? Can you find any gaps in your coverage where you don't address a key issue about your topic?

Angle. Have you shown what is new about your topic or what has changed recently? Have you connected your paper to any recent events or changes in our culture? Have you uncovered any unexpected or surprising issues that complicate or challenge your own views?

Purpose. Is your purpose clear in the introduction of your paper, and have you achieved that purpose by the conclusion? Does your purpose need to be more focused?

Chapter 2 discusses these issues in depth if you would like more strategies for shaping your topic, angle, and purpose.

Think About Your Readers (Again) and the Context

As you drafted your paper, chances are good that you gained a better understanding of your readers' expectations, values, and attitudes. Now try to put yourself in your readers' place to imagine how they will react to your ideas and the way you have expressed them. Be sure to consider whether your readers are academics or a more general audience, as in Brad's case.

Expectations. Have you given readers all the information they need to make a decision? What additional information do they need if they are going to agree with you? Are there any places in your paper where you can cut out information that goes beyond what the readers need to know?

Values. Are your readers' values different from yours? If so, have you anticipated their values and how their values might cause them to react differently to your ideas than you would? Can you add anything that would appeal to their sense of values or help build trust between you and them?

Attitudes. Have you adjusted the text to fit your primary readers' attitude about your topic? If they have a positive attitude about your topic, have you reinforced that attitude? If they have a negative attitude, have you given them good reasons to think differently about your topic?

Now look at the context for your document. Again, it's likely that you have developed a stronger understanding of the place, medium, and social-political issues that will influence how your readers receive and interpret your ideas.

Place. How will the physical place in which readers experience your document shape how they read it? What will they see, hear, and feel? What is moving in this place, and who will be there? How will the history and culture of this place shape how readers will interpret what you are saying?

Medium. How does the technology you used to present the information shape how people read it? Paper documents are received differently than onscreen documents. Information provided as presentations, videos, and podcasts will also be understood in unique ways.

Social and Political Influences. What current social, economic, and political trends are in play with your topic and readers? How will your ideas affect your readers' relationships with others or their economic and political concerns?

If you need more help profiling your readers and understanding the contexts in which they will use your document, turn to Chapter 3, "Readers, Contexts, and Rhetorical Situations."

Level 2: Substantive Editing

Watch Office Hours Series: Revising

When doing "substantive editing," you should look closely at the content, organization, and design of your document. Read through your paper again, paying attention to the following issues:

Determine Whether You Have Enough Information (or Too Much)

Your paper needs to have enough information to support its claims and explain your ideas to readers, but you don't want to include more content than you need.

- ❐ Does your thesis statement (usually in the introduction and/or the conclusion) describe what you're achieving in this paper?
- ❐ Are your claims in the body of the paper expressed completely and accurately? Could you express them in a more prominent, precise, or compelling way?
- ❐ Can you find any places where your ideas need more support or where your claims need more evidence drawn from sources?
- ❐ Are there any digressions? Can you trim the text down?

If you need more information or sources to back up your ideas, turn to Chapter 22, "Finding Sources and Collecting Information."

Reorganize Your Work to Highlight Major Ideas

Your readers will expect your document to conform to the genre's typical organizational pattern. This does not mean mechanically following a formula, but it does mean that your document should reflect the features your readers will expect in this genre.

❏ Does your paper have each of the sections that are usually included in this genre? If not, are you making a conscious choice to leave out a section or merge it with something else?

❏ Does your introduction do its job according to the conventions of the genre? Does it draw your readers in, introduce them to the topic, state the purpose and main claim, and stress the importance of the subject?

❏ Are your main ideas prominent enough? If not, can you move these main ideas to places where your readers are more likely to see them?

❏ Does the conclusion do its job according to the conventions of the genre? Does it restate the main point of the whole paper, re-emphasize the importance of the topic, and offer a look to the future?

❏ Do the introduction and conclusion echo each other? If not, can you adjust your introduction and conclusion so they are clearly talking about the same topic, angle, and purpose?

Chapter 16 discusses introductions and conclusions, and Chapter 17 discusses paragraphing and sections.

Look for Ways to Improve the Design

Review how your document looks, focusing on whether the design is a good fit for your readers. The design should make your text easier to read and more attractive.

❏ Does the design of the document match your readers' expectations for the genre? Is the visual "tone" of the design appropriate for this genre?

❏ Keeping in mind the differing requirements for academic and popular writing, does the text look inviting, interesting, and easy to read? Can you use page design, images, or colour to make it more attractive and inviting to your readers?

❏ Have you used the design principles of balance, alignment, grouping, consistency, and contrast to organize and structure the page layout?

❏ Have you used graphics and charts to reinforce and clarify the written text while adding a visual element to the document?

Chapter 14, "Designing," offers some helpful strategies for improving the design of your document.

Ask Someone Else to Read Your Work

Substantive editing is a good time to ask others to review your work. Ask a friend or someone from your class to read through your text. Tell him or her to concentrate on content, organization, and design. For now, your editor can ignore any typos or grammatical errors, because right now you need feedback on higher-level features and problems in the text.

For example, Figure 15.4 shows some helpful substantive editing comments from Rachel, a person in Brad's class, on his second draft. Brad has made significant

North America Is Addicted to Oil

When gasoline prices rose dramatically in the summer of 2008, North Americans whined and complained. They called for more oil to be pumped from the arctic, from the shores of California and Florida, from the oil sands in Alberta. They yelled at gas station attendants and wrote angry letters to newspapers and members of their respective governments.

But it's not as though we didn't see this coming. For years, economists, conservationists, and political leaders have been telling the North American public that the cheap ride on oil would be coming to an end. The demand for oil was continually going up, especially with emerging economies like those in China, India, and Brazil demanding more oil. Yet, people kept buying big cars and commuting longer and longer distances. It's not as though we weren't warned.

> Back up these claims with cites from sources.

North America is a junkie, and oil is our heroin. In this proposal, I would like to show how treating oil as an addiction can help us get out of this terrible situation and perhaps even save the planet.

> Your thesis statement is clear, but it could be less blunt.

How do we stop being addicted to oil? As someone who stopped smoking, I know just how difficult it can be to break an addiction. After smoking for almost three years, I decided that I wanted to quit. One of my friends gave me a book written by psychologist Stanton Peele called *Seven Tools to Beat Addiction*, which I will discuss below.

> I noticed that you don't really have a section that discusses the problem. Instead, you just go straight to the solution. Maybe you should spend a little more time talking about the causes and effects of the problem.

Values: Build a foundation of values—We need to have conversations about what we value as North Americans. Right now, our societies are running on consumerism, greed, and selfishness. We need to build or rebuild core values in which the community's needs balance with the desires of the individual.

(continued)

FIGURE 15.4 Substantive Editing

Brad revised his first draft for a peer review session the next day. Here is the second draft and substantive editing comments from Rachel in his writing group.

(continued)

Motivation: Activate our desire to quit—Major political parties and governments need to reach consensus on this issue and then work together to solve it. We cannot kick the habit if one party or the other is telling us we don't really have a problem.

> *This is cool, but some outside support would make it stronger.*

Reward: Weigh the costs and benefits of addiction—Governments need to commission scientific studies that show North Americans the real costs of oil, such as the costs to our health, our environment, and the militaries we need to protect our flow of the drug. Only then will we be able to truly measure the benefits of getting off the junk.

> *A chart or graph would support what you are saying here.*

Resources: Identify strengths and weaknesses—Our nations need to recognize that our scientific, technological, and manufacturing capabilities would allow us to make a relatively quick conversion to other forms of energy, like solar, wind, and nuclear. Our weaknesses, however, include short-sighted thinking and selfishness.

> *This list could be designed better to make it more readable.*

Support: Get help from those nearest to us—Like any addict, North America is going to need support. Certainly, our Allies in Europe and Asia would be willing to help. They're recovering addicts too.

> *Some quotes from sources would make this part much stronger.*

A Mature Identity: Grow into self-respect and responsibility—North America has been behaving like a young addict who doesn't care for himself and lacks responsibility for his actions. These nations need to mature and start taking on adult priorities, such as caring for others, making tough decisions, and protecting those who are weaker than us.

Higher Goals: Pursue and accomplish things of value—Our addiction has caused us to give up on many of those ideals that made us strong in the first place. We're cutting exploration, innovation, diplomacy, and creativity, so we can continue our flow of the

FIGURE 15.4 Substantive Editing

drug. It's time to get back to what North America once was—a beacon of democracy and prosperity. Once the drug is out of our system, we can start to think about the future again, rather than just our next fix.

Let's be honest. Getting ourselves off oil is going to be hard and a little painful. It's a life change, and we are going to be tested. But the benefits of ending our oil addiction are enormous. We will save money, our health, and improve our security. We've taken the first step. We admitted we have a problem. Now, let's do something about it.

Perhaps you can expand on the benefits of doing this. More discussion of the benefit might help win over your readers.

Overall, Brad, I really like your paper. Comparing North America's need for oil to a drug addiction really helped me see the problem we have. Your purpose seems clear enough, and I think I understand your main point. One big problem is that you make some pretty big claims that aren't really supported with evidence in your paper. As a reader, I need some evidence before I can really be convinced of the problem and need for a solution.

improvements to his first draft (shown in Figure 15.2). Rachel's thorough comments will help him improve it even more, because they highlight the proposal's weaknesses in content, organization, and design.

Level 3: Copyediting

Copyediting involves improving the "flow" of your text by making it *clear, concise, consistent,* and *correct* (sometimes called the "Four Cs" by professional copyeditors). When you are copyediting, focus exclusively on your document's title and headings, paragraphs, and sentences. Your ideas need to be as clear as possible and stated as concisely as possible. Also, make sure your ideas are consistent and that your facts are accurate.

Review Your Title and Headings

Your title should grab the reader's attention, or, in the case of academic essays, identify the topic and approach. The headings in your document should help the reader quickly grasp your ideas and understand how the document is structured.

- ❐ Is the title unique and/or informative? If your readers saw the title alone, would they be interested in reading your paper?
- ❐ Do the headings accurately reflect the information that follows them?
- ❐ Do the headings grab the readers' attention and bring them into the text?
- ❐ Are the headings consistent in grammar and parallel to each other in structure?

You can learn more about using effective titles and headings in Chapter 12, "Organizing and Drafting," and Chapter 14, "Designing."

Edit Paragraphs to Make Them Concise and Consistent

Work through your document paragraph by paragraph, paying attention to how each one is structured and how it works with the paragraphs around it.

As you read through each paragraph, ask yourself these questions:

- ❐ Would a transition sentence at the beginning of the paragraph help make a bridge from the prior paragraph?
- ❐ Would transitions help bridge any gaps between sentences in the paragraph?
- ❐ Is each paragraph unified? Does each sentence in the paragraph stick to a consistent topic? Do any sentences seem to stray from the paragraph's claim or statement?
- ❐ Does each paragraph logically follow from the paragraph that preceded it and does it prepare readers for the paragraph that follows?
- ❐ If the paragraph is long or complex, would it benefit from a "point sentence" at its end that states or restates the paragraph's overall point?

Of course, there are exceptions to these guidelines. If you are using an "open-form genre" (e.g., narrative), your paragraphs may be designed to lead your readers from one moment to the next or one event to the next.

Revise Sentences to Make Them Clearer

After you reshape and refine each paragraph, focus your attention on the clarity and style of individual sentences.

- ☐ Are the subjects of your sentences easy to locate? Do they tend to be placed early in the sentence where your readers can easily find them?

- ☐ Do the verbs express the action of the sentence? Can you remove any passive verbs (e.g., *is, was, be, has been*) by putting an action verb in its place?

- ☐ Can you eliminate any unnecessary prepositional phrases?

- ☐ If writing for a general audience, are your sentences breathing length? Are any sentences too long (i.e., do they take longer than one breath to say out loud)?

In Chapter 13, "Choosing a Style," you can find some "plain style" techniques for improving the clarity of your sentences while making them more concise.

Revise Sentences to Make Them More Descriptive

Now, work on giving your sentences more impact and power.

- ☐ Do your sentences use vivid detail to help readers visualize what you are writing about? Can you use sight, hearing, smell, taste, and feel to enhance the experience of reading your sentences?

- ☐ Would any similes, metaphors, or analogies help your readers to understand or visualize what you are talking about?

- ☐ Do your sentences generally use a consistent tone and voice? Can you describe in one word the tone you are trying to set in your paper? Do your sentences achieve that tone?

Level 4: Proofreading

Proofreading is the final step in editing your document, during which you should search for any typos, grammatical errors, spelling mistakes, and word usage problems. Proofreading takes patience and practice, but it is critical to successful writing.

These proofreading strategies will help you catch those kinds of errors:

Read Your Writing Out Loud

Your ear will often detect problems that slip past your eyes. When reading your paper out loud, you need to pay attention to every word. Errors that may slip by when reading silently really stick out when reading aloud.

Read Your Draft Backwards

By reading your draft backwards, sentence by sentence, you can concentrate on the words rather than their meaning. You will find yourself noticing any odd sentence constructions and misspelled words.

Read a Hard Copy of Your Work

If you have been drafting and editing onscreen, reading a printed hard copy will help you to see your writing from a fresh perspective. You might even try changing the font or line spacing to give the printed out text a different look.

Know Your Grammatical Weaknesses

If you know you tend to make certain grammatical mistakes, devote one proofreading pass just to those issues. For instance, if you have trouble with *its* versus *it's*, or trouble with run-on sentences, devote one entire proofreading session to that kind of mistake, looking only for it.

Use Your Spellchecker

Spellcheck has become a reliable tool over the years. It can flag most annoying typos and spelling errors. You should not, however, rely exclusively on your spellchecker for proofreading. Instead, read through your document looking for possible spelling problems. If you aren't sure whether a word is being spelled or used correctly, then use your word processor's dictionary to look it up.

Peer Review: Asking for Advice

The keys to productive peer review are focus and honesty. Writers need to tell their reviewers specifically what kind of help they want. For example:

- This is an early draft, so don't pay any attention to the grammar and wording. Look at my ideas and my claim. Could they be stronger or sharper?

- My readers are high school students who are considering skipping post-secondary studies. Do you think this draft addresses their needs and answers the questions they would have?

- My claim is X. What can I do to make sure that it comes through clearly and persuasively?

- Please look at the introduction closely. Do I introduce the topic and engage the reader's interest?

Encourage your reviewers to be honest about your draft. You need them to do more than say "I like it," "It looks good," or "I would give it an A." Ask them to be as tough as possible, so you can find places to improve your writing.

As we have seen in this chapter, an editor cannot handle all four levels of revising and editing at the same time. As a writer, you should determine which level of edit is most helpful at this point. For instance, you do not want someone nitpicking about grammar issues when you are still figuring out your basic ideas and the document's overall approach. You also do not want someone telling you that your angle and purpose are completely wrong when your work is due in 30 minutes and all you want is proofreading.

Editors and writers need to communicate about what kind of feedback they want. At all levels, you should tell the writer about gaps and problems. But you should never forget that writers also need to understand what's working well in their documents.

Level 1: Global Revison. At this level, question and challenge the writer's basic approach to the topic, angle, and purpose. Check to see whether the writer has appropriately adapted the document to the readers' expectations, values, and attitudes.

Level 2: Substantive Editing. Help the writer rethink the document's content, organization, and design. Review the content for both strengths and possible gaps. Examine the organization and tell the writer whether each part of the document does the job it needs to. Look at the overall design to see what elements could be rethought.

Level 3: Copyediting. Edit the style for clarity, persuasion, and consistency. Look closely at the title, headings, paragraphs, and sentences to make sure they are clear, concise, consistent, and correct.

Level 4: Proofreading. When proofreading, look for mistakes. Do not simply make the changes for the writer. Instead, you should point out problems so that the writer can see them. In a writing class, however, the writer should decide what needs to be changed in the final draft.

Write your responses to these questions on a sheet of paper or in an e-mail, so the author has something concrete to work with when revising the draft. As always, be sure to point out both strengths and places for improvement.

Ready to finish your document? Follow the "Four Levels of Editing" to revise and edit your text like a professional.

REVISE Globally (Level 1)

Revision means "re-visioning" the text. Challenge your draft's topic, angle, and purpose. Then think further about your readers and the contexts in which they will read or use your document.

EDIT the Content, Organization, and Design (Level 2)

Substantive editing involves looking closely at the content, organization, and design of your document. Determine whether you have enough (or too much) content. Then make sure the organization of your document highlights your major ideas. Also, look for ways you can improve the design.

COPYEDIT Paragraphs and Sentences (Level 3)

Copyediting involves improving the "flow" of your text by making it *clear, concise, consistent*, and *correct*. Review your title and headings to make sure they are meaningful and consistent. Work paragraph by paragraph to make the text concise and consistent. Then revise the style of your sentences to make them clear and descriptive.

PROOFREAD Your Work (Level 4)

As a last step, proofreading is your final opportunity to catch any errors, like typos, grammatical errors, spelling mistakes, and word usage problems. To help you proofread, try reading your writing out loud, reading the draft backwards, and reading a hard copy of your work. Be aware of your grammatical weaknesses and look for those specific errors. Meanwhile, use your computer's spellchecker to catch any smaller errors.

ASK Someone Else to Review Your Work

By now, you are probably unable to see your document objectively. So have someone else look over your work and give you an honest assessment. Your professor may even give you time to "peer review" each other's writing.

QUICK START GUIDE

1. On the Internet, find a document that seems to be poorly edited. With your group, discuss the impact that the lack of editing has on you and other readers. What do the errors say about the author and perhaps the company or organization he or she works for?

2. Choose a grammar rule with which you have problems. Explain in your own words what the rule is (use the "Handbook" section of this book for help). Then explain why you have trouble with it. Why do you have trouble remembering to follow it during composing?

3. With your group, create a simile or analogy that sums up how you see the differences among the levels of editing, from global revision to local editing (proofreading). For example, you might say, "Global editing is like _____, while substantive editing is like _____." Or, you might complete the sentence: "The overall progression from global editing to proofreading is like moving from _____ to _____."

1. On your own or with a colleague, choose a draft of your writing and decide which level of revising and editing it needs. Then, using the appropriate section in this chapter, walk through the steps for editing the document at that level.

2. Write a brief e-mail explaining the main differences between the levels of revising and editing to someone unfamiliar with the concept.

3. Find a text on the Internet that you think is poorly written. Using the four levels of editing, read through the text four separate times. Each time, explain what you would need to do to the text to make it stronger.

1. **Edit a text from someone in your class.** Exchange drafts with another person or within a small group during peer review. In addition to the draft itself, write a memo to your reviewers telling them exactly what you'd like them to focus on. Use the language from this chapter (level 1, level 2, global, local, etc.) and define as precisely as you can what you think might be an issue.

2. **Copyedit a text onscreen with Track Changes.** Find a rough draft (one of your own, a colleague's, or something from the Internet) and use Track Changes to do a level 3 edit (copyediting) on it. When you have finished, write an e-mail to your professor explaining your edits.

MyCompLab

For support in meeting this chapter's objectives, follow this path in MyCompLab:

Student Resources → Writing → The Writing Process → Revising. Review the Instruction and Multimedia resources about revising and editing; then complete the Exercises and click on Gradebook to measure your progress.

4 Strategies
for Shaping
Ideas

PART OUTLINE

CHAPTER 16

Drafting Introductions and Conclusions   322

CHAPTER 17

Developing Paragraphs and Sections   331

CHAPTER 18

Using Basic Rhetorical Patterns   343

CHAPTER 19

Using Argumentative Strategies   357

CHAPTER 20

Working Collaboratively with Other Writers   376

These chapters go way beyond just tips and tricks. Instead, you will learn time-tested STRATEGIES *for arranging your ideas and writing with strength and authority.*

16

Drafting Introductions and Conclusions

┌─ **In this chapter, you will learn how to:** ─────────────

- start your papers with clear, engaging introductions appropriate to the genre you are writing in.
- catch your readers' attention with a grabber, lead, or discussion of existing research.
- finish your papers with strong conclusions.

└──

Introductions and conclusions are important because they are the places where the readers are paying the most attention. If readers don't like or get what they need from your introduction, chances are good that they won't like the rest of your text either. And, if they don't like how your paper ends, they will be left with doubts about what you had to say.

In this chapter, you are going to learn some easy-to-use strategies for writing great introductions and conclusions. By mastering some basic "moves" that are commonly made in introductions and conclusions, you can learn how to write powerful, engaging openings and closings for your texts.

Drafting Introductions

Put yourself in your readers' place. Before you start reading, you probably have some questions: "What is this? Why was this sent to me? What is this writer trying to get me to believe or do? Is this important? Do I care about this?" Your readers will be asking the same kinds of questions when they begin reading your text.

Five Introductory Moves

Your introduction should answer your readers' questions up front by making some or all of the following five introductory moves:

Move 1: Identify your topic.

Move 2: State your purpose.

Move 3: Offer background information on your topic.

Move 4: State your main point. In shorter papers (less than eight pages) this will likely be your thesis statement.

Move 5: Stress the importance of the topic to your readers.

These opening moves can be made in just about any order, although a thesis is typically placed near the end of the introduction. Only moves 1, 2, and 4 are really needed for a successful introduction, because these moves tell readers what you are writing about, why you are writing, and what you want to explain or prove. The other two moves will help your readers familiarize themselves with the topic. Here is a sample introduction that uses all five moves:

The Negative Influence of Contemporary Advertising on the Health of North American Youth: Analyzing the Promotion of Ideal Body Images and Substance Abuse

Sahil Sidhu

According to the American Academy of Pediatrics (AAP), a typical child in the United States is exposed to an estimated 40,000 commercials per year (AAP, as cited in Perse, 2006). Considering this, and the fact that children are much more likely than adults to be affected by messages in advertising (AAP, 2004), the influence of commercial media on modern youth must be analyzed. Although there are certain advertisements that attempt to safeguard the health of adolescents, such as those that discourage drinking while driving, other advertisements portray alcohol and tobacco consumption as an acceptable and fashionable lifestyle choice. Moreover, the media's representation of the ideal woman as unrealistically tall and thin has well-documented negative effects on female self-esteem (Ahern et al., 2011). Research has consistently shown that advertising damages the physical and mental health of North American adolescents. Thus, despite some limited positive effects, contemporary advertising has a predominantly negative influence on the health of North American youth, particularly through the promotion of the ideal body and the consumption of alcohol and tobacco.

> Background information and startling statistic.

> Topic and purpose identified.

> Importance of topic stressed.

> Main point or thesis stated.

In this introduction, the author *identifies the topic* (advertising's effects) and purpose up front and then offers some *background information*. In the next sentences, he *stresses the importance of the topic* with some data. Then he finishes the introduction by stating his *main point*.

Generally, it is a good idea to put your paper's main point, or thesis, at the end of the introduction, but you don't need to put it there. In the sample introduction above, for example, the writer could easily move the sentences around to put the main point earlier if that seemed to work better.

Using a Grabber to Start Your Introduction

To catch readers' attention, some writers like to use a *grabber* or *hook* at the beginning of their introduction. A grabber can gently spark your readers' curiosity, or it can capture them with a compelling statement and shout, "Listen to me!" Here are some good grabbers you can use:

Ask an Interesting Question. A question draws readers into the text by prompting them for an answer.

> Have you ever thought about becoming a professional chef? The training is rigorous and the work can be difficult, but the rewards are worth it.

State a Startling Statistic. An interesting statistic can immediately highlight the importance of the topic.

> A recent survey shows that 73 percent of teens in Oakville have smoked marijuana, and 23 percent report using it at least once a week ("Weed" A3).

Make a Compelling Statement. Make a statement that challenges readers at the beginning of the text.

> Unless we take action now on global warming, we are likely to see massive storms and rising ocean levels that will drown coastal cities.

Begin with a Quotation. A quote is a good way to pique your readers' curiosity.

> That great Canadian Pierre Trudeau once said, "The attainment of a just society is the cherished hope of civilized man." Today, it seems like our fellow citizens have forgotten what a just society might stand for.

Use Dialogue. Dialogue offers a quick way to bring your readers into the story you are telling.

> One morning at breakfast, I heard a couple of other students from my dorm talking about the terrorist attacks on September 11th. One of them said, "September 11th was just like when the Germans bombed Pearl Harbor." The other gave a confused look and asked, "You mean the Chinese, right? The Chinese bombed Pearl Harbor." That's when I came to the troubling conclusion that many people my age have a dangerously flawed grasp of history.

The best grabber is one that (1) identifies your topic, (2) says something that intrigues your readers, and (3) makes the point of your paper in a concise way.

Using a Lead to Draw in the Readers

You can also use a lead (also spelled "lede") to introduce your text. A lead is the first one or two paragraphs of a news story in a magazine, newspaper, or website. Like a grabber, the aim of a lead is to capture the readers' attention while giving them good reasons to continue reading. Here are some commonly used types of leads:

Scene Setter. A scene setter describes the place in which something important or interesting happened.

> The young men wade through thigh-high grass beneath the firs and ponderosa pines, calmly setting the forest on fire. With flicks of the wrist, they paint the landscape in flame. The newborn fires slither through the grass and chew into the sagging branches. Every few minutes a fire ignites, flames devouring it in a rush of light, the roar of rockets. It is over in seconds. Only a smoking skeleton remains. (Neil Shea, "Under Fire")

Anecdote. An anecdote starts out the introduction with an interesting true story that happened to the author or someone else.

> My second-grade teacher never liked me much, and one assignment I turned in annoyed her so extravagantly that the red pencil with which she scrawled "See me!" broke through the lined paper. Our class had been asked to write about a recent field trip, and, as was so often the case in those days, I had noticed the wrong things. (Tim Page, "Parallel Play")

Case Histories. A case history lead tells two to three very short true stories about different people who have had similar problems or experiences.

> Fred Jenkins never thought he was the kind of person to declare bankruptcy. He was a successful businessman with money in the bank. When his wife found out that she had ovarian cancer, though, his bank accounts were soon emptied by the costs of her care. Mira Johanson took a different path to bankruptcy. She racked up $24,000 in credit card debt because she bought a house she couldn't afford. When she was laid off at Gerson Financial, she could no longer make the minimum payments on her credit cards. Then, with her credit in ruins, she could not refinance her mortgage. Her personal finances collapsed, causing her to lose everything.

Personal Sketch. Articles that are about a person often start out with a description of the person and a small biography.

> In mid-January 1959, Fidel Castro and his comrades in revolution had been in power less than a month. Criticized in the international press for threatening summary justices and execution for many members of the government

of ousted dictator Fulgencio Batista, Castro called on the Cuban people to show their support at a rally in front of Havana's presidential palace.

Castro, 32, wore a starched fatigue cap as he faced the crowd. With him were two of his most trusted lieutenants, Camilo Cienfuegos, unmistakable in a cowboy hat, and Ernesto (Che) Guevara in his trademark black beret. (Guy Gugliotta, "Comrades in Arms")

The lead comes before your main point (i.e., your thesis) in the introduction. A lead will make the introduction a bit longer than usual, and it will draw your readers into your text and encourage them to keep reading.

Using the State of Existing Research

The previous suggestions apply to writing for general audiences and many (such as the use of questions, statistics, quotations, and case histories) also apply to academic essays. However, academic essays use an additional approach to draw in their specialized readers, namely situating their work in relation to existing research debates. In order to do this, academic writers seek to identify the current state of research on their topic and then situate their texts within the key debates. This convention ensures that their work will be important and of interest to those specialized readers in the field. Often, identifying research debates leads into an academic literature review, which you can find discussed in Chapter 5. Here is an example of a student writer using this approach:

Description of existing research.

Identification of debate.

Presentation of research as responding to the debate.

Research shows that gay and bisexual adolescents are repeatedly subjected to harassment and discrimination. Their peers ostracize them for not conforming to society's heterosexual expectations (Grossman, D'Augelli, & Frank, 2011) and, like many minorities, they experience academic difficulties, suffer from substance abuse, and are prone to self-harm and suicide (Smith, 2004). While research seems conclusive on the negative effects that minority status entails, debate persists about how best to address these problems and change social attitudes. Analysis of the recent "It Gets Better" media campaign suggests a new set of possibilities. This campaign takes a revolutionary attitude to issues of lesbian, gay, bisexual, and transgender (LGBT) discrimination by making discrimination socially unacceptable, and it unites members of the North American LGBT community in ways that previous campaigns did not.

Drafting Conclusions

When you are in a university or college lecture, what happens when your professor says, "In conclusion. . . ," or "Finally," or "Here is what I really want you to take away from today's lecture"? Everyone in the audience wakes up and starts paying close attention. Why? Because everyone knows the professor is going to state his or her main points.

The same is true of the conclusion at the end of your document. When your readers arrive at the conclusion, they will start paying closer attention because they know you are going to state your main points.

Here are five moves that you could make in your conclusion:

Move 1: Signal clearly that you are concluding.

Move 2: Restate your main point.

Move 3: Stress the importance of your topic again.

Move 4: Call your readers to action.

Move 5: Look to the future.

Your conclusion should be as short as possible, and it should be similar to your introduction in content and tone. In your conclusion, you need to bring readers back around to the beginning of your argument, showing them that you have achieved your purpose. For example, consider Sahil Sidhu's conclusion:

> In conclusion, this paper demonstrates that the negative influences of contemporary advertising on the health of North American youth greatly outweigh the positive influences; it does so by analyzing the impact of ads that portray ideal body images, underage smoking, and underage drinking. For example, promotion of ideal appearances can lead to the development of body dissatisfaction, kidney stones, anorexia, and bulimia. Similarly, the influence exerted by tobacco and alcohol advertising on youth can lead to cancer, drug use, and a greater tendency to drink and drive. On the other hand, studies show that modern advertising can have a positive effect on the health of adolescents through campaigns that discourage tobacco usage and drinking while driving. Currently, though, these positive examples pale in comparison to the overall negative impact of advertising. Considering this, media education must be directed toward North American youth; adolescents need to be taught to resist the enticing messages put forth by modern advertising. The preservation of their health depends on it.

Conclusion signalled.

Main point restated.

Call to action.

Importance of topic and look to the future stated.

This conclusion makes all five concluding moves in one brief paragraph. First, the author *signals that he is concluding* in the first sentence with the phrase, "In conclusion."

Phrases that signal a conclusion include the following:

In the end,	In brief,	As a whole,
Put briefly,	Overall,	In closing,
Ultimately,	In summary,	To finish up,
To sum up,	Finally,	On the whole,

Then the author stresses the *importance of the topic* by returning to the main argument. The return to this key idea, which started in the introduction, also brings the reader around to the beginning of the argument, making it feel whole. This return to the issues stated in the opening is sometimes called a *framing device*. Framing works particularly well with the academic identification of research debates. In essays that use existing research as a framing device, writers will conclude with an explanation of how they responded to previous work.

A *call to action* and the *look to the future* appear in the final sentences. Pairing the look to the future with a call to action gives it more power because the author is stating it directly and telling readers what should be done.

You don't need to include all five of these concluding moves in your document, and they don't need to appear in any specific order. If you find yourself writing a conclusion that goes longer than one or two paragraphs, you might move some of the information into the body of the paper.

Here are some basic strategies for writing an introduction and conclusion for your paper.

DIVIDE Your Argument into a Beginning, Middle, and End

Nonfiction documents should have an introduction (tell them what you are going to tell them), a body (tell them), and a conclusion (tell them what you told them).

DRAFT Your Introduction

A typical introduction includes up to five moves: (1) identify your topic, (2) state your purpose, (3) offer background information on your topic, (4) state your main point, and (5) stress the importance of the topic.

DEVELOP a Grabber, Lead, or Research Discussion for Your Introduction

Your introduction will need to capture the readers' interest right away. So use a question, intriguing statistic, compelling statement, interesting story, or quotation to hook them.

DRAFT Your Conclusion

A conclusion should make up to five moves: (1) signal that you are concluding, (2) restate the main point, (3) re-emphasize the importance of the topic, (4) call for action, and (5) look to the future.

VERIFY That Your Introduction and Conclusion Work Together

The introduction and conclusion should work together, containing similar information, restating your main point, and using a similar tone. Often, the conclusion will complete a story that was started in the introduction. Here is also where the main point of the paper should be repeated once again.

1. Find a document on the Internet and identify its introduction and conclusion. With a group of people in your class, talk about whether you think the introduction and conclusion are effective in this text.

2. With your group, find an example of each kind of grabber and lead listed in this chapter. Print out or copy your examples and label which kind of grabber or lead they use.

3. Look closely at four conclusions from four different sample texts. With your group, rank the conclusions from best to worst. What aspects of some of the conclusions made them superior to the others?

1. Find an argument or other text that you have enjoyed reading this term. Then write a one page rhetorical analysis in which you discuss the structure of the text. Explain how the text's introduction, body, and conclusion work.

2. Find a text that you think has a weak introduction and/or conclusion. Diagnose the structural problems with the text's introduction and conclusion. What could the author have done better to build a stronger introduction and/or conclusion?

1. **Evaluate the organization of a reading.** Choose a reading from this book and write a two page structural analysis of it. Using the criteria described in this chapter, analyze its introduction, body, and conclusion to determine whether they are well organized and whether they are the appropriate length.

2. **Describe the qualities of a good Internet article lead.** Internet readers are notoriously impatient, and they make quick decisions about whether to click to something else. Find three different kinds of leads used in articles on the Internet. Write a brief evaluation in which you discuss how the electronic medium changes the way readers enter the text.

MyCompLab

For support in meeting this chapter's objectives, follow this path in MyCompLab:

Student Resources → Writing → The Writing Process → Drafting. Review the Instruction and Multimedia resources about introductions and conclusions; then complete the Exercises and click on Gradebook to measure your progress.

Developing Paragraphs and Sections

In this chapter, you will learn how to:

- write a paragraph with an effective topic sentence and support.
- get paragraphs to flow from one sentence to the next.
- make sections out of related groups of paragraphs.

Paragraphs and sections help your readers understand at a glance how you have structured your ideas. Good paragraphs and sections help your readers figure out your main points and how you are supporting them.

A paragraph's job is actually rather straightforward: a paragraph presents a claim or statement, and then it supports or proves that claim or statement with facts, reasoning, examples, data, anecdotes, quotations, or descriptions. A paragraph isn't just a bunch of sentences that seem to fit together. Instead, a solid paragraph is a unit that is built around a central topic, idea, issue, or question. There are no hard-and-fast rules for writing paragraphs in terms of length or structure. A paragraph's length and structure need to fit its purpose and the genre you are using.

A section is a group of paragraphs that supports a common idea or claim. A section offers a broad claim and then uses a series of paragraphs to support or prove that claim. Longer post-secondary papers and most workplace documents are usually carved up into a few or several sections so they are easier to read.

In this chapter, you will learn how to develop great paragraphs and sections that will make your writing stronger and better organized.

Creating a Basic Paragraph

Paragraphs tend to include up to four elements: a *transition*, a *topic sentence, support sentences,* and a *point sentence.* The diagram in Figure 17.1 shows where these kinds of sentences usually appear in any given paragraph. And, here is a typical paragraph with these four elements highlighted:

> The amount of plastic the world consumes annually has steadily risen over the past seventy years, from almost nil in 1940 to closing in on six hundred billion pounds today (transition). We became plastic people really just in the space of a single generation (topic sentence). In 1960, the average American consumed about thirty pounds of plastic products (support). Today, we're each consuming more than three hundred pounds of plastics a year, generating more than three hundred billion dollars in sales (support). Considering that lightning-quick ascension, one industry expert declared plastics "one of the greatest business stories of the twentieth century" (Scheer, 2010) (point sentence). (Susan Freinkel, *Plastics: A Toxic Love Story*)

Transition or Transitional Sentence (Optional)

👁—[Watch
Common
Grammar
Errors: 15.
Transitions

The purpose of a transition or transitional sentence is to make a smooth bridge from the prior paragraph to the current paragraph. These kinds of transitions are especially useful when you want to shift or change the direction of the discussion.

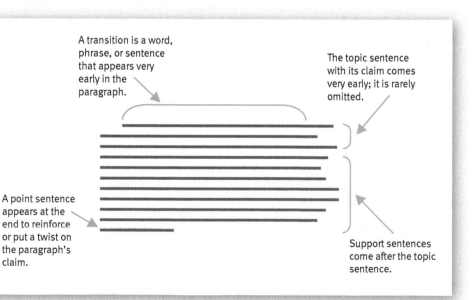

FIGURE 17.1
The Shape of a Paragraph

Although paragraphs vary in terms of function and structure, the core of a paragraph includes the topic sentence with a claim followed by support sentences. Transition and point sentences can, in many cases, improve the flow of the paragraph.

A transition is a word, phrase, or sentence that appears very early in the paragraph.

The topic sentence with its claim comes very early; it is rarely omitted.

A point sentence appears at the end to reinforce or put a twist on the paragraph's claim.

Support sentences come after the topic sentence.

A transition, if needed, should appear at the beginning of the paragraph. It might be as brief as a single word or phrase (e.g., *finally, in the past*) or as long as a complete transitional sentence. A transitional sentence might ask a question or make an obvious turn in the discussion:

> If fast food is causing North America's expanding waistlines, what are our options for counteracting the power of fast food over young people?

A question like this one sets up the topic sentence that would likely follow it. Here is a transitional sentence that makes an obvious turn in the discussion:

> Before moving ahead, though, we first need to back up and discuss some of the root causes of poverty in Canada.

This type of transitional sentence turns the readers' attention to a new issue while setting up the paragraph's claim (topic sentence).

A transitional word or phrase can also make an effective bridge between two paragraphs. Here are some transitional words and phrases that you can try out:

For example	Nevertheless	While it may be
To illustrate	At the same time	true that
For this reason	To summarize	Above all
As an illustration	While this may or	In addition
Besides	may not be true	With this in mind
Of course	Equally important	For this purpose
In the past	As a result	To this end
In the future	Consequently	At this point
The next step	Meanwhile	Subsequently
In any event	In contrast	Whenever . . .
On the whole	Despite . . .	Occasionally
Likewise	Rather	Inevitably
Accordingly	At last	Admittedly
In conclusion	All of a sudden	Under these
More specifically	Suddenly	conditions
In the same way	In the meantime	In this way
In other words	At any rate	On the other
Specifically	At least	hand
On the contrary	Even though	

Transitional words and phrases can lead off a paragraph's transitional sentence, or they can be used to start out a paragraph's a topic sentence.

Topic Sentence (Needed)

A topic sentence announces the paragraph's subject and makes a statement or claim that the rest of the paragraph will support or prove.

> A good first step would be to remove fast food options from junior high and high school lunch programs.

> Debt on credit cards is the greatest threat to the Canadian family's financial security.

In most paragraphs and almost every academic paragraph, the topic sentence will be the first or second sentence. You may have been told in the past that a topic sentence can be put anywhere in a paragraph. That's true. But if you want your reader to understand the paragraph's subject and identify its key statement or claim quickly, put that topic sentence up front.

Of course, there are always exceptions to any guideline. If you are telling your readers a story or leading them toward a controversial or surprising point, your topic sentence might arrive at the end of the paragraph. For example, here is a paragraph in which the topic sentence appears at the end, because the author is showing how something changed over time:

> My second grade homeroom teacher was a young graduate from a missionary school. When she found out I spoke English, she began to practice her English on me. One day she used English when asking me to run an errand for her. As I turned to close the door behind me, I noticed the puzzled faces of my classmates. I had the same sensation I had often experienced when some stranger in a crowd would turn on hearing me speak English. I was more intensely pleased on this occasion, however, because I suddenly felt that my family language had been singled out from the family languages of my classmates. Since we were not allowed to speak any dialect other than Standard Chinese in the classroom, having my teacher speak English to me in class made English an official language of the classroom. I began to take pride in my ability to speak it (topic sentence). (Min Zhan Lu, "From Silence to Struggle")

In some paragraphs, like this narrative paragraph, the topic sentence can appear at the end.

Support Sentences (Needed)

Support sentences make up the body of most paragraphs. These sentences provide examples, details, reasoning, facts, data, quotations, anecdotes, definitions, descriptions, and anything else needed to back up the paragraph's topic sentence. Support sentences usually appear after the topic sentence.

> The fast food chains feed off the sprawl of Colorado Springs, accelerate it, and help set its visual tone (topic sentence). They build large signs to attract motorists and look at cars the way predators view herds of prey (support). The chains thrive on traffic, lots of it, and put new restaurants at intersections

where traffic is likely to increase, where development is heading but real estate prices are still low (support). Fast food restaurants often serve as the shock troops of sprawl, landing early and pointing the way (support). Some chains prefer to play follow the leader: when a new McDonald's opens, other fast food restaurants soon open nearby on the assumption that it must be a good location (support). (Eric Schlosser, *Fast Food Nation*)

Point Sentence (Needed)

Point sentences state, restate, or amplify the paragraph's main point at the end of the paragraph. They often link the paragraph's claim to the main argument or thesis of the essay. A point sentence is especially useful in longer paragraphs when you want to reinforce or restate the topic sentence of the paragraph in different words.

> Of the many ways to fail on a dating website, not posting a photo of yourself is perhaps the most certain (topic sentence). . . . A man who does not include his photo gets only 60 percent of the volume of e-mail response of a man who does; a woman who doesn't include her photo gets only 24 percent as much. A low-income, poorly educated, unhappily employed, not very attractive, slightly overweight, and balding man who posts his photo stands a better chance of gleaning some e-mails than a man who says he makes $200,000 and is deadly handsome but doesn't post a photo. There are plenty of reasons someone might not post a photo—he's technically challenged or is ashamed of being spotted by friends or is just plain unattractive—but as in the case of a brand-new car with a For Sale sign, prospective customers will assume he's got something seriously wrong under the hood (point sentence). (Steven Levitt and Stephen Dubner, *Freakonomics*)

As shown in the paragraph above, a point sentence is a good way to stress the point of a complex paragraph. The topic sentence at the beginning of the paragraph states a claim and the point sentence drives it home.

Getting Paragraphs to Flow (Cohesion)

Getting your paragraphs to flow is not difficult, but it takes a little practice. Flow, which is also called *cohesion*, is best achieved by paying attention to how each paragraph's sentences are woven together. You can use two techniques, *subject alignment* and *given-new chaining*, to achieve this feeling of flow.

Subject Alignment in Paragraphs

A well-written paragraph keeps the readers' focus on a central subject, idea, issue, or question. For example, the following paragraph does not flow well because the subjects of the sentences are inconsistent:

Watching people at the park on a Saturday afternoon is a true pleasure. Frisbee golf is played by a group of students near the trees. Visiting with each other are dog owners with their pets running around in playful packs. Picnic blankets have been spread out, and parents are chatting and enjoying their lunch. The playground is full of children sliding down slides and playing in the sand.

One way to get a paragraph to flow is to align the paragraph's sentences around a common set of subjects.

Watching people at the park on a Saturday afternoon is a true pleasure. Near the trees, a group of students play frisbee golf. Off to the side, dog owners visit with each other as their pets run around in playful packs. Parents chat and enjoy their lunch on spread-out picnic blankets. On the playground, children slide down slides and play in the sand.

This revised paragraph flows better (it is coherent) because the subjects of the sentences are all people. In other words, the paragraph is about the people at the park, so making people the subjects of the sentences creates the feeling that the paragraph is flowing.

To make your paragraphs flow, first decide what the paragraph is about. Then revise its sentences so they use a consistent set of subjects. Subject alignment means keeping a consistent set of subjects, not the same subject, through most or all of the paragraph.

Given-New in Paragraphs

Another good way to create flow is to use something called "given-new chaining" to weave the sentences together in a paragraph. Here's how it works.

Each sentence in the paragraph should start out with something that appeared in the prior sentence (called the "given"). Then the remainder of the sentence offers something that the readers didn't see in the prior sentence (called the "new"). That way, each sentence takes something given from the prior sentence and adds something new.

Recently, an art gallery exhibited the mysterious paintings of Irwin Fleminger, a modernist artist whose vast Mars-like landscapes contain cryptic human artifacts. One of Fleminger's paintings attracted the attention of some young school children who happened to be walking by. At first, the children laughed, pointing out some of the strange artifacts in the painting. Soon, though, the strange artifacts in the painting drew the students into a critical awareness of the painting, and they began to ask their bewildered teacher what the artifacts meant. Mysterious and beautiful, Fleminger's paintings have this effect on many people, not just schoolchildren.

In this paragraph, the beginning of each sentence takes something from the sentence before it. This creates a given-new chain, causing the text to feel coherent and flowing.

A combination of subject alignment and given-new chaining will allow you to create good flow in your paragraphs while using a rich variety of sentence structures to keep the text interesting.

Deciding on Paragraph Length

The length of a paragraph should be determined by three things: the genre you are using, your readers, and the amount of support you need to back up the paragraph's topic sentence. The medium of your text will also influence paragraph length, because electronic texts and newspapers often use smaller paragraphs to help readers scan and read quickly.

Each genre tends to use paragraphs that are tailored to its readers' expectations and reading styles. For instance, a research paper is usually read carefully for evidence, so paragraphs in research papers tend to be longer. Quite differently, paragraphs in a movie review are usually short, because readers tend to read these documents quickly for the overall assessment.

The key to determining a paragraph's length is to look at the topic sentence. Then make sure your paragraph has enough support sentences to back up that claim or statement.

Supersized Paragraphs

When used properly, long paragraphs signal depth of thought and coverage. Since the purpose of a paragraph is to support one statement or prove one claim, a long paragraph signals to the reader that

- the paragraph's claim or statement is very complex, requiring lots of support;

- the author is cramming many ideas together into one extended paragraph; or

- the author feels the need to handle an idea in great depth.

Supersized paragraphs are appropriate for analytical treatises or reflective thinking on a difficult topic, but they can be quite difficult for readers who are not committed to a deep reading of the text.

Rapid-Fire Paragraphs

Small paragraphs are easier and quicker to process, making it more likely that your readers will actually read each whole paragraph. These kinds of paragraphs are most useful in reviews and position papers published in newspapers or on news webpages. They are also useful in narrative or creative writing when you want to describe a scene with lots of action. Rapid-fire paragraphs speed up the reader's pace. However, small paragraphs also signal to the readers that

- the paragraph's claim or statement is simple, requiring minimal support;
- the author doesn't have enough support to back up the paragraph's claim or statement; or
- the author hasn't thought very deeply about this issue.

If you find yourself writing a series of short rapid-fire paragraphs, you might look closer at these paragraphs to determine whether you need to fill them out with more support. Or you might consider combining two or three smaller paragraphs into a larger paragraph that supports a larger claim or statement.

Paragraph Length Variety

Paragraphs within a document should be generally similar in size throughout the text, with some variation in length. Occasionally, though, you can use a short paragraph to highlight an important point. When you suddenly use a very short paragraph, it grabs your readers' attention because it *contrasts* with other paragraphs. Visually, readers will understand instantly (before they read the first word) that a paragraph will be different from the other paragraphs in content, tone, or direction.

So when you want an idea or claim to stand out, consider placing it in a very brief paragraph—like this one. You will grab your readers' attention.

Organizing a Section

A section is a group of paragraphs that supports a major point in your text. When used properly, sections break a larger document into manageable portions. They also provide readers with a bird's-eye view of the document, allowing them to take in the gist of a longer document at a glance.

Opening, Body, Closing

Like a paragraph, a section usually supports or proves a major statement or claim. This statement or claim tends to be placed at the beginning of the section, often in a brief *opening paragraph*. Then the *body paragraphs* in the section each contribute something to support that statement or claim. Finally, an optional closing paragraph or final sentence can be used to restate the major statement or claim that the section was supporting or trying to prove.

Organizational Patterns for Sections

When organizing a section, begin by asking yourself what you want to achieve. Then identify a pattern that will help you structure and fill out that space. Figure 17.2 on page 340 shows a variety of patterns that you might consider when organizing sections in your text. These are some of the most common patterns, but others, including variations of the ones shown here, are possible.

Using Headings in Sections

Headings are especially helpful for marking where sections begin and end. They can help you and your readers make transitions between larger ideas. Also, they give readers an overview of the structure of the document.

All headings within a certain level should follow consistent word patterns. A consistent wording pattern might use gerunds (*-ing* words), questions, or statements.

Inconsistent Headings	Performance Enhancement
	Is Performance Enhancement Unethical?
	Kinds of Performance Enhancement
Consistent Headings Using Gerunds	Defining Performance Enhancement
	Understanding the Ethics of Performance Enhancement
	Determining the Downside
Consistent Headings Using Questions	What Is Performance Enhancement?
	What Are the Risks?
	What's Really the Issue Here?
Consistent Headings Using Claims	Cognitive Performance Enhancement Is Possible
	Enhancement Will Improve Student Performance
	A Better National Conversation Is Needed

Headings should also be specific, clearly signalling the content of the sections that follow them.

Unspecific Headings	Fast Food
	The High School Scene
	Solutions
Specific Headings	Fast Food and High School Students: A Bad Mix
	The Effects of Fast Food on Health and Performance
	Alternatives to Fast Food

Using Sections and Paragraphs Together

A well-organized document is a structure that contains structures (sections) that contain structures (paragraphs) that contain structures (sentences). The purpose of a paragraph is to support or prove a statement or claim. The purpose of a section is to

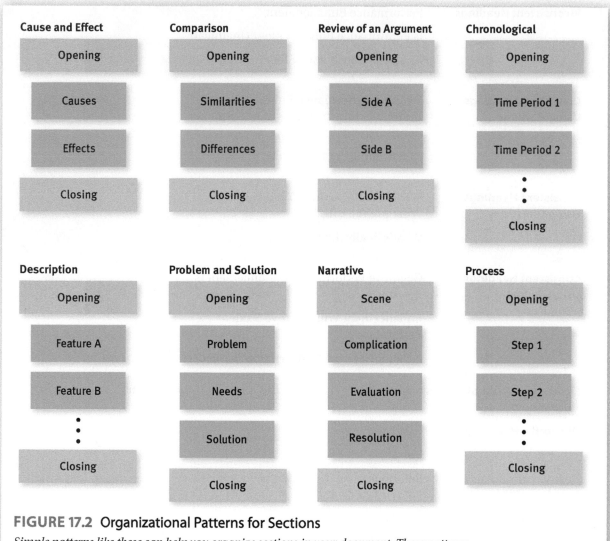

FIGURE 17.2 Organizational Patterns for Sections

Simple patterns like these can help you organize sections in your document. These patterns should not be followed mechanically.

use a series of paragraphs to support a larger claim. The sections, altogether, support the thesis or main point of the document.

If you learn how to write solid paragraphs and sections, you will find that the structures of paragraphs and sections will help you figure out what you need to include in each part of your document. That will save you time, while improving your writing dramatically.

Here are some basic strategies for creating clear, logical paragraphs and sections in your documents.

IDENTIFY the Four Kinds of Sentences in a Paragraph

A typical paragraph has a *topic sentence, support sentences,* and a *point sentence.* As needed, a paragraph can also include a *transition sentence,* word, or phrases.

STATE Each Paragraph's Topic Sentence Clearly

A topic sentence announces the paragraph's subject—the central idea or issue covered in the paragraph. Your topic sentences should make a statement or claim that the rest of the paragraph will support or prove.

DEVELOP Support Sentences for Each Paragraph

Support sentences make up the body of most paragraphs. These sentences provide examples, details, reasoning, facts, data, anecdotes, definitions, descriptions, and anything else that backs up the paragraph's topic sentence.

DECIDE If a Transition Sentence or Transition Is Needed

If the prior paragraph is talking about something significantly different from the current paragraph, you might consider using a transition sentence or transitional word or phrase to bridge the gap.

USE a Point Sentence to Link Your Support to Your Claims

Use a point sentence to state or restate the paragraph's main point. Usually, the point sentence makes a claim that is similar to the topic sentence at the beginning of the paragraph.

DETERMINE Whether Your Paragraph's Length Is Right

The length of your paragraphs depends mostly on your subject matter and your readers. Long paragraphs suggest depth but may look hard to read. Short paragraphs are easier to read but may suggest that the claims are not fully supported.

COMBINE Paragraphs into Sections

Larger documents should be carved into sections. A typical section has an opening paragraph and body paragraphs. A closing paragraph is optional.

1. In studies of high school students' writing, researchers have found that inexperienced writers tend to place topic sentences at the end of their paragraphs, not the beginning. Why do you think inexperienced writers compose this way?

2. In this chapter, you learned that topic sentences should usually appear at the beginning of a paragraph and occasionally at the end. Can you think of any situations in which burying the topic sentence in the middle of the paragraph would be a good idea?

3. With your group, choose a reading in Part 2 of this book and pull its paragraphs apart, identifying their topic sentences, support sentences, transition sentences, and point sentences.

Try
This
Out

1. Go to the Internet and collect some interesting paragraphs. Identify the topic sentence and support sentences in each paragraph. If transition sentences and point sentences are used, highlight them, too. In a presentation to your class, choose one of your paragraphs and show how it works.

2. Find a badly written paragraph in a printed or online text. First, improve the flow of the paragraph by aligning the subjects of the sentences. Second, use given-new strategies to revise the paragraph's sentences. Finally, use a combination of subject alignment and given-new strategies to improve its flow. Which of these methods (subject alignment, given-new, or a combination) worked best?

3. Using your library's databases, find a scholarly article that is divided into sections. Look at each section carefully to determine what patterns they are following. Which patterns for sections described in this chapter are most common? Are the sections following any patterns that aren't shown in this chapter?

Write
This

1. **Diagnose and solve a paragraph's organizational problems.** Find a paragraph that has a confusing organization (one of your own, a colleague's, or something from the Internet). Diagnose the problems with this paragraph using the guidelines in this chapter. Then write a one page analysis of the paragraph in which you explain its problems and offer two to five suggestions for improving it.

2. **Use a computer to revise the structure of a section.** Find a poorly organized, multiple page document on the Internet that is divided into sections. Revise the organization of one section so that it includes a clear opening paragraph and body paragraphs. Write an e-mail to the document's author (you don't have to actually send it) in which you discuss the problems with the original section and describe your strategy for improving it.

┌─ MyCompLab ─

For support in meeting this chapter's objectives, follow this path in MyCompLab:

Student Resources → Writing → The Writing Process → Drafting. Review the Instruction and Multimedia resources about writing body paragraphs; then complete the Exercises and click on Gradebook to measure your progress.

CHAPTER

18

Using Basic
Rhetorical
Patterns

In this chapter, you will learn how to:

- use rhetorical patterns to develop your ideas.
- organize paragraphs and sections into familiar patterns.
- combine rhetorical patterns to make sophisticated arguments.

When drafting, writers will often use *rhetorical patterns* to arrange their ideas into sections and paragraphs. Rhetorical patterns or modes are familiar forms and strategies that help you to develop and organize information in ways your readers will easily comprehend. Teachers of rhetoric, like Aristotle, called these patterns *topoi*, or commonplaces. *Topoi* (from the Greek word "place") are familiar patterns or strategies that you can use in a variety of situations. Academics in particular use these reasoning patterns to better understand the parts of a topic. If you follow these patterns, you can feel confident that you are thinking like an academic and reasoning in ways that will result in solid evidence for academic papers.

Rhetorical patterns are not formulas to be followed mechanically or in isolation. You can alter, bend, and combine these patterns to fit your purpose and the genre of your text. Chapter 6, for instance, offers examples of these patterns used in analysis.

Narrative

A narrative describes a sequence of events or tells a story in a way that illustrates a specific point.

Narratives can be woven into just about any genre. In reviews, literary analyses, and rhetorical analyses, narrative can be used to summarize or describe what you are analyzing. In proposals and research papers, narratives can be used to re-create events

FIGURE 18.1 The Narrative Pattern

Narratives tend to have these five parts. Parts can be moved or removed to fit the rhetorical situation.

and give historical background on a topic. While academic writers thus use narrative, keep in mind that they do so sparingly and for specific purposes. You do not want to simply re-tell a story in an academic paper, but use narrative and description to identify the key issues and events that you will go on to analyze.

The diagram in Figure 18.1 shows the typical pattern for a narrative. When telling a story, writers will usually start out by *setting the scene* and *introducing a complication* of some kind. Then the characters in the story *evaluate the complication* to figure out how they are going to respond. They then *resolve the complication*. At the end of the narrative, the writer *states the point* of the story, leading into original analysis.

Consider, for example, the following paragraph, which follows the narrative pattern:

As I write this, my faculty's email server has just recovered from a day-long outage that sent my immediate network of colleagues into more than a bit of a tizzy (scene). In the midst of a hectic teaching term, with grant applications and reference letters due, not to mention the usual busyness of academic life (complications), most of us found it pretty hard to cope with even a brief interruption in our lines of communication (evaluation). For many, the immediate recourse—not surprisingly—was to Facebook, where we could not only commiserate (and commiserate we did!) but could also share important bits of information that would allow us to get on with our day (resolution). That almost automatic recourse to Facebook suggests just how ubiquitous social networking technology has become in the academic world (point)....

—Michael O'Driscoll, "Introduction: Face/Book/Net/Work: Social Networking and the Humanities," *English Studies in Canada* 36.4 (2010): 1-3

The narrative pattern is probably already familiar to you, even if you didn't know it before. This is the same pattern used in television sitcoms, novels, and just about any story. In nonfiction writing, though, narratives are not "just stories." They help writers make specific points for their readers. The chart in Figure 18.2 shows how narratives can be used in a few different genres.

✳–[Explore
Description 4:
Mars
Pathfinder
Rover
(interactive)

Description

Description allows writers to portray people, places, and objects. Descriptions often rely on details drawn from the five senses—seeing, hearing, touching, smelling, and tasting. In situations where the senses don't offer a full description, writers can turn to other rhetorical devices to deepen the readers' experience and understanding.

Objective of Genre	Use of Narrative
In a **proposal,** use a story to explain a problem, its causes and effects.	In a proposal about food safety, a writer motivates the reader to care about the issue by telling the story of a girl who died from food poisoning.
In a **review,** summarize a movie's plot for readers.	In a movie review of a new romantic comedy, the writer gives an overview of the movie's main events, without giving away how the conflict in the movie was resolved.
In a **literary analysis,** use a historical narrative to offer background information on the text.	In a literary analysis, the writer tells an interesting story about the poet whose poem is being analyzed. This story offers insight into the meaning of the poem.

FIGURE 18.2 Using Narratives

In academic analyses, for instance, writers may use argumentative features to help them observe and explain all the parts of a topic. In academic papers, description, like narrative, sets up or leads into further analysis. It is rarely an end in itself, but a way of identifying key features of a topic.

Describing with the Senses

Like you, your readers primarily experience the world through their senses. So when you need to describe someone or something, start out by considering your subject from each of the five senses:

What Does It Look Like? List its colours, shapes, and sizes. What is your eye drawn toward? What makes your subject visually distinctive?

What Sounds Does It Make? Are the sounds sharp, soothing, irritating, pleasing, metallic, harmonious, or erratic? What effect do these sounds have on you and others?

What Does It Feel Like? Is it rough or smooth, hot or cold, dull or sharp, slimy or firm, wet or dry?

How Does It Smell? Does your subject smell fragrant or pungent? Does it have a particular aroma or stench? Does it smell fresh or stale?

How Does It Taste? Is your subject spicy, sweet, salty, or sour? Does it taste burnt or spoiled? What foods taste similar to the thing you are describing?

If you are describing a scene or a person, punctuate your description with surprising or contrasting details.

Objective of Genre	Use of Description
In a **rhetorical analysis,** describe the text and its key features.	In an analysis of an advertisement, the writer begins by describing the ad's subject matter and main message.
In a **proposal,** describe a plan or a product.	A team of proposal writers uses description to show how a new playground would look in a local park.
In a **research paper,** describe the laboratory setup for an experiment.	The methodology section of a scientific research paper describes how a laboratory experiment was put together, allowing the readers to verify and replicate it.

FIGURE 18.3 Using Descriptions

Describing with Vocabulary and Rhetoric

In addition to the senses, writers often make note of specialized language choices and rhetorical or argumentative strategies. If you require further description, particularly in an academic writing situation, consider the following:

Vocabulary. What words are used in the text? What are their connotations (associations) and denotations (defined meanings)? How do they establish a tone? What audience do they seek to address?

Argument. What kinds of arguments are made in the text? Does it use *logos, ethos,* or *pathos*? Does it sufficiently support its claims? Do you see any flaws in the logic?

Description is commonly used in all genres. The chart in Figure 18.3 shows how descriptions could be used in several kinds of writing situations.

Explore
Extended Definition: Diabetes Circular (interactive)

Definition

A definition states the exact meaning of a word. Definitions explain how a particular term is being used and why it is being used that way. They are especially helpful for clarifying ideas and explaining important concepts.

Sentence definitions, like the ones in a dictionary, typically have three parts: the term being defined, the category in which the term belongs, and the distinguishing characteristics that set it apart from other things in its category.

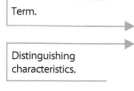
Term.

Distinguishing characteristics.

Cholera is a potentially lethal illness caused by the bacterium *Vibrio cholerae*, with symptoms of vomiting and watery diarrhea.

Category.

An *extended definition* is longer than a sentence definition. An extended definition usually starts with a sentence definition and then continues to define the term further. An extended definition is typically found near the beginning of a text. It both clarifies how the term will be used throughout the paper and provides one focus for the ensuing discussion. You can extend a definition with one or more of the following techniques:

Word Origin (Etymology). Exploring the historical origin of a word can provide some interesting insights into its meaning.

> According to the *Online Etymology Dictionary*, the word *escape* comes from the Old French word "eschaper," which literally meant "to get out of one's cape, leave a pursuer with just one's cape."

Examples. Giving examples of how the word is used can put its meaning into context for readers. Examples, of course, provide important forms of evidence in many other contexts.

> For example, when someone says he is "between jobs," it means he is unemployed.

Negation. When using negation, you explain something by telling readers what it is not.

> St. John's wort is not a stimulant, and it won't cure all kinds of depression. Instead, it is a mild sedative.

Division. You can divide the subject into two or more parts, which are then defined separately.

> There are two kinds of fraternities. The first kind, a "social fraternity," typically offers a dormitory-like place to live near a campus, as well as a social community. The second kind, an "honorary fraternity," allows members who share common backgrounds to network and support fellow members.

Similarities and Differences. When using similarities and differences, you compare and contrast the thing being defined to other similar things.

> African wild dogs are from the same biological family, *Canidae,* as domestic dogs, and they are similar in size to a labrador. Their coats, however, tend to have random patterns of yellow, black, and white. Their bodies look like those of domestic dogs, but their heads look like those of hyenas.

Analogy. An analogy compares something unfamiliar to something that readers would find familiar.

> Your body's circulatory system is similar to a modern Canadian city. Your arteries and veins are like roads for blood cells to travel on. These roadways contain white blood cells, which act like provincial police patrolling for viruses and bacteria.

Objective of Genre	Use of Definition
In a **literary analysis,** explain a literary concept.	When writing a literary analysis, the writer defines words like "irony" or an important concept in the novel or poem.
In a **rhetorical analysis,** define a rhetorical term that helps explain why something is persuasive.	A person critiquing an advertisement defines the word *"pathos"* to help her explain how emotion is used to sway an audience.
In a **research paper,** clarify an important technical term.	In a research paper about the great apes, the writer defines what a bonobo is and how it is different from other apes.

FIGURE 18.4 Using Definitions

The chart in Figure 18.4 shows how definitions can be used in a variety of genres.

Classification

Classification allows you to place objects and people into groups, so they can be discussed in greater depth. A classification can take up a single paragraph, or it might be used to organize an entire section (Figure 18.5). There are three basic steps to using classification to organize a paragraph or section:

Step One: List Everything That Fits into the Whole Class

List all the items that can be included in a specific class. Brainstorming is a good tool for coming up with this kind of list.

If you discuss all of these items individually, you will bore your readers to tears. So you need to find a way to break this long list down into smaller classifications. Move to step two.

FIGURE 18.5 Using Classifications

Objective of Genre	Use of Classification
In a **review,** identify common subgenres.	A reviewer uses classification to identify where a new vampire movie fits in the horror movie genre.
In a **position paper,** identify main points.	A writer of a position paper on movie venues will categorize aspects of watching in the theatre under either positive or negative.
In a **research paper,** divide a number of species into smaller subspecies.	A researcher uses classification to describe a family of insects.

Step Two: Decide on a Principle of Classification

The key to classifying something is to come up with a *principle of classification* that helps you do the sorting. For example, let's imagine you are classifying all the ways to stop smoking. You would list all the methods you can find. Then you would try to sort them into categories:

Nicotine replacement—nicotine patch, nicotine gum, sprays, inhalers, lozenges, nicotine fading.

Lifestyle changes—exercise daily, eat healthy snacks, break routines, distract yourself, set up rewards, keep busy.

Medical help—acupuncture, hypnosis, antidepressants, counselling, support group.

Smoking-like activities—chew gum, drink hot tea, breathe deeply, eat vegetables, eat nuts that need to be shelled.

Step Three: Sort into Major and Minor Groups

If you choose an effective principle of classification, you should be able to sort or divide the items from your brainstorming list cleanly into the major and minor categories you came up with. In other words, an item that appears in one category should not appear in another. Also, no items on your list should be left over. These processes of classifying and dividing work together to group items and clarify your major ideas in a paper.

Cause and Effect

Exploring causes and effects is a natural way to discuss many topics. When we try to figure out why something happened, we automatically look for its causes. Then, we try to study its effects. When using this rhetorical pattern, identify both causes and effects, and then explain *how* and *why* specific causes led to those effects. See Chapter 6 for more discussion on using cause and effect in analysis.

Some cause and effect explanations are clearly identifiable, while others are arguable, meaning that people disagree about what causes the event and its effects. Figure 18.6 outlines the three main kinds of cause and effect explanations and explains how they could be used in different genres.

Even when describing a complex cause and effect scenario, you should try to present your analysis as clearly as possible, as in this explanation of tornado formation:

Although scientists still do not completely understand the causes behind the formation of tornadoes, most agree on this basic pattern. Three ingredients must be present: a large mass of warm moist air, a large mass of cold dry air,

Objective of Genre	Kind of Cause and Effect		Use of Cause/Effect
In a **position paper**, argue that one event has led to a certain outcome.	*Simple cause and effect*: One thing causes something else.	[ ] → causes → [ ]	Governments should lower interest rates because when interest rates go up (cause), consumer spending goes down (effect).
In a **research paper**, explain the cause of something.	*Cause/effect chains*: An effect becomes the cause of another effect.	[ ] → causes → [ ] → causes → [ ]	The recent disaster in Japan occurred because a massive slippage along the Earth's crust (cause 1) created an enormous undersea earthquake (effect). This set in motion a tsunami (cause 2), which engulfed thousands of square miles in the area, leading to massive destruction and the deaths of 200,000 people (effect).
In a **proposal**, explain how your plan will lead to good results.	*Multiple causes and effects*: A set of causes leads to a set of effects.	combine to cause	In a plan to redesign your institution's cafeteria, you propose to (1) transform the existing food court into a more pleasant eating area, (2) create a café that offers a local, healthy, and affordable menu, and (3) create a store offering similar products (causes). This will lead to increased business, customer satisfaction, and sustainability (effects).

FIGURE 18.6 Three Kinds of Cause and Effect, and Examples of Using Cause and Effect

and a violent collision between the two. During springtime in central North America, enormous masses of warm moist air can move rapidly northeastward from the Gulf of Mexico into what has become known as "tornado alley." When the warm air collides with the cold air, thunderstorms are almost always produced. However, if the rapidly moving warm air slides under the cold air and gets trapped beneath, a tornado can occur. Because warm air is lighter than cold air, the warm-air mass will try to form something like a "drain" in the cold-air mass that would allow the warm air to shoot through. If this happens, a vortex of air develops, sucking everything on the ground upward at enormous velocities, causing the strongest winds produced anywhere in nature, up to 300 miles (483 kilometres) per hour. These powerful winds sometimes accomplish the unbelievable, such as uprooting enormous trees and driving pieces of straw through wooden planks.

Comparison and Contrast

Comparison and contrast allows you to explore the similarities and differences between two or more people, objects, places, or ideas. When comparing and contrasting, you should first list all the characteristics that the two items have in common. Then list all the characteristics that distinguish them from each other.

You can then show how these two things are similar to and different from each other. There are two main patterns used to organize comparison and contrast material: *block* and *alternating*. In the block pattern, information is divided into two main groups. For example, you could discuss all the similarities and then all the differences, or all the points about topic one and then all those about topic two. As an example of block comparison and contrast, see the paragraph that follows:

The differences between first-degree and second-degree murder can seem subtle. Both are forms of homicide, which is defined as taking another person's life. Also, in both types of murder, the perpetrator intentionally killed the victim. First-degree murder happens when the perpetrator planned in advance to kill someone. He or she wanted to murder someone else, made a plan, and carried out the act. Usually, he or she then tried to cover up the murder. First-degree murder can also refer to a killing that was not specifically planned but that takes place in the context of another serious crime, such as sexual assault or kidnapping. Second-degree murder happens when the alleged killer did not plan in advance to murder or physically harm the victim. For example, a burglar commits second-degree murder if he intentionally kills a security guard who discovers him committing the crime. In this case, the burglar did not set out to kill the security guard, but he did it on purpose when he was discovered.

Compares the two forms of murder to show their basic similarities.

Contrasts the two forms of murder to show their subtle differences.

In the alternating pattern, information is classified into major points and then both topics are discussed under each point. In the following piece of student writing, the author identifies three main topics and contrasts big box stores with family-run businesses in relation to each:

The proliferation of "big box" or large retail stores, typically located on the outskirts of mid-sized urban centres, has generated strong community-based reactions. Some people feel that these stores are exploitive, while others feel that they offer middle-class Canadian families better retail opportunities than more traditional family-run businesses do. While there are compelling arguments on both sides of the family-run versus box store debate, three key

Identifies topic and debate.

> Contrasts box stores and family businesses under the first topic of service.

> Contrasts box stores and family businesses under the second topic of price.

> Contrasts box stores and family businesses under the third topic of effect on communities.

issues must be taken into consideration. First, service levels vary significantly between the two. Smaller, family-based businesses are able to establish relationships with consumers and offer considerate, knowledgeable service. Box stores, on the other hand, employ a shifting workforce of often less-knowledgeable workers. In addition, the size of those businesses means that customer service can be hard to obtain. Second, prices tend to differ markedly, with box stores able to buy in large quantities so that they offer consumers much lower prices. Small, family-based businesses do not carry the same clout with suppliers and must sell at higher prices in order to sustain a reasonable profit level. Finally and perhaps most controversially, the effects on communities are widely debated. Small, family businesses are typically located downtown and are perceived to create a better sense of community, lessen consumers' environmental footprints (since they do not have to drive great distances to the store), and treat workers more equitably. Box stores have been accused of destroying communities because they do not encourage personal relationships, have a larger negative impact on the environment and, in cases like that of WalMart, exploit workers fairly regularly. Sadly, the real issue in this debate seems to be whether price takes precedence over service and community, and that is a question on which society at large must take a moral stand.

Comparison and contrast is a useful way to describe something by comparing it to something else. Or you can use it to show how two or more things measure up against each other. Figure 18.7 describes how comparison and contrast can be used in a variety of genres.

Combining Rhetorical Patterns

Rhetorical patterns can be combined to meet a variety of purposes. For example, you can embed a comparison and contrast within a narrative. Or you can use a classification within a description. In other words, you shouldn't get hung up on a particular

Objective of Genre	Use of Comparison and Contrast
In a **rhetorical analysis** of an ad, compare and contrast an innovative recent ad with a more conventional ad.	A writer contrasts one of Dove's "Real Beauty" ads featuring a real-life model with a fashion ad featuring a very thin, tall, professional model to better demonstrate Dove's more realistic approach to beauty.
In a **proposal,** compare the plan to successful plans used in the past.	While pitching a plan for a new dog park, a proposal writer shows that similar plans have worked in other cities.
In a **position paper,** contrast an opponent's plan to the one being supported.	An economist argues against more government spending, contrasting growth in the 1960s with the 2008-2010 recession.

FIGURE 18.7 Using Comparison and Contrast

pattern as *the* way to make your point. You can mix and match these rhetorical patterns to fit your needs. All of the readings in *Writing Today* use combinations of rhetorical patterns, so you should turn to them for examples.

Also remember from Chapter 6 that many topics undergo development and change. You may need to adapt the rhetorical patterns you use to account for this process. For instance, if you are discussing an essay that initially asserts social media has become widely used but then builds on that to raise concerns about privacy, you will need to describe not only the wide uses of social media but at a later point describe the privacy issues that may occur. Here is a final example that uses several rhetorical devices in combination to discuss an Old Spice commercial, a topic that you will quickly see involves a sequence rather than a static set of events:

> The establishing shot of "The Man Your Man Could Smell Like" shows actor Isaiah Mustafa in a bathroom, dressed only in a towel and holding a bottle of Old Spice body wash. In a commanding voice, he addresses a female audience, saying, "Ladies, look at me, look at your man. Look at me, look at your man. Sadly, he isn't me . . ." (Old Spice, 2009). Quickly, the scene changes to a yacht where Mustafa promises his audience diamonds and tickets to "that thing you love" before moving to a final visual of a beach where he claims "anything is possible" with Old Spice body wash (Old Spice, 2009). The ad makes an effective pathos appeal, both in its sexual depiction of Mustafa and in its increasingly hyperbolic promises to give the viewer anything she desires, and so effectively revitalizes Old Spice's image.
>
> — *Narrative of the commercial's sequence.*
>
> — *Classification under pathos and image advertising, and division into its two main forms of appeal.*
>
> Image advertising is designed to shift people's perceptions, and this is clearly occurring in the Old Spice ad. "The Man Your Man Could Smell Like" creates a sexy, confident image by presenting a bare-chested Mustafa throughout, showing off his toned physique. His authoritative baritone and imperative commands further stress his masculine confidence. This image is in contrast with the way Old Spice was positioned in previous ad campaigns. Earlier ads showed the product as appropriate for older men and stressed its traditional values, while the new campaign seeks to create a younger, sexier image and so entice a new set of consumers. Indeed, the exaggerated promises throughout the ad are designed to appeal to the sensibilities of younger viewers, who are aware of how ads manipulate viewers and so are likely to enjoy this ad's humorous exploitation of that.
>
> — *Examples of how the ad creates an image.*
>
> — *Comparison and contrast with previous ads.*
>
> — *Description of intended audience and appeal.*

Here are some easy ways to start using and combining basic rhetorical patterns in your writing.

NARRATE a Story

Consider places in your writing where you can tell a story. Set the scene and then introduce a complication. Discuss how you or others evaluated and resolved the complication. Then tell readers the main point of the story.

DESCRIBE People, Places, or Objects

Consider your subject from your five senses: sight, sound, touch, smell, and taste. Pay special attention to language, rhetoric, and features that make your subject unique or interesting to your readers.

DEFINE Your Words or Concepts

Look for any important words or concepts in your writing that need to be defined in greater depth. A sentence definition should have three parts: the term, the category, and distinguishing characteristics. To extend the definition, try learning about the word's history, offer examples of its usage, use negation to show what it isn't, divide the subject into two or more parts, or discuss its similarities and differences with other things.

CLASSIFY Items by Dividing Them into Groups

If you are discussing something large or complex, list all its parts. Then use a principle of classification to sort that list into two to five major groups. Each group can be divided further into minor groups.

USE Cause and Effect to Explain How and Why Something Occurs

Examine your subject in terms of causes and effects. When analyzing a problem, explain what has caused it. When proposing a solution, describe how your plan will lead to positive results.

COMPARE and Contrast Things

Find something that is similar to your subject. List all the similarities between the two items. Then list all the differences. Describe their similarities and differences.

MIX It Up!

Rhetorical patterns are not recipes or formulas to be mechanically followed. You can combine these patterns in ways that enhance their strengths. Most well-developed paragraphs use several of these strategies together.

1. Have each member of your group find two print examples of one of the basic rhetorical patterns discussed in this chapter and give a brief presentation in which he or she shows how the examples illustrate the pattern.

2. Basic rhetorical patterns, such as comparison and contrast or classification and division, are sometimes used as structures for essays. With your group, discuss and list the advantages and disadvantages of using these patterns to learn how to write whole documents.

Talk About This

1. Pick a place where you can sit undisturbed for half an hour. Write down everything you hear, feel, smell, and taste. Do *not* write down what you see. Then try to write a one page description of the place where you were sitting. Try not to include any visual elements. Instead, use only your other senses to describe the place.

2. Pick two things that are similar in most ways but different in some important ways. Write two one-paragraph comparison and contrasts of these two things using each of the patterns, block and alternating, shown above. Which pattern worked best for your comparison and contrast, and why?

3. With your group, create a concept map that classifies the men and women at your university with the aim of better identifying student service needs. When you are finished, discuss whether it is possible to appropriately sort people into groups without resorting to stereotypes.

Try This Out

1. **Examine something using five different strategies.** Think of something you know a lot about but with which others are unfamiliar. Using basic rhetorical patterns (narrative, description, definition, classification, cause and effect, and comparison and contrast), help someone who knows little about your topic to understand it.

2. **Find rhetorical patterns on the Internet.** Write a two page rhetorical analysis of an online article in which you identify these basic rhetorical patterns and discuss how they are used.

3. **Do an extended definition.** Choose a term you think will be useful in relation to an essay topic you are working on (it should be a key term that not everyone might be familiar with or that is used in a specialized way). Remember, an extended definition will begin with the sentence definition, and then may employ any of the following: etymology, examples, division, negation, and comparison/contrast with a similar term. You can develop the extended or contextual aspect by searching an appropriate library database for essays that use the word in context or by consulting a scholarly encyclopedia. Remember to cite any sources that you use.

MyCompLab

For support in meeting this chapter's objectives, follow this path in MyCompLab:

Student Resources → Writing → Writing Purposes. Review the Instruction and Multimedia resources about the basic rhetorical patterns; then complete the Exercises and click on Gradebook to measure your progress.

Using Argumentative Strategies

In this chapter, you will learn how to:
- determine the source and nature of an arguable claim.
- use reasoning, authority, and emotion to support your argument.
- identify and avoid argumentative fallacies.

For some people, the word *argument* brings up images of fingerpointing, glares, outbursts, or quiet resentment. Actually, these aren't arguments at all. They are quarrels. When people quarrel, they no longer listen to each other or consider each other's ideas.

An argument is something quite different. An argument involves making reasonable claims and then backing up those claims with evidence and support. The objective of an argument is not to "win" and prove you have the truth. Instead, your primary goal is to persuade others that you are *probably* right. Arguments rarely end with one side proving the other side wrong. Instead, both sides strive to persuade others that their position is stronger or more beneficial, perhaps reaching agreement in the middle.

In university or college and in the professional world, arguments are used to think through ideas and debate uncertainties. Arguments are about getting things done by gaining the cooperation of others. In most situations, an argument is about agreeing as much as disagreeing, about cooperating with others as much as competing with them. The ability to argue effectively will be an important part of your success in post-secondary courses and in your career.

Argument can be used in any genre, but it is more prominent in some than in others. Forms of narrative writing, for example, do not typically make straightforward arguments, because they are primarily based on personal experience or historical facts. Other genres, such as reviews, evaluations, literary analyses, rhetorical analyses, proposals, and research papers, are much more argumentative because their authors are deliberately trying to persuade readers to accept a particular view or idea.

In this chapter, you will learn some helpful strategies for persuading people to accept your ideas. You can use these strategies to argue effectively with your friends and family. They are also useful for arguing about important issues in university and college and in the workplace.

What Is Arguable?

((•●[**Listen** Audio Lesson Section 1: Big Ideas— Constructing an Argument

Let's begin by first discussing what is "arguable." Some people will say that you can argue about anything. And in a sense, they are right. We *can* argue about anything, no matter how trivial or pointless.

"I don't like chocolate."	"Yes, you do."
"The Battle of the Plains of Abraham occurred in 1759."	"No, it didn't."
"It really bugs me when I see a pregnant woman smoking."	"I think pregnant women should have the right to make their own decisions."

These kinds of arguments are rarely worth the time and effort. Of course, we can argue that our friend is lying when she tells us she doesn't like chocolate, and we can challenge the historical fact that the Battle of the Plains of Abraham occurred in 1759. (Anything is arguable.) However, debates over *personal judgments,* such as liking or not liking chocolate or subjective reactions to pregnant women smoking, quickly devolve into "Yes, No!" kinds of quarrels. Meanwhile, debates about *proven facts*, like the year the Battle of the Plains of Abraham occurred, can be resolved by consulting a trusted source. To be truly arguable, a claim should exist somewhere between personal judgments and proven facts (Figure 19.1).

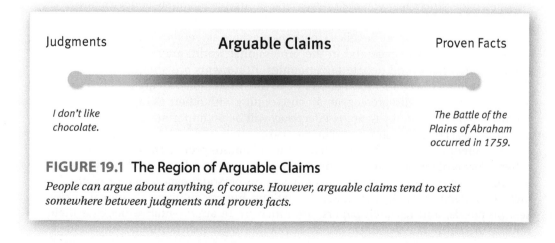

Judgments	**Arguable Claims**	Proven Facts
I don't like chocolate.		*The Battle of the Plains of Abraham occurred in 1759.*

FIGURE 19.1 The Region of Arguable Claims
People can argue about anything, of course. However, arguable claims tend to exist somewhere between judgments and proven facts.

Arguable Claims

When laying the groundwork for an argument, you need to first define an arguable claim that you will try to persuade your readers to accept as probably true. For example, here are two arguable claims on two sides of the same topic:

Arguable Claim:

Canada made a mistake when it refused to join the 2003 war against Iraq because that refusal damaged Canada–US relations and hindered the international effort to remove Saddam Hussein's dangerous dictatorship.

Arguable Claim:

Despite US criticisms, Canada was justified in refusing to participate in the 2003 invasion of Iraq, because that invasion was based on faulty intelligence suggesting Saddam Hussein possessed weapons of mass destruction.

These claims are "arguable" because neither side can prove that it is factually right nor that the other side is factually wrong. Meanwhile, neither side is based exclusively on personal judgments. Instead, both sides want to persuade you, the reader, that they are *probably* right.

When you develop and draft your argument, your goal is to support one side to the best of your ability, but you should also imagine opponents who will be presenting a different position. Keeping your opponents in mind will help you to clarify your ideas, generate support, and identify any weaknesses in your argument. Then, when you draft your argument, you will be better able to show readers that you have considered both sides fairly.

If, on the other hand, you realize that there really isn't another credible side to your argument or that the other side is extremely weak, then you may not have an arguable claim in the first place.

Four Sources of Arguable Claims

Once you have a rough idea of your arguable claim, you should refine and clarify it. Toward this end, it is helpful to figure out what kind of arguable claim you are trying to support. Arguable claims generally arise from four different sources: issues of definition, causation, evaluation, and recommendation (Figure 19.2).

Issues of Definition. Some arguments hinge on how to define an object, event, or person. For example, here are a few arguable claims that debate how to define something:

Animals, like humans, are sentient beings who have inalienable rights; therefore, killing and eating animals is an unethical act.

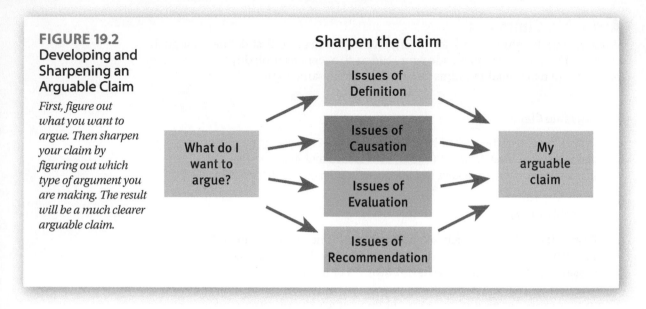

**FIGURE 19.2
Developing and
Sharpening an
Arguable Claim**

*First, figure out
what you want to
argue. Then sharpen
your claim by
figuring out which
type of argument you
are making. The result
will be a much clearer
arguable claim.*

Sharpen the Claim

What do I want to argue? → Issues of Definition · Issues of Causation · Issues of Evaluation · Issues of Recommendation → My arguable claim

The terrorist acts of September 11, 2001, were an unprovoked act of war, not just a criminal act. Consequently, the United States was justified in declaring war on Al-Qaeda and its ally, the Taliban government of Afghanistan.

A pregnant woman who smokes is a child abuser who needs to be stopped before she further harms her unborn child.

Issues of Causation. Humans tend to see events in terms of cause and effect. Consequently, we often argue about whether one thing caused another.

The main cause of boredom is a lack of variety. People become bored when nothing changes in their lives, causing them to lose their curiosity about the people, places, and events around them.

Advocates of gun control incorrectly blame the guns when an event such as the École Polytechnique massacre happens. Instead, we need to look at the sociological and psychological causes of violence, such as mental illness, prejudice, and the shooters' histories of aggression.

Pregnant mothers who choose to smoke are responsible for an unacceptable number of birth defects in children.

Issues of Evaluation. We also argue about whether something is *good* or *bad, right* or *wrong,* or *better* or *worse.*

The movie *The Pirates of the Caribbean* is better than the classic pirate movie, *Captain Blood,* because Johnny Depp plays a more realistic pirate than Errol Flynn's overly romantic portrayal.

The current Canadian taxation system is unfair, because the majority of taxes fall most heavily on people who work hard and corporations who are bringing innovative products to the marketplace.

Although both are dangerous, drinking alcohol in moderation while pregnant is less damaging to an unborn child than smoking in moderation.

Issues of Recommendation. We also use arguments to make recommendations about the best course of action to follow. These kinds of claims are signalled by words like "should," "must," "ought to," and so forth.

Bombardier should convert its Quebec factory to renewable energy sources, like wind, solar, and geothermal, using the standard electric grid only as a backup supply for electricity.

The meat industry is heavily subsidized by the Canadian taxpayer; therefore, we recommend removing all subsidies, making vegetarianism a financially viable choice.

We must help pregnant women to stop smoking by developing smoking-cessation programs that are specifically targeted toward this population.

To refine and sharpen your arguable claim, you should figure out which of these four types of arguable claims you are making, as shown in Figure 19.2. Then revise your claim to fit neatly into one of the four categories.

Using Reason, Authority, and Emotion

Once you have developed an arguable claim, you can start figuring out how you are going to support it with evidence. There are three types of evidence you might use to support your position: reason, authority, and emotion (Figure 19.3). A solid argument will usually employ all three types of evidence; however, one type will usually be the dominant mode of argument.

Greek rhetoricians like Aristotle originally used the words *logos* (reason), *ethos* (authority), and *pathos* (emotion) to discuss these three kinds of evidence. See Chapters 11 and 6 for how to use these concepts in prewriting and rhetorical analyses.

Reason (*Logos*)

Reasoning involves appealing to your readers' common sense or beliefs.

Logical Statements. The first type of reasoning, logical statements, allows you to use your readers' existing beliefs to prove they should agree with a further claim. Here are some common patterns for logical statements:

If . . . then. "If you believe X, then you should also believe Y."

Either . . . or. "Either you believe X or you believe Y."

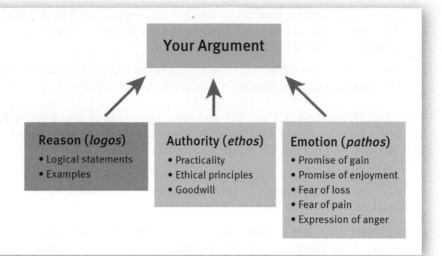

FIGURE 19.3
Three Types of Evidence for Supporting an Argument

Three types of evidence can be used to support an argument: reason, authority, and emotion.

Your Argument

Reason (*logos*)
• Logical statements
• Examples

Authority (*ethos*)
• Practicality
• Ethical principles
• Goodwill

Emotion (*pathos*)
• Promise of gain
• Promise of enjoyment
• Fear of loss
• Fear of pain
• Expression of anger

Cause and effect. "X causes Y." or "Y is caused by X." (See Figure 19.4.)

Costs and benefits. "The benefits A, B, and C show that doing X is worth the costs."

Better and worse. "X is better than Y." or "X is worse than Y."

Examples. The second type of reasoning, examples, allows you to illustrate your points or demonstrate that a pattern exists.

"For example." "For example, in 1994 . . ." "For instance, last week . . ." "To illustrate, there was the interesting case of . . ." "Specifically, I can name two times when . . ."

Personal experiences. "Last summer, I saw . . ." or "Where I work, X happens regularly." Be cautious about using this kind of example as your primary form of evidence in academic writing, since academics prefer objective, expert data.

Facts and data. "According to our experiment, . . ." or "Recently published data show that . . ."

Patterns of experiences. "X happened in 2000, 2004, and 2008. Therefore, we expect it to happen again in 2012." "In the past, each time X happened, Y has happened also."

Quotes from experts. "Dr. Jennifer Xu, a scientist at Los Alamos National Laboratory, recently stated . . ." or "In his 2009 article, historian George Brenden claimed . . ."

FIGURE 19.4 A Cause and Effect Argument

In this advertisement from Health Canada, the primary argument strategy is cause and effect (i.e., smoking hurts unborn babies, or "X causes Y"). The argument also uses emotion (pathos).

Authority (*Ethos*)

Authority involves using your own experience or data from credible sources to support your arguments. In academic writing in particular, published research by experts on your topic is considered compelling evidence. Another way to strengthen your authority is to demonstrate your practicality, ethical principles, and goodwill. These three types of authority were first mentioned by Aristotle as a way to strengthen credibility with readers, and these strategies still work well today.

Practicality. Show your readers that you are primarily concerned about solving problems and getting things done, not lecturing or theorizing. Where appropriate, admit that the issue is not simple and cannot be fixed easily. You can also point out that reasonable people can disagree about the issue. Being "practical" involves being realistic about what is possible, not idealistic about what would happen in a perfect world. In academic papers, reliability as a researcher can also be a way of demonstrating your authority. So be sure to proofread your writing and to verify your data in order to portray yourself as a trustworthy scholar.

Ethical Principles. Demonstrate that you are arguing for an outcome that meets a firm set of ethical principles. An ethical argument can be based on any of three types of ethics:

- *Rights:* Using human rights or constitutional rights to back up your claims.

- *Laws:* Showing that your argument is in line with civic laws.

- *Utilitarianism:* Arguing that your position is more beneficial for the majority.

Goodwill. Demonstrate that you have your readers' interests in mind, not just your own. Of course, you may be arguing for something that benefits you. So show your readers that you care about their needs and interests, too. Show them that you understand their concerns and that your position is a "win-win" for both you and them.

Emotion (*Pathos*)

Using emotional appeals to persuade your readers is appropriate if the feelings you draw on are suitable for your topic and readers. An example that draws on readers' experiences can be a more persuasive kind of evidence than an example that is foreign to readers. Keep in mind, though, that this kind of evidence is used sparingly in academic papers, which rely on reason and authority, not emotion, as primary forms of support. Promises of gain or threats of loss are often perceived as fallacies or weak forms of argument in academic contexts. They are, however, widely used in popular writing and advertising. As you develop your argument, think about how your and your readers' emotions might influence how their decisions will be made.

Begin by listing the positive and negative emotions that are associated with your topic or with your side of the argument.

Promise of Gain. Demonstrate to your readers that agreeing with your position will help them gain things they need or want, like trust, time, money, love, advancement, reputation, comfort, popularity, health, beauty, or convenience.

Promise of Enjoyment. Show that accepting your position will lead to more satisfaction, including joy, anticipation, surprise, pleasure, leisure, or freedom.

Fear of Loss. Suggest that not agreeing with your opinion might cause the loss of things readers value, like time, money, love, security, freedom, reputation, popularity, health, or beauty.

Fear of Pain. Imply that not agreeing with your position will cause feelings of pain, sadness, frustration, humiliation, embarrassment, loneliness, regret, shame, vulnerability, or worry.

Expressions of Anger or Disgust. Show that you share feelings of anger or disgust with your readers about a particular event or situation.

Use positive emotions as much as you can, because they will build a sense of happiness and goodwill in your readers (Figure 19.5). Generally, people like to feel good and believe that agreeing with you will bring them gain, enjoyment, and happiness.

Negative emotions should be used sparingly. Negative emotions can energize your readers and spur them to action. However, you need to be careful not to threaten or frighten your readers, because people tend to reject bullying or scare tactics. Any feelings of anger or disgust you express in your argument must be shared by your readers, or they will reject your argument as too harsh or reactionary.

FIGURE 19.5
**Using Emotions
in an Argument**

*This advertisement
uses emotional
appeals to influence
readers.*

Avoiding Argumentative Fallacies

An argumentative or, as it is sometimes termed, a logical fallacy is an error in reasoning. As much as possible, you want to avoid fallacies in your arguments, because they are weaknesses that your opponents can exploit. Plus, they can keep you from gaining a full understanding of the issue because fallacies usually lead to inaccurate or ambiguous conclusions.

Figure 19.6 defines and gives examples of common argumentative fallacies. Watch out for them in your own arguments. When an opponent uses a fallacy, you can attack it as a weak spot in his or her argument.

Fallacies tend to occur for three primary reasons:

False or Weak Premises. In these situations, the author is overreaching to make a point. The argument uses false or weak premises (bandwagon, *post hoc* reasoning, slippery slope, or hasty generalization) or it relies on comparisons or authorities that don't exist (weak analogy, false authority).

Irrelevance. The author is trying to distract readers by using name calling (*ad hominem*) or bringing up issues that are beside the point (red herring, *tu quoque, non sequitur*).

Ambiguity. The author is clouding the issue by using circular reasoning (begging the question), arguing against a position that no one is defending (straw man), or presenting the reader with a limited choice of options (either/or).

Argumentative Fallacy	Definition	Example
Ad Hominem	Attacking the character of the arguer rather than the argument.	"Mary has no credibility on the smoking ban issue, because she was once a smoker herself."
Bandwagon (*Ad Populum*)	Suggesting that a person should agree to something because it is popular.	"Over one thousand people have decided to sign up, so you should too."
Begging the Question	Using circular reasoning to prove a conclusion.	"Conservatives believe in hard work and strong values. That's why most Canadians are conservative."
Either/Or	Presenting someone with a limited choice, when other choices are possible.	"We either buy this car now, or we spend the rest of the year walking to school."
Straw Man	Arguing against a position that no one is defending.	"Letting children play soccer on a busy highway is wrong, and I won't stand for it."
Weak Analogy	Making an improper comparison between two things that share a common feature.	"Paying taxes to the government is the same as handing your wallet over to a mugger in the park."
Post Hoc Reasoning	Arguing that one event caused another when they are unrelated.	"Each time my roommate is out of town, it causes my car to break down and I can't get to work."
Hasty Generalization	Using a part to make an inaccurate claim about a whole.	"The snowboarder who cut me off proved that all snowboarders are rude."
Slippery Slope	Suggesting that one event will automatically lead to a chain of other events.	"If we allow them to legalize marijuana, soon we will have a nation of drug addicts."
Red Herring	Saying something that distracts from the issue being argued about.	"So, because books can now be found on the Internet, you're suggesting we burn our libraries?"
False Authority	Defending a claim with a biased or untrustworthy source.	"My mother read my paper, and she thinks it deserves an A."
Non Sequitur	Stating a conclusion that does not follow from the premises.	"Watching *30 Rock* each week will make you smarter and more popular."
Tu Quoque	Improperly turning an accusation back on the accuser.	"If you cared about global warming, as you claim, you wouldn't have driven a car to this meeting."

FIGURE 19.6 Common Argumentative Fallacies

Argumentative fallacies do not prove that someone is wrong about a topic. They simply mean that the person is using weak or improper reasoning to reach his or her conclusions. In some cases, especially in advertising, fallacies are used on purpose. The advertiser wants to slip a sales pitch past the audience. Savvy arguers can also use argumentative fallacies to trip up their opponents. You should learn to recognize these fallacies so you can counter them when necessary.

Rebuttals and Refutations

Because we argue *with* others in an effort to gain their understanding and cooperation, you need to anticipate how your opponents and your readers will feel about your claims and your support. You need to imagine their possible objections or misunderstandings. After all, something that sounds like a good reason to you may not sound so convincing to your reader. See Chapter 8 for an example of a rebuttal related to climate change.

Summarize Your Opponents' Position Objectively

If you're discussing something "arguable," then there must be at least one other side to the issue. So you should demonstrate that you understand that other side before you offer a rebuttal or try to counter it. If you ignore the other side, your readers will think you are either unfairly overlooking potential objections or you just don't understand the other side of the argument. One way to disarm your opponents is to summarize their position objectively early in your argument.

Summarizing your opponents' position does three things for your argument. First, it lays out some specific points that you can then argue against or refute when you state your side of the argument. Second, it takes away some of your opponents' momentum, because they will not have anything new to offer the readers. Third, it will make you look more reasonable and well-informed about the issue you are arguing about.

Recognize When the Opposing Position May Be Valid

Your opponents probably aren't completely wrong. There are likely to be situations, both real and hypothetical, where the other side may be valid. For example, let's say you are arguing that the North American automobile industry needs to convert completely to manufacturing electric cars within twenty years. Your opponents would argue that this kind of dramatic conversion is not technically or economically feasible.

To disarm your opponents, you could name a few situations in which they are correct:

> Converting fully to electric vehicles within twenty years may not be possible in some circumstances. For example, it is unlikely that large trucks, like semitrailers, will be able to run on electricity two decades from now because batteries will not be strong enough to provide the amount of energy required to move their weight for long distances. Meanwhile, even if we stopped manufacturing

gasoline-powered vehicles immediately, they would still be on the road for decades, requiring gas stations and mechanical repair. We cannot, after all, ask all drivers to immediately switch over to electric vehicles, especially if they cannot afford it.

By identifying situations in which your opponents' position may be valid, you give some ground to your opponents while putting boundaries around their major points.

Concede Your Opponents' Minor Points

When you concede a minor point, you are acknowledging that your opponents' viewpoints or objections are valid in a limited way, while highlighting a potential weakness in your own position. In these cases, you should candidly acknowledge this limitation and address it fairly.

For instance, if you were arguing that the federal government should use taxpayer money to help the auto industry develop electric cars, you could anticipate two objections to your argument:

- Production of electric cars cannot be ramped up quickly because appropriate batteries are not being manufactured in sufficient numbers.
- Canada's electric grid could not handle millions of new electric cars being charged every day.

These objections are important, but they do not undermine your whole argument. Instead, you should concede that they are problems while demonstrating that they are problems that can be fixed.

It is true that the availability of car batteries and the inadequacy of Canada's electricity grid are concerns. As Stephen Becker, a well-respected consultant to the auto industry, points out, "car manufacturers are already experiencing a shortage of batteries," and there are no plans to build more battery factories in the future (109). Meanwhile, as the CBC has reported, existing utilities are not designed for the added demands of electric cars. Nick Beck, director of Transportation Energy Technology at Natural Resources Canada, cautions, "Neighbourhood transformers that convert electricity to the right voltage before it enters people's homes aren't designed for the kind of load created by a number of cars all drawing large amounts of power from the grid at the same time, and they may fail, causing neighbourhood power outages" (qtd. in CBCNews).
    However, there are good reasons to believe that these problems, too, can be dealt with if the right measures are put in place. First, if investors had more confidence that there would be a steady demand for electric cars, and if the government guaranteed loans for new factories, the growing demand for batteries would encourage manufacturers to bring them to market (Vantz 12). Second, experts have been arguing for years that Canada needs to invest in an updated electricity grid that will meet our increasing needs for electricity. We already need to build a better grid, because the current grid *is* too fragile, even

for today's needs. Moreover, it will take years to build a fleet of 20 million cars. During those years, the electric grid can be rebuilt.

By conceding some minor points, you weaken their effectiveness. By anticipating your opponents' arguments, you can minimize the damage to your own argument.

Refute or Absorb Your Opponents' Major Points

In some situations, your opponents will have one or two major points that cannot be conceded without undermining your argument. In these situations, you should study each major point to understand why it is a threat to your own argument. Is there a chance your opponents have a good point? Could your argument be flawed in some fundamental way?

If you still believe your side of the argument is stronger, you have a couple of choices at this point. First, you can refute your opponents' major point by challenging its factual correctness. It helps to look for a "smoking gun" moment in which your opponents make a mistake or overstate a claim.

Critics of electric cars argue that the free market should determine whether electric cars and the infrastructure to support them should be built. They argue that the government should not determine which automotive technologies survive and thrive. This kind of argument goes against the historical record. The Canadian government has always been involved in building roads, railways, and airports. For decades, it has given tax breaks to support the manufacturing of gasoline vehicles. We are simply asking for these supports to be shifted in ways that will meet future needs, not the needs of the past.

In other situations, you should absorb your opponents' arguments by suggesting that your side of the argument is necessary or is better for the majority.

The skeptics are correct that the conversion from gasoline cars to electric cars will not be easy and may even be economically painful. At this point, though, we have little choice. Our dependence on oil, which is something we all agree is a problem, is a threat to our economic and environmental future. Our planet is already experiencing the negative effects of global climate change, which could severely damage the fragile ecosystems on which we depend for food, air, and water. We aren't talking about lifestyle choices at this point. We are talking about survival.

When absorbing your opponents' major points, you should show that you are aware that they are correct but that the benefits of your position outweigh its costs.

Qualify Your Claims

In an argument, you will be tempted to state your claims in the strongest language possible, perhaps even overstating them.

Overstatement

The government must use its full power to force the auto industry to develop and build affordable electric cars for the North American consumer. The payoff in monetary and environmental benefits will more than pay for the investment.

Qualified Statement

Although many significant challenges must be dealt with, the government should begin taking steps to encourage the auto industry to develop and build affordable electric cars for the North American consumer. The payoff in monetary and environmental impact could very well pay for the effort and might even pay dividends.

When qualifying your statements, you are softening your position a little. This softening gives readers the sense that they are being asked to make up their own minds on the matter. Few people want to be told that they "must" do something or "cannot" do something else. If possible, you want to avoid pushing your readers into making an either/or, yes/no kind of decision, because they may reject your position altogether.

Instead, remember that all arguments have grey areas. No one side is absolutely right or wrong. Qualifying your claims allows you to give the impression that your side has some flexibility and allows you to take a more objective, academic tone. You can use the following words and phrases to qualify your claims:

unless	even though	in some cases
would	reasonably	almost certainly
in all	probably	often
probability	not including	although
except	plausibly	most likely
perhaps	possibly	may
usually	aside from	could
if	in most	if possible
maybe	circumstances	might
frequently	conceivably	should

You can also soften your claims by acknowledging that you are aware of the difficulties and limitations of your position. Your goal is to sound reasonable while advocating for your side of the argument.

Using an Argumentative Form

Many of the principles discussed in this chapter have been used for a long time to construct arguments in courts of law, in political speeches, and of course in essays and books. Certain forms have developed over time that help writers develop claims, support those claims, and rebut opposing views. You may find it useful to follow one of these forms, although you can certainly incorporate the principles we have discussed into your essays in other ways as well. Here are the three most common argumentative forms.

Classical Argument Form

Classical argument form has been used for over two thousand years to structure ideas and convince listeners. The North American legal system is based on elements of this form. It involves what Richard Coe, professor at Simon Fraser University and author of several influential texts on form and rhetoric, terms an "antagonistic" approach, meaning that classical rhetoricians seek victory over their opponents. If your purpose is to convince your readers and prove opposing views wrong, then using the five elements of this form may help you do that.

Introduction and Thesis Statement. Identifies the topic and states the thesis or argumentative position clearly and polemically.

> Environmental pollution causes a number of health problems and should be reduced through government and citizen action.

Background Information. Sets forth the facts and defines key terms.

> Background information for an essay on the relation between environmental pollution and health problems could include facts on the nature of environmental pollution, statistics on its increase, and an identification of the main forms of pollution.

Evidence. Presents your research and analysis supporting the thesis; consider arranging for emphasis.

> Supporting evidence for the relationship between environmental pollution and health problems would include studies on the connections between asthma, allergies, cancer, and pollution.

Rebuttal: Anticipates other viewpoints and demonstrates their flaws.

> The cost of reducing pollution is negligible and easily overcome.

Conclusion. Summarizes and considers a final appeal.

> Evidence shows that we need to reduce pollution and create a cleaner world for the next generation.

Rogerian Form

Not all arguments benefit from an antagonistic approach. When you are seeking to create consensus on an issue, for instance, you may wish to negotiate rather than prove your opponents wrong. In these situations, Rogerian form may be a more help-ful structure. Psychologist Carl Rogers (1902–1987) proposed that "threat hinders communication," and rhetoricians have since used his ideas to develop the following four-step argumentative approach:

Introduction and Thesis Statement. Identifies the topic and "frames" the thesis as a problem to be solved or as developing from a point of consensus.

> We all want cleaner air and better health; therefore, environmental pollut-ants must be reduced.

Acknowledgement of the Opposing Position. States the opposition briefly to establish an unbiased, reasonable tone. You may acknowledge elements of common ground, but keep your thesis or argumentative position clear (in other words, explain the other side, but do not agree with it).

> The cost of reducing pollution may cause an economic recession, but this change is nevertheless essential in order to preserve our health.

Statement of Your Position. Provides evidence and reasons in support of your thesis.

> Research proves environmental pollutants cause asthma and allergies, as well as contributing to the development of cancer.

Statement of How Readers Would Benefit by Moving Toward Your Position. Returns to your thesis and argumentative "frame," explaining how you have solved the problem or reached a greater point of consensus.

> The costs of reducing pollution can be overcome through planning and tech-nology, while the health benefits are significant. Reducing pollution will benefit everyone in the long term.

The Toulmin Model

Philosopher Stephen Toulmin (1922–2009) developed this form to evaluate moral reasoning. It is often useful for analyzing others' arguments as well as constructing valid claims within paragraphs or sections of an essay. It follows three main steps:

Claim. Presents a statement that must be verified. In essay writing, this may be your thesis statement.

> Air pollution causes health problems.

Support. Provides reasons and evidence, usually organized from broad to more specific.

Studies quantify increased rates of asthma, respiratory allergies, and lung cancer in major North American cities.

Warrant. Shows the logic or reasoning which links claim and support.

North American cities have higher rates of air pollution due to cars, manufacturing, and energy requirements, so the increased rates of asthma, respiratory allergies, and lung cancer in these places are likely due to air pollution.

Rebuttals are sometimes, although not always, included in Toulmin form to further strengthen the claim. They typically follow the main warrants.

Here are some strategies for becoming more effective at argument.

DEVELOP an "Arguable Claim"

An arguable claim is a statement that exists between personal judgments and proven facts. It should also be a claim that others would be willing to dispute.

IDENTIFY the Source of Your Arguable Claim

Arguable claims tend to emerge from four types of issues: issues of definition, causation, evaluation, and recommendation. You can sharpen your claim by figuring out what kind of issue you are arguing about.

FIND Reason-Based Evidence to Back Up Your Claims

Reasoning consists of using logical statements and examples to support your arguments.

LOCATE Authoritative Evidence to Back Up Your Claims

You can use your own experience if you are an expert, or you can draw quotes from other experts who agree with you. You should also build up your authority by demonstrating your practicality, ethical principles, and goodwill toward readers.

USE Emotional Evidence to Back Up Your Claims if Appropriate

Identify any emotions that shape how your readers will be influenced by your argument. If you are writing for a non-academic audience, you can use promise of gain, promise of enjoyment, fear of loss, fear of pain, and expressions of anger and disgust to influence them.

COUNTER or Disarm Your Opponents

There are a variety of ways to counter or weaken your opponents' argument through rebuttal and refutation including (a) summarizing their position objectively, (b) identifying limited situations in which the opposing position may be valid, (c) conceding your opponents' minor points, (d) refuting or absorbing your opponents' major points, and (e) qualifying your claims.

AVOID Argumentative Fallacies and Consider Whether an Argumentative Form Would Be Helpful

Look for fallacies in your argument and locate them in your opponents' existing arguments. An argumentative fallacy is a weak spot that should be addressed in your own work and can be exploited in your opponents' arguments. Consider whether Toulmin, classical, or Rogerian forms might help you structure your argument.

1. With a group of people from your class, talk about how you usually argue with your friends and family. When are arguments productive? At what point do they become quarrels?

2. Discuss whether each of the following claims is "arguable." Explain why each is or is not arguable.

   a. I always like to bring a water bottle with me when I work out at the gym.

   b. The Edmonton Oilers were Canada's favourite team during the 1980s.

   c. The major message behind the television show *Family Guy* is that it's okay to act rudely, obscenely, and irresponsibly.

   d. Multiculturalism has been a success, revitalizing Canadian culture and encouraging continued growth.

3. With your group, identify five reasons why arguing can be useful, productive, or even amusing.

Talk About This

1. On the Internet, find a fairly short opinion article about an issue that interests you. Identify its main claim and determine which kind of evidence (*logos, ethos,* or *pathos*) is most dominant.

2. Find three different websites that persuade people to stop smoking. Compare and contrast their argument strategies. In a presentation, show why you think one website is more persuasive than the others.

3. With a group of three or four people from your class, divide up the list of fallacies in Figure 19.6 (on page 366). Then find or create examples of these fallacies. Share your examples with other groups in your class.

Try This Out

1. **Generate four claims and four counterclaims.** Choose an issue that you care about and develop an "arguable claim" from each of the sources of arguable claims discussed in this chapter (i.e., definition, causation, evaluation, recommendation). Then, for each of these arguable claims, develop a counterclaim that an opponent might use to argue against your positions.

2. **Find the fallacies in an advertisement.** Find an advertisement on television that uses one or more argumentative fallacies to support its points. In a two page ad critique (see pages 99–100), draw attention to the fallacies and use them as weak spots to undermine the advertisement.

Write This

MyCompLab

For support in meeting this chapter's objectives, follow this path in MyCompLab:

Student Resources → Writing → Writing Purposes → Writing to Argue or Persuade. Review the Instruction and Multimedia resources about writing arguments; then complete the Exercises and click on Gradebook to measure your progress.

20

Working Collaboratively with Other Writers

In this chapter, you will learn how to:

- work productively in groups and teams.
- assign specific roles to team members.
- understand and overcome conflicts that can arise in collaborative work.

In your post-secondary studies and throughout your career, you will be asked to collaborate with other people on a variety of projects. Working in teams allows people to concentrate their personal strengths and take advantage of each other's abilities. Working with others also helps you to be more creative and take on more complex, longer projects.

Computers and the Internet have significantly increased our ability to collaborate with others. You probably already use e-mail, texting, mobile phones, blogs, microblogs, social networking sites, chat, and virtual worlds to keep in touch with your friends and family. In your career, you will use these same kinds of communication tools to interact with people at your office, across the country, and throughout the world.

In your classes and in the workplace, collaboration will tend to take on two forms:

Working in Groups. Groups involve people who are working on separate but related assignments. Each member of the group shares his or her ideas and research, and everyone helps review and edit each other's work. Each person completes and hands in his or her own assignment.

Working in Teams. Teams involve people who are working on the same project. Each member of the team is responsible for completing one or more parts of the project, and the team hands in one common assignment or set of assignments.

In this chapter, you will learn how to work productively in groups and teams, and you will learn some strategies for avoiding and overcoming the negative aspects of working with others.

Working with a Group of Other Writers

In your classes, professors will regularly ask you to work in groups. Often, these groups are informal, made up of the people who happen to be sitting near you in class that day. Your professor may also put you into a group with people who are working on a similar topic or who have a major similar to yours.

Choosing Group Roles

When you are put into a group, each person should choose a role:

Facilitator. The facilitator is responsible for keeping the group moving forward toward completing the task. His or her responsibility is to make sure the group stays on task, always keeping an eye on the clock. When the group goes off on a tangent or becomes distracted, the facilitator should remind the group members what they are trying to achieve and how much time is left to complete the task. When the group runs out of new ideas, the facilitator should prompt discussion by summarizing the group's major points and asking individuals to respond to those ideas.

Scribe. The scribe takes notes on what the group says or decides. These notes can be shared among the group members, helping everyone remember what was decided. If the group runs out of issues to talk about, the scribe should look back through the notes to pick out topics that could benefit from more discussion.

Innovator. The innovator should feel free to come up with new and unique ideas that help the group see the issue from other perspectives. The innovator should look for ways to be creative and different, even though he or she might come up with something that the rest of the group will probably not agree with.

Designated Skeptic. The designated skeptic's job is to keep the group from reaching easy consensus on issues. He or she should bring up concerns that someone else might use to raise doubts about what the members of the group have decided.

These roles should be rotated among the group members. Give everyone a chance to be a facilitator, scribe, innovator, and skeptic.

Figuring Out What the Group Needs to Do

Soon after your professor puts you into groups, you can warm up by answering the following questions:

What Is Our Primary Goal? Figure out exactly what your group is being asked to accomplish. The facilitator of the group can state what he or she thinks the task is. Other members of the group can elaborate on or sharpen that statement until everyone settles on a common goal.

What Else Should We Achieve? Sometimes your professor will ask your group to achieve a few secondary goals, too. Figure out what they are and have the scribe write them down.

How Much Time Do We Have? With your goals listed, figure out how much time you can devote to each one. Accomplishing the primary goal will usually take up the most time, but save some time for those secondary goals.

What Are We Expected to Deliver? When time is up, what is the group supposed to have finished? Does the professor expect someone to summarize the group's ideas for the class? Does the group need to produce something on paper to be handed in?

Who Will Speak for Our Group? Pick someone who can speak for the group when the activity is over. This choice should be made early, so the designated speaker can think about what he or she is going to say. This responsibility should rotate among group members, so one person doesn't end up always speaking for the group.

These questions are designed to get everyone on the same page. Otherwise, your group might waste time because you aren't sure what you are doing and what you are supposed to deliver.

Getting the Work Done

Now it's time to go to work. Here are some of the ways your group can work together to help each other succeed:

Generate Ideas. Your group can brainstorm ideas and help each other see different perspectives on issues. Any prewriting technique, such as concept mapping, listing, or brainstorming, can be used by the group to generate ideas. The scribe should write down the ideas while the other group members talk.

Serve as a Sounding Board. The people in your group can serve as a forum for talking out your ideas for an assignment and figuring out your angle on the project. The group's facilitator should ask each person in the group to take turns sharing his or her ideas. Then, after each person speaks, every group member should say something positive about the speaker's project and offer at least one suggestion for improving it.

Discuss Readings. Your group will be asked to discuss the course readings to figure out the meaning of the text and its implications. Each person should be asked to contribute. Meanwhile, the designated skeptic should keep the group from reaching quick consensus about what a reading means. Your professor will likely ask each group to offer a brief report to the class about your discussion.

Review Works-in-Progress. Members of your group can read and comment on your writing, helping you strengthen and clarify your ideas. You can rotate papers among members of the group. If time allows, each member of the group might take a turn reading someone else's paper out loud. While listening, other members of the group should take notes about the paper's strengths and what could be improved.

Working with a Team

Throughout your post-secondary career, especially in advanced courses for your major, you will be asked to work on team projects. Working in teams usually involves developing one project (i.e., a document, presentation, product, experiment) that your team will hand in together. To be successful, you and your team members will need to set goals and deadlines, negotiate with each other, divide up the work, and overcome disagreements.

One helpful way to successfully work as a team is to use the "Four Stages of Teaming" that were developed by management guru Bruce Tuckman (Figure 20.1). Tuckman noticed that successful teams tend to go through four predictable stages when working on a project:

Forming. Getting to know each other, defining goals, describing outcomes, setting deadlines, dividing up the work.

Storming. Experiencing disagreements, sensing tension and anxiety, doubting the leadership of the team, experiencing conflict, feeling uncertain and frustrated.

Norming. Forming consensus, revising the project's goals, refining expectations of outcomes, solidifying team roles.

Performing. Sharing a common vision, delegating tasks, feeling autonomous, resolving conflicts and differences in constructive ways.

These are the stages for *successful* groups. Some groups break down at the storming stage, while other groups never reach the performing stage. The secret to working in teams is recognizing that these stages are normal—including storming—and knowing what to do at each stage.

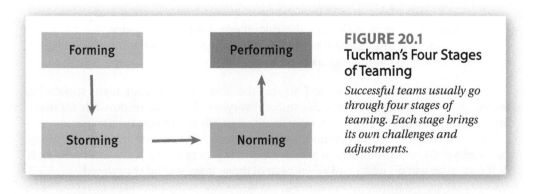

FIGURE 20.1
Tuckman's Four Stages of Teaming

Successful teams usually go through four stages of teaming. Each stage brings its own challenges and adjustments.

Forming: Planning a Project

When your team is first formed, you should give team members an opportunity to get to know each other and figure out the expectations of the project. When starting a new project, people are usually excited and a little anxious because they are uncertain about the professor's and the other team members' expectations.

Hold a Planning Meeting.   Your first task should be to plan the project and set some deadlines. To help you get started, do some or all of the following:

- ❐ Ask all team members to introduce themselves.
- ❐ Define the purpose of the project and its goals.
- ❐ Describe the expected outcomes of the project.
- ❐ Identify the strengths and interests of each team member.
- ❐ Divide up the work.
- ❐ Create a project calendar and set deadlines.
- ❐ Agree on how conflicts will be solved when they arise (because they will).

Choose Team Responsibilities.   Each member of the team should be given a specific role on the project. When writing a collaborative document, here are four roles that your team might consider assigning:

Coordinator. This person is responsible for maintaining the project schedule and running the meetings. The coordinator is not the "boss." Rather, he or she is responsible for keeping people in touch and keeping the project on schedule.

Researchers. One or two group members should be assigned to collect information. They are responsible for digging up material at the library, running searches on the Internet, and coordinating any empirical research.

Editor. The editor is responsible for the organization and style of the final document. He or she identifies missing content and places where the document needs to be reorganized.

Designer. This person designs the document, keeping audience and purpose in mind. If appropriate, he or she gathers images from the Internet, creates graphs and charts, and takes photographs.

Notice that there is no "writer" in this list. Everyone on your team should be responsible for writing part of the document. Everyone should be responsible for reading and responding to all the parts, even those originally written by another person.

It is all right if your team seems a little uncertain at the beginning. When forming, you and your team should try to sketch out what you're doing, why you're doing it that way, who will do what, and when each of those tasks will be completed.

Storming: Overcoming Differences

Conflict is a normal part of any team project, so you need to learn how to manage the conflicts that come up. In fact, one of the reasons your professors put you into work teams is so you can learn how to manage conflict in constructive ways. Conflict may seem uncomfortable at the time, but it can lead to new ideas and more creativity.

Here are some strategies and tips for managing conflict:

Run Efficient Meetings. Choose a facilitator for the meeting and decide up front what will happen, what will be achieved, and when it will end. At the end of each meeting, each team member should state what he or she will do on the project before the next meeting.

Encourage Participation from Everyone. Each team member should have an opportunity to contribute ideas and opinions. No one should be allowed to sit back and let the others make decisions. Also, no one should dominate the meeting, cutting off the ideas of others.

Allow Dissent (Even Encourage It). Everyone should feel welcome to disagree or offer alternative ideas for consideration. In fact, dissent should be encouraged, because it often leads to new and better ways of completing the project.

Mediate Conflicts. Conflicts will come up, and people are going to grow irritated and even angry with each other. When conflicts happen, give each side time to consider and state their position. Then identify the two to five *issues* that the two sides disagree about. Rank these issues from most important to least. Address each of these issues separately, and try to negotiate a solution to the conflict.

Motivate Any Slackers. Slackers can kill the momentum of a team and undermine its ability to finish the project. If someone is slacking, your team should make your expectations clear to that person as soon as possible. Often, slackers simply need a straightforward list of responsibilities.

Conflict is normal and inevitable. When you see conflict developing in your team, remind yourself that the team is just going through the storming stage of the teaming process. You are going to experience plenty of conflict in advanced classes and in your career, so here is a good place to practise managing it.

Norming: Getting Down to Work

The storming stage can be frustrating, but soon afterward your team will usually enter the norming stage. Norming gives your group an opportunity to refine the goals of the project and finish the majority of the work.

Revise Project Goals and Expected Outcomes. At a meeting or through e-mail, your team should look back at the original goals and outcomes you identified during the planning stage. Sharpen your goals and clarify what your team will complete by the end of the project.

Adjust Team Responsibilities.   Your team should redistribute the work so the burden is shared fairly among team members. Doing so will raise the morale of the group and allow more work to be done in the time allowed.

Revise the Project Calendar.   More than likely, unexpected challenges and events have put your team a little behind schedule. So spend some time with your team working out some new deadlines. These deadlines will need to be firmer than the ones you set in the forming stage.

Hold Regular Meetings.   Your team should meet once or twice a week, depending on your timeline. Each person in the team should bring something new to each meeting.

Use Online Collaborative Tools.   You can't always meet face to face, but you can still collaborate. Online collaborative software such as *Google Docs* allows team members to view the document's editing history, revert to previous versions of a document, and even work on the same document simultaneously. When you do work together online, it's best to also have a voice connection.

Keep in Touch with Each Other.   Depending on the project deadline, your group should be in touch with each other every day or every other day. Texting or e-mailing works well. If you aren't hearing regularly from someone, give that person a call. Regular contact will help keep the project moving forward.

Conflict will still happen during the norming stage. That's normal. Talk any issues out. The conflicts, however, should be less frustrating during the norming stage, because your group will have a clearer sense of the project's goals, each other's roles, and the expected outcomes.

Performing: Working as a Team

When performing, each team member recognizes and understands the others' talents, needs, and capabilities. During the performing stage, your team is doing more than just trying to finish the project. Now, everyone on the team is looking for ways to improve the project, leading to higher-quality results (and more satisfaction among team members).

This is as much as we are going to say about performing in this book. Teams usually need to be together for several months before they reach this stage. If your team in a class reaches the performing stage, that's fantastic. If not, that's fine too. The performing stage is a goal you should work toward in your advanced classes and in your career, but it's not typical in an undergraduate writing course.

Here are some useful strategies and tips that will help you get going on a group or team project.

CHOOSE Group Member Roles

A group works best when each person chooses a specific role. Some popular roles include facilitator, scribe, innovator, and designated skeptic.

DETERMINE What the Group Is Being Asked to Do

Talk with your group about its main goal and other objectives, while determining how much time is available, what is expected of the group, and who will speak for the group.

PURSUE Goals by Doing a Variety of Activities

Your group can be used to generate new ideas, serve as a sounding board, discuss readings, and review and edit each other's work.

REMEMBER That Teams Go Through Stages

When working on a team project, keep in mind that teams go through four stages: forming, storming, norming, and performing.

PLAN the Team Project

While forming, hold a planning meeting and have each team member choose his or her responsibilities on the project.

WORK Through Any Conflicts

When the team reaches the storming phase, work on running good meetings, encouraging participation from everyone, allowing dissent, mediating conflict, and motivating any slackers.

RETHINK the Team's Goals and Roles

After storming, teams usually enter a norming phase in which project goals are modified and team roles are adjusted.

IMPROVE Your Team's Quality

Teams that are together for a long time reach the performing stage, allowing them to concentrate on improving quality and satisfaction.

1. With a group in class, discuss the positive and negative experiences you have had while working in groups or teams. Describe two or three specific things group members can do to get a struggling group back on track.

2. In your group, discuss situations in which slackers have hurt a project you were working on. What are some ways to remove slackers from a project if they won't get to work?

3. What are some of the qualities of a successful sports team? How do the leaders of the team behave? How do the others on the team contribute?

1. Using the Internet to do research, list five ways in which you will need to use collaborative skills to be successful in your chosen career path. Write a brief report in which you discuss what kinds of collaborative work happens in your field.

2. With a team of people in your class, pick a topic that you are all interested in. Then, in less than an hour, put together a visual report on that topic. While your team is working, pay attention to how each person contributes to the project. Before your next class, each person in the group should write two to three paragraphs describing (a) what happened, (b) what went well, and (c) what could have gone better. Compare experiences with your team members.

3. Research the future of virtual offices, telecommuting, and teleworking. In a brief report, explain how new media and technology will change how people work and how people will communicate with each other.

1. **Imagine that your classroom is a workplace.** With a group in your class, evaluate your writing class as a workplace. Write a proposal for restructuring the classroom as an effective and collaborative workplace. In your report, explain whether or not you think this kind of change would be a good idea.

2. **Use an online collaborative tool.** Write a pitch to your professor in which you advocate for the use of online collaborative tools in your writing class.

MyCompLab

For support in meeting this chapter's objectives, follow this path in MyCompLab:

Student Resources → Writing → Writing Purposes → Writing to Argue or Persuade. Review the Instruction and Multimedia resources about writing arguments; then complete the Exercises and click on Gradebook to measure your progress.

PART **5** Doing
Research

PART OUTLINE

CHAPTER 21
Starting Research   388

CHAPTER 22
Finding Sources and Collecting Information   398

CHAPTER 23
Quoting, Paraphrasing, and Citing Sources   415

CHAPTER 24
Using MLA Style   429

CHAPTER 25
Using APA Style   454

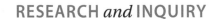

RESEARCH *and* INQUIRY

are the keys to discovery. In these

chapters, you will learn how

to do thoughtful and thorough research,

discovering answers to the questions

that intrigue you.

21

Starting Research

- develop your own dependable "research process" that will help you inquire into topics that interest you.
- devise a "research plan" for your projects that allows you to stay on schedule and keep track of sources and information.
- assess whether sources are reliable and trustworthy.

Research is a systematic inquiry into a topic, using hands-on experience, factual evidence, and secondary sources to inquire, explore, and understand something that interests you. Research is used to do three important things:

- **Inquiring:** A researcher gathers information in order to investigate an issue and explain it to other people.

- **Advancing knowledge:** Researchers, especially scientists, collect and analyze facts to increase or strengthen our knowledge about a subject.

- **Supporting an argument:** In some situations, research can be used to persuade others and support a particular side of an argument while gaining a full understanding of the opposing view.

Research requires much more than a visit to the library to pick up a few books or articles that agree with your pre-existing opinion. It involves more than simply using the first page of hits from an Internet search engine like *Google*. Instead, research, and particularly academic research, is about pursuing truth and developing knowledge.

In this chapter, you will learn how to develop your own "research process" that will help you inquire into topics that interest you. Using a dependable research process will allow you to write and speak with authority, because you will be more confident about the reliability of your sources. Always remember that finding sources is easy—especially on the Internet—but it's critical that you find good sources that provide information you can trust. A reliable research process will actually save you time in the long run while helping you find more useful and trustworthy sources of information.

This chapter is about getting your research process started. Then, in Chapter 22, "Finding Sources and Collecting Information," we will go into more depth about how to find and generate information with online, print, and empirical sources.

Starting Your Research Process

Watch Office Hours: Narrowing the Topic

A reliable research process, as shown in Figure 21.1, is "recursive," which means the researcher collects sources and modifies the working thesis in a cyclical way. The process ends when the working thesis fits the facts available.

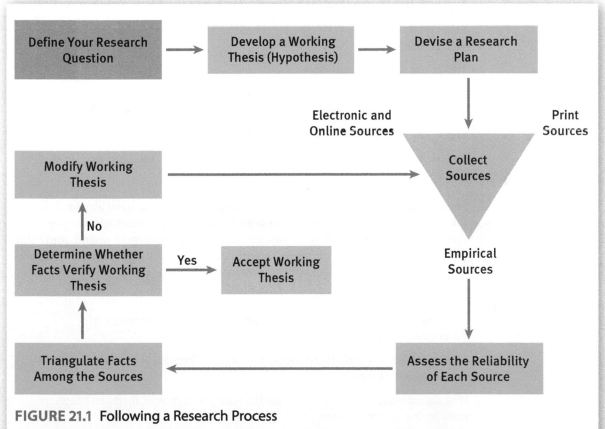

FIGURE 21.1 Following a Research Process

A reliable research process will save you time and energy. Each source you collect will lead you to other sources. Keep looping until you collect the information you need to draft your paper.

When starting your research, you should do three things:

1. Define a *research question* and sharpen it.

2. Develop a *working thesis* or *hypothesis* that offers your best guess about how you will answer the research question.

3. Devise a *research plan* to help you systematically collect the information needed to answer your research question and determine whether your working thesis is verifiable.

Step One: Define Your Research Question

Your research question names the topic you are studying and states specifically what you want to find out about that topic. Write down the exact question your research will try to answer:

Topic: Immigrants and the economy.

Research Question: Is the flow of immigrants into Canada helping or harming our economy?

Topic: The possibility of bioterrorism.

Research Question: Is bioterrorism (the release of "super-viruses" or deadly airborne pathogens) a real threat to our health, or is it mostly media hype?

Topic: The oddity of wearing shorts and flipflops in wintertime.

Research Question: Why do some people wear shorts and flipflops, even in the middle of winter?

Notice that in moving from topic to research question, you have already begun to narrow down your research. The best research questions are short and simple.

Once you have written down a research question, you should spend some time sharpening it. The research questions mentioned above, for example, are a little too broad for a typical university or college research paper. Here are sharper versions of these questions:

Are immigrants having a positive or negative effect on the economy of Vancouver, British Columbia?

Is bioterrorism a real threat to people in southern Ontario, or is it just another media-generated frenzy?

Why do some students at Simon Fraser University always wear shorts and flipflops, even in the middle of winter?

These sharper research questions will help you narrow the scope of your research, saving you time and effort by allowing you to target the best kinds of sources and information.

Step Two: Develop a Working Thesis

After defining your research question, you should then develop a *working thesis*, which is also called a "hypothesis" in some fields. Your working thesis is your best guess about how you will answer your research question.

In one sentence, try to write down your overall claim about your topic. For example, here are some working theses based on the research questions above:

> I believe immigration helps the Vancouver economy by attracting low-wage labour, thus keeping costs down; but immigrants also use up valuable public resources and take jobs away from citizens who already live here.

> In Ontario, we need to be on guard against bioterrorism because we spend much of the winter confined indoors, increasing the chances that viruses will spread from person to person.

> Some Simon Fraser students wear shorts and flipflops in winter because they prefer light, comfortable clothing, and they can keep warm by staying inside and walking from building to building across campus.

As you do your research, it is likely your working thesis will change, eventually becoming the main claim for your project. If possible, boil your working thesis down into one sentence. If you require two or three sentences to state your working thesis, your topic may be too complex or broad.

Step Three: Devise a Research Plan

Before you begin collecting sources, set aside a little time to sketch out your *research plan*. Your research plan should describe the kinds of sources you will need to collect to answer your research question. Your plan should also describe how you are going to collect these sources and your deadlines for finding them. Your professor may ask you to submit a research plan at an early stage of the research project. A typical research plan has these elements:

- Research question
- Working thesis
- Results of start-up research
- Description of electronic, online, print, and empirical sources available
- Schedule for conducting and completing the research
- Bibliography

Even if your professor does not ask for a research plan, you should spend some time considering each of these items in order to better target sources and streamline your research.

Doing Start-Up Research

Now that you have created a research question, working thesis, and research plan, you're ready to start tracking down sources and collecting information. Some researchers find it helpful to begin by doing an hour of "start-up" research. This kind of research will help you to gain an overall view of the topic, figure out the various sides of the issue, and identify the kinds of sources available.

In Chapter 22, "Finding Sources and Collecting Information," we will talk about doing formal research, which is much more targeted and structured. For now, though, let's look at some good ways to do start-up research:

Surf the Internet. Put your research question or its keywords into *Google, Yahoo!,* or *Ask.com.* See what pops up. Jot down notes about the kinds of information you find. Identify some of the major issues and people involved with your topic and take note of any key sources of information that you might want to look up later. Remember, though, that if you have been asked to use scholarly sources you will not likely use any of these Internet sources in the final paper. They can help you get started by giving an overview of your topic, but be sure to turn to academic sources for your actual assignment.

Look Through Online Encyclopedias. Major online encyclopedias include *Wikipedia, MSN Encarta,* or *Encyclopaedia Britannica Online.* Again, note the major issues and people involved with your topic. Identify key terms and any controversies about your topic.

    One note: Professors probably won't let you cite online encyclopedias like *Wikipedia* or *Encyclopaedia Britannica* as authoritative sources, because the entries are often written by nonexperts. Nevertheless, online encyclopedias are useful for gaining a quick overview of your topic and finding sources that are authoritative. That's why they can be especially helpful when doing start-up research.

Browse Your Library's Catalogue. Log on to your school's online library catalogue and type in keywords to see what kinds of materials are available on your topic. Write down the names of any authors and titles that look like they might be helpful. In some cases, your library's catalogue can e-mail your selections to you.

Start-up research should take you an hour or less. Your goal is to gain an overall sense of your topic, not to make up your mind or form your final opinion. At this point, keep your options open and don't become too occupied by one source or perspective.

Watch Office Hours: Evaluating Sources

Assessing a Source's Reliability

All information is not created equal. Some people who claim to be "authorities" are downright wrong or even dishonest. Even more problematic are people who have agendas or biases, and whose print and online writings aren't always honest or truthful about the facts. To assess the reliability of your sources, consider these questions:

Is the Source Credible?

To determine whether a source's author and publisher are trustworthy, you should use an Internet search engine to check out their backgrounds and expertise. If you can find little or no information about the author or publisher—or if they have questionable credentials or reputations—you should avoid using the source and look for something more reliable. If your professor has asked you to use scholarly sources, then the authors should be just that—scholars working in a field related to your topic.

How Biased Are the Author and the Publisher?

All sources have some bias because authors and publishers have their own ideas and opinions. When you are assessing the reliability of a source, consider how much the author or publisher *wants* the information to be true. If it seems like the author or publisher would only accept one kind of answer from the outset (e.g., "smoking does not cause cancer"), the information should be considered too biased to be a reliable source. On the other hand, if the author and publisher were open to a range of possible conclusions, you can feel more confident about using the source. Academics have general ethical obligations to approach a topic objectively, although it is still useful to evaluate scholarly sources for biases and/or conflicts of interest.

How Biased Are You?

As a researcher, you need to keep your own biases in mind as you assess your sources. Try viewing your sources from alternative perspectives, even (or especially) perspectives you disagree with. Knowing your own biases and seeing the issue from other perspectives will help you gain a richer understanding of your topic.

Is the Source Up to Date?

Depending on your topic, information can quickly become obsolete. In some fields, like cancer research, information that is only a few years old might already be out of date. In other fields, like geology, information that is decades old might still be usable today. So pay attention to how rapidly the field is changing. Consult your professor or a research librarian about whether a source can be considered up to date.

Can You Verify the Information in the Source?

You should be able to confirm your source's information by consulting other, independent sources. If a source is the only one that offers information that you want to use, you should treat it as unverified and use it only cautiously, if at all. If multiple sources offer the same or similar kinds of information, then you can use each source with much more confidence.

Evaluating Your Sources: A Checklist

- ☐ Is the source reliable?

- ☐ How biased are the author and the publisher?

- ☐ How biased are you?

- ☐ Is the source up to date?

- ☐ Can you independently verify the information in the source?

Managing Your Research Process

When you finish your start-up research, you should have enough information to create a schedule for completing your research. A research schedule will help you finish the project in manageable chunks. At this point, you should also start a bibliographic file to help you keep track of your sources.

Creating a Research Schedule

You might find "backward planning" helpful when creating your research schedule. Backward planning means working backward from the deadline to today, filling in all the tasks that need to be accomplished. Here's how to do it:

1. On your screen or a piece of paper, list all the tasks you need to complete for the research project.

2. On your calendar, set a deadline for finishing your research. You should also fill in your deadlines for drafting, designing, and revising your project.

3. Work backwards from your research deadline, filling in the tasks you need to accomplish and the days on which each task needs to be completed.

Online calendars like those from *Scrybe, Google,* or *Yahoo!* are great tools for making research schedules. Your mobile phone or computer might have calendar applications already installed. A low-tech paper calendar still works well, too, for scheduling your research project.

Starting Your Bibliography File

One of the first tasks on your research schedule should be to set up a file on your computer that holds a working bibliography of the sources you find. Each time you find a useful source, add it to your bibliography file.

Minimally, as you find sources, make sure you record all the information needed for a full bibliographic citation (you will learn how to cite sources in Chapters 24, "Using MLA Style," and 25, "Using APA Style"). That way, when you are ready to create your works-cited or references page at the end of your paper, you will have a list of your sources ready to go.

Following and Modifying Your Research Plan

You should expect to modify your research plan as you move forward with the project. In some cases, you will find yourself being pulled away from your research plan by interesting facts, ideas, and events that you didn't know about when you started. For the most part, that is all right. Let your research take you wherever the facts lead you.

While researching, check in regularly with your research question and working thesis to make sure you are not drifting too far away from your original idea for the project. Or, you might need to adjust your research question and working thesis to fit some of the sources or new issues you have discovered.

When Things Don't Go as Expected

Research is a process of inquiry—of exploring, testing, and discovering. You are going to encounter ideas and issues that will require you to modify your approach, research question, or working thesis. Expect the unexpected and move forward.

Roadblocks to Research. You may not be able to get access to all the sources you had planned on using. For example, you might find that the expert you wanted to interview is unavailable or doesn't want to talk to you, or that the book you needed is checked out or missing from the library, or that you simply cannot find certain data or information. Don't give up. Instead, modify your approach and move around the roadblock by exploring related sources, trying other databases, or, if warranted, applying data found in a general source to your particular topic.

Information and Ideas That Change Your Research Question or Working Thesis. You might find something unexpected that changes how you see your topic. For instance, sources might not support your working thesis after all. Or, you might find that a different, more focused research question is more interesting to you. Rather than getting distracted or disappointed, look at this as an opportunity to discover something new. Modify your research question or working thesis and move forward.

These temporary roadblocks can be frustrating, but these inevitable surprises can also make research fun. If research were just mechanical plugging and chugging, then we wouldn't need to do it in the first place.

Use these guidelines to begin your research process.

UNDERSTAND Why Writers Do Research

Keep in mind that the purpose of research is to inform and support your ideas. Research is not just a regurgitation of others' ideas.

DEFINE Your Research Question

Name your topic and state your research question as specifically as possible. This is the question that your research will help you answer. Improve the efficiency of your research by sharpening that research question as much as possible.

DEVELOP a Working Thesis

In a single sentence, write down your working thesis. This is your best guess, or "hypothesis," for what you think will be your main claim.

DO Some "Start-Up" Research

Take half an hour to an hour to scan the kinds of sources available and get an overall sense of the various views on your research question. This informal start-up can include the Internet, online encyclopedias, or your library's online catalogue.

DEVISE Your Research Plan

Avoid the temptation to just dive in. Take a little time to make a written plan that describes your research question, working thesis, start-up research results, your schedule, and an early bibliography.

CREATE a Schedule

Use "backward planning" to break your research into manageable chunks. After listing all the tasks you will need to complete, work backward from your deadline, filling in the tasks and the days they need to be completed.

KEEP a Bibliography File

Keep a computer file of your working bibliography and maintain it. Your readers will need this bibliographic information to see where your sources can be found.

EXPECT the Unexpected

As you find new information, you will want to modify your research approach, research question, and working thesis. This is all part of the research process.

1. List five possible research questions that you find personally interesting. Then turn each of your research questions into a working thesis. With a small group, talk about these research questions and your working theses. Do group members have any ideas about how you could narrow your research?

2. With a small group, develop a research question on a topic that is interesting to all of you. Go online and use a variety of keywords to explore that topic. What are some possible answers to the research question?

3. In class, discuss what kinds of sources you think are most reliable. Do you believe online sources can be as reliable as print sources? When are hands-on empirical sources, like interviews or surveys, better than online and print sources?

1. Do about thirty minutes of start-up research on something that interests you. In an e-mail, describe to your professor what kinds of issues you will face if you want to do some formal research on this topic.

2. In a brief memo to your professor, describe your research plan for your next project. Explain why you think specific types of sources will be most helpful and why other kinds of sources probably will not be helpful.

3. On the Internet, find three sources of information that you would consider "heavily biased." Write an evaluation of these sources, explaining why you consider them biased and perhaps unreliable as sources.

1. **Create a research plan.** Write a full research plan. Identify your research question and your working thesis, show the results of your start-up research, and identify the kinds of sources you plan to target.

2. **Start a research journal.** Keep a journal while you do research for your next assignment. Keep track of the kinds of research you did and the amount of time you devoted to those activities. Determine what kinds of research yielded the most useful information and what kinds of research cost you too much time.

MyCompLab

For support in meeting this chapter's objectives, follow this path in MyCompLab:

Student Resources → Research → The Research Assignment. Review the Instruction and Multimedia resources about evaluating sources; then complete the Exercises and click on Gradebook to measure your progress.

22

Finding Sources and Collecting Information

Now that you have figured out your working thesis and research plan, you are ready to start collecting sources. In this chapter, you will learn how to collect a variety of *primary* and *secondary* sources that will help you inquire into your topic and find useful information. The ability to collect reliable sources will be critical to doing useful, dependable research in university or college and in the workplace.

Evaluating Sources with Triangulation

When doing any kind of research, you should try to draw information from a variety of perspectives. If you rely on just one type of source, especially the Internet, you risk developing a limited or inaccurate understanding of your topic. To avoid this problem, *triangulate* your research by looking for information from three different types of sources:

Print sources (academic and other): Database articles, books, journals, magazines, newspapers, government publications, reference materials, and microform/microfiche.

Electronic and online sources: Websites, CD-ROMs, listservs, television, radio, podcasts, videos, and blogs.

Empirical sources: Personal experiences, field observations, interviews, surveys, case studies, and experiments.

Together, these three types of sources are called the *research triangle* (Figure 22.1). Here's how the research triangle works. If you collect similar facts from all three kinds of sources, the information you found is probably reliable. If you gather comparable facts from only two points of the triangle, your findings are probably still reliable but open to some doubt. However, if you can only find facts from one point on the triangle, then you probably need to do more research to back up your findings.

Of course, finding similar information in all three types of sources doesn't make something true. It just means the information is probably trustworthy. Triangulation is a good way to evaluate your sources and corroborate the facts you uncover about your topic. Keep in mind that "facts" and the "truth" are more slippery than we like to admit.

Also, remember that there are always at least two sides to any issue. In fact, academics often look for areas of debate to help establish and define a research position. So don't just look for sources that support your working thesis. Instead, use triangulation to find sources that also challenge what you believe. Even if you completely disagree with one of your sources, the argument it makes might give you a stronger understanding of your own position.

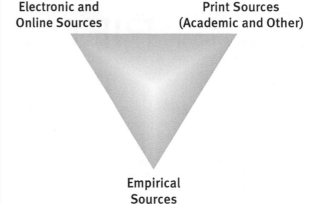

FIGURE 22.1 The Research Triangle

Triangulating your sources is a good way to ensure that you are drawing information from a variety of places. If you find similar information from all three corners of the triangle, it is probably reliable.

Using Primary and Secondary Sources

Researchers tend to distinguish between two types of sources: *primary sources* and *secondary sources*. Both kinds are important to doing reliable research.

Primary Sources. These are the actual records or artifacts, such as letters, photographs, videos, memoirs, books, or personal papers, that were created by the people involved in the issues and events you are researching (Figure 22.2). Primary sources can also include any data or observations collected from empirical research. If you are writing a literary analysis, the poem, story, novel, or play you are analyzing is considered a primary source.

Secondary Sources. These are the writings of scholars, experts, and other knowledgeable people who have studied your topic. For example, scholarly books by historians are secondary sources because their authors analyze and reflect on events from the past. Secondary sources can include books, academic journals, magazines, newspapers, and blogs.

Patricia Belanger née Burrows
Daughter of an English War Bride
Andes
March 24, 1944

R.M.S.P. "ANDES." (TRIPLE-SCREW 15,620 TONS GROSS). SOUTH AMERICAN SERVICE.

Source: The ship *Andes*. Photograph. *Canadian Museum of Immigration at Pier 21.* Web. 10 Aug. 2012.

I came to Canada with my mother, Phyllis (Coffill) Burrows, on the troop ship, Andes. We embarked from Liverpool on March 16, 1944, arriving in Halifax on March 24, 1944. My father, Cameron Burrows, a native of Chatham, Ontario, joined the Canadian Signal Corps and was posted to England. He met my mother there and they were married in Hammersmith, London, on February 16, 1941—I arrived on December 27, 1941. My father was subsequently wounded in action in Sicily and was transferred into a hospital in North Africa to recuperate.

Although I remember nothing of the trip, my mother tells me that she could not believe all the fresh fruit and bacon and eggs for breakfast, having suffered through all the rationing. She told me she was enjoying her first real breakfast in years when I piped up and said, "Mummy, I'm going to be sick!" And I was. Apparently, there were many returning troops on the Andes but very few women and children. I always marvel that we even made it to Canada through the North Atlantic with the war still in full swing.

Patricia Belanger as an infant with her mother.

Source: Private photograph.

I made my first trip back to England with my mother in 1961 and we spotted a model of the troop ship Andes in a storefront window in Trafalgar Square. Three Christmases ago, through a lot of diligent research, I managed to track down photographs of the Andes and had one blown up and framed for my mother and dad for Christmas. It hangs in a place of honour over their fireplace. She could not believe it when she saw it. My mother was one of the original members of a war brides club formed in Chatham, Ontario. For years, it was a very active group, but through time it disbanded. However, my mother still retains her friendships with those who have not passed away.

I consider it unique to have been a "war child." I am very proud of both my British and Canadian heritage and in fact carry both EEC and Canadian passports.

Source: Patricia Belanger, "Patricia Belanger née Burrows, Daughter of an English War Bride," *Andes,* 24 Mar. 1944. *Canadian Museum of Immigration at Pier 21.* Web, 10 Aug. 2012.

FIGURE 22.2 Primary Sources of Information

Primary sources were created by the people involved in the events you are studying or through empirical research.

Finding Electronic and Online Sources

401

For most research projects in university or college, you will usually rely on secondary sources. However, you should always look for opportunities to collect information from primary sources because they allow you to get closer to your topic than secondary sources.

Finding Electronic and Online Sources

The Internet is a good place to start doing research on your topic. Keep in mind, though, that the Internet is only a starting place for your research. You will need to triangulate, using print and empirical sources to support anything you find on the Internet.

Using Internet Search Engines

Search engines let you use keywords to locate information about your topic. If you type your topic into *Google, Yahoo!,* or *Ask,* the search engine will return dozens or even millions of links. A handful of these links will be useful, and the vast majority of them will not.

With a few easy tricks, though, you can target your search with some common symbols and strategies. For example, let's say you are researching how sleep deprivation affects students. You might start by entering the phrase:

sleep and students

With this generic subject, a search engine will pull up millions of webpages that might refer to this topic. Of course, there is no way you are going to have time to look through all those pages to find what you need, even if the search engine ranks them for you.

So you need to target your search to pull up only the kinds of materials you want. Here are some tips for pulling up better results:

Use Exact Words. Choose words that exactly target your topic, and use as many as you need to sharpen your results. For example,

sleep deprivation effects on students test taking

Use the Plus (+) Sign. If you put a plus sign in front of words, that tells the search engine to only find pages that have those exact words in them.

sleep +deprivation effects on +students +test +taking

Use the Minus (–) Sign. If you want to eliminate any pages that refer to things you don't want to see, you can use the minus sign to eliminate pages that refer to them.

sleep deprivation +effects on students +test +taking –insomnia –apnea

Use Quotation (" ") Marks. If you want to guarantee that the search engine will find specific phrasings on websites, you can use quotation marks to target those phrases.

"sleep deprivation" +effects on students and "test taking" –insomnia –apnea

Use Wildcard Symbols. Some search engines have symbols for "wildcards," like ?, *, or %. These symbols are helpful when you know most of a phrase, but not all of it.

"sleep deprivation" +effects on students and "test taking" neural* behavioural* –insomnia –apnea

These search engine tips will help you pull up the pages you need. Figure 22.3 shows the results of an Ask.com search using the phrase

"sleep deprivation" +effects on students and "test taking" –insomnia –apnea.

Something to remember is that the first items pulled up by search engines are usually *sponsored links*. In other words, these companies paid to have their links show up at the top of your list. Most search engines highlight these links in a special way. For example, they are highlighted in blue by Ask.com in Figure 22.3. You might find these links useful, but you should keep in mind that the sponsors are biased because they want to sell you something.

Using the Internet Cautiously

Watch Evaluating Sources: Interactive Tutorial

You already know that information from the Internet can be unreliable. In fact, many of the so-called "facts" on the Internet are really just opinions and hearsay

FIGURE 22.3
Targeting Your Search

In this search, the use of symbols has helped narrow the search to useful pages.

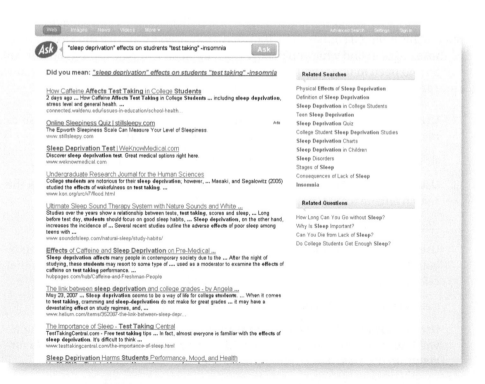

with little basis in reality. Also, many quotes that appear on the Internet have been taken out of context or corrupted in some way. So you need to use information from the Internet critically and even skeptically. Don't get fooled by a professional-looking website, because a good Web designer can make just about anything look professional.

Chapter 21, "Starting Research," offers some questions for checking the reliability of any source. Here are some additional questions you should use to challenge Internet sources:

- Can you identify and trust the author(s) of the source?

- What organization is this source associated with and why is it publishing this information?

- What does the source's author or organization have to gain from publishing this information?

- Does the source clearly distinguish between opinions and independent facts?

- Does the source fairly discuss two or more sides of the issue?

- Does the source use other independent sources to back up claims and can you access those sources?

- Does the information seem too incredible, too terrible, or too good to be true?

- Has the website been updated recently?

The Internet has plenty of useful, reliable information, but there is also a great amount of junk. It's your responsibility as a researcher to critically decide what is reliable and what isn't.

Using Documentaries and Television/Radio Broadcasts

Multimedia resources such as television and radio broadcasts are available online through network websites as well as sites like *YouTube* and, if you pay to subscribe, *Netflix*. Depending on who made them, documentaries and broadcasts can be reliable sources. If the material is from a trustworthy source, you can take quotes and cite these kinds of electronic sources in your own work.

Documentaries. A documentary is a nonfiction movie or program that relies on interviews and factual evidence about an event or issue. The National Film Board of Canada website (www.nfb.ca) offers many documentaries online. A documentary can be biased, though, so check into the background of the person or organization that made it.

Television Broadcasts. Cable channels and news networks like the Canadian Broadcasting Corporation, the History Channel, the National Geographic Channel, and the Biography Channel are producing excellent broadcasts that are reliable and can be cited as support for your argument. Programs on news channels that feature just one or two highly opinionated commentators are less reliable because they tend to be sensationalistic and are often biased.

Radio Broadcasts. Radio broadcasts, too, can be informative and authoritative. Public radio broadcasts, such as the Canadian Broadcasting Corporation, offer well-researched stories on the air and at their websites. On the other hand, political broadcasts like *Adler Online* or, in the US, *The Rush Limbaugh Show* can slant news and manipulate facts. You cannot rely on these broadcasts as main sources in your argument.

Using Wikis, Blogs, and Podcasts

As a general rule, you should not use wikis, blogs, or podcasts as your main sources for academic research projects, because they are too opinion-based and their "facts" are often unreliable. Nevertheless, they are helpful for defining issues and pointing you toward more established sources.

Wikis. You probably already know about *Wikipedia,* the most popular wiki, but a variety of other wikis are available, like *WikiHow, Wikibooks,* and *Wikitravel.* Wikis allow their users to add and revise content, and they rely on other users to back-check facts. On some topics, such as popular culture (e.g., television programs, music, celebrities), a wiki might be the best or only source of up-to-date information. On more established topics, however, you should always be skeptical about the reliability of their information. Your best approach is to use these sites primarily for start-up research on your topic and to help you find other, more reliable sources.

Blogs. Blogs can be helpful for exploring a range of opinions on a particular topic. However, even some of the most established and respected blogs like *The Huffington Post, Mashable,* and *The Big Picture* are little more than opinionated commentaries on the day's events. Like wikis, blogs can help you identify the issues involved with your topic and locate more reliable sources, but most of them are not reliable sources themselves.

Podcasts. Most news websites offer podcasts, but the reliability of these sources depends on who made the audio or video file. Today, anyone with a video camera or digital tape recorder can make a podcast, even a professional-looking podcast, so you need to carefully assess the credibility and experience of the person who made it. Many top universities and researchers in the world, however, are now creating and sharing podcasts online. *iTunes U* has a variety of informative and trustworthy podcasts available and *TED.com* has a number of talks by international academics.

On just about every topic, you will find plenty of people on the Internet who have opinions. The problem with online sources is that just about anyone can create or edit them. That's why the Internet is a good place to start collecting sources, but you need to also collect print and empirical sources to back up what you find.

Finding Print Sources

With such easy access to electronic and online sources, people sometimes forget to look for print sources on their topic. That's a big mistake. Print sources or online versions of print sources are typically the most reliable forms of information on a topic.

Locating Books at Your Library

Finding useful books on your topic at your campus or local public library is actually rather easy. More than likely, your library's website has an online search engine that you can access from any networked computer (Figure 22.4). This search engine will allow you to locate books in the library's catalogue. Meanwhile, your campus library will usually have research librarians on staff who can help you find useful print sources. Ask for them at the Information Desk.

Books. The most reliable information on your topic can usually be found in books. Authors and editors of books work closely together to check their facts and gather the best information available. So books tend to be more reliable than websites. Many books are also now available in electronic format. The downside of books is that they tend to become outdated in fast-changing fields.

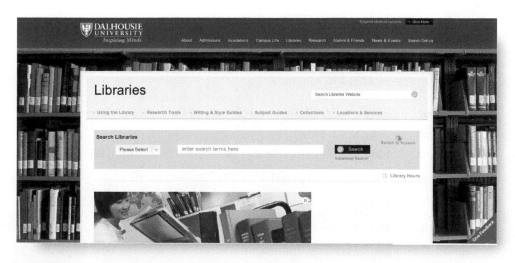

FIGURE 22.4 Searching Your Library's Catalogue

Your library's catalogue is easy to search online. Here is the University of Dalhousie library's webpage for searching its catalogue. Finding books is almost as easy as using a search engine to find information on the Internet.

Government Publications. The Canadian government produces an amazing amount of printed material on almost any topic you could imagine. Government websites, like *Government of Canada Publications,* are a good place to find these sources. Your library probably collects many of these materials because they are usually free or inexpensive.

Reference Materials. The reference section of your library collects helpful reference tools, such as almanacs, directories, encyclopedias, handbooks, and guides. These reference materials can help you find facts, data, and information about people, places, and events. You'll find that your school library will have many of these resources available in an electronic format.

Right now, entire libraries of books are being scanned and put online. Out-of-copyright books are appearing in full-text versions as they become available. Meanwhile, versions of copyrighted books are searchable, allowing you to see excerpts and identify pages on which you can locate the specific information you need.

Finding Articles at the Library

At your library, you can also find articles in academic journals, magazines, and newspapers. These articles can be located using online databases or periodical indexes available through your library's website. If your library does not have these databases available online, you can find print versions of them in your library's "Reference" or "Periodicals" areas.

Academic Journals. Articles in academic journals are usually written by scientists, professors, consultants, and subject matter experts (SMEs). These journals will offer some of the most exact information available on your topic. To find journal articles, you should start by searching in a *periodical index* related to your topic. Some of the more popular periodical indexes include:

ArticleFirst. Business, humanities, medicine, popular culture, science, and technology

EBSCOhost. Academic, business, science, psychology, education, liberal arts

ERIC. Education research and practice

Humanities Index. Literature, history, philosophy, languages, communication

LexisNexis. News, business, medical, and legal issues

OmniFile. Education, science, humanities, social science, art, biology, and agriculture

PsycINFO. Psychology and related fields

Web of Science. Physics, chemistry, biology, and life sciences

IEEE Xplore. Engineering and science

Magazines. You can find magazine articles about your topic with the *Readers' Guide to Periodical Literature*, which is likely available through your campus library's website. Print versions of the *Readers' Guide* should be available in your library's periodical or reference rooms. Other useful online databases for finding magazine articles include *Find Articles, MagPortal,* and *InfoTrac.*

Newspapers. For research on current issues or local topics, newspapers often provide the most recent information. At your library or through its website, you can use newspaper indexes to search for information. Past editions of newspapers are often stored on microform or microfiche, which can be read on projectors at your campus library. Some of the more popular newspaper indexes include *ProQuest Newspapers, Canadian Newstand, LexisNexis,* and *EBSCOhost.*

Doing research at your campus or local public library is almost as easy as doing research on Internet search engines. You will find that the librarians working there can help you locate the materials you need. While at the library, you will likely stumble across useful materials you didn't expect, and the librarians might be able to help you find materials you would never have found on your own.

Using Empirical Sources

Empirical sources include observations, experiments, surveys, and interviews. They are especially helpful for confirming or challenging the claims made in your electronic, online, and print sources. For example, if one of your electronic or online sources claims that "each day, students watch an average of five hours of television but spend less than one hour on their coursework," you could use observations, interviews, or surveys to confirm or debunk that statement. Remember that when completing empirical research, you must obtain ethical approval from your institution's ethics committee.

Interviewing People

Interviews are a great way to go behind the facts to explore the experiences of experts and regular people. Plus, interviewing others is a good way to collect quotes that you can add to your text. Here are some strategies for interviewing people:

Prepare for the Interview

1. **Do your research.** You need to know as much as possible about your topic before you interview someone about it. If you do not understand the topic before going into the interview, you will waste your own and your interviewee's time by asking simplistic or flawed questions.

2. **Create a list of three to five factual questions.** Your research will probably turn up some facts that you want your interviewee to confirm or challenge.

3. **Create a list of five to ten open-ended questions.** Write down five to ten questions that cannot be answered with a simple "yes" or "no." Your questions should urge the interviewee to offer a detailed explanation or opinion.

4. **Decide how you will record the interview.** Do you want to record the interview as a video or make an audio recording? Or do you want to take written notes? Each of these methods has its pros and cons. For example, audio recording captures the whole conversation, but interviewees are often more guarded about their answers when they are being recorded.

5. **Set up the interview.** The best place to do an interview is at a neutral site, like a classroom, a room in the library, or perhaps a café. The second best place is at the interviewee's office. If necessary, you can do interviews over the phone.

Conduct the Interview

1. **Explain the purpose of your project and how long the interview will take.** Start out by explaining to the interviewee the purpose of your project and how the information from the interview will be used. Also, tell the interviewee how long you expect the interview will take.

2. **Ask permission to record.** If you are recording the interview in any way, ask permission to make the recording. First, ask if recording is all right before you turn on your recorder. Then, once the recorder is on, ask again so you record the interviewee's permission.

3. **Ask your factual questions first.** Warm up the interviewee by asking questions that allow him or her to confirm or deny the facts you have already collected.

4. **Ask your open-ended questions next.** Ask the interviewee about his or her opinions, feelings, experiences, and views about the topic.

5. **Ask if he or she would like to provide any other information.** Often people want to tell you things you did not expect or know about. You can wrap up the interview by asking, "Is there anything else you would like to add about this topic?"

6. **Thank the interviewee.** Don't forget to thank the interviewee for his or her time and information.

Interview Follow-Up

1. **Write down everything you remember.** As soon as possible after the interview, describe the interviewee in your notes and fill out any details you couldn't write down during the interview. Do this even if you recorded the interview.

2. **Get your quotes right.** Clarify any direct quotations you collected from your interviewee. If necessary, you might e-mail your quotes to the interviewee for confirmation.

3. **Back-check the facts.** If the interviewee said something that was new to you or that conflicted with your prior research, use electronic, online, or print sources to back-check the facts. If there is a conflict, you can send an e-mail to the interviewee asking for clarification.

4. **Send a thank you note.** Usually an e-mail that thanks your interviewee is sufficient, but some people prefer to send a card or brief letter of thanks.

Using an Informal Survey

Informal surveys are especially useful for generating data and gathering the views of many different people on the same questions. Many free online services, such as *SurveyMonkey* and *Zoomerang,* allow you to create and distribute your own surveys. They will also collect and tabulate the results for you. Just remember that if you are distributing or publishing the results, ethics regulations may apply. Here is how to create a useful, though not a scientific, survey:

1. **Identify the population you want to survey.** Some surveys target specific kinds of people (e.g., post-secondary students, women from ages 18–22, medical doctors). Others are designed to be filled out by anyone.

2. **Develop your questions.** Create a list of five to ten questions that can be answered quickly. Surveys typically use four basic types of questions: rating scales, multiple choice, numeric open-ended, and open-ended. Be aware that qualitative or descriptive data will be harder to analyze. Figure 22.5 shows examples of all four types.

3. **Check your questions for neutrality.** Make sure your questions are as neutral as possible. Don't lead the people you are surveying with biased or slanted questions that fit your own beliefs.

4. **Distribute the survey.** Ask a number of people to complete your survey, and note the kinds of people who agree to do it. Not everyone will be interested in completing your survey, so remember that your results might reflect the views of specific kinds of people.

5. **Tabulate your results.** When your surveys are returned, convert any quantitative responses into data. In written answers, pull out phrases and quotes that seem to reflect how the people you surveyed felt about your topic.

Professional surveyors will point out that your informal survey is not objective and that your results are not statistically valid. That's fine, as long as you are not using your survey to make important decisions or support claims about how people really feel. Your informal survey will still give you some helpful information about the opinions of others.

Doing Field Observations

Conducting a field observation can help you generate ideas and confirm facts. Field observations involve watching something closely and taking detailed notes. They are often used in the natural and social sciences. For instance, you might make field observations on student behaviour during finals week.

1. **Choose an appropriate location (field site).** You want to choose a field site that allows you to see as much as possible, while not making it obvious that you are watching and taking notes. People will typically change their behaviour if they think someone is watching them.

**FIGURE 22.5
Types of Survey
Questions**

*Make sure your questions
are easy to understand to
help your survey takers
provide answers quickly
and accurately.*

Rating Scales

Going skiing is a good Spring Break activity.

Strongly Agree	Agree	Disagree	Strongly Disagree	No Opinion
☐	☐	☐	☐	☐

Multiple Choice

In what region did you spend most of your childhood?

☐ Maritimes
☐ Ontario or Quebec
☐ Prairies

☐ Yukon, Northwest Territories, or Nunavut
☐ West Coast
☐ Other

Numeric Open-Ended

How many times have you gone downhill skiing in your life? _____

Text Open-Ended

What do you enjoy most about skiing in British Columbia?

_____
_____
_____
_____

2. **Take notes in a two-column format.** A good field note technique is to use two columns to record what you see. On the left side, list the people, things, and events you observed. On the right side, write down how you interpret what you observed.

3. **Use the Five-W and How questions.** Keep notes about the *who, what, where, when, why,* and *how* elements that you observe. Try to include as much detail as possible.

4. **Use your senses.** Take notes about the things you see, hear, smell, touch, and taste while you are observing.

5. **Pay attention to things that are moving or changing.** Take special note of the things that moved or changed while you were observing, and what caused them to do so.

When you are finished taking notes, spend some time interpreting what you observed. Look for patterns in your observations to help you make sense of your field site.

Developing an Annotated Bibliography

Your professor may ask you to prepare an *annotated bibliography* that summarizes and assesses the sources you collected. An annotated bibliography is an alphabetical list of your sources that briefly summarizes and occasionally assesses the value of each one. Figure 22.6 shows part of an annotated bibliography that includes online, print, and empirical sources. A complete annotated bibliography, with additional instructions for developing it, can be found in Chapter 10.

Entries in an annotated bibliography are typically formatted according to an established documentation style (see Chapter 24, "Using MLA Style," and Chapter 25, "Using APA Style").

As you research your topic, an annotated bibliography will help you to accomplish several important tasks:

- **Keep track of your sources,** allowing you to remember what each source contained and how it related to your project.

- **Keep a brief summary of commentary on each source,** so you can quickly locate the exact information you need to support a claim or argument in your document.

- **Consider each source in depth** and figure out how it fits into your research project.

Your professors will also use annotated bibliographies to review the kinds of sources you are collecting and make suggestions about other possible sources or to ensure that you are collecting a variety of sources.

Creating an annotated bibliography is not difficult. First, list your sources alphabetically, using MLA or APA documentation style. Then summarize each source in a brief paragraph. The first sentence in your summary should state the purpose of the source. The remaining sentences should express its major points. Conclude with a brief evaluation of how each source fits into your research project. See Chapter 10 for more in-depth instructions.

As you write your entries, be especially careful to avoid plagiarism. If you take a quote or even ideas from the source, carefully label them with page numbers and the necessary quotation marks. This is especially important in a research project, because as you draft your text, you may forget which words and ideas in your annotated bibliography originally came from your source. You might innocently use them in your work, thinking they were your own.

FIGURE 22.6
Excerpt from an Annotated Bibliography

In this excerpt from an annotated bibliography, the writer has used MLA documentation style to list her sources. Then, for each source, she offers a summary and a paragraph that comments on how the source relates to her research project.

Holman, Virginia. "Not Like My Mother." *Prevention* 60.3 (2008): 59-62. Print.

In this article, the author describes her childhood experiences as her mother became schizophrenic, and she discusses how she freed herself from fears about suffering a similar fate. She shows how her mother's mental illness had profound effects on her life, challenging her to live her life differently than her mother. The author realizes that her mother's mental illness made her stronger, and that she inherited many of her mother's positive qualities.

Commentary: This article offers a helpful first-person view into schizophrenia that reflects some of my own experiences with my brother Paul's illness. Holman's mother is similar in many ways to Paul. She is fine on her medications, but goes off them occasionally, creating havoc for the family. I can use this article to illustrate the effects of schizophrenia on family members.

Mahler, James. Personal interview. 8 Apr. 2010.

Professor Mahler, a nationally recognized expert on schizophrenia at the University of Minnesota, made the point that schizophrenia is especially challenging because of the behaviour it brings about. Schizophrenics, he told me, are often paranoid, thinking others are watching them, stalking them, or trying to hurt them. He pointed out that medication often doesn't completely remove these thoughts. Medications only hold them in check. So family members of the schizophrenic often feel they need to modify their behaviour to avoid triggering symptoms. This behaviour modification can have profound effects on how family members relate to the schizophrenic and to each other.

Commentary: This interview really helped me connect the dots among my other sources. Professor Mahler answered my family-related questions in ways that went beyond the clinical answers that are available in articles.

Reliable research involves collecting sources from a variety of electronic, online, print, and empirical sources.

TRIANGULATE Your Sources

Make sure your research plan will allow you to triangulate your sources. Collect electronic, print, and empirical sources that will allow you to confirm or challenge any facts or information you find.

SEARCH Online Sources

Use Internet search engines, listservs, podcasts, and other online sources to collect information on your subject. As you are searching, consider the reliability of each source. A professional-looking website does not mean the source is reliable.

FIND Documentaries or Broadcasts About Your Topic

You can download documentaries and broadcasts online. Your library may have documentaries you can borrow as well.

READ Books on Your Topic

You can access many books through your library's online catalogue. Books are often the most reliable sources of information.

USE Indexes and Databases to Find Articles

Access indexes and databases through your library's website to find articles in academic journals, magazines, and newspapers.

TRY Empirical Methods to Gather Information

You can interview experts, conduct surveys, or do field observations to confirm or challenge the online and print sources you have gathered about your topic.

LOOK for Gaps in Your Information

Each source you find will raise more questions. When you notice gaps, do some more research to fill them.

DEVELOP an Annotated Bibliography

An annotated bibliography will help you keep track of your sources and consider them in more depth.

1. With your group, discuss your plans for triangulating two or three sources for your research project.

2. In a small group, talk about which kinds of sources you believe will be most helpful for your research. Depending on your topic, you will find different kinds of information helpful.

3. How reliable is the Internet as a source of information for your research? With a group in your class, come up with a list of ten ways you could back-check an Internet source.

1. Using your library's website, locate at least five books and five articles for your next assignment. Create an annotated bibliography using either MLA or APA citation style.

2. Using an Internet search engine, locate ten sources of information on your topic. Try using symbols in the search engine (+, –, "") to target your searches and find the most useful information available. Write an evaluation in which you discuss the ten best sources you found.

3. Choose one of the empirical tools discussed in this chapter (i.e., interview, survey, or field observation). Create the materials you would need to use this tool for your own research. Write a brief explaining your empirical tool to your professor and discuss the kinds of results you hope it will yield.

1. **Learn how professionals do research.** Using the Internet, research how people in your field of study do their own research. In a report, discuss your field's research practices.

2. **Find some suspicious sources.** Locate three to five online sources on your topic that you consider suspicious or misleading. Write a brief report that explains why you consider these electronic sources to be suspicious and how people can determine whether a source on this topic is reliable or not.

MyCompLab

For support in meeting this chapter's objectives, follow this path in MyCompLab:

Student Resources → Research → The Research Assignment. Review the Instruction and Multimedia resources about finding sources; then complete the Exercises and click on Gradebook to measure your progress.

Quoting, Paraphrasing, and Citing Sources

> **In this chapter, you will learn how to:**
>
> - quote, paraphrase, and summarize your sources in a research context.
> - frame quotes, paraphrases, and summaries in your texts.
> - avoid plagiarizing the works and ideas of others.

In post-secondary studies and in the workplace, you need to do more than simply collect sources when you're doing research. You also need to take the next step and engage with your sources, *using* them to develop your ideas and support your claims. As Chapter 21, "Starting Research," explained, research allows you to extend the work of others and advance your ideas with greater efficiency, clarity, authority, and persuasiveness. This chapter explains how to incorporate that research into your own writing.

When you use sources to inform and support your ideas, your writing has more authority. Also, by engaging with the ideas of others, you enter a larger conversation about those ideas within a particular discipline or profession.

When using a quotation, you are taking a key word, phrase, or passage directly from a source. A direct quote conveys the original text's immediacy and authority while capturing its tone and style.

When paraphrasing, you are explaining a specific idea or describing a specific portion of the source using your own words and your own sentence structures. Typically, your paraphrase will be about the same length as the material you are using from the source. Unlike a direct quotation, paraphrase allows you to clarify or draw attention to a particular issue or point in the original. That way, you can show readers how the author's ideas fit in with your overall work.

When summarizing, you are describing the major ideas of a source in your own words. Often you will summarize not only *what* authors say but *how* they say it. For instance, you might describe their reasoning process or the evidence they cite. A summary should be much shorter than the original, and it should be structured so that the major points you want to make about your source stand out. Chapter 4 offers an in-depth explanation of how to write a summary; here we expand on its uses in research writing.

This chapter will show you how to incorporate the ideas and words of others into your work while giving appropriate credit. Chapters 24 and 25 will show you how to cite your sources properly using MLA and APA documentation styles.

Common Knowledge: What You Don't Need to Cite

Some information doesn't need to be cited. Common knowledge includes widely known facts that can be found in a variety of sources. For instance, the following are all common knowledge or facts and would not need to be cited:

- George Stroumboulopoulos is host of *George Stroumboulopoulos Tonight*.
- Toronto is the largest city in Ontario in terms of population.
- The anterior cruciate ligament is one of the four major ligaments in the human knee; it connects the femur to the tibia.

Common knowledge does not need to be cited because it belongs to everyone. If you aren't sure whether something is common knowledge, you should go ahead and cite it.

Quoting

When quoting an author or speaker, you are importing their exact words into your document and placing quotation marks around those words. It sounds pretty easy, but you can confuse your readers or even get yourself in trouble if you don't properly incorporate and cite the words of others. In some cases, you could be accused of plagiarism. Here are some ways to quote properly using the source text in Figure 23.1 as a reference.

Brief Quotations

A brief quotation takes a word, phrase, or sentence directly from an original source. Always introduce and give some background on quotations: do not expect them to make your point themselves. Note that even brief quotations require citations in academic contexts.

The point is that books and video games represent two very different kinds of learning. When you read a biology textbook, the content of what you read is what matters. Reading is a form of explicit learning. When you play a video game, the value is in how it makes you think. Video games are an example of collateral learning, which is no less important.

Being "smart" involves facility in both kinds of thinking—the kind of fluid problem solving that matters in things like video games and I.Q. tests, but also the kind of crystallized knowledge that comes from explicit learning. If Johnson's book has a flaw, it is that he sometimes speaks of our culture being "smarter" when he's really referring just to that fluid problem-solving facility. When it comes to the other kind of intelligence, it is not clear at all what kind of progress we are making, as anyone who has read, say, the Gettysburg Address alongside any Presidential speech from the past twenty years can attest. The real question is what the right balance of these two forms of intelligence might look like. *Everything Bad Is Good for You* doesn't answer that question. But Johnson does something nearly as important, which is to remind us that we shouldn't fall into the trap of thinking that explicit learning is the only kind of learning that matters.

In recent years, for example, a number of elementary schools have phased out or reduced recess and replaced it with extra math or English instruction. This is the triumph of the explicit over the collateral. After all, recess is "play" for a ten-year-old in precisely the sense that Johnson describes video games as play for an adolescent: an unstructured environment that requires the child actively to intervene, to look for the hidden logic, to find order and meaning in chaos.

One of the ongoing debates in the educational community, similarly, is over the value of homework. Meta-analysis of hundreds of studies done on the effects of homework shows that the evidence supporting the practice is, at best, modest. Homework seems to be most useful in high school and for subjects like math. At the elementary-school level, homework seems to be of marginal or no academic value. Its effect on discipline and personal responsibility is unproved. And the causal relation between high-school homework and achievement is unclear: it hasn't been firmly established whether spending more time on homework in high school makes you a better student or whether better students, finding homework more pleasurable, spend more time doing it. So why, as a society, are we so enamored of homework? Perhaps because we have so little faith in the value of the things that children would otherwise be doing with their time. They could go out for a walk, and get some exercise; they could spend time with their peers, and reap the rewards of friendship. Or, Johnson suggests, they could be playing a video game, and giving their minds a rigorous workout.

FIGURE 23.1 Source Text

This excerpt from Malcolm Gladwell's article "Brain Candy" will be used in this chapter to demonstrate quoting, paraphrasing, and summarizing.

Words. If an author uses a word in a unique way, you can put quotes around it in your own text. After you tell your reader where the word comes from, you don't need to continue putting it inside quotation marks.

> **Acceptable quotation:** Using Gladwell's terms, some important differences exist between "explicit" learning and "collateral" learning (36).

> **Unacceptable quotation:** Using Gladwell's terms, some important differences exist between explicit learning and collateral learning (36).

Phrases. If you want to use a whole phrase from a source, you need to put quotation marks around it. Then weave the quote into a sentence, making sure it flows with the rest of your writing.

> **Acceptable quotation:** Tomorrow's educators need to understand the distinction between, as Gladwell puts it, "two very different kinds of learning" (36).

> **Unacceptable quotation:** Tomorrow's educators need to understand the distinction between, as Gladwell puts it, two very different kinds of learning (36).

Sentences. You can also bring entire sentences from another source into your document. Use a *signal phrase* (e.g., "As Gladwell argues,") or a colon to indicate that you are quoting a whole sentence.

> **Acceptable quotation:** As Gladwell argues, "Meta-analysis of hundreds of studies done on the effects of homework shows that the evidence supporting the practice is, at best, modest" (36).

> **Acceptable quotation:** "Meta-analysis of hundreds of studies done on the effects of homework," as Gladwell argues, "shows that the evidence supporting the practice is, at best, modest" (36).

> **Unacceptable quotation:** Meta-analysis of hundreds of studies done on the effects of homework shows that the evidence supporting the practice is, at best, modest, according to Gladwell.

> **Acceptable quotation using a colon:** Gladwell summarizes the research simply: "Meta-analysis of hundreds of studies done on the effects of homework shows that the evidence supporting the practice is, at best, modest" (36).

> **Unacceptable quotation using a colon:** Gladwell summarizes the research simply: Meta-analysis of hundreds of studies done on the effects of homework shows that the evidence supporting the practice is, at best, modest.

Long Quotations

Occasionally, you may need to quote a source at length. A quote that is longer than four lines of text (MLA style) or forty words (APA style) should be formatted as a *block quote*. A block quote indents the entire quotation to separate it from your normal text. No quotation marks are used, and the citation appears at the end of the quote, outside the final punctuation mark.

A child is unlikely to acquire collateral learning through books or studying for the SAT exams, Gladwell explains. They do acquire it through play, even playing video games:

> The point is that books and video games represent two very different kinds
> of learning. When you read a biology textbook, the content of what you
> read is what matters. Reading is a form of explicit learning. When you play
> a video game, the value is in how it makes you think. Video games are an
> example of collateral learning, which is no less important. ("Brain" 2)

In asserting that collateral learning "is no less important" than explicit learning, Gladwell implies that American education may be producing students who are imbalanced—with too much content knowledge and too little facility in dealing with unstructured situations, the kinds of situations that a person is likely to face every day of his or her working life.

Author introduces the quotation with context and a signal phrase.

Block quote.

Author explains what the quote means.

Use block quotes only when the original quotation cannot be paraphrased and must be preserved in its full length. Don't expect a long quotation to make your point for you. Instead, use the quote to support the point you are making.

Paraphrasing and Summarizing

When paraphrasing or summarizing, you are putting someone else's ideas into your own words. In some situations, using a paraphrase or summary is preferable to using a quote. In contexts where the content is more important than the actual wording (such as occurs in many scientific scholarly papers), it is often advisable to paraphrase or summarize. Using too many quotations can make a text look choppy and might lead the reader to think that you are just stitching together other people's words. Paraphrasing allows you to maintain the tone and flow of your writing.

There are three main differences between a summary and a paraphrase:

- A summary often covers the entire content of the source, while a paraphrase handles only a portion of it.

- A summary organizes the source's main ideas in a way that may modify the source's organization. A paraphrase follows the organization of the original.

- A summary is shorter than the original, while a paraphrase is about the same length as the portion of the text being paraphrased.

For a full discussion of summary, be sure to consult Chapter 4.

Paraphrasing

The goal of paraphrasing is to explain and describe a portion of the source's text in your own words. A paraphrase is usually about the same length or a little shorter than the material being paraphrased. For example, the writers of the following acceptable and unacceptable paraphrases are trying to describe Gladwell's distinction between "explicit" and "collateral" learning.

Acceptable Paraphrase

Gladwell explains that we can think of intelligence (or "smart," as he calls it) as having two related but distinct dimensions (36). On the one hand, there is the intelligence dimension we associate with storing, accessing, and reproducing information and with the ability to solve certain kinds of problems. This is the kind of intelligence a person gets from reading books and, generally, from school—what Gladwell calls "explicit" learning. Then there's another kind of intelligence that we get through "collateral" learning. When people develop this kind of intelligence, they have the practical know-how needed to enter a confusing, complex, chaotic situation and quickly and perhaps intuitively develop a hierarchy of what needs to be done, how it should be done, and when it should be done. Both kinds of intelligence are important, Gladwell assures us, but we probably need to think long and hard about the "right balance" between them.

In this acceptable paraphrase, the writer used primarily her own words. When she used exact words from Gladwell's article, she placed them inside quotations. Now let's look at a paraphrase that is too close to the original source:

Unacceptable Paraphrase

Gladwell explains that being smart requires two kinds of thinking. When a person reads a textbook, a magazine, or a manual of some kind, he or she is engaging in explicit learning. Here the crystallized knowledge that comes from the content of what you read is what matters. Playing video games is an example of collateral learning. Here the value lies in how the game makes you think and results in adaptable problem-solving skills. Although many people think that explicit learning is the only kind that matters, both kinds of smart are important (36).

The highlighted words and phrases are taken directly from Gladwell's article. Even though the writer explicitly cites the source of these ideas, too many words are lifted directly from the source without quotation or attribution. If the writer felt it was important to use these exact words and phrases, she should have placed them inside quotation marks and cited them.

When paraphrasing, don't allow your own voice to be overwhelmed by your source's tone or voice. Notice how the unacceptable paraphrase has almost the same voice as the original source. In the acceptable paraphrase, the writer's voice comes through clearly. Her paraphrase is accurate even as she uses her own words.

Summarizing

Remember that when you summarize someone else's work, you are capturing the source's principal idea or ideas. A summary often goes beyond a source's major points to explain the source's structure; its tone, angle, or purpose; its style; its underlying values; or the persuasive strategies it uses to drive home its points. In the following summaries, the writers address the main idea in Gladwell's review: the right balance between "explicit" and "collateral" learning. See Chapter 4 for a discussion of the steps involved in creating an effective summary.

Acceptable Paragraph-Length Summary

In the final portion of "Brain Candy," Gladwell accepts Johnson's argument that video games can help develop valuable capacities and extends it further, suggesting that we overvalue "explicit" learning and undervalue "collateral" learning, which happens when people play video games. But the real issue, Gladwell tells us, is not whether students are getting better at collateral learning or whether collateral learning is important. "The real question," asserts Gladwell, "is what the right balance of these two forms of intelligence might look like" (36). We need to discuss this question, Gladwell suggests, because many of the decision-makers in education seem to be proceeding as if explicit learning is all that matters without a healthy debate. We have failed to acknowledge, Gladwell reminds us, that play (even or *especially* playing video games) also results in an important kind of intelligence.

Notice how this summary focuses on an explicit point and makes it prominent.

An unacceptable summary usually relies too much on the wording of the original text, and it often does not prioritize the most important points in the source text.

Unacceptable Summary

In the final portion of "Brain Candy," Gladwell accepts Johnson's argument that playing video games is valuable because of how it makes you think and extends it further, asking what the right balance between these two forms of intelligence would look like. Gladwell explains that books and video games deliver two very different kinds of learning (36). When you read, it's the content that matters. Reading is a form of explicit learning. Playing a video game is valuable because of the way it makes you think. Collateral learning is no less important than explicit learning. But the real question, Gladwell tells us, is figuring out the right balance of these two forms of intelligence. We need to discuss this question, Gladwell suggests, because many of the decision-makers in education seem to be proceeding as if explicit learning is all that matters without a healthy debate. For example, a number of elementary schools have eliminated recess and replaced it with math or English (36). They have also increased the amount of homework, even though nobody knows whether spending more time on homework in high school makes you a better student or whether better students spend more time on their homework. Gladwell concludes by saying that as a society, we are so enamoured of homework because we do not understand the value of the things that children would otherwise be doing with their time. This is the triumph of the explicit over the collateral.

The highlighted phrases in this example show places where the summary uses almost the same wording as the original text. In this example, this writer has engaged in what is becoming known as "patchwriting." Writing scholar Rebecca Moore Howard defines patchwriting as "copying from a source text and then deleting some words, altering grammatical structures, or plugging in one synonym for another" (xvii). Patchwriting is a form of plagiarism, which is discussed later in this chapter.

Framing Quotes, Paraphrases, and Summaries

Your readers need to easily see the boundaries between your work and the material you are taking from your sources. To help them identify these boundaries, you should properly *frame* your quotations, paraphrases, and summaries by using signal phrases and *citations*, and by making *connections* to your own ideas (Figure 23.2).

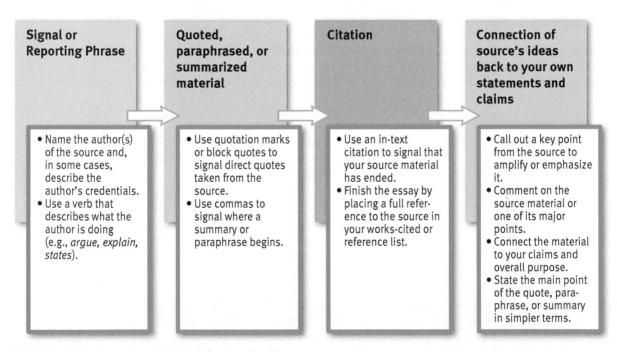

FIGURE 23.2 Framing Material from a Source

Material taken from a source should be clearly framed with a signal or reporting phrase, a citation, and a connection to your own statements and claims.

Signal or Reporting Phrase. Remember from Chapter 4 that a signal or reporting phrase indicates where the source material came from. The words "as" and "in" are often at the heart of a signal phrase (e.g., "As Gladwell argues," "In his article 'Brain Candy' Gladwell states").

Direct Quotation. Material quoted directly from your source should be separated from your own words with commas, quotation marks, and other punctuation to indicate which words came directly from the source and which are your own.

Citation. A citation allows readers to find the exact page or website of the source. In MLA or APA documentation style, an in-text citation is used to cite the source. In other documentation styles, you might use a footnote or endnote. See Chapters 24 and 25 for end reference formats.

Connection. When you connect the source's ideas to your ideas, you will make it clear how the source material fits in with your own statements and claims.

Figure 23.2 offers a diagram that colour codes these features. The following three examples use these colours to highlight signal or reporting phrases, source material, citations, and connections.

As Malcolm Gladwell reminds us, many American schools have eliminated recess in favour of more math and language studies, favouring "explicit" learning over "collateral" learning (36). This approach is problematic, because it takes away children's opportunities to interact socially and problem-solve, which are critical skills in today's world.

Speculating about why we so firmly believe that homework is critical to academic success, Gladwell suggests, "Perhaps because we have so little faith in the value of the things that children would otherwise be doing with their time" (36). In other words, Gladwell is arguing that we are so fearful of letting children play that we fill up their time with activities like homework that show little benefit.

Studies show that the careers of the future will rely heavily on creativity and spatial recognition, which means people who can think with the right side of their brain will have the advantage (Pinker, 2006, p. 65). If so, we need to change our educational system so that we can strengthen our abilities to think with both sides of the brain, not just the left side.

As shown in this example, the frame begins with a signal or reporting phrase. These phrases typically rely on an action verb that signals what the author of the source is trying to achieve in the material that is being quoted, paraphrased, or summarized. Figure 23.3 provides a helpful list of verbs you can use to signal quotes, paraphrases, and summaries.

The frame typically ends with a connection showing how the source material fits into your overall discussion or argument. Your connection should do one of the following things for your readers:

FIGURE 23.3
Verbs for Signal or Reporting Phrases

Use verbs like these to introduce quotations, paraphrases, and summaries.

accepts	accuses	acknowledges
adds	admits	advises
agrees	alleges	allows
analyzes	announces	answers
argues	asks	asserts
believes	charges	claims
comments	compares	complains
concedes	concludes	confirms
considers	contends	countercharges
criticizes	declares	demonstrates
denies	describes	disagrees
discusses	disputes	emphasizes
explains	expresses	finds
grants	holds	illustrates
implies	insists	interprets
maintains	notes	objects
observes	offers	points out
proclaims	proposes	provides
quarrels	reacts	reasons
refutes	rejects	remarks
replies	reports	responds
reveals	shows	states
suggests	supports	thinks
urges	writes	

- Call out a key point from the source to amplify or emphasize it.

- Expand on the source material or one of its major points.

- Connect the source material to your claims and overall purpose.

- Rephrase the main point of the source material in simpler terms.

When handled properly, framing allows you to clearly signal the boundaries between your source's ideas and your ideas.

Watch Office Hours: Avoiding Plagiarism

Avoiding Plagiarism

The Council of Writing Program Administrators defines plagiarism this way:

> **In an instructional setting, plagiarism occurs when a writer deliberately uses someone else's language, ideas, or other original (not common-knowledge) material without acknowledging its source.**

In post-secondary settings, plagiarism is a form of academic dishonesty, the same as cheating on an exam, and it can lead to a failing grade on an assignment or even for the class. In the workplace, plagiarism is a form of copyright infringement in which one person illegally takes the ideas or words of someone else without their permission. Copyright infringement can lead to costly lawsuits and the firing of any employee who commits it.

Plagiarism is not always intentional. Sometimes writers forget to copy down their sources in their notes. Sometimes they forget where specific ideas came from. But even if you plagiarize accidentally, you may find yourself in serious trouble with your professors, your university, or your employer. So it is crucial that you understand the kinds of plagiarism and learn to avoid them.

Academic Dishonesty

The most obvious form of plagiarism occurs when someone hands in work that is not his or her own. Everyone, including your professors, knows about "cheater websites" that sell or give away post-secondary papers. Everyone also knows about "borrowing" someone else's paper. And everyone knows it's easy to cut and paste a sample paper from the Internet. (If you found it, chances are good your professor will find it, too.)

And yet, some students still foolishly try to get away with these kinds of plagiarism. Your professors aren't naive and they often have online tools to help them trace sources. If you hand in a paper that's not your own, you're being dishonest. When students get caught, they often fail the class, which looks bad on their transcripts and is very difficult to explain to future employers or graduate school admissions committees. They might even be expelled. This kind of plagiarism is clearly intentional and few people will have sympathy for someone who is so obviously cheating.

Ironically, people who buy, download, or copy papers often spend more time and energy finding the paper and worrying about the consequences of getting caught than they would if they just wrote the paper in the first place.

Patchwriting

Patchwriting was mentioned earlier in this chapter. Usually, patchwriting happens when someone cuts and pastes one or more paragraphs from a webpage or other source and then alters words and sentences to make them look like his or her own.

When done intentionally, patchwriting is clearly a form of academic dishonesty, because the writer is presenting someone else's ideas as his or her own without attribution. Some students have even tried to patchwrite an entire paper. They cut and paste several paragraphs from one source or a variety of sources. Then they add some transitions and a few of their own sentences, while altering the words and sentences from the original. As a result, little of the paper is based on their own ideas. This kind of dishonesty, when caught, usually leads to a failing grade on the paper and for the class.

Patchwriting can happen unintentionally, especially when a writer copies sentences or paragraphs from a source and then forgets the material was taken from somewhere else. The writer might even cite the source, not realizing that the text they included is too close to the original. Unfortunately, your professor cannot tell whether you were intentionally being dishonest or just made an honest mistake.

To avoid patchwriting, make sure you carefully identify your sources in your notes. Clearly mark any direct quotes taken from your sources with quotation marks, brackets, or some other kind of distinguishing mark. Then, when you use these materials in your document, make sure you quote, paraphrase, and summarize them using proper citations.

Ideas and Words Taken Without Attribution

In university and college and in the workplace, you will often need to use the exact ideas, words, phrases, or sentences from a source. When you do this, *you must correctly quote and cite that source.* That is, you must place those words inside quotation marks (or block quote them) and provide a citation that tells your reader precisely where you got those words. If you use ideas, words, phrases, or sentences without attribution, you could be charged with academic dishonesty or copyright infringement.

Sometimes it is difficult to determine whether someone else owns the ideas that you are using in your document. If you aren't sure, cite the source. Citing a source will only add support to your work, and it will help you avoid being accused of plagiarism.

The Real Problem with Plagiarism

No doubt, plagiarism is easier than ever with the Internet. It's also easier than ever to catch someone who is plagiarizing. Your professors can use *Google* too, and they have access to plagiarism checking websites like *Turnitin.* They also often have access to collections of prior papers that were handed in.

If you plagiarize, there is a good chance you will get caught, and the price will be steep. But the real problem with plagiarism is that you are cheating yourself. You're probably paying many thousands of dollars for your education. Cheating robs you of the chance to strengthen your communication skills and prepare for advanced courses and your career.

Of course, there is pressure to do well in your classes, and you don't always have enough time to do everything you want. In the end, though, doing your own work will help you improve and strengthen your mind and abilities. Don't miss that opportunity.

Here are some helpful guidelines for quoting, paraphrasing, and summarizing sources and avoiding plagiarism.

DECIDE What to Quote, Paraphrase, or Summarize

Ask yourself what kinds of materials should be quoted, summarized, or paraphrased in your document. To guide your decision, keep your readers' needs and the genre in mind.

INCLUDE Short Quotations and Cite Them Properly

Any words, phrases, or sentences should be placed in quotation marks and cited with MLA or APA documentation style.

USE Block Quotes for Longer Quotations

If a quote is longer than four lines (MLA style) or forty words (APA style) or contains more than one sentence, set it off in a block quote. A block quote indents the quotation to separate it from the normal text.

PARAPHRASE Important Sources and Cite Them

A paraphrase puts someone else's ideas into your own words. Paraphrases are usually about the same length or a little shorter than the original. Make sure you do not use words from the original text unless you quote them. Paraphrases need to be cited.

SUMMARIZE Sources with Important Ideas and Cite Them

A summary captures the principal ideas of a source by summarizing the entire work or a major portion of it. Summaries are shorter than paraphrases, and they usually present the source's main ideas from most important to least important.

USE Signal or Reporting Phrases and Verbs to Mark Quotes, Paraphrases, and Summaries

A *signal phrase* uses words like "as" or "in" to highlight for the readers where a source is being referenced. A variety of *signal verbs* can also highlight the beginning of a quote, paraphrase, or summary.

DON'T Plagiarize Intentionally or Unintentionally

Plagiarism, whether intentional or unintentional, is a form of academic dishonesty. It involves using someone else's words or ideas without giving them proper credit. Intentional plagiarism usually leads to a failing grade for the paper and the course. Don't do it.

1. What kinds of research have you done in the past, and how did you incorporate sources into your work? How do you think research in your post-secondary studies will be handled differently?

2. Look at the example of "patchwriting" on pages 421–422. Discuss how you can avoid patchwriting in your own work.

3. With your group, discuss how professors should keep students from plagiarizing, and what should be done when someone does plagiarize.

1. Choose a television commercial and try to paraphrase it and summarize it. How challenging is it to do this accurately?

2. Choose three quotations from a source and practise incorporating them into something you are writing for this class. Be sure to use a signal or reporting phrase.

3. Choose three paragraphs from a source and purposely create an inappropriate "patchwritten" text. Then transform your patchwritten text into an appropriate paraphrase. As you rewrite the text, pay attention to the kinds of alterations you need to make.

1. **Summarize a source.** Choose a source text and write down a single sentence that summarizes the source's main point in your own words. Now write a one paragraph summary of the source, highlighting its major ideas. Finally, turn your one paragraph summary into a multiple paragraph summary that includes quotes and citations.

2. **Explain how to handle plagiarism.** Write a brief position paper in which you discuss how universities should handle plagiarism in the age of the Internet. Offer some ideas about how professors can steer students away from the temptation to plagiarize.

MyCompLab

For support in meeting this chapter's objectives, follow this path in MyCompLab:

Student Resources → Research → The Research Assignment. Review the Instruction and Multimedia resources about integrating sources; then complete the Exercises and click on Gradebook to measure your progress.

24

Using MLA Style

In this chapter, you will learn how to:

- use MLA parenthetical citations in your academic papers.
- create bibliographic entries for a works-cited list.
- prepare a works-cited list in MLA style.

Modern Language Association (MLA) documentation style helps you to keep track of your sources, while showing your readers where you found the supporting information in your document. MLA style is most commonly used in the humanities (i.e., English, history, philosophy, languages, art history). This style is also used in other scholarly fields because of its flexibility and familiarity.

In the previous chapter, you learned how to quote, paraphrase, and cite your sources. In this chapter, you will learn how to use MLA style to reference your sources and create a list of "Works Cited" at the end of your document. The models of MLA citations shown here are the ones most commonly used in post-secondary settings and in the workplace. If you cannot find a model that fits the source you are trying to cite, you should turn to the *MLA Handbook for Writers of Research Papers*, 7th ed. (2009). Be sure your MLA Handbook is the seventh edition (the most recent version), because MLA formats changed in 2009 to better accommodate online publication requirements.

On the Internet, an increasing number of online citation generators are available, or your word-processing software may include one. We recommend using these online tools because they can help you quickly generate MLA-style documentation. However, you should always make sure the generator is following the most up-to-date MLA documentation style. Also, double-check all citations to make sure they were created correctly.

Parenthetical Citations

When citing a source with MLA style, you first need to include a *parenthetical reference*. A parenthetical reference appears in the text of your document, usually at the end of the sentence where the information that you used from another source appears. For example:

> Archeologists have shown that wild dogs diverged from wolves about ten thousand years ago (Jones 27).

> For example, in *The Robber Bride* , Atwood depicts the response of second-wave feminism to postfeminism (Tolan 46), through the complex interactions of three friends with an aggressive vampire, Zenia, who has recently returned from the dead.

Note: For a key to the colour highlighting used here and throughout this chapter, see the bottom of page 431.

As shown here, a parenthetical reference includes two important pieces of information: the source's name (usually an author's name), a single space with no comma, and the page number from the source where the information appeared. The first parenthetical reference above signals to readers that the information in this sentence was taken from page 27 in a work from someone named " Jones ." The second parenthetical reference signals that its information can be found on page 46 in a source written by someone named " Tolan ."

If readers want to, they can then turn to the "Works Cited" at the end of the document to see the full citation, which will look like this:

> Jones, Steve. *Darwin's Ghost.* New York: Ballantine, 2000. Print.

> Tolan, Fiona. "Sucking the Blood Out of Second Wave Feminism: Postfeminist Vampirism in Margaret Atwood's *The Robber Bride.*" *Gothic Studies* 9.2 (2007): 45-57. Print.

In other words, the parenthetical reference and the full citation work together. The reference points readers to the works-cited list, where they can find the information needed to locate the source.

When the Author's Name Appears in the Sentence

You don't always need to include the author's name in the parenthetical reference. If you name the author in the sentence, you only need to provide the page number in parentheses. For example:

According to Steve Jones, a genetic scientist, archeologists have shown that wild dogs diverged from wolves about ten thousand years ago (27).

In her recent article, Tolan (46) argues that Atwood's *The Robber Bride* is really an allegory of postfeminism, in which three second-wave feminists are confronted with the anxieties brought about by the postfeminist backlash.

Typically, a parenthetical reference appears at the end of the sentence, but as shown above, it can also appear immediately after the name of the source.

If the first part of your sentence draws information from a source but the remainder of the sentence represents your own thoughts, you should put the reference immediately after the source's material is used. For example:

Glassner argues that naive Americans are victimized by a news media that is engaged in "fear-mongering" and other scare tactics (205), but I believe the American people are able to distinguish between real news and sensationalism.

Citing More Than One Source in the Same Sentence

If you want to cite multiple sources that are basically saying the same thing, you can use one parenthetical reference, separating the sources with semicolons:

In Canada, as in most nations, socio-economic disparities in educational attainment have persisted despite decades of reform (Shavit and Blossfeld 24 ; Deng and Treiman 392).

If you are citing more than one source in the same sentence but they are making different points, you should put the parenthetical reference as close as possible to the information taken from each source. For example:

Some historians view Cicero as a principled defender of the dying Roman Republic (Grant 29), while others see him as an idealistic statesman who stood helplessly aside as the Republic crumbled (Everett 321).

Citing a Source Multiple Times

In some situations, you will need to cite a source multiple times. If your document continues using a single source, you only need to include the page number in following references as long as no other source comes between them.

New owners often misread the natural signals from their new puppy (Monks 139). One common problem is *submissive urination* in which a puppy shows submission by peeing when greeted. Owners often mistakenly believe the puppy is doing something wrong or defiant, when the puppy is really trying to signal submission. In other words, punishing the dog for submissive urination is exactly the wrong thing to do, because it only encourages the puppy to be even more submissive, resulting in even more puddles on the floor (140).

In the example above, the full parenthetical reference is included early in the paragraph. The second reference, which is only a page number, is clearly referring back to the source in the first reference.

However, if another source is cited between two parenthetical references to the same source, the author's name from the first source would need to be repeated in a subsequent reference. For example:

New owners often misread the natural signals from their new puppy (Monks 139). One common problem is *submissive urination* in which a puppy shows submission by peeing when greeted. Owners often mistakenly believe the puppy is doing something wrong or defiant, when the puppy is really trying to signal submission (Kerns 12). In other words, punishing the dog for submissive urination is exactly the wrong thing to do, because it only encourages the puppy to be even more submissive, resulting in even more puddles on the floor (Monks 140).

In the example above, the author includes " Monks " in the last sentence's reference because the reference "(Kerns 12)" appears between the two references to the source written by Monks .

Other Parenthetical References

A wide variety of parenthetical references are possible. Figure 24.1 shows models of some common parenthetical references that you might need to use. Choose the one that best fits your source. If none of these models fits the source you are trying to cite, you can use combinations of these models. If you still cannot figure it out, turn to the *MLA Handbook* for help.

Preparing the List of Works Cited

Your list of works cited appears at the end of your document. In this list, you should include full citations for all the sources you cited in your document. A typical entry includes features like the name of the author, the name of the text, the place where it

Type of Source	Example Parenthetical Reference
Single author	(Gerns 12)
Single author, multiple pages	(Barnes 5-9) or (Barnes 34, 121) *The hyphen signals a range of pages. The comma suggests similar information can be found on two different pages.*
Two authors	(Hammonds and Gupta 203)
Three authors	(Gym, Hanson, and Williams 845)
More than three authors	*First reference:* (Wu, Gyno, Young, and Reims 924) *Subsequent references:* (Wu et al. 924)
Multiple sources in same reference	(Yu 34; Thames and Cain 98; Young, Morales, and Cato 23) *The semicolon divides the sources.*
Two or more works by the same author	(Tufte, *Visual* 25) and (Tufte, "Powerpoint" 9) *The first prominent word in the source's title is used. Italics signals a book, while quotation marks signal an article.*
Different authors with the same last name	(M. Smith 54) and (A. Smith 34) *The first letter abbreviates each author's first name.*
Corporate author	(NASA 12) or Alb. Beef Prod. 232) *Abbreviate as much of the corporate name as possible. Periods are needed with abbreviations that are not known acronyms.*
No author for book	(*Handling* 45) *Use the first prominent word in the title and put it in italics.*
No author for journal article or newspaper article	("Genomics" 23) *Use the first prominent word in the title and put it in quotation marks.*
No author for newspaper article	("Recession" A4) *The letter "A" is the section of the newspaper and the number is the page.*
Quoted in another source	(qtd. in Franks 94) *"qtd." stands for "quoted."*

FIGURE 24.1
Types of MLA Parenthetical References

(continued)

Author Title Publication Online Source

(continued)

FIGURE 24.1
Types of MLA
Parenthetical
References

Type of Source	Example Parenthetical Reference
Webpage or other document with no pagination	(Reynolds, par. 3) *"par." stands for paragraph, as counted down from the top of the page. The comma separates the name from the paragraph number.*
Webpage or other document with no author and no pagination	("Friendly," par. 7) *Put the first prominent word in the title in quotes, with "par." standing for the paragraph, as counted down from the top of the page. The comma separates the title from the paragraph number.*

Not all possible parenthetical references are shown here. If you have a unique source that doesn't fit these examples, you can usually figure out how to cite it by combining the above reference models. If you still cannot figure out how to cite your source, turn to the *MLA Handbook* for help.

was published, the medium in which it was published, and the date it was published. For example, here are three different entries from three different types of sources:

Chew, Robin. "Charles Darwin, Naturalist, 1809-1882." *Lucidcafe*. Robin Chew. n.d. Web. 27 Aug. 2012.

Poresky, Louise. "Cather and Woolf in Dialogue: The Professor's House to the Light House." *Papers on Language and Literature* 44.1 (2008): 67-86. Print.

Ross, Sinclair. *As For Me and My House*. Toronto: McClelland & Stewart, 1957. Print.

Only sources you reference in your document should appear in your works cited. The works-cited list is not a bibliography of all the sources you found on your topic. It is only a list of sources that you actually used in the document.

In a works-cited list, the entries are listed in alphabetical order by the authors' last names. When the author's name is not known, the work is alphabetized by the first prominent word in its title. When alphabetizing, ignore words like *The, A,* or *An* if they are the first word in the title.

Including More Than One Source from an Author

If your works-cited list includes two or more sources from the same author, only the first entry should include the author's name. Afterward, entries should use three hyphens instead of the name. Multiple entries from one author should be alphabetized by the first prominent words in the titles.

Murphy, James. *Rhetoric in the Middle Ages: A History of Rhetorical Theory from Saint Augustine to the Renaissance*. Berkeley, CA: U of California P, 1974. Print.

---. *A Short History of Writing Instruction: From Ancient Greece to Modern America.* 2nd ed. Mahwah, NJ: Erlbaum, 2001. Print.

--- ed. *Three Medieval Rhetorical Arts.* Berkeley: U of California P, 1971. Print.

Murphy, James, Richard Katula, Forbes Hill, and Donovan Ochs. *A Synoptic History of Classical Rhetoric.* 3rd ed. Mahwah, NJ: Erlbaum, 2003. Print.

As shown above, if a single author is also listed as a coauthor for another entry, you should include the full name again without the three hyphens.

Formatting a List of Works Cited

According to MLA guidelines, it is standard to start the works-cited list on a new page with the centred heading "Works Cited" appearing at the top (Figure 24.2). Entries are then listed double-spaced, in hanging indent format, which means the first line of each entry is not indented, but the rest of the lines are indented a half inch (1.25 cm).

In professional texts, however, your works-cited list should match the design of your document. The "Works Cited" heading should be consistent with other headings. If you are single-spacing the rest of your document, the works-cited list should be single-spaced, too, perhaps with spaces between entries.

Torres 12

Works Cited

Barber, Paul. *Vampires, Burial, and Death.* New Haven, NJ: Yale UP, 1989. Print.

Bluestein, Gene. *Poplore: Folk and Pop in American Culture.* Amherst: U of Massachusetts P, 1994. Print.

Keyworth, Donald. "Was the Vampire of the Eighteenth Century a Unique Type of Undead Corpse?" *Folklore* 117.3 (2006): 1-16. Print.

Todorova, Maria. *Imagining the Balkans.* Oxford: Oxford UP, 1996. Print.

FIGURE 24.2 Formatting a List of Works Cited

MLA style requires that the heading "Works Cited" be centred on the page. The margins should be one inch (2.5 cm) on all sides. The entries should be double-spaced.

Author Title Publication Online Source

Citing Sources in the List of Works Cited

The following examples of MLA citations are based on the guidelines in the *MLA Handbook for Writers of Research Papers* (7th ed., 2009). This list is not comprehensive. However, we have included models of the most common kinds of entries in a works-cited list. You can use these examples as models for your own citations. If you do not find a model for a source, you should turn to the *MLA Handbook*.

MLA List of Works Cited

Journals, Magazines, and Other Periodical Publications

1. Article, Journal with Volume and Issue Numbers
2. Article, Journal with Issue Number Only
3. Article, Edited Book
4. Article, Magazine
5. Article, Newspaper
6. Article, Author Unknown
7. Article, CD-ROM
8. Editorial
9. Letter to the Editor
10. Review

Books and Other Nonperiodical Publications

11. Book, One Author
12. Book, Two Authors
13. Book, Three Authors
14. Book, Four or More Authors
15. Book, Corporate or Organization Author
16. Book, Edited Collection
17. Book, Translated
18. Book, Author Unknown

19. Book, Second Edition or Beyond
20. Book, in Electronic Form
21. Document, Government Publication
22. Document, Pamphlet
23. Foreword, Introduction, Preface, or Afterword
24. Sacred Text
25. Dissertation, Unpublished

Web Publications

26. Website, Author Known
27. Website, Corporate Author
28. Website, Author Unknown
29. Article from an Online Periodical
30. Article from an Online Scholarly Journal
31. Periodical Article Accessed Through a Database (Web)
32. Blog Posting
33. Wiki Entry
34. Podcast

Other Kinds of Sources

35. Film or Video Recording
36. Television or Radio Program

37. Song or Audio Recording

38. CD-ROM

39. Personal Correspondence, E-Mail, or Interview

40. Work of Art

41. Print Advertisement

42. Commercial

43. Speech, Lecture, or Reading

44. Map

45. Cartoon

Citing Journals, Magazines, and Other Periodical Publications

Citations for periodicals, such as journals, magazines, and other regularly published documents, need to include on the article itself as well as the publication information. The title of the article should appear in quotation marks. The volume number and issue number appear after the title of the periodical. The page numbers follow the year the work was published.

A citation for a journal, magazine, or other periodical publication includes the following features:

1. Name of the author, corporation, or editor with last name first

2. Title of the work in quotation marks

3. Name of the periodical in italics

4. Volume number and issue number

5. Date of publication (year for scholarly journal; day, month, year for other periodicals)

6. Range of page numbers for whole article

7. The medium in which the work was published ("Print" for a journal, periodical, or newspaper)

    ①   ②   ③   ④   ⑤   ⑥

Author. "Article Title." *Journal Title* Date or Volume.Issue (Year): page numbers.

    ⑦

Medium of publication.

1. Article, Journal with Volume and Issue Numbers

Jovanovic, Franck. "The Construction of the Canonical History of Financial Economics." *History of Political Economy* 40.2 (2008): 213-42. Print.

2. Article, Journal with Issue Number Only

Lee, Christopher, "Enacting the Asian Canadian." *Canadian Literature* 199 (2008): 28-44. Print.

3. Article, Edited Book

Goodheart, George. "Innate Intelligence Is the Healer." *Healers on Healing*. Ed. Richard Carlson and Benjamin Shield. New York: Putnam, 1989. 53-57. Print.

4. Article, Magazine

Zakaria, Fareed. "Obama's Vietnam: How to Salvage Afghanistan." *Newsweek* 9 Feb. 2009: 36-37. Print.

5. Article, Newspaper

Tait, Carrie. "Tapping Oil Reserves Poses Risk." *Globe and Mail* 29 Mar. 2012, national ed.: B7. Print.

6. Article, Author Unknown

"The Big Chill Leaves Bruises." *Albuquerque Tribune* 17 Jan. 2004: A4. Print.

7. Article, CD-ROM

Hanford, Peter. "Locating the Right Job for You." *The Electronic Job Finder*. San Francisco: Career Masters, 2001. CD-ROM.

8. Editorial

"A Vital Boost for Education." Editorial. *New York Times* 4 Feb. 2009, New York ed.: A30. Print.

9. Letter to the Editor

Wilson, Derek. Letter. *National Post* 21 Mar. 2012, national ed.: A13. Print.

10. Review

Leonhardt, David. "Chance and Circumstance." Rev. of *Outliers,* by Malcolm Gladwell. *New York Times* 30 Nov. 2008: New York ed.: BR9. Print.

Citing Books and Other Nonperiodical Publications

Books and other nonperiodical publications are perhaps the easiest to list in the works-cited list. A book citation will have some of the following features:

1. Name of the author, corporation, or editor with last name first (add "ed." or "eds." if the work is listed by the name of the editor)

2. Title of the work

3. City where the work was published

4. Publisher

5. Year of publication

6. Medium of publication

①   ②   ③   ④   ⑤   ⑥

Author. *Title.* City of publication: Publisher, year of publication. Medium of publication.

11. Book, One Author

Ambrose, Stephen. *Band of Brothers*. 3rd ed. New York: Simon, 2001. Print.

12. Book, Two Authors

Brett, Michael, and Elizabeth Fentress. *The Berbers: The Peoples of Africa*. Malden: Wiley-Blackwell, 1996. Print.

13. Book, Three Authors

Fellman, Michael, Daniel E. Sutherland, and Lesley J. Gordon. *This Terrible War: The Civil War and Its Aftermath*. New York: Longman, 2007. Print.

14. Book, Four or More Authors

Huss, Bernhard, Marc Mastrangelo, R. Scott Smith, and Stephen M. Trzaskoma. *The Unknown Socrates*. New York: Bolchazy-Carducci, 2002. Print.

15. Book, Corporate or Organization Author

American Psychiatric Association. *Diagnostic and Statistical Manual of Mental Disorders*. 4th ed. Washington: APA, 1994. Print.

16. Book, Edited Collection

Mueller-Vollmer, Kurt, ed. *The Hermeneutics Reader*. New York: Continuum, 1990. Print.

17. Book, Translated

Dostoevsky, Fyodor. *Notes from Underground*. 2nd ed. Trans. Michael Katz. New York: Norton, 2001. Print.

18. Book, Author Unknown

Physical Science. New York: McGraw, 1998. Print.

19. Book, Second Edition or Beyond

Kottak, Conrad. *Anthropology: The Exploration of Human Diversity*. 12th ed. New York: McGraw, 2008. Print.

20. Book, in Electronic Form

Darwin, Charles. *On the Various Contrivances by Which British and Foreign Orchids Are Fertilised by Insects*. London: Murray, 1862. Web. 1 Jan. 2008.

21. Document, Government Publication

Arguin, Paul M., Phyllis E. Kozarsky, and Ava W. Navin, eds. *Health Information for International Travel 2007-2008: The Yellow Book*. St. Louis: Centers for Disease Control, 2007. Print.

22. Document, Pamphlet

Parks Canada. *Canada's National Parks and National Historic Sites: Directory for the Travel Trade*. Ottawa: Parks Canada, 1999. Print.

23. Foreword, Introduction, Preface, or Afterword

Parker, Hershel. Foreword. *Moby Dick*. By Herman Melville. Evanston: Northwestern UP, 2001. xiii-xvi. Print.

24. Sacred Text

The New Oxford Annotated Bible. 3rd ed. New York: Oxford UP, 2001. Print.

25. Dissertation, Unpublished

Charlap, Marie-Helene. "Once with Women, Now with Women: A Qualitative Study of Identity." Diss. New York U, 2008. Print.

Citing Web Publications

Conventions for citing Web publications continue to evolve. In the most recent update of the *MLA Handbook* (2009), Web addresses (URLs) have been removed. When possible, you should include two dates: the date the material appeared on the Internet, and the date you accessed the material. If you cannot find the first date, then put *n.d.* for "no date." If you cannot find the publisher of the information, put *N.p.* for "no publisher." See Figures 24.3 to 24.5 for help locating information.

26. Website, Author Known

Nagel, Michael. "Biography." *The Official Mark Twain Website*. CMG Solutions, n.d. Web. 2 Feb. 2009.

27. Website, Corporate Author

Environment Canada. Enforcement. *Wildlife Enforcement*. Environment Canada, 20 Feb. 2012. Web. 27 Aug. 2012.

FIGURE 24.3 CITATION MAP: Citing All or Part of a Website

A citation for a Web publication will have some or all of the following features:

① Name of the author, corporation, editor, webmaster with last name first

② Title of the work (in quotation marks if an article; italicized if a stand-alone work)

③ Name of the website in italics if different than the title of the work

④ Publisher of the website. (If not available, use *N.p.* for "no publisher.")

⑤ Date of publication, including day, month, year. (If not available, use *n.d.* for "no date.")

⑥ The medium in which the work was published ("Web" for websites)

⑦ Date on which you accessed the website

①	②	③	④
Author of page or document.	"Title of document" or *Title of Page*.	*Title of Overall website*.	Publisher of

⑤	⑥	⑦
website, or N.p., date of publication, or n.d.	Medium of publication.	Date of your access.

①	②	③	④	⑤	⑥	⑦
Mills, Elinor.	"FAQ: Demystifying ID Fraud."	*CNET*.	CBS Interactive,	5 May 2009.	Web.	10 May 2009.

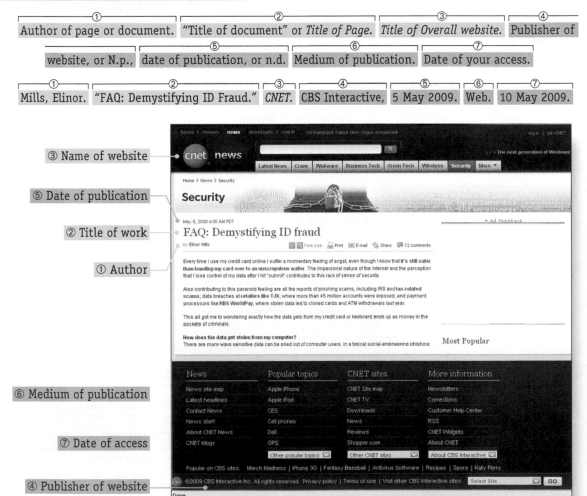

③ Name of website

⑤ Date of publication

② Title of work

① Author

⑥ Medium of publication

⑦ Date of access

④ Publisher of website

Author Title Publication Online Source

FIGURE 24.4 CITATION MAP: **Citing a Scholarly Journal on the Web**

A citation for an article from a scholarly journal on the Web includes the following features:

① Name of the author, last name first

② Title of the work in quotation marks

③ Name of the journal in italics

④ Volume number and issue number

⑤ Date of publication (year for scholarly journal)

⑥ Range of page numbers for whole article

⑦ The medium in which the work was published

⑧ Your date of access

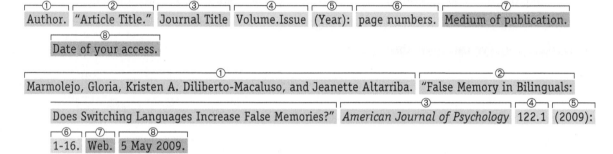

Author. "Article Title." Journal Title Volume.Issue (Year): page numbers. Medium of publication. Date of your access.

Marmolejo, Gloria, Kristen A. Diliberto-Macaluso, and Jeanette Altarriba. "False Memory in Bilinguals: Does Switching Languages Increase False Memories?" *American Journal of Psychology* 122.1 (2009): 1-16. Web. 5 May 2009.

④ Volume, issue

③ Name of journal

⑤ Date of publication

Can. Psychiatry 2012;57(3):184–191

⑥ Page numbers available on PDF

② Title of work

Original Research

Substances Used in Completed Suicide by Overdose in Toronto: An Observational Study of Coroner's Data

① Authors

Mark Sinyor, MD, MSc[1]; Andrew Howlett, MD[1]; Amy H Cheung, MD, MSc, FRCPC[2]; Ayal Schaffer, MD, FRCPC[3]

[1] Resident, Department of Psychiatry, University of Toronto and Sunnybrook Health Sciences Centre, Toronto, Ontario. Correspondence: 2075 Bayview Avenue, Toronto, ON M4N 3M5; mark.sinyor@utoronto.ca.

[2] Associate Professor, Department of Psychiatry, University of Toronto and Sunnybrook Health Sciences Centre, Toronto, Ontario.

[3] Associate Professor, Department of Psychiatry, University of Toronto, Toronto, Ontario; Head, Mood and Anxiety Disorders Program, Sunnybrook Health Sciences Centre, Toronto, Ontario.

Key Words: antidepressant, opioid, overdose, over-the-counter medication, suicide, Toronto

Received May 2011, revised, and accepted August 2011. Portions of these data were presented as a paper at the Canadian Psychiatric Association Annual Conference in Toronto, Ontario, in September 2010.

Objective: To identify the substances used by people who die from suicide by overdose in Toronto and to determine the correlates of specific categories of substances used.

Method: Coroner's records for all cases of suicide by overdose in Toronto, Ontario, during a 10-year period (1998 to 2007) were examined. Data collected included demographic data, all substances detected, and those determined by the coroner to have caused death. Logistic regression analyses were used to examine demographic and clinical factors associated with suicide by different drug types.

Results: There were 397 documented suicides by overdose (mean age 49.1 years, 50% female). Most substances detected were psychotropic prescription medications ($n = 245$), followed by other prescription medications ($n = 143$) and over-the-counter (OTC) medications ($n = 83$). More than one-half of all suicides by overdose were determined to have only one specific substance as the cause of death ($n = 206$). In suicides where only one class of substance was present in lethal amounts, OTC medication ($n = 48$), opioid analgesics ($n = 44$), and tricyclic antidepressants ($n = 44$) were most common.

⑦ Medium of publication

⑧ Date of access

From *Canadian Journal of Psychology*. Copyright © 2012

FIGURE 24.5 CITATION MAP: Citing a Scholarly Journal from a Database

A citation for an article from a scholarly journal accessed through a database includes the following features:

① Name of the author, last name first

② Title of the work in quotation marks

③ Name of the journal in italics

④ Volume number and issue number

⑤ Date of publication (year for scholarly journal)

⑥ Range of page numbers for whole article

⑦ Name of database

⑧ Medium of publication

⑨ Your date of access

Author. "Article Title." *Journal Title* Volume.Issue (Year): page numbers. *Database.* Medium of publication. Date of your access.

McGee, Elizabeth, and Mark Shevlin. "Effect of Humor on Interpersonal Attraction and Mate Selection." *Journal of Psychology* 143.1 (2009): 67-77. *Academic Search Premier.* Web. 4 Apr. 2009.

⑦ Name of database

② Title of work

① Authors

⑥ Page numbers

④ Volume, issue

⑤ Date of publication

③ Name of journal

⑧ Medium of publication

⑨ Date of access

Author Title Publication Online Source

28. Website, Author Unknown

"CBC Budget Cut by $115M Over 3 Years." *CBC.ca*. CBC-Radio Canada, 29 March 2012. Web. 30 March 2012.

29. Article from an Online Periodical

Leier, Andrew. "How Martian Winds Make Rocks Walk." *ScienceDaily*. ScienceDaily, 12 Jan. 2009. Web. 4 Feb. 2009.

30. Article from an Online Scholarly Journal

Ochiagha, Terri. "The Literary Fantastic in African and English Literature." *CLCWeb* 10.4 (2008): n. pag. Web. 5 Feb. 2009.

31. Periodical Article Accessed Through a Database (Web)

Sklansky, David. "Police and Democracy." *Michigan Law Review* 103.7 (2005): 1699-1830. *JSTOR*. Web. 5 Feb. 2009.

32. Blog Posting

Callahan, Alex. "Why Leadership Campaigns are Messier Than Elections." *The Huffington Post Canada*. HuffingtonPost.ca, 23 Mar. 2012. Web. 26 Mar. 2012.

33. Wiki Entry

"Galileo Galilei." *Wikipedia*. Wikimedia, n.d. Web. 5 Feb. 2009.

34. Podcast

"Interview with Neil Gaiman." *Just One More Book*. N.p., 27 Jan. 2009. Web. 3 Feb. 2009.

Citing Other Kinds of Sources

There are many other kinds of sources you will consult in your research. Especially for performances, you may choose to begin a citation with either an artist's name, a director or producer's name, or the title of the work. Consult the *MLA Handbook* for specific examples.

1. Title of the work (italics for a complete work; quotation marks for a work that is a segment, episode, or part of a whole) OR name of a specific performer, director, writer, etc. (last name, first name)

2. Title of the program, in italics, if applicable

3. Name of the network that aired or produced the work

4. Call letters and city of the station that aired the work, if available

5. Date of broadcast (day, month, year)

6. The medium of the work (e.g., television, radio, DVD, CD, film)

35. Film or Video Recording

Fiddler on the Roof. Dir. Norman Jewison. Prod. Norman Jewison. The Mirisch
    Production Company, 1971. Film.

Harris, Rosalind, perf. *Fiddler on the Roof.* Dir. Norman Jewison. The Mirisch
    Production Company, 1971. Film.

36. Television or Radio Program

"Episode 18." Narr. Rick Mercer. *Rick Mercer Report.* CBC. 12 Mar. 2012. Web.
    29 Aug. 2012.

37. Song or Audio Recording

Myer, Larry. "Sometimes Alone." *Flatlands.* People's Productions, 1993. CD.

38. CD-ROM

Lilley, Linda, Scott Harrington, and Julie Snyder. *Pharmacology and the Nursing
    Process Companion CD.* 5th ed. St. Louis: Mosby, 2007. CD-ROM.

39. Personal Correspondence, E-Mail, or Interview

Schimel, Eric. Personal interview. 12 Dec. 2008.

40. Work of Art

Vermeer, Johannes. *Girl with a Pearl Earring.* N.d. Oil on canvas. Mauritshuis, The
    Hague.

41. Print Advertisement

Rogers. Advertisement. *Moneysense.* December 2011. Print.

42. Commercial

Toyota. Advertisement. MSNBC. 5 Feb. 2009. Television.

43. Speech, Lecture, or Reading

Johnston, David. "Speech from the Throne." Parliament Buildings, Ottawa. 3 June
    2011. Address.

Author Title Publication Online Source

44. Map

"Japan." Map. *Rand McNally World Atlas.* New York: Rand, 2004. 31. Print.

45. Cartoon

Adams, Scott. "Dilbert." Comic strip. *Journal and Courier* (Lafayette) 8 Apr. 2009: C8. Print.

A Student's MLA-Style Research Paper

The document starting on the next page uses MLA citation style. You can use this document to observe how an author uses MLA citation style under real conditions, including parenthetical references and a list of works cited.

MyCompLab

For support in meeting this chapter's objectives, follow this path in MyCompLab:

Student Resources → Research → Citing Sources. Review the Instruction and Multimedia Resources about MLA style; then complete the Exercises and click on Gradebook to measure your progress.

Turnbow 1

Katelyn Turnbow

Professor Thompson

English 102

6 May 2009

MLA does not require a separate title page, although many professors suggest you use one.

Lives Not Worth the Money?

The idea of a forgotten disease is almost absurd—a disease for which a cure is available and effective but never given a chance to work. We are often of the belief that human life is invaluable, that it cannot be bought with money, and that a sick person should be treated whether he is an enemy or a friend, poor or rich. In reality, however, the cures that do not make money for some manufacturer are simply not made at all. According to the World Health Organization (WHO), one need only look at African sleeping sickness. There is a cure, but the victims who would benefit from the drug are poor and considered "unprofitable" by the pharmaceutical industry. It remains, however, a drug company's ethical responsibility to care for people its drugs can save, even when helping them is not profitable.

Thesis statement

African sleeping sickness, also known as Human African Trypanosomiasis or HAT, was discovered in 1902 and kills more than 50,000 people a year. These victims, however, are often forgotten because they are poor and live in sub-Saharan Africa, not a prosperous Western nation (see Fig. 1). The disease is caused by a parasite and transmitted to humans by the Tsetse fly. Some villages in the region report that sleeping sickness is the "first or second cause of mortality," and that it is "even ahead of HIV/AIDS" (WHO). WHO estimates that on top of the 17,616 cases reported in 2005, about 50,000–70,000 cases were never diagnosed.

Specific statistics from credible sources provide credibility for the paper's arguments.

Sleeping sickness manifests in two distinct stages. The haemolymphatic stage (blood-lymph node) occurs shortly after exposure to the parasite and causes headache, fever, joint pain, and itching (WHO).

Turnbow 2

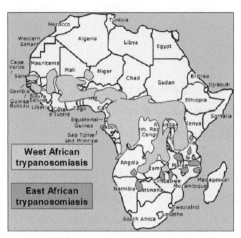

Fig. 1. Distribution of West African or Gambian Sleeping Sickness and East African or Rhodesian Sleeping Sickness.
Source: Richard Hunt/Microbiology and Immunology On-line; *www.microbiologybook.org* University of South Carolina.

The neurological stage follows, occurring months or even years after initial infection (see Fig. 2). This phase begins when the deadly parasite invades its host's central nervous system (CNS) and is accompanied by a large array of neurological symptoms including confusion, loss or disturbance of the senses, personality changes, and decreased coordination as well as the "disturbance of the sleep cycle which gives the disease its name" (WHO). Sleeping sickness is always fatal if not treated, and by the time the disease reaches its neurological stage, it is usually too late (WHO).

Effective treatments for sleeping sickness have been available since 1921, but they are dangerous and extremely painful. If diagnosed and treated in the early stages, sleeping sickness responds well to Pentamidine or, in extreme cases, Suramin. Both drugs, while sometimes

Maps, illustrations, and photographs should be placed in the paper where they provide the most support for in-text arguments.

Turnbow 3

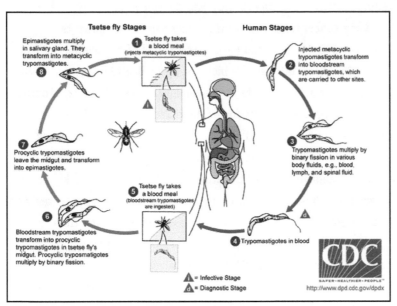

Fig. 2. Life Cycle of *T.b. gamienese* and *T.b. rhodesiense.*
Source: Alexander J. da Silva and Melanie Moser; *Centers for Disease Control Public Health Image Library;* n.d.; Web; 27 Apr. 2009.

accompanied by serious side effects such as heart and kidney failure, are fairly safe and inexpensive (WHO). Victims in the CNS stage of HAT, however, have for a long time been treated with a drug called Melarsoprol. Melarsoprol is widely available and cheap, but is derived from arsenic, and, acting as the potent poison that it is, can kill 5–20 percent of patients. The drug is also excruciatingly painful, described by many victims as "fire in the veins" ("Sleeping Sickness"). Although Melarsoprol "wouldn't pass a single ethical or drug-safety test" in the developed world, it is still used in Africa because it is the only treatment readily available to victims of this fatal but neglected disease (Gombe).

It is surprising, then, to learn that a new and highly effective treatment was developed almost 40 years ago. The chemotherapy drug,

When there is no author, use an abbreviated title of the article.

defluoro-methyl-ornithine (DFMO), was developed in the 1970s but failed as a cancer treatment, causing only hair loss in patients (Wickware 908-09). It would have been the end of the pharmaceutical, but in 1983, New York parasite biologist Cyrus Bacchi discovered DFMO's effectiveness on the later stage of sleeping sickness (Shah 22). Shortly after this discovery, Belgian doctor Henri Taelman used DFMO to treat an infected woman who had already fallen into a coma, and, almost miraculously, DFMO brought the woman out of her coma within 24 hours. Dr. Taelman renamed the drug eflornithine, but it quickly became known as the "resurrection drug" because it was "so effective at reviving even comatose patients" (Wickware 909; McNeil A1). Other than the highly toxic Melarsoprol, eflornithine is the only drug effective against late-stage Trypanosomiasis (McNeil A1). In addition to a much lower drug-induced mortality rate, eflornithine has fewer and milder side effects than Melarsoprol, and patients who receive eflornithine are more than twice as likely to survive the year following treatment as those treated with the older drug (Chappuis et al. 748-50).

It is clear that the drug is sorely needed by those who suffer the formidable symptoms of sleeping sickness. Despite this, eflornithine was very short-lived. The pharmaceutical company, Sanofi-Aventis, halted production of the resurrection drug in 1995 along with two other anti-trypanosome drugs (Wickware 909). A drug aimed toward treatment of diseases in poor countries was simply "not considered to be a profitable venture to many pharmaceutical companies" (Thomas). This attitude left groups such as WHO and Doctors without Borders struggling to control the disease and save their dying patients without the drugs they needed to do so. Once again these organizations were forced to rely on Melarsoprol, which seemed almost as likely to kill patients as it was to save them (Jackson and Healy 6).

When quoting more than one author, separate the information with a semicolon.

When a work has more than three authors, use the name of the first author listed followed by "et al." meaning "and others."

Turnbow 5

Although WHO, Doctors without Borders, and similar groups petitioned Aventis to continue production of the drug that would save thousands, it was not until 2001 that production of eflornithine resumed. Aventis had found a new use for the "resurrection drug"—hair removal. The company was once again mass producing eflornithine as an ingredient in a $54-a-tube facial hair removal cream for women. Aventis was even generous enough to donate 60,000 doses to WHO so that its doctors could treat HAT in sub-Saharan Africa (Jackson and Healy 6). Although this in itself was good, the company's reasons for doing so are less admirable. It placed "money before all" in all of its decisions, showing the "crass commodification of health" by an industry that was once "driven by a motive to improve human health" (Gombe). It is clear from the initial decision to halt production and Aventis's willingness to donate the drug only after a more cost-efficient use for it was found, that the company only helps others when it can make money by being kind. WHO's agreement with Aventis is only guaranteed for five years and the contract will expire soon (Chappuis et al. 751). The drug is already in short supply, and WHO can only afford to give it to those victims who survive their dose of arsenic and still need to be treated with the safer and more effective alternative (Etchegorry et al. 958). Aventis claims that the drug is "corrosive and destroys the equipment used to make it," suggesting that the pharmaceutical giant will once again refuse help to those in need and charge WHO and Doctors without Borders $70.00 a dose (McNeil A1). This is a price that neither organization can afford and that is far out of reach for the thousands of indigent victims who suffer from trypanosomiasis every year (McNeil A1).

Lifestyle drugs currently account for over "eighty percent of the world's pharmaceutical market," while companies are "ignoring diseases, like sleeping sickness and malaria, that affect only the poor" (McNeil

The topic sentence at the beginning of each paragraph should state your point.

Illustrations that support your point (topic sentence) can include quotations, statistics, figures, and other evidence.

The end of the paragraph should explain the significance of the point with illustrations for the reader, and support the paper's thesis.

Turnbow 6

A1). While I understand that pharmaceutical companies are big businesses committed to raising profits, it is unfortunate that the "$406 billion dollar global industry" feels it cannot spare its extra doses of eflornithine, a gesture that would save so many human lives (Shah 20).

The beginning of the conclusion is a summary of the key arguments, which also reflects the thesis claim.

A pharmaceutical company, which specializes in manufacturing medical products, should have at least some commitment to treating those who suffer from strategically forgotten diseases. Because it manufactures treatments for diseases and makes billions of dollars from health care, Aventis has an unspoken responsibility for the people it can afford to save and must continue to provide the drug to the organizations that devote all of their time and money to fighting diseases in developing countries. Unlike a vial of chemicals, no price tag can be placed on a human life. Our responsibility is the same, even if those we help cannot give us anything in return. Here, there are truly no excuses.

Turnbow 7

Works Cited

Chappuis, Francois, Nitya Udayraj, Kai Stietenroth, Ann Meussen, and Patrick A. Bovier. "Eflornithine Is Safer Than Melarsoprol for the Treatment of Second-Stage Trypanosoma Brucei Gambiense Human African Trypanosomiasis." *Clinical Infectious Diseases* 41.5 (2005): 748-51. Print.

Etchegorry, M. Gastellu, J. P. Helenport, B. Pecoul, J. Jannin, and D. Legros. "Availability and Affordability of Treatment for Human African Trypanosomiasis." *Tropical Medicine and International Health* 6.11 (2001): 957-59. Print.

Gombe, Spring. "Epidemic, What Epidemic: Treating Sleeping Sickness." *Bulletin of Medicus Mundi Switzerland.* Medicus Mundi Switzerland, Apr. 2004. Web. 12 Apr. 2009.

Jackson, Nicolette, and Sean Healy. "Facial Hair Cream to the Rescue." *New Internationalist* (2002): 6. Print.

McNeil, Donald G., Jr. "Cosmetic Saves a Cure for Sleeping Sickness." *New York Times* (2001): A1. *EBSCOhost.* Web. 28 Apr. 2009.

Shah, Sonia. "An Unprofitable Disease." *The Progressive* Sept. 2002: 20-23. Print.

"Sleeping Sickness." Doctors without Borders. 2009. Web. 12 Apr. 2009.

Thomas, Susan L. "African Sleeping Sickness." *Insect Science at Boston College.* 1 Mar. 2002. Web. 12 Apr. 2009.

Wickware, Potter. "Resurrecting the Resurrection Drug." *Nature Medicine* 8.9 (2002): 908-09. *EBSCOhost.* Web. 28 Apr. 2009.

World Health Organization. "African Trypanosomiasis." WHO, Aug. 2006. Web. 27 April 2009.

25

Using APA Style

In this chapter, you will learn how to:

- use APA parenthetical citations in your academic papers.
- create bibliographic entries for a references list.
- prepare a references list in APA style.

American Psychological Association (APA) documentation style, like MLA style (Chapter 24), is a method for keeping track of your sources, while letting readers know where you found the support for your claims. APA style is commonly used in the social sciences, physical sciences, and technical fields.

In this chapter, you will learn how to use APA style to reference your sources and create a list of "References" at the end of your document. The models of APA citations shown here are the ones most commonly used in post-secondary settings and in the workplace. For more information on APA style, consult the *Publication Manual of the American Psychological Association,* 6th ed. (2010).

Parenthetical Citations

When citing a source with APA style, you first need to include a parenthetical citation. A parenthetical citation appears in the text of your document, usually at the end of the sentence where the information that you used from another source appears. For example:

Children see the world from a different perspective than adults, making the divorce of their parents especially unsettling (Neuman, 1998, p. 43).

Among Africa's other problems, the one that is most significant may be its lack of reliable electrical energy (Friedman, 2008, p. 155).

As shown here, a full parenthetical citation includes three important pieces of information: the source's name (usually an author's name), the year in which the source was published, and the page number from the source where the information appeared.

If readers want to, they can then turn to the list of "References" at the end of the document to see the full citation, which will look like this:

Neuman, G. (1998). *Helping your kids cope with divorce the sandcastles way.* New York, NY: Random House.

Friedman, T. (2008). *Hot, flat, and crowded.* New York, NY: Farrar, Straus, & Giroux.

In other words, the parenthetical citation and the full reference work together. The parenthetical citation points readers to the reference list, where they can find the information needed to locate the source.

Note: For a key to the colour highlighting used here and throughout this chapter, see the bottom of this page.

APA style also allows you to refer to a whole work by simply putting the author's name and the year of the source. For example:

Genetics are a new frontier for understanding schizophrenia (Swaminathan, 2008).

Autism and psychosis have been shown to be diametrical disorders of the brain (Crespi & Badcock, 2008).

These parenthetical references without page numbers are common in APA style, but not in MLA style. Remember that if you are quoting or referring to a specific page in either style, you must include page numbers.

In situations where you are specifically highlighting a study or author, you should move the full parenthetical reference up in the sentence:

According to one study (Adreason & Pierson, 2008), the cerebellum plays a key role in the onset of schizophrenia.

Three books (Abraham & Llewellyn-Jones, 1992; Boskind-White & White, 2000; Burby, 1998) have tried to explain bulimia to nonscientists.

When the Author's Name Appears in the Sentence

If you name the author in the sentence, you only need to provide the year of the source and the page number in parentheses. The year should follow the name of the source, and the page number is usually placed at the end of the sentence. For example:

Author   Title   Publication   Online Source

Neuman (1998) points out that children see the world from a different perspective than adults, making the divorce of their parents especially unsettling (p. 43).

Friedman (2008) argues that Africa's most significant problem may be its lack of electrical energy (p. 155).

If one part of your sentence draws information from a source but the remainder of the sentence states your own thoughts, you should put the reference immediately after the source's material is used. For example:

As Dennett (1995) points out, scientists are uncomfortable with the idea that nature uses a form of reason (p. 213), but I think we must see nature as a life form that is looking out for its best interests.

Citing More Than One Source in the Same Sentence

In APA style, it is common to cite multiple sources making the same point, separated with semicolons:

Several researchers (Crespi & Badcock, 2008; Shaner, Miller, & Mintz, 2004, p. 102; Swaminathan, 2008) have shown the toll that schizophrenia takes on a family.

In the sentence above, the writer is referring to the whole work by Crespi and Badcock and Swaminathan, but she is only referring to page 102 in the article by Shaner, Miller, and Mintz.

If you are citing more than one source in the same sentence but they are making different points, you should put the parenthetical reference as close as possible to the information taken from each source. For example:

Depression is perhaps one of the most common effects of bulimia (McCabe, McFarlane, & Olmstead, 2004, p. 19), and this depression "almost always impairs concentration" (Sherman & Thompson, 1996, p. 57).

Citing a Source Multiple Times

In some situations, you will need to cite a source multiple times. If your document continues using a single source, some editors and professors prefer that you include only the page number in subsequent references as long as no other source comes between them.

The side effects of brain tumour treatment can include fatigue, brain swelling, skin irritation, ear congestion, hair loss, depression, and eye irritation (Black, 2006, p. 170). For women and some men, the loss of their hair is perhaps the most disturbing because it draws looks and questions from others, and it is the most outward sign of their illness. Depression, however, perhaps needs the most attention because it often requires patients to take antidepressants and stimulants to maintain a normal life (p. 249).

In the example above, the full parenthetical citation is included early in the paragraph. The second reference, which is only a page number, is clearly referring back to the source in the first reference.

However, the *Publication Manual of the APA* and other editors and professors require that you cite the source in full on each use. This is an area of debate in APA style, and you will want to ask you professors about their preference.

In all situations, if another source is cited between two parenthetical citations to the same source, the author's name from the first source would need to be repeated in a subsequent reference. For example:

The side effects of brain tumour treatment can include fatigue, brain swelling, skin irritation, ear congestion, hair loss, depression, and eye irritation (Black, 2006, p. 170). For women and some men, the loss of their hair is perhaps the most disturbing because it draws looks and questions from others, and it is the most outward sign of their illness. In her memoir, Becker (2003) discusses moments when she obsessed about hiding the incision where the tumour was removed (p. 231). Depression, however, perhaps needs the most attention because it often requires patients to take antidepressants and stimulants to maintain a normal life (Black, 2006, p. 249).

In the example above, the author includes a full parenthetical reference to Black in the final sentence of the paragraph, because the reference to Becker (2003) appears between the first and second references to Black.

Other Parenthetical References

Figure 25.1 shows models of some common parenthetical citations. Choose the one that best fits your source. If none of these models fits the source you are trying to cite, you can use combinations of these models. If you still cannot figure it out, turn to the APA's *Publication Manual.*

Preparing the List of References

Your list of references appears at the end of your document. In this list, you should include full citations for all the sources you cited in your document. A typical entry includes features like the name of the author, the date of publication, the title of the text, and the place of publication. For example, here are three different entries from three different types of sources:

FIGURE 25.1
Types of APA
Parenthetical
References

Type of Source	Example Parenthetical Reference
Single author	(Gerns, 2009, p. 12)
Single author, multiple pages	(Barnes, 2007, pp. 5–9) or (Barnes, 2007, pp. 34, 121)
	The dash signals a range of pages. The comma suggests similar information can be found on two different pages. The "pp." signals multiple pages.
Two authors	(Hammonds & Gupta, 2004, p. 203)
	The ampersand (&) is used instead of "and."
Three authors	(Gym, Hanson, & Williams, 2005, p. 845)
	The ampersand (&) is used instead of "and."
More than three authors	*First reference:* (Wu, Gyno, Young, & Reims, 2003, p. 924)
	Subsequent references: (Wu et al., 2003, p. 924)
Six or more authors	*First and subsequent references:* (Williamson et al., 2004, p. 23)
Multiple sources in the same reference	(Thames & Cain, 2008; Young, Morales, & Cato, 2009; Yu, 2004)
	The semicolon divides the sources.
Two or more works by the same author	(Tufte, 2001, p. 23) and (Tufte, 2003)
	The author's name is used with the date.
Two or more works by the same author in the same year	(Tufte, 2001a, p. 23) and (Tufte, 2001b, p. 11)
	The "a" and "b" signal two different works and will appear in the list of references also.
Different authors with the same last name	(M. Smith, 2005, p. 54) and (A. Smith, 2007, p. 34)
	The first letters abbreviate each author's first name.
Corporate author	(National Aeronautics and Space Administration [NASA], 2009, p. 12) or (Alberta Beef Producers, 2006, p. 232)
	Well-known acronyms, such as NASA, can be put in brackets the first time and then used in any following parenthetical references. (NASA, 2009, p. 14)

Type of Source	Example Parenthetical Reference
No author for book	(*Handling Bulimia,* 2004, p. 45) *Use the full title of the source in italics.*
No author for journal article or newspaper article	("Genomics as the New Frontier," 2008, p. 23) *Put the full title in quotation marks.*
No author for newspaper article	("Recession," 2009, p. A4) *The letter "A" is the section of the newspaper and the number is the page.*
Cited in another source	(as cited in Franks, 2007, p. 94)
Webpage or other document with no pagination	(Reynolds, 2006, para. 3) *"para." stands for "paragraph," as counted down from the top of the page.*
Webpage or other document with no author and no pagination	("Friendly," 2008, para. 7) *Put the first prominent word in the title in quotes with "para." standing for "paragraph," as counted down from the top of the page.*

Not all possible parenthetical references are shown here. If you have a unique source that doesn't fit these examples, you can usually figure out how to cite it by combining features of the above reference models.

Servan-Schreiber, D. (2008). *Anti-cancer: A new way of life.* New York, NY: Viking.

Crespi, B., & Badcock, C. (2008). Psychosis and autism as diametrical disorders in the social brain. *Behavior Brain Science, 31*(3), 241–261.

Chew, R. (2008, February 1). Charles Darwin, naturalist, 1809–1882. *Lucidcafe.* Retrieved from http://www.lucidcafe.com/library/96feb/darwin.html

Only sources you reference in your document should appear in your References. The reference list is not a bibliography of all the sources you found on your topic. It is only a list of sources that you actually cited in the document.

In a reference list, the entries are listed in alphabetical order, by the authors' last names. When an author's name is not known, the work is alphabetized by the first prominent word in its title. When alphabetizing, ignore words like *The, A,* or *An* if they are the first word in the title.

VAMPIRES IN HOLLYWOOD   12

References

Arthen, I. (2005, December 9). Real vampires. *FireHeart, 2*. Retrieved
    from http://www.earthspirit.com/fireheart/fhvampire.html

Barber, P. (1989). *Vampires, burial, and death*. New Haven, CT: Yale UP.

Bluestein, G. (1994). *Poplore: Folk and pop in American culture*. Am-
    herst, MA: University of Massachusetts Press.

Keyworth, D. (2006). Was the vampire of the eighteenth century a
    unique type of undead corpse? *Folklore, 117*(3), 1–16.

FIGURE 25.2
Formatting a List of References

The APA Publication Manual *specifies that the heading "References" be centred on the page. The margins should be one inch (2.5 cm) on all sides. The entries should be double-spaced.*

If you are listing two works by the same author in the same year, they should be alphabetized by the first prominent words in their titles and then distinguished by "a," "b," "c" and so on (e.g., 2007 a , 2007 b , 2007 c).

Formatting a List of References in APA Style

According to APA guidelines, it is standard to start the reference list on a new page with the heading "References" appearing centred at the top (Figure 25.2). Entries are then listed double-spaced, in hanging indent format, which means the first line of each entry is not indented, but the rest of the lines are indented a half inch (1.25 cm).

In professional texts, however, your reference list should match the design of your document. The "References" heading should be consistent with other headings. If you are single-spacing the rest of your document, the reference list should be single-spaced, too, perhaps with spaces between entries.

Citing Sources in the List of References

The following list is not comprehensive. However, we have included models of the most common kinds of entries in a reference list. You can use these examples as models for your own citations. If you do not find a model for a source, you should turn to the APA's *Publication Manual,* 6th edition (2010). Note that in the APA manual you will find online periodicals covered within the same section as print periodicals. We discuss them in a separate section here to help you understand the elements required for online sources.

APA List of References

Journals, Magazines, and Other Periodical Publications

1. Article, Journal with Continuous Pagination
2. Article, Journal without Continuous Pagination
3. Article, Edited Book
4. Article, Magazine
5. Article, Newspaper
6. Article, Author Unknown
7. Article, CD-ROM
8. Review

Books and Other Nonperiodical Publications

9. Book, One Author
10. Book, Two Authors
11. Book, Three or More Authors
12. Book, Corporate or Organization Author
13. Book, Edited Collection
14. Book, Translated
15. Book, Author Unknown
16. Book, Second Edition or Beyond
17. Book, Dissertation or Thesis
18. Book, in Electronic Form
19. Document, Government Publication
20. Document, Pamphlet

Web Publications

21. Website Corporate Author
22. Website Author Unknown
23. Article from an Online Periodical
24. Scholarly Journal Article with a Digital Object Identifier (DOI)
25. Scholarly Journal Article
26. Podcast

Other Kinds of Sources

27. Film or Video Recording
28. Television or Radio Program
29. Song or Audio Recording
30. CD-ROM
31. Personal Correspondence, E-Mail, or Interview

Citing Journals, Magazines, and Other Periodical Publications

A citation for a journal, magazine, or other periodical publication includes the following features:

1. Name of the author, corporation, or editor; last name first, followed by initial of first name and any middle initials

2. Date of publication (year for scholarly journal; year, month, day for other periodicals)

3. Title of the work, not enclosed in quotation marks (capitalize only first word, proper nouns, and any word that follows a colon)

4. Title of the periodical in italics (capitalize all significant words)

5. Volume number (italicized) and issue number (not italicized, but enclosed in parentheses). If each issue begins with page 1, include the issue number.

6. Range of page numbers for whole article

    ①   ②   ③   ④   ⑤

Author. (Date of publication). Title of article. *Title of Journal, volume number*
          ⑤   ⑥

(issue number), page numbers.

1. Article, Journal with Continuous Pagination

Boren, M. T., & Ramey, J. (1996). Thinking aloud: Reconciling theory and practice. *IEEE Transactions on Professional Communication, 39,* 49–57.

2. Article, Journal without Continuous Pagination

Stirling, I., & Parkinson, C. L. (2006). Possible effects of climate warming on selected populations of polar bears. *Arctic, 59*(3), 261–275.

3. Article, Edited Book

Katz, S. B., & Miller, C. R. (1996). The low-level radioactive waste siting controversy in North Carolina: Toward a rhetorical model of risk communication. In G. Herndl & S. C. Brown (Eds.), *Green culture: Environmental rhetoric in contemporary America* (pp. 111–140). Madison, WI: University of Wisconsin Press.

4. Article, Magazine

Appenzeller, T. (2008, February). The case of the missing carbon. *National Geographic,* 88–118.

5. Article, Newspaper

Tait, C. (2012, March 29). Tapping oil reserves poses risk. *Globe and Mail,* p. B7.

6. Article, Author Unknown

The big chill leaves bruises. (2004, January 17). *Albuquerque Tribune,* p. A4.

7. Article, CD-ROM

Hanford, P. (2001). Locating the right job for you. *The electronic job finder* [CD-ROM]. San Francisco, CA: Career Masters.

8. Review

Leonhardt, D. (2008, November 30). Chance and circumstance. [Review of the book *Outliers*, by Malcolm Gladwell]. *New York Times*, p. BR9.

Citing Books and Other Nonperiodical Publications

A book citation will have some of the following features:

1. Name of the author, corporation, or editor with last name first (include "(Ed.)" or "(Eds.)" if the work is listed by editor)

2. Year the work was published, in parentheses (if unknown, use *n.d.* for "no date")

3. Title of the work, in italics (capitalize only first word, proper nouns, and any word that follows a colon)

4. City and province or state, or country where the work was published (use standard Canada Post abbreviations for provinces or states; spell out the full names of countries outside of Canada or the United States)

5. Publisher

①   ②   ③   ④
Author. (Year of publication). *Title of work*. City and province or state (or country)
⑤
of publication: Publisher.

9. Book, One Author

Jones, S. (2001). *Darwin's ghost: The origin of species updated*. New York, NY: Ballantine Books.

10. Book, Two Authors

Pauling, L., & Wilson, E. B. (1935). *Introduction to quantum mechanics*. New York, NY: Dover Publications.

11. Book, Three or More Authors

Newnan, D. G., Eschenbach, T. G., & Lavelle, J. P. (2008). *Engineering economic analysis* (10th ed.). Oxford, England: Oxford University Press.

12. Book, Corporate or Organization Author

American Psychiatric Association. (1994). *Diagnostic and statistical manual of mental disorders* (4th ed.). Washington, DC: Author.

13. Book, Edited Collection

Mueller-Vollmer, K. (Ed.). (1990). *The hermeneutics reader.* New York, NY: Continuum.

14. Book, Translated

Habermas, J. (1979). *Communication and the evolution of society* (T. McCarthy, Trans.). Boston, MA: Beacon Press.

15. Book, Author Unknown

Handbook for the WorkPad c3 PC Companion. (2000). Thornwood, NY: IBM.

16. Book, Second Edition or Beyond

Williams, R., & Tollet, J. (2008). *The non-designer's web book* (3rd ed.). Berkeley, CA: Peachpit.

17. Book, Dissertation or Thesis

Simms, L. (2002). *The Hampton effect in fringe desert environments: An ecosystem under stress* (Unpublished doctoral dissertation). University of New Mexico.

18. Book, in Electronic Form

Darwin, C. (1862). *On the various contrivances by which British and foreign orchids are fertilised by insects.* London, England: John Murray. Retrieved from http://pages.britishlibrary.net/charles.darwin3/orchids/orchids_fm.htm

19. Document, Government Publication

Greene, L. W. (1985). *Exile in paradise: The isolation of Hawaii's leprosy victims and development of Kalaupapa settlement, 1865 to present.* Washington, DC: U.S. Department of the Interior, National Park Service.

20. Document, Pamphlet

Parks Canada. (1999). *Canada's national parks and national historic sites: Directory for the travel trade.* Ottawa, ON: Author.

Citing Web Publications

In APA style, citations for Web documents do not need to include your date of access if you can provide a publication date. However, you do need to provide either the URL from which a source was retrieved or a Digital Object Identifier (DOI). When including a URL or DOI, always insert a break *before* a slash, period, or other punctuation mark.

FIGURE 25.3 CITATION MAP: Citing Part or All of a Website

A citation for a Web publication will have some or all of the following features:

① Name of the author, corporation, organization, editor, or webmaster. For authors and editors, last name first followed by initials.

② Date of publication, in parentheses (year, month, date). If no date is given, write (n.d.) to indicate "no date."

③ Title of the individual page, document, or article.

④ Title of the Website, in italics.

⑤ Retrieval information: date retrieved if the source information is likely to change (e.g., a wiki) and the site's URL; do not add a period at the end of the URL.

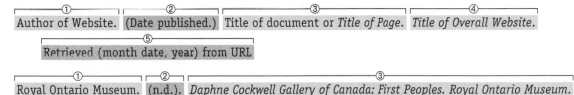

Author of Website. (Date published.) Title of document or *Title of Page*. *Title of Overall Website.*
Retrieved (month date, year) from URL

Royal Ontario Museum. (n.d.). *Daphne Cockwell Gallery of Canada: First Peoples. Royal Ontario Museum.*
Retrieved June 30, 2012, from http://www.rom.on.ca/exhibitions/wculture/index.php

② Date of publication
① Author (organization)
⑤ Date retrieved and URL
④ Title of website
③ Title of page

FIGURE 25.4 CITATION MAP: Citing a Journal Article with a DOI

An article with a DOI retrieved from a database does not require either the database name or your date of retrieval as part of your citation. A citation for such an article does need to include the following features:

① Name of the author (last name, initials)

② Publication date

③ Title of article

④ Title of the journal in italics

⑤ Volume number in italics, and issue number (in parentheses, not italicized)

⑥ Page numbers

⑦ Digital Object Identifier. (It is easiest to cut and paste the DOI directly from the original document into your text.)

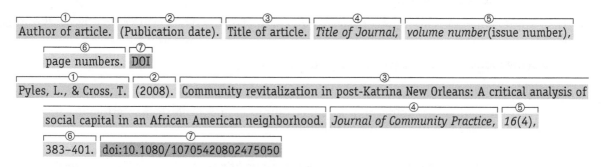

Author of article. (Publication date). Title of article. *Title of Journal, volume number*(issue number), page numbers. DOI

Pyles, L., & Cross, T. (2008). Community revitalization in post-Katrina New Orleans: A critical analysis of social capital in an African American neighborhood. *Journal of Community Practice, 16*(4), 383–401. doi:10.1080/10705420802475050

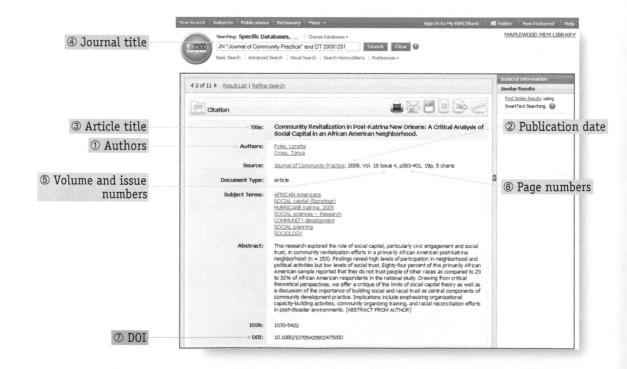

④ Journal title

③ Article title

① Authors

⑤ Volume and issue numbers

⑦ DOI

② Publication date

⑥ Page numbers

21. Website, Corporate Author

Environment Canada. (2011). *Wildlife enforcement.* Retrieved from
http://www.ec.gc.ca/alef-ewe/default.asp

22. Website, Author Unknown

Clara Barton: Founder of the American Red Cross. (n.d.). *American Red Cross Museum.*
Retrieved from http://www.redcross.org/museum/history/claraBarton.asp

23. Article from an Online Periodical

Vaitheeswaran, V. (2009, April 16). Medicine goes digital. *The Economist.* Retrieved
from http://www.economist.com/specialreports

24. Scholarly Journal Article with a Digital Object Identifier (DOI)

Blake, H., & Ooten, M. (2008). Bridging the divide: Connecting feminist histories
and activism in the classroom. *Radical History Review, 2008* (102), 63–72.
doi:10.1215/01636545-2008-013

25. Scholarly Journal Article

The APA no longer requires you to include the name of a database from which
you retrieve a journal article. Use the DOI, if available, for such an article.

Ankers, D., & Jones, S. H. (2009). Objective assessment of circadian activity and
sleep patterns in individuals at behavioural risk of hypomania. *Journal of
Clinical Psychology, 65,* 1071–1086. doi:10.1002/jclp.20608

26. Podcast

Root, B. (2009, January 27). *Just one more book* [Audio podcast]. Retrieved from
http://www.justonemorebook.com/2009/01/27/interview-with-neil-gaiman

Citing Other Kinds of Sources

A variety of other sources are available, each with their own citation style. The citations for these sources tend to include most of the following types of information:

1. Name of the producers, writers, or directors with their roles identified in parentheses (Producer, Writer, Director)

2. Year of release or broadcast, in parentheses

3. Title of the work (italics for a complete work; no italics for a work that is a segment, episode, or part of a whole)

4. Name of episode (first letter of first word capitalized)

5. Title of the program (italicized)

6. Type of program (in brackets), e.g., [Film], [Television series], [Song]

7. City and province or state, if in Canada or the US, or country where work was produced

8. Distributor of the work (e.g., HBO, Miramax, New Line Productions)

9. Retrieval information, for works accessed online

27. Film or Video Recording

Jackson, P. (Director), Osborne, B., Walsh, F., & Sanders, T. (Producers). (2002). *The lord of the rings: The fellowship of the ring* [Motion picture]. Hollywood, CA: New Line Productions.

28. Television or Radio Program

Moscovitch, H. (Writer). (2011). Episode 103 [Radio series episode]. In G. Nelson, A. Pettle, A. Moodie, & J. Sherman (Creators), *Afghanada*. Toronto, ON: CBC Radio.

29. Song or Audio Recording

Myer, L. (1993). Sometimes alone. On *Flatlands* [CD-ROM]. Ames, IA: People's Productions.

30. CD-ROM

Geritch, T. (2000). *Masters of renaissance art* [CD-ROM]. Chicago, IL: Revival Productions.

31. Personal Correspondence, E-Mail, or Interview

In APA style, personal correspondence is not listed in the reference list. Instead, the information from the correspondence should be given in the parenthetical citation:

This result was confirmed by J. Baca (personal communication, March 4, 2004).

A Student's APA-Style Research Paper

The document starting on the next page uses APA style for parenthetical citations and the references list. The student writer followed her professor's requirements for formatting her paper; formatting guidelines in the APA *Publication Manual* are intended for submissions to professional journals.

MyCompLab

For support in meeting this chapter's objectives, follow this path in MyCompLab:

Student Resources → Research → Citing Sources. Review the Instruction and Multimedia Resources about APA style; then complete the Exercises and click on Gradebook to measure your progress.

RUNNING HEAD: ORGANIC FOOD BETTER THAN CONVENTIONAL FOOD?   1

Is Organically Produced Food Better in Terms of Nutrition, Sensory
Appeal, and Safety Than Conventionally Produced Food?

Coralee Miller

University of Guelph Professor Krause Nutrition 445

The *Publication Manual of the APA* and some professors request that "Running Head" precede the abbreviated title on the *first page only*. Others, however, find this unnecessary.

Title page formatted in APA style with abbreviated title as running head. For a professional paper, the writer's affiliation replaces the school and course information.

ORGANIC FOOD BETTER THAN CONVENTIONAL FOOD?   2

Is Organically Produced Food Better in Terms of Nutrition, Sensory
Appeal, and Safety Than Conventionally Produced Food?

> Researched
> information on
> consumer
> preferences.

Over the last decade, the organic food industry has grown rapidly.
Many consumers are seeking out healthier alternatives in their lives,
particularly when it comes to food. Most consumers of organic food
purchase organic as opposed to conventional foods because of their belief
that organic foods are healthier, safer, and taste better (Magkos, Arvaniti,
& Zampelas, 2006). Another reason for choosing organic foods is the belief
that organic food production is less harmful to the environment and more
sustainable (Bourn & Prescott 2002). Many claims to support these beliefs

> Research question.

have been made, but is organic food actually scientifically proven to be
better than conventional food? This essay argues that, despite consumer

> Thesis clearly stated.

perceptions, organically produced food is not significantly more
nutritious, appetizing, or even safer than conventionally produced food.

Organic food is produced using agricultural methods that avoid
synthetic fertilizers, pesticides, growth hormones, antibiotics, genetic

> Multiple sources are
> separated by a
> semicolon.

engineering, and feed additives (Magkos et al., 2006; Winter & Davis, 2006).
Instead, organic farming relies on crop rotations, animal manures, legumes,
green manures, organic wastes, and biological pest control to produce food
that is acceptable for the commercial market (Magkos et al., 2006). During
the production of organic animal products, animals must eat 100% organic
feed in order for products from those animals to be considered organic
(Winter & Davis, 2006). Organic food must be produced in accordance with
standards set out by certifying agencies through the many stages of
production. In the United States, any product that is labelled "100%
organic" must contain only organic ingredients. Products with the label

> This paragraph
> offers an extended
> definition of organic
> food.

"organic" must be made with a minimum of 95% organic contents, and the
remaining 5% are also regulated (Winter & Davis, 2006). All products with
ingredients that are 95% organic or higher may use the United States
Department of Agriculture (USDA) organic seal (Winter & Davis, 2006).

ORGANIC FOOD BETTER THAN CONVENTIONAL FOOD?   3

While no official statements have declared organic food to be healthier than non-organic food, the majority of people who buy organic food believe that it is safer and provides greater health benefits (Bourn & Prescott, 2002; Zhao, Chambers, Matta, Loughin, & Carey, 2007). Though not yet confirmed, a current theory argues that some organic food consumers may reap psychological and even physical benefits due to their belief organic is healthier (Magkos et al., 2006). This health belief may, in essence, produce a placebo effect. The majority of organic food buyers are women, which is likely because women are the primary grocery shoppers in most households and are therefore more informed about organic products than men (Yiridoe, Bonti-Ankomah, & Martin, 2005). Yiridoe et al. (2005) also state that younger consumers are more inclined to choose organic products than the older generation, which could be due to their preference for chemical-free and environmentally friendly lifestyles. Some consumers, while looking to buy organic, purchase conventional foods instead because they find organic foods too expensive or their availability too limited (Yiridoe et al., 2005). Other consumers may not buy organic because they are not well informed about it, and some consumers are skeptical of how strict organic regulations actually are (Yiridoe et al., 2005). Although significant research has examined why people do or do not buy organic food, most of the findings indicate that decisions are based on lifestyle or economic choices rather than factual information.

Nutritive Differences

One of the biggest reasons consumers cite for buying organic is the assumption that organic foods have higher nutritional content and will provide greater health benefits (Bourn & Prescott, 2002). While a variety of studies have been done focusing on a limited number of macronutrients and micronutrients, the general consensus is that

---

Claim or topic sentence.

When author's name appears in the sentence summarizing an entire article, only year is cited parenthetically.

Summary of existing research on consumer attitudes.

Point sentence.

Main headings are centred and bold.

ORGANIC FOOD BETTER THAN CONVENTIONAL FOOD?   4

additional, larger, and more highly controlled studies must be completed

Claim on the
inconclusiveness of
nutritional benefits.

before any results prove conclusive (Bourn & Prescott, 2002; Magkos et
al., 2006). The inconclusive results obtained from nutrient value studies
comparing organic versus conventional foods may be partly attributed to
the many additional aspects of farming that can affect the nutrient
content (Bourn & Prescott, 2002). Some of these factors include
genetics, environment soil type, management practices, and handling,
processing, and storing methods (Bourn & Prescott, 2002). Studies on
nutrient content have shown that organic foods tend to have lower
nitrogen and nitrate contents than their conventionally produced

Multiple authors
listed on a first
reference.

counterparts (Herencia, García-Galavís, Dorado, & Maqueda, 2011).
Although high amounts of dietary nitrate have been associated with
gastric cancer in animals, evidence to support this effect in humans is
lacking (Magkos et al., 2006). Additionally, the consumption of
vegetables has been shown to be protective against gastric cancer,
independent of whether vegetables have a high or low nitrate content
(Magkos et al., 2006). Nutrient studies to date are limited, because they
do not determine the bioavailability of the proposed additional nutrients
(Bourn & Prescott, 2002). A particular type of produce may technically
have a higher nutritive content, but unless the higher content of the
nutrients corresponds with an increased bioavailability, it is of little

Summary of the
research showing
little nutritional
benefit.

significance. Bourn & Prescott (2002) remind their readers that even if a
person's diet is predominately organic, if the diet is unbalanced, any
potential benefits of organic food are likely to be negated.

Sensory Quality Differences

Claim or topic
sentence.

Many consumers purchase organic food because they believe it
appeals more to their senses than conventional food does. In particular,
consumers believe that organic food tastes better than conventional
food. Bourn & Prescott (2002) suggest consumer expectation that
organic food will taste better may be due to the belief that more

ORGANIC FOOD BETTER THAN CONVENTIONAL FOOD? 5

expensive products are of higher quality or that chemicals in conventional foods impart unpleasant tastes. Though many subjects of sensory quality tests enter with the belief that organic produce tastes better than conventional produce, findings from these studies reveal that neither food category was unanimously preferred over the other (Bourn & Prescott, 2002; Zhao et al., 2007). Again, many factors contribute to the appeal of the final product, and without strict controls over these factors, sensory quality study results may be invalid. The belief that organic produce tastes better may simply be due to the "organic" label (Bourn & Prescott, 2002). Bourn and Prescott (2002) found that subjects showed a preference for products with the label "organic" over unlabelled products, even when the products were the same. Much of the research surrounding taste preference has resulted in conflicting evidence, so generalizations cannot yet be made.

Point sentence summarizing the subjective appeal of organic food.

Safety Differences

Perhaps the biggest issue surrounding the choice of organically produced over conventionally produced food is safety. While safety may be considered in terms of environmental safety or production safety, this section will focus on safety with regard to food consumption. Three areas of food safety will be discussed: pesticide use, toxin content, and pathogenic contamination. Because of the limited pesticide use in organic food production, organic food does, in fact, have much lower levels of pesticide residue than conventionally grown food. However, residue amounts on conventionally grown food are generally far below the maximum limit at which food is still considered safe to eat (Magkos et al., 2006). Furthermore, organically produced food is unlikely to remain completely free of pesticide throughout its entire production cycle. Organic crops may become contaminated by runoff water from ponds or neighbouring non-organic fields, contaminated groundwater, pesticide spray via wind drift, or cross-contamination during transport, processing,

Transition and initial claim regarding pesticide levels.

ORGANIC FOOD BETTER THAN CONVENTIONAL FOOD?   6

and storage (Magkos et al., 2006). Over the past decade, the amount of pesticides used on conventional crops has dropped dramatically (Magkos et al., 2006). This trend is likely to continue, but even now the difference in amounts of pesticide residue found on conventional and organic food seems insignificant. The variation in amount of residue between the two types of production may, in fact, be less than the variation between two crops using the same technique (Magkos et al., 2006). Magkos et al. (2006) suggest that it is not chemical residue that poses the greatest risk of contamination but rather microbial content, as demonstrated by recent food-borne disease outbreaks.

Toxin formation has been a major concern in relation to food production. One hypothesis regarding toxin formation suggests that organic plants are more susceptible to stress than their conventional counterparts (Winter & Davis, 2006). This proposed stress, caused by attacks from insects, weeds, and plant pathogens, is the result of limited use of insecticides, herbicides, and fungicides. Stress from these factors may cause the plants to increase their own chemical defences (Winter & Davis, 2006). These chemical defences, though sometimes seen as causing a beneficial increase of antioxidants, may also result in elevation of other metabolites that may be toxic rather than helpful (Winter & Davis, 2006). While these toxins are natural, to suggest that a toxin is safer than a pesticide simply because it is "natural" is illogical. Organic farmers sometimes use breeds that are more pest-resistant in place of pesticides. Studies have revealed that this practice can cause adverse health effects. For example, under stressful conditions such as fungal attack, celery plants can synthesize metabolites that increase their pest-resistance but are also known to cause contact dermatitis in humans (Winter & Davis, 2006). Magkos et al. (2006) suggest that the US population may be at greater risk from an unbalanced intake of

---

Point sentence on the extended summary of Magkos et al.'s study.

Claim regarding toxin levels in organic produce.

ORGANIC FOOD BETTER THAN CONVENTIONAL FOOD?   7

nutrients than from the potential increased intake of toxic substances. Various practices to reduce plant stress are used in both organic and conventional production, so the generalization that organic plants face greater stress may soon be incorrect (Winter & Davis, 2006). Currently, however, the toxin production of organic plants must be considered a potential safety issue.

Some studies have shown a greater prevalence of bacterial organisms in organic chickens compared to their conventional equivalents; Magkos et al. (2006) suggest that this observation may be due to organic chickens' free access to soil and water. In contrast, conventional flocks are kept contained, and thus, controlled. It has been suggested that organic food is at greater risk of animal fecal contamination because of its heavy use of manure as fertilizer (Bourn & Prescott, 2002). These claims may be unsubstantiated; certified organic producers must adhere to strict specifications regarding the use of animal manure, but conventional producers (who also use animal manure frequently) do not have such requirements (Bourn & Prescott, 2002). Due to this difference in regulations, conventional growers may not treat animal manure for bacterial contamination as thoroughly as organic growers do. Regardless, organic food may be at greater risk for fecal contamination as a result of the increased interaction between crops and animals. Because pesticides are prohibited, organic crops may come in more frequent contact with animals, and subsequently their feces (Bourn & Prescott, 2002). One final reason that people may believe organic food poses a higher risk for bacterial contamination is that organic is often associated with the term "'natural," which in some cases means unprocessed. Pasteurization, however, is permitted for organic food because it uses heat rather than chemicals (Bourn & Prescott, 2002). Despite claims of greater microbial contamination,

Point sentence on how preceding evidence shows toxin levels may in fact be greater in organic food.

Claim regarding bacterial levels in organic food.

Point sentence on the inconclusive claims regarding the bacterial risks of organic food.

ORGANIC FOOD BETTER THAN CONVENTIONAL FOOD?   8

current studies are not conclusive as to whether organic food poses a greater microbial risk (Winter & Davis, 2006).

Conclusion

Organic food continues to gain popularity in the diet choices of North Americans, and this increasing demand for organic food will foster further research to investigate organic food claims. Results from recent studies have neither substantiated nor dismissed current claims made about the healthiness and safety of organic food, and these claims remain controversial. When the USDA standards came into effect, the USDA Secretary clarified that organic certification was a production philosophy and organic labelling did not imply a superior product (Winter & Davis, 2006). The difficulty with publicizing findings from single studies is that their results are not sufficient to make adequate recommendations and often mislead the public (Magkos et al., 2006). Safe production practices are required for all commercially produced food, whether organic or conventional (Bourn & Prescott, 2002). The number of factors that affect attributes of food, such as growing conditions, management practices, transportation, and storage, make it difficult to conduct a "perfect" controlled study (Bourn & Prescott, 2002). Based on current literature, it does not appear that organically produced food is significantly more nutritious, appealing, or safe than conventionally produced food.

Conclusion on how research shows organic food is neither better nor worse than conventional food.

References

Bourn, D., & Prescott, J. (2002). A comparison of the nutritional value, sensory qualities, and food safety of organically and conventionally produced foods. *Critical Reviews in Food Science and Nutrition, 42*(1), 1–34. doi:10.1080/10408690290825439

Herencia, J. F., García-Galavís, P. A., Dorado, J. A. R., & Maqueda, C. (2011). Comparison of nutritional quality of the crops grown in an organic and conventional fertilized soil. *Scientia Horticulturae, 129*(4), 882–888. doi:10.1016/j.scienta.2011.04.008

Magkos, F., Arvaniti, F., & Zampelas, A. (2006). Organic food: Buying more safety or just peace of mind? A critical review of the literature. *Critical Reviews in Food Science and Nutrition, 46*(1), 23–56. doi:10.1080/10408690490911846

Winter, C. K., & Davis, S. F. (2006). Organic foods. *Journal of Food Science, 71*(9), 117–124. doi:10.1111/j.1750-3841.2006.00196.x

Yiridoe, E. K., Bonti-Ankomah, S., & Martin, R. C. (2005). Comparison of consumer perceptions and preference toward organic versus conventionally produced foods: A review and update of the literature. *Renewable Agriculture and Food Systems, 20*(4), 193–205. doi:10.1079/RAF2005113

Zhao, X., Chambers, E., Matta, Z., Loughin, T. M., & Carey, E. E. (2007). Consumer sensory analysis of organically and conventionally grown vegetables. *Journal of Food Science, 72*(2), 87–91. doi:10.1111/j.1750-3841.2007.00277.x

References begin on a new page. All cited works are included and listed in alphabetical order by author.

DOI is included whenever available.

6 Getting Your Ideas Out There

PART OUTLINE

CHAPTER 26

Using the Internet   480

CHAPTER 27

Creating a Portfolio   488

CHAPTER 28

Succeeding on Essay Exams   498

CHAPTER 29

Presenting Your Work   509

Your thoughts and ideas deserve a wider audience. **GET YOUR WRITING OUT THERE** *for others to discuss, debate, and respond. These chapters will show you how to take your writing public.*

26

Using the
Internet

In this chapter, you will learn how to:

* create a social networking site.
* start your own blog.
* contribute an article to a wiki and upload a video.

Today people are reading and writing more than ever. They write e-mails, keep up with current events on websites, update their *Facebook* profiles, share their opinions on blogs, and create podcasts and *YouTube* videos. They are texting with their friends and microblogging with *Twitter*.

In this chapter, you will learn how to use the Internet and new media to put your writing out in the public sphere. There are now more ways than ever to publicize your writing and make an impact on the world through your words.

Is This Writing?

Maybe you are wondering if some of the new media tools we will discuss in this chapter can still be considered writing. Blogging looks like writing, but what about social networking sites or video sharing sites? Can we still call that writing?

We live in a time of great technological change, so we need to expand and change our understanding of what it means to "write" and be "literate." This kind of revolution has happened before. When the printing press was introduced in Europe in the fifteenth century, it also dramatically changed people's ideas about what writing looked like. Before the printing press, "writing" meant handwritten texts, such as letters, written records, and ornate illuminated books. The printing press democratized the written word, giving the public access to ideas and texts that were once available only to a privileged few. Then society's understanding of writing changed to fit the new technology.

More than likely, the monks working in the scriptoriums of medieval Europe would have been mystified and anxious about the kinds of writing that we take for granted today. Mass-produced books, newspapers, magazines, junk mail, brochures, posters, and other kinds of writing would have seemed very odd and even threatening to them. They would have seen computers as a form of magic or even witchcraft.

So it's not surprising that today we wonder whether these new media tools are really forms of writing. More than likely, within your lifetime, writing will change in ways that make it look very different than it does now. The new technologies described in this chapter are only the beginning of that change. Also remember that many forms of online writing are popular rather than academic, so you will want to write with the appropriate audience in mind.

Creating a Social Networking Site

Let's start with the easiest way to go public with your writing—creating a profile on a social networking website like *Facebook, MySpace, Google+, Bebo, LinkedIn,* or *Spoke*. The first four, *Facebook, MySpace, Google+,* and *Bebo,* can help you connect and stay in touch with your friends and other kindred souls. Increasingly, these social networking sites are being used by nonprofit organizations, political movements, and companies to stay in touch with interested people. For example, your college or university may have a *Facebook* or *MySpace* site that lets you keep in touch with what is happening on campus.

LinkedIn and *Spoke* are career-related social networking sites that will help you connect with colleagues, business associates, and potential employers.

Choose the Best Site for You

Each social networking site is a little different. As you choose which site is best for you, think about your purpose for having a social networking site. Right now, you probably just want to keep in touch with your friends. But as you move through your post-secondary studies and into the workplace, your site may become a way to network with other people in your field and share your ideas. Also think about the kinds of writing you want to do. Some social networking sites are better at supporting longer genres of writing, such as analyses, reviews, position papers, and other kinds of extended texts.

Be Selective About Your "Friends"

Carefully select your "friends." It's tempting to add everyone you know, but that isn't the best approach. Again, think about the purpose of your site. You can only keep in touch with a certain number of people, so be selective. You don't want so-called "friends" writing things on your wall that would make you look bad to important people at your university or to future employers.

Add Regularly to Your Profile

Write regularly on your site and keep it up to date. Express your opinions. Share your ideas. Discuss current events or your passions. However, don't put any private information on your profile, such as contact information or anything that would allow a stranger to track you down. Any pictures you put on your page should be appropriate for anyone to see (because they will).

Start thinking of your site as more than a way to keep in touch with friends. Your site will likely evolve into a tool for staying in touch with people in your academic field, other professionals and clients, and people in your community. It will be less about what you did last weekend and more about your long-term interests, your career, and how you're making a difference in the world.

Starting Your Own Blog

A blog is a website in which a writer keeps a public journal of his or her experiences, thoughts, and opinions. Blogs are usually made up of words and sentences, but there are also an increasing number of photo blogs, video blogs, and audio blogs.

Choose a Host Site for Your Blog

Don't pay for a blogging site. Some popular free blogging sites include *Blogger, Wordpress, Blogsome,* and *Moveable Type.* Each one has strengths and weaknesses, so you might look at them all to determine which one will fit your needs and reach the people you want to speak to. Another kind of blog is a "microblog," which only allows a small number of words per post. *Twitter* was the groundbreaking microblogging site, but other microblogging services are now available.

Begin Your Blog

Once you pick a host site, it will ask you for some basic information, such as your name, your blog's name, and an e-mail address. You will then be shown a menu of templates that are available (Figure 26.1). Pick one that fits your personality and the kinds of topics you want to discuss on your blog.

Compose, Edit, and Publish Your Ideas. On your blogging site, you will see tabs or buttons on the screen that allow you to "compose," "edit," and "publish" your comments. Type some of your thoughts into the Compose screen and hit the Post or Publish button. Your words should appear on your blog. Keep adding more comments when you feel the urge.

Personalize Your Blog

Blogging sites will allow you to add photographs, profiles, polls, newsreels, icons, and other gadgets to your blog's layout. Pick features that are appropriate for the kind of blog you want to create, and don't go overboard. You don't want the extra stuff on your site to distract readers from your ideas and arguments.

FIGURE 26.1 Choosing a Blog Template

The template you choose for your blog should fit your personality and the kinds of topics you want to discuss on your blog.

Let Others Join the Conversation. The initial settings for your blogging site will strictly control access to your blog. You and you alone will be able to post comments on your blog. As you grow more comfortable with your blog, though, you might want to loosen up your settings to allow others to write comments. If so, you should first decide who will be able to make comments on your blog.

When starting out, only allow "registered users" (i.e., people who you give permission to comment on your blog) to add comments. Some bloggers set their blog to allow "anyone" to comment. That's risky, because strangers and spammers may contribute posts that annoy or embarrass you. If you allow *everyone* to comment, you will need to spend a great amount of time cleaning up your blog.

As you are blogging, keep in mind that your blog is a public site. In other words, anyone can read what you have put on your page. So keep the blog interesting, and don't say anything that puts you in a bad light. Always remember that current or future employers may discover your blog, so you want to only say things that you would say directly to your current or future boss. Plus, always remember that you can be sued for writing slanderous or libellous things about other people. So keep it clean and truthful.

Writing Articles for Wikis

Wikis are collaboratively written Internet sites that allow users to add and edit content. *Wikipedia* is, of course, one of the more popular wikis. It is an online encyclopedia that allows users to add, edit, and manage information on just about any topic. Other wikis are also popular, such as *eHow, wikiHow, Wikitravel, CookbookWiki, ProductWiki, Uncyclopedia,* and *Wikicars.* Your professors may ask you to add material to one of these popular wikis or contribute to a wiki dedicated to your class.

Like any user, you have the ability to add articles to these wikis and edit the existing content. Here's how to add an article to the wiki of your choice:

Write the Article

Like any kind of writing, you should begin by thinking about your topic, angle, purpose, readers, and the contexts in which your article will be needed or used. Research your topic thoroughly, draft the article, and edit it carefully. Include any appropriate graphics. You should also have your sources available, so they can be listed in "References," "External Links," and "Further Reading" sections of the article. It is best to write your wiki article with a word processor. This will allow you to do all the drafting and revising needed before you add it to the wiki.

Above all, you want to make sure your article is interesting and factually accurate. If your article is about something trivial or mundane, the wiki administrator will simply delete it. If your article is factually inaccurate, other wiki users will rewrite your work.

Remember, though, that this correction process can take time. If you are using a wiki for your research, it is best to verify the information using another source.

Add Your Article to the Wiki

Look for the button on the wiki that says, "Create an article" or "Start the X article" in which X is the name of your topic. Most wikis will expect you to have an account if you want to add an article. Once you log in, the wiki will provide a box where you can cut and paste your article from your word processor.

Edit and proofread your article. Then click the Save Page button. At this point, your article will be added to the wiki.

Other people can revise and edit your article, so you should return to your article periodically to make sure someone hasn't altered it to say something inaccurate. You might even be pleasantly surprised to find that someone has expanded your article, providing information you didn't know about.

Putting Videos and Podcasts on the Internet

You can upload videos to websites like *YouTube, MySpace Videos, MSN Video, Yahoo! Video, Joost,* and *Metacafe.* Some popular podcasting sites include *Podcast Alley, iTunes, Digg,* and *Podcast Pickle.* Here is how to put your video or podcast on one of these sites.

Create Your Video or Record Your Podcast

Making a video or podcast takes some preparation if you want to make something worth watching or hearing. As with any kind of writing, you should first consider your topic, angle, purpose, readers, and the contexts in which your video or podcast will be experienced. Then invent the content and draft a script. Think of the most appropriate background or scenery for your video.

Above all, don't bore your audience. Good planning and tight scripting will allow you to make something worth watching or listening to.

Edit Your Work

Edit your work with video or sound editing software. Some good video editing software packages include *Corel VideoStudio, Microsoft Movie Maker, Adobe Premiere, Final Cut,* and *iMovie.* The most common sound editing software packages for editing podcasts include *Adobe Audition, Audacity, GarageBand,* and *Cubase.* One or more of these editing tools may have already been preloaded onto your computer, so look for them in your applications before you buy something new.

Upload Your Video or Podcast

If your video or podcast is ready to be uploaded, then go to the "upload" link in your account. The site will ask you for a title and description, as well as some keywords called "tags." Try to include as many keywords as you can. That way, people who are searching the website will be more likely to come across your video or podcast.

Again, always remember that these sites are public. So don't show, do, or say anything that is illegal, unethical, or embarrassing. Be very careful not to give too much personal information. Even if you put limits on who can access your videos and podcasts, someone else, including your friends, might share them with others.

The social media tools you use to manage your personal life can be powerful platforms for sharing your ideas and arguments with a much larger community. Here's what you can do with these tools.

CREATE Your Profile on a Social Networking Site

Choose the social networking site that is most appropriate for your lifestyle and thoughts. Pick one that has the audience you most want to reach.

BLOG About What Matters to You

You're more likely to update your blog often—and write with a passion that engages and involves readers—if you choose a topic of ongoing personal interest.

SHARE Your Online Compositions

Post your work for others to see. But be strategic about who can see or follow you and how (or if) others can comment or participate on your site.

PARTICIPATE in Knowledge Making on a Wiki Site

Share what you're learning in school by writing entries for wikis—or by correcting erroneous information. Be sure your information is accurate, well-researched, and useful to others.

BROADCAST Your Ideas to the World

Use video and audio recording technologies to capture places, events, and people of interest to you and the community. Upload your work to a site where it can be widely shared and discussed.

1. With your group in class, talk about the different ways you use the new media tools discussed in this chapter. Discuss how these media tools have changed the way people communicate in your lifetime.

2. How are social networking sites, blogging, and audio and video sharing changing the workplace? How do members of your group expect new media to shape their careers?

3. Do you think people learn social skills online that they can use elsewhere? Or, are social media actually harmful to people's abilities to interact in the real world?

1. If you already have a social media site, revise it in ways that would make it appealing (or at least acceptable) to a future employer or your professor.

2. With a group of people from your class, shoot a small video or record a podcast. Upload the video or podcast to a video sharing website and send a link to your professor.

3. With a group in your class, think of a topic that interests all of you. Then, using three different wikis, read the articles written about that topic. What facts do these wiki articles have in common? What facts are different or missing from one or more of the articles? How do the articles approach the topic from different angles, and what do they choose to highlight?

1. **Learn about a new media tool.** Write a review of one of the new media tools discussed in this chapter. Discuss its future and how you think it will affect your life and your career.

2. **Write your ideas in a blog.** For two weeks, keep a blog in which you write about anything that interests you. Then write an e-mail to your professor in which you explain why you did or didn't enjoy blogging, and whether you think you will continue blogging in the future.

MyCompLab

For support in meeting this chapter's objectives, follow this path in MyCompLab:

Student Resources → Writing → Writing Samples. Review the Multimedia resources about websites; then complete the Exercises and click on Gradebook to measure your progress.

27

Creating a Portfolio

In this chapter, you will learn how to:

- collect and select your materials for your portfolio.
- write a reflection on your work.
- present your materials for academic and career-related purposes.

P ortfolios include selections of your best work, packaged for people who need to understand or evaluate your background, abilities, knowledge, and potential. They also give you a chance to reflect on your writing, leading to deeper, more permanent learning. As a student, you may be asked to create a portfolio for a specific course, or you may be required to compile a collection of your work as a "capstone" to your studies in your major.

Your portfolio will also be an important part of your job application package, because it allows you to show interviewers examples of your work. After you are hired, your portfolio may be used to track your professional development and determine whether you receive a raise or a promotion.

Two Basic Kinds of Portfolios

There are two basic types of portfolios: *learning portfolios* and *showcase portfolios*.

Learning Portfolios. Learning portfolios focus on your progress toward mastering specific knowledge and abilities. Your learning portfolio is like a movie that leads your readers through a course or your post-secondary career to witness the progress you have made. Your portfolio shows where you started and where you are now, demonstrating what you have learned. Learning portfolios include finished documents, and they often include drafts of work and brainstorming notes.

Showcase Portfolios. Showcase portfolios display only finished products that demonstrate your work at its best. They are designed to highlight the knowledge and abilities

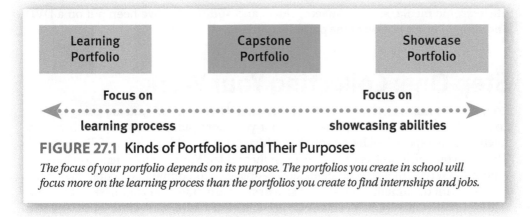

FIGURE 27.1 Kinds of Portfolios and Their Purposes

The focus of your portfolio depends on its purpose. The portfolios you create in school will focus more on the learning process than the portfolios you create to find internships and jobs.

that you have mastered to this point in your career. They are like a snapshot that provides a rich and detailed depiction of your skills and know-how at the present moment.

A third kind of portfolio, usually called a "capstone portfolio" is a hybrid of these two (Figure 27.1). Like a learning portfolio, a capstone portfolio is designed to show your progress toward mastering specific knowledge and abilities. However, capstone portfolios usually do not include drafts or notes because they are designed to show your work at its best.

Getting Started on Your Portfolio

Creating a portfolio is not difficult, but it does take some time and planning. Here are four simple steps to follow:

1. **Collect** your work in an ongoing "archive" folder on your computer's hard drive or in a file folder. Each item in your portfolio is called an *artifact*.

2. **Select** those artifacts that best exemplify the knowledge and ability you want your portfolio to exhibit. Your selections depend on who will be viewing your portfolios and why.

3. **Reflect** on what is in the portfolio. Usually professors or supervisors will ask you to write a brief reflection that introduces and reviews the materials in your portfolio.

4. **Present** the portfolio as a complete package. Depending on how it will be used, your portfolio might be print, online, or multimedia.

Your portfolio should include a wide collection of artifacts, including anything you want to show your readers. It should include documents, of course, but it might also include photographs, presentations, and projects. It could also include a variety of electronic media, such as images, video, and audio that have been put on a DVD and slipped into a pocket of the portfolio or folder.

Step One: Collecting Your Work

Your archive is like a storehouse of raw material. Here is where you are going to keep copies of your work until you need them for your portfolio. To start your archive, you might create a special folder on your hard drive called "Archive" or "Portfolio Archive." Then, as you finish projects, save a copy in that folder. Your school might also have an e-portfolio service that gives students storage space on its computers for their materials.

For print documents, you should also designate a drawer in your desk or file cabinet for archive materials. Keep any projects, awards, letters, or other career-related documents in this drawer. Then at the end of each semester, you can look through these items and decide what to add to your portfolio and what to file for later use.

Right now, early in your post-secondary career, is the best time to create an archive. That way, you can get into the habit of saving your best work. An added benefit to starting your archive right now is that you will always know where your best work is stored. The worst time to start an archive is when you are getting ready to graduate. At that point, much of your best work will have been forgotten, lost, or thrown out.

Archiving for a Specific Course

In some courses, your professor will require you to complete a portfolio that shows your work from the class. Make sure you understand what kinds of materials you will need to save for your portfolio. Some professors will ask that you save everything, from notes, to drafts, to polished copies. Other professors may just want final versions of your work in the portfolio. Here are some things you might be asked to save:

- All notes, including class notes, brainstorming, freewrites, journalling, and so on

- Rough drafts, informal writing, responses, and perhaps your professors' written comments on your drafts

- Peer review, both reviews you've done for others and reviews others have done for you

- Final drafts

- Other electronic material, such as images, multimedia, blogs, web-based discussions, and so on

Archiving for Your Post-Secondary Career

Your department or school may ask you to create a portfolio at various stages of your program. For instance, at the end of your second or third year, your institution may require you to submit a portfolio that illustrates your ability to write well and think critically. Your department or program may require you to create a portfolio that shows you are ready to be admitted to the major. And at the end of your undergraduate years, you may be asked to create a capstone portfolio that illustrates what you have accomplished in your major field of study.

Items that you should save for this portfolio include the following:

- Awards or recognition of any kind
- Letters of reference from professors
- Scholarship letters and letters of acceptance
- Materials and evaluations from internships, co-ops, or jobs
- Copies of exams (preferably ones you did well on)
- Evidence of participation in clubs or special events and volunteer work

You never know what you might need, so keep anything that might be useful. If you regularly save these materials, you will be amazed at how much you did while you were in school.

Archiving for Your Professional Career

Employers often ask job applicants to bring a professional portfolio to interviews to present their work. It is also common for professionals to maintain a portfolio for promotions, performance reviews, and job searches. A professional portfolio is likely to include these materials:

- Reflective cover letter that introduces the portfolio by describing your career goals, education, work experiences, skills, and special abilities
- Résumé
- Examples of written work, presentations, and other materials such as images, links to websites, and so on
- Diplomas, certificates, and awards
- Letters of reference

For job interviews, you should create two versions of your professional portfolio. The first version, which you should never give away, should hold all your original materials. The second version, called a "giveaway portfolio," should have copies of your materials that you can leave with interviewers.

Step Two: Selecting the Best Artifacts

Once you have created an archive, it's time to actually begin the process of creating a portfolio. Keep in mind that a single archive can supply the material for any number of portfolios, each with a different purpose and audience.

Start by considering which artifacts in your archive will allow you to achieve your portfolio's purpose and meet the needs of your readers. Select items carefully because the best examples of your work need to stand out, not get buried in a stack of documents. Your professors may specify a certain number of documents, for instance, to promote the habit of selecting judiciously. A prospective employer will likely only have time to review a small number of items. Choose a handful of key documents that help you achieve your purpose and catch your reader's interest.

Step Three: Reflecting on Your Work

You may be asked to write two kinds of reflections for your portfolio, depending on how it will be used:

Learning-Focused Reflections. These reflections tell the story of your progress in a class or an academic program. They show that you have mastered certain knowledge and abilities. They also give you a chance to understand the course objectives more thoroughly and to master the course content even more completely.

Mastery-Focused Reflections. These reflections focus more on demonstrating how well you have mastered certain bodies of knowledge and abilities. In this kind of reflection, your readers want you to explain what you can do and how well you can do it.

Your Reflection as an Argument

Like any argument, your reflection should state a claim and provide support for that claim. Whether you are creating a learning portfolio or a showcase portfolio, your reflection needs to state an overall claim (i.e., a main point or thesis). Then the reflection should use the items in the portfolio as evidence to support your claim.

Demonstrating these features, Figure 27.2 shows a learning-focused reflection written by a student for a first-year writing course. Notice how this reflection makes a claim about the writer's experience, knowledge, and abilities, and then goes on to point readers toward specific places in the portfolio where they can find evidence that supports that claim. This reflection, for a writing course portfolio, focuses on process and progress.

Step Four: Presenting Your Materials

How you present your work is very important. So when assembling your portfolio, don't just throw your materials into a manila envelope or fasten them together with a binder clip. That looks sloppy and unprofessional. You need to present your materials in an organized and attractive way, so your readers can find the documents they want to see. A three-ring binder or a nice folder would work well. Another option is to create an electronic or e-portfolio that you can put on the Internet or on a disc.

MEMORANDUM

Date: December 2, 2012

To: Greg Evans

From: Josh Kotobi

Subject: Portfolio Memo

English 101 helped me improve my writing in every way, including my rhetoric, grammar, style, and understanding of genres and how to use them. The class objectives included learning about many different genres, and how to present ideas, information, and arguments in each genre. In this cover letter, I will explain my progress and learning in terms of each of the five learning goals for the course.

Reading and Analysis

We read a variety of literary and other writing, and we worked on summarizing, interpreting, evaluating, and synthesizing the ideas in these writings. These activities expanded our writing skills as we learned how to write in different genres and styles. The close analysis of each of these texts allowed us to better understand what constitutes effective writing and ineffective writing.

I believe that the documents that show my progress and ability best in this area are the first and final drafts of my position paper. In the first draft, I just dismissed David Brooks's whole argument. I barely mentioned it, and then didn't even deal with his points. But in the final draft, you'll see that on the first two pages, I summarize, paraphrase, and quote David Brooks's article about marriage. I worked

> States purpose and main point.

> Highlights learning goals and uses documents to support claims.

(continued)

FIGURE 27.2 A Student's Learning-Focused Reflection

This reflection, created for a course in first-year writing, exemplifies one approach to the cover letter. The student's professor asked for cover letters that described students' learning progress in terms of the five main course goals.

FIGURE 27.2
A Student's Learning-Focused Reflection

(continued)

very hard to explain his arguments fairly, and I even conceded two points that were very strong. Even so, I went on to use my analysis of his argument to position my own. I didn't just bounce off Brooks's argument—I incorporated it into mine to make my position stronger.

[Kotobi goes on to discuss the other learning goals of the course, omitted here.]

All in all, bit by bit, week by week, I made progress with my writing. The first draft of my first paper, as you can see, was really bad. I was just writing automatically without even thinking. But I think you'll find that as the semester progressed, I wrote more thoughtfully as I learned to frame problems and use the ideas of the authors I read. I'm very pleased about the progress I've made and feel much better about doing well in the rest of my courses.

> Finishes with main point and looks to the future.

For a Specific Course. Most portfolios for a single course are organized chronologically from the earliest documents to the most recent documents. Your reflection should appear first as an introduction to the portfolio. And if you are asked to include drafts of papers, you should put them *behind* the final versions, not in front of them.

For a Capstone Course. A portfolio for a capstone course can be organized in a variety of ways. You could organize it by courses in your major, giving each course its own part and arranging the parts in numerical order. Or you could organize the portfolio by genres (i.e., reviews, analyses, reports, proposals, and so on). Drafts are not typically included in capstone portfolios.

For a Job Application Packet. Portfolios used for job searches typically follow the organization of a résumé. After your reflection, you should include parts like Education, Related Coursework, Work Experience, Skills, Awards, and Activities. Each part should have its own divider with a tab.

If you will be presenting your portfolio in person (e.g., in an interview or to a group), you should organize your material in a way that helps you verbally explain your background and experiences. It should also look professional and purposeful.

Creating an E-Portfolio

Increasingly, people are going electronic with their portfolios. Making an e-portfolio is not difficult, especially if you know how to create a basic website or if you have access to an e-portfolio service at your university.

Electronic portfolios have several advantages:

- They can be accessed from anywhere there is a networked computer, including a professor's or interviewer's office.

- They can include multimedia texts such as movies, presentations, and links to websites you have created.

- They can include scanned-in documents that show comments that others have handwritten on your work.

- They provide interactivity for the reader. For example, the reflective letter can link directly to the documents in the portfolio or to items on the Internet.

- They include materials and links to information that would not typically be found in a nonelectronic portfolio. For example, you might put links to your university and academic department to help interviewers learn about your educational background.

- They can be updated easily, while older versions can be archived.

- They provide customized access features so that different readers can or cannot see specific parts of the portfolio.

- They eliminate copying costs.

Some e-portfolio services even allow you to maintain an electronic archive from which you can create a virtually limitless number of e-portfolios, each targeted for a specific purpose and audience.

Keeping Your Portfolio Up to Date

This term, your professor may be asking you to create a portfolio only for your writing class. Right now, though, would be a good opportunity to also create an archive for your portfolio that you can use throughout your post-secondary career and beyond.

Each semester, spend a little time keeping your portfolio up to date. Add items that show your knowledge and abilities. Archive documents that have been eclipsed by better work. Look for chances to create documents that fill out any gaps in your portfolio. You can also find opportunities to add to your portfolio by joining clubs, doing volunteer work, and completing internships or co-ops.

It only takes an hour or so each term to keep your portfolio up to date, but you will be thankful you did, especially when you are nearing graduation and starting to look for a job.

Use this guide to help you begin and complete your portfolio.

COLLECT Your Work in an Archive

Get into the habit of saving your documents and projects in an archive. For a specific course, you may want to save *everything,* from notes to rough drafts to final drafts, from print documents to audio files to images to movies. For a capstone portfolio in the middle or at the end of your academic career, you will want to save a variety of examples of your best work. Some schools allow you to store your work in an electronic archive.

SELECT the Works for a Specific Type of Portfolio

When you have a specific type of portfolio in mind, start selecting the works from your archive that will help you to achieve your purpose and that will be most useful for your readers.

REFLECT on What the Portfolio Shows: Your Learning Process, Your Abilities, and Your Experience

Every portfolio needs some kind of reflection or cover letter that introduces readers to the portfolio. In your reflection, make your argument about what the portfolio shows by pointing out to readers what they should notice.

PRESENT Your Portfolio

If you're using a binder or folder for your portfolio, include a table of contents and tabbed section dividers. If you're creating an e-portfolio, use an attractive webpage design, links, and an easy-to-use navigation system.

KEEP Your Portfolio Up to Date

Revisit your portfolio at the end of each term. It will be useful when you begin your job search. Many professionals maintain an ongoing portfolio for career development, promotions, and new opportunities.

1. Brainstorm the development of a portfolio for this course or another course. Describe to your group how you would collect, select, reflect on, and present your work.

2. In your group, discuss the differences between a learning and a showcase portfolio. Which are you most comfortable with? Which do you think would be most appropriate for this course?

3. Imagine that your major requires that you create a capstone portfolio, including what you learned and how you learned it. Make a list of the kinds of artifacts that you will want to have saved for this portfolio, with a brief explanation of what each artifact would show about you.

Talk About This

1. Analyze the rhetorical situation for a job interview portfolio. Briefly, write down notes that define the topic, angle, purpose, readers, and contexts for this kind of portfolio. Also, discuss how the rhetorical situation might change to suit different kinds of job interviews.

2. Go online and find an e-portfolio created by a university or college student. What kinds of artifacts are included? Is there anything surprising about the documents or projects the student has included? How is the portfolio organized and designed? Does the organization make things easy to find?

3. Go online and find at least two professional e-portfolios from people who are pursuing a career like the one you want to pursue. What is included in their portfolios? How well does the cover letter introduce and explain the contents of the portfolio?

Try This Out

1. **Create a mini-portfolio.** With your most recent assignment in this course, create a mini-portfolio that charts your progress from prewriting through drafts and feedback to final drafts. Write a cover letter in which you reflect on your writing process for this assignment. In your reflection, make a claim about your learning and support it.

2. **Critique an e-portfolio on the Internet.** Find an interesting e-portfolio on the Internet. Write a three page rhetorical analysis in which you analyze its effectiveness. How does the author use reasoning (*logos*) to demonstrate his or her knowledge and abilities? How does he or she build up a sense of authority (*ethos*)? Where, if any-place, does the author use emotion (*pathos*) to add personality to the portfolio?

Write This

> ## MyCompLab
>
> For support in meeting this chapter's objectives, follow this path in MyCompLab:
>
> Portfolio → Portfolio Building Tips. Review the Instruction and Multimedia resources about building a portfolio; then select Build a New Portfolio to build your own portfolio.

28

Succeeding on
Essay Exams

In this chapter, you will learn how to:

- prepare yourself to succeed on an essay examination.
- begin the exam with confidence, while budgeting your time.
- organize your ideas so you can answer questions quickly and effectively.

Taking essay exams can be a little stressful, but once you learn a few helpful strategies, they will be much easier. You can succeed on essay exams by using some of the time-tested rhetorical strategies you have already learned in this book.

Keep in mind that professors use essay exams to evaluate how well you understand the course materials, how you organize ideas, and whether you can apply what you learned. Exams give you opportunities to demonstrate higher-order thinking skills, such as interpreting ideas, applying concepts to new situations, analyzing solutions, synthesizing knowledge, and evaluating beliefs. They are another way of demonstrating your knowledge and expressing your ideas to an audience.

This chapter will help you succeed by showing you what to expect in essay exams and providing strategies that will help you prepare for and write them. You will learn a four-stage process for doing well on essay exams: preparing, starting the exam, answering the questions, and finishing the exam (Figure 28.1).

Preparing for an Essay Exam

Studying course materials closely and taking good notes during lectures are important first steps for succeeding on exams. Be sure to review key readings and check to see if sample exams are available. In addition, though, you should prepare for an essay exam by *being active* with the material. Here are some strategies for doing so:

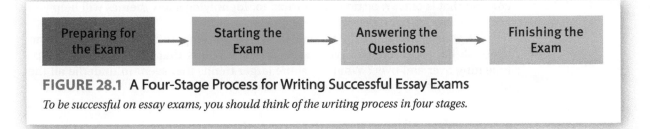

FIGURE 28.1 A Four-Stage Process for Writing Successful Essay Exams

To be successful on essay exams, you should think of the writing process in four stages.

Work in Study Groups

In your class or at your residence, find two to five other dedicated students who are willing to meet regularly to study together and collaborate on projects. It helps to find group members who understand the material both better than you and not as well as you. People who have already mastered the material can help you strengthen your own understanding. Likewise, when you help others learn course content, you strengthen your own understanding of the material.

Set up a regular time and place to meet with your study group, perhaps one to three times a week. Your university's student union, library, or a local café can be good places for regular meetings.

Ask Your Professor About the Exam

You can often improve your chances of succeeding on an exam by asking your professor about it during class or office hours. Your professor may be willing to provide you with sample questions or examples from previous tests. However, professors don't like it when students "grade grub" by constantly asking, "Will this be on the test?" Instead, ask more open-ended questions like these:

- What kinds of questions are likely to appear on the exam?

- What kinds of things do you expect us to be able to do on the exam?

- How many questions will be on the exam, and how long should each take to answer?

- How do you think we should prepare for this exam?

- Can you give us a list of five to ten concepts or key ideas that we should master for this exam?

- Can you describe what a typical answer to the exam question would look like?

One or two questions like these will almost always be welcome.

Pay Attention to Themes

As you look over your lecture notes and textbook, look for thematic patterns to help you organize and remember the course material. A theme is a consistent idea or concept that is often repeated or returned to. Identifying a few themes will help you keep all those facts and details together in your mind.

Ask yourself, what are the fundamental ideas and topics that your professor and textbook have focused on? What are some key points that your professor keeps repeating over and over? What are some larger trends that seem to underlie all the ideas and concepts you have learned in this class?

Create Your Own Questions and Rehearse Possible Answers

Come up with your own questions that you think might appear on the exam and generate responses to them. You can rehearse your responses a few different ways:

- **Talk to yourself:** Mentally run through your responses and, if possible, say your answers out loud.

- **Talk to others:** Talk through answers with members of your study group.

- **Outline or plan out responses:** By yourself or with others, use outlines to map out possible responses. Then express your answers orally or in writing (on paper, your computer, or a whiteboard).

- **Simulate the actual exam:** Write a response or two within a set amount of time. If you have test anxiety and tend to go blank before an exam, try to practise in the actual classroom where you will be taking the test (classrooms are often empty in the evening).

Starting Your Essay Exam

So the professor has just handed you the exam. Now what? First, take a deep breath and relax. Second, avoid the impulse to just dive right in.

Review the Exam Quickly to Gain an Overall Picture

Take a moment to review the whole exam. Pay attention to the kinds of questions, how much time is recommended for each, and how many points each is worth. Pay special attention to the questions that are worth the most because you will want to leave extra time for them.

As you read each question, jot down a few quick notes or a brief outline and move on to the next question. These notes and outlines have two benefits: first, they help you warm up by putting your ideas down on the page before you start writing, and second, they will show your professor where you were going with each answer even if you run out of time. Your professor won't give you full credit for an outline, but he or she might give you partial credit if you were answering the question correctly.

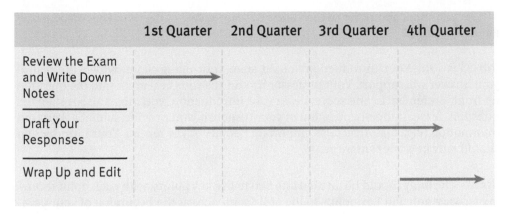

FIGURE 28.2 Budgeting Your Time

Don't just dive in and start writing. Take some of your total time to plan your answers, and be sure to leave time at the end to write conclusions and do some final insertions, editing, and proofreading.

Budget Your Time

Allocate your time properly, so you can answer all the questions. As shown in Figure 28.2, it might help to think in quarters about the time available for your essay exam. Spend a portion of the first quarter considering each question, jotting down some notes, and outlining a possible answer for each question. Devote the second and third quarters to actually drafting your answers one by one. Save some of the fourth quarter for revising, editing, and proofreading.

Answering an Essay Exam Question

When answering an essay exam question, your goal is to demonstrate how much you *know* about the course material and what you can *do* with it. So for most essay exam questions, you will want to keep the organization and style of your response fairly simple and straightforward while demonstrating your mastery of essay format.

Organize Your Answer

Remember that an essay exam answer should always have an introduction, body, and conclusion. That advice might sound obvious, but under pressure, people often forget these three parts. Instead, they just start writing everything they know about the topic. This often leads to a jumble of facts, names, and concepts that are hard to understand.

As you think about the organization of your answer, keep the basic structure of an essay in mind:

Introduction. Your introduction should state your main claim, which the rest of your answer will support. Your professor should see your best answer to the question up front, preferably in one sentence. In your introduction, you might also restate the question, forecast the organization of your response, and provide some background information (e.g., historical facts, important people, or key terms). Your introduction should only be a few sentences.

Body. The body should be divided into two to five key points, with each point receiving a paragraph. Put key points in the topic sentences at the beginning of your paragraphs. Then support each key point with facts, data, reasoning, and examples. Usually, you will find that the professor is asking you to do one of the following things:

- *Explain* a historical event, story plot, or process (narrative or summary).
- *Describe* something or explain how it works (description).
- *Define* something (definition).
- *Divide* something into groups or types (classification).
- *Compare* two or more things (comparison and contrast).
- *Argue* for or against (summary of both sides, argument for one).
- *Solve* a problem (description of problem and argument for a solution).

Once you know what your professor is asking you to do, the structure of your answer will become much more obvious.

Conclusion. Briefly indicate that you are wrapping up (e.g., "In conclusion,") and restate your main point. If time allows, you may also want to describe the implications of your response, state the significance of the problem, or make a prediction about the future.

Above all, keep your answers simple and straightforward. Your professor isn't expecting you to come up with a new theory or an amazing breakthrough. He or she is looking for evidence that you have mastered the materials and can do something with what you have learned.

Finishing Your Essay Exam

Save a little time at the end of the exam for revising and editing. You won't have much time, so focus on completeness and clarity.

Checklist for Revising and Editing Essay Exams

- ☐ Reread each prompt to make sure you answered the question.
- ☐ Look for any missing key points and determine if you have time to add them.
- ☐ Check whether your ideas are clear and easy to follow.
- ☐ Emphasize key terms and concepts by inserting them or highlighting them.
- ☐ Proofread for grammatical errors, spelling mistakes, and garbled handwriting.

Remember, you will gain nothing by racing through the exam and being the first person out the door. You won't look any smarter, and your professor really won't be that impressed. So you may as well use all the time available to do the best job you can.

One Student's Essay Exam

To demonstrate some of the ideas from this chapter, here is a typical essay exam response written by a student. His answer is clear and straightforward. The organization is basic, and the style is plain. It's not perfect, but it achieves the student's goals of showing that he understands the course materials and can do something with that information.

Essay Prompt: In your opinion, which world region or subregion has the greatest potential to improve its development status over the course of your lifetime? Why? What environmental, human, and/or economic resources could it depend on in this process?

Shane Oreck

Question 3B

Prominently identifies which question he is answering.

The region that has the greatest potential to improve is Latin America. The reasons for this are: its natural resources, technological potential, tourism potential, and human resources.

First, countries within Latin America have a bounty of natural and biological resources. If these countries eventually become able to excavate these minerals in a more efficient manner, then their economy will boom. In the Amazon, many countries are looking toward this uncharted area in hopes of finding biological sources that will help in the areas of science and health. So with time and ingenuity, hopefully this will help Latin America's economy as well.

Introduction restates the question, makes a clear main claim, forecasts the answer, and uses keywords from lectures and readings.

<table>
<tr>
<td>

Each body paragraph begins with a strong topic sentence that announces a key point.

</td>
<td>

Second, because Latin America is so close to more technologically advanced countries, they have a great potential for technological advancement. This would be better accomplished through a new trade pact with countries in North America and even Russia. If Latin America can make trade a more viable source of income, then the economy will probably boom, bringing with it technological advance and outside sources that could be of importance for these countries.

</td>
</tr>
<tr>
<td>

The writing style is simple and straightforward.

</td>
<td>

Third, tourism has great potential because of Latin America's beautiful oceans, views, landscapes, historical attractions, and architecture. They do face difficulties in terms of modern facilities and safety for Western guests, but if they can create the infrastructure, then, like Mexico, they could enjoy substantial economic relief from the money generated. Some Latin American countries, like Brazil, are already enticing travellers into their areas.

Lastly, Latin America has a vast array of human resources. Although current educational resources are lacking, these countries are heavily populated. With improved educational opportunity and greater availability of birth control (so that women can plan families and enjoy educational opportunities as well), the people of Latin America would be an enormous untapped resource in which to revitalize the region, economically and culturally.

</td>
</tr>
<tr>
<td>

The conclusion wraps up with its main point and a look to the future.

</td>
<td>

It's true also that many other regions of the world, including China and India, would be candidates for greatest potential for improving their development status. But because of its location, abundance of mineral and biological resources, trade and technological potential, tourism, and human resources, Latin America certainly has the potential for creating a bright future. Besides, Latin America has been so poorly developed for so long, it seems due for a resurgence.

</td>
</tr>
</table>

Pay attention to the straightforward nature of this exam answer. The student used a simple organizational pattern, with a clear introduction, body, and conclusion. The main points are easy to locate in the paragraph's topic sentences. Specific and meaningful facts, details, and reasoning are used to support claims. As demonstrated in this essay exam, your goal is to keep your answers simple, demonstrating that you know the material and can use it to make an argument. Figure 28.3 shows some other typical essay exam questions and a few strategies for answering them.

FIGURE 28.3 Sample Essay Exam Questions

Knowing: Understanding the Course Material

Question Cues	Strategy	Examples
Knowing • explain • define • describe • classify • compare	Know the major ideas, dates, events, places, and so on.	**Deaf Studies** Describe the events surrounding the 1880 Milan conference. What were the historical, educational, and philosophical themes that emerged at this conference? Who were the key players and what were their positions? What was the significance for Deaf culture? (12 points) **History** Bradbury describes ten major causes of the Industrial Revolution. List five of them and explain how each contributed to the industrialization of Europe. (5 points) **Sociology** Explain the difference between participant and nonparticipant research, how each is used in sociological research, and for what purposes each is used.
Understanding • summarize • explain • compare	Grasp the meaning of important ideas, facts, and theories. Compare two ideas, positions, or theories.	**Developmental Psychology** Compare the stages of personality development according to Piaget and Erikson. **Management** Identify whether each of the following scenarios is best described as a differential cost, opportunity cost, or sunk cost. (5 points each)

Doing: Applying, Analyzing, Synthesizing, and Evaluating Course Material

Question Cues	Strategy	Examples
Applying • explain • describe • compare • solve	Use information, methods, concepts, and theories in new contexts to solve problems, discover relationships, or illustrate concepts.	**Cost Management** The Pointilla T-Shirt Company produces high-quality casual apparel for a name-brand company in the United States. Management needs an analysis of their product and period costs so they can develop plans for controlling them. Given the following costs, calculate the total product and period costs. . . . **Art History** Use an iconographical analysis to describe the qualities, nature, and history of the statue pictured below.
Analyzing • explain • define • classify	Recognize patterns; interpret causes and effects; identify components.	**Canadian Literature** Compare the essays on Sinclair Ross's *As For Me and My House* by literary critics Lorraine McMullen and Andrew Lesk. How does each critic explain the characters' relationships? How do those differing interpretations indicate changing social norms? **Nursing** Explain the difference between *glycemic index* and *glycemic load* to two audiences: (1) a class of first-year medical students (who have a good understanding of biochemistry), and (2) the parents of a child with diabetes (who have an eighth grade education and do not know, for instance, the difference between carbohydrates, proteins, and fat). (30 minutes)

(continued)

FIGURE 28.3 Sample Essay Exam Questions
(continued)

Question Cues	Strategy	Examples
Synthesizing • combine • create • develop a plan • argue for or against	Generalize from facts; combine knowledge from different areas; make predictions; draw conclusions.	**Literature** Consider Sinclair Ross's novel *As For Me and My House* and Margaret Atwood's discussion of Canadian literature in *Survival*. Apply Margaret Atwood's definition of Canadian identity, which we discussed in class, to Ross's book and decide whether *As For Me and My House* is in fact archetypal Canadian literature or not. Be sure to state Atwood's definition and describe at least three aspects of the novel that support your position. **Pharmacy** The chemical formulas and structures for Pharmaceutical A and Pharmaceutical B are shown in the figure below. Explain from a biochemical perspective what would happen if the two drugs were taken simultaneously. In your response, be sure to identify the relevant function groups present in each compound, classify each pharmaceutical, relate some of the structural features of the compound to physical and chemical properties, and discuss the consequences of confusing the two drugs.
Evaluating • assess • argue for or against • solve	Compare and evaluate ideas, models, theories, or plans.	**Introductory Earth Sciences** Describe how the geology, climate, and biology (focusing on plants and animals) of London, England, have changed from the Late Triassic Period to the present. Use the figures below depicting the drift of the continents and apply your knowledge of plate tectonics, climatology, and paleobiology to support your answer. **Geography** In your opinion, which world region or subregion has the greatest potential to improve its development status over the course of your lifetime? Why? What environmental, human, and/or economic resources could it depend on in this process?

Essay exams can be challenging, but you will be more successful if you prepare properly. To do your best, follow these steps.

PREPARE for the Exam

Take good notes on lectures and readings, but also consider the key themes and issues that your professor keeps returning to. Form and regularly meet with a study group. Go to your professor and ask what the exam will look like, and what he or she wants to see in an exam response.

START the Exam

First read through the entire text to get the big picture, making note of how much time you have and the point value for each question. Budget your time so you can outline some answers, write out the exam, and revise and edit.

ANSWER the Questions

Make sure you understand what each question is asking you to do (explain, describe, define, classify, compare, argue for or against, or solve a problem). As you write, stay focused and try to maintain a simple, straightforward organization and style.

FINISH Up with Revising and Editing

Reread the questions and make sure your responses answer them. Make any adjustments needed and highlight places where you address the question directly. Save some time for proofreading.

1. Individually, freewrite an answer to this question: What is hard about writing essay exams? After you've written your response, discuss your answer with your group and come up with three strategies for making essay exams more manageable.

2. In a group or in an informal written response, examine the student example in this chapter. Explain why its structure is appropriate for an essay exam.

3. In a group, talk about the essay exam response *as a genre*. What other genres does it resemble and in what ways?

1. As an informal writing assignment, create at least two essay exam prompts for another course you are taking. Share them with your group.

2. Find a textbook that has questions at the end of the chapters and choose one question that you think could be on an essay exam. Make an outline of how you would respond to that question on an essay exam. Discuss your outline with your group.

3. Type "sample essay exam" into an Internet search engine and locate three examples of essay exam questions. Analyze these questions and explain what kinds of content, organization, and style would be appropriate in an answer.

1. **Write a practice essay exam.** As practice, write an essay exam response to a prompt created by your professor. When you are finished, compare your response with those of your classmates.

2. **Argue for or against essay exams in post-secondary institutions.** Write a letter to the editor of your campus newspaper. In your letter, argue for or against the use of essay exams as a way of testing students. If you are arguing against using essay exams, what would be a suitable replacement for them?

MyCompLab

For support in meeting this chapter's objectives, follow this path in MyCompLab:

Student Resources → Writing → Writing Samples. Review the Multimedia resources about websites; then complete the Exercises and click on Gradebook to measure your progress.

Presenting Your Work

> **In this chapter, you will learn how to:**
> - get started on developing your presentation.
> - organize your presentation with a good introduction, body, and conclusion.
> - deliver your presentation with confidence and style.

You will need to make public presentations in your university or college courses and in the workplace. More and more, professors are asking students to present their projects to an audience. And almost any professional career will require you to present information, ideas, and opinions. Your ability to speak effectively in front of an audience will be an important cornerstone of your success.

In fact, public speaking is becoming more important as new technologies, like video streaming and video conferencing, become common features of the modern workplace. These new media make it possible to present the material in real time and answer your audience's questions.

Most genres go hand in hand with public presentations. For instance, in the workplace it is common for people to present proposals and reports to their clients. In your advanced courses, you will be asked to present analyses, position papers, proposals, and research papers.

In this chapter, we are going to show you some easy strategies for turning your documents into public presentations. If you learn and practise a few simple techniques, your presentations will be more effective.

Getting Started

Because this book is about writing, not public speaking, we are going to assume that you have already written a document that you need to turn into a presentation. Now it is time to take that written text and repurpose it into a presentation for an audience.

Ask a Few Key Questions to Get Started

Solid preparation is the key to successful public speaking. A good way to start preparing is to ask the Five-W and How questions:

- *What* do I want to accomplish with my presentation?
- *Who* will be in my audience and what do they need?
- *Why* am I presenting this information to this audience?
- *Where* will I be giving my presentation?
- *When* will I be asked to speak?
- *How* should I give the presentation?

Answer each of these questions separately. Your answers will give you an overview of what you need to do to prepare for your presentation.

Something to keep in mind is that your audience wants more from you than just the information in your document. After all, if they wanted to, they could just read it. So why do they want you to present it to them instead? A presentation gives members of your audience a chance to interact with you and ask questions. That interaction is also valuable for you as a researcher, since it will give you feedback on your work. (This is one reason why academics present their work publicly.) Your audience wants to see you in action. They want you to *perform* the material for them.

Ask yourself how you can make your presentation more interactive, more visual, and more entertaining than your original written text.

Choose the Appropriate Presentation Technology

Think about what technology will be available and which would fit your presentation. The technology you choose depends on the audience's expectations and the place where you will be giving your talk.

Each kind of presentation technology offers advantages and disadvantages. Figure 29.1 describes some of the advantages and disadvantages of each.

Allot Your Time

If you are new to speaking in public, a five- to ten-minute presentation might sound like a lifetime. The time, though, will go fast. A ten-minute presentation, for example, is only the equivalent of a four or five page paper. So you will need to budget your time carefully to avoid going over the time allowed.

Figure 29.2 on page 512 shows how to budget the time for a presentation with three major topics. Of course, if your paper has fewer or more than three topics, you should make adjustments in the times allowed for each one. These time limits are flexible guidelines, not rigid rules.

FIGURE 29.1
Pros and Cons
of Presentation
Technologies

	Advantages	Disadvantages	Genres
Computer with Digital Projector	• Can be dynamic, particularly if you use one of the new online presentation programs such as *Prezi* • Allows for animation and sound • Creates a more formal atmosphere	• Requires a darkened room, which might inconvenience your audience • Diverts attention from the speaker to the screen • Computers are not completely reliable	Reviews, Literary Analyses, Rhetorical Analyses, Position Papers, Proposals, and Research Papers
Overhead Projector	• Projectors are available in most workplaces and classrooms • Easy to print transparencies from most home printers	• May seem static and somewhat outdated • Need to manually change transparencies during your presentation	Literary Analyses, Rhetorical Analyses, Position Papers, Proposals, and Research Papers
Whiteboard, Chalkboard, Notepad	• Allows speaker to create visuals on the spot • Audience pays more attention because speaker is moving	• Cannot be used with a large audience • Writing on board requires extra time • Ideas need to be transferred clearly to the board	Position Papers, Proposals, and Research Papers
Poster Presentation	• Allows audience to see whole presentation • Presents highly technical information clearly • Allows audience to ask specific questions	• Cannot be presented to more than a few people • Can be hard to transport	Reviews, Literary Analyses, Rhetorical Analyses, Position Papers, Proposals, and Research Papers
Handouts	• Help reinforce major points • Can offer more detail, data, and statistics • Audience has something to take home	• Handing them out can be distracting in large presentations • Audience members may read the handouts instead of listening to the talk	Reviews, Literary Analyses, Rhetorical Analyses, Position Papers, Proposals, and Research Papers

**FIGURE 29.2
Allotting Your
Presentation
Time**

*When planning
your presentation,
allot your time
carefully to scale
your talk to the
time allowed.*

	5-Minute Presentation	10-Minute Presentation	20-Minute Presentation
Introduction	Half a minute	1 minute	1–2 minutes
Topic 1	1 minute	2 minutes	5 minutes
Topic 2	1 minute	2 minutes	5 minutes
Topic 3	1 minute	2 minutes	5 minutes
Conclusion	Half a minute	1 minute	1 minute
Questions and Answers	1 minute	2 minutes	3 minutes

Explore
Presentation
Proposal 1

Organizing Your Presentation's Content

The organization of your presentation will typically follow the genre you are using to organize your document. Your talk should have a clear beginning, middle, and end. That advice might seem rather obvious, but public speakers regularly forget to properly introduce their talk to the audience, or they abruptly end without summing up their main points.

There is an old speechmaking saying you should commit to memory: *Tell them what you're going to tell them. Tell them. Tell them what you told them.*

In preparing your content, don't simply read your written essay and, if you have created visual aids, don't simply read your slides or handouts. The best presentations are ones in which the presenter talks spontaneously from a brief outline or set of notes. Those notes should contain the presentation's key points and examples and follow the structural suggestions below.

Introduction: Tell Them What You're Going to Tell Them

The introduction of your talk is almost always the most critical part of your whole presentation. At the beginning of your speech, you have a small window—perhaps a minute or two—to capture the audience's attention while stating your topic, purpose, and main point. If you don't grab the audience at this point, they may tune out for the rest of your talk.

A shorter presentation with a brief introduction will make two or three of the following moves, while a long introduction might include all six:

Identify your topic. Tell your audience what your presentation is about.

State the purpose of your presentation. Explain what you are going to do in your talk.

State your main point. Tell them what you want to prove or support.

Stress the importance of your topic to the audience. Explain why this issue is important to them and why they should pay attention.

Offer background information on the subject. Provide enough information to familiarize the audience with your topic.

Forecast the structure of your talk. Tell them how your talk will be organized.

Even if you are naturally funny, starting your presentation with a joke is risky. The problem with jokes is that they often flop, and they can be offensive in ways you might not anticipate.

Instead of telling a joke, think of a good *grabber* to start out your speech. A grabber states something interesting or challenging that captures the audience's attention. Some effective grabbers include:

A rhetorical question: "Do you ever wonder why child actors tend to have personal problems when they become adults?"

A startling statistic: "A recent survey shows that 74 percent of women students report that they have been sexually harassed at this university. Meanwhile, 43 percent of male students report they have been harassed."

A compelling statement: "If nothing is done about global climate change, it is likely that polar bears will become extinct in the wild during our lifetime."

An anecdote: "Last year, I finally climbed my first mountain over 14,000 feet. In many ways, climbing that mountain affirmed to me that I had triumphed over the injuries I sustained in Afganistan two years before."

A show of hands: "Let's see a show of hands. How many of you voted in the last federal election?"

A good grabber identifies your topic while giving your audience a little something to think about.

The Body of Your Talk: Tell Them

The body of your presentation is where you are going to state your major points and support them with facts, reasoning, examples, data, quotations, and any other forms of proof you can offer.

In most situations, the body of your presentation should follow the same pattern as the body of your document. Divide your text into two to five major issues that you want to discuss with the audience. If you try to cover more than five topics, you risk overwhelming the audience with more new information than they can handle. So organize the body of your talk to feature the most important things you want them to remember.

Here's a good strategy that might help you strip down your talk to something you can handle in a small amount of time. Look through your document and ask yourself, "What does my audience *need* to know about this topic to make a decision?" Then cross out any material that goes beyond need-to-know information.

Conclusion: Tell Them What You Told Them

People make this mistake all the time. They finish the body of their talk. Then they shrug their shoulders and say something like, "That's all I have to say. Any questions?" This kind of abrupt ending feels awkward, and it misses an opportunity to drive home the presentation's main point.

Here's a better way to handle your conclusion. Once you clearly signal that you are about to conclude, you will have the audience's heightened attention for the next two minutes. Take advantage of this by repeating your main point in a clear and memorable way. A typical conclusion will include some or all of the following moves:

Signal clearly that you are concluding. Make an obvious transition that signals the end of your talk, such as "Let me wrap up now" or "Finally."

Restate your main point. Tell your audience exactly what you have been trying to explain or prove in your talk.

Re-emphasize the importance of your topic to the audience. Be clear about why the audience should care about your topic. Answer their "Why should I care?" questions.

Call the audience to action. If you want the people in your audience to do something, tell them what you think they should do. Be specific about the actions you want them to take.

Thank the audience. When you are finished, don't forget to say, "thank you." This phrase signals the audience that your presentation is done, and it usually prompts them to give you some applause.

Remember to keep your conclusion brief. Once you say something like, "In conclusion," you have one or two minutes to finish up. If you ramble beyond a couple of minutes, your audience will be annoyed.

Question and Answer

At the end of your talk, you should be prepared to answer a few questions from the audience. The question and answer period offers you a good opportunity to interact with the audience and clarify your ideas. During the question and answer period, you should be ready to answer three types of questions:

A Request for Clarification or Elaboration. These types of questions are opportunities to reinforce some of your key points. When you field this kind of question, start out by rephrasing it for the audience. Rephrasing will allow you to put the issue in your own words and state it loudly enough for the whole audience to hear. Then answer the question, expanding on the information you provided in your talk.

A Challenging Question. Occasionally, an audience member will ask a question that challenges the information you provided in your talk. Here is a good three-step strategy for answering these kinds of questions:

1. **Rephrase the question.** State the question in terms that will allow you to answer it in ways that reflect your own beliefs.

2. **Validate the question.** Tell the audience that you understand the questioner's concerns and even share them.

3. **Elaborate and move forward.** Explain that the course of action you are supporting is preferable because it addresses the issue more appropriately or seems more reasonable.

The Heckling Question. In rare cases, an audience member will want to heckle you with hostile questions. In these cases, you need to recognize that the questioner is *trying* to sabotage your presentation. He or she wants you to become flustered. Don't let the heckler do that to you. After trying your best to answer one or two questions from a heckler, simply say, "I'm sorry you feel that way. Perhaps we can meet after my talk to discuss your concerns." Then look away from that person. Usually, someone else in the audience will ask a question and you can move on.

When the question and answer period is over, you should briefly thank the audience again. This will usually prompt another round of applause.

Designing Your Visual Aids

Visual aids will help you clarify your ideas and illustrate your main points for the audience. Perhaps the best way to create visual aids is to make slides with the presentation software (*PowerPoint*, *Keynote*, or *Presentations*) that came with your word-processing software. Online presentation software is also becoming available and will allow you to easily access Internet material during your talk.

Explore
Presentation 1:
Slides from
Presentation
(interactive)

Format Your Slides

Whether you are presenting in a large lecture hall with a projector or to a few people with a poster presentation, slides are some of the best visual aids available (Figure 29.3). Here are some strategies for formatting your slides:

- Title each slide with an action-oriented heading.

- Put five or fewer major points on each slide. If you have more than five major points, divide that topic into two slides.

- Use left-justified text for most items on your slides. Centred text should only be used for the titles of your slides.

- Use dark text on a white or light background whenever possible. Light text on a dark background can be difficult to read.

- Use bulleted lists of phrases instead of paragraphs or sentences.

- Use photos, icons, and graphics to keep your slides fresh and active for the audience. Make sure your graphics look good on the screen. Increasing the size of a web-based graphic, for example, can make the image look blurry or grainy.

FIGURE 29.3
Creating Slides

Shown here are a title slide and a body slide from a research paper repurposed as a presentation. The graphics add a strong visual identity to the slides.

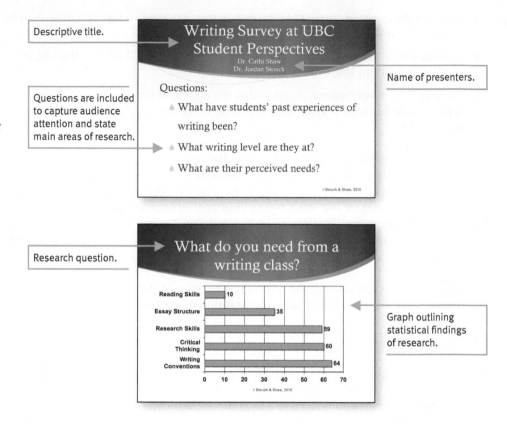

Descriptive title.

Questions are included to capture audience attention and state main areas of research.

Name of presenters.

Research question.

Graph outlining statistical findings of research.

You will be tempted to pack too much material onto each slide. Effective slides, like the ones shown in Figure 29.3, need to be simple and easy to interpret. You don't want your audience trying to puzzle out the meaning of your complicated slides instead of listening to your talk.

Delivering Your Presentation

How you deliver your talk will make a significant impact on your audience. The usual advice is to "be yourself" when you are speaking in public. Of course, that's good advice for people who are comfortable speaking in front of an audience. Better advice is to "be the person the audience expects." In other words, like an actor, play the role that fits your topic and your audience.

Body Language

Ideally, the movements of your body should help you reinforce your message and maintain the audience's attention.

Dress Appropriately. Your choice of clothing needs to reflect your audience's expectations and the topic of your talk. Even when you are presenting to your classmates, you should view it as an opportunity to practise your workplace and professional demeanor. Dress as though you are presenting in a professional workplace, not as if you were simply going to class.

Stand Up Straight. When speakers are nervous, they tend to slouch, lean, or rock back and forth. This looks unprofessional and makes it difficult to breathe calmly. Instead, keep your feet squarely under your shoulders with knees slightly bent. Keep your shoulders back and down and your head up to allow good airflow. If your shoulders are forward and up, you won't get enough air and the pitch of your voice will seem unnaturally high.

Use Open Hand and Arm Gestures. For most audiences, open hand and arm gestures will convey trust and confidence. Avoid folding your arms, keeping your arms at your sides, or putting both hands in your pockets, as these poses will convey a defensive posture that audiences do not trust.

Make Eye Contact. Everyone in the audience should believe you made eye contact with him or her at least once during your presentation. If you are nervous about making eye contact, look at the audience members' foreheads instead. They will think you are looking them directly in the eye.

Move to Reinforce Major Points or Transitions. If possible, when you make important points, step forward toward the audience. When you make transitions in your presentation from one topic to the next, move to the left or right. Your movement across the floor will highlight the transitions in your speech.

Voice and Tone

As you improve your presentation skills, you should start paying more attention to your voice and tone.

Speak Lower and Slower. When speaking to an audience, you will need to speak louder than you normally would. As your volume goes up, so will the pitch of your voice, making it sound unnaturally high to the audience. By consciously lowering your voice, you should sound just about right. Also, nerves may cause you to speak too quickly. Silently remind yourself to speak slowly.

Use Pauses to Reinforce Your Major Points. Each time you make a major point, pause for a moment to let the audience commit it to memory.

Use Pauses to Eliminate Verbal Tics. Verbal tics like "um," "ah," "like," "you know," "OK?" and "See what I mean?" are nervous habits that fill gaps between thoughts. If you have a verbal tic, train yourself to pause when you feel like using one of these sounds or phrases. Before long, you will find them disappearing from your speech.

Minimize How Often You Look Down at Your Notes. You should try to look at your notes as little as possible. When you look down at your notes, your neck bends, restricting your airflow and lowering your volume. Plus, notes can become a distracting "safe place" that keeps you from engaging visually with your audience.

Practising and Rehearsing

You should leave plenty of time to practise your presentation out loud. Even better advice, though, is to "rehearse" what you are going to say and how you are going to say it. Rehearsal allows you to practise your presentation in a more realistic setting.

Practise, Practise, Practise

Practising involves speaking your presentation out loud to yourself. As you are working through your presentation verbally, you should memorize its major points and gain a sense of its organization and flow. While practising, you should:

- Listen for any problems with content, organization, and style.
- Edit and proofread your visuals and handouts.
- Decide how you are going to move around as you deliver the speech.
- Pay attention to your body language and voice.

If you notice any problems as you are practising your presentation, you can stop and fix them right away.

Rehearse, Rehearse, Rehearse

The secret to polishing your presentation is to rehearse it several times. Unlike practice, rehearsal means giving the presentation from beginning to end *without stopping*. As much as possible, you want to replicate the experience of giving your real talk. After each rehearsal session, you should make any revisions or corrections.

Recruit friends to listen as you rehearse your presentation. They will provide you with a live audience, so you can gauge their reactions to your ideas. Ideally, they will also give you constructive feedback that you can use to improve the presentation. Another possibility is recording your presentation, with either audiovisual or just audio.

Practising will help you find any major problems with your talk, but rehearsal will help you turn the whole package into an effective presentation.

Here are some helpful guidelines for developing and giving presentations.

ANSWER the Five-W and How Questions About Your Presentation

Think about the who, what, where, when, why, and how issues that will shape the content, organization, style, and design of your presentation.

CHOOSE the Appropriate Presentation Technology

Depending on the size of your audience and the room in which you will be speaking, consider what kind of presentation technology would best allow you to present your ideas.

ORGANIZE Your Ideas

More than likely, the genre of your document offers a good organization for your talk. Remember to "Tell them what you're going to tell them. Tell them. Tell them what you told them."

DESIGN Your Visual Aids

Slides work well for most presentations. Use presentation software, such as *PowerPoint, Prezi, Keynote,* or *Presentations,* to convert your paper into a colourful and interesting set of slides. If slides aren't appropriate, you should look into the possibility of using a whiteboard or handouts.

THINK About Your Body Language

Consider issues like how you will dress, and how you will stand and move when you are presenting. Practise making eye contact with people.

IMPROVE Your Voice and Tone

Work on speaking lower and slower, while using pauses to reinforce your major points. Also, use pauses to eliminate any verbal tics, such as "um," "ah," "like," and "you know."

PRACTISE and Rehearse

Ultimately, practice and rehearsal are the best ways to improve and polish your presentation. Use practice to help you revise your talk and correct errors. Use rehearsal to polish your presentation and make it as persuasive as possible.

1. In a small group, share your opinions about what works well in a presentation. Discuss effective and ineffective presenters (coaches, teachers, public speakers). What traits made these people effective or ineffective as public speakers?

2. Find a video clip online of a particularly problematic speech. Imagine that you and your group are this person's speaking coach. Being as helpful as possible, what advice would you give this person to improve his or her future presentations?

3. With your group, choose three things from this chapter that you would like to use to improve your presentation skills. Then take turns presenting these three things to your "audience."

1. Find a speech on a video website (*TED.com* is one good source). In a brief rhetorical analysis, discuss the strengths and weaknesses of the presentation. Specifically, pay attention to the content, organization, style, and use of visuals in the presentation.

2. Outline a two minute speech on a subject that you know well. Then, without much further thought, give a presentation to a small group of people from your class. Practise making the six introductory moves mentioned in this chapter and the five concluding moves.

3. Using presentation software, turn one of the papers you wrote for this class into slides. Break your paper down into major and minor points, and add pictures and illustrations that will help your audience visualize your ideas. Print out your slides and look for any inconsistencies in wording or places where you could reorganize.

1. **Evaluate a public presentation.** Attend a public presentation on your campus. Instead of listening to the content of the presentation, pay attention to how it was organized and presented. Then write a review of the presentation. Use the presentation strategies described in this chapter to discuss the strengths and weaknesses of the speaker and his or her talk.

2. **Repurpose a written text into a presentation.** Choose a major project for this course or another one and turn it into a presentation. Choose the appropriate presentation technology. Make sure you develop an introduction that captures your audience's attention. Divide the body of your paper into two to five major topics. Then develop a conclusion that stresses your main points and looks to the future. When you have finished creating your talk, spend some time practising and rehearsing it. Your professor may ask you to present your talk in class.

MyCompLab

For support in meeting this chapter's objectives, follow this path in MyCompLab:

Student Resources → Writing → Writing Samples. Review the Multimedia resources about presentations; then complete the Exercises and click on Gradebook to measure your progress.

PART 7

Handbook

PART OUTLINE

1 Sentences 524

2 Verbs 540

3 Pronouns 545

4 Style 550

5 Punctuation,
Mechanics, and
Spelling 554

Do you have questions about grammar, usage, or spelling? Look no further. Your questions will be answered in this **HANDBOOK**.

This handbook is a reference tool for questions about English grammar and usage. It focuses on the sentence as the basic material of written and spoken discourse. It avoids grammatical jargon as much as possible, but it does define terms where they are necessary for understanding important concepts and problems. Refer to this guide while writing and when your professor suggests sections for you to study. It will help you write correctly, clearly, and with an appropriate style. Note that some of the examples demonstrate academic citations as well as grammar concepts.

1. **Sentences,** *524*
   1A Fragments, *524*
   1B Comma Splices, *528*
   1C Fused Sentences, *530*
   1D Parallelism, *531*
   1E Coordination and
      Subordination, *532*
   1F Mixed Sentences, *534*
   1G Shifts, *534*
   1H Dangling and Misplaced
      Modifiers, *536*
   1I Restrictive and Nonrestrictive
      Modifiers, *537*
   1J Adjectives and Adverbs, *539*

2. **Verbs,** *540*
   2A Tense, *540*
   2B Voice, *541*
   2C Mood, *542*
   2D Subject-Verb Agreement, *543*

3. **Pronouns,** *545*
   3A Pronoun Case, *545*
   3B Pronoun Reference, *547*

3C Pronoun Agreement, *548*
3D Relative Pronouns, *549*

4. **Style,** *550*
   4A Conciseness, *550*
   4B Appropriate Language, *552*

5. **Punctuation, Mechanics, and
   Spelling,** *554*
   5A End Punctuation, *554*
   5B Semicolon, *555*
   5C Comma, *556*
   5D Colon, *559*
   5E Dash, *560*
   5F Quotation Marks, *560*
   5G Other Marks, *561*
   5H Capitalization, *562*
   5I Abbreviation, *563*
   5J Apostrophe, *564*
   5K Italics, *565*
   5L Hyphens, *566*
   5M Numbers, *567*
   5N Spelling, *568*

1 Sentences

Every sentence has at least one subject and at least one verb, begins with a capital letter, and ends with end punctuation (a period, question mark, or exclamation point). In university or college writing and beyond, you will be asked to communicate complex ideas. You may need to try out new sentence patterns to connect those ideas, and that may lead you to make some sentence errors. Use this handbook to help you understand the wide variety of sentence types while avoiding grammatical errors.

1A Fragments

Sentence fragments are errors in which partial sentences are treated as complete sentences—begun with a capital letter and ended with a period. The fragment may be a subordinate clause, a phrase, or a combination of subordinate elements. What makes each a fragment is that it lacks a subject or a verb, or that it begins with a subordinating word. Only independent clauses can make independent statements.

Subordinate Clause Fragment

Recognition.   A subordinate clause has a subject and a verb but is not an independent clause because it includes a subordinate connector.

Some common subordinating connectors, grouped by function, include:

Time: *after, before, once, since, until, whenever*

Place: *where, wherever*

Cause: *as, because, since*

Contrast: *although, even though, though, while*

Condition: *even if, if*

Result: *in order that, so, so that*

Alternative: *than, whether*

Relative pronouns, such as *who, whom, whose, whatever, why,* and *unless,* can also be subordinate connectors.

Any clause beginning with one of these words is *subordinate* and should not be written as a sentence. Here are examples of clause fragments (italicized):

Research shows that university students are widely and extensively using social media. *Which often interferes with their academic achievement* (Jacobsen and Forste 279).

Norway's Lapps are believed to be a nomadic people of Asian heritage. *Who follow reindeer herds through Norway's cold, rugged land.*

Because winters in interior BC are not as cold or as long as they once were. The mountain pine beetle has spread and caused significant damage to forest habitats.

Correction.   There are two main ways of correcting clause fragments: (1) attaching them to the preceding or following sentence, and (2) removing or changing the subordinating connector. These sentences illustrate both types of correction:

Research shows that university students are widely and extensively using social media. *This practice* often interferes with their academic achievement (Jacobsen and Forste 279). The subordinating word of the fragment is changed.

Norway's Lapps are believed to be of Asian heritage—nomadic people who follow reindeer herds through Norway's cold, rugged land. The fragment is connected to the sentence with a dash.

Because winters in interior BC are not as cold or as long as they once were, the mountain pine beetle has spread and caused significant damage to forest habitats. *The fragment is connected to the following sentence with a comma.*

Phrase Fragment

Phrase fragments lack a subject, a verb, or both. The most common phrases written as fragments are *verbal phrases* and *prepositional phrases.*

Recognition. A *verbal phrase* is a word group made up of a verb form and related modifiers and other words. As opposed to *verb phrases,* which are made up of verb parts (such as *has been gone*), a verbal phrase is constituted with a *verbal,* a word formed from a verb but not functioning as a verb. *Going,* for example, is a verbal, as is *gone.*

There are three kinds of verbals: gerunds, participles, and infinitives. Gerunds end in *-ing;* participles end in either *-ing* (present) or *-ed* (regular past); infinitives are usually introduced by *to.* Here are a few examples of how verbals are formed from verbs:

Verb	Present Participle and Gerund	Past Participle	Infinitive
snap	snapping	snapped	to snap
look	looking	looked	to look
want	wanting	wanted	to want
go	going	gone	to go
has	having	had	to have

Verbals function primarily as adjectives and nouns, most often in verbal phrases.

In the following examples, the italicized verbal phrases are fragments because they are written as sentences:

Eero Saarinen designed the 630-foot Gateway Arch for the St. Louis riverfront. *Imagining a giant stainless steel arch.* *Participial phrase modifying Eero Saarinen*

Critics said that cranes could not reach high enough. *To lift the steel sections into place.* *Infinitive phrase modifying high*

Saarinen knew that precision was of utmost importance. In *building the arch.* *Gerund phrase as object of preposition In*

Correction. Verbal phrase fragments can be corrected in one of two ways: (1) by connecting them to a related sentence, or (2) by expanding them into a sentence. Both ways are illustrated below:

Eero Saarinen designed the 630-foot Gateway Arch for the St. Louis riverfront. *He imagined a giant stainless steel arch.* *The verbal fragment is expanded to a sentence.*

Critics said that cranes could not reach high enough *to lift the steel sections into place.* *The verbal fragment is connected to a related sentence.*

Saarinen knew that precision was of utmost importance in *building the arch.*
The gerund phrase, object of the preposition *In*, is connected to a related sentence.

Recognition.   A *prepositional phrase* is a word group made up of a preposition and its object. Together they contribute meaning to a sentence, usually modifying a noun or a verb. Like subordinating conjunctions, prepositions show relationships, such as time, place, condition, and cause. Common prepositions include *about, above, among, below, but, by, in addition to, into, like, from, out of, past, regarding, toward,* and *until.*

In the following examples, prepositional phrases have been written as sentences and are therefore fragments:

Social networking sites are a popular form of online communication. *Like e-mail and online discussion groups.*

Norway is a land of natural beauty. *From its fjord-lined coast to frigid Lapland.*

Correction.   Prepositional phrase fragments can also be corrected (1) by connecting them to a related sentence, or (2) by expanding them into a sentence.

Social networking sites are a popular form of online communication, *like e-mail and online discussion groups.*
or *Like e-mail and online discussion groups*, social networking sites are a popular form of online communication. The prepositional phrase is connected to a related sentence.

Norway is a land of natural beauty. *Its charm extends from its fjord-lined coast to frigid Lapland.* The prepositional phrase is expanded into a sentence.

Incomplete Thoughts

Sometimes fragments are simply errors in punctuation—the writer uses a period when a comma or no punctuation would be correct. A more difficult type of fragment to correct is the incomplete thought, such as this one:

A large concrete dock 50 feet short of a wooden platform anchored in the middle of the bay.

With fragments of this sort, the writer needs to insert the missing information. The reader doesn't know what happens—what the dock does or what is done to it. The fragment might be revised like this:

A large concrete dock *juts out, stopping* 50 feet short of a wooden platform anchored in the middle of the bay.

Acceptable Fragments

You probably encounter fragments every day. Titles are often fragments, as are answers to questions and expressions of strong emotion.

Titles: *Gates of Fire: An Epic Novel of the Battle of Thermopylae*

Answer to question: "How many sources does this essay cite?" "Eight."

Expression of strong emotion: "What a great concert!"

And much advertising uses fragments:

> Intricate, delicate, exquisite. Extravagant in every way.

> Another successful client meeting. Par for the course.

Finally, writers quoting spoken words might use fragments:

> Claire asked Erin, "Why would you do that?"

> Erin shrugged. "Because."

Common as they are in everyday life, fragments are usually unacceptable in academic or workplace writing, because incomplete thoughts can confuse a reader and detract from the clarity of the work. When you do choose to use a fragment, you should do it intentionally, and only after carefully considering your readers and the effect that you want to achieve.

Watch
Common Grammar Errors: 1. Five Ways to Fix a Comma Splice Error

1B Comma Splices

Comma splices consist of two independent clauses (clauses that can stand alone as sentences) improperly joined together by a comma as one sentence. Here are two examples:

> The economy of Algeria is in trouble, many citizens blame the government.

> The death of any soldier is tragic, however, death by friendly fire is particularly disturbing.

Recognition.   The first step in avoiding comma splices is to identify them. Because they happen only in sentences with at least two independent clauses, you can test your sentences by substituting periods for commas. If you end up with two complete sentences, you probably have a comma splice. In testing the first of the two preceding examples we come up with the following result:

> The economy of Algeria is in trouble.

> Many citizens blame the government.

Both of these clauses obviously qualify as complete sentences, so they must be independent clauses. They therefore cannot be connected with a comma. Remember this simple rule of punctuation: *Periods and commas are not interchangeable.* If a period is correct, a comma is not.

Correction.   You can revise comma splices using five different strategies.

1. Separate the independent clauses using a comma and a *coordinating conjunction*. There are seven—and *only* seven—coordinating conjunctions. As a memory aid, their first letters spell F-A-N-B-O-Y-S:

for	but
and	or
nor	yet
	so

To correct a comma splice, begin the second independent clause with one of these conjunctions preceded by a comma. For example:

The economy of Algeria is in trouble, *and* many citizens blame the government.

2. Separate the independent clauses using a semicolon (with or without a transitional adverb). Semicolons are often interchangeable with periods and therefore can be used to separate independent clauses. For example:

The economy of Algeria is in trouble; many citizens blame the government.

The death of any soldier is tragic; *however,* death by friendly fire is particularly disturbing.

In the second example, *however* is a transitional adverb. Unlike coordinating conjunctions, *transitional adverbs* are not conjunctions and so do not join sentence elements. They do, however, connect ideas by showing how they relate to one another. Like conjunctions, they can show addition, contrast, result, and other relationships. Some of the most common transitional adverbs are *also, in addition, next, finally, for example, however, meanwhile, therefore,* and *then.*

A semicolon should always precede the transitional adverb that begins the second independent clause. A comma usually follows the transitional adverb, although in some instances, as in the following example, the comma is omitted:

Air bags deflate within one second after inflation; *therefore* they do not interfere with control of the car.

Some comma splices result when writers use transitional adverbs as if they were coordinating conjunctions. If you have trouble distinguishing transitional adverbs from coordinating conjunctions, remember that none of the coordinating conjunctions is longer than three letters, and all of the transitional adverbs are four letters or longer. Also, keep in mind that transitional adverbs are movable within the sentence while coordinating conjunctions are not; for example, the preceding example could be rewritten as:

Air bags deflate within one second after inflation; they do not *therefore* interfere with control of the car.

3. Make one of the independent clauses subordinate to the other by inserting a subordinating conjunction. When one of the clauses explains or elaborates on the other, use an appropriate subordinating conjunction to make the relationship between the two clauses more explicit (see 1A Fragments). Consider the following comma splice and its revision:

The research remains inconclusive, further studies on media influence will be necessary.

Because the research remains inconclusive, further studies on media influence will be necessary.

4. Rewrite one of the independent clauses as a modifying phrase. A *modifying phrase* serves as an adjective or adverb within a sentence. By rewriting one of the independent clauses as a phrase, you can eliminate unneeded words. For example, consider the following comma splice and its revision:

The researchers explained their findings, they were emphatic about the implications of their research.

The researchers explained their findings, emphasizing the implications of their research. Here *emphasizing the implications of their research* modifies the verb *explained*.

5. Punctuate each independent clause as a separate sentence. No law of grammar, punctuation, or style says you must present the two independent clauses together within one sentence. The example from before is perfectly acceptable written as follows:

The economy of Algeria is in trouble. Many citizens blame the government.

It may be to your advantage to divide long and/or complex independent clauses into separate sentences. Doing so may help convey your meaning to readers more clearly.

((•—[**Listen**
Audio
Lesson
Section 1:
Big Ideas—
Correcting
Common
Errors:
Fragments
and Run-On
Sentences

1C Fused Sentences

Fused sentences, sometimes called *run-on sentences,* are similar to comma splices. However, instead of a comma between the two independent clauses, there is no punctuation; the two independent clauses simply run together. For example:

The United States has 391 lawyers per 100,000 people Japan has only 23 attorneys per 100,000 (Ramseyer and Rasmussen 5).

The World Cup is the most popular sporting event in the world you would never know it based on the indifferent response of the average American.

((•—[**Listen**
Audio
Lesson
Section 2:
Practice
Questions—
Correcting
Common
Errors:
Fragments
and Run-On
Sentences

Recognition.   Unlike the comma splice, there is no punctuation in the fused sentence to guide you to the end of the first independent clause and the beginning of the second. As a result, it can be more challenging to identify independent clauses within fused sentences, particularly if the sentence also contains modifying phrases or dependent clauses set off by commas. The best way to do this is to read from the beginning of the sentence (reading aloud may help) until you have found the end of the first independent clause. Consider the following example:

Even though the results were inconclusive at this point, the long term nature of the study was noted it received considerable media attention.

This fused sentence contains a subordinate clause (*Even though the results were inconclusive at this point*) attached to one of the two independent clauses (*the long term nature of the study was noted* and *it received considerable media attention*).

Correction.   Revise fused sentences using any one of the same five strategies for correcting comma splices (see 1B Comma Splices, for more information on each strategy).

1. Separate the independent clauses using a comma and a coordinating conjunction. For example:

   The United States has 391 lawyers per 100,000 people, *but* Japan has only 23 attorneys per 100,000 (Ramseyer and Rasmussen 5).

2. Separate the independent clauses using a semicolon (with or without a transitional adverb). For example:

   The United States has 391 lawyers per 100,000 people; Japan has only 23 attorneys per 100,000 (Ramseyer and Rasmussen 5).

   The World Cup is the most popular sporting event in the world; *however,* you would never know it based on the indifferent response of the average American.

3. Make one of the independent clauses subordinate to the other by inserting a subordinating conjunction. The newly formed dependent clause should explain the remaining independent clause. For example, consider the following fused sentence and its revision:

   I run a marathon my feet get sore.

   Whenever I run a marathon, my feet get sore.

4. Rewrite one of the independent clauses as a modifying phrase. Remember, modifying phrases act as adjectives or adverbs. Consider the following fused sentence and its revision:

   Multiculturalism is often debated among scholars they fear it leads to isolation within migrant communities.

   Multiculturalism is often debated among scholars, who fear it leads to isolation within migrant communities. Here, the phrase *who fear* modifies the noun *scholars.*

5. Punctuate each independent clause as a separate sentence. As with comma splices, you can write the independent clauses (and their related phrases and dependent clauses) as separate sentences. Indeed, this is often the easiest way to handle fused sentences. For example:

   Even though the results were inconclusive at this point, the long term nature of the study was noted. It received considerable media attention. Here, the subordinate clause is attached to the first independent clause and the second independent clause stands on its own.

1D Parallelism

Correctly used parallelism results when two or more grammatically equivalent sentence elements are joined. The sentence elements can be nouns, verbs, phrases, or clauses. (See 1E Coordination and Subordination.)

👁—⌐**Watch**
Common Grammar Errors: 17. Lack of Parallel Structure

Parallelism becomes a problem when dissimilar elements are joined in pairs, in series, in comparisons using *than* or *as,* or in comparisons linked by correlative conjunctions. Consider the following examples of faulty parallelism:

The student did not like written assignments or taking notes during class. The two elements in the pair are not parallel.

Media negatively influences adolescents in three ways: by lowering self-esteem, by offering false body images, and it leads to eating disorders. The last of the three elements in the series is not parallel.

Michael decided to complete his degree next semester rather than studying abroad for another year. The two elements compared using *than* are not parallel.

My sister not only lost the race but also her leg got hurt. The two elements compared by the correlative conjunction *not only . . . but also* are not parallel. Other correlative conjunctions include *both … and, either . . . or, neither . . . nor, whether . . . or,* and *just as . . . so.*

Faulty parallelism can be corrected in various ways:

The student did not like *writing* assignments or taking notes during class. Word form was changed in the first element to make it parallel to the second.

Media negatively influences adolescents in three ways: by lowering self-esteem, by offering false body images, and *by creating* the pre-conditions for eating disorders. The last element was rewritten to make it parallel with the others in the series.

Michael decided to complete his degree next semester rather than *to study* abroad for another year. The verb form of the second element is changed from a participle to an infinitive to make it parallel with the verb form in the first element.

My sister not only lost the race but also *hurt her leg*. The second element was rewritten to make it parallel with the first element.

1E Coordination and Subordination

When dealing with complex ideas, you will often need to explain relationships among things, ideas, places, people, events, and so forth. Sometimes you will choose to explain those relationships within a single sentence. Most sentence relationships involve either coordination or subordination. That is, sentence elements are either grammatically equal to other elements (coordination) or grammatically dependent on other parts (subordination). For example, two independent clauses in a sentence are coordinate; but in a sentence containing an independent clause and a dependent clause, the dependent clause is subordinate (indeed, dependent clauses are also called subordinate clauses).

Coordination

When two or more equivalent sentence elements appear in one sentence, they are coordinate. These elements can be words, phrases, or clauses. Only parallel elements can be coordinated: verbs linked with verbs, nouns with nouns, phrases with phrases, and clauses with clauses (see 1D Parallelism). For example:

Broccoli and *related vegetables* contain beta-carotene, a substance that may reduce the risk of heart attack. Two nouns are joined by a coordinating conjunction.

The researchers *studied, noted,* and *analyzed* the results of their survey. Three parallel verbs are joined in a series with commas and a coordinating conjunction.

American medical devices are equally remarkable, *giving life to those with terminally diseased organs, giving mobility to those crippled with arthritic joints and deadened nerves,* and even, miraculously, *restoring the sense of hearing to those deprived of it.* (*Atlantic.*) The participial (verbal) phrases are joined by commas and a final coordinating conjunction. Also, embedded in the second participial phrase, two coordinate noun phrases are joined by a coordinating conjunction: *arthritic joints and deadened nerves.*

The term "Big Bang" is common usage now with scientists, but it originated as a sarcastic rejection of the theory. Two independent clauses are joined by a comma and a coordinating conjunction.

Subordination

If all sentence elements were grammatically equivalent, the sameness would be tedious. Subordinate elements show where the emphasis lies in sentences and modify elements with independent clauses. A subordinate element—either a phrase or clause—is dependent on the element it modifies for its meaning. At the same time, it often provides a fuller meaning than could be achieved exclusively through the use of independent elements. For example:

For walking and jogging, the calorie expenditure is greater for people of greater body weight. The subordinate element is a prepositional phrase modifying *is greater.*

Increasing both speed and effort in aerobic activities, the exerciser burns more calories. The subordinate element is a verbal phrase modifying *exerciser.*

Because sedentary people are more likely to burn sugar than fat, they tend to become hungry sooner and to overeat. Subordinate clause modifying the verb *tend.*

People *who exercise on a regular basis* change certain enzyme systems *so that they are more likely to burn fat than sugar.* There are two subordinate clauses, one beginning with *who* and modifying *People,* and one beginning with *so that* and modifying the verb *change.*

Effective writing has both coordination and subordination—coordination that sets equivalent elements side by side, and subordination that makes some elements dependent on others. These useful writing tools can be used often or rarely, depending on the rhetorical situation, the genre, and the style you choose to use.

1F Mixed Sentences

A mixed sentence is a problem that occurs when two or more parts of a sentence do not make sense together. It is called faulty predication when a subject and predicate are mismatched. This kind of problem usually occurs when writers are striving to express complex relationships.

The following mixed sentences are common in everyday speech and may not seem inconsistent to you. Indeed, in casual speech they are usually accepted. In standard written English, however, they qualify as grammatical errors.

By lax government regulations made it possible for the oil spill to occur. The prepositional phrase *By lax government regulations* is treated as the subject of the verb *made*. Prepositional phrases cannot serve as subjects.

Just because the candidate once had a drinking problem does not mean he will not be a good mayor now. The adverb clause *because the candidate once had a drinking problem* is treated as the subject of the verb *does not mean*. Adverbs modify verbs and adjectives and cannot function as subjects.

A CAT scan is when medical technicians take a cross-sectional X-ray of the body. The adverb clause *when medical technicians take a cross-sectional X-ray of the body* is treated as a complement of the subject *CAT scan*—another function adverbs cannot serve.

The reason I was late today is because my alarm clock broke. The subject, *reason,* is illogically linked with the predicate, *is because. Reason* suggests an explanation, so the predicate, *is because,* is redundant.

Revise mixed sentences by ensuring that grammatical patterns are used consistently throughout each sentence. For cases of faulty predication, either revise the subject so it can perform the action expressed in the predicate or revise the predicate so it accurately depicts an action performed by the subject. When you are writing, avoid these patterns: *is when*, *is where*, and *The reason . . . is because.*

There are often many ways to revise mixed sentences. In each of the following revisions, the grammatical patterns are consistent and the subjects and predicates fit together logically:

Lax government regulations made it possible for the oil spill to occur.

Just because the candidate once had a drinking problem, we cannot conclude that he will not be a good mayor.

A CAT scan is a cross-sectional X-ray of the body.

The reason I was late today is that my alarm clock broke.

1G Shifts

Shifts occur when writers lose track of their sentence elements. Shifts occur in a variety of ways:

In person

In music, where left-handed people seem to be talented, the right-handed world puts *you* at a disadvantage. Shift from *people,* third person, to *you,* second person.

In tense

Even though many musicians *are* left handed, instruments *had been designed for right handers.* Shift from present tense to past perfect.

In number

A left-handed *violinist* has to pay extra to buy *their* left-handed violin. Shift from singular to plural (be particularly aware of this shift when making references to unspecified readers, viewers, or researchers).

In mood

Every time the *violinist played, she could always know* when her instrument was out of tune. Shift from the indicative mood, *violinist played,* to the subjunctive mood, *she could always know.*

In voice

The sonata *was being practised* by the violinists in one room while the cellists *played* the concerto in the other room. Shift from the passive voice, *was being practised,* to the active voice, *played.*

In discourse type

She said, *"Your violin is out of tune,"* and that *I was playing the wrong note.* Shift from the direct quotation, *"Your violin is out of tune,"* to the indirect quotation, that *I was playing the wrong note.*

Once you recognize shifts, revise them by ensuring that the same grammatical structures are used consistently throughout the sentence:

In music, where left-handed *people* seem to be talented, the right-handed world puts *them* at a disadvantage.

Even though many musicians *are* left handed, instruments *have been designed* for right handers.

Left-handed *violinists* have to pay extra to buy *their* left-handed violins.

Every time the violinist *played,* she *knew* when her instrument was out of tune.

The violinists *practised* the sonata in one room while the cellists *played* the concerto in the other room.

She said, *"Your violin is out of tune and you are playing the wrong note."*

((•●—Listen
Dangling and
Misplaced
Modifiers

1H Dangling and Misplaced Modifiers

Dangling and misplaced modifiers are words and word groups that are phrased or positioned in ways that make the meaning of a sentence unclear and sometimes even ludicrous. They are most commonly verbal phrases, prepositional phrases, and adverbs. Here are examples:

> *Reading carefully*, the shark appears unjustly villainized in popular culture. The dangling verbal phrase appears to relate to *shark*, but of course sharks do not read.

> *To extend lead out of the eversharp pencil,* the eraser cap is depressed. The dangling verbal phrase implies that *the eraser cap* does something.

> The eversharp pencil is designed to be used permanently, *only periodically replacing the lead*. The dangling verbal phrase implies that the pencil replaces the lead.

> Dr. Roy *only* wrote one book. The misplaced adverb should precede *one*.

> Defining one's terms *clearly* strengthens one's argument. *Clearly* is a "squinting" modifier which could, confusingly, apply to either *defining one's terms* or *strengthening one's argument*.

Errors of this type are difficult for writers to recognize because to the writers they are not ambiguous.

Recognition.   Verbal phrases always have implied but unstated subjects. In other words, somebody or something is performing the action of the verbal phrase, but the phrase itself does not say who or what. For clarity, that implied subject should be the same as the subject of the sentence or clause. In the first example above, the implied subject of *Reading* is not *the shark*. In the second example, the implied subject of *To extend* is not *the eraser cap*. And in the third example, the implied subject of *replacing* is not *the pencil*. Also check passive voice, because in a passive sentence the subject is not the doer of the action. In the second example, the dangler can be corrected when the verb, changed from passive to active voice, tells who should depress the eraser (see correction that follows).

Correction.   The way to correct dangling and misplaced modifiers depends on the type of error. Misplaced modifiers can often be moved to a more appropriate position:

> Dr. Roy wrote *only* one book.

> *Clearly* defining one's terms strengthens one's argument.

Dangling modifiers usually require some rewording:

> *After one carefully reads relevant newspaper and magazine reports*, the shark appears unjustly villainized in popular culture. The dangling verbal phrase is converted to a clause.

To extend lead out of the eversharp pencil, *depress the eraser cap.* The main clause is revised so that *you* is the implied subject of *depress* (as it is for *To extend).*

The eversharp pencil is designed to be used permanently, *only periodically needing the lead replaced.* The dangling verbal phrase is revised so that the implied subject of *needing* is *pencil.*

1l Restrictive and Nonrestrictive Modifiers

Some modifiers are essential to a sentence because they *restrict,* or limit, the meaning of the words they modify; others, while adding important information, are not essential to the meaning of a sentence. The first type is called restrictive and the second nonrestrictive. The terms usually refer to subordinate clauses and phrases. Here are examples of restrictive and nonrestrictive modifiers:

Restrictive

People *who plan to visit Europe* should take time to see Belgium. Relative clause modifying and identifying *People.*

The industrialized country *between the Netherlands and France on the North Sea* is constitutionally a kingdom. Prepositional phrases modifying and identifying *country.*

The Kempenland was thinly populated *before coal was discovered there.* Subordinate clause modifying *was populated* and giving meaning to the sentence.

Language and cultural differences have created friction *that has existed for centuries.* Relative clause modifying and identifying *friction.*

Nonrestrictive

Belgium has two major populations: the Flemings, *who live in the north and speak Flemish,* and the Walloons, *who live in the south and speak French.* Two relative clauses, the first modifying *Flemings* and the second modifying *Walloons.*

With Brussels in the middle of the country, both groups inhabit the city. Prepositional phrases, together modifying *inhabit.*

NATO's headquarters is in Brussels, *where it has been since its beginning in 1950.* Subordinate clause modifying *Brussels.*

Covering southeastern Belgium, the sandstone Ardennes mountains follow the Sambre and Meuse rivers. Participial (verbal) phrase modifying *mountains.*

These examples illustrate several aspects of restrictive and nonrestrictive modifiers:

1. They *modify* a word in the clause or sentence; they therefore function as adjectives or adverbs.
2. They can appear at the beginning, somewhere in the middle, or at the end of a sentence or clause.

3. Most types of subordinate elements can be either restrictive or nonrestrictive.

4. Whether a clause or phrase is restrictive or nonrestrictive depends on its function in the sentence.

5. Restrictive elements are not set off with punctuation; nonrestrictive elements are set off with commas (and sometimes dashes).

If you think the distinction between restriction and nonrestriction is not worth making, consider the following sentences, the first restrictive and the second nonrestrictive:

> This agreement shall continue for five years from the date it is made and thereafter for five year terms unless and until it is terminated by one year's notice by either party.

> This agreement shall continue for five years from the date it is made, and thereafter for five year terms, unless and until it is terminated by one year's notice by either party.

Set off with commas, the nonrestrictive *unless and until* clause indicates that the agreement can be terminated at any point (even during the first five years) with one year's notice. In the first sentence, however, the clause does restrict, or limit, the meaning of *unless and until* to subsequent five year terms, but not the initial five year agreement. A clause similar to this example created a well-known real-life error in 2006 in Atlantic Canada, which ended up costing Rogers telecommunications over two million dollars (a good reason to use restrictive and nonrestrictive clauses accurately). Often only the writer knows the intended meaning and therefore needs to make the distinction by setting off, or not setting off, the modifier.

Here are a few guidelines that might help you in making this fine distinction:

1. A modifier that modifies a proper noun (one that names a person or thing) is usually nonrestrictive, because the name is sufficient identification. Notice *Flemings* and *Walloons* in the previous example.

2. A *that* clause is almost always restrictive.

3. Adverbial subordinate clauses (those beginning with subordinating conjunctions such as *because* and *when*) are almost always restrictive and are usually not set off with commas when they appear at the end of their sentences. If they appear at the beginning of sentences, they are almost always set off with commas.

4. A nonrestrictive modifier at the beginning of a sentence is followed by a comma, one at the end is preceded by a comma, and one in the middle is enclosed with two commas.

Here is a final set of examples in which the first nonrestrictive *who* clause, set off with commas, suggests that all students are planning careers in international aid and should volunteer abroad (clearly unlikely). The second restrictive *who* clause limits the meaning to only students who are planning careers in international aid (a more likely meaning):

Students, who are planning careers in international aid, should consider volunteering abroad.

Students who are planning careers in international aid should consider volunteering abroad.

1J Adjectives and Adverbs

((•—Listen Comparatives and Superlatives

Adjectives and adverbs, often called *modifiers,* modify nouns and verbs. Adjectives modify nouns; that is, they describe, limit, explain, or alter them in some way. Adverbs modify verbs, adjectives, and other adverbs, telling more than the words by themselves would tell: drive *carefully* (adverb modifying a verb), *unexpectedly* early (adverb modifying an adjective), drive *very* carefully (adverb modifying an adverb). Adverbs usually tell how, where, when, and how much.

Adjectives and adverbs occasionally present some problems for writers. Be careful not to use adjectives when adverbs are needed, as in this incorrect sentence:

The governor suspected that the legislators were not taking him *serious.* The sentence element receiving modification is the verb *were not taking* yet the modifier *serious* is an adjective, which can only modify nouns. The correct modifier for this sentence is the adverb *seriously.* (If you are not sure whether a word is an adjective or an adverb, check your dictionary, which should identify parts of speech.)

Another problem in form concerns the *comparative* and *superlative* degrees. The comparative form of adjectives and adverbs shows a greater degree between two things, as in these correct sentences:

Your argument is *stronger* than mine. Adjective comparing *your argument* and *mine.*

Your essay makes an argument *better* than mine does. Adverb comparing how the two *make* an argument.

The comparative degree is formed by adding *-er* to shorter adjectives and adverbs (*strong, stronger; hard, harder*). Longer words are preceded by *more* (*beautiful, more beautiful; seriously, more seriously*). Do not use *-er* with *more* (not *more harder*).

The superlative form shows a greater degree among three or more things, as in these correct sentences:

This is the *best* argument I have ever read. Adjective comparing the present argument to all other arguments the writer has read.

Your essay makes the argument *best* of all essays I have read. Adverb comparing how all essays the writer has read make arguments.

The superlative degree is formed by adding *-est* to shorter adjectives and adverbs (*strong, strongest; hard, hardest*). Longer words are preceded by *most* (*beautiful, most beautiful; seriously, most seriously*). Do not use *-est* with *most* (not *most strongest*).

Do not use adjectives and adverbs gratuitously, just to fill space or because you think you ought to. They are effective only when they add meaning to a sentence.

2 Verbs

Verbs are the core of a sentence; together with subjects, they make statements. Verbs often tell what the subject is doing:

> The company *agreed* to plead guilty to criminal charges.

> Nearly every miner *can name* a casualty of black lung disease.

Another common function of verbs is to link subjects to complements:

> Fort Nelson *is* a community of 5,000 in the north of British Columbia.

Sometimes the verb tells something about the subject, as the following passive verb does:

> Casualties of mining *cannot be measured* only by injuries.

Through changes in form, verbs can tell the time of the action (past, present, future), the number of the subject (singular or plural), and the person of the subject (first person, *I, we;* second person, *you;* third person, *he, she, it, they*).

Watch
Common Grammar Errors: 11. Wrong Verb Tense or Verb Form

2A Tense

Writers can encounter problems with verbs because verbs, unlike most other words in English, have many forms, and a slight shift in form can alter meaning. Notice how the meanings of the following sentences change when the verbs change:

> The concert *starts* at 8:15 p.m.

> The concert *started* at 8:15 p.m.

The first verb implies that the concert has not yet begun; the second, that it had already begun. Observe how the verb *vanish* changes in the following sentences to indicate differences in time, or *tense:*

Present:	Many agricultural jobs *vanish.*
Past:	Many agricultural jobs *vanished.*
Future:	Many agricultural jobs *will vanish.*
Perfect:	Many agricultural jobs *have vanished.*
Past Perfect:	Many agricultural jobs *had vanished.*
Future Perfect:	Many agricultural jobs *will have vanished.*

Omitting an *-ed* ending or using the wrong helping verb can give readers a false message.

Helping (Auxiliary) Verbs.   It is also important to use a form that is a *finite,* or an actual, verb. In the following example, the word that appears to be a verb (italicized) is not a finite verb:

> The amphibian species *dying* in the rainforest.

The word *dying* docs not havc one of the primary functions of verbs—telling the time of the action, called *tense*. The time of the occurrence could have been the past (*the amphibian species were dying*), the present (*the amphibian species are dying*), or the future (*the amphibian species will be dying*). We also don't know whether the writer meant one species or many. The *-ing* form is a *verbal* and requires a helping, or auxiliary, verb to make it finite, or able to tell time: words such as *am, is, are, was, were* (forms of *be*). Other helping verbs are *do* (*Do* you *want* the paper? She *doesn't want* the paper) and *have* (I *haven't seen* the paper; *has* she *seen* it?).

Irregular Verbs.   Most verbs change forms in a regular way: *want* in the present becomes *wanted* in the past, *wanting* with the auxiliary *be* (i.e., *is wanting*), and *wanted* with the auxiliary *have* (i.e., *have wanted*). Many verbs change irregularly, however—internally rather than at the ending. Here are a few of the most common irregular verbs:

Base Form	Past Tense	Present Participle	Past Participle
be (is, am, are)	was, were	being	been
come	came	coming	come
do	did	doing	done
drink	drank	drinking	drunk
give	gave	giving	given
go	went	going	gone
grow	grew	growing	grown
lie	laid	lying	lain
see	saw	seeing	seen
take	took	taking	taken
teach	taught	teaching	taught
throw	threw	throwing	thrown
wear	wore	wearing	worn
write	wrote	writing	written

Check your dictionary for the forms of other verbs you suspect may be irregular.

The verb form that is perhaps the most troublesome is the *-s* form in the present tense. This form is used for all singular nouns and the pronouns *he, she,* and *it*. (See 2D Subject-Verb Agreement.)

2B Voice

Listen
Passive versus
Active Voice

English sentences are usually written in the active voice, in which the subject of the sentence is the doer of the action of the verb:

Scott misplaced the file folder. *Scott,* the subject of the sentence, performed the action, *misplaced.*

With the passive voice, the doer of the action is the object of a preposition or is omitted entirely:

The file folder was misplaced by Scott. *File folder* is now the subject of the sentence.

The file folder was misplaced. The person doing the action is not named.

As a writer, you need to decide whether to use the active or passive voice. The passive voice requires more words than the active voice, it can hide the doer, and its overuse reduces clarity and increases confusion. This is why you may have been told that you should *never use the passive voice.*

Choose the passive voice when it is appropriate to the genre and to your readers' needs. For genres such as rhetorical and literary analyses, you will probably choose active voice because readers of these genres usually want to know who is doing what to whom. In other situations, you may choose to use the passive voice, either because you do not know the doer's identity or because the doer's identity is unimportant or obvious to the reader. When writing a lab report in a chemistry course, for instance, your reader does not need to be told who specifically combined the chemicals. Finally, the passive voice can be useful if you want to keep the subjects consistent within a paragraph.

But unless you have good reason to use the passive voice, avoid it. First, look for passive voice by noting *by* phrases near the ends of your sentences. If you find any, determine whether the subject of your sentence performs the action of your verb. If not, revise the sentence so that it does. Another way to find occurrences of the passive voice is to look for forms of *be: am, is, are, was, were, been, being.* Not all these verbs will be passive, but if they function as part of an action verb, determine whether the subject performs the action. If it does not, and if your sentence would be clearer with the subject performing the action, revise to the active voice.

2C Mood

English verbs are stated in one of three moods: indicative, imperative, and subjunctive. In most writing and speaking, the most commonly used mood by far is the *indicative mood*, which is used to make statements, to ask questions, and to declare opinions. For example:

Not many people today *think* the world *is* flat. Makes a statement.

Does anybody today *think* the world is flat? Asks a question.

Members of the Flat Earth Society *should re-evaluate* their thinking. Declares an opinion.

Verbs in the *imperative mood* issue commands, requests, or directions. Imperative verbs never change form. When the subject of an imperative verb is not explicitly identified, it is understood to be *you.*

Hand in your exams now. Issues command.

Please *complete* this report by tomorrow morning. Issues request.

Turn right at the light and *drive* for another two blocks. Issues directions.

Verbs in the *subjunctive mood* communicate wishes, make statements contrary to fact, list requirements and demands, and imply skepticism or doubt. They usually appear in clauses introduced by *if, that, as if,* and *as though.* Use the base form of the verb for the present tense subjunctive. For the past tense subjunctive of the verb *be,* use *were* for all subjects.

> She wishes that corporations *were* more environmentally responsible.
> Communicates wish.

> If the world *were* to end tomorrow, we would not have to pay taxes anymore.
> Makes statement contrary to fact.

> The summons requires that potential jurors *arrive* punctually at 8:00 a.m. and *sign* in with the court clerk. Lists requirements.

> He presents himself as if he *were* an expert on medieval literature. Implies skepticism.

Be sure to select the correct verb forms to express indicative, imperative, and subjunctive moods.

2D Subject-Verb Agreement

Clauses are made of subjects and verbs plus their modifiers and other related words. A fundamental principle of usage is that verbs agree with their subjects. In most cases, this principle presents no problem: You say "Birds *have* feathers," not "Birds *has* feathers." But not all sentences are this simple. Before getting into the problem areas, consider first that errors in subject-verb agreement occur only with present tense verbs and the verb tenses that use present tense forms of helping verbs (such as *have* and *be*). And, except for the irregular verb *be* (with its forms *am, is, are, was, were*), the problem centres on third-person singular verbs with their *-s* ending. Here is the problem illustrated. Notice that only the verbs in the third-person singular are different. Unfortunately, all nouns are third person and, when singular, require this form in the present tense.

	Present		**Present Perfect**	
	Singular	**Plural**	**Singular**	**Plural**
First person	I work	we work	I have worked	we have worked
Second person	you work	you work	you have worked	you have worked
Third person	he (she, it) works	they work	he (she, it) has worked	they have worked

It is the *-s* form, then, that you need to watch for to avoid errors in subject-verb agreement. Here are some issues that may cause problems.

Intervening Subordinate Element

When a subject and a verb are side by side, they usually do not present a problem. Often, however, writers separate them with subordinate elements, such as clauses, prepositional or verbal phrases, and other elements. The result may be a subject-verb agreement error. The following sentence illustrates this problem:

> The realization that life is a series of compromises never occur to some people.
> The subject is *realization,* a singular noun, and should be followed by the singular

((•⃝ **Listen** Audio Lesson Section 1: Big Ideas— Correcting Common Errors: Subject-Verb Agreement and Parallel Structure

((•⃝ **Listen** Audio Lesson Section 2: Practice Questions— Correcting Common Errors: Subject-Verb Agreement and Parallel Structure

((•⃝ **Listen** Subject-Object Agreement and Subject-Complement Agreement

verb *occurs*. The corrected sentence would read "The realization that life is a series of compromises never occurs to some people."

Subject Complement

Subject complements follow some verbs and rename the subject, although they are not always in the same number as the subject. Because a singular subject may have a plural complement, and vice versa, confused writers might make the verb agree with the complement instead of the subject. Here's an example:

> **The result of this mistake are guilt, low self-esteem, and depression.** The subject is *result*, not *guilt, low self-esteem,* and *depression*; the singular subject should be followed by the singular verb *is*. The corrected sentence would read "The result of this mistake is guilt, low self-esteem, and depression."

Compound Subject

Two or more words may be compounded to make a subject. Whether they are singular or plural depends on their connector. Subjects connected by *and* and *but* are plural, but those connected by *or* and *nor* are singular or plural depending on whether the item closer to the verb is singular or plural. Here are examples:

> **The young mother and the superior student *are* both candidates for compulsive perfectionism.** Two subjects, *mother* and *student,* are joined by *and* and take a plural verb.

> **Promotions or an employee award *tells* the perfectionist he or she is achieving personal goals.** When two subjects, *promotions* and *award,* are joined by *or,* the verb agrees with the nearer one; in this sentence, a singular verb is required.

> **An employee award or promotions *tell* the perfectionist he or she is achieving personal goals.** Here the plural verb, *tell,* agrees with *promotions,* the closer of the two subjects.

Indefinite Pronoun as Subject

Indefinite pronouns are defined and listed under 3C Pronoun Agreement. Although these words often seem plural in meaning and are sometimes even used as plural in casual speech, most of them are singular grammatically. When indefinite pronouns are the subjects of sentences or clauses, their verbs are usually singular. Here are examples:

> **Everyone *has* at some time worried about achieving goals.** The singular indefinite pronoun *everyone* takes a singular verb, *has*.

> **Each car and truck on the highway *was* creeping along on the icy pavement.** The singular indefinite pronoun, *each,* requires a singular verb, *was*.

> **Neither of us *is* going to worry about being late.** The singular indefinite pronoun, *neither,* takes a singular verb, *is*.

Nevertheless, some of us *are* going to be very late. The indefinite pronoun *some* (like *all, any,* and *none*) is singular or plural depending on context; compare "Some of the book *is* boring."

Inverted Sentence Order

Inverted sentence order can confuse your natural inclination toward subject-verb agreement. Examples of inverted order are questions, plus sentences beginning with *there.* Sentences like these demand closer attention to agreement.

Have the results of the test come back yet? The plural subject, *results,* takes a plural verb, *have.*

There *are* many special services provided just for kids at hotels, ski lodges, and restaurants. The plural subject, *services,* takes a plural verb, *are. There* is never a subject; it only holds the place for the subject in an inverted sentence.

Intervening Relative Clause

Subordinate clauses that begin with the relative pronouns *who, which,* or *that* present special problems in subject-verb agreement. Their verbs must agree with their own subjects, not with a word in another clause. These subordinate clauses demand special attention because whether the pronouns are singular or plural depends on their antecedents. These sentences illustrate agreement within relative clauses:

Every person who *attends* the baseball game will receive a free cap. *Who,* the subject of *attends,* means "person," a singular noun.

John is one of the few people I know who *study* amphibians. *Who,* the subject of *study*, means "people," a plural noun.

John is the only one of all the people I know who *studies* amphibians. *Who* in this sentence means "one."

3 Pronouns

Pronouns can have all the same sentence functions as nouns; the difference is that pronouns do not have the meaning that nouns have. Nouns name things; a noun stands for the thing itself. Pronouns, however, refer only to nouns. Whenever that reference is ambiguous or inconsistent, there is a problem in clarity.

3A Pronoun Case

Case is a grammatical term for the way nouns and pronouns show their relationships to other parts of a sentence. In English, nouns have only two case forms: the regular form (the one listed in a dictionary, such as *year*) and the possessive form (used to show ownership or connection, such as *year's*; possessive nouns are discussed in 5J Apostrophe).

Watch
Common Grammar Errors: 6. Pronoun Case Problems

Pronouns, however, have retained their case forms. Here are the forms for personal and relative pronouns:

	Subjective	Objective	Possessive
Personal	I	me	my, mine
	you	you	your, yours
	he	him	his
	she	her	her, hers
	it	it	its
	we	us	our, ours
	they	them	their, theirs
Relative	who	whom	whose
	whoever	whomever	whosever

Notice, first, that possessive pronouns, unlike possessive nouns, do not take apostrophes—none of them. Sometimes writers confuse possessive pronouns with contractions, which do have apostrophes (such as *it's,* meaning *it is* or *it has;* and *who's,* meaning *who is;* for a further discussion, see 5J Apostrophe).

Another problem writers sometimes have with pronoun case is using a subjective form when they need the objective or using an objective form when they need the subjective.

Subjective Case.   Use the subjective forms for subjects and for words referring to subjects, as in these examples:

Among the patients a nutritionist sees are the grossly overweight people *who* have tried all kinds of diets. *Who is subject of the verb have tried in its own clause.*

They have a life history of obesity and diets. *They is the subject of have.*

He and the patient work out a plan for permanent weight control. *He and patient are the compound subjects of work.*

The patient understands that the ones who work out the diet plan are *he* and the nutritionist. *He and nutritionist refer to ones, the subject of the clause.*

Notice that pronoun case is determined by the function of the pronoun in its own clause and that compounding (*he and the patient*) has no effect on case.

Objective Case.   Use the objective forms for objects of all kinds:

"Between *you* and *me,*" said the patient to his nutritionist, "I'm ready for something that works." *You and me are objects of the preposition between.*

An exercise program is usually assigned to the patient for *whom* dieting is prescribed. *Whom is the object of the preposition for.*

The nutritionist gives *her* a suitable alternative to couch sitting. *Her is the indirect object of gives.*

Modest exercise combined with modest dieting can affect *him or her* dramatically. *Him or her is the direct object of can affect.*

Having advised *them* about diet and exercise, the nutritionist instructs dieters about behavioural change. *Them is the object of the participle having advised.*

Notice again that the case of a pronoun is determined by its function in its own clause and is not affected by compounding (*you and me*).

Possessive Case.   Use the possessive forms to indicate ownership. Possessive pronouns have two forms: adjective forms (*my, your, his, her, its, our, their*) and possessive forms (*mine, yours, his, hers, its, ours, theirs*). The adjective forms appear before nouns or gerunds; the possessive forms replace possessive nouns.

The patient purchased *his* supplements from the drug store *his* nutritionist recommended. *Adjective form before nouns.*

His swimming every day produced results faster than he anticipated. *Adjective form before gerund.*

His was a difficult task to accomplish, but the rewards of weight loss were great. *Possessive form replacing possessive noun.*

3B Pronoun Reference

Personal and relative pronouns (see list under 3A Pronoun Case) must refer unambiguously to their antecedents or previous references. Pronouns and antecedents must agree.
   Ambiguous pronoun reference may occur in various ways:

- More than one possible antecedent.
- Adjective used as intended antecedent.
- Implied antecedent.
- Too much separation between antecedent and pronoun.

Here are sentences in which the pronouns do not clearly refer to their antecedents:

The immunologist refused to admit fraudulence of the data reported by a former colleague in a paper *he* had cosigned. *More than one possible antecedent. He could refer to immunologist or to colleague.*

In Carolyn Chute's book *The Beans of Egypt, Maine, she* treats poverty with concern and understanding. *Adjective used as intended antecedent (possessive nouns function as adjectives). In this case, Carolyn Chute's modifies book and cannot serve as an antecedent of the pronoun she.*

It says in the newspaper that the economy will not improve soon. *Implied antecedent. There is no antecedent for it.*

Watch
Common
Grammar
Errors: 5.
Pronoun
Reference
Problems

In Vancouver *they* have bike lanes through the downtown core. Implied antecedent. There is no antecedent for *they*.

Faulty pronoun reference is corrected by clarifying the relationship between the pronoun and its intended antecedent. Observe how the example sentences have been revised:

The immunologist refused to admit fraudulence of the data reported by a former colleague in a paper *the immunologist* had cosigned. *The immunologist* replaces the unclear pronoun *he*.

In *her* book *The Beans of Egypt, Maine, Carolyn Chute* treats poverty with concern and understanding. The possessive pronoun *her* replaces the possessive noun and refers to the noun subject, *Carolyn Chute*.

The newspaper reports that the economy will not improve soon. The unclear pronoun *it* is replaced by its implied antecedent, *newspaper*.

Vancouver has bike lanes through the downtown core. The unclear pronoun *they* is replaced by *Vancouver*.

3C Pronoun Agreement

Some pronoun errors occur because the pronoun and its antecedent do not agree. Pronouns must agree with their antecedents in number, person, and gender. (See the list of pronouns in 3A Pronoun Case.)

Compound Antecedents

Problems sometimes occur with compound antecedents. If the antecedents are joined by *and,* the pronoun is plural; if they are joined by *or,* the pronoun agrees with the nearer antecedent. Here are examples of correct usage:

In the pediatric trauma centre, the head doctor and head nurse direct *their* medical team. The pronoun *their* refers to both *doctor* and *nurse*.

The head doctor or the head nurse directs *his or her* team. The pronouns *his or her* refer to the closer antecedent, *nurse* (because the gender of the nurse is not known, the neutral alternatives are used).

The head doctor or the other doctors give *their* help when it is needed. The pronoun *their* agrees with the closer antecedent, *doctors*.

Indefinite Pronouns as Antecedents

A particularly troublesome kind of agreement is that between personal or relative pronouns and *indefinite pronouns*. As their name implies, indefinite pronouns do not refer to particular people or things; grammatically they are usually singular but are often intended as plural. Some common indefinite pronouns are *all, any, anybody, each, either, everybody, neither, no one, nothing, one, some, somebody,* and *something*.

Like nouns, these pronouns can serve as antecedents of personal and relative pronouns. But because most of them are grammatically singular, they can be troublesome in sentences. Here are examples of correct usage:

Everyone in the trauma centre has *his or her* specific job to do. **or** All the personnel in the trauma centre have *their* specific jobs to do. The neutral, though wordy, alternative *his or her* agrees with the singular indefinite pronoun *everyone*. Despite what you may have heard in casual usage, in an academic paper it is incorrect to write *"Everyone in the trauma centre has their specific job to do"* because you are following the singular indefinite pronoun *everyone* with the plural *their*. The second sentence illustrates the use of the plural when gender is unknown. *All*, like the indefinite pronouns *some, any, none, most,* and *more*, can be either singular or plural depending on the sentence.

Each of them does *his or her* job efficiently and competently. **or** *All* of them do *their* jobs efficiently and competently. *Each* is singular, but *all* can be either singular or plural, depending on context (compare *"All* literature has *its* place").

Shifts in Person

Agreement errors in *person* are shifts between *I* or *we* (first person), *you* (second person), and *he, she, it,* and *they* (third person). These errors are probably more often a result of carelessness than of imperfect knowledge. Being more familiar with casual speech than formal writing, writers sometimes shift from *I* to *you*, for example, when only one of them is meant, as in this sentence:

My interpretation of the advertisement focuses on its *pathos* appeal, which is so well done it makes *you* forget that the ad is really selling a product. The person represented by *you* was not present. The writer means *me*.

See also 1G Shifts.

3D Relative Pronouns

((•─[**Listen**
Couple Who versus Couple That—
Relative Pronoun Agreement

Use relative pronouns to introduce clauses that modify nouns or pronouns. Personal relative pronouns refer to people. They include *who, whom, whoever, whomever,* and *whose*. Nonpersonal relative pronouns refer to things. They include *which, whichever, whatever,* and *whose*.

Use *which* to introduce nonrestrictive clauses and *that* to introduce restrictive clauses (see 1I Restrictive and Nonrestrictive Modifiers). Use *who* to refer to the subject of the sentence and *whom* to refer to an object of the verb or preposition. Following are examples of common errors:

The lawyer *that* lost the case today went to Osgoode Hall law school. Uses impersonal relative pronoun *that*.

Conflict between the two parties led to the lawsuit *that* was finally settled today. The relative pronoun *that* introduces a nonrestrictive clause that modifies *lawsuit*. Nonrestrictive clauses supply extra information to the sentence, not defining information.

The case resulted in a ruling, *which* favoured the plaintiff. The relative pronoun *which* introduces a restrictive clause that modifies *ruling*. Restrictive clauses supply defining information.

Later, the lawyer *whom* lost the case spoke with the jurors *who* we had interviewed. The first relative pronoun *whom* refers to the subject *lawyer* while the second relative pronoun *who* refers to the object of the verb *had interviewed*.

Once you recognize relative pronoun errors, it is usually easy to fix them:

The lawyer *who* lost the case today went to Osgoode Hall law school.

Conflict between the two parties led to the lawsuit, *which* was finally settled today.

The case resulted in a ruling *that* favoured the plaintiff.

Later, the lawyer *who* lost the case spoke with the jurors *whom* we had interviewed.

4 Style

There is no such thing as "correct style." Style is a choice you make as a writer in response to the rhetorical situation. In Chapter 13, "Choosing a Style," you learned several strategies for using style in ways that are appropriate for your purpose, readers, and genre. Here, you will learn strategies for writing with clarity and conciseness. You will also learn strategies for recognizing when certain kinds of language are and are not appropriate.

4A Conciseness

Watch
Common
Grammar
Errors: 19.
Wordiness
and
Redundancy

Nobody wants to read more words than necessary. Concise writing shows that you are considerate of your readers. You do not need to eliminate details and other content to achieve conciseness; rather, you cut empty words, repetition, and unnecessary details.

In the following passage, all the italicized words could be omitted without altering the meaning:

In the final analysis, I feel that the United States should have converted to the *use of the* metric system *of measurement* a long time ago. *In the present day and age,* the United States, except for Borneo and Liberia, is the *one and* only country in the *entire* world that has not yet adopted this measurement system.

You may choose to repeat key words when you are striving for a certain effect (such as setting a tone or establishing character), but take care to avoid pointless repetition, which only bores and slows down your readers.

Follow these guidelines to achieve conciseness in your writing:

1. **Avoid redundancy.** Redundant words and expressions needlessly repeat what has already been said. Delete them when they appear in your writing.

2. **Avoid wordy expressions.** Phrases such as *In the final analysis* and *In the present day and age* add no important information to sentences and should be removed and/or replaced.

3. **Avoid unnecessary intensifiers.** Intensifiers such as *really, very, clearly, quite,* and *of course* usually fail to add meaning to the words they modify and therefore are often unnecessary. Delete them when doing so does not change the meaning

of the sentence, or when you could replace the words with a single word (for instance, replacing *very good* with *excellent*).

4. **Avoid excess use of prepositional phrases.** The use of too many prepositional phrases within a sentence makes for wordy writing. Always use constructions that require the fewest words.

5. **Avoid negating constructions.** Negating constructions using words such as *no* and *not* often add unneeded words to sentences. Use shorter alternatives when they are available.

6. **Use the passive voice only when necessary.** Passive constructions require more words than active constructions (see 2B Voice). They can also obscure meaning by concealing the sentence's subject. When there is no good reason to use the passive voice, choose the active voice.

Here are more examples of wordy sentences that violate these guidelines:

If the two groups *cooperate together,* there will be *positive benefits* for both. Uses redundancy.

There are some people *who* think the metric system is un-American. Uses wordy expression.

The climb up the mountain was *very* hard on my legs and *really* taxed my lungs and heart. Uses unnecessary modifiers.

On the eleventh day of December in 1997, Western leaders signed the Kyoto Accord *in Japan for protocols going into effect in 2005.* Uses too many prepositional phrases.

She *did not like* hospitals. Uses negating construction when a shorter alternative is available.

The door *was closed* by that man over there. Uses passive voice when active voice is preferable.

Corrections to the wordy sentences above result in concise sentences:

If the two groups cooperate, both will benefit. This correction also replaces the wordy construction *there will be . . . for both* with a shorter, more forceful alternative.

Some people think the metric system is un-American.

The climb up the mountain was hard on my legs and taxed my lungs and heart.

On 11 December 1997, Western leaders signed the Kyoto Accord, which went into effect in 2005.

She hated hospitals.

That man over there closed the door.

4B Appropriate Language

Effective writers communicate using appropriate language; that is, language that:

1. Suits the genre and rhetorical situation (topic, angle, purpose, readers, context).
2. Avoids sexist usage.
3. Avoids bias and stereotype.

Suitability

The style and tone of your writing should be suitable to your rhetorical situation and the genre you have chosen. Some situations require *formal language.* Formal language communicates clearly and directly with a minimum of stylistic flourish. Its tone is serious, objective, and often detached. Formal language avoids slang, pretentious words, and unnecessary technical jargon. *Informal language,* on the other hand, is particular to the writer's personality or social group and assumes a closer and more familiar relationship between the writer and the reader. Its tone is casual, subjective, and intimate. Informal language can also employ slang and other words that would be inappropriate in formal writing.

Keep in mind that what counts as suitable language always depends on the rhetorical situation you are facing and the genre you are using. Pretentious words might be appropriate if you were writing a parody of someone you feel is pretentious. Certain technical jargon would be not only suitable but also preferable in a technical report written for readers who are experts in the field. Slang could get across just the message you want in a casual genre, in which you want to identify with a particular group that uses particular terms. Formal language conveys the professional tone you want in academic writing. Use your genre know-how and rhetorical awareness to help you decide when a certain kind of language is or is not suitable.

As informal language is rarely used within most academic, technical, or business settings, the following examples show errors in the use of formal language:

The director told the board members to *push off.* Uses informal language.

Professor Oyo *dissed* Marta when she arrived late to his class for the third time in a row. Uses slang.

The *aromatic essence* of the gardenia was intoxicating. Uses pretentious words.

The doctor told him to take *salicylate* to ease the symptoms of *viral rhinorrhea.* Uses unnecessary jargon.

Employing formal language correctly, these examples could be revised as follows:

The director told the board members to leave.

Professor Oyo spoke disrespectfully to Marta when she arrived late to his class for the third time in a row.

The scent of the gardenia was intoxicating.

The doctor told him to take aspirin to ease his cold symptoms.

Sexist Usage

Gender-exclusive terms such as *policeman* and *chairman* are offensive to many readers today. Writers who are sensitive to their audience, therefore, avoid such terms, replacing them with expressions such as *police officer* and *chairperson* or *chair*. Most sexist usage in language involves masculine nouns, masculine pronouns, and patronizing terms.

Masculine Nouns.   Do not use *man* and its compounds generically. For many people, these words are specific to men and do not account for women as separate and equal people. Here are some examples of masculine nouns and appropriate gender-neutral substitutions:

Masculine Noun	Gender-Neutral Substitution
mailman	mail carrier
businessman	businessperson, executive, manager
fireman	firefighter
man-hours	work hours
mankind	humanity, people
manmade	manufactured, synthetic
salesman	salesperson, sales representative, sales agent
spokesman	spokesperson, representative

Using gender-neutral substitutions often entails using a more specific word for a generalized term, which adds more precision to writing.

Masculine Pronouns. Avoid using the masculine pronouns *he, him,* and *his* in a generic sense, meaning both male and female. This can pose some challenges, however, because English does not have a generic singular pronoun that can be used instead. Consider the following options:

1. Eliminate the pronoun.

   Every writer has an individual style. Instead of Every writer has his own style.

2. Use plural forms.

   Writers have their own styles. Instead of A writer has his own style.

3. Use *he or she, one,* or *you* as alternates only sparingly.

   Each writer has his or her own style. Instead of Each writer has his own style.

   One has an individual writing style. Instead of He has his own individual writing style.

   You have your own writing style. Instead of A writer has his own style.

Please note that academic writing avoids the "you" pronoun as overly casual.

Patronizing Terms.   Avoid terms that cast men or women in gender-exclusive roles or imply that women are subordinate to men. Here are some examples of biased or stereotypical terms and their gender-neutral substitutions:

Biased/Stereotypical Term	Gender-Neutral Substitution
lady lawyer	lawyer
male nurse	nurse
career girl	professional, attorney, manager
coed	student
housewife	homemaker
stewardess	flight attendant
cleaning lady	housecleaner

Biases and Stereotypes

Biased and stereotypical language can be hurtful and can perpetuate discrimination. Most writers are sensitive to racial and ethnic biases or stereotypes, but writers should also avoid language that shows insensitivity to age, class, religion, disability, and sexual orientation. The accepted terms for identifying groups and group members have changed over the years and continue to change today. Avoid using terms that have fallen into dis- use such as *Indian* or *Oriental;* instead, use accepted terms such as *aboriginal* or *Asian.*

((•• ⌐Listen Audio
Lesson
Section 1: Big
Ideas—
Punctuation
and
Mechanics

5 Punctuation, Mechanics, and Spelling

Punctuation is a system of signals telling readers how the parts of written discourse relate to one another. Punctuation provides readers with cues for interpreting the writer's words as the writer intended them to be understood.

This section discusses punctuation used within and at the ends of sentences. Other marks, those used within words (apostrophes, hyphens, italics, and slashes), are also explained later in this section.

((•• ⌐Listen
Audio Lesson
Section 2:
Practice
Questions—
Punctuation
and
Mechanics

5A End Punctuation

A period is the normal mark for ending sentences. A question mark ends a sentence that asks a direct question, and an exclamation point ends forceful assertions.

Period .

Sentences normally end with a period.

> Studies suggest that eating fish two or three times a week may reduce the risk of heart attack. Statement.

> Eat two or three servings of fish a week. Mild command.

> The patient asked whether eating fish would reduce the risk of heart attack. Indirect question.

Avoid inserting a period before the end of a sentence; the result will be a fragment (see 1A Fragments). Sentences can be long or short; their length does not determine their completion. Both of the following examples are complete sentences:

Eat fish. Mild command; the subject, you, is understood.

In a two-year study of 1,000 survivors of heart attack, researchers found a 29 percent reduction in mortality among those who regularly ate fish or took a fish oil supplement. Statement; one sentence.

Question Mark   ?

A sentence that asks a direct question ends in a question mark.

How does decaffeinated coffee differ from regular coffee?

Do not use a question mark to end an indirect question:

The customer asked how decaffeinated coffee differs from regular coffee.

With quoted questions, place the question mark inside the final quotation marks:

The customer asked, "How does decaffeinated coffee differ from regular coffee?"

Exclamation Point   !

The exclamation point tells readers that the sentence should be interpreted as forceful or dramatic.

Fire!

Shut that door immediately!

Because they give the impression of shouting, exclamation points are rarely needed in formal business and academic writing.

5B Semicolon   ;

Listen
Semicolons

Semicolons are mainly used for connecting two independent clauses.

Dengue hemorrhagic fever is a viral infection common to Southeast Asia; it kills about 5,000 children a year.

Sometimes the second clause contains a transitional adverb (see 1B Comma Splices):

Dengue has existed in Asia for centuries; *however,* it grew more virulent in the 1950s.

Do not use a comma where a semicolon or period is required; the result is a comma splice (see 1B Comma Splices). In contrast, a semicolon used in place of a comma may result in a type of fragment (see 1A Fragments):

In populations where people have been stricken by an infectious virus, survivors have antibodies in their bloodstreams; *which prevent or reduce the severity of subsequent infections.* The semicolon makes a fragment of the *which* clause.

Do not confuse the semicolon with the colon (see 5D Colon). While the semicolon connects independent clauses, a colon ordinarily does not.

The semicolon is also used to separate items in a series when the items contain internal commas:

Scientists are researching the effects of staphylococcus bacteria, which cause infections in deep wounds; influenza A virus, which causes respiratory flu; and conjunctivitis bacteria, which have at times caused fatal purpuric fever.

((•—[**Listen**
Commas
Between
Coordinate
Adjectives

5C Comma   ,

The comma is probably the most troublesome mark of punctuation because it has so many uses. Its main uses are explained here.

Compound Sentences.

A comma joins two independent clauses connected with a coordinating conjunction (see 1B Comma Splices):

Martinique is a tropical island in the West Indies, *and* it attracts flocks of tourists annually.

Do not use the comma between independent clauses without the conjunction, even if the second clause begins with a transitional adverb:

Faulty: Martinique is a tropical island in the West Indies, it attracts flocks of tourists annually. Two independent clauses with no conjunction creates a comma splice.

Faulty: Martinique is a tropical island in the West Indies, consequently it attracts flocks of tourists annually. Two independent clauses with a transitional adverb creates a comma splice.

Introductory Sentence Elements.

Commas set off a variety of introductory sentence elements, as illustrated here:

When the French colonized Martinique in 1635, they eliminated the native Caribs. Introductory subordinate clause.

Choosing death over subservience, the Caribs leaped into the sea. Introductory participial (verbal) phrase.

Before their death, they warned of a "mountain of fire" on the island. Introductory prepositional phrase.

Subsequently, the island's volcano erupted. Introductory transitional adverb.

Short prepositional phrases sometimes are not set off with commas:

In 1658 the Caribs leaped to their death.

Sometimes, however, a comma must be used after a short prepositional phrase to prevent misreading:

Before, they had predicted retribution. Comma is required to prevent misreading.

Nonrestrictive and Parenthetical Elements.

Words that interrupt the flow of a sentence are set off with commas before and after. If they come at the end of a sentence, they are set off with one comma.

In this class are nonrestrictive modifiers (see 1I Restrictive and Nonrestrictive Modifiers), transitional adverbs (see 1B Comma Splices), and a few other types of interrupters. Here are examples:

This rugged island, *which Columbus discovered in 1502,* exports sugar and rum. Nonrestrictive *which* clause; commas before and after.

A major part of the economy, *however,* is tourism. Interrupting transitional adverb; commas before and after.

Tourists, *attracted to the island by its climate,* enjoy discovering its culture. Interrupting participial (verbal) phrase (see 1A Fragments); commas before and after.

A popular tradition in Martinique is the Carnival, *which occurs just before Lent each year.* Nonrestrictive *which* clause; one comma.

Martinique is an overseas department of France, *a status conferred in 1946.* An absolute, ending the sentence (participial phrase plus the noun it modifies).

Series
Commas separate items in a series:

Martiniquans dance to *steel drums, clarinets, empty bottles, and banjos.* Four nouns.

Dressing in colourful costumes, dancing through the streets, and thoroughly enjoying the celebration, Martiniquans celebrate Carnival with enthusiasm. Three participial (verbal) phrases.

Martinique has a population of over 300,000, its main religion is Roman Catholicism, and its languages are French and Creole dialect. Three independent clauses.

Various sentence elements can make up a series, but the joined elements should be grammatically equivalent (see 1D Parallelism, which discusses faulty parallelism). Common practice calls for a comma before the conjunction joining the last item in the series, often called the "serial comma" or the "Oxford comma."

Quotations
Commas set off quoted sentences from the words that introduce them:

"A wise man," says David Hume, "proportions his belief to the evidence."

According to Plato, "Writing will produce forgetfulness" in writers because "they will not need to exercise their memories." The second clause is not set off with a comma.

"*X* on beer casks indicates beer that paid ten shillings duty, and hence it came to mean beer of a given quality," reports *The Dictionary of Phrase and Fable.*

Quotations introduced with *that* and other connectors (such as *because* in the second sentence here) are not set off with commas. Commas at the end of quotations go inside the quotation marks.

Coordinate Adjectives

Commas separate adjectives that equally modify a noun:

> The Canada Food Guide was designed as a *meaningful, memorable* way to represent the ideal daily diet. Two adjectives modify the noun *way* equally.

When you're not sure about using a comma, try inserting the coordinating conjunction *and* between the two adjectives to see if they are truly coordinate (*meaningful and memorable*). Do not use a comma between adjectives that are not coordinate or between the last adjective and the noun being modified. (See also 1J Adjectives and Adverbs.)

Addresses and Dates

Use a comma to separate city and province in an address, but not to set off the postal code:

> Maple Ridge, British Columbia V2X 2R0 *or* Maple Ridge, BC V2X 2R0

In a sentence, a province name is enclosed in commas:

> The letter from Maple Ridge, British Columbia, arrived by express mail.

Dates are treated similarly:

> January 5, 1886 *but* 5 January 1886

> The events of January 5, 1886, are no longer remembered. When other punctuation is not required, the year is followed by a comma.

Commas to Avoid

Some people mistakenly believe that commas should be used wherever they might pause in speech. A comma does mean pause, but not all pauses are marked by commas. Use a comma only when you know you need one. Avoid the following comma uses:

1. To set off restrictive sentence elements:

   > People, *who want a balanced diet,* can refer to the Canada Food Guide. The restrictive *who* clause is necessary to identify *people* and should not be set off with commas.

2. To separate a subject from its verb and a preposition from its object:

   > People who want a balanced diet, can refer to the Canada Food Guide. The comma following the *who* clause separates the subject, *people,* from its verb, *can refer to.* Treat the noun phrase (*People who want a balanced diet*) as if it were a single word.

   > The food guide recommends consuming food from grains, *such as,* bread, cereals, rice, and pasta. The preposition *such as* should not be followed by a comma.

3. To follow a coordinating conjunction (see 1B Comma Splices):

> The food guide describes a new approach to a balanced diet. But, some people do not choose to follow it. The coordinating conjunction *but* should not be set off with a comma.

4. To separate two independent clauses (see 1B Comma Splices) not joined with a coordinating conjunction:

> The guide recommends fewer servings of dairy and meat products, therefore consumers would buy less of these higher-priced foods. The comma should be replaced with a semicolon (5B).

5. To set off coordinate elements joined with a coordinating conjunction:

> Vegetables and fruits are emphasized, *and should be eaten several times a day.* The coordinating conjunction *and* joins a second verb, *should be eaten,* not a second independent clause; therefore no comma is needed.

5D Colon :

Colons connect two sentence parts, as a hinge connects a door to its frame. Colons tell readers that a second part of the sentence is coming and that the second part will complement the first part by providing either: (1) a list that has been anticipated in the first part, or (2) an explanation, restatement, or elaboration of the first part:

> The space shuttle *Challenger* lifted off on January 28, 1986, with a seven-member crew: Francis R. Scobee, Michael J. Smith, Ronald E. McNair, Ellison S. Onizuka, Judith A. Resnik, Gregory B. Jarvis, and Christa McAuliffe. The list explains *crew.*

> A twelve-member investigating team discovered the cause of the disaster: a leak in one of the shuttle's two solid-fuel booster rockets. The phrase explains *the cause of the disaster.*

Do not use colons interchangeably with semicolons (see 5B Semicolon). Semicolons separate two independent clauses that are closely related (see 1B Comma Splices). Colons ordinarily are followed by a phrase or phrases, but they can be followed by an independent clause:

> A twelve-member investigating team discovered the cause of the disaster: a leak was found in one of the shuttle's two solid-fuel booster rockets. Both sides of the colon contain an independent clause.

Avoid using colons after verbs and prepositions (see 1A Fragments):

> The two causes of the O-ring failure were cold temperatures and design deficiencies. No colon after *were.*

> The commission investigating the disaster noted a number of failures in communication, such as one within the National Aeronautics and Space Administration. No colon after *such as.*

Colons have a few other set uses:

Time:	10:15 a.m.
Salutation in a business letter:	Dear Patricia Morton:
Biblical reference:	Genesis 2:3

5E Dash   —

The dash separates sentence elements like a comma, but suggests greater emphasis:

> In *The War of the Worlds* (1898), science fiction writer H. G. Wells described an intense beam of light that destroyed objects on contact—the laser.

It is also used to set off a nonrestrictive sentence element (see 1I Restrictive and Nonrestrictive Modifiers) that might be confusing if set off with commas:

> A number of medical uses—performing eye surgery, removing tumours, and unclogging coronary arteries—make the laser more than a destructive weapon. The three explanatory items separated by commas are set off from the rest of the sentence with dashes.

Like commas that set off nonrestrictive elements within a sentence, dashes are often used in pairs—at the beginning of the interruption and at the end.

A dash is sometimes used in place of a colon when a colon might seem too formal or when you want your reader to pay special attention to what follows the dash:

> Besides its medical uses, the laser serves many other functions—reading price codes, playing compact audio discs, and sending telephone messages.

Use the dash with caution; overuse defeats the purpose of giving special emphasis to special parts of your writing. Overuse might also give readers the impression that you aren't familiar with alternative means of punctuation or are being overly casual.

Note that a dash (sometimes more specifically called an "em dash") has the width of the capital letter "M"; it is much wider than a single hyphen.

5F Quotation Marks   " "

The main use for quotation marks is to set off direct quotations:

> Professor Charlotte Johnson announced, "Interdisciplinary science is combining fields of scientific knowledge to make up new disciplines."

> "Biochemistry," she went on to say, "combines biology and chemistry."

Quotations within quotations are marked with single quotation marks:

> "The term 'interdisciplinary science' thus describes a change in how processes are investigated," she concluded.

Use quotation marks correctly with other punctuation marks. Periods and commas (see 5C Comma) always go inside the end quotation marks; colons and semicolons almost always go outside the quotation. Dashes, question marks, and exclamation points go inside or outside depending on meaning—inside if the mark applies to the quotation and outside if it applies to the surrounding sentence:

"Do you know the various branches of the physical sciences?" asked Professor Johnson. Question mark goes inside quotation marks because it applies to the quotation.

Did the professor say, "Histology deals with tissues and cytology with the fine structures of individual cells"? Question mark goes outside quotation marks because it applies to the surrounding sentence, not the quotation.

Do not use quotation marks to set off indirect quotations:

The professor said that histology and cytology are different branches of study.

Also, do not use quotation marks when you are using a long quotation. Instead, place the quoted material in its own block of text that is all indented and omit the quotation marks. If you are using APA style, indent quoted material that is more than forty words in length. If you are using MLA style, indent quoted material that requires four or more lines of your paper. (See Chapter 23, "Quoting, Paraphrasing, and Citing Sources," for more information on properly formatting long quotes.)

Another use for quotation marks is to enclose titles of works that are not published separately, including short stories, poems, songs, chapters, and essays:

"You Are a Man," by Richard Rodriguez

"The Incident," by Countee Cullen

Do not enclose titles of your own essays in quotation marks when they are in title position. (See 5K Italics for treatment of titles of works that are published separately.)

Quotation marks are sometimes used to indicate to readers that you are using a word or phrase in a special sense, but be careful not to overuse this function:

The "right" way to do a thing is not always the best way.

5G Other Marks

Parentheses ( )

Parentheses enclose interrupting elements, setting them off from the rest of the sentence or discourse with a greater separation than other enclosing marks such as commas and dashes. They usually add explanatory information that might seem digressive to the topic.

The Particle Beam Fusion Accelerator *(PBFA II)* is a device designed to produce energy by fusion. Parentheses set off an abbreviation that will henceforth be used in place of the full term.

The PBFA II stores up to 3.5 million joules of energy. *(One joule is the amount of energy expended by a one-watt device in one second.)* Parentheses set off an explanation framed as a complete sentence.

Parentheses are always used in pairs. They might have internal punctuation (as in the second example), but marks related to the sentence as a whole go outside the parentheses. Parentheses are almost never preceded by a comma. Note the following example:

During fusion *(joining of two atomic nuclei to form a larger nucleus),* mass is converted to energy. Parenthetical element is followed by a comma, showing that it relates to *fusion*. If it had been preceded by a comma, it would appear, illogically, to relate to *mass*.

Brackets [ ]

Square brackets have limited uses and are not interchangeable with parentheses. Their most common use is to indicate to the reader that the writer has inserted words into quoted material:

Describing the Great Depression, Frederick Lewis Allen says, "The total amount of money paid out in wages *[in 1932]* was 60 percent less than in 1929." The words *in 1932* were not part of the original text.

Some writers use brackets to enclose brief parenthetical material within parentheses:

Jules Verne (*Journey to the Center of the Earth* [1864]) described giant apes and a vast subterranean sea at the core of the earth. The date of publication is parenthetical to the title of the book.

Ellipsis Dots   . . .

Ellipsis dots (spaced periods) are used in quotations to indicate where words have been omitted. Three spaced dots mark omissions within a sentence. If the omission comes at the end of your sentence but not at the end of the original sentence, use four spaced periods.

One of the legacies of the Great Depression, says Frederick Lewis Allen, is that "if individual Americans are in deep trouble, . . . their government [should] come to their aid." Words following a comma in the original sentence are omitted within the sentence. The brackets enclose an inserted word.

This idea, adds Allen, "was fiercely contested for years. . . ." Allen's sentence did not end at *years,* where the quoted sentence ends.

Make sure that the omitted words do not distort the meaning of the original selection.

5H Capitalization

The rules for capitalization are relatively fixed. Following are examples of situations calling for capitalization.

1. Beginning of a sentence:

   In 1929, the gross national product of Canada fell dramatically.

2. Proper names or nouns:

   With the onset of the *Great Depression, Prime Minister Mackenzie King* at first tried to reassure provincial and municipal governments. Historical period or event; person.

   Farmers in *Saskatchewan*, manufacturers in *Ontario*, and teachers in *Quebec* all organized labour movements. Place.

The Great Depression was part of a worldwide collapse, ending only with *World War II.* Historical period or event.

In 1935, *Prime Minister R. B. Bennett* set up the *Canadian Wheat Board* to aid Canadian farmers. Person; institution.

Jell-O, Pepsi, Rice Krispies Trade names.

Aunt Beatrice, Grandmother Dietz, Dad Relationships when they are part of the name; but not *my dad* and *my aunt and uncle.*

3. Titles:

Death at an Early Age, by Jonathan Kozol; *The Dancing Wu Li Masters: An Overview of the New Physics,* by Gary Zukav. Capitalize first and last words, words following colons, and all other words except articles (*a, an,* and *the*) and conjunctions and prepositions of fewer than five letters (*and, but, in, by,* etc.).

Avoid capitalizing common nouns; for example:

For many people, the *winter* of 1902 was bleak. Seasons.

Many people moved *south* to a warmer climate. Compass directions.

My *great-grandparents* were among those who moved. Relationships.

Simon Waterson was a *professor of history* at the time. Titles that are not part of proper names.

5I Abbreviation

While abbreviations are part of the language, not all are acceptable in all circumstances. A general guideline is that they are less common in formal prose than in less formal circumstances. The following examples are arranged from most acceptable to least acceptable in written prose.

Titles with proper names

Dr. Paul Gordon   Paul Gordon, Ph.D.
George Grossman, Jr.

Times and dates

11:15 A.M. *or* 11:15 a.m.   53 BCE   371 CE

Names of organizations and countries

NATO   CIA   NBC

Most countries and provinces have adjectival forms (e.g., Canadian), but the United States is an exception. In formal writing, use *US* as an adjective (*in a US city*) and *United States* as a noun (*a city in the United States*).

Latin abbreviations (write out except in source citations and parenthetical comments)

etc.   and so forth (*et cetera*—applies to things)
i.e.   that is (*id est*)
e.g.   for example (*exempli gratia*)
cf.   compare (*confer*)
et al.   and others (*et alii*—applies to people)
N.B.   note well (*nota bene*)

Abbreviations to be avoided in most prose

The school board not bd. met on Tuesday not Tues. February not Feb. **3.**

William not Wm. Townsend was a guest lecturer in the economics not econ. class.

Townsend arrived from Fredericton, New Brunswick not NB, late last night.

Consult your dictionary when you have questions about specific abbreviations.

<table>
<tr><td>

⊙─┐**Watch**
Common
Grammar
Errors: 14.
Misusing the
Apostrophe

</td><td>

5J Apostrophe   ʼ

The apostrophe has two main uses in English—to mark possessive nouns and to show contractions—plus a few specialized uses. Avoid all other uses.

Possessive Nouns

Ownership or connection is marked on nouns with apostrophes:

</td></tr>
</table>

Norton's résumé is short and concise. The résumé belongs to Norton.

This week's newsletter will be a little late. The newsletter of this week

The article's title is confusing. The title of the article

To make nouns possessive, follow one of these steps:

1. For singular nouns, add *'s* (*nature* + *'s* = *nature's*; *Tess* + *'s* = *Tess's*).
2. For plural nouns ending in *s*, add *'* (*strangers* + *'* = *strangers'*).
3. For plural nouns not ending in *s*, add *'s* (*men* + *'s* = *men's*).

Do not use apostrophes to make nouns plural. (See 5N Spelling.) And do not use apostrophes with possessive and relative pronouns. (See 3A Pronoun Case.) For example:

The *Harris's* are in Florida. Incorrectly uses apostrophe to make the noun *Harris* plural.

The family lost *it's* home in the fire. Incorrectly uses apostrophe with the pronoun *it* to make it possessive.

Contractions

Apostrophes stand in place of omitted letters in contractions:

doesn't	does not
isn't	is not
I'd	I would
you've	you have
it's	it is *or* it has
who's	who is *or* who has
let's	let us
we'll	we will

Because contractions reflect a casual style, they are usually not acceptable in formal writing. Do not confuse the contracted *it is* (*it's*) and *who is* (*who's*) with the possessive pronouns *its* and *whose*. (See 3A Pronoun Case.)

Special Uses

Plurals of letters, numbers, and words used as terms

I am hoping to get all *A*'s this year.

The memo had four misspelled *there*'s. See 5K Italics, which discusses italicizing words used as terms.

All the *7*'s are upside down in the 1990s catalogue. The plural for years is usually formed without apostrophes.

Omitted letters or numbers

We'll never forget the summer of *'78*. Restrict to informal writing.

"Be *seein'* ya," Charlie said. Dialect in quoted speech.

5K Italics

Italic type, which slants to the right, has specialized uses.

Titles of works published independently

The Atlantic Monthly (magazine)

Alias Grace (book)

Leaves of Grass (book-length poems)

The National Post (newspaper)

This Hour Has 22 Minutes (television program)

The Rez Sisters (play)

Ships, aircraft, spacecraft, and trains

Challenger (spacecraft)

Leasat 3 (communications satellite)

San Francisco *Zephyr* (train)

Italics are also used for words, letters, and numbers used as themselves in a sentence:

The process of heat transfer is called *conduction*.

The letter *e* is the most commonly used vowel.

Many people consider *13* to be an unlucky number.

Italics can also be used for emphasis:

"I said, '*Did* you buy the tickets?' not '*Would* you buy the tickets?'"

Although underlining was used as a substitute for italics in the past, writers generally avoid it nowadays because underlining is used for other purposes (for example, to indicate a hyperlink in Web and other electronic writing).

5L Hyphens   -

Hyphens have three main uses: to divide words at the ends of lines, to form compound words, and to connect spelled-out numbers.

Dividing Words

There are three general rules to remember when using hyphens to divide words at the ends of lines: (1) always divide between syllables, (2) don't divide one-syllable words, and (3) don't divide words so that only two letters carry over to the second line. Consider the following examples:

After the results came back, the doctor sat me down and explained my *condition*.

While they could not cure the condition, at least they could alleviate its *symptoms*.

In the end, after months of waiting and mountains of legal fees, the court*ruled* against him. Incorrectly divides the one-syllable word *ruled*.

Needless to say, when the court ruled against him, he was not *particularly* pleased. Incorrectly divides the word *particularly* so that only the last two letters carry over to the second line.

Forming Compound Words

Knowing when to hyphenate compound words can be tricky because some compound words can be written as single words (for example, *graveyard* or *postmaster*) while others can be written as two separate words (for example, *place kick* or *executive secretary*). Complicating matters further, compound adjectives take hyphens when they precede nouns but not when they follow nouns. Here are some examples of the correct and incorrect use of hyphens:

My *ex-husband* is a *pro-Liberal* campaigner. Use hyphens after the prefix *ex-* and any prefix placed before a proper name, in this case *pro-* before *Liberal*. In general, though, most words formed with prefixes are written as one word; for example, *antisocial* or *multicultural*.

The web-site revealed that her brother in law had published several short stories. This sentence contains two hyphenation errors. First, the compound word web-site should be written as a single word, website. Second, the compound noun *brother in law* should be hyphenated as *brother-in-law*.

The *secretary treasurer* advised the group to invest in the *rapidly-growing company*. This sentence contains two hyphenation errors. First, the compound noun *secretary treasurer* requires a hyphen. Second, compounds consisting of an adverb ending in *-ly* (such as *rapidly*) and an adjective or participle (such as *growing*) are not hyphenated.

Connecting Spelled-Out Numbers

Use hyphens to link compounds of spelled-out numbers and to link numbers to nouns. For example:

twenty-fifth time	six-year-old
three-metre statue	35-year-old
900-hectare ranch	

Whenever you have a question about dividing words and hyphenating compound words, use your dictionary. Dots usually mark syllables, and hyphens mark hyphenated compounds.

5M Numbers

Numbers can be spelled out or written as numerals. When to employ one style or the other depends on the writing context. In most academic writing in the humanities, and indeed in most writing geared for a general audience, numbers are usually spelled out. In the sciences, however, numbers are usually written as numerals.

Unless you are asked to follow different conventions, use the following guidelines to handle numbers in writing:

1. Spell out numbers requiring two words or less and write numerals for numbers requiring three or more words. In practice, this means you will write out numbers *one* to *ninety-nine* and write numerals for *100* and above.

2. Spell out numbers that begin sentences. For long numbers this can lead to awkward sentences. In such instances, you should consider revising the sentence to move the number away from the beginning of the sentence so it can be written in numerals.

3. Make exceptions for numbers used in special figures. In these instances, numbers are usually written as numerals. Special figures of this type include days and years; pages, chapters, and volumes; acts, scenes, and lines; decimals, fractions, ratios, and percentages; temperatures; addresses; statistics; and amounts of money.

Consider the following examples:

The company mailed *twenty-one* parcels yesterday.

She bought *900* hectares of ranch land with her lottery winnings.

One hundred and fifty-two cows drowned in the flood.

The Battle of Vimy Ridge began on April *9, 1917*.

You will find the answer on page *87* in Chapter *5*.

The famous "To be, or not to be" soliloquy appears in act *3*, scene *1* of *Hamlet*.

The temperature reached *40°*C yesterday.

The suspect resided at *221* Dolores Street, apartment *3B*.

The winning margin was *2* to *1*.

With tax, the umbrella cost $*15.73*.

5N Spelling

Your word processor's spellchecker will flag most misspelled words and suggest alternatives, but it will often miss unintended homonyms (for instance, accepting *Brutish Literature* when you meant to type *British Literature*). Because you should not rely solely on a spellchecker, here is a review of the most useful and dependable rules of spelling.

Doubling a Final Consonant

When adding a suffix such as *-ing* or *-ed* to a word that ends in a consonant, double the final consonant to keep the internal vowel short; for example, *permit, permitted; stop, stopped*. Double the final consonant when all three of the following are true:

1. The word ends in a consonant preceded by a vowel.

2. The word is one syllable or the accent is on the final syllable. Please note that Canadian spelling does occasionally double the consonant for two-syllable words with the accent on the first syllable, such as "travelling," "cancelling," and "labelling." Consult a Canadian dictionary if in doubt.

3. The suffix begins with a vowel.

Here are some other examples:

hop	hopped	begin	beginning
sit	sitting	prefer	preferred
put	putting	occur	occurrence
win	winner	recap	recapped

Words Containing *ie* or *ei*

The familiar rhyme about using *ie* or *ei* is true most of the time—enough times that it is worth remembering: *i* before *e* except after *c* when the sound is long *e*. Thus, words such as these follow the rule:

receive	believe	weight
ceiling	chief	beige
conceited	siege	eight

There are a few common exceptions: *caffeine, either, neither, seize,* and *weird*. Another common word that the rule does not address is *friend* (spelled *i* before *e*, but the sound is not long *e*).

Final *e*

To add an ending to a word that ends in a silent *e,* drop the *e* when the ending begins with a vowel:

believe + able = believable   believe + ed = believed

move + able = movable   move + ment = movement

hope + ing = hoping   hope + ful = hopeful

When the consonant preceding the final *e* is a soft *c* or *g,* the *e* is dropped only when the ending begins with *e* or *i:*

change + ing = changing   change + able = changeable

notice + ing = noticing   notice + able = noticeable

manage + er = manager   manage + ment = management

nice + er = nicer   nice + ly = nicely

Final *y*

To add an ending to a word with a final *y* preceded by a consonant, change the *y* to *i* except when your ending is -*ing:*

happy + ly = happily   study + ing = studying

apply + es = applies   apply + ing = applying

vary + ous = various   vary + ing = varying

try + ed = tried   try + ing = trying

When the final *y* is preceded by a vowel, keep the *y:*

play + ed = played   play + ful = playful

employ + ed = employed   employ + ment = employment

but

say + s = says   say + d = said

pay + ment = payment   pay + d = paid

Never change the *y* when adding an ending to a proper noun: *the Barrys.*

Plurals

Plural nouns ordinarily have an *s* ending:

boy + s = boys   car + s = cars

Words that end in *ch, s, sh, x,* or *z* require -*es:*

box + es = boxes   church + es = churches

Words ending in *o* are a little more troublesome. If the *o* is preceded by a vowel, add *s:*

radio + s = radios   video + s = videos

If the *o* is preceded by a consonant, ordinarily add -*es:*

hero + es = heroes   potato + es = potatoes

A few common words take either *s* or -*es* (check your dictionary before you choose):

tornados, tornadoes   zeros, zeroes   volcanos, volcanoes

Some words form their plurals internally or do not have a plural form. Do not add an *s* to these words:

child, children	deer, deer
man, men	fish, fish
mouse, mice	moose, moose

Compound words ordinarily have an *s* at the end of the compound:

textbook, textbooks	snowshoe, snowshoes
text edition, text editions	

But when the first word of the compound is the main word, add the *s* to it:

sisters-in-law	attorneys-general

Whenever you are in doubt about the correct plural ending, check your dictionary.

Homonyms

Some of the most troublesome words to spell are homonyms, words that sound alike but are spelled differently. Here is a partial list of the most common ones:

accept, except	maybe, may be
affect, effect	of, 've (have)
already, all ready	passed, past
cite, sight, site	than, then
forth, fourth	their, there, they're
it's, its	to, too, two
know, no	whose, who's
lead, led	your, you're

A few other words, not exactly homonyms, are sometimes confused:

breath, breathe	lightning, lightening
choose, chose	loose, lose
clothes, cloths	precede, proceed
dominant, dominate	quiet, quite

Check the meanings of any sound-alike words you are unsure of in your dictionary.

MyCompLab

For support on grammar and usage questions, click on Grammar in MyCompLab:

Select your topic and review the Instruction and Multimedia resources; then complete the Exercises and click on Gradebook to measure your progress.

Credits

Photos

Text and Illustrations

Index

A

A heads, 294
abbreviations, 563–564
absorbing opposing points, 369
abstractions, 45, 46*f*
abstracts
    defined, 40
    in research paper, 212, 223
academic dishonesty, 425
academic essay, 210. *see also* research paper
academic expectations, 64, 70, 73
academic journals, 406
academic proposal, 191–192
access points, 288
accuracy, in summary, 47
active voice
    benefits of, 226
    the "doer" as subject, 277–278
    shifts in, 535
    use of, 541–542
ad hominem, 366*f*
ad populum, 366*f*
addresses, 558
adjectives
    coordinate adjectives, 558
    defined, 539
Adler Online, 404
admission of limitations, 92, 261
Adobe Audition, 485
Adobe Premiere, 485
adverb clauses, 534
adverbs
    comparative degree, 539
    functions of, 534, 539
    hyphenation of, 567
    as misplaced modifier, 536
    transitional adverbs, 529, 555, 556, 557
advertisements
    ad critique, 99–100
    MLA documentation style, 445
afterword, 440
agreement
    pronoun-antecedent agreement, 548–549
    subject-verb agreement. *see* subject-verb agreement
aircraft, 566
alignment, 288, 290–291, 301
alphabetization
    in references list, 459–460
    in works cited list, 434
alternating pattern, 351–352
am, 542
ambiguity, 365
American Psychological Association (APA). *see* APA style

analogies
    as argument technique, 156, 366*f*
    defined, 347
    as descriptive technique, 282
analyzing
    context, 31–33
    literary analysis. *see* literary analysis
    reader analysis worksheet, 30*f*
    rhetorical analysis. *see* rhetorical analysis
    rhetorical situation, 10, 11*f*
    for summary, 42
Andrews, Jennifer ("Rethinking Canadian and American Nationality"), 140–142
anecdotes, 325, 513
anger, 364
angle
    defined, 19
    defining question, 16
    developing, 23
    and global revision, 308
    identifying, 19, 34, 181, 218–219
annotated bibliography, 227–229, 411–412
antagonistic approach, 371
antecedents, 547–548
APA references list
    alphabetization, 459
    article
        in journals, 461–462
    articles
        author unknown, 462
        on CD-ROM, 463
        in edited books, 462
        in magazines, 462
        in newspapers, 462
        from online periodical, 467
        review, 463
        from scholarly journal, 467
    books
        author unknown, 464
        corporate author, 464
        dissertation, unpublished, 464
        edited collection, 464
        in electronic form, 464
        features of, 463
        multiple authors, 463
        one author, 463
        organization as author, 464
        second edition or beyond, 464
        thesis, 464
        translation, 464
    broadcasts, 467–468
    CD-ROMs, 468
    citation map, 465

APA references list (*Continued*)
  documents, 464
  e-mail, 468
  example of, 455
  films, 468
  formatting of, 460
  government publications, 464
  interviews, 468
  multiple works in same year, 460
  pamphlets, 464
  periodicals, 461–462
  personal correspondence, 468
  preparing, 457, 459–460
  radio broadcasts, 468
  recordings, 468
  songs, 468
  student sample, 477
  television broadcasts, 468
  videos, 468
  websites
    author unknown, 467
    corporate author, 467
    features of, 465
    online periodical, 467
    scholarly journal with DOI, 467
APA style
  for block quotes, 419, 427, 561
  parenthetical citations
    author name in sentence, 455–456
    author name repeated, 457
    described, 454–455
    elements of, 455
    location of, 455
    multiple citations of single source, 456–457
    multiple source in sentence, 456
    and reference list, 455
    types of, 458–459*f*
  references list. *see* APA references list
  student sample, 468–477
apostrophes
  and contractions, 546, 565
  and possessive case, 546, 564
  special uses, 565
  uses of, 564
appeal to experts, 92, 261, 362
appeals of authority (*ethos*)
  in argument, 363–364, 374
  defined, 91
  as heuristic, 261, 263*f*
  in rhetorical analysis, 92
appeals of emotion (*pathos*)
  in argument, 364, 365*f*, 374
  as heuristic, 262, 263*f*
  in rhetorical analysis, 91, 92–93

appeals of reasoning (*logos*)
  in argument, 361–362, 374
  as heuristic, 261, 263*f*
  in rhetorical analysis, 91
appropriate language, 99, 552–554
archive, 489, 490–491, 496
are, 542
arguable, 358
arguable claims
  defined, 374
  developing and sharpening, 360*f*
  examples of, 359
  explained, 359
  issues of causation, 360
  issues of definition, 359–360
  issues of evaluation, 360–361
  issues of recommendation, 361
  region of, 358*f*
  sources of, 359–361, 374
argument. *see also* position paper
  arguable, 358–358
  arguable claims
    defined, 374
    developing and sharpening, 360*f*
    examples of, 359
    explained, 359
    issues of causation, 360
    issues of definition, 359–360
    issues of evaluation, 360–361
    issues of recommendation, 361
    region of, 358*f*
    sources of, 359–361, 374
  argumentative fallacies. *see* argumentative fallacies
  argumentative form, 370–373
  articulating, 46–47
  authority (*ethos*), 363–364, 374
  causation, 360
  and counterargument, 157
  defined, 357
  emotion (*pathos*), 364, 365*f*, 374
  ethical principles, 363
  evaluation, 360–361
  evidence, 361–364
  examples, use of, 362
  explained, 148
  features of, 150
  goodwill, 364
  organization model, 149
  persuasive style techniques, 156
  practicality, 363
  reasoning (*logos*), 361–362, 374
  rebuttal and refutation, 367–370
  recommendation, 361
  and reflection, 492

in research paper, 224
structure of, 45, 46*f*
student sample, 150–151
and thesis statement, 20
in various genres, 357
argumentative fallacies
    ambiguity, 365
    avoiding, 365, 374
    false premises, 365
    irrelevance, 365
    and rebuttal, 157
    types of, 366*f*
    weak premises, 365
argumentative form
    classical argument form, 371
    Rogerian form, 371–372
    Toulmin model, 372–373
argumentative research paper, 210, 218
articles
    APA documentation style, 467
    finding, 406–407
    MLA documentation style, 437–438
artifact, 489
attitude, readers', 30–31, 35, 308
attribution, 426
Audacity, 485
audience. *see* readers
author, research of, 123
authoritative tone, 190, 190*f*
authority (*ethos*)
    in argument, 363–364, 374
    defined, 91
    as heuristic, 261, 263*f*
    in rhetorical analysis, 92
author's voice, 281
auxiliary verbs, 540–541

B
B heads, 294
back-checking, 159, 408
background information, 64–65, 73, 125
backward planning, 394, 396
balance, 155, 288, 288–290, 301
bandwagon, 366*f*
bar charts, 299
"Bare-Knuckled Knockout" (Johnson), 74–75
be, 542
Bebo, 481
been, 542
begging the question, 366*f*
being, 542
believing, 66
better and worse, 362
bias
    in sexist language, 554

in sources, 393
and stereotypes, 554
your own, 393
bibliography
    annotated bibliography, 411–412
    vs. references list, 459
    working bibliography, 394, 396
    vs. works cited list, 434
block pattern, 351
block quotes, 419–420, 427, 535
Blogger, 482
blogs
    defined, 482
    as exploratory writing, 263, 264*f*
    host sites, 482
    MLA documentation style, 444
    for research, 404
    template, 483*f*
    and topics, 486
    writing your own, 482–483
Blogsome, 482
body language, 516–517, 519
body of document
    drafting, 270
    in essay exam, 502
    of literary analysis, 125–126
    in presentation, 513
    of research paper, 212, 224–225
books
    APA documentation style, 463–464
    locating, 405
    MLA documentation style, 438–439
"Borders" (King), 132–139
"Boys and Violence" (Feder, Levant, & Dean), 239–251
brackets, 562
brainstorming
    for common expectations, 63*f*
    for costs-benefits analysis, 185*f*
    defined, 259
    for points of contention, 152*f*
    on topic, 220*f*
brief reader profile, 27–28, 35
broadcasts
    APA documentation style, 467–468
    on Internet, 485, 486
    MLA documentation style, 444–445
    radio, 404
    television, 403–404

C
C heads, 294
calendar, 382
call to action, 328, 514
Canadian Newsstand database, 183
capitalization, 562–563

capstone portfolio, 489, 494
case, defined, 545
case history, 325
catalogue, 392, 405
causation, 360
cause and effect
    in argument, 362, 363*f*
    defined, 94
    described, 349
    and genres, 350*f*
    kinds of, 350*f*
    organizational pattern, 340*f*
CD-ROMs
    APA documentation style, 463, 468
    MLA documentation style, 438
cf., 564
chalkboard, 511*f*
challenging questions, 514–515
character, getting into, 281
characters, exploration of for literary analysis, 122
charts, 158, 296–300
chronological description
    organizational pattern, 340*f*
    in review, 67
chronology, 224
citation generators, 429
citation map
    scholarly journal from database, 443*f*
    scholarly journal on the Web, 442*f*
    web site, 441*f*
citations. *see also* APA style; MLA style
    citation generators, 429
    common knowledge, 416
    in-text parenthetical citations, 225
    in literary analysis, 130
    and paraphrases, 427
    parenthetical citations, 430–432
    purpose of, 423
    in research paper, 225
    and summaries, 427
    in summary, 49
    types of, 423
claims
    vs. opinions, 154
    supporting with evidence, 159
classical argument form, 371
classification
    defined, 93
    and genres, 348*f*
    steps in, 348–349
clauses
    independent clauses
        and colons, 559
        and comma splices, 528–530
        and comma usage, 556, 559

and fused sentences, 530–531
    and semicolons, 555
subordinate clauses
    defined, 525
    as fragments, 525–526
climax, 122
Coe, Richard, 371
collaborative online tools, 382
collaborative writing, 376–377. *see also* group writing; team writing
colons
    avoiding, 559
    vs. dashes, 560
    defined, 559
    with quotation marks, 560
    vs. semicolons, 555, 559
    uses of, 560
columns, 290
comma splices, 528–530
commas
    with addresses, 558
    avoiding, 558–559
    in compound sentences, 556
    with coordinate adjectives, 558
    and coordinating conjunctions, 531, 559
    with dates, 558
    and independent clauses, 559
    with introductory sentence elements, 556
    with nonrestrictive parenthetical elements, 538, 556–557
    Oxford comma, 557
    vs. periods, 528
    with quotation marks, 558, 560
    with quotations, 556–558
    and restrictive sentence elements, 558
    serial comma, 557
    in series, 555–556, 557
    splices, 528–530
    uses of, 556–558
common expectations, 58, 62–64, 63*f*, 71, 73
common knowledge, 416
commonplace, 343
comparative degree, 539
comparison and contrast
    defined, 94
    described, 351
    and genres, 352*f*
    organizational pattern, 340*f*
    patterns of, 351–352
comparisons using *than* or *as*, 532
compelling statement, 324, 513
complete argument, 20
complication, 344
compound antecedents, 548
compound sentences, 556
compound subjects, 544

compound words, 566–567, 570
concept map
    to analyze problem, 182*f*
    on authoritative tone, 190*f*
    example of, 257*f*
    explained, 257–258
    for proposal, 183, 184*f*
    for research plan, 221*f*
    for topic, 18*f*
conciseness, 550–551
conclusion
    of academic proposal, 191
    drafting, 270, 326–328, 329
    in essay exam, 502
    of literary analysis, 118, 126, 131
    of position paper, 150, 155
    of presentation, 513–514
    of proposal, 171, 189
    of research paper, 225
    of review, 68
    of rhetorical analysis, 87, 98
    signalling expressions, 327
    student sample, 327
    style of, 126–127
condensing, 47. *see also* summary
conflict, 381, 383
conjunctions
    coordinating conjunctions
        and comma usage, 556, 559
        list of, 528
    correlative conjunctions, 532
    subordinating conjunctions, 529, 531
connection, to material from a source, 423
connectors, 525
consistency
    in design, 288, 292–294, 301
    in headings, 292, 293–294, 338–339
    in lists, 292
context
    analyzing, 31–33, 34
    defined, 31
    defining question, 16
    and design, 288
    and global revision, 308–309
    importance of, 33*f*
    medium, 32, 309
    and place, 31, 309
    social and political influences, 32–33, 309
    and summary, 45–46, 51
    theoretical context, 123–124
contractions, 546, 565
contrast, 288, 301
CookbookWiki, 484
coordinate adjectives, 558
coordinating conjunctions

and comma usage, 556, 559
    list of, 528
coordination, 532–533
coordinator, 380
copyediting
    defined, 303, 313, 318
    descriptive material, 315
    paragraphs, 314
    and peer editing, 317
    sentences, 314–315
    titles and headings, 314
copyright law, 65, 296, 424–425
Corel VideoStudio, 485
correlative conjunctions, 532
costs-benefits analysis
    in argument, 362
    brainstorming, 185*f*
    defined, 171
    figuring out, 184, 194
    showing the reader, 188–189
Council of Writing Program Administrators, 424
counterargument, 157
cover page, 229
Creative Commons, 296
credentials, 92, 261
credibility (*ethos*)
    in argument, 363–364, 374
    as heuristic, 261, 263*f*
    in rhetorical analysis, 91, 92
credibility of sources, 383
Cubase, 485
cubing, 262–263
cultural metaphor, 285
cultural studies, 124
cultural values, 29–30

D
Dailey, Kate ("Friends with Benefits"), 161–164
dangling modifiers, 536–537
dashes
    vs. colons, 560
    and nonrestrictive modifiers, 538
    with quotation marks, 560
    uses of, 560
data, 362
date accessed, 440, 441
dates, 558, 563
Davies, P. S. W. ("Media Influence on the Body Image. . ."),
    81–82
Dean, James ("Boys and Violence"), 239–251
deconstruction, 124
definition
    and arguable claims, 359–360
    defined, 93, 346
    extended definition, 346–347

definition (*Continued*)
  and genres, 348*f*
  parenthetical definition, 156, 227
  sentence definition, 156, 227, 346
  techniques, 347
  of unfamiliar terms, 156
degree, 539
deliverables, 188
description
  defined, 93, 344
  editing, 315
  feature-by-feature, 67
  and genres, 346*f*
  organizational pattern, 340*f*
  of review subject, 67
  with rhetoric, 346
  with the senses, 345
  with vocabulary, 346
descriptive headings, 158
design
  access points, 288
  alignment, 288, 290–291, 301
  balance, 288, 288–290, 301
  columns, 290
  consistency, 288, 292–294, 301
  and context, 288
  contrast, 288, 294–295, 301
  and genre, 287
  Gestalt theory of design, 288
  graphs, diagrams, and charts, 158, 296–300, 301
  grouping, 288, 291–292, 301
  headings, 158
  labelling, 296, 297*f*
  lists, 192
  of literary analysis, 128
  photography and images, 295–296
  of position paper, 157–158, 160
  of presentation slides, 515–516
  principles of, 288
  of proposal, 192, 194
  and purpose, 287–288
  and readers, 288
  of research paper, 229–230, 232
  of review, 71
  of rhetorical analysis, 100–101
  and substantive editing, 310
  typefaces, 292–293
  white space, 192, 292
designated skeptic, 377
designer, 380
details
  vs. abstractions, 45
  sensory, 68–69
diagrams, 158, 299, 299–300, 300*f*
dialogue, as introduction, 324

differences, 347
Digg, 485
Digital Object Identifier (DOI), 465
digital projector, 511*f*
digressions, 158
direct quotation, 423
discourse type, shifts in, 535
disgust, 364
dissent, 381
dissertation, unpublished
  APA documentation style, 464
  MLA documentation style, 440
division, of topic, 93, 347
documentaries, 403
documentation. *see* APA style; MLA style
documents
  APA documentation style, 464
  MLA documentation style, 440
doubting, 66
drafting
  conclusion, 326–328, 329
  every day, 272, 274
  introduction, 322–326, 329
  literary analysis, 124–126, 131
  position paper, 154–155, 160
  proposal, 184–190
  research paper, 223–226, 232
  review, 66–68, 73
  rhetorical analysis, 102
  summary, 46–47, 51
  using genres to organize ideas, 269–270, 274
  and writer's block, 272–273, 274

E
e-portfolio, 490, 495
-ed as word ending, 526, 540, 568
editing
  copyediting, 303, 313–315
  in essay exam, 503, 507
  global revision, 303, 304–309
  levels of, 303, 304*f*
  of literary analysis, 130, 131
  peer editing, 316–317
  of position paper, 158–159, 160
  proofreading
    defined, 303, 315, 318
    and peer editing, 317
    of proposal, 192
    of research paper, 230–231
    of review, 72
    strategies for, 315–316
  of proposal, 192–193, 194
  of research paper, 230–231, 232
  of review, 71–72, 73
  of rhetorical analysis, 101, 102

software for, 485
substantive editing, 303, 309–313
of summary, 49–50
videos or podcasts, 485
editor
letter to, 438
of writing team, 380
editorials, MLA documentation style, 438
e.g., 564
eHow, 484
either. . . or, 361, 366*f*
electronic documents, reader use of, 32
electronic sources
blogs, 404
documentaries, 403
finding, 401–405
Internet search engines, 401–402
podcasts, 404
radio broadcasts, 404
reliability of, 403
television broadcasts, 403–404
types of, 398
wikis, 404
ellipsis dots, 562
em dash. *see* dashes
emotion
appeals of emotion (*pathos*)
in argument, 364, 365*f*, 374
as heuristic, 262, 263*f*
in rhetorical analysis, 91, 92–93
eight basic emotions, 92–93
as proof, 92–93
emphasis, 566
empirical sources
field observation, 409–411
interview, 407–408
for position paper, 153
for proposal, 183
for rhetorical analysis, 94
survey, 409
types of, 398, 407
encyclopedias, 392
enjoyment, promise of, 364
-er as word ending, 539
essay exam
answering exam question, 501–502, 507
finishing, 502–503
four-stage process, 499*f*
preparing for, 498–500, 507
and professor, 499
purpose of, 498
rehearsing for, 500
reviewing questions at start, 500–501, 507
revising and editing, 503, 507
sample questions, 505*f*

starting, 500–501, 507
student sample, 503–504
and study groups, 499
and themes, 499–500
and time management, 501, 507
-est as word ending, 539
et al., 564
etc., 564
ethical principles, in argument, 363
ethics, and surveys, 409
ethos
in argument, 363–364, 363–364, 374
defined, 91
as heuristic, 261, 263*f*
in rhetorical analysis, 92
etymology, 347
evaluation, in argument, 360–361
evidence, types of, 362*f*
exact words, 401
exam. *see* essay exam
example
defined, 94
as definition, 347
as evidence, 362
Excel, 296
exclamation points, 554, 555, 560
executive summary, 172–180
expectations, readers', 27, 28–29, 35, 308
experience
as proof, 92, 261, 362
as research, 66, 73
expert evidence, 92, 261, 362
exploratory writing
blogging, 263
defined, 256
explained, 267
exploratory draft, 264–265
journaling, 263
microblogging, 264
and presentation software, 265, 266*f*
expository research paper, 210, 218
expression of good will, 92, 261
extended definition, 346–347
extended reader profile, 28–31
external proposal, 171
eye contact, 517

F
F-A-N-B-O-Y-S, 528
Facebook, 264, 481
facilitator, 377
false authority, 366*f*
false premises, 365
fear of loss, 364
fear of pain, 364

Featherstone, Liza ("What's a Girl to Read?"), 103–105
feature-by-feature description, 67
Feder, June ("Boys and Violence"), 239–251
feminism, 124
field observation, 65, 409–411
figures of speech
    analogy, 156, 282, 347, 366*f*
    metaphor, 156, 190, 282–283, 285
    onomatopoeia, 283, 285
    simile, 156, 190, 282
Final Cut, 485
first-level headings, 294
first person, 226, 540, 543, 549
five senses, 260
Five-W and How questions
    explained, 259–260
    in field observation, 410
    for presentations, 510, 519
    and reader profiles, 27–28
    and reviews, 64–65
footers, 230, 292
foreword, 440
formal language, 552
formal style, 49
formalism, 124
forming, 379, 380
"Forty Years of Struggle and Still No Right to Inuit Education in Nunavut" (Rasmussen), 195–202
fragments
    acceptable fragments, 527–528
    defined, 524
    incomplete thoughts, 527
    phrase fragments, 526–527
    and punctuation, 555
    subordinate clause fragments, 525–526
    types of, 525
framing device, 328
framing material from a source, 422–424
freewriting, 19, 20*f*, 258–259
friends, 481
"Friends with Benefits" (Dailey), 161–164
fused sentences, 530–531
future perfect tense, 540–541
future tense, 540–541

G
gain, promise of, 364
GarageBand, 485
gender-neutral substitution, 553, 554
gender studies, 124
generalization, 366*f*
genres. *see also* specific genres
    choosing, 22, 23
    defined, 4–5, 13
    and design, 287

    in education and career, 12, 13
    flexibility of, 5, 13
    as guiding concept, 10–11
    know-how, 13
    literary genres, 121
    in movies, 6–7
    and paragraph length, 337
    and passive voice, 542
    popular vs. academic, 8–9
    and the rhetorical situation, 33–34
    subgenres, 121
    and use of cause and effect, 350*f*
    and use of classification, 348*f*
    and use of comparison and contrast, 352*f*
    and use of definition, 348*f*
    and use of description, 346*f*
    and use of narrative, 345*f*
    usefulness of, 5–6
    using genres to organize ideas, 269–270, 274
    in writing, 7–9
    and writing process, 9–11, 13
gerunds
    defined, 526
    in headings, 338–339
    and possessive pronouns, 547
Gestalt theory of design, 288
gestures, 517
Giltrow, Janet, 42
given-new chaining, 336
global revision
    and angle, 308
    and context, 308–309
    defined, 303, 318
    and peer editing, 317
    and purpose, 308
    and readers, 308
    student sample, 305–306*f*, 307*f*
    and topic, 308
good moral character, 92, 261
goodwill, 364
Google+, 481
Google Docs, 382
government publications
    APA documentation style, 464
    finding, 406
    MLA documentation style, 440
grabbers, 324, 513
Graff, Gerald, 42
grammatical weaknesses, 315
grant proposal, 171
graphics
    design principles, 296–300, 301
    for position paper, 158
    for proposal, 192
    for reviews, 73

graphs, 298–299
group writing. *see also* team writing
    defined, 376
    determining goals, 383
    questions to answer, 377–378
    roles, 377, 383
    strategies for, 378–379
grouping, 288, 291–292, 301

H
handouts, 511*f*
hard copy, 315
hasty generalization, 366*f*
headers, 230, 292
headings
    consistency in design, 292, 293–294
    consistency in word patterns, 338–339
    descriptive headings, 158
    editing, 314
    levels of, 293–294
    meaningful headings, 192, 229
    in sections, 338–339
    specificity of, 339
heckling questions, 515
helping verbs, 540–541
heuristics
    cubing as, 262
    defined, 256, 267
    and *ethos*, 261
    five senses as, 260
    and *logos*, 261
    and *pathos*, 262
    proofs as, 260–262
    questioning as, 259–260
    types of, 259–262, 267
Hill, R. J. ("Media Influence on the Body Image..."), 81–82
historical context, 96–97
historical setting, 123
homonyms, 570
hook, 324
Howard, Rebecca Moore, 422
hyphens, 566–567
hypothesis, 391

I
ideas, development of
    cubing, 262–263
    exploratory writing
        blogging, 263
        defined, 256
        explained, 267
        exploratory draft, 264–265
        journaling, 263
        microblogging, 264
        and presentation software, 265, 266*f*

        heuristics, 259–262, 267
    prewriting
        benefits of, 267
        brainstorming. *see* brainstorming
        concept map. *see* concept map
        defined, 256
        freewriting, 258–259
        importance of, 266
        storyboarding, 259
        techniques, 257–259
    strategies for, 256
identification with reader, 92
i.e., 564
ie vs. *ei*, 568
if... then, 361
illustration, 94
images, 295–296
imitation, 281
iMovie, 485
imperative mood, 542
Impress, 265
incomplete thoughts, 527
indefinite pronouns
    as antecedents, 548–549
    list of, 548
    and subject-verb agreement, 544
independent clauses
    and colons, 559
    and comma splices, 528–530
    and comma usage, 556, 559
    and fused sentences, 530–531
    and semicolons, 555
indexes
    newspaper index, 407
    periodical index, 153, 406
indicative mood, 542
indirect questions, 554, 555
indirect quotations, 535, 561
infinitives, 526
informal language, 552
informal style, 49
information
    background information, 64–65, 73, 125
    personal, 92, 261, 362, 485
    quantity of, 309
    researching. *see* research
    sources. *see* sources
-ing as word ending, 526, 541, 568
innovator, 377
inquiry
    academic expectations, 64
    common expectations, 62–64
    for literary analysis, 121–123, 131
    for position paper, 152–153
    for proposal, 181–182, 183–184

inquiry (*Continued*)
   for research paper, 218–221
   for review, 62–64
   for rhetorical analysis, 91–93
   for summary, 44–45, 51
   uses of proofs, 91–93
insider language, 92, 261
intensifiers, 550
internal proposal, 171
Internet
   blogs, 482–483, 486
   caution in using, 402–403
   citing. *see* APA style; MLA style
   podcasts, 32, 404, 444, 484–485
   search engines, 401–402
   social media, 481–482, 486
   surfing, 392
   videos, 484–485
   wikis, 404, 444, 484–484, 486
   writing for, 480–481
interpretive claims, 125*f*
interpretive question
   and background information, 125
   clarity of, 130
   finding, 121
   and interpretive claims, 125*f*
   purpose of, 116
   stating, 131
interrupters, 557
intervening subordinate element, 543
interviews
   APA documentation style, 468
   conducting, 408
   follow-up, 408
   MLA documentation style, 445
   for opposing viewpoint, 153
   preparing for, 407–408
   as research, 65
introduction
   in academic proposal, 191
   anecdote, 325
   case history, 325
   citing, 440
   drafting, 270, 322–326, 329
   in essay exam, 502
   five introductory moves, 322–324
   grabber, 324
   hook, 324
   lead, 325–326
   in literary analysis, 118, 131
   personal sketch, 325–326
   in position paper, 150, 154
   in presentation, 512–513
   in proposal, 171, 185
   in research paper, 212, 224

   in review, 66–67
   in rhetorical analysis, 87, 95
   scene setter, 325
   state of existing research, 326
   student sample, 326
irregular verbs, 541
irrelevance, 365
is, 542
is when, 534
is where, 534
issue number
   in references list, 466
   in works cited list, 437
issues
   of causation, 360
   of definition, 359–360
   of evaluation, 360–361
   recommendation, 361
   in research paper, 224
italics
   for titles, 465, 565
   uses of, 565
   for website name, 441
iTunes, 485
iTunes U, 404

J
jargon, 92, 190, 227, 261, 552
job application portfolio, 494
Johnson, Brian D. ("Bare-Knuckled Knockout"), 74–75
jokes, 513
Joost, 484
journalistic questions
   explained, 259–260
   in field observation, 410
   for presentations, 510, 519
   and reader profiles, 27–28
   and reviews, 64–65
journals
   APA documentation style, 461–462, 467
   as exploratory writing, 263
   MLA documentation style, 437–438
   as sources, 406

K
Kendrick, James ("The Many Shades of Red"), 76–79
KeyNote, 32, 265, 296, 515
King, Thomas ("King"), 132–139
Kingston, Anne ("Outraged Moms, Trashy Daughters"), 52–53

L
labelling, 296, 297*f*
language
   appropriate, 99, 552–554
   exploration of for literary analysis, 123

formal, 552
informal, 552
patronizing terms, 554
sexist usage, 553–554
suitability, 552
Latin abbreviations, 564
Lawrie, Z. ("Media Influence on the Body Image. . ."), 81–82
laws, 363
lead, 325–326
learning-focused reflections, 492, 493f
learning portfolio, 488
lede, 325–326
"Letter to the Editor on Climate Story" (Walker & Roberts), 165–166
letters (alphabetic), omitted, 565
letters (personal), citing, 445, 468
letters to the editor
    argument in, 161–164
    MLA documentation style, 438
Levant, Ronald F. ("Boys and Violence"), 239–251
library
    articles, locating, 406–407
    books, locating, 405
    Canadian Newsstand database, 183
    catalogues, 392, 405
    government publications, 406
    periodical index, 153
    Readers' Guide, 153
    reference materials, 406
    search engines, 405
    website of, 153
line graphs, 298
linear process, 94
LinkedIn, 481
listing. *see* brainstorming
lists
    consistency in design, 292
    as design feature, 192
    parallelism in, 557
    punctuation with, 555–556, 557
literary analysis
    body of, 125–126
    citations in, 130
    conclusion, 118, 126, 131
    content development, 121–124
    and definition, 348f
    designing, 128
    explained, 116
    features of, 118
    inquiry, 121–123, 131
    introduction, 118, 125, 131
    and narrative, 345f
    organization model, 117
    organizing and drafting, 124–126, 131
    personal response, 127

quotations in, 118, 126, 127, 130
readers' expectations, 28
reading response, 128, 129f
research, 123–124, 131
revising and editing, 130, 131
vs. rhetorical analysis, 116
student sample, 118–120
summary in, 118
support for interpretation, 118
literary present tense, 126–127
literature review, 70–71, 191. *see also* review
logical fallacies, 365–367, 366f, 374
logical statements, 361–362
logos
    in argument, 361–362
    as heuristic, 261, 263f
    in rhetorical analysis, 91
look to the future, 68, 189, 225, 270, 328
loss, fear of, 364

M
magazines
    APA documentation style, 462
    finding, 407
    MLA documentation style, 437–438
main argument, 20
Martin, Emily ("The Egg and the Sperm"), 106–112
Marxism, 124
masculine nouns and pronouns, 553
Mashable, 404
mastery-focused reflections, 492
"Media Influence on the Body Image. . ." (Lawrie, Sullivan, Davies, & Hill), 81–82
mediation, 381
medium
    as reader context, 32, 35, 309
    types of, 32
meetings, 380, 381, 382
Metacafe, 484
metaphors, 156, 190, 282–283, 285
microblogs, 264
Microsoft Movie Maker, 485
minus (–) sign, 401
misplaced modifiers, 535–536
mixed sentences, 534
MLA Handbook for Writers of Research Papers, 7th ed., 429
MLA style
    for block quotes, 419, 427, 561
    online citation generators, 429
    parenthetical citations
        author name in sentence, 430–431
        described, 430
        elements of, 430
        example of, 430
        location of, 430

MLA style (*Continued*)
    multiple citations of single source, 431–432
    multiple source in sentence, 431
    types of, 432, 433*f*
    and works cited list, 430
  student sample, 446–453
  works cited list. *see* MLA works cited list
MLA works cited list
  advertisements, 445
  alphabetization, 434
  articles
    in books, 438
    on CD-ROM, 438
    from database, 444
    editorials, 438
    features of, 437
    in journals, 437
    letter to the editor, 438
    in magazines, 437–438
    in newspapers, 438
    in online periodical, 444
    in online scholarly journal, 444
    in periodicals, 437–438
    reviews, 438
  audio recordings, 445
  blogs, 444
  books
    afterword, 440
    author unknown, 439
    corporate author, 439
    edited collection, 439
    in electronic form, 440
    features of, 438–439
    foreword, 440
    introduction, 440
    multiple authors, 439
    one author, 439
    organization as author, 439
    preface, 440
    sacred texts, 440
    second edition or beyond, 440
    translation, 439
  broadcasts, 444–445
  cartoons, 446
  CD-ROMs, 445
  citation maps
    scholarly journal from database, 443*f*
    scholarly journal on the Web, 442*f*
    web site, 441*f*
  commercials, 445
  described, 432, 434
  dissertations, unpublished, 440
  documents
    government publications, 440
    pamphlets, 440

    e-mail, 445
    films, 445
    formatting of, 435
    interviews, 445
    lectures, 445
    maps, 446
    multiple sources from one author, 434–435
    n.d., 440
    N.p., 440
    online journals, 442*f*
    performances, 444–445
    personal correspondence, 445
    podcasts, 444
    preparing, 432, 434
    print advertisements, 445
    quotation marks in, 437
    radio broadcasts, 445
    readings, 445
    sacred texts, 440
    songs, 445
    speeches, 445
    student sample, 453
    television broadcasts, 445
    videos, 445
    websites
      author known, 440
      author unknown, 444
      corporate author, 440
      features of, 441
    wikis, 444
    works of art, 445
Modern Language Association (MLA). *see* MLA style
modifiers
  adjectives and adverbs, 539
  dangling and misplaced, 535–536
  restrictive and nonrestrictive, 537–539
  unnecessary modifiers, 551
modifying phrases, 530, 531
mood
  shifts in, 535
  types of, 542–543
more, 539
most, 539
Moveable Type, 482
movies, genres in, 6–7
MSN Video, 484
MySpace, 481
MySpace Videos, 484

N
names, 563
narrative
  defined, 343–344
  and genres, 345*f*
  organizational pattern, 340*f*

pattern of, 343–344
in process analysis, 94
N.B., 564
n.d., 440, 465
negation, 347, 551
new criticism, 124
new historicism, 124
new media. *see* Internet
newspapers
APA documentation style, 462
finding, 407
MLA documentation style, 438
nominalization, 226–227, 278–279
non sequitur, 366*f*
nonpersonal relative pronouns, 549
nonrestrictive modifiers, 537–539, 556–557
norming, 379, 381–382
notepad, 511*f*
nouns
function of, 545
masculine, 553
possessive case, 564
proper nouns, 562
N.p., 440
number, shifts in, 535
numbers
compounds, 567
omitted, 565
plural of, 565
spelled out, 567–568
used as themselves, 566

O
objective case, 546–547
omitted letters or numbers, 565
online citation generators, 429
online sources
APA documentation style, 464, 465–467
blogs, 404
encyclopedias, 392
finding, 401–405
Internet search engines, 401–402
MLA documentation style, 440–444
podcasts, 404
reliability of, 403, 413
for research, 94, 153, 182
types of, 398
wikis, 404
onomatopoeia, 283, 285
opinion vs. claim, 154
organization models
argument, 149
literary analysis, 117
position paper, 149
proposal, 170

research paper, 211
review, 59
rhetorical analysis, 86
summary, 41
organizing and drafting
literary analysis, 124–126, 131
position paper, 154–155, 160
proposal, 184–190
research paper, 223–226, 232
review, 66–68, 73
rhetorical analysis, 102
summary, 46–47
using genres to organize ideas, 269–270
originality, in summary, 47
outline
creating, 270–271
for research methodology, 222*f*
starter outline, 271*f*
"Outraged Moms, Trashy Daughters" (Kingston), 52–53
overhead projector, 511*f*
overstatement, 370
Oxford comma, 557

P
pace, changing, 70
page numbers
in parenthetical citations, 455, 457
in references list, 466
in works cited list, 437
in your documents, 158, 230, 292
pain, fear of, 364
pamphlets
APA documentation style, 464
MLA documentation style, 440
paper documents, reader use of, 32
paragraphs
cohesion, 335–336
creating, 332–335
defined, 331
editing, 314
elements of, 332, 341
flow of, 335–336
given-new chaining, 336
length of, 337–338, 341
point sentences, 335, 341
rapid-fire paragraph, 337–338
and sections, 339–340, 341
shape of, 332*f*
subject alignment, 335–336
supersized paragraph, 337
support sentences, 334–335, 341
top-down style, 156, 226
topic sentences, 334, 341
transitions, 332–333, 341
variety in, 338

parallelism
    and coordination, 532
    within sentences, 531–532
    in series, 557
paraphrasing
    citing, 427
    described, 415
    of description, 420
    examples of, 420
    framing, 422–424
    order of, 225
    vs. summarizing, 419
parentheses, 561–562
parenthetical citations
    APA documentation style, 454–457
    MLA documentation style, 430–432
parenthetical definition, 156, 227
participation, 381
participles, 526, 541
passive voice
    avoiding, 226, 277, 551
    and dangling and misplaced modifiers, 536
    and genres, 542
    identifying, 542
    shifts in, 535
    use of, 278, 542
past perfect tense, 540–541
past tense, 540–541
patchwriting, 422, 425–426
pathos
    in argument, 364, 365*f*, 374
    as heuristic, 262, 263*f*
    in rhetorical analysis, 91, 92–93
patronizing terms, 554
peer editing
    copyediting, 317
    global revision, 317
    in group work, 379
    proofreading, 317
    of proposal, 192
    and specificity, 316–317
    student sample, 310–313
    substantive editing, 310–313, 317
perfect tense, 540–541
performances, MLA documentation style, 444–445
performing, 379, 382
periodical index, 153, 406
periodicals
    APA documentation style, 461–462
    MLA documentation style, 437–438
periods
    vs. commas, 528
    defined, 554
    with quotation marks, 560

uses of, 554
permission, for photographs and images, 296
person
    shifts in, 535, 549
    and subject-verb agreement, 543
personal correspondence
    APA references list, 468
    MLA works cited list, 445
personal credentials, 92, 261
personal experience, 92, 261, 362
personal information, 92, 261, 362, 485
personal judgments, 358
personal pronouns, 546
personal response, in literary analysis, 127
personal sketch, 325–326
personal values, 29
persuasive style techniques, 156
photographs, 295–296
phrase fragments, 526–527
phrases, quoting, 418
pie charts, 299
place, as context, 31, 35, 309
plagiarism
    academic dishonesty, 425
    attribution, 426
    avoiding, 424–426
    defined, 424
    patchwriting, 425–426
    real problem with, 426
    and voice, 281
plain style
    described, 285
    guidelines for, 276–281
    for position paper, 155, 160
planning meeting, 380
plot, exploration of for literary analysis, 122
plurals, 565, 569–570
Plurk, 264
plus (+) sign, 401
Plutchik, Robert, 92
Podcast Alley, 484
Podcast Pickle, 485
podcasts
    creating for Internet, 484–485
    MLA documentation style, 444
    reader use of, 32
    for research, 404
point sentences, 335, 341
points of contention, 152–153
points of interest, 224
political trends, 33, 35, 309
portfolio
    archives, 489, 490–491, 496
    artifacts, selecting, 491–492, 496

for capstone course, 494
collecting your work, 490–491
e-portfolio, 490, 495
getting started, 489–490
for job application, 494
kinds of, 488–489
presenting, 492–495, 496
reflecting on, 492, 493*f*, 496
for specific course, 494
steps in, 490–495
updating, 495, 496
position paper
balance, 155
and cause and effect, 350*f*
and classification, 348*f*
and comparison and contrast, 352*f*
conclusion, 150, 155
content development, 152–153
designing, 157–158, 160
explained, 148
features of, 150
inquiry, 152–153
introduction, 150, 154
organization model, 149
organizing and drafting, 154–155, 160
readers' expectations, 28
rebuttal, 157
research for, 153
revising and editing, 158–159, 160
student sample, 150–151
style of, 155–156
and summary, 154
understanding the issue, 154
possessive case
nouns, 564
pronouns, 546, 547, 564
post-colonialism, 124
post hoc reasoning, 366*f*
poster presentation, 511*f*
posture, 517
PowerPoint, 32, 265, 296, 515, 519
practicality, 363
preface, 440
premises, false or weak, 365
prepositional phrases
commas with, 556
defined, 526, 527
eliminating, 279
excess use of, 551
as fragments, 526
not serving as subjects, 534
in plain style, 279
prepositions, 527
present perfect tense, 543

present tense, 540–541, 543
presentation technology
choosing, 510, 519
pros and cons of, 511*f*
slide formatting, 515, 516*f*
software, 265, 266*f*, 515
types of, 511*f*
Presentations, 515, 519
presentations
and appropriate dress, 517
and body language, 516–517, 519
body of, 513
challenging questions, 514–515
conclusion, 513–514
delivering, 516–518
and eye contact, 517
formatting slides, 515–516
and gestures, 517
heckling questions, 515
importance of, 509
introduction, 512–513
organization of, 512–515, 519
and posture, 517
practising, 518, 519
question and answer period, 514–515
questions to answer in preparation, 510, 519
reader use of, 32
rehearsing, 518, 519
technology for. *see* presentation technology
and time management, 510, 512*f*
and visual aids, 515–516, 519
voice and tone, 517–518, 519
pretentious words, 552
prewriting
benefits of, 267
brainstorming. *see* brainstorming
concept map. *see* concept map
defined, 256
freewriting, 258–259
importance of, 266
storyboarding, 259
techniques, 257–259
Prezi, 519
primary sources
defined, 399
examples of, 400*f*
principle of classification, 349
print sources
academic journals, 406
articles, 406–407
books, 405
finding, 404–407
government publications, 406
at library, 405–406

print sources (*Continued*)
    magazines, 407
    newspapers, 407
    reference materials, 406
    for research, 46, 94, 153, 182–183
    types of, 398
problem and solution, 340*f*
process analysis
    defined, 94
    organizational pattern, 340*f*
procrastination, 273
ProductWiki, 484
project calendar, 382
promise of enjoyment, 364
promise of gain, 364
pronouns
    agreement, 548–549
    and antecedents, 547–548
    case, 545–547
    case forms, 546
    forms for, 546
    function of, 545
    indefinite pronouns, 544, 548
    masculine pronouns, 553
    objective case, 546–547
    personal pronouns, 546
    possessive case, 546, 547, 564
    pronoun reference, 547–548
    relative pronouns, 525, 546, 549–550
    and shifts in person, 549
    subjective case, 546
proofreading
    defined, 315, 318
    design, 303
    and peer editing, 317
    of proposal, 192
    of research paper, 230–231
    of review, 72
    strategies for, 315–316
proofs, types of, 91, 260–261
proper names or nouns, 562
proposal
    academic proposal, 191–192
    analyzing problem, 181–182, 194
    and cause and effect, 350*f*
    and comparison and contrast, 352*f*
    concept map, 182*f*
    conclusion, 171, 189
    content development, 181–184
    costs-benefits analysis, 184, 188–189, 194
    and description, 346*f*
    designing, 192, 194
    developing a plan, 183–184
    drafting, 194
    explained, 169
    features of, 171

    grant proposal, 171
    identifying problem, 181, 194
    internal vs. external, 171
    introduction, 171, 185
    and narrative, 345*f*
    organization model, 170
    organizing and drafting, 184–190
    plan section, 183, 187–189, 187*f*, 194
    problem section, 183–184, 186–187, 186*f*
    readers' expectations, 28
    research, 182–183, 184, 194
    revising and editing, 192–193, 194
    solicited vs. unsolicited, 171
    student sample, 172–180
    style of, 190
    types of, 171
proven facts, 358, 362
Publication Manual of the American Psychological Association,
    6th ed. *see* APA style
punctuation
    with addresses, 558
    apostrophes. *see* apostrophes
    brackets, 562
    colons. *see* colons
    commas. *see* commas
    dashes, 538, 560
    with dates, 558
    defined, 554
    ellipsis dots, 562
    end punctuation, 554–555
    exclamation points, 554, 555, 560
    hyphens, 566–567
    and nonrestrictive modifiers, 538
    parentheses, 561–562
    periods. *see* periods
    question marks, 554, 555, 560
    quotation marks. *see* quotation marks
    with quotations, 557–558
    semicolons. *see* semicolons
    in series, 555–556, 557
purpose
    defined, 20
    defining question, 16
    and design, 287–288
    and genre, 22*f*
    and global revision, 308
    identifying, 20–21, 34
    writing, 23

Q
qualified statement, 370
qualifying terms, 370
Quattro Pro, 296
question and answer period, 514–515
question marks
    defined, 554

with quotation marks, 555, 560
use of, 555
questions
factual questions, 407, 408
Five-W and How questions
explained, 259–260
in field observation, 410
for presentations, 510, 519
and reader profiles, 27–28
and reviews, 64–65
indirect questions, 554, 555
as introduction, 324
journalistic questions. *see* journalistic questions
open-ended questions, 407, 408
quotation marks
with indirect quotations, 535
with other punctuation, 555, 558, 560
and search engines, 401
single quotation marks, 560
uses of, 560–561
in works cited list, 437
quotations
block quotes, 419–420, 427, 535
brief quotations, 416–418
commas with, 556–558
described, 415, 416
direct quotations, 423
as evidence, 362
formatting of, 225
framing, 422–424
indirect quotations, 535, 561
as introduction, 324
in literary analysis, 118, 126, 127, 130
long quotations, 418–419, 427, 535
paraphrasing, 419–420
phrases, 418
and quotation marks, 416, 560
within quotations, 560
sentences, 418
verifying, 408
words, 418
R
radio broadcasts
APA references list, 468
MLA references list, 445
as sources, 404
rapid-fire paragraph, 337–338
Rasmussen, Derek ("Forty Years of Struggle and Still No Right to Inuit Education in Nunavut"), 195–202
reader analysis worksheet, 30*f*
reader profiles
brief, 27–28, 35
elements of, 27*f*
extended, 28–31
reader analysis worksheet, 30*f*
readers' attitudes, 30–31

readers' expectations, 28–29
readers' values, 29–31
readers
defining question, 16
and design, 288
identification with, 92, 261
profiling, 34. *see* reader profiles
specialized, 326
readers' attitudes, 30–31, 308
readers' expectations, 27, 28–29, 308
Readers' Guide, 153, 407
readers' values, 29–31, 308
reading backwards, 315
reading out loud, 315
reading response, 128, 129*f*
readings
"Bare-Knuckled Knockout" (Johnson), 74–75
"Borders" (King), 132–139
"Boys and Violence" (Feder, Levant, & Dean), 239–251
"Forty Years of Struggle and Still No Right to Inuit Education in Nunavut" (Rasmussen), 195–202
"Friends with Benefits" (Dailey), 161–164
"Letter to the Editor on Climate Story" (Walker & Roberts), 165–166
"Media Influence on the Body Image . . ." (Lawrie, Sullivan, Davies, & Hill), 81–82
"Outraged Moms, Trashy Daughters" (Kingston), 52–53
"Rethinking Canadian and American Nationality" (Andrews & Walton), 140–142
Summary of David Bartholomae's "Inventing the University" (Stouck & Shaw), 54–55
"Tell the Awful Truth" (Saier & Trevors), 203–206
"The CNN Effect Revisited" (Robinson), 233–238
"The Egg and the Sperm" (Martin), 106–112
"The Many Shades of Red" (Kendrick), 76–79
"What's a Girl to Read?" (Featherstone), 103–105
reasoning (*logos*)
in argument, 361–362, 374
as heuristic, 261, 263*f*
in rhetorical analysis, 91
rebuttal
absorbing opposing points, 369
conceding points, 368–369
example of, 165–166
methods of, 374
qualifying claims, 369–370
refuting opposing points, 369
strategies for, 157
summarizing opposing view, 367
validity of opposing view, 367–368
recommendation, 361
red herring, 366*f*
redundancy, 279–280, 550, 551
reference materials, 406
reflections, 492, 493*f*, 496
refutation, 369

registered users, 483
regular verbs, 541
relative clauses, 545
relative pronouns
    case forms, 546
    function of, 549–550
    list of, 549
    as subordinate connectors, 525
reliability of sources, 392–394
reporting expressions
    for material from a source, 423, 424*f*
    in summary, 48–49
research
    annotated bibliography, 227–228
    background information, 64–65, 73
    cyclical nature of, 223*f*
    empirical sources
        field observation, 409–411
        interview, 407–408
        for position papers, 153
        for proposals, 183
        for rhetorical analysis, 94
        survey, 409
        types of, 398, 407
    and experience, 66, 73
    field observation, 65
    interview, 65
    for literary analysis, 123–124, 131
    online sources
        APA documentation style, 464, 465–467
        blogs, 404
        encyclopedias, 392
        finding, 401–405
        Internet search engines, 401–402
        MLA documentation style, 440–444
        podcasts, 404
        for position papers, 153
        for proposals, 182
        reliability of, 403, 413
        for rhetorical analysis, 94
        for summaries, 46
        types of, 398
        wikis, 404
    for position papers, 153, 160
    print sources
        academic journals, 406
        articles, 406–407
        books, 405
        finding, 404–407
        government publications, 406
        library, 405–406
        magazines, 407
        newspapers, 407
        for position papers, 153
        for proposals, 182–183

reference materials, 406
    for rhetorical analysis, 94
    for summaries, 46
    types, 398
    for proposals, 182–183, 184, 194
    purposes of, 388, 396
    for research papers, 221–223, 232
    and review, 64–66
    for rhetorical analysis, 94–95, 102
    roadblocks to, 395
    for summaries, 45–46, 65
    and summary, 51
research papers
    abstract, 223
    argumentative research paper, 210, 218
    body of, 212, 224–225
    and cause and effect, 350*f*
    and classification, 348*f*
    conclusion, 212, 225
    content development, 218–223
    and definition, 348*f*
    and description, 346*f*
    designing, 229–230, 232
    explained, 210
    expository research paper, 210, 218
    features of, 212
    inquiry, 218–221
    introduction in, 212, 224
    organization model, 211
    organizing and drafting, 223–226, 232
    readers' expectations, 28
    references or works cited, 226
    research for, 221–223, 232
    research question, 219
    revising and editing, 230–231, 232
    student sample, 212–217
    style of, 226–227, 232
    thesis statement, 224
research plan, 221–222, 391, 395, 396
research process
    defining a question, 390, 396
    and hypothesis, 391
    managing, 394
    outlined, 389*f*
    plan, devising, 391, 396
    plan, following and modifying, 395, 396
    recursive nature of, 389–390
    scheduling, 394, 396
    and source reliability, 392–394
    start-up research, 392, 396
    steps in, 390–391
    and working thesis, 391, 395, 396
research question
    defining, 390, 396
    developing, 219, 232

modifying, 395
research schedule, 394, 396
research triangle, 399
researcher, 380
restrictive modifiers, 537–539, 558
"Rethinking Canadian and American Nationality" (Andrews & Walton), 140–142
retrieval information, 465
reviews
    academic expectations, 64, 70, 73
    APA documentation style, 463
    and classification, 348f
    common expectations, 58, 62–64, 63f, 71, 73
    conclusion, 68
    content development, 62–66
    designing, 71
    discussion of strengths and shortcomings, 67–68
    features of, 60
    graphics, 73
    introduction, 66–67
    literature review, 70–71
    MLA works cited list, 438
    and narrative, 345f
    organization model, 59
    organizing and drafting, 66–68, 73
    overview, 58
    pace of, 70
    readers' expectations, 28
    research, 64–66
    revising and editing, 71–72, 73
    student sample, 60–62
    style of, 68–70, 73
    subject, description of, 67
    tone of, 69, 71
revising and editing
    copyediting, 303, 313–315
    in essay exam, 503, 507
    global revision, 303, 304–309
    levels of, 303, 304f
    of literary analysis, 130, 131
    peer editing, 316–317
    of position paper, 158–159, 160
    proofreading
        defined, 303, 315, 318
        and peer editing, 317
        of proposal, 192
        of research paper, 230–231
        of review, 72
        strategies for, 315–316
    of proposal, 192–193, 194
    of research paper, 230–231, 232
    of review, 71–72, 73
    of rhetorical analysis, 101, 102
    software for, 485
    substantive editing, 303, 309–313

of summary, 49–50
videos or podcasts, 485
rhetorical analysis
    ad critique, 99–100
    analysis of the text, 98–98
    and comparison and contrast, 352f
    conclusion, 87, 98
    content development, 91–95
    and definition, 348f
    and description, 346f
    designing, 100–101
    explanation of rhetorical concepts, 95–96
    features of, 87
    historical context, 96–97
    inquiry, 91–93
    introduction, 87, 95
    vs. literary analysis, 116
    organization model, 86
    organizing and drafting, 95–98, 102
    purpose of, 85
    readers' expectations, 28
    research, 94–95, 102
    revising and editing, 101, 102
    rhetorical patterns, 93–94
    strategies for, 100
    student sample, 87–90
    style of, 99, 102
    summary, 96–97
rhetorical patterns
    cause and effect, 94, 349–351, 354
    classification, 93, 348–349, 354
    combining rhetorical patterns, 352–353, 354
    comparison and contrast, 94, 351–352, 354
    defined, 343
    definition
        with analogy, 347
        and division, 347
        etymology, 347
        with examples, 347
        explained, 93, 346–347
        extended definition, 346, 354
        and genres, 348f
        with negation, 347
        parenthetical definition, 156, 227
        sentence definition, 156, 227, 346, 354
        similarities and differences, 347
    description, 93, 344–346, 354
    narrative, 343–344, 345f, 354
    types of, 93–94
rhetorical question, 513
rhetorical situation
    elements of, 16, 17f, 26
    and genres, 33–34
rights, 363
roadblocks to research, 395

Roberts, David ("Letter to the Editor on Climate Story"), 165–166

Robinson, Piers ("The CNN Effect Revisited"), 233–238

Rogerian form, 371–372

Rogers, Carl, 372

rough draft, 305–306*f*

run-on sentences, 530–531

S

-*s* as word ending, 543

sacred texts, MLA documentation style, 440

Saier Jr., M. H. ("Tell the Awful Truth"), 203–206

sans serif fonts, 292–293

scene setter, 325, 344

scribe, 377

search engines, 401–402

second-level headings, 294

second person, 540, 543, 549

secondary sources, 399

sections
    components of, 338
    defined, 331
    headings in, 338–339
    organizing, 338–339, 340*f*
    and paragraphs, 339–340, 341
    purpose of, 338

semicolons
    vs. colons, 555, 559
    with independent clauses, 529, 531
    in lists, 555–556
    vs. periods, 529
    with quotation marks, 560
    use of, 555–556

senses, 260, 345, 410

sentence definition, 156, 227, 346

sentence fragments
    acceptable fragments, 527–528
    defined, 524
    incomplete thoughts, 527
    phrase fragments, 526–527
    and punctuation, 555
    subordinate clause fragments, 525–526
    types of, 525

sentences
    adjectives and adverbs, 539
    comma splices, 528–530
    compound sentences, 556
    concise, 226
    coordination, 532–533
    dangling and misplaced modifiers, 536–537
    defined, 524
    editing, 314–315
    flow of, 99, 159
    fragments, 524–528
    fused sentences, 530–531
    introductory sentence elements, 556
    inverted order, 545
    length of, 99, 190, 280–281
    mixed sentences, 534
    and parallelism, 531–532
    point sentences, 335, 341
    quoting, 418
    shifts in, 534–535
    subject of. *see* subject of sentence
    subject-verb agreement, 543–545
    support sentences, 334–335, 341
    topic sentences, 230, 334, 341

serial comma, 557

series, 555–556, 557

serif fonts, 292–293

setting, 122

sexist usage, 553–554

Shaw, Cathi (Summary of David Bartholomae's "Inventing the University"), 54–55

shifts, 535, 549

ships, 566

show of hands, 513

showcase portfolio, 488–489

signalling expressions
    for conclusion, 327
    for material from a source, 51, 423, 424*f*, 427
    in summary, 48–49

similarities and differences, 347

similes, 156, 190, 282

single quotation marks, 560

skeptic, designated, 377

slackers, 381

slang, 552

slides, 515–516

slippery slope, 366*f*

social media, 481–482, 486

social trends, 33, 35, 309

social values, 29

software
    concept mapping software, 258
    for graphs, 296
    online citation generators, 429
    online collaborative software, 382
    for podcast editing, 485
    presentation software, 168, 265, 266*f*, 297, 515
    spreadsheet software, 297
    for video editing, 485

solicited proposal, 171

sounding board, 378

sources
    and bias, 393
    citing/quoting, 225. *see also* APA style; MLA style
    credibility of, 383
    currency of, 393
    electronic sources

blogs, 404
documentaries, 403
finding, 401–405
Internet search engines, 401–402
podcasts, 404
radio broadcasts, 404
reliability of, 403
television broadcasts, 403–404
types of, 398
wikis, 404
empirical sources
field observation, 409–411
interview, 407–408
for position paper, 153
for proposal, 183
for rhetorical analysis, 94
survey, 409
types of, 398, 407
evaluating, 394, 398–399
online sources
APA documentation style, 465–467
blogs, 404
finding, 401–405
Internet search engines, 401–402
MLA documentation style, 440–444
podcasts, 404
for position papers, 153
for proposals, 182
reliability of, 403, 413
for rhetorical analysis, 94
types of, 398
wikis, 404
primary, 399
print sources
academic journals, 406
articles, 406–407
books, 405
finding, 404–407
government publications, 406
at library, 405–406
magazines, 407
newspapers, 407
for proposals, 182–183
reference materials, 406
for research, 94, 153
for summaries, 46
types of, 398
reliability of, 392–394, 403, 413
secondary, 399
triangulating, 182, 398–399, 413
verifying information, 393
spacecraft, 566
speech. *see* presentations
spellchecker, 316, 568
spelling

doubling final consonants, 568
final *e*, 569
final *y*, 569
homonyms, 570
plurals, 569–570
Spoke, 481
spreadsheet software, 297
square brackets, 562
start-up research, 392, 396
statistics, as introduction, 324, 513
storming, 379, 381
storyboarding, 259
Stouck, Jordan (Summary of David Bartholomae's "Inventing the University"), 54–55
straw man, 366*f*
structure
of argument, 45, 46*f*, 149
of literary analysis, 117
of position paper, 149
of proposal, 170
of research paper, 211
of review, 59
of rhetorical analysis, 86
of summary, 41, 48–49
student samples
APA references list, 477
APA style, 468–477
argument, 150–151
conclusion, 327
essay exam, 503–504
global revision, 305–306*f*, 307*f*
introduction, 326
literary analysis, 118–120
MLA style, 446–453
MLA works cited list, 453
peer editing, 310–313
position paper, 150–151
proposal, 172–180
research paper, 212–217
review, 60–62
rhetorical analysis, 87–90
substantive editing, 311–313
summary, 43–44
style
conciseness, 550–551
defined, 276
developing, 73
formal vs. informal, 49
improving, 284
for literary analysis, 126–127
plain style
described, 285
guidelines, 276–281
for position papers, 155, 160
for position papers, 155–156, 160

style (*Continued*)
    for proposals, 190
    for research papers, 226–227, 232
    for reviews, 68–70
    for rhetorical analysis, 99, 102
    for summaries, 49
    top-down style, 156, 226
subject alignment, 335–336
subject complements, 544
subject of sentence
    and clarity, 277
    compound subjects, 544
    and the "doer", 277
    position in sentence, 278
    understood subject, 555
subject of writing. *see* topics
subject-verb agreement
    and compound subjects, 544
    and indefinite pronouns, 544
    and intervening relative clause, 545
    and intervening subordinate elements, 543
    and inverted sentences, 545
    and subject complements, 544
subjective case, 546
subjunctive mood, 542–543
subordinate clause fragments, 525–526
subordinate clauses, 525–526
subordinating conjunctions, 529, 531
subordinating connectors, 525
subordination, 532, 533
substantive editing
    defined, 303, 318
    and design, 310
    and information quantity, 309
    peer editing, 310–313, 317
    reorganizing to highlight ideas, 309–310
    student sample, 311–313
Sullivan, E. A. ("Media Influence on the Body Image..."), 81–82
summarizing a source
    citing, 427
    described, 416, 421–422
    examples of, 421–422
    framing, 422–424
    order of, 225, 427
    vs. paraphrasing, 419
summary
    in argument, 367
    basic approach, 51
    content development, 44–46
    detail, level of, 47
    executive summary, 172–180
    length of, 47
    in literary analysis, 118, 126
    objective summary, 150
    organization model, 41

    organizing and drafting, 46–47
    overview, 42
    in position paper, 150, 154
    readers' expectations, 28
    in research paper, 224
    of review subject, 67
    revising and editing, 49–50
    in rhetorical analysis, 96–97
    structuring, 48–49
    student sample, 43–44
    style of, 49
    uses of, 40
Summary of David Bartholomae's "Inventing the University" (Stouck & Shaw), 54–55
superlative degree, 539
supersized paragraph, 337
support sentences, 334–335, 341
survey
    creating, 409
    online services, 409
    questions, types of, 410*f*
    as research, 65
symbolism, 122–123
synthesizing to find common ground, 66

T
tables, 299, 300*f*
team writing. *see also* group writing
    defined, 376
    forming, 379, 380
    improving, 383
    norming, 379, 381–382
    performing, 379, 382
    planning meeting, 380, 383
    responsibilities, 380, 382, 383
    rethinking goals, 381, 383
    stages of, 379, 383
    storming, 379, 381
technical terms, 227
TED.com, 404
television broadcasts
    APA references list, 468
    MLA works cited list, 445
    as sources, 403–404
"Tell the Awful Truth" (Saier & Trevors), 203–206
tenses
    and auxiliary verbs, 540–541
    explained, 540–541
    and irregular verbs, 541
    list of, 540
    literary present tense, 126–127
    shifts in, 535
    subject-verb agreement, 543–545
text
    analysis of, 98–98

defined, 85
The Big Picture, 404
"The CNN Effect Revisited" (Robinson), 233–238
"The Egg and the Sperm" (Martin), 106–112
The Huffington Post, 404
"The Many Shades of Red" (Kendrick), 76–79
the reason . . . is because, 534
The Rush Limbaugh Show, 404
theme
    and essay exams, 499–500
    exploration of for literary analysis, 122
theoretical context, 123–124
thesis. *see also* thesis statement
    defined, 20
    refining, 130, 222
    in research paper, 219
thesis statement
    defined, 21
    for literary analysis, 125, 130, 131
    for research papers, 224, 232
    revising, 230
    working thesis, 391, 395, 396
third-level headings, 294
third person, 540, 543, 549
time management
    in essay exam, 501, 507
    for presentations, 510, 512*f*
times, 563
titles
    abbreviations of, 563
    capitalization of, 563
    editing, 314
    and italics, 465, 565
    personal, 563
    and quotation marks, 437, 561
    and typeface, 293
to as part of infinitive, 526
tone
    authoritative, 190
    exploration of for literary analysis, 123
    objective, academic, 226
    in presentation, 517–518, 519
    in proposal, 190
    in review, 69, 71
    in summary, 51
    and voice, 281
top-down paragraphs, 156, 226
topic sentences, 230, 334, 341
topics
    debatable, 160
    defining question, 16
    and global revision, 308
    identifying, 17–19, 23, 34
    mapping, 18
    narrowing, 23, 131, 181, 218

topoi, 343
Toulmin model, 372–373
Toulmin, Stephen, 372
trains, 566
transitional adverbs, 529, 557
transitional sentences. *see* transitions
transitions
    editing, 314
    need for, 341
    purpose of, 332–333
    transitional words and phrases, 333
translation
    APA documentation style, 464
    MLA works cited list, 439
Trevors, J. T. ("Tell the Awful Truth"), 203–206
triangulate, 182, 398–399, 413
tropes
    analogy, 156, 282
    defined, 282
    metaphor, 156, 190, 282–283
    onomatopoeia, 283, 285
    simile, 156, 190, 282
tu quoque, 366*f*
Tuckman, Bruce, 379
Tumblr, 264
Twitter, 264, 482
typefaces, 292–293

U
Uncyclopedia, 484
underlining, 566
unsolicited proposal, 171
utilitarianism, 363

V
values, readers', 29–31, 35, 308
verb phrases, 526
verbal phrases
    defined, 526
    as fragments, 526
    and implied subjects, 536
verbal tics, 517
verbals
    and auxiliary verbs, 541
    defined, 526
verbs
    action in, 278
    auxiliary verbs, 540–541
    functions of, 540
    helping verbs, 540–541
    irregular verbs, 541
    position in sentence, 278
    regular verbs, 541
    for signalling expressions, 424*f*
    singular and plural, 543

verbs (*Continued*)
    tenses. *see* tenses
    in thesis statements, 21*f*
vertical alignment, 290–291
videos
    creating for Internet, 484–485
    reader use of, 32
visual aids, 515–516, 519. *see also* graphics
vocabulary, 346
voice, author's
    establishing your own voice, 281, 285
    in presentation, 517–518, 519
    in summary, 51
voice, grammatical
    active vs. passive, 226, 277–278, 541–542
    shifts in, 535
volume number
    in references list, 466
    in works cited list, 437

W

Walker, Russ ("Letter to the Editor on Climate Story"), 165–166
Walton, Priscilla L. ("Rethinking Canadian and American Nationality"), 140–142
was, 542
weak analogy, 366*f*
weak premises, 365
weight, 288–290
were, 542
"What's a Girl to Read?" (Featherstone), 103–105
white space, 192, 292
whiteboard, 511*f*
Wikibooks, 404
Wikicars, 484
wikiHow, 404, 484
Wikipedia, 404, 484

wikis
    MLA documentation style, 444
    for research, 404
    writing for, 484–484, 486
Wikitravel, 404, 484
wildcard symbols, 402
word origin, 347
Wordpress, 482
words
    etymology, 347
    quoting, 418
    used as terms, 565, 566
    used in special sense, 561
wordy expressions, 550, 551
working thesis, 391, 395, 396
works cited list. *see* MLA works cited list
writer's block, 272–273, 274
writing concepts, 480–481
writing process. *see also* specific elements
    description with tropes. *see* tropes
    drafting introductions, bodies, and conclusions, 270
    drafting through writer's block, 272–273
    establishing your voice, 281
    and genres, 9–11
    heuristics, 259–262
    organizing and drafting. *see* organizing and drafting
    outlining, 270–272
    prewriting. *see* prewriting
    revising and editing. *see* revising and editing
    steps in, 10, 11*f*
    style, development of. *see* style
writing style. *see* style

Y

Yahoo! Video, 484
YouTube, 484